STRATEGIES FOR NAVIGATING

GRADUATE SCHOOL

AND BEYOND

KEVIN G. LORENTZ II
DANIEL J. MALLINSON
JULIA MARIN HELLWEGE
DAVIN PHOENIX
J. CHERIE STRACHAN

apsa
AMERICAN
POLITICAL
SCIENCE
ASSOCIATION

AMERICAN POLITICAL SCIENCE ASSOCIATION

Designed by Madelyn L. Dewey

Photo Credits
Cover: Graphic design/cover art by Madelyn L. Dewey.
Section Photographs (edited by Madelyn L. Dewey): Section I photograph (Fizkes/Getty Images Plus), Section II photograph (Prostock-Studio/Getty Images Plus), Section III photograph (Artisteer/Getty Images Plus), Section IV photograph (monkeybusinessimages/Getty Images Plus), Section V photograph (JLco—Julia Amaral/Getty Images Plus), Section VI photograph (Fizkes/Getty Images Plus), Section VII photograph (Scyther5/Getty Images Plus), Section VIII photograph (fizkes/Getty Images Plus), Section IX photograph (PeopleImages/Getty Images Plus).

ISBN (Soft Cover): 978-1-878147-74-5

Table of Contents*

Preface

John Ishiyama .... **xix**

1 | Nevertheless, We Persisted: Pathways Through Grad School (Introduction)

Kevin G. Lorentz II, Daniel J. Mallinson, Julia Marin Hellwege, Davin Phoenix, and J. Cherie Strachan **1**

> This chapter offers some background about the inspiration for the project, the editors' brief narratives of their time in graduate school, and brief overviews of the sections of this volume.

Section I: The Application Process

2 | How to Get In: A Roadmap for Navigating Decision-Making and the Application Process

Kelly Piazza, Chris Culver, and Lynne Chandler-Garcia **11**

> This chapter discusses decisions regarding whether, when, and where to go to graduate school, then offers guidance on how to navigate the application process. It encourages prospective students to find programs that match their goals and effectively communicate their personal and professional narrative through the application materials.

3 | Financial Concerns: Taking on Student Loans, Graduate Assistant Positions, and Funding Considerations

Courtney N. Haun and Jennifer Schenk Sacco **17**

> This chapter identifies financial considerations and identifies some ways students can mitigate financial woes. Financial planning should be done before deciding on a graduate program, and this chapter provides guiding questions to help prospective students weigh their options.

4 | Don't You Forget About Me: The Application Process and Choosing a Program

Tara Chandra, Patricia C. Rodda, and William D. Adler **23**

> This chapter discusses the process of selecting a PhD program once prospective students have been admitted. The authors articulate a systematic approach to assessing the best program fit, making the most out of visit day, and looking beyond rankings to think about quality-of-life issues in graduate school. This chapter also includes advice for students who are choosing between master's and PhD programs.

Please note that, unless otherwise stated, all authors contributed equally to their respective articles.

5 | Seasoned Professionals Applying to and Navigating Doctoral Programs

Marty P. Jordan, Erika Rosebrook, and Eleanor Schiff **27**

> This chapter speaks to seasoned professionals looking to leave the public, nonprofit, or private sectors after a lengthy tenure and pursue a PhD. The authors review several considerations to weigh in returning to academia and highlight the challenges and advantages that older graduate students face when applying to and navigating doctoral programs.

Section II: On Campus

6 | Moving Beyond the One-Shot Orientation: Understanding and Making the Most of Ongoing Orientations

Anthony Petros Spanakos and Mishella Romo Rivas **35**

> This chapter advocates an ongoing process of orientation, going beyond the one-off orientation that is usually used for graduate students, full-time and adjunct faculty alike.

7 | Building a Supportive Mentoring Network

Mary Anne S. Mendoza and Samantha A. Vortherms **41**

> Building a successful mentoring network is a key strategy for thriving in graduate school both personally and professionally. This chapter lays out the who, what, where, when, how, and whys of building your own network.

8 | Speak of the Devil and (S)he Appears: The Role of Academic Administrators During Graduate School and Beyond

Lauren C. Bell **47**

> This chapter offers a "who's who" of administrators on college and university campuses, explains some of the reasons that tensions often exist between faculty members and administrators, and offers graduate students a guide for interacting with administrators during their time in graduate school and as they navigate the academic job market.

9 | When Do Titles Matter and Why? A Guide for Graduate Students in Political Science

Meg K. Guliford, Meena Bose, and Dan Drezner **53**

> This chapter provides guidance on using titles versus first names for faculty in multiple graduate school settings.

10 | Relax! They're Important, But Not Defining Choices: Choosing Your Subfield and Committees

Mike Widmeier and Joseph B. Phillips **57**

> This chapter gives some advice on how to choose your subfield specialization and how to get the most out of a dissertation committee.

11 | Does an Internship Have Value for Political Science Graduate Students?

Susan E. Baer **63**

> This chapter discusses tensions and benefits related to completing an internship as a graduate student and offers recommendations and reflection based on my internship experience as a political science doctoral student.

12 | The Explicit, Implicit, and Unknown: Comprehensive Exams

Samantha R. Cooney and David O. Monda **69**

> The purpose of this chapter is to discuss the strategies, opportunities, and challenges of preparing to successfully pass Comprehensive Exams at the graduate level.

13 | Selecting an Adviser: Professsional and Personal Considerations

Chris Macaulay, Mary McThomas, and Alisson Rowland **75**

> This chapter provides guidance for graduate students in selecting their adviser, outlining the many positive and negative factors for students to consider, suggesting resources to help in their consideration, and addressing potential inequities in this process.

14 | Getting Started on the Doctoral Dissertation

Brady Baybeck **81**

> Your dissertation will be a self-directed original research project that will consume a considerable amount of your waking hours. No wonder it is intimidating to get started! This chapter provides a concrete path for moving forward on your dissertation prospectus (and other projects).

15 | The Doctoral Dissertation and MA Thesis: Managing the Process, Your Life, and Your Data

Michael Widmeier and Dessi Kirilova **87**

> This chapter reviews chronologically the key phases of the capstone-type projects in which graduate programs typically culminate. We review elements which a dissertation and a master's thesis have in common (selecting a topic, collecting data, navigating relationships with advisors and other expectations) and highlight the ways in which they differ. The chapter also includes a special discussion of data management strategies since this underappreciated and rarely taught set of simple good practices can help keep graduate students on track during the course of their independent work.

16 | Balancing Pregnancy, Parenthood, and Graduate School

Kimberly Saks McManaway, Regina Bateson, Marty P. Jordan, Karen Kedrowski, and Kyle

Harris **95**

> This chapter offers some advice and resources for graduate students who are currently or considering becoming parents. The authors discuss the decision to give birth to or adopt children; review different considerations such as breastfeeding, parental leave, childcare, job searches, and other supports; and provide suggestions for balancing the demands of parenting and academia.

17 | Practicing Effective Time Management

Samantha A. Vortherms and Coyle Neal **107**

> This chapter discusses strategies for time management. We argue that the key to successful time management is knowing your priorities, knowing yourself, and investing in yourself.

Section III: Professional Development— Scholarship

18 | Professional Norms: Clearing a Barrier to Developing Meaningful Relationships

Benjamin Isaak Gross, Kevin M. Kearns, and Evan M. Lowe **115**

This chapter discusses professional norms. We argue that learning and practicing professional norms is not only essential for professional success, but also shapes political science as a discipline. Also, we offer advice to graduate students on how to best learn and practice good professional norms.

19 | Balancing Expectations for Research Transparency: Institutional Review Boards, Funders, and Journals

Mneesha Gellman, Matthew C. Ingram, Diana Kapiszewski, and Sebastian Karcher **121**

This chapter considers benefits of and challenges to pursuing research transparency and identifies strategies for achieving openness and engaging productively with key institutional stakeholders on transparency-related issues.

20 | Fieldwork

Kelebogile Zvobgo, Charmaine N. Willis, Myunghee Lee, Anne-Kathrin Kreft, and Ezgi Irgil **129**

This chapter discusses defining, navigating, planning, and conducting fieldwork. It engages theory and praxis to offer answers to questions that graduate students puzzle over about fieldwork.

21 | How to Conference

Kimberly N. Turner, Christina Boyes, Elizabeth Bennion, and James Newman **135**

This chapter provides advice regarding strategies and approaches to attending academic conferences. The chapter addresses networking, presenting your research, which conferences to attend and why. The chapter provides specific advice from the perspective of recently finished graduate students and seasoned professors.

22 | Hidden Expenses in Graduate School: Navigating Financial Precarity and Elitism

Devon Cantwell-Chavez and Alisson Rowland **143**

This chapter discusses "hidden" expenses of graduate school and cultural components of funding, such as reimbursement, to help students anticipate less obvious expenses throughout their program. We also offer templates for conference expense tracking, a conference budgeting guide, and a guide for finding supplemental conference and workshop funds.

23 | Show Me the Money: Information, Strategies, and Guidelines for Applying to Grants and Fellowships in Graduate School

Angie Torres-Beltran, Cameron Mailhot, Elizabeth Dorssom, and Christina Boyes **149**

This chapter aims to "pull back the curtain" on a portion of the hidden curriculum of academia by providing an overview of what external grants and fellowships are, the purposes they can serve during one's graduate career, and a few strategies and tradeoffs to consider when applying for these funding sources.

24 | Political Science Publications: Charting Your Own Path

Shane Nordyke **155**

This chapter outlines the variety of publication types prevalent in Political Science. It also discusses some of the advantages and disadvantages of each for scholars.

25 | Turning Term Papers into Articles: Paths to a Productive Peer-Review Process

Michael P. A. Murphy **161**

> This chapter discusses how term papers can become peer reviewed articles, including "contribution-first writing," finding your audience, practical strategies for journal selection, and potential pitfalls on the path to a productive peer-review process!

26 | Managing Online Harassment in the Academy

Seth Masket, Angela Ocampo, and Jennifer Victor **167**

> This chapter offers some practical advice for scholars who encounter rude, threatening, or anti-social behavior in their professional online activity.

27 | To Twitter or Not to Twitter

Elizabeth (Bit) Meehan and Salah Ben Hammou **171**

> This chapter provides an overview of political science Twitter: why scholars use Twitter, what they use it for, and how to protect your safety online. We offer practical guidance and considerations for graduate students in deciding whether to use Twitter.

Section IV: Professional Development— Teaching

28 | Serving as a Graduate Teaching Assistant: Tips and Strategies

Zoe Nemerever and Bianca Rubalcava **181**

> This chapter outlines the roles and expectations of teaching assistants and discusses resources and strategies for a successful and rewarding experience.

29 | Preparing for the First Solo Teaching Experience: An Alternative to Learning as You Go

Christina Boyes, Mario Guerrero, Matt Lamb, and Mary Anne S. Mendoza **187**

> This chapter addresses course preparation and common situations which arise before, during, and after teaching your first course.

30 | Resources for Teaching Excellence: APSA's Education Section and the TLC

Megan Becker, Elizabeth A. Bennion, Colin M. Brown, and Eric Loepp **195**

> APSA provides several opportunities for graduate students to learn more about the practice of pedagogy in political science. This chapter introduces the Political Science Education Section and Teaching and Learning Conference as fora for learning new teaching methods, networking with other teacher-scholars, and discovering more about the process of publishing the scholarship of teaching and learning (SoTL).

Section V: Professional Development— Service

31 | Academic Service and Flourishing

Anthony Petros Spanakos and Ignangeli Salinas-Muniz **203**

> Service can be an area where graduate students can experience happiness, belonging, and intellectually productive challenges. It can also be overwhelming and draw students away from their primary area of research. What strategies and opportunities are best?

32 | Towards a More Holistic Graduate Experience: Professional Service to the Discipline

Courtney N. Haun and Ivy A. M. Cargile **209**

We address the various opportunities available for graduate students to provide service to the larger discipline at national, regional, and local levels along with some of the potential benefits and disadvantages.

33 | Community, Solidarity, and Collective Power: The Role of Graduate Student Organizations and Graduate Worker Unions

Samantha R. Cooney, Patrick J. Gauding, Anna A. Meier, and Kevin Reuning **215**

In addition to being students, graduate students are often employees of their universities. This chapter addresses how graduate worker unions and student organizations can provide sources of solidarity, community, and empowerment as grads navigate the demands of low-paying and exploitative jobs.

Section VI: Professional Development—The Job Market

34 | Expect the Unexpected: Choices and Challenges in the Political Science PhD Job Market

Bobbi G. Gentry, Kyla K. Stepp, and Jeremiah J. Castle **223**

This chapter provides an overview of the job market for political science PhDs, emphasizing that a variety of trends have contributed to a decline in tenure-track positions and a growth in post-docs, visiting positions, and "alt-ac" careers. We also provide an overview of the timing and structure of the academic market.

35 | Mental Health and the Job Market

Anna A. Meier, Adnan Rasool, and Annelise Russell **228**

This chapter focuses on protecting mental health while looking for an academic job. We address the uniquely stressful components of the academic job market and what you and your institution can do to protect your well-being during the job search.

36 | What Your PhD Advisors Can't Tell You Because They Don't Know: Landing a Job at a Student-Focused Institution

Karen M. Kedrowski **232**

This chapter provides strategies for applying and interviewing at student centered institutions, with advice that your PhD advisors may not be able to provide because they may not have worked at such institutions.

37 | A Commitment to Teaching, Learning, and Student Advocacy: Community College Careers

LaTasha Chaffin DeHaan, Josh Franco, Verónica Reyna, and Randy Villegas **237**

In this chapter we will examine the mission, vision, and values of community colleges along with their economic and educational impact in the United States. We will additionally address how community colleges are among the most diverse educational institutions in the United States and offer one of the most rewarding and fulfilling careers that political science graduate students can consider.

38 | More than Reordering the Cover Letter: Preparing for Careers at Small Liberal Arts Colleges

Kelly Bauer and Shamira Gelbman **243**
> This chapter offers guidance for political science graduate students considering faculty careers at small liberal arts colleges, providing details about a day in the life of a SLAC professor and suggesting how graduate students might prepare themselves for this job market.

39 | Preparing for a Career at a Regional Comprehensive University

Elizabeth A. Bennion, Monica E. Lineberger, and Eric D. Loepp **249**
> This chapter discusses a genuine perspective of the academic career at a Regional Comprehensive University (RCU). Making the point that RCU's are teaching-oriented, not teaching-exclusive, the authors argue that while these positions are rarely candidates' first choice, they offer fulfilling careers with balance between research, teaching, and service.

40 | Succeeding at a Research-Intensive Institution (R1 or R2)

Karen M. Kedrowski and Benjamin Melusky **255**
> This chapter provides advice for success at research intensive institutions, including formulating an application, interviewing, developing a research trajectory, and making the most of the pre-tenure review.

41 | Pushing the Boundaries of Your PhD: Exploring Careers Outside the Ivory Tower

Danielle Gilbert, S.R. Gubitz, Jennifer Kavanagh, and Kelly Piazza **261**
> This chapter highlights the diversity of career options open to political science PhDs, in particular those outside of tenure track jobs at major research universities and small liberal arts colleges. The chapter describes the advantages, disadvantages, and how to prepare for teaching opportunities at the US military service academies and professional military education institutions; pre-collegiate education positions; policy-focused jobs at think tanks, nonprofits, and in government; and private sector jobs.

42 | Weighing Up the Options: The Adventure of an Academic Career Outside of the United States

Dale Mineshima-Lowe, Pablo Biderbost, and Guillermo Boscán Carrasquero **271**
> This chapter considers one's career prospects in political science beyond the US. Drawing on our collective experiences (in Spain and the United Kingdom), we offer some insights about pursuing academic opportunities (studying and careers) outside the United States.

43 | Making a Statement: Research, Teaching, and Diversity Statements for the Academic Job Market

Kelly Bauer, Colin M. Brown, Melissa L. Sands, and Maricruz Ariana Osorio **277**
> This chapter discusses the research, teaching, and diversity statements commonly requested for faculty position applications. We suggest that writing these statements can play an important role in developing one's academic identity and plotting a forward trajectory and offer reflective prompts to support applicants' writing process.

44 | A Limited Time Offer: Exploring Adjunct, Visiting, and Fixed-Term Positions

Austin Trantham, Connor J.S. Sutton, Margaret Mary Ochner, and Jennifer E. Lamm **283**

As the availability of tenure-track appointments continues to decline, more graduate students will serve in non-tenure track (NTT) positions. This chapter provides practical advice for those considering NTT appointments from the authors' collective experiences, including strategies for success in these positions.

45 | The Academic Interview/Marathon

Christopher Macaulay and Michelle D. Deardorff **289**

This chapter explores the interview process and includes advice on how to prepare for an on-campus interview, navigate the interview itself, and succeed once the interview is complete. This includes helpful advice for interviewees and perspective from individuals on both sides of the interview experience.

46 | You Have an Academic Job Offer…Now What? Negotiating Advice from Two Perspectives

William O'Brochta and Lori Poloni-Staudinger **295**

This chapter describes the process of receiving, negotiating, and accepting a job offer with perspectives from both a faculty member and a dean.

47 | Started from the Bottom, Now We're Here: Navigating the Job Market Without a "Top Tier" PhD

Rachel E. Finnell and Alexandra T. Middlewood **301**

This chapter offers advice to graduate students who are not part of "top tier" PhD programs on tackling the job market by discussing the quandary with program rankings, providing considerations for setting beneficial goals, offering guidance on creating and utilizing academic networks, and discussing the teaching versus research debate.

48 | Getting "Us" a Job: The Two+ Body Problem and the Academic Job Market

Tyler P. Yates **307**

This chapter provides advice to academics on the job market who must not only consider their own job prospects and future but those of a partner—who may or may not also be an academic. This includes tips to prepare for the application process, suggestions for navigating potential job offers, and possible short-term and long-term solutions for the two+ body problem.

Section VII: Climate and Culture in the Department and Profession

49 | Climate and Culture in Political Science: Diversifying our Institutions, Methods, and Identities to Combat Implicit Bias and Microaggressions

Natasha Altema McNeely, LaTasha Chaffin DeHaan, and Verónica Hoyo **315**

In this chapter, we argue the foundation for implicit biases and microaggressions is the deep-rooted notion that a "prototypical" model of Political Science exists; be it in the form of a university or department, a type of political scientist, a particular focus field and a best career path. We explore the pervasive effects of a monolithic approach of one-size-fits all to our institutions, our methods and our identities in light of the intersectionality of graduate students' lived experiences and personal realities.

50 | Feeling Like a Fraud: Imposter Syndrome in Political Science

Thomas S. Benson, Bobbi G. Gentry, and Sarah Shugars **323**

Imposter syndrome can present feelings of intellectual self-doubt—among other things—and it is not experienced equally or in a universal manner, with intersectional identities able to shape and compound how imposter syndrome is experienced. This chapter offers numerous recommendations to help manage imposter syndrome for oneself or to help others.

51 | Discrimination and Sexual Assault: Resources and Options for Responding and Reporting

Devon Cantwell-Chavez, Asif Siddiqui, and Christina Fattore **329**

This chapter provides definitions for sexual assault and discrimination, an in-depth walk-through of the process for reporting these issues, and resources for bystanders and receiving disclosures of these issues. Furthermore, we discuss the shortcomings and failures of existing structures and offer a menu of options for care and healing.

52 | Sexual Harassment in Academia: What Every Graduate Student Should Know

Rebecca Gill and Valerie Sulfaro **343**

This chapter offers definitions of sexual harassment and sexual coercion, assesses the scope of the problem within the discipline and the consequences of harassment, and provides a comprehensive review of options to pursue in response to experiences of sexual harassment.

53 | What Do You Need to Know About the Culture of Overwork?

Thomas S. Benson **355**

This chapter offers insights and resources into the culture of overwork in the discipline and how prospective and current political science graduate students can navigate the challenges associated with this culture. Advice is provided for students at different stages and for those with different identities.

Section VIII: Strategies for Addressing Implicit Bias, Harassment, and Assault

54 | Concerns for BIPOC Students and Scholars and a Model for Inclusive Excellence

Aleena Khan, Jair Moreira, Jessica S. Taghvaiee, and Andrea Benjamin **363**

This chapter identifies several concerns underrepresented racial/ethnic students and scholars face in the field of political science including: the lack of representation of BIPOC students and faculty; the climate of departments and programs; and the personal hardships students may face in navigating graduate school such as experiencing imposter syndrome, macro- or micro-aggressions, and intersectional experiences. We conclude with recommendations for both students and institutions to address some of the systemic issues outlined in this chapter.

55 | Political Science & LGBTQ Identity: Thoughts & Suggestions for LGBTQ Graduate Students

Monique Newton, Brian F. Harrison, and Edward F. Kammerer, Jr. **371**

The purpose of this chapter is to discuss some of the challenges and opportunities that come with pursuing a PhD from two perspectives: as an LGBTQ person and as someone who wants to conduct research on LGBTQ-related topics.

56 | Gender and the Political Science Graduate Experience: When Leaning In Isn't Enough

Maya Novak-Herzog, Alisson Rowland, Kimberly Saks McManaway, and Tabitha Bonilla **379**

This chapter considers the differential experience of woman-identifying individuals in graduate school by discussing teaching research and service. It suggests potential strategies to navigate obstacles and build community to move beyond lean-in narratives that can sometimes further penalize women in political science.

57 | Concerns for International Graduate Students in Political Science

Thomas S. Benson and Silviya Gancheva **387**

This chapter draws attention to the challenges faced by international graduate students in the United States and provides information on how students at different stages can deal with these challenges. Notably, we—as two international graduate students—provide advice on applications, finances, immigration, housing, language, cultural norms in education, teaching, and the job market.

58 | Teaching as an International Graduate Student

Irmak Yazici **393**

This chapter addresses the unique challenges international graduate students of political science face as teaching assistants and/or instructors and provides a roadmap on how to overcome these challenges whilst making successful progress towards dissertation research and writing.

59 | Religious Minorities and the Graduate School Experience

Sierra Davis Thomander and Andrea Malji **397**

This chapter provides strategies and resources for students who face challenges as members of minority religions, broadly defined, covering issues such as calendar differences, dietary restrictions, and discrimination. Aspiring allies of religious minorities will also benefit from reading this chapter.

60 | Concerns for First-Gen Political Science Graduate Students

Thomas S. Benson and T. Mark Montoya **405**

This chapter focuses on identifying the challenges faced by first-generation (first-gen) political science graduate students. We stress that while not all first-gen experiences are identical, we can highlight solutions for first-gen political science graduate students by calling to mind assets-based approaches that deviate from the existing focus on deficiencies.

61 | Disabilities and Chronic Health Issues

Eun A Jo, Sally Friedman, and Alan Babcock **411**

This chapter documents some common challenges for students with disabilities and chronic health issues and identifies possible resources (institutional, legal, and social) that students may seek out in their respective departments, universities, and beyond. In doing so, we hope to acknowledge the unique needs of students with disabilities as well as inform, based on our lived experiences, how academia as a whole may better accommodate those needs.

Section IX: Health and Wellness in Graduate School

62 | Why You're Doing This: Sustaining Joy and Inspiration in the Scholarly Vocation
Yuna Blajer de la Garza, Patrick J. Egan, and Sarah Shugars **419**

Why should you pursue a PhD in political science? Because few other careers provide the range of remarkable and enjoyable opportunities to be intellectually creative, to work independently, and to make contributions to society as the vocation of political science scholarship.

63 | No Rapunzel in This Ivory Tower: Finding Your Collective and Overcoming Academic Isolation

Devon Cantwell-Chavez, Siobhan Kirkland, Hannah Lebovits, Maricruz Ariana Osorio, Natalie Rojas, Rosalie Rubio, Sarah Shugars, Rachel Torres, and Rachel Winter **425**

Graduate school can be a lonely and isolating time. This chapter explores some of the institutional and systemic reasons that lead to graduate students—especially those who are underrepresented in the profession—to feel isolated. Additionally, we provide examples of strategies for coping and thriving in the face of the reality of isolation. Furthermore, we provide recommendations to the profession for how we can reduce circumstances that lead to isolation for students during their graduate education.

64 | Health and Well-Being in Graduate School: Preventing Burnout

Thomas S. Benson and Christina Boyes **431**

Health and well-being constitute critical components of graduate students' success and potential issues like burnout, chronic stress, depression, fatigue, and imposter syndrome threaten to undermine such success. In turn, this chapter provides strategies on how students can manage their health and well-being, including advice for those who are already struggling and those seeking to prevent these issues arising.

65 | Things that Can Go "Wrong": Finding Our Own Way in Graduate School

Misbah Hyder, Dana El Kurd, Felicity Gray, Devon Cantwell-Chavez, and Alisson Rowland **437**

While facing obstacles in graduate school—such as changing your dissertation topic and/or advisor, transferring programs, taking a leave of absence, or working multiple jobs—it might feel like something has gone "wrong." This chapter challenges that framing and guides how to make choices when plans change.

66 | Should I Stay or Should I Go? Making the Decision to Leave Your Graduate Program

Carmen J. Burlingame **445**

Written from the perspective of someone who did leave their PhD program, this chapter provides recommendations on tangible steps to have the most success when transitioning from academia—including completing requirements for a terminal master's, following through on previous commitments to colleagues, and identifying transferable skills into the workforce.

67 | Rest in Graduate School: Boundaries, Care-Taking Labor, Racial Capitalism, and Ill Health

Pyar Seth and Alexandra De Ciantis **449**

This chapter foregrounds the prioritization of rest and well-being through a critique of academic overwork infused by racial capitalism.

68 | Mental Health and Well-Being in Grad School: Dealing with Isolation, Depression, Anxiety, and Turmoil

Nasir Almasri and Dana El Kurd **455**

Graduate students exhibit significant levels of depression and anxiety. This chapter discusses what we know about mental health struggles among graduate students and offers strategies that can help mitigate potentially negative mental health experiences during graduate school.

69 | Health and Well-Being in Graduate School: Counseling and Other Resources

Mikaela Karstens and Anne M. Whitesell **463**

This chapter discusses the importance of mental healthcare in grad school and identifies numerous resources and strategies students can use to meet their emotional and psychological needs.

Contributor Biographies **469**

List of Tables and Figures

Chapter 3

Table 1: Template for Comparing Program Costs and Funding 20

Chapter 7

Figure 1: Mentoring Relationships 42

Chapter 8

Figure 1: Who's Who? A Summary of Key Administrative Titles and Positions 48

Chapter 16

Table 1: Parental Leave Policies for the top 40 Political Science PhD Programs in the US 99
Table 2: Childcare Facilities & Monthly Costs for top 40 Political Science PhD Programs in the US 100
Table A: Appendix—On Campus Resources for Graduate Students who are Pregnant or Parents 102-103

Chapter 22

Figure 1: Guaranteed Funds Per Year, Political Science PhD Programs 145

Chapter 23

Table 1: Stages, Purpose, Types, and Examples of External Grants and Fellowships 150

Chapter 25

Figure 1: Belcher's Ten Types of Claims to Significance 162
Table 1: Strategies to Consider for Putting an Article's Contribution in Context of a Given Journal 163

Chapter 32

Table 1: Organizations Graduate Students Can Pick From 211

Chapter 44

Figure 44.1 Common Characteristics of NTT Positions 284
Figure 44.2 Dos and Don'ts for NTT Positions 287

Chapter 51

Table 1: Summary of Discrimination Response and Reporting Options 335
Table 2: Summary of Sexual Assault Response and Reporting Options 338

Chapter 54

Table 1: Psychology and Social Science Doctorate Recipients by Sex, Ethnicity, and Race 2020 364

Preface

University of North Texas & Past-President of the American Political Science Association

---

This book is something I needed when I first entered graduate school in the 1980s. I was basically clueless. My story is very similar to the stories that the editors of this volume recount. I had no idea what graduate school was like and was poorly prepared to be a successful political science graduate student. At the time I first entered graduate school, I had the wrongheaded assumption that political science was like "contemporary history" which had been told to me by one of my professors at my undergraduate institution. I thought graduate school was just an extension of undergraduate (which, frankly, I skated through). Man, was I wrong!

As this book so rightly points out, not everyone comes to graduate school with the same amount of academic cultural capital. My story is not so different than the experiences recounted in this book. Many questions face students like me who had no idea what graduate school was. I went to Bowling Green State University as an undergraduate—it was the only school I had applied to, because it was not very far, but far enough from my home in Parma, Ohio. I majored in political science and history (I was more a historian than I was a political scientist) and then decided I would go to the University of Michigan to study Russian history (and got an MA in Russian and East European Studies). Something happened to me at U of M, and I realized I wanted to be a political scientist (of all things!), so I ended up entering Michigan State University's PhD program in political science (again, the only school I applied to).

When I arrived in the fall of 1985, I was confronted by the fact that I knew virtually nothing about political science. I did not know anything about research, nor what a seminar was, and barely knew there was something called regression. I did not know what an assistantship was, and I knew nothing about financial aid or scholarships, nor how to navigate the program. Fortunately, I did not incur debt, largely because I worked as a short order cook in addition to my assistantship throughout graduate school (although that was not a smart thing to do). I must say it was a rough time for me. I was also beset with a terrible sense of being an imposter.

All of those challenges I faced are addressed in this book. Issues covered include how to apply in a smart way to a variety schools (not doing what I did) and how to leverage a better assistantship deal than I did. This book offers advice on how to take full advantage of the orientations (unlike me) and how to build a network of mentors and colleagues (who helped me a lot). This volume also offers great advice on how do deal with administration and where to go for help.

There is great advice provided in this book that talks about structuring your class work to help develop your research ideas, that eventually develops into a dissertation topic and a research agenda. There is also an extensive discussion about how to prepare for the comprehensive examinations (as well as guidance as to how to pass those exams).

One of the most important choices that a graduate student can make in preparation to tackle the dreaded thesis or dissertation is the selection of their major advisor, someone who is notable scholar, but also someone the student can work with. There is also very valuable advice offered as to the process by which a dissertation or thesis is put together ranging from selecting a topic, writing a prospectus, collecting data, navigating relationships with advisors and other expectations. And what to do after you are finished (such as figuring out conferencing and the publishing game). Perhaps most importantly, the book covers how to prepare for teaching. When I was a graduate student, I was thrown into a class, and I learned how to teach on my own. This book provides insights on how one prepares to teach. And finally, and perhaps most importantly, how to get a job in academia and beyond.

But there is also personal advice such as balancing parenthood and graduate school, maintaining your health and wellness, and resources that are available on campuses that are often not known about. And significantly, what can the student do if they are victims of harassment.

This book is the most comprehensive resource available to prospective and current graduate students to date. It should be required reading for any student who is taking professionalization workshops or courses in our departments. My life would have been so much easier had this book been available when I was a student. I believe it will have lasting impact on the next generation of graduate students in political science.

Acknowledgements

The editors would first and foremost like to thank all the amazing authors who responded with enthusiasm to our call for proposals. Many of these authors were matched by us and had never collaborated before, but the product has been nothing short of impressive. Books like this can take years to finally pull off and, thanks to our contributors, this book was brought from concept to completion in a single year. We also must thank APSA for their support of this idea. We particularly want to thank Jon Gurstelle and Kim Mealy for their help in all stages of this process—from conceptualization to production. We also appreciate Bennett Grubbs for streamlining this collaboration via APSA Educate and APSA Preprints. The research support provided by the University of South Dakota was also imperative in our endeavor to complete this project. We would like to thank USD students Cohl Turnquist, Aaron Vlasman, and Israt Jahan for their administrative assistance, and Carson Sehr and Madelyn Dewey for editorial assistance.

1 | Nevertheless, We Persisted: Pathways Through Grad School

Kevin G. Lorentz II[1], Daniel J. Mallinson[2], Julia Marin Hellwege[3],
Davin L. Phoenix[4], & J. Cherie Strachan[5]

1. Saginaw Valley State University 2. Penn State Harrisburg
3. University of South Dakota 4. University of California, Irvine 5. The University of Akron

G raduate school is often a new and daunting venture for students. Concepts unique to graduate school such as a "comprehensive exam," "probationary status," or even the Dean of Graduate Studies might be unfamiliar to some graduate students. It is important to recognize that not every student enters graduate school with the same level of academic cultural capital—the accumulation of knowledge, behaviors, and skills that demonstrate social status and cultural competence (Bourdieu 1973).

Research has found that some demographics are more likely to have academic cultural capital when it comes to graduate education—namely white, male students born to at least one parent with a graduate degree. These students begin graduate school better equipped to deal with its challenges because of accumulated social, financial, and cultural resources. First generation and minoritized students often have lower, if any, cultural capital, and therefore face greater obstacles to success (Gardner and Holley 2011; Gildersleeve, Croom, and Vasquez 2011; Holley and Gardner 2012).

A major advantage of cultural capital is greater awareness of the vast hidden curriculum in graduate school. Without cultural capital, it can be easy for students to become lost in the face of a new, high-stakes, graduate-level environment. This edited volume will help students to uncover the hidden curriculum of graduate school and provides the resources necessary for students to navigate it.

Our volume owes gratitude to Jessica McCrory Calarco's book *A Field Guide to Grad School: Uncovering the Hidden Curriculum*, a review of which inspired this project (Mallinson 2022). The idea for this volume emerged, as projects often do, with a conversation between colleagues. Cherie Strachan was serving her final year as reviews editor for the *Journal of Political Science Education* when Dan Mallinson submitted his review of Calarco's book. Dan and Cherie emailed back and forth about how helpful her volume was, as well as how they wished such a resource had been available back when they entered graduate school. As the pair had been, respectively, a female student and a first-generation student, they had faced implicit bias and discrimination that they had not anticipated and had not been prepared to handle.

After several exchanges, Dan and Cherie zeroed in on how they might improve upon Calarco's slim volume based on their own experiences. First, they thought students would benefit from a more in-depth guide specifically tailored to the discipline of political science. Second, they realized that the distinct experiences and needs of minoritized, first-gen, and women students in our discipline are not addressed enough in current discourse. These two realizations inspired this volume in the interest of providing an important service to all of our future colleagues, but also in helping to recruit and retain a more diverse array of students into political science graduate programs. Political science has a well-documented problem with retention of women and minoritized faculty linked to the pernicious "hidden curriculum" as well as structural problems in the discipline and higher education (Bates, Jenkins, and Pflaeger 2012; Bos, Sweet-Cushman, and Schneider 2019; Brown et al. 2020; Crawford and Windsor

2021; Mitchell and Hesli 2013; Lavariega Monforti and Michelson 2008; Windsor, Crawford, and Breuning 2021). If the discipline hopes to fix what is now a game of chutes and ladders which affects diverse scholars in our discipline (Windsor, Crawford, and Breuning 2021), recruiting and retaining more diverse graduate students seems a likely place to start.

Eventually, Dan and Cherie concluded that if such a graduate school resource were to exist, they would probably need to take the initiative to make it happen. Even though both were burdened by teaching during a pandemic (as many of us were) and busy with other academic projects and important life events (one with a new baby on the way, the other with an empty nest while starting a new job), they managed to find good colleagues to help with an edited collection. They then pitched the project to APSA and ensured that the final volume included the major topics that they hoped to pass on to grad students.

The process moved quickly. Dan and Cherie recognized their limitations, not only in terms of time and energy but in terms of their own intersectional identities and ability to ensure that the call for chapters resonated with people across all segments of the discipline at all stages of their careers. They reached out to colleagues known for their dedication to student mentorship and disciplinary service as well as for their commitment to diversity, equity, and inclusion. They were so happy when these colleagues—Julia Marin Hellwege, Davin Phoenix, and Kevin Lorentz—enthusiastically signed up for this project. They all agree that this volume may well be one of the most important contributions to the discipline that they will make over the course of their collective careers.

When this group pitched the project to APSA, they were met with support and encouragement. This project owes a debt of thanks to Director of Publishing Jon Gurstelle and Senior Director of Diversity and Inclusion Kimberly Mealy for their early support and for their help with revising and improving upon the initial prospectus and call for chapters. The response to the call for chapters was overwhelming. There are 150 authors on this project, and together they allow for a broad representation of the overarching political science discipline. We also owe a debt of gratitude to Madelyn Dewey for her expert work in formatting the book and designing the cover.

Editors' Own Experiences

Kevin: Much to the annoyance of my spouse, I love to bring along a guidebook whenever we visit someplace new. My husband always says this takes the "fun" out of exploring, but I find even a short preview makes me better prepared to take in the sights and sounds. Looking back, I think I should have consulted a guidebook before entering graduate school; unfortunately, one tailored to the political science graduate journey just didn't exist.

That desire (and need) led me to jump at the opportunity to edit this book. In preparation, I created a list of "things I wish I knew" before starting my graduate school career. Topping that list, not surprisingly, were items like understanding the application process better, selecting an advisor, and having a better idea of the academic and non-academic job markets. True, I did learn on the fly, and I was fortunate to have great mentors and peers along the way to share their wisdom and experience. It just would have been great to know some of this information before I dove in!

But my list also included advice that I desperately wished I had known before entering my first graduate program. I wish someone had told me the importance of a graduate program's "fit." I wish I knew just how stressful graduate school was—mentally, emotionally, and financially. On more than one occasion, too, I just didn't know how to handle something, and certainly didn't know what resources (if any) may have been available to me. That's part of this book's goal: to help you navigate the "hidden curriculum," or the stuff that they don't tell you about graduate school.

This isn't to say that I have regrets about graduate school. In fact, I look back on those six years fondly. I was fortunate to work with numerous people who are now dear friends, colleagues, and research collaborators. I have a professional network that spans the breadth of political science, and all the support that comes with such a network, too. (Indeed, I'm co-editing this volume with a former mentor!) I learned a lot (academically, personally, and professionally). And my career today wouldn't be possible without my graduate degree.

So, if I can provide one piece of advice? It doesn't hurt to bring a guide(book) along your graduate school journey. I wish you the best and much success!

Dan: I'm a first generation kid all around. Neither of my parents went to college, nor did they know anything about graduate school. I'm one of those "Limbo" kids (Lubrano 2004) growing up in a majority white suburban, and largely wealthy, school district with blue collar parents. My dad had his own construction business before a major heart attack pushed him into a white collar job as a building inspector. My mom also worked a "white collar" job, but as an administrative assistant. Steady paychecks meant that we didn't face some of the financial uncertainties that blue collar families face, but my parents still acted their roots. Then, my dad died when I was 13 and things became less secure. I cycled through a series of dream careers in high school—pastor, electrical engineer, lawyer, airman—all of which required at least a college degree. To this day I cannot even explain why I applied to the six undergraduate institutions that I did (and not others), but I can say that I had no idea what I was doing.

That lack of confidence that I'm taking the right steps follows me to this day. I decided in my undergraduate years that I wanted to teach political science at a college, but no PhD programs wanted me that first go around. When applying to grad school the first time, I balanced prestige (meaning I had heard of the place…), which was (somewhat) more obvious, and geographic location, but I received little guidance about what a good PhD program would be. I had no idea how to find one that fit me well. Hell, I didn't even know what I wanted from my academic career beyond wanting to teach. All I knew was that I needed a PhD. The second time I applied, after obtaining my masters, I was more successful, but equally clueless about how academia actually worked. I chose to go to Penn State because my stipend would stretch further there due to cost of living (blue collar roots, woot) and I was wooed by their recruitment weekend. I had no idea of Penn State's standing or its "placement" record. I had a vague idea that I wanted to do state politics, but not who I wanted to work with. I managed to figure things out as I went along, but I also didn't face many of the disadvantages that others experience in graduate school (racism and sexism, among others).

Even now, on the tenure track, I continue to feel in "Limbo;" out of place. There is still a hidden curriculum everywhere. I know very little about wine or fine liquor like my colleagues (and bosses) with white collar backgrounds. I'm still trying to navigate balancing the expectations of others (I'm on the tenure track) with what I want to invest my time in. I am still drawn to free food, just like I was as a graduate student. When I travel to a conference, I am very careful to make sure I stay under budget and I basically ignore any opportunities that would require me to pay out of pocket. I hate wearing a suit and feel more comfortable in blue jeans. My wife cuts the whole family's hair. I'm taking up woodworking as a hobby, like my dad.

Each step of the way in my academic journey has felt like groping around in the dark for clues to what I should be doing and what is valued. It has worked out for me and my journey has been largely positive. I thrived personally in grad school. I met my wife and we had our first son. I had a stronger community among fellow grad students then, than I do now among peers. But I know first-hand such positives are not the case for everyone. I have seen students abused (mentally, verbally, emotionally), discouraged, and neglected. I have seen bad program culture harm people and ruin careers before they even started. My goal in this book is to advance the work going on throughout our discipline to make the culture better. Some days it feels like things are advancing, then others it feels like we're moving backwards. But perhaps the most gratifying thing that I have heard over and over as we've worked on this book is "I wish I had this in grad school." The book does not pretend to cover every nook and cranny of the hidden curriculum, but I hope it improves even one student's grad school experience.

Julia: When I was in first grade, we were asked what we wanted to be when we grew up. I said I wanted to be a professor. When prompted as to how one might become a professor, I reportedly answered: "first you go to school for a long time, then you go to more school, and then you write a book." My mom always wondered how I would have known about graduate school or writing a dissertation given that I had no friends or family in academia. Unfortunately, by the time I was ready to apply for graduate school, I still did not know much more about how graduate school works.

As an immigrant in the United States and a first-generation college graduate, I didn't know much about how to achieve my goal to become a professor. I did know that higher education in the United States is expensive and so part of my decision on where I ultimately attended college (Colorado Mesa University) was to have a relatively cheaper option (than my first choice) so I could afford to go to graduate school. Not knowing that I could apply directly to a PhD program, I applied for a master's program first. I recall making a phone call to check in on my application and to introduce myself. The professor on the other end said they weren't sure about my application: "Sure, you have a great GPA, but it's not like you went to Michigan." I remember feeling deflated, but once I was finally accepted, I was determined to prove myself.

The students in the master's program were regularly ignored and dismissed, especially students like myself who had no funding. It was generally assumed that we were not interested in continuing to the PhD program. Further, my early advisor and comprehensive exam committee chair was a new professor, leaving me with little guidance. By the time I was admitted to the PhD program, starting my third year, few of the faculty members knew who I was. I was lucky that a senior faculty member took me under her wing and had me assigned as her graduate assistant. In the coming year, I thought I was excelling in the program. My advisor was encouraging on my "field paper," and I was feeling very confident…until he left. The department chair assured me that after summer break, I would be able to defend my paper and move forward. Come fall, he told me he had no recollection of the conversation and that the other likely faculty member who could advise me was not on board with my paper. Long story short, I abandoned my project, changed sub-fields entirely, and got a new advisor.

The second half of my graduate school experience was smoother than the beginning. I thoroughly enjoyed the work I did; however, the work was substantial. I had 40 hours of assistantships and teaching assignments. I also served as our department's graduate student association president and was the primary caretaker for my younger brother who was a young teenager at the time. While I can confidently say that I made many friends in grad school, there was also significant turmoil. From fellow students who called on the department chair to resolve office conflicts rather than resolving them as adults, to faculty members suggesting some of the students, with me in the lead, were ostracizing other students because they are Latino—all the while not recognizing me as a Latina—to faculty treating students as pawns in their conflicts, arguing we were being "overworked" despite us earning not only pay but publication credit.

Yes. Graduate school is hard, and navigating graduate school was not easy. However, and as I told my husband at one of those lower points, in my view my worst day doing what I do, still felt (and still feels today) better than I can imagine my best day doing anything else. I love my job today. I had a great experience on the job market because of the experiences and opportunities I had in graduate school. Of course, my favorite memories from graduate school were those long Saturdays at the Flying Star restaurant working away the day with my very best friends, with piles of books and papers around us, bouncing ideas, lamenting, and writing Stata code and sentences intermittently. Navigating graduate school was certainly more than just "going to school" and "writing a book," although, at the end of the day, it also was just that.

Davin: When I think back to my grad school experience, I'm frankly taken back by how unprepared I was for what I was getting myself into. How hard can it be, I thought, so naively. I got through college pretty well, pitfalls and all. This is just the next step up from that right? Oh, how very wrong.

My grad school experience gave me some of my most cherished relationships, and some moments when I've never felt more isolated. Some momentous triumphs, and some of my darkest hours. When my journey ended, I felt a satisfying payoff to many years' worth of sacrifices, exhaustive work, and lessons learned. But a non-trivial portion of my time in grad school was spent "floating"—drifting from one tentpole to another without a clear sense of my larger research trajectory, without confidence that I belonged in my program or the discipline.

To get out of this rut, I had to step out of my comfort zone and admit to myself and trusted advisers and peers that I felt adrift. Work with my adviser to develop a concrete action plan for learning the "hidden curriculum" of how to navigate this unknown world. Lean on my support system in a way that was scary because it made me feel so vulnerable, but ultimately necessary.

I know that many people advancing through a PhD program face the same challenges. And these are especially pronounced for folks like me who are first-generation or carrying one or more identities that are underrepresented or underserved within the discipline. I hope this guidebook can reassure people that they're not alone in facing these challenges, help them craft proactive strategies to deal with them in a healthy manner, and surface some of the structural issues within graduate programs that perpetuate inequities, increasing our collective sense of urgency to work in concert to eradicate them. Lofty goals? Yes. But if we can help people avoid floating and feel like they're navigating their journey on solid ground, we've done a good thing.

Cherie: As much as I lament not having access to a collection like this one when I was a political science graduate student, I don't think it was possible to produce such a volume in the mid-1990s. At that point, advice about how to pursue a graduate degree was passed down from political science faculty to those they chose to mentor. And we were not self-reflective enough either in academia writ large or as a discipline to realize that, simply given the weight of demographics, this informal practice largely meant older white men of means mentoring younger white men of means, in a self-perpetuating loop. I know that I personally, as a woman with a working-class socioeconomic status, would not have gone on to earn a doctorate if one of those men, Dan Shea, now chair of the Department of Government at Colby College, had not only encouraged me to do so—but was also incredibly generous with his time—mentoring me, teaching me how to apply to doctoral programs, and writing me letters of recommendation. What kind of career and life would I have had, if serendipity had not intervened, and if Dan had not been hired to fill an assistant professor line when I was an MA student earning a certificate in applied politics at The University of Akron? I don't know where I would be, but it certainly would not have entailed a fulfilling career as a tenured full professor of political science.

Yet mentoring students who don't fit the "typical" political science demographic profile should not be left to chance encounters with professors who see their potential and mentor them. Moreover, mentoring from even the most generous white men at the time could not have addressed elements of the "hidden curriculum" that disrupt the learning experiences and career trajectories of women and those with minoritized and intersectional identities. It can be challenging and risky for minoritized and women professors to address issues of implicit bias, discrimination, and harassment directly. This was especially the case prior to social activism like the #MeToo Movement. Those who did speak up were subject to social and professional sanctions, as many academics, like those in so many other professions, were just not ready to admit that inclusion and equity were a problem. Stories were not shared openly, which not only limited the ability to mentor students with intersectional identities, but also limited the ability to seek policy changes that helped institutions of higher education and professional associations adopt effective reforms.

Hence, the only "direct" advice I received along these lines was from a professor from my undergraduate program, who upon learning I planned to go on for a PhD, simply warned me that women in political science needed to "be careful," especially at conferences. I got my first hint of what that meant two weeks into my doctoral program, when the only two advanced women students in the entire program dragged me aside to give me advice on navigating (i.e., avoiding being misogynistically berated and/or physically harassed) by a certain professor on campus. Other issues I learned to navigate on my own. When I started to attend conferences, for example, I quickly noticed that at least some of my male colleagues would not ask serious questions about my research and current projects, until after learning that I was not only married, but also very happily married and monogamous. I adapted and quickly began to lead with this information when I met new colleagues, immediately dropping clues about my happily married status into informal conversations. In doing so, I found a solution that worked for me personally, but to do so, I leveraged my privilege as a cisgender, heterosexual, married woman to create an informal remedy that was not available to many others.

We may not be perfect, but the discipline has come a long way since the 1990s. APSA has a code of conduct and an ombudsperson, and there are now enough diverse tenured professors in our discipline that the tide has shifted. At least some people can risk telling their stories—like those I shared above—

without worrying that their efforts to transform the discipline through transparency will be career-ending. In the 1990s, this project would simply not have been possible because there were too few BIPOC and women and other minoritized faculty to write the chapters, and even fewer who would have risked their career to openly and honestly address issues related to diversity, equity, and inclusion. Yet in 2022, we were inundated with brave colleagues willing to provide blunt, pragmatic advice gleaned from their own lived experiences. I am grateful that my career has spanned this transformation of academia and political science. I hope that the edited collection we offer here will help to further lay bare the "hidden curriculum" of graduate school and, by doing so, will result in a more welcoming and inclusive educational and professional experiences for us all.

Plan of the Book

The chapters that follow address both common situations that graduate students will encounter (e.g., the application process; navigating classes, exams, and the dissertation; securing a job post-degree), but also the "hidden" curriculum less likely to be openly talked about: how to deal with harassment, discrimination, implicit biases, and other obstacles to diversity, equity and inclusion in the discipline and academia. Each chapter is written as a short encyclopedic entry, giving you a quick summary of the topic and advice and resources for how to navigate challenges associated with it. Given the guidebook nature of this project, authors offer up an insider's account, synthesizing standing empirical literature and anecdotal accounts. Each chapter also contains references to other chapters in the guide, and we encourage you to consult chapters in the volume as they become relevant to you throughout your graduate school journey.

The book proceeds as follows: first, the volume surveys the application process, including how to choose a graduate program, how to finance your graduate degree, filling out applications, and special considerations for seasoned professionals returning to school. Next, several chapters discuss what happens after you're admitted to a graduate program, from orientation to the dissertation. These chapters run the gauntlet of your graduate school journey and also discuss how to manage your personal life alongside your academic studies. The next three sections cover the most common professional development pursuits: scholarship, teaching, and service. Contributors provide best practices, tips, and suggestions for how to bolster your research credentials, prepare for your first teaching experience, and how you can engage in the larger discipline as a graduate student.

We then turn to discussing the job market and the various careers that are available to you post-graduation. Some chapters discuss how to prepare for specific careers in academia but also outside of the academe, while others provide guidance on how to prepare job applications and build your professional network beyond your graduate program cohort. The next two sections discuss more of the "hidden" curriculum, including the prevailing culture in your graduate school and the larger profession. Chapters explore concerns for various minoritized and underrepresented populations, offering anecdotes, recommendations, and resources, should you need them. Finally, the volume concludes with a larger discussion about managing your health (physical, emotional, and mental) and well-being in graduate school.

References

Bates, Stephen, Laura Jenkins, and Zoe Pflaeger. 2012. "Women in the Profession: The Composition of UK Political Science Departments by Sex." *Politics* 32(3): 139-152.

Bourdieu, Pierre. 1973. "Cultural Reproduction and Social Reproduction." In *Knowledge, Education, and Cultural Change*, ed. Richard Brown, 71-112. London: Routledge.

Bos, Angela L., Jennie Sweet-Cushman, and Monica C. Schneider. 2019. "Family-Friendly Academic Conferences: A Missing Link to Fix the 'Leaky Pipeline'?" *Politics, Groups, and Identities* 7(3): 748-758.

Brown, Nadia E., Yusaku Hoiuchi, Mala Htun, and David Samuels. 2020. "Gender Gaps in Perceptions of Political Science Journals." *PS: Political Science & Politics* 53(1): 114-121.

Calarco, Jessica McCrory. 2021. *A Field Guide to Grad School*. Princeton, NJ: Princeton University Press.

Crawford, Kerry F. and Leah C. Windsor. 2021. *The PhD Parenthood Trap*. Washington, DC: Georgetown University Press.

Gardner, Susan K. and Karri A. Holley. 2011. "'Those Invisible Barriers are Real': The Progression of First-Generation Students Through Doctoral Education." *Equity & Excellence in Education* 44(1): 77-92.

Gildersleeve, Ryan Evely, Natasha N. Croom, and Philip L. Vasquez. 2011. "'Am I Going Crazy?': A Critical Race Analysis of Doctoral Education." *Equity & Excellence in Education* 44(1): 93-114.

Holley, Karri A. and Susan Gardner. 2012. "Navigating the Pipeline: How Socio-Cultural Influences Impact First-Generation Doctoral Students." *Journal of Diversity in Higher Education* 5(2): 112-121.

Lavariega Monforti, Jessica and Melissa R. Michelson. 2008. "Diagnosing the Leaky Pipeline: Continuing Barriers to the Retention of Latinas and Latinos in Political Science." *PS: Political Science & Politics 41(1): 161-166.*

Mallinson, Daniel J. 2022. "Review of A Field Guide to Grad School: Uncovering the Hidden Curriculum." *Journal of Political Science Education* 17(sup1): 981-982.

Mitchell, Sara McLaughlin and Vicki L. Hesli. 2013. "Women Don't Ask? Women Don't Say No? Bargaining and Service in the Political Science Profession." *PS: Political Science & Politics* 46(2): 355-369.

Windsor, Leah Cathryn, Kerry F. Crawford, and Marjike Breuning. 2021. "Not a Leaky Pipeline! Academic Success is a Game of Chutes and Ladders." *PS: Political Science & Politics* 54(3): 509-512.

The Application Process

2

How to Get In: A Roadmap for Navigating Decision-Making and the Application Process

Kelly Piazza,[1] Chris Culver,[1] & Lynne Chandler-Garcia[1]

1. United States Air Force Academy*

*DISCLAIMER: The views expressed in this article, book, or presentation are those of the author and do not necessarily reflect the official policy or position of the United States Air Force Academy, the Air Force, the Department of Defense, or the U.S. Government. PA#: USAFA-DF-2022-7

KEYWORDS: Master's, Doctoral Degree, Curriculum Vitae.

Whether to Go to Graduate School

Students sometimes pursue graduate school as a default step post-undergraduate education because they are uncertain about the future, afraid that the job market is poor (see Chapter 34), or are looking to defer academic loans. While the prospect of graduating from college can be daunting, it is important that you carefully consider your career aspirations before applying to graduate school. There are a variety of degree programs and educational paths that differentially prepare students for their career goals.

Master's Versus Doctoral Degrees

The first decision you need make is between applying to a *master's* and a *doctoral degree* program. Often, students see these degrees as steppingstones on the same path. While this perception may be grounded in truth in some cases, these degree programs often provide students with distinct experiences, training, and opportunities with different career paths in mind. A master's degree in political science or in a related professional, interdisciplinary degree program (public policy, public administration, or international affairs) prepares you to apply your understanding of the discipline in practical arenas as a consumer—rather than as a producer—of knowledge. This degree type and associated training is desirable for several careers in government service at the federal, state, and local levels as well as for jobs at non-profits, think tanks, and in international affairs. Graduates of political science master's programs can also find positions as lobbyists, consultants, and journalists, just to name a few. Put bluntly, master's degree programs are often specifically designed to prepare students for employment outside of academics or research.

A doctoral degree in political science prepares you well to be a producer of political knowledge through systematic research. This degree type and associated training are especially desirable for careers as an educator, researcher, or analyst. If these are your goals, you should strongly consider applying directly to a doctoral program, many of which do not require or even award master's degrees.

Determining whether to apply to a master's or doctoral degree program requires both meaningful introspection about your personal strengths and aspirations as well as research about educational requirements of desired careers. Too often, students view degrees with a hierarchical mindset and a goal to get to the "top," without recognizing the different purposes that they serve. In some fields, the median earnings for those with professional master's degrees are higher than those with doctoral degrees, and this is particularly true in the social sciences. Instead of trying to reach the "top" of the degree chain, consider your long-term career aspirations and choose the path that is most likely to help you achieve them.

When to Go to Graduate School

After deciding whether to apply to master's or doctoral degree programs, the second decision is when to go to graduate school, accounting for both financial and family planning considerations. Some students prefer to enter graduate school immediately following graduation from their undergraduate institution, while others decide to enter the job market and then return to school in later career stages. In the following, we explore the advantages and disadvantages of various timing decisions.

Advantages of Going Early

There are several advantages to entering graduate school early in one's life. Going to graduate school immediately following college can be a good decision for those whose desired careers require a master's or PhD as the minimum education.

If you participated in a rigorous undergraduate research program and are confident about the specific topics you wish to study (and about the relevance of these topics to your career aspirations), you might find it advantageous to continue your studies without a break.

Pursuing graduate school immediately after college is also beneficial in the sense that you will maintain the momentum of the student mindset. Students who are fresh from undergrad might not be as intimidated by the substantial amount of reading and writing required.

Students applying to graduate school immediately after college likely have current relationships with faculty members who can write letters of recommendation and provide guidance on the choice of program and school. If you delay graduate school, be sure to ask your undergraduate professors for letters of recommendation before graduating so that your professors remember and can comment on personal attributes such as class participation and outstanding assignments.

Recognizing the significant time commitment of graduate education, students who want to finish graduate school before starting a career or a family may find it advantageous to complete graduate work as soon as possible. A master's degree in political science usually takes a full-time student one and a half to two years and a part-time student three to four years. A doctoral degree in political science usually takes those with a master's degree an additional four to seven years and those without a master's degree six to 10 years, on average, with some students taking even longer depending on how long dissertation research takes.

Advantages of Waiting

There are also many good reasons to wait and take some years off between college and graduate school. Prospective students who begin graduate school with some work experience under their belts are often better able to tailor their graduate studies towards their career goals. Additionally, classes may be more meaningful when you have work experiences that relate to the material under study. Students without professional experience might find themselves wandering and sampling classes, which can be expensive in terms of time and money.

Practically speaking, waiting a year or two provides more time to study for the GRE, visit universities, and make connections with potential future professors. These connections can be extremely important because many admissions committees are looking for students who have already identified professors under whom they would like to work.

Another good reason to wait to apply to graduate school is to build the time management skills, maturity, and emotional strength required to complete a graduate degree. Time management skills are imperative when a research paper is due the same week an 800-page book is assigned, and 50 undergraduate papers need to be graded (a workload not uncommon for political science graduate students, especially in doctoral programs). Additionally, some younger students may find themselves at a disadvantage in the classroom when political debates become heated and even fierce. Older students, who have had more "real world" experiences, are often more capable of being assertive in the classroom while maintaining the professionalism needed to engage in academic debate. This type of emotional intelligence developed through work experience may also be helpful in handling the rejections that inevitably come with submitting work to political science journals and conferences.

Finally, a primary reason for entering the workforce before graduate school is to earn and save money. Graduate school can be expensive and having a nest egg can be advantageous. (For additional discussions about applying to graduate later in life, see Chapter 5. See also Chapter 17 for further tips and suggestions regarding time management.)

Financial Considerations

When deciding whether to attend graduate school, financial considerations are paramount. A master's or doctoral degree has the potential to increase your future earnings. While those holding a master's degree in political science are likely to make significantly more than those with a bachelor's degree, the pay differential between a master's degree and a doctoral degree depends on the occupation. University professors with a PhD in political science tend to make substantially more than those with a conventional master's degree in political science, but in other occupations such as within the government, a PhD might not equate to better income.

While future payoffs are important to consider, so is the current cost of the degree. Tuition costs vary widely among institutions, with some programs costing as little as $20,000 and others costing as much as $50,000. Carefully research tuition costs as well as fees. Opportunities for fellowships, research assistantships, and teaching assistantships may also be available and can help cover costs. You should also consider the amount of student loan debt that will accumulate through the course of graduate studies. Before deciding to enter a graduate program, it is critical to review your financial standing and budget for the next two to ten years. Students with families will have special budgetary considerations.

Family Considerations

Deciding to attend graduate school should be a part of your larger plans for life, which include your career and family. Some potential students decide to go to graduate school before starting a family to focus on academia. Others, however, do not want to defer having a family for the extended time it takes to complete a graduate degree, especially a PhD. Thus, deciding to undertake graduate school with a family requires special considerations. Chapter 16 provides an in-depth analysis of these special considerations, so we will just provide some overarching and general guidance here: it is important to weigh family needs and priorities in the decision-making process and to recognize that graduate school is costly, both from a financial and time perspective; post-graduate school career opportunities (especially on the tenure track) may require geographic flexibility and sacrifice.

Where to Go to Graduate School

After deciding whether to apply to master's or doctoral degree programs and determining the "right time" to pursue graduate studies, the third decision involves selecting specific programs that align with your career goals and reflect timing considerations. As you research potential graduate programs, your goal should not be to find the best program as determined by reputable program rankings, but to find the program that is the best fit for your career goals, financial and family considerations, and personal interests or strengths. When you find programs that are a good fit, you will likely start to develop the excitement and motivation that will carry you through the application process.

How to Go to Graduate School

The Application Process and Components

There are several important components of political science graduate school applications. Although the specific requirements vary across schools and programs, most require, at minimum, a cover letter, a *curriculum vitae* (CV), a personal statement, a writing sample, and letters of recommendation. As you begin to prepare these materials, there are several important considerations to keep in mind.

First, unlike most undergraduate admission committees that sort through tens of thousands of applications with standardized and objective processes, most political science graduate program admissions committees evaluate applications with a more personal and potentially subjective process. These committees are not always looking for the "best" candidate as determined by standard, objective measures, but rather for the candidates that effectively communicate that they are the best fits for their program and faculty. The best way for applicants to find success in this process is to be authentic in communicating their goals and, particularly, the alignment between their goals and the program to which they are applying.

Second, you should acknowledge that the admissions committee is trying to learn who you are, but that they only have your application from which to work. In most cases, these committees will make determinations without ever meeting you in person. Even in the rare cases where they use interviews, committees will decide whether to conduct interviews based on the contents of your application.

These first two points require you to adopt a narrative-oriented approach to how you build your application. Your goal is not just to develop a collection of stand-alone application components but rather to leverage these components to craft a narrative. Your narrative should tell a story of who you are, what you have done, where you are going, and how your degree program of interest fits into that story. Through your cover letter, CV, essays, and all the other components of your application, you'll need to build a picture of your narrative in the minds of the committee members who are reading it. They are trying to distinguish between the students who only get good grades and the students who will enhance the reputation of their institution while bringing authentic intellectual curiosity to their classrooms and research. That decision is often not just based on a collection of accolades, accomplishments, or objective measures (though these are all important), but on a mental picture of who you are and where you are going as communicated on paper. You'll need to start by figuring out the answers to those questions for yourself before communicating that narrative through your application components.

As you craft this narrative, you should not shy away from communicating parts of your identity that have shaped your goals, values, perspectives, and experiences. Like many other areas in society, the discipline of political science has historically underrepresented minoritized groups, but many programs are actively looking to cultivate a more diverse student and faculty population that better represents the society in which we live. Those from minoritized populations or with intersectional identities that have authentically shaped their experience should feel comfortable communicating the connection between their identity and their academic and professional plans. You can also lean into your identity as you communicate the fit between your narrative and your program of interest. Chapters 54 through 61 will discuss in more depth concerns, thoughts, suggestions, and challenges for students from various backgrounds.

Third, it is important to develop drafts of each of the application materials early on in your process to provide ample time for edits and revision. Use the remaining time before application due dates to better tailor your materials to each school to which you are applying, and to capitalize on the limited space provided in each document to craft a unique and comprehensive narrative for the committee to evaluate. It is similarly important to select and communicate school and program, subfield, and/or concentration selections with letter of recommendation writers early so that they, too, have ample time to prepare thoughtful letters of recommendation tailored for each application.

The following subsections outline important, but perhaps not obvious, application material considerations learned through years of advising undergraduate students applying for graduate studies in political science.

The Cover Letter

The cover letter should serve as an introduction to your application and should consist of a one-page overview of the content that you will elaborate upon in additional application materials. More pointedly, the cover letter should: (1) include a brief introduction to you, the applicant, (2) identify the particular program, subfield, and/or concentration to which you are applying, (3) describe your academic and professional goals while positing that these have motivated your decision to apply, (4) describe the experiences that you have had that have prepared your for success in the selected program, subfield, and/or concentration, and (5) thank the committee for their consideration and provide your contact information for the committee to use to reach you with any outstanding questions.

The Curriculum Vitae (CV)

The curriculum vitae (CV) should outline your education, employment and professional experience, awards and selection for honorable programs, academic achievements and conference participation, extracurricular activities, service experiences, and academic references in separate, clearly distinguished sections. Through each of these sections, you have the opportunity to convince those evaluating your application of your preparedness for graduate studies.

Through our experience advising graduate student applicants, we have found that a common shortcoming of curricula vitae is the use of undefined acronyms and the lack of sufficient explanations of programs, positions, and experiences, assuming committee familiarity. With this mind, we strongly recommend that you solicit feedback prior to submission. If the person reviewing your application raises questions about acronyms, programs, positions, or experiences, this should signal to you that your document requires some additional attention before submission. Relatedly, you should use descriptions of content on your curriculum vitae to highlight your preparedness for graduate studies on the basis of content and disciplinary exposure, technical training (e.g., research methods and language proficiencies), professional and leadership experience, etc.

In terms of other general advice, we strongly urge applicants to use consistent and visually appealing formatting, to eliminate pre-college content, and to use reverse chronological ordering of content within sections.

The Personal Statement

The personal statement should consist of a narrative that addresses the following questions in sequence:
- Who are you?
- What are your academic or professional goals?
- How will graduate studies at the specific school (and in the particular program to which you are applying) equip you with the training and experience necessary to help you achieve your professional goals?

In your response to these questions, you should convince those evaluating your application of the sincerity of your interest in and ability to succeed in their program, as well as the alignment between the program that you are applying for and your academic and professional aspirations, and the unique and diverse qualities and perspectives that you will bring to their program.

A well-crafted personal statement requires deep introspection, iterative drafts, and the soliciting and incorporation of feedback. To get you started, we recommend considering the following prompts:
- What shapes your identity?
- Briefly describe one moment in your life when you were the best version of yourself.
- Fill in the blank: In ten years, I want to be _____.
- What is one thing you could do today to make your world a slightly better place?
- If you had your senator's ear and one minute to propose a policy or law that could make the United States a better nation, what would you propose?
- What have you accomplished?

The Writing Sample

The writing sample provides the search committee with an opportunity to evaluate your ability to think critically about big questions in political science, develop research questions informed but unanswered by existing literature, construct and execute an appropriate research design, identify implications of research findings and directions for future research, and communicate effectively in writing.

While it is not essential for the writing sample to reflect the research interests that you espouse in your cover letter and personal statement, alignment may help to signal the sincerity of your academic passions as communicated in other application materials.

Letters of Recommendation

Most graduate school applications require applicants to submit several letters of recommendation to accompany application materials prepared by you, the applicant. It is important to select letter writers who know you well on both a professional and personal level, have the bandwidth to write you a high-quality letter, have knowledge of and expertise in political science, and are detail oriented. While your letter writers are ultimately responsible for drafting this application component, there are several things that you can do to ensure that your letter writers are well positioned to craft letters that reflect positively on you as a candidate and are aligned with the application materials that you have put together.

First, it is important to discuss specific school and program selections with your letter writers and to provide them with your rationale for selecting these school and program selections (verbally and in the writing of your own application materials). This fosters alignment across all application materials, resulting in a cohesive application package. Second, writing letters of recommendation, when done well, can be a time-consuming task. It is important that you give those agreeing to write you letters of recommendation ample time to put together tailored letters for the different schools and programs to which you are applying. Third, your letter writers likely have many other obligations on their plates. It is important to provide your letter writers with regular reminders of upcoming deadlines to ensure that your applications are complete for submission deadlines.

Conclusion

Prospective political science graduate students should engage in deep introspection to determine whether or not graduate studies are appropriate based on career aspirations, timing, and financial and family considerations. If, on the basis of these factors, you decide to pursue graduate studies, it is important to select programs that inspire excitement and motivation throughout the application process. It is important to develop application materials early and with feedback that adequately reflect the narrative of who you are, what you have done, where you are going, and how your degree program of interest fits into that story. When done well, you should be confident in the quality of your application and your prospects for admission. Good luck!

3

Financial Concerns: Taking on Student Loans, Graduate Assistant Positions, and Funding Considerations

Courtney N. Haun[1] & Jennifer Schenk Sacco[2]

1. Samford University 2. Quinnipiac University

KEYWORDS: Financial Pitfalls, Funding Opportunities.

Introduction

Financial concerns can arise when it comes to covering the costs of a graduate program in political science and landing a job post-graduation. This chapter aims to identify ways students can mitigate financial challenges by considering their personal financial situations and the circumstances of their prospective academic institutions. Common experiences during graduate school have also revealed the need to highlight issues that can hinder academic and career success, such as student exploitation. Time is a valuable commodity, and students should consider the amount of time spent completing a program and other prospective obligations that come along with the journey to degree completion, such as graduate assistantships. We argue that financial planning is of great importance before committing to a political science graduate program. In the following, we will discuss the potential financial burden of graduate school, financing options and pitfalls, and strategies for avoiding a high debt burden for graduate studies.

Graduate School Costs and Future Pay

In the United States (US), the average cost of a political science graduate program is estimated at $20,000 per year (Warren 2021). Students who pursue this degree option typically enter the workforce in a government setting (50% in 2020), or a professional, scientific, and technical services setting (21% in 2020) (BLS 2020). Payscale (2021) has reported that average salaries for master's degrees in political science, public administration, and public policy range from $65,000–$72,000 a year, and a PhD in political science has an average annual wage of $85,000. BLS (2020) data shows that employment for political scientist jobs is expected to grow 9% from 2020–2030, equating to roughly 600 new positions and totaling 7,600 for projected employment. In addition to the sticker price and expected future salary, it is essential to compare the cost of living in the city you are considering, as it makes a difference in the lifestyle you will be able to afford and/or the amount you need to borrow while completing your degree. Major metro and coastal areas are generally significantly more expensive than outlying areas. Consulting an online cost of living calculator such as the one provided by Bankrate[1] is essential to understand the true cost of your degree.

Future Prospects

Three-quarters of all faculty positions are not on the tenure track, according to a 2018 analysis by the American Association of University Professors (Flaherty 2018). In 1980, 70% of faculty were tenured or tenure-eligible. Today, 75% are not tenure eligible, and 47% hold "part-time" positions (AFT 2020). Not having the protection of tenure means less academic freedom and reliance on year-to-year or short multi-year contracts, even if the compensation is sufficient. Tenure track positions are more common at research-focused institutions, but they still only make up about one-third of faculty at those institutions (Flaherty, 2018). Life as contingent faculty can entail challenging situations, making it even harder to pay down debt accrued during a graduate program (see Chapter 44). According to a 2019 survey of contingent faculty, the American Federation of Teachers (2020) reports that one-third of the 3,076 contingent faculty respondents earned less than $25,000 a year, placing them below the poverty line for a family of four. Only 15% reported they could comfortably cover their basic monthly expenses, fewer than half had access to employer-provided health insurance, and nearly one-fifth relied on Medicaid. Additionally, 41% reported they do not know if they will have a teaching position until one month before the start of an academic year, 75% work on term-to-term appointments, and 37% report they cannot see a path to retirement, though 64% of respondents were over the age of 50. Almost 40% of contingent faculty responded that they had been teaching in higher education for more than 15 years (AFT 2020).

Financial Packages

Full funding packages for political science PhD students generally span a fixed number of years (four¬ to five), and may include some combination of tuition, a monthly living stipend, medical insurance, funding for study materials, and/or travel stipend. In addition to such benefits, contracts may require maintenance of a minimum GPA and teaching of undergraduates (Warren 2021). In 2017, 53.5% of doctoral students received some sort of financial assistance (Warren 2021). Sources of funding for graduate degrees that do not require repayment are fellowships, scholarships, stipends, grants, and assistantships (though you "repay" assistantships by working). Other public and private loans require repayment, and thus should be minimized to the greatest extent possible. It takes an average of four to eight years to complete a PhD in political science. Even students who enter with full funding packages may need to find other sources once those initial packages run out. Many dissertating students take on teaching assistantships and/or apply for funding from external agencies after an initial research fellowship ends.[2] Be aware, teaching assistantships may lengthen your time in graduate school and thus increase the total cost of your degree, as they are time spent not working on a dissertation nor earning a full-time salary. However, as the market for full-time positions after graduation has become more competitive, teaching experience and evidence of teaching effectiveness is widely expected for full-time applicants. Other sources of income for graduate students include tutoring, family support, and part-time jobs. While part-time jobs and tutoring may be necessary to keep you afloat financially, they may also impede progress on your degree and are unlikely to be of benefit to you on your curriculum vitae.

Loan Pitfalls

One of the biggest possible *financial pitfalls* is that, unlike undergraduate loan programs, the federal Grad Plus loan program, created in 2005, has no fixed limit on what you can borrow (Korn and Fuller 2021). You can even borrow for living expenses on top of tuition and fees. Because of this, loan amounts can grow very steeply over the course of four to eight years of doctoral studies. This loan program is what makes offering master's degrees so enticing to universities—students have a way to pay for them, albeit with borrowed money. For the first time, in 2020-2021, graduate students are on track to borrow as much as undergraduate students in the same year (NCES 2018). Average total loan balances (including undergraduate debt, excluding Parent PLUS loans) for students who complete a PhD in any field outside of education doubled between 1999-2000 and 2016-2017, from $48k to $99k in inflation-adjusted dollars (NCES 2018). In 2015-2016, 44% of those who successfully completed a PhD program had graduate debt, while 53% of master's degree completers had debt, reflecting lower institutional support for master's education (IES 2020).

Grad Plus loans can go into payment forbearance when your annual earnings are low, but the interest will continue to grow, so the amount you owe after graduation may grow significantly if your income does not support repayment in a given year, and your future monthly payment will go up if the accrued interest is added to the principal that you owe. Moreover, you will owe even more interest on the higher principal amount. A deferment is a similar suspension of payments for a time; however, you do not accrue interest during deferment. An income-driven repayment plan may make more sense, as your principal will not grow with unpaid interest and you will maintain your eligibility toward eventual loan forgiveness; however, you will owe taxes on the benefit.[3]

In 2015, the Department of Education imposed "gainful employment" rules on for-profit institutions, such that if the ratio of average debt to average salary two years post-graduation was too high, students could no longer use federal student loans to attend, effectively capping the amount a student could borrow for for-profit graduate education. There is no such limit on borrowing imposed on nonprofit graduate institutions, however (Petersen 2021). Large, untenable education debt has real and extensive consequences well beyond the time when a person is in school. It can make home buying, marriage, children, moving to a different location (such as abroad) and even retirement financially unthinkable for some, and this is particularly something to be wary of when considering some of the common career placements for aspiring academics (see above).

Given the possible debt and career prospects for those with graduate degrees in almost all academic fields, including political science, it is important to keep finances at the front of your mind when choosing to attend a graduate program. If you have decided that a graduate degree in political science is still for you, here are some strategies for minimizing the financial burden of the degree.

How to Think Through Your Financial Situation

All students have differing financial situations that play a role in their graduate school education and the *funding opportunities* they seek. Some students may not be as worried about covering the cost of tuition and other expenses because of support from those in their personal network. Others may be more concerned about incurring costs because they will be solely responsible for the financial burden. Of course, many students fall in between the financial freedom and financial burden poles of this continuum. Asking yourself the following questions is a great first step:

- How many years will it take to complete the program?
- What are the projected costs of living in the region?
- How can I minimize my expenses (having a roommate, living further away, giving up a car)?
- How much am I willing/able to pay for a graduate program? How much debt, if any, have I already incurred during undergraduate studies?
- How much debt am I willing/able to go into? What will my future monthly payments look like?[4] What is a realistic salary and monthly budget after graduation?
- How can I supplement any funding gaps that may exist? What are my funding options? (See hypothetical example in table below).

After thinking through these questions, you should have a better idea of your personal financial situation. The next step is considering what is being offered to you by graduate programs.

Graduate schools also have differing financial situations. Tuition, fee rates, and funding available to students vary substantially from program to program. Some programs may have strong financial packages to offer prospective students (e.g., research fellowships or graduate assistantships), while others may have none. Funding, or lack thereof, is a significant factor potential students should consider when selecting a graduate program. The answers to the questions above as well as the loan calculating tools provided (see endnote 4) can be used to evaluate which programs should be considered and which may fall lower on the list of options.

When researching the possibility of graduate assistantships, you should collect information about how long the funding will last if awarded the position (contracted year-to-year, length of the program, etc.). It is important to uncover the responsibilities and time expectations that fall within the potential position as well. For example, some assistantships require 20–30 hours weekly of research or teaching responsibilities while completing the program. This can quickly become a heavy workload alongside course completion, comprehensive exam preparation, and other responsibilities as a student. We suggest asking yourself the following questions and weighing these dynamics accordingly:

- How many years does the package cover?
- What type and amount of work is expected in exchange?
- If I do not complete my degree by the end of the last funded year, are there additional internal funding possibilities when I am ABD?

Another step students should consider taking is exploring funding options further to create an action plan. This can be as simple as creating a list of programs you are interested in and then writing out the funding options that are available in those programs. For each program, you could write out the funding options available at the program, department, and college or university level. The funding options can include scholarships, discounted tuition rates, teaching and/or research assistantships, as well as other means. *Table 3.1* is a hypothetical example that can be used as a template to lay out options.

Table 3.1: Template for Comparing Program Costs and Funding

Programs of Interest	Tuition Cost	Program Funding	Department Funding	College/ University Funding
First Choice: Castle University–Master of Public Administration Program	$20K/per year	Graduate Assistantships (tuition only) three years covered one course as teaching assistant	Travel to Conferences (1 per academic year)	N/A
Second Choice: Saturn College–Master of Public Administration Program	$30K/per year	N/A	N/A	Potential Scholarships (competitive and differs annually)

Much funding information can be found online; however, it would be beneficial for you to meet with the program coordinator or director for more funding details. You should record all information based on what is available online and during meetings. This information can be used to rank the programs of interest with your individual financial situation in mind.[5]

External Funding

Luckily, there are more funding options than what your prospective graduate program does or does not offer. Other options include but are not limited to grant opportunities, external scholarships, part-time jobs, tutoring, and fellowships. You can and should explore these options in tandem to internal funding. Depending on the tuition costs and personal financial situations, you can determine the amount of funding needed and address opportunities accordingly. With both internal and external funding options, planning well in advance will help you to become more competitive in the application process. In fact, external funding applications often have early deadlines, and even internal assistantship or fellowship funding often requires students to apply and be accepted to their graduate program earlier than students not seeking funding. Additionally, knowing the financial options can help to determine the monetary gap that may exist and how it can be supplemented.

The following list of sources, although not exhaustive, provides information about potential external funding options for current and future political science graduate students. To evaluate your options, we suggest creating a similar table (as provided above) but for external funding. Resources for finding external funding include:

- Fellowships: The Ohio State University, Department of Political Science: https://polisci.osu.edu/graduate/current-students/external-funding
- Scholarships: The Scholarship System, Political Science Scholarships: https://thescholarshipsystem.com/blog-for-students-families/the-ultimate-list-of-political-science-scholarships/
- Grants: CollegeGrants.org, Political Science Grants: https://www.collegegrants.org/building-bridges-utilizing-political-science-college-grants.html
- Loans: The Office of US Department of Education, Federal Student Aid: https://studentaid.gov/understand-aid/types/loans

Student-loan debt surpasses credit card debt in the US and has become the second largest category of consumer debt (Friedman 2020). After looking into all financial options, we recommend that you consider loans as a last resort, even if that means attending your second or third choice program rather than your most desired school, because for most people, student debt can be a significant stumbling block for many years after graduation.

A Word of Caution About Exploitation

It is unfortunate but important to recognize that because finances can be so tight for graduate students, and because working relationships with mentors can be so close and the power differential so large, the potential for exploitation of students in graduate school can be high. In 2016 when an international graduate student at Columbia University reported to the university that they may need to drop out of school because of their tuition costs and the cost of living, the student was informed through official channels that university president Lee Bollinger hires students to walk his dogs, Arthur and Lucy (Korn and Fuller 2021).[6] But students being asked to provide personal services to faculty members is common, and while it can be mutually beneficial, students may not feel free to decline without fearing retribution. Pet care, house sitting, and personal errand running are common "opportunities" presented to students by their mentors. While this can be a way to make additional funds which faculty know students need, it is less common for professors to consult the schedules and availability or interests of the students they are soliciting. In an open labor market, "applicants" do not fear academic and personal retribution for refusing to accept work. As a student, this is something you may need to navigate, and if you become a faculty member in the future, it is incumbent upon you to recognize the potential that you are exploiting a student with an offer to make more money. A better way to proceed would be to post a listing of what services you are seeking with the terms (pay, hours, timing, location, tasks) upfront, and let students submit their own names for the tasks and recognize that if your preferred student(s) does not apply, there may be valid reasons for that.

Conclusion

There is much to consider financially when deciding to pursue a political science graduate program. This chapter highlights how financial planning can be used to outline graduate program options, their costs, and avenues to minimize debt through funding options such as graduate assistantships and scholarships. Although borrowing money is an option to help cover educational expenses, this can be a major pitfall in terms of paying back the debt with job outlook and average salaries in mind. Investing in a graduate education has many benefits; however, you can be better prepared to weigh the costs of this education by considering financing options as well as other barriers (i.e., exploitation) that can occur in pursuit of a graduate degree. It is important to be cognizant of the financial implications of furthering your education. There are systemic dynamics and cultural norms about education that can obscure some genuine pitfalls that have been created by both policy and circumstance in the academy. Be realistic about your financial future and weigh your choices accordingly.

Endnotes

1   There are multiple cost of living calculators to be found online, but Bankrate offers a nicely detailed one: https://www.bankrate.com/calculators/savings/moving-cost-of-living-calculator. aspx.

2   Sallie Mae maintains a database of external graduate school scholarships: https://www.salliemae. com/student-loans/graduate-school-information/graduate-school-scholarships/

3   See for more info: https://studentaid.gov/manage-loans/lower-payments/get-temporary-relief

4   For a federal student loan calculator to estimate your payments, see: https://studentaid.gov/loan-simulator/.

5   The Wall Street Journal has created an excellent tool to compare debt to financial prospects for some institutions and degrees which may help you to compare the financial implications of similar degrees at different schools: https://www.wsj.com/articles/is-a-graduate-degree-worth-the-debt-check-it-here-11626355788

6   Pres. Bollinger stated that this was never intended to supplant university support, just provide extra spending money.

References

American Federation of Teachers. 2020. An Army of Temps: AFT 2020 Adjunct Faculty Quality of Work/Life Report. https://www.aft.org/highered/resources/army-temps (Accessed November 22, 2021).

Bureau of Labor Statistics. 2020. US Department of Labor, Occupational Outlook Handbook, Political Scientists, https://www.bls.gov/ooh/life-physical-and-social-science/political-scientists.htm (Accessed October 31, 2021).

Flaherty, Colleen. 2018. "A Non-Tenure Track Profession?" *Inside Higher Ed*. October 12, 2018. https://www.insidehighered.com/news/2018/10/12/about-three-quarters-all-faculty-positions-are-tenure-track-according-new-aaup (Accessed November 15, 2021).

Friedman, Zack, 2020. Student loan debt statistics in 2020: A record $1.6 trillion. *Forbes Magazine*. https://www.forbes.com/sites/zackfriedman/2020/02/03/student-loan-debt-statistics/?sh=204ef416281f (Accessed November 28, 2021).

IES. 2020. "Digest of Education Statistics." Institute of Education Sciences, National Center for Education Statistics. https://nces.ed.gov/programs/digest/d20/tables/dt20_332.45.asp. (Accessed October 31, 2021).

Korn, Melissa, and Andrea Fuller. 2021. "'Financially Hobbled for Life': The Elite Master's Degrees that Don't Pay Off," *The Wall Street Journal*. July 8, 2021 https://www.wsj.com/articles/financially-hobbled-for-life-the-elite-masters-degrees-that-dont-pay-off-11625752773?st=ef9geqi4tustpkl&reflink=desktopwebshare_permalink (Accessed October 31, 2021).

NCES 2018. "Trends in Student Loan Debt for Graduate School Completers." National Center for Education Statistics. https://nces.ed.gov/programs/coe/pdf/coe_tub.pdf (Accessed October 31, 2021).

Payscale. 2021. https://www.payscale.com/research/US/Degree, (Accessed October 31, 2021).

Petersen, Anne Helen. 2021. "The Master's Trap: What makes a graduate program predatory?" Culture Study. July 21, 2021. https://annehelen.substack.com/p/the-masters-trap (Accessed October 31, 2021).

Wall Street Journal. 2021. "Is a Graduate Degree Worth the Debt? Check It Here" https://www.wsj.com/articles/is-a-graduate-degree-worth-the-debt-check-it-here-11626355788 (Accessed on November 15, 2021).

Warren, Christiane. 2021. "What is the Cost of a Doctorate Degree?" Study.com. January 7, 2021. https://study.com/articles/How_Much_Does_a_Doctorate_Degree_Cost.html (Accessed October 4, 2021).

4

Don't You Forget About Me: The Application Process and Choosing a Program

Tara Chandra[1], Patricia C. Rodda[2], & William D. Adler[3]

1. University of California, Berkeley 2. Carroll University 3. Northeastern Illinois University

KEYWORDS: Terminal MA, PhD Programs.

Which Should I Choose? Terminal MA Versus PhD Programs

In considering graduate programs, you will need to decide whether to do a terminal master's degree, where you get just that degree at the end, or apply directly to a PhD program. Some people thinking about graduate school often assume that doing a PhD immediately after completing their undergraduate work is the quickest and safest choice. The underlying assumption is that it will be faster than doing a terminal masters' degree prior to a PhD. However, this is not necessarily true.

A terminal masters' program can offer a wide variety of benefits. For some students, it provides an opportunity to explore potential tracks within the discipline of political science prior to entering a PhD program. Although many have already decided on a particular concentration before applying to graduate programs, for others they may need some coursework at the graduate level before finalizing their chosen specialty. Importantly, this is not a negative—taking the time to choose your specialty correctly can be a crucial step in preparing for a successful career and can save time later, when being uncertain of your specialty can result in taking unneeded coursework.

On the other side, another key question that every individual needs to weigh is whether a terminal masters' degree in a particular specialty can be beneficial before starting a PhD program. Some masters' programs are designed to focus on specific areas of emphasis, such as an MPA or MPP. Those planning to do policy-focused PhD studies may find one of these degrees to be an asset. For some PhD departments, having that masters' degree already in hand can be a positive, demonstrating that the applicant can succeed at the graduate level. This is especially true if you've already taken the time at the MA level to consider your specialty and chosen direction in a doctoral program and can effectively communicate that in your applications.

Having said all of this, for many students entering directly into a PhD program may be the right choice. If you are already certain of your concentration and have planned out a field of study, there may be no reason to do a terminal masters' first. Starting a PhD immediately can indeed be quicker if you already are certain of where you want your career to go. PhD programs also tend to offer funding in the form of assistantships, which include tuition, a small stipend, and health insurance (more on funding in Ch. 3).

As we discuss below, personal concerns, such as location and proximity to family, will often be crucial in making your decision. Staying in the right location may necessitate picking a program that is not your first choice for other reasons, at least temporarily. If this means starting in a terminal MA program, it's best to think of this as an opportunity to learn more and prepare for doctoral work, rather than as a disappointment.

Where Should I Apply? Pragmatism and Quality of Life

Everyone has their own advice for how you should choose a graduate program. Most of this advice is valid and you should talk to as many people willing to give you that advice as possible. However, the advice you might receive can also be contradictory, confusing, or patronizing. More importantly, most of the advice currently available to graduate students in all fields, not just political science, fails to consider a key element in the decision-making process: you. So, in this section, we address how to wade through the well-intentioned advice you may receive and still make a choice that fits the kind of life and career you desire.

Most advice offered by graduate programs, undergraduate advisors, and other online sources focus on the pragmatic side of the application process. This advice focuses on choosing programs based on your academic and professional goals. This advice is critical. Once you have made the decision to go to graduate school, you want to aim for the best program for your subfield and ultimate career goals. Since there is so much publicly available information on these topics, we have chosen a few of what we feel are the most important, confusing, or often overlooked suggestions for choosing a program from a pragmatic perspective.

First, as Dr. Daniel Nexon says, "check your ego at the door" (Nexon 2012). Acceptance rates at all graduate programs are quite low. Each school and program have their own idiosyncratic process for deciding which students to accept. Yes, there are some common denominators: GRE scores, your written materials, and the fit between your research interests and those of the faculty. However, the exact weight and influence of each of these elements differs between schools, programs, and even years. Many decisions about whether to admit you to a specific program end up being made for reasons over which you have no control: the availability of funding that year, the number of applications received, or specific faculty members planning on going on sabbatical in the coming years. All of this means that, perhaps the most important piece of pragmatic advice that we can give you is to put together the very best application you can, apply to programs that you think best fit your needs, and then let the chips fall where they may. Easier said than done. But take a breath, hit submit, and try to let it go if you can.

Second, make sure all your application materials do two things: demonstrate you understand what political science and your specific subfield involve and that you are prepared for further study in this field. Applicants often want to include stories that demonstrate their passion for or fascination with political science. While potentially interesting, these stories do not communicate to an admissions committee anything about your ability to succeed in or add to their program. So, instead, you should focus—and ask your letter writers to focus—on demonstrating your knowledge of the field, especially your chosen subfield, the skills you have acquired to date that have prepared you to move on to graduate school, and how attending that specific program will allow you to build on those skills and enter the profession for which you are aiming (whether it is academia, policy, or something else). Your application materials are also where you should address, as directly as possible, anything in your profile that might lead a committee to question the strength of your application—lower GRE scores, a major or degree in something other than political science, or a return to academia after an extended period away.

Third, diversify. Do not pin all your hopes on any one thing—any one school, faculty member, or program. As you consider each program, look for all the different aspects that will help you reach your specific career goals. You should be able to identify more than one faculty member with whom you could work, skills (like methods training, internships, or teaching) in which that program excels, and resources offered by the department, program, or school (like curriculum design courses or conference funding). In the years it will take you to complete your degree, your department will change; faculty will leave, new courses will be offered, or leadership will turn over. The better prepared you are to be flexible and alter your path to completing your degree regardless of these changes, the more likely you will be to succeed and get out of your department, program, and school what you need to build your desired career.

This is where most sources giving advice to potential graduate students stop. From our perspective, however, this misses a key element that should influence your decision: your quality of life. Graduate school—whether you attend a terminal masters' program or a PhD program—is a multi-year commitment. To be successful in a graduate program over these multiple years, you should consider what you need in your life to be happy, healthy, and avoid burning out. So, at multiple points in this process, you should take some time to sit and really think about what gives you a high quality of life. This last part of our advice is probably the hardest to give because it truly is unique to each of you. Here are just a few things you should consider as you contemplate your quality of life:

- How far are you willing to be from your family and/or friends?
- What is your relationship status? If you are single, think about what the dating scene might be like in different locations. If you are in a relationship, will your partner come with you? If so, what opportunities are there for them in each location?
- What is the cost of living? If that cost is not covered by your program funding, will you be able to live as comfortably as you need?
- Depending on your identity or interests, will you feel safe, welcomed, and included in the location of the program? For those who are members of a marginalized community, such as LGBTQ+ or BIPOC, this question can be especially important.

Where Should I Go? Making the Final Decision

Unlike the mountain of advice you can find about where and how to apply to graduate programs, when it comes to selecting the program to attend, the prevailing advice is often "go to the best program you get into." But what does "best" really mean? In this final section, we suggest that "best" can look different to each person and that the process for selecting a graduate program ought to be more rigorous than selecting a program based solely on ranking.

Assuming that students are choosing from more than one program, we recommend thinking carefully about all the facets of graduate life that might be important for any individual student—available funding, the department's approach to graduate mentorship and professional development, methodological plurality, faculty diversity, flexibility of requirements, ability to take courses across disciplines, and broader department culture—and investigate them thoroughly before deciding. You likely did much of this research during the application phase, but take some time to review that information, contact current graduate students, and ask critical questions of the department, program, and school.

One of the first ways to begin a thorough investigation of graduate programs is, of course, to attend the program's visit day, and we highly recommend that students attend the visit day for every program to which they are admitted. There is no better way to get a sense of a department than being physically present. Visit days allow students to meet potential mentors and future committee members and to assess whether their teaching, research, and mentoring approach is a good fit for a given individual. They are an opportunity to observe the top layer of a department and its culture. If you are not able to attend every visit day, use the information you already know about each program to prioritize which ones you should attend. For those you cannot attend, be sure to do the extra homework of reaching out to current graduate students for their take on the program.

Visit days should also be about looking for intangible cues—do current students in the program seem happy? Are they gathering in shared spaces to co-work, or do they seem isolated and competitive with each other? The graduate student culture is a huge component of student life and making sure that the environment is supportive, friendly, and inclusive will go a long way to ensuring success in graduate school. Stop and talk to graduate students you meet who are not officially part of visit day and ask how they like the department and what they wish they had known before they started. Meet with as many current students in the program as possible, especially—and this cannot be emphasized enough—students who are advisees of any faculty member you are considering as an advisor.

After visit day, we recommend continuing your outreach with current graduate students in the program. Remember, students who are further along in the program are often not present at visit day, as they may be away from campus conducting fieldwork or in a phase of their program where they do not need to be on campus regularly. Connecting with these 'older' graduate students, who have had several years of experience in the program, will provide you with vital information about the department's culture, history, and any recent or upcoming changes that might affect the graduate experience. When speaking with current students, aim to have an honest and open conversation while resisting the urge to engage in gossip. But knowing if a potential advisor will be going on leave, leaving the department altogether, or if they are simply not a great advisor, is critical to making the right decision.

You should also be open with current students and faculty about the other programs you are considering, as it is possible that a given program simply is not a good fit for an individual, or that there is a faculty member in another department who would, for substantive or methodological reasons be a better advisor. The 'right' fit with an advisor is not just substantive or methodological though. Trying to get a sense of how they advise—how intensely they like to control their students' research questions, methods etc., as well as how often they are willing to meet, how quickly they respond to student emails, how many drafts of student work they will read, and how they support their students in finding funding for research—is very important to determining whether a given advisor will be the best fit for you.

One final thing you should consider is how flexible departmental culture and requirements are if (as is likely), your research topic changes. One of the most beautiful things about graduate school is how much your understanding of the world is broadened by exposure to many different types of research on a multitude of topics, and it is not unlikely that your proposed research will change between the time you apply and your (usually) third year when you write and defend your prospectus. You can account for this by talking in detail with program staff and graduate advisors to understand how flexible the program is in allowing students to get a master's in another department, if there are certificate programs available, and whether committee members from outside the department are allowed to sit on students' committees. The bureaucratic nitty-gritty may seem irrelevant at the beginning of your program, but if your research becomes focused on a particular method, topic, or area of the world that your chosen department cannot support wholly, then the ability to get expert advice or training from outside the department becomes even more critical.

Overall, the main takeaway of this section should be that the process of selecting a program—just on academic merits, even before considering all the other facets of life that are very important to a healthy and successful graduate experience—should be in-depth and rigorous. You should talk to students at all levels, faculty, and staff in every program you are seriously considering, and do your best to get a clear sense of life in the department before making a final decision that will have lifelong professional and personal consequences.

Conclusion

Applying to graduate school can seem like a daunting prospect, perhaps made even more difficult by all the various and contradictory advice you may get. This chapter is designed to focus on the needs of each individual prospective graduate student, and what is important to you in planning your graduate education and your career. Although some things will remain constant for all potential graduate students—writing strong application materials, a statement of interest that shows you understand the field and what role you want to play in it, taking GREs—many other factors will come into play and those can vary widely. Whether you want to start at a terminal masters' program or enter a PhD program directly, where you want to live, what type of environment is right for you, are decisions that ultimately only you can make.

5 | Seasoned Professionals Applying to and Navigating Doctoral Programs

Marty P. Jordan[1], Erika Rosebrook[1], & Eleanor Schiff[2]

1. Michigan State University 2. The Pennsylvania State University

KEYWORDS: Tangible and Intangible Costs, Direct Pathway Students.

Introduction

Although positive attempts have been made to assess the gender, racial, and ethnic composition of incoming doctoral students (e.g., APSA 2018), we know very little as a discipline about the breadth and depth of professional experience that applicants bring to their graduate studies. Most incoming PhD students are either direct pathway students (coming straight from undergraduate studies) or have taken a year or two in the workforce before starting graduate school (Mosyjowski et al. 2017). Students with significant work experience (greater than five years) returning to pursue a doctoral degree (i.e., returning students) are the exception rather than the norm. These seasoned professionals generally encounter different challenges than students who matriculate directly or soon after undergraduate study. As they consider graduate school, seasoned practitioners may have to weigh opportunity costs, financial considerations, cultural re-entry issues, work-life balance, familial and community obligations, among other factors. Beyond these tradeoffs, prospective students with extensive applied experience will also have to navigate the application process, take the GRE, secure letters of recommendation, and evaluate different departmental environments. Despite these challenges, seasoned pros can leverage their experience, skills, maturity, and professionalism when applying, executing coursework, establishing research agendas, and connecting the dots between the theoretical and applied worlds of politics. Indeed, doctoral students with ample work experience offer something special to academic units and political science in terms of having a broader perspective in applying real-world political experiences to academia. We hope this chapter serves as a resource detailing what we wish we knew then when we applied for and attended graduate school as seasoned professionals. Collectively, we three authors amassed 36 years of practitioner experience in the public, nonprofit, and for-profit arenas before deciding to pursue doctoral degrees and become academicians. One of us worked at the White House and in the federal bureaucracy. One of us labored with local and state governments. And one of us spent time with international nonprofits and a publicly traded global company. Of course, these musings reflect our finite experiences. Others with different intersectional identities may testify to divergent accounts and offer distinctive guidance. Still, we offer some suggestions for seasoned professionals as they consider PhD applications, navigate graduate studies, and contribute to their academic departments.

Deciding to Pursue a Doctoral Degree and Navigating the Application Process

Deciding to leave the workforce after an extended tenure and pursue a PhD is no simple quandary. There are multiple considerations to weigh. For instance, there are opportunity costs to changing careers. Seasoned professionals may be near or at the peak of their careers. Many have already completed a terminal master's or JD. Professionally, they have built a reputation, established a network, gained valuable applied skills, and made recognizable contributions to their industries. Opting to earn a doctoral degree may mean surrendering these hard-won connections and positions of influence. It can be humbling to go from having a personal office, benefitting from an assistant, managing subordinates, or serving as the point person on multiple projects to starting anew as a student. The authors of this chapter experienced such whiplash as we went from the White House, a governor's office, and corporate boardrooms to being students without a title and sharing office space.

There are financial considerations too. Becoming a pupil again will likely result in a sizable pay cut, an extended pause in retirement contributions, and a loss of other pecuniary perks and benefits. The average graduate student stipend in political science ranges from $14,000 to $30,000 per year (ProFellow 2020). As a result, students may have to take out education loans to cover the cost of living, childcare, or other financial obligations. All these monetary sacrifices may not be worth it to some considering that the average salary for assistant professors is $67,000 per year (Zippia 2021), with Research I universities paying more and lower-tier public universities and liberal arts colleges compensating less. Still, your doctorate may carry more value in the governmental and private sectors, and the professional freedom of academia is refreshing.

Beyond these *tangible costs* are *intangible* ones, such as culture and work-life balance. Doctoral studies are a significant undertaking. Work weeks as long as 60 hours are common. Little time is left for family, friends, and extracurricular activities. Most students take five to seven years to complete their degrees. In addition, academia lends itself to a set of highly intelligent but highly critical individuals. Such spaces replete with high achieving individuals can make for a difficult environment to shine and thrive. Being at the top of your game in industry will not necessarily translate to success in higher education. All of this makes for a mentally, emotionally, and physically taxing journey. We further discuss the practical and cultural challenges for seasoned professionals seeking a PhD later in this chapter.

However, pursuing a doctorate has many advantages as well. A mid-career transition may be a welcome and needed change for one's self-actualization, priorities, and goals. Moreover, universities are centers of rich intellectual stimulation and innovation. It is an extraordinary privilege to be paid (albeit a minimal amount) to learn, teach, and research—all to build new knowledge and advance the discipline. Graduate studies also offer schedule flexibility which may suit one's preferred lifestyle, familial responsibilities, or personal circumstances. As we highlight later in the chapter, there are ways to leverage your professional experience to benefit your academic pursuits. Ultimately, we believe the career change was worth the opportunity costs, but we understand if others make different calculations. Regardless, this decision is more than a job change, and we strongly encourage prospective doctoral students to fully evaluate the tradeoffs in the context of one's personal circumstances to decide what is best.

Once you have decided to pursue doctoral studies, you can turn your attention to identifying where and how to apply. For starters, you may need to (re-)take the GRE. Fortunately, a fair number of programs are abandoning the GRE requirement because standardized tests are not good predictors of academic success and are especially punitive for low-income students, many of whom are disproportionately people of color. Still, most programs require GRE scores to assess applicants' verbal, quantitative, or writing abilities. Of course, working full-time may not afford much free time to study for the GRE. Despite the commitment and cost, we recommend enrolling in a GRE-prep course. It provides structured practice and teaches strategies to answer questions efficiently and effectively, especially for those more distant from their undergraduate test-taking years. Moving up a few percentiles in GRE results could mean the difference between admittance or not, or a university fellowship or not. GRE scores may be an especially important heuristic for admission committees as they are not always able to assess professional experience objectively and consistently (Jackman 2017; King et al. 2008; Michel et al. 2019;

Posselt 2014).

Determining where to apply may require weighing geographic, partner, familial, financial, or other considerations.[1] Direct pathway students tend to have greater flexibility in applying to the highest-ranked programs where they are competitive and can field competing offers. Meanwhile, seasoned professionals are typically older and more likely to be in long-term relationships, expectant or current parents, have a mortgage and significant financial commitments, or have established social networks or long-term community ties. These obligations make it challenging to cast a wide net. Anecdotally, each chapter author here only applied to two programs at most. Importantly, the decision to pursue a doctoral degree does not affect you alone. Instead, the pursuit will likely impact your partner, child(ren), family members, or friends. Therefore, robust communication about the positives and negatives of earning a PhD with the key people in your life is essential.

Nonetheless, applicants with an extensive resume can leverage their professional experience when writing their personal and research essays. These statements are sales pitches for the value add you will bring to the department, university, and discipline (see Chapter 43). It is worth the effort to help admission committees connect your applied experience and academic goals. For example, experience fundraising or managing budgets may benefit you in applying for research grants. Time spent working in a legislative office or lobbying affords you a front-row seat to better understand the practical aspects of the policymaking process. Working as an attorney gives insights into judicial decision making. Years dedicated to international sales and marketing are an excellent primer for research in international political economy. A long-term stint with a foreign aid agency has readied you to study comparative politics. Professionalism, maturity, executive function, substantive understanding, and applied skills are valuable in higher education. Seasoned professionals should highlight their lived and professional experiences, articulating how such experience has made them see political and policy phenomena of interest in new ways. Doing this well may yield admittance along with a university scholarship, fellowship, or more competitive aid package.

A final piece of the application process is securing someone to write you a letter of recommendation. Programs typically require at least three strong references. While it certainly is acceptable to ask one or two members of your professional network to submit a letter on your behalf, at least one letter writer should be a faculty member from your undergraduate, master's, or law school studies. Depending on the amount of time since graduation, this may be more challenging for some than others. If you are able, it is wise to maintain regular contact (e.g., checking in at least once a year) with an academic mentor. Even if it has been an extended time, it is worth reaching out to a professor you admired and performed well for, reminding them of your academic excellence, and updating them on your current endeavors. If you do most of the work of summarizing your past and recent accolades for them, and how your experience in their class shaped the perspective you'll bring to graduate study, they will be more likely to commit to writing the letter.

Whether you are admitted into one or more programs, we encourage you to attend open houses and meet with departmental faculty and other doctoral students. During these visits, you can get a sense of the departmental culture. You may be able to negotiate your financial package, securing additional dollars or guaranteed summer funding. You may want to assess how many other doctoral students bring extensive work experience to the table. It might help if you inquired how professional and lived experiences are valued by faculty. You could ask about program expectations and flexibility concerning your other obligations and commitments. Finally, you should determine whether you can find or foster the community of peers and support you will need to weather a long, exacting, and worthwhile journey.

Challenges for Seasoned Professionals

Once you have decided to enter a PhD program, returning students face a different set of challenges than their direct pathway peers, but they also enjoy some key advantages.

Challenges that we have identified for older students are both practical and cultural. Practically, many returning students have more demands on their personal time than direct pathway students. Many are married or partnered off and may have children or parents to care for. Many seasoned professionals also have entrenched financial or community commitments. Such obligations can present additional time management challenges when juggling the intense pressure and workload of a PhD program. Given the profile of typical doctoral students, most PhD programs are not designed to accommodate these added responsibilities and thus may not offer the same resources a traditional workplace would. Therefore, we recommend investigating the culture and formal support options available in a program for your circumstances.

Practical challenges are also coupled with cultural challenges for seasoned professionals returning to academia. Returning students can be significantly older than their cohort peers, perhaps even ten to twenty years older. Because of the age gap and likely unshared interests, it can be challenging to make friends, bond as a group, and persevere through difficult coursework and comprehensive exams. While PhD work is largely individualized, the early years of study can necessitate intense collaboration within the cohort to succeed. Returning students can sometimes feel on the periphery of the cohort due to the age gap and cultural displacement, making the first couple of years potentially more isolating.

Another conceivable cultural challenge for returning students is interacting with and working for faculty that are in fact their age peers. Returning students are professionals, but faculty may not be aware of their extensive career experience, achieved skillsets, or knowledge base. Beyond that, a large power gap exists between students and faculty. This can leave some faculty (and other graduate students) not fully recognizing or utilizing the talents and perspectives of these returning students.

Further, returning students with real-world professional experience often witness a surprising disconnect between theories in political science and applied realities in the political arena. How politics is practiced is more nuanced than summative regression analyses. The ivory tower can sometimes engage in too many thought experiments devoid of the benefit of reality. Seasoned professionals can offer substantive insights on political institutions and behavior, provide historical context, propose more valid measures, or offer concrete examples to buttress or refute key theories. Returning students can help bridge that gap, but only if faculty and other graduate students are open to this practical experience.

Advantages for Seasoned Professionals

In spite of these practical and cultural challenges, seasoned professionals enjoy some advantages over their younger peers. A PhD program is long and grueling for most students, regardless of age. Many direct pathway students are exemplar students, making graduate studies a sensible choice. With this success, however, can come mental anguish particularly if the student is struggling with a course, comprehensive exams, a dissertation, or other service responsibilities. Many direct pathway students' identities are tied to their academic performance. It can be shocking, even debilitating for some to receive poor marks, encounter significant criticism from faculty, or experience failure. Students that drop out of doctoral programs do so for a host of reasons (Paterson 2016), but having one's confidence married to school performance is a central one as it affects a student's psychological wellbeing.

Of course, returning students also experience criticism, failure, and challenges in graduate school. But generally, these students have greater maturity, a more solidified sense of self, and past experience to shoulder faculty criticism or program challenges with less mental anguish. Being chastised in the halls of Congress, losing a legal case, failing to close a large sale, or other such events can steel returning students for possible admonitions. Additionally, since returning students are proven professionals, it can be easier for them to treat graduate studies like a job and set healthy work boundaries. Likewise, returning students made the choice to return to academia. This deliberate decision can help returning students persevere even when the immediate woes of data collection or the marathon of dissertation writing can seem daunting. Studies show that doctoral students with extensive industry experience tend to harbor greater motivation and drive for their research agenda (Mosyjowski 2017). Having a long-term outlook and keeping life in perspective can serve as an asset for returning students over their direct pathway peers.

One of the challenges of graduate school for all students is carving out individual space for research and contributions to the field. Professional experience offers returning students unique opportunities to develop distinct research perspectives, withstand the peculiarities of the academic work environment, and establish leadership roles in the classroom and professional organizations.

Seasoned professionals bring a wealth of insight into addressing one of political science's main issues: measuring and understanding political and social phenomena. In many ways, professional experience is lived in the gap between rules and systems as they are written and as they are experienced. Years working in a local government, for a nonprofit, or on the Hill not only produce a network of contacts who are willing to sit for interviews or aid research efforts, but they also yield an understanding of data and the processes that produce such evidence.

Many of us who have encountered academic research before entering academia have experienced reading a journal article and questioning the authors' understanding of budget data, committee votes, or policy cases. Or, if the authors do have a handle on the topic, the writing can be esoteric or difficult for non-academics to engage. It can be difficult to remember during the disorienting process of graduate school, where you are being socialized to the academic culture of research, but your experience is a robust foundation for scholarship and your past experience writing for a lay audience is an advantage. We recommend maintaining some contact with your network and colleagues outside of higher education throughout your doctoral studies as a reminder of the value your experience can add to your academic endeavors and deep understanding of the political world.

This hard-earned knowledge and professional networks also make life easier as instructors in the classroom. While anecdotes are only singular data points, they are invaluable in finding ways for students to connect applied political phenomena and their own experience to larger theories and concepts. Sharing examples of how things "really work" illustrates the tradeoffs required in governing and the value and limitations of political science in explaining real-world decisions and results. For direct pathway students, those examples can take years to develop, but as a seasoned professional, you have access to those cases and can more easily adapt to what resonates best with students.

You can also easily tap professional networks to bring in speakers or guests that can give different perspectives or offer additional connections to classroom and academic material. For people who are accustomed to work that is more communal or positively impacts the community, the individualism of graduate study can be especially difficult. Teaching offers an opportunity to maintain that aspect of your professional skillset and continue to contribute beyond research.

Finally, there are other advantages to entering graduate school with experience in professional settings. Compared to traditional workplaces, academia will likely be a culture shock. There may be limited supervisory oversight, few personnel policies, or great freedom for tenured faculty. Interactions occur one-on-one in situations with large power imbalances and little supervision, and classroom environments are largely subject to individual faculty preferences. In this environment, harassment and other toxic behaviors can be prevalent and difficult to address (see Chapter 52 on harassment and options for responding). Direct pathway students may not even recognize the severity of a problem without past examples to serve as a comparison.

Seasoned professionals likely have experience navigating, or even administering systems of accountability in large organizations. They also presumably have a better understanding of what is and is not acceptable in professional interactions. This can allow you to take a leadership role in addressing harmful situations and creating healthier cultures, using tools gained outside of academia to facilitate discussions and foster accountability within units and throughout the profession.

Conclusion: Beyond Graduate School and Final Thoughts

Deciding to embark on the strenuous, though rewarding, adventure of doctoral education is a major decision for any student. But it is especially so for seasoned professionals. The opportunity costs of leaving an established career to begin anew in an academic setting can be daunting. The three of us succeeded in making the transition and are glad that we did, but we all faced quite different challenges than direct pathway students during the application process and navigating graduate school. We have tried to enumerate some of the cultural and personal challenges that seasoned professionals may encounter in pursuing academic work and encourage you to think about what your future goals are and how obtaining a PhD is beneficial for your long-term plans.

Most academic departments define their success by how many of their PhD graduates place in a tenure-line post at a Research 1 university. However, there are other options for political science PhDs. For example, think tanks, consulting companies, data science organizations, advocacy groups, policy-makers, governmental agencies, private firms, and many other entities welcome trained political scientists. Academia is not the only path. And with universities trimming their budgets, reducing the number of available tenure-track lines, and turning to non-permanent faculty to fill the gaps, remembering that an array of options is available offers flexibility and opportunities to seasoned professionals for successful arenas after graduate school (See Chapter 41 on non-traditional options).

In the final analysis, the three of us made big choices and gambled in some ways with our careers in pivoting out of established arenas into the unknowns of academia. For all of us, the sacrifice was worth it. Higher education is less about spending 40 hours chained to a desk than about the intellectual freedom to create new knowledge, focus on meaningful societal challenges, and touch students' lives. It is always tempting to think about "what if" and "where would I be" had we chosen not to pursue PhDs. But even though the road was arduous, the journey has been valuable. We wish all seasoned professionals considering this path the best of luck in deciding whether to pursue a political science doctoral degree.

Endnotes

1   The late Tom Carsey (2020) offers some excellent advice for deciding among different doctoral programs.

References

American Political Science Association (APSA). 2018. "2016–2017 APSA Graduate Placement Survey: Incoming Students Report." https://preprints.apsanet.org/engage/api-gateway/apsa/assets/orp/resource/item/61015b730b093e2830e42b7a/original/2018-2020-apsa-graduate-placement-survey-incoming-students-report.pdf.

Carsey, Thomas M. 2020. *Tom's Comments: Advice about Graduate School, Finding a Job, Reaching Tenure in Political Science and Other Social Sciences, and All of the Steps in Between.* University of North Carolina at Chapel Hill. https://politicalscience.unc.edu/wp-content/uploads/sites/186/2020/09/Toms-Comments-Carsey-book-9-7-2020.pdf.

Jackman, Simon. 2017. "What Do We Learn from Graduate Admissions Committees? A Multiple Rater, Latent Variable Model, with Incomplete Discrete and Continuous Indicators." *Political Analysis* 12 (4): 400–424. https://doi.org/10.1093/pan/mph026.

King, Gary, John Bruce, and Michael Gilligan. 2008. "The Science of Political Science Graduate Admissions." Political Science and Politics 26 (January). https://doi.org/10.2307/419549.

Michel, Rochelle S., Vinetha Belur, Bobby Naemi, and Harrison J. Kell. 2019. "Graduate Admissions Practices: A Targeted Review of the Literature." ETS Research Report Series 2019 (1): 1–18. https://doi.org/10.1002/ets2.12271.

Mosyjowski, Erika A. 2017. "Drivers of Research Topic Selection for Engineering Doctoral Students." *International Journal of Engineering Education* 33 (4): 1283–96. https://digitalcommons.kettering.edu/cgi/viewcontent.cgi?article=1204&context=mech_eng_facultypubs.

Mosyjowski, Erika A., Shanna R. Daly, Diane L. Peters, Steven J. Skerlos, and Adam B. Baker. 2017. "Engineering PhD Returners and Direct-Pathway Students: Comparing Expectancy, Value, and Cost." *Journal of Engineering Education* 106 (4): 639–76. https://doi.org/10.1002/jee.20182.

Patterson, Te-Erika. 2016. "Why Do So Many Graduate Students Quit?" *The Atlantic.* July 6, 2016. https://www.theatlantic.com/education/archive/2016/07/why-do-so-many-graduate-students-quit/490094/.

Posselt, Julie R. 2014. "Toward Inclusive Excellence in Graduate Education: Constructing Merit and Diversity in PhD Admissions." *American Journal of Education* 120 (4): 481–514. https://doi.org/10.1086/676910.

ProFellow. 2020. "Fully Funded PhD Programs in Political Science." March 17, 2020. https://www.profellow.com/fellowships/fully-funded-phds-in-political-science/.

Zippia. 2020. "Average Assistant Professor Of Political Science Salary 2021: Hourly and Annual Salaries." May 18, 2020. https://www.zippia.com/assistant-professor-of-political-science-jobs/salary/.

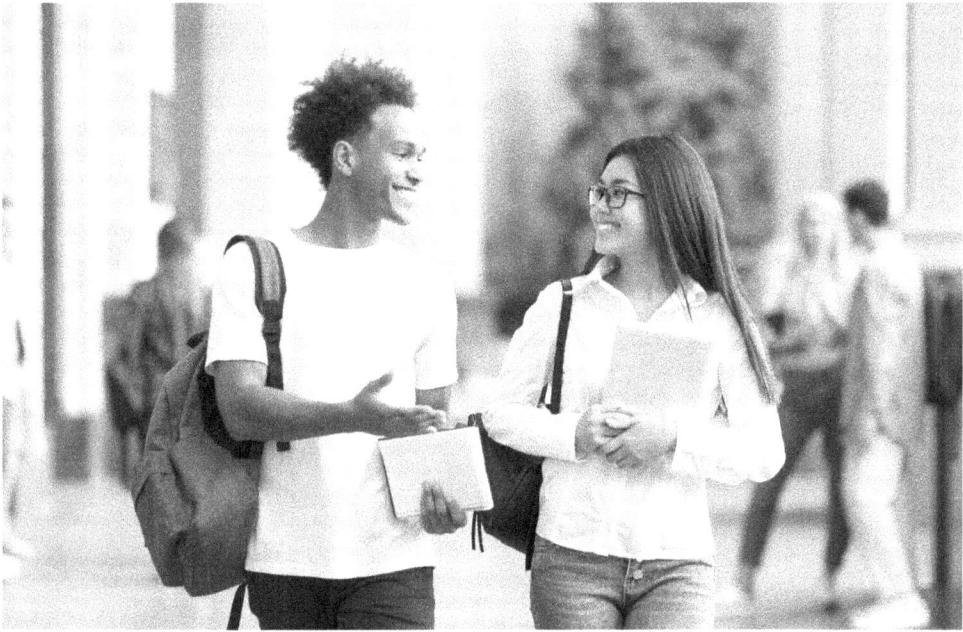

On Campus

6

Moving Beyond the One-Shot Orientation: Understanding and Making the Most of Ongoing Orientations

Anthony Petros Spanakos[1] & Mishella Romo Rivas[2]

1. Montclair State University 2. Princeton University

KEYWORDS: Orientations, Culture of Overwork.

Introduction

Every graduate program has an orientation for incoming students, and many institutions of higher education have a similar orientation session for new faculty. Additionally, political science departments often host an annual check-in event for adjunct faculty. Yet, little long-term programming is developed and delivered for returning students or tenure track and fixed term faculty. The limited programming is unfortunate because a one-shot orientation cannot adequately introduce students and faculty to their colleagues, universities, and disciplines, nor does it ensure they are connected to mentors who can help them thrive. Orientations, as they are generally offered, are time-limited events that aim to answer big general questions—many of which do not arise until the person has been at the institution for some time—and it is assumed that, once oriented, the new person will find or be found by a mentor or will do well enough without one. To respond to these conditions, we argue that an orientation should be an ongoing process into the complex environment in which all people share responsibilities for welcoming and getting to know others. If orientation is limited to a single office and a one-time event, it is more likely to simply answer questions on a prepared checklist rather than truly help situate a person in a particular field or space. This is especially so in universities and academic departments. The diversity of people within and entering mean that there is no single, complete list of data a new person should know. Rather, a person is entering a dynamic environment with different persons, relationships, offices, and responsibilities. Since this chapter recommends a vision of orientation that is ongoing, reflective, and mindful of representation and inclusion (Mealy 2009; Mealy 2018; Tormos-Aponte and Velez-Serrano 2020; Yanow 2020), it contributes to research that emphasizes the importance of early efforts by both students and faculty to establish proactive relationship-building and to facilitate early professionalization into the field (Fugate, Jaramillo, and Preuhs 2002; Hu, Kuh, and Li 2008). This vision is supplemented with practical behavioral suggestions based on the authors' experiences as graduate students, adjunct faculty, full-time faculty, and department chair. This chapter will also explain what orientation should be and why this is something that must be understood as occurring over time, with varying people, and in multiple spaces. It will also make recommendations for students and faculty which will help build the practices and expectations that can make orientation an ongoing activity.

Orientation as One-Off and On-Going

Orientations are generally one-off events in which introductions are made, slides are shown and, possibly, some icebreaking activity takes place and libations are eventually enjoyed. Orientations have generally moved from addressing traditional academic topics (e.g., questions about comprehensive exams), administrative (e.g., a flow chart in the department and college) and organizational (e.g., unions) matters to also include social (e.g., relevant social groups) and emotional (e.g., relevant support offices) and psychological (e.g., mental health and other services) ones. This approach would be adequate if new students and faculty were entering largely familiar settings and expectations. Yet, moving from an undergraduate or graduate experience, the working world, or even a faculty position at another university is not so simple. Indeed, while all universities and departments have strategic plans, visions, by-laws, and a wide range of supporting committees and departments they vary significantly in reach, import, and dynamism and such variation can have a significant impact on one's ability to excel in a department and personally flourish. The types of services, expectations, strengths, weaknesses, challenges, and opportunities provided by the various levels of administration within the university are heightened by particularities of the personalities who occupy formal and informal positions in the department. Thus, while any department is likely to have some support at the library or inclusion initiatives, the personnel, types, range, and effectiveness of programs vary considerably.

In most orientations, departments or universities introduce new members of the academic community to a broad set of topics, people, and offices but, inevitably, the new members witness little more than short presentations and receive business cards.[1] They can hardly address the issues that emerge in any depth, and they rely on the person to remember the names and functions of various offices. Unfortunately, there is a time gap between when one learns of, say, who handles internal grants or complaints, and when a relevant situation emerges. Additionally, staff change, funding wanes and swells, and offices get reorganized, repurposed, or collapsed into other units. As such, the checklist from day one easily fades behind the most pressing responsibilities of grading hundreds of student papers, pursuing publication, and participating in academic service. When a department maintains the orientation process open it signals to graduate students and faculty that their membership in the community is something to be taken seriously over time, not a concern raised before the semester and 'real work' emerges. The following sections offer recommendations for graduate students and early career scholars in working with the department to keep the orientation process dynamic.

During Graduate School

While the previous section addressed a view of how departments usually think of and practice orientation, this section offers a more bottom-up discussion and considers what the student can and should do regardless of what the *status quo* is in the department. One of the most important insights about offering advice with the privilege of hindsight is that we are aware that graduate school can be most fruitful when students take on a proactive approach to developing research within their department and outside of it. The subsequent sections aim to support this claim.

Proactive Relationship-Building

Usually, when graduate students take the first step in relationship building within their department, they are most likely to seek out people who are similar to them in terms of subfield, thematic, regional, and methodological preferences. This goes against the mantra repeated at many orientations that students should leave silos and comfort zones and should reinvigorate research questions with fresh perspectives. Yet, students are also expected to hit the ground running and to work on comprehensive exams or qualifying papers in their second or third years. Students and faculty work backwards and expect relationships with qualifying paper readers to develop in year one. The recommendations below offer guidance on ways to overcome the temptation of strategic relationship building to help students get the most of the opportunities and resources within their department:

- Students can request information on the office hours of faculty with whom they have had class and with those who they have not had class early on in the program. This is important since graduate students who know that office hours are intended to provide a regular and permanent space for faculty-student interaction and build social capital are more proactive and tend to develop relationships with one or more faculty members early (Guerreo and Rod 2013; Pascarella et al. 2000).[2]

- The department can recommend workshops, events, and lectures organized by students and faculty in other subfields and students ought to make an effort to participate in a few of these each semester. It is precisely in these areas when students are not motivated to build a network for strategic reasons that they are often most capable of learning a more general lesson about the craft of scholarship or the way the field works.
- Students can follow up with visiting scholars or professors engaged in organizing low-stakes events. This will allow students to build a network and continue to learn about research, scholars, and methods that students might have otherwise missed when operating within events organized by their primary subfields.
- Students should begin writing and researching preliminary ideas from early seminar papers sooner rather than later. Indeed, taking on this task is fruitful since it may also facilitate interactions with faculty earlier and can prompt ideas for review essays or short research notes that can generate long term projects. Engaging in these exercises can also help students begin to think about how classic paradigms in the field interact with emerging and cutting-edge research.

All in all, these recommendations encourage students to take the lead. While some faculty make initial efforts to orient, mentor, and welcome students, many still expect graduate students to take the first step in establishing a professional relationship. Of course, this expectation creates difficulties for first year students, who may be reluctant to go to office hours without a specific class-related question and are unlikely to see classroom professors as advisors with whom they could discuss general questions. Ideally, in a department where all faculty take on some responsibility for welcoming new students and are cognizant of a responsibility for continual orientation of students, students will be able to recognize how faculty will look out for students (Hesli and Fink 2003).[3] However, sometimes this proactive effort is not wholly institutionalized and as such, after reading this guidebook students should have actionable recommendations to take the lead in helping the department faculty and administration produce and reproduce the practices that help orientation remain an ongoing process in different arenas. If students manage to achieve this, with support of the department, they will likely discover unexpected connections and wisdom (Munck and Snyder 2007), and also to get to know the people, the chief resources of the department, who can contribute to helping the student learn new literature, gain new perspectives, and experiment with different types of material. These gains all contribute to the scholarly development and success of graduate students.

Early and Continued Exposure to Professionalization into the Field

In addition to proactive relationship building, orientation as an ongoing process should not simply introduce students to a department but also to a field and one of the most important ways to experience and understand political science is to participate in academic conferences. Often graduate students are advised to refrain from participating in these events until they have concrete research questions, plans, and contributions to the field. Faculty should encourage students in graduate classes to consider coordinating a panel at a local political science conference as the experience helps students develop a sense of community, builds oral presentation skills, motivates students to make research meaningful for an audience beyond a classroom, and exposes them to feedback.[4] These are very clear and actionable ways in which all faculty can be part of an ongoing orientation process. (For more insight on conference attendance, see chapter 21). Below we offer some actionable recommendations for students to take the lead in early professionalization:

- Attend conferences early and in person, so as to learn experientially what it means to "do" political science and build a scholarly network. Initial participation might be simply as a member of an audience or as a poster session presenter. But there is also little harm in presenting research and honestly communicating to an audience that research is preliminary and you look forward to receiving comments. Perhaps the most important part of this task for students is to learn the Platonic lesson of knowing what they do not know.

- Network with peers who are asking similar research questions and are in a similar subfield. This is quite important since it is often difficult to find students with a similar research agenda within one's own department, particularly when the department is small or returning graduate students are not present in the department.
- Co-author with future colleagues within or outside other departments while in graduate school. This can be quite helpful for students once they have begun to work on their dissertation, including by helping students overcome the intense isolation that accompanies a narrowly focused research process. During the dissertation process which appears so solitary, faculty can also be helpful in guiding students about how to set up boundaries during co-authorship and how to make the best of a collaborative experience. That is, faculty can continue to orient their students.

In the aggregate, the experience of early professionalization gives students a more accurate image of critical aspects of the profession than would participation as a student in a classroom. While COVID-19 has facilitated opportunities for virtual events, it is still advisable to prioritize attending conferences in person. In hallways, book exhibits, and cafes nearby participants make unexpected connections, follow up on insightful questions asked during question-and-answer periods, meet people whose research they know or who are at departments where faculty of interest work, and they do so as they walk from one room to the next or on the way to get a warm drink or to explore the city where the conference is situated. These are places where some of the most important orientation takes place.

Faculty Orientation

This section extends our approach of orientation as an ongoing process to early stages in an academic career. Adjunct faculty, often advanced graduate students, tend to receive no orientation or have an informal and brief one in their interview with the hiring person or committee. Many departments host once a year (some once a semester) meetings where adjunct faculty and the relevant director meet to discuss the upcoming semester. Adjunct faculty often only meet the tenure-line faculty who they actively seek out, who teach in the classroom near them, or who occupy a relevant office (e.g., chair). Not only does this limit the ability of the faculty member to know the department, and thus to advise students, but it can be jarring when the department selects a new chair or graduate program director.

Recently, a number of universities have implemented one semester or one-year orientations for new full-time faculty. These programs involve monthly meetings, are led by a senior faculty member, often supported by other veteran faculty as mentors. The program usually consists of addressing in more depth and with more participation issues that might ordinarily be raised in a typical orientation (e.g., the dean of students speaks about what his or her office does, interventions for struggling students, etc.). For example, a November workshop on student success and assessment could allow faculty, new and veteran, to discuss mid-term assignments as a community, build fellowship, and come up with potentially long-term strategies.

As with any orientation program, these programs end. A faculty member after one year may understand quite a bit of the department and university and know where and to whom one should go for particular information, but there is still much to be learned. Some will be capable of figuring this out, using contacts made, and finding new resources over time. But many, unintentionally, retrench into classes and research and easily lose track of the sense of participating in a community. This is true at the departmental and university level. It is not unusual for faculty members in the same department who like and respect each other to see each other only once a month at department meetings, and for faculty members who once met in a first-year experience to see each other every few months or years. Associate professors are, on average, the least satisfied and most anxious (Jacobs and Winslow 2004). It is at this stage in the career, and lives, of many where there is a particular need for re-orientation.[5] Normally, if leaders think about this issue, it is thought of as a question of mentoring,[6] but it is deeper than this and is best addressed by a department and university commitment to continually offering opportunities for faculty of different ranks and disciplines to learn about how they and others participate in disciplines and a broader professional academic field that undergoes change.

Departments should develop their own ongoing orientation activities to facilitate the regular participation of faculty trained in different generations and with different methodological and thematic preferences in discussions about the field, where it is, and where it should be. This can help with some of the potential challenges associated with faculty searches. Pairing faculty up with others in the department (and rearranging the pairs every year or two) for ongoing orientation and mentoring can be very helpful. Putting aside departmental resources to support jointly authored papers between faculty and faculty and students can also help foster relationships and belonging. Another way to institutionalize opportunities for ongoing orientation for faculty is to hold faculty presentations and workshops which are meant to either let a faculty member walk through the reasoning for studying a specific issue or to teach and give insight into a particular methodology or literature. Rather than having faculty presenting 'finished' products for review (important for other reasons), allowing faculty to explore and publicly deliberate on why "X" is of interest and how they think it can be studied or to share and teach colleagues are moments in which greater awareness of colleagues and the field can be developed.

Conclusion: Enjoying the Valleys of Learning

One of the most insightful recommendations received from a former colleague during orientation was to enjoy the valleys of learning. Indeed, this is a recommendation for students, professors, and administrators alike. The wisdom in the expression lends itself to many situations without one specific mechanism for application of the insight. One lesson from more than two decades as an academic is that frustration in research and teaching is normal but can be productive as well as disabling. In class, one of us reminds students that almost all of the time spent on a paper is spent figuring out what one wants to argue vis-a-vis extant literature, while writing the paper can be done in a short time. Yet, scholars tend to feel they have accomplished something only when they see words on a page. Frustration is bound to emerge, and it is important to remind students that much learning does not produce immediately obvious standards of success, such as a paper, publication, or grant. Students need a strategy for building a successful career while navigating academia's *culture of overwork* (for more insight into this culture, see chapter 53.)

Anticipating these highs and lows, understanding how common they are in the field and profession, experiencing them with a concerned cohort of fellow students and engaged faculty all enrich the graduate experience and help overcome the challenges faced. These challenges are real as usually only 26–27% of graduate students in doctoral programs in political science make it to ABD status (APSA 2021, 9). Additionally, roughly 32% of students land a tenure track position after graduating (APSA 2021, 10).[7] (Chapter 66 provides insight into the decision to leave graduate school, while chapters 41 and 42 detail ways to pursue careers outside of academia.) Orienting students early and in an ongoing fashion can best provide students with information, activities, networks, and confidence that can lead to success and happiness in graduate school and beyond.

Endnotes

1   The great challenge of an orientation is that it aims to convey wisdom that was learned over time, in dialogue and struggle, in edited form, separated from lived experience. The role time plays in becoming a member of a community was attested to in Aristotle's *Eudemian Ethics* where "fellowship," "the special task of political science" is understood as something that occurs only after trials over time (EE 1234b22-23, 1237b/1238a3).

2   Those who do not know about office hours or face an 'imposter syndrome' are less likely to seek out faculty unless there is a problem, and even then only after the problem has snowballed that the student feels overwhelmed. Underrepresented students who are among the first in their family and social circle to enter graduate school are more likely to struggle with proactive engagement with faculty (Gable 2021). This difficulty is driven by misperceptions about office hours, which can be accentuated if students have one or two bad experiences either during their time as

undergraduates or as graduate students.

3   One practice that is especially helpful is to ask students in office hours, 'how are your other classes going?' and 'how has your first/second/third year been going?' Questions which move the discussion to the student's general experience outside of your class together can open up space for students to feel more comfortable and ask different questions which can be fundamental to the student's success, professional development, and personal flourishing. Although faculty often feel rushed, they should be very careful to model academic engagement in office hours: office hours should not be seen as responding to student questions, but as opportunities to learn about the students and understand how better to direct their attention and studies.

4   There are, of course, some conferences that are more inviting for undergraduate and graduate student participation and faculty should share information with students about these conferences.

5   Had they been consciously participating in orientation over time, perhaps they would be less anxious.

6   When one of us began a mentor program, an associate professor asked about whether this was only for new or assistant professors. The program was designed for all faculty, and it matched assistant professors and lecturers with associate professors, associate professors with full professors.

7   This is the 11-year average that was provided by APSA before the COVID pandemic. However, in the 2018-2019 year, the average was 28.40%, down about 5 percentage points (p. 10).

References

APSA. 2021. "APSA Graduate Placement Report: Analysis of Political Science Placements for 2018-2020." American Political Science Association. https://preprints.apsanet.org/engage/api-gateway/apsa/assets/orp/resource/item/61649e5d8b620d1d574c4b7f/original/apsa-graduate-placement-report-analysis-of-political-science-placements-for-2018-2020.pdf (Accessed December 6, 2021), 1-23.

Jacobs, Jerry A. And Sarah E. Winslow. 2004. "Overworked Faculty: Job Stresses and Family Demands." *The ANNALS of the American Academy of Political and Social Science*. November.

Fugate, Gregory A., Patricia A. Jaramillo, and Robert R. Preuhs. 2001. "Graduate Students Mentoring Graduate Students: A Model for Professional Development." *PS: Political Science & Politics* 34 (1): 132–33.

Gable, Rachel. 2021. *The Hidden Curriculum: First Generation Students at Legacy Universities.* Princeton: Princeton University Press.

Guerrero, Mario and Alisa Beth Rod. 2013. "Engaging in Office Hours: A Study of Student-Faculty Interaction and Academic Performance." *Journal of Political Science Education* 9 (4): 403-416.

Hesli, Vicki L., Evelyn C. Fink, and Diane M. Duffy. 2003. "The Role of Faculty in Creating a Positive Graduate Student Experience: Survey Results from the Midwest Region, Part II." *PS: Political Science & Politics* 36 (4): 801-804.

Hu, Shouping, George D. Kuh, and Shaoqing Li. 2008. "The Effects of Engagement in Inquiry-Oriented Activities on Student Learning and Personal Development." *Innovative Higher Education* 33 (2): 71–81.

Mealy, Kimberly A. 2018. "American Political Science Association Diversity and Inclusion Report." Washington, DC: American Political Science Association.

Mealy, Kimberly A. 2009. "Supporting Education, Professional Development, and Diversity." *PS: Political Science & Politics* 42 (1): 1 (supplement).

Munck, Gerardo L., and Richard Snyder, eds. 2007. *Passion Method and Craft in Comparative Politics.* Baltimore, MD: Johns Hopkins University Press.

Pascarella, Ernest. T., Christopher T. Pierson, Gregory C. Wolniak, and Patrick T. Terenzini. 2004. "First-Generation College Students: Additional Evidence on College Experiences and Outcomes." *Journal of Higher Education* 75 (3): 249-284.

Tormos-Aponte, Fernando and Mayra Velez-Serrano. 2020. "Broadening the Pathway for Graduate Students in Political Science." *PS: Political Science & Politics* 53 (1): 145–46.

Yanow, Dvora. 2020. "'Mentoring,' Past and Present." *PS: Political Science & Politics* 53 (4): 770–74.

7 Building a Supportive Mentoring Network

Mary Anne S. Mendoza[1] & Samantha A. Vortherms[2]

1. California State Polytechnic University, Pomona 2. University of California, Irvine

KEYWORDS: Near-Peers, Formal Mentoring, Informal Mentoring, General Mentors, Subject Experts, Methodological Experts, Faculty Advocate, Readers.

Introduction

Mentors come in many forms, but all mentors provide various forms of support over the course of our graduate careers. Building a supportive network of faculty, near-peer, and peer mentors both inside your department and the political science community more broadly helps you advance your career and makes the often-challenging process of graduate school easier. Mentors provide a range of support, including direct career advice, research guidance, emotional support, and a sense of belonging. Developing a supportive network is important for all graduate students but is particularly beneficial for graduate students from under-represented backgrounds, as mentors can provide a sense of belonging in an alienating environment and open doors to important resources. In this chapter, we outline the who, what, where, when, why, and how of building a mentoring network. We argue that you should think of mentorship not as a single relationship between yourself and your advisor, but broadly as a network for support that provides guidance from a variety of sources. We highlight the types of roles mentors can play and provide advice on where to find mentors and existing resources to help you build the support you need to thrive in graduate school and your career.

Who, What, and Why Mentorship?

Building a mentoring network starts with understanding who "counts" as a mentor. In general, mentors are people we trust to provide advice based on their expertise and experience. Academic advisors, and faculty in our department, are often clear candidates for mentors. But these are not the only people that graduate students can turn to for advice. In some cases, graduate students may need multiple mentors for different things and faculty advisors should not be the only source of mentorship for everything. *Near-peers*—graduate students in older cohorts and postdoctoral fellows—can also be mentors, especially since they understand how to navigate the formal and informal expectations of the program. Peers in the same cohort can also serve as a mentor because they are colleagues with potentially valuable insight and the shared experience of graduate school. Mentoring involves "sharing experiences, hardships, and knowledge to help others to grow, advance and carry on a legacy" (Marino 2020, 748). This means that mentors are all of those around you who provide support based on their past experiences.

Mentorship is often framed as a formal affair where students and faculty are assigned to each other, but not every university sets junior scholars up with mentors. Similarly, most faculty who are willing to work with you are unlikely to proactively seek out mentees and establish a mentorship relationship.

This is not because they are uninterested, but because of busy workloads. Therefore, understanding the formal and informal ways that mentorship occurs is useful for junior scholars trying to find mentors.

Formal mentoring—which occurs as an established relationship between a faculty member or senior graduate student and their assigned graduate student—has stated objectives. One prime example is your academic advisor and committee members who, at the very least, provide feedback on your research and sign off on your progress through the degree. Other examples of formal mentorship can be found through opportunities in your department, university, or field when you sign up for a mentor and are matched with a volunteer.

Informal mentoring, however, happens more organically and may not always have stated objectives. An informal mentor can be a faculty member not on your committee or a graduate student (near-)peer. These may also be individuals you meet at conference panels, receptions, or doing research. Informal mentoring usually develops naturally as you build professional and personal relationships.

Approaches to Mentorship

Many students begin their graduate programs with one model of mentorship in mind. They see advisors as intellectual sculptors while expecting guidance and direction from one source. In reality, this is only one form of mentorship. Moreover, it is often not the most effective for all students. Three of the most common forms of mentoring relationships are the master-apprentice model, the hierarchical model, and the network model (*Figure 7.1*).

Figure 7.1: Mentoring Relationships

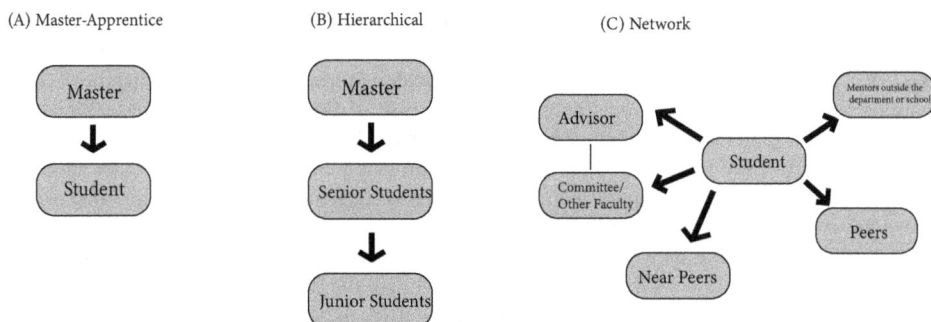

(A) Master-Apprentice

Master → Student

(B) Hierarchical

Master → Senior Students → Junior Students

(C) Network

Advisor, Committee/Other Faculty, Student, Mentors outside the department or school, Peers, Near Peers

The master-apprentice model ties the student to one mentor who provides all of the mentoring and support the student needs. The hierarchical model builds on this by creating a hierarchy of scholars based on experience within the advisor's group. Lastly, in the network model, students approach a variety of people for mentoring; thus, it is the broadest model.

While there is no one-type-fits-all model, we believe the network model is the most beneficial for most students. By broadening your mentoring network, you have greater avenues for support and can create a community to support you through the different challenges and phases of graduate school.

Roles Mentors Play

Mentors play a variety of roles throughout your career, both during and after graduate school, including these common roles:

General mentors include your advisor and committee members or those in your department who have a direct say over the progress of your career. An advisor provides the most direct feedback on one's work and career progress. Other faculty members, on and off your committee, can also advise you on a wide variety of topics such as setting deadlines for timely completion of program requirements, providing direction on research papers, or resolving in-classroom difficulties when teaching.

A subject expert is someone who knows your research area well. Subject experts are helpful at directing you to case-specific literature and understanding your case or topic more broadly.

Methodological experts are mentors who can help you complete your research design or approach. These mentors help you identify appropriate methodological approaches, gain skills for methods, and review results.

A *faculty advocate* uses their position to advocate for your interests or individual concerns. Advocates often know you or your situation well. We contend that advocates serve to ensure that you, as a person, are valued beyond your research input. Universities can have complex systems of governance and advocates help you navigate the institutional structures that exist to provide you with the best support.

Readers are people willing to read your work and give you substantive feedback at different stages. Final products, whether dissertation chapters, articles, or books, never get published without the feedback of multiple readers. In earlier years, readers largely come from your institution, but in later years it is helpful to have readers from outside your department to provide new perspectives. Faculty members can all be readers, but near-peer and peer mentors are also invaluable. If you are particularly concerned about your work being "ready" to submit somewhere, near-peer mentors can help you address early-stage problems so that your advisors can focus on higher-level feedback. Students from under-represented groups benefit disproportionately from peer mentoring through reading and writing groups (Cassese and Holman 2018). Readers can be further broken down by the type of feedback they give.

- *Napkin Readers* help you brainstorm, such as sketching out an argument on a napkin over a coffee. They are great at asking questions about your ideas and push you to think about your work in a different light.
- *The Cheerleader* is good at positive reinforcement. Many times, the Cheerleader can see your work contextualized in ways that you cannot, identifying how your research speaks to a broader audience.
- *The Critic* is a reader who provides a hard-hitting assessment of your work. They identify weaknesses in your argument or methodological approach while also helping you overcome them.
- *The Specialist* knows your area of study well. They provide the first "sniff" test—an informal reality check—of an idea or an argument.
- *Line-by-Line readers* help us polish language and clarify our arguments. They are willing (and able!) to read your writing closely to edit grammar while also helping clarify language so your argument comes across clearly.
- *Older sibling mentors* are graduate students in advanced cohorts who have already experienced the stages of the program that lie ahead of you. These mentors provide invaluable institutional knowledge ranging from logistical questions, such as how to get conference travel reimbursed, to what it's like working with certain faculty members. Older sibling mentors have been there, in your department, and can share their experiences.

Graduate school and academic life is challenging for any number of reasons. One of the essential peer-mentor roles is that of emotional supporters. While some graduate students are prone to competition, the role of an emotional support mentor is to listen empathetically, make space for your concerns, and validate your experiences. Graduate students from other institutions can be especially valuable sources of emotional support, since they can empathize with your experience without knowing the members of your department as intimately.

Accountability mentors are those who help keep you on track and get your work done, so that projects move forward. There are many ways to do accountability groups in graduate school: sitting down to write together, email check-ins, sharing to-do lists, or setting deadlines and follow-ups. Find a way that works for you and surround yourself with people who help you keep your momentum up.

Why it Matters

Mentors provide information about the broad process of graduate school and developing as a scholar because they have been there. Mentors gained their experience through learning from or collaborating with others and can introduce you to other scholars in the field, point out useful resources, and identify other potentials for your research. Based on their experiences, they help mentees overcome obstacles and prevent unnecessary challenges. For example, research shows engaging in mentoring networks improves women's likelihood of obtaining a faculty position (Argyle and Mendelberg 2020). Peer mentoring also improves professional, learning, social, and psychological outcomes for students (Fugate, Jaramillo, and Preuhs 2001; Lorenzetti et al. 2019).

Mentors can provide invaluable insight into how to navigate unknown experiences, such as the importance of having an elevator speech or what to do if a more senior person is being untoward at a reception. Students, especially from under-represented backgrounds, may not always have the privilege of knowing the expected behaviors in certain situations, making this knowledge sharing even more important. For some students, mentors can also help them navigate and challenge the limits of how to "present" oneself, especially when academia places additional expectations on students of color or LGBTQ+ individuals. This volume includes several chapters on concerns for individuals of particular groups, please see the section on strategies for addressing implicit bias, harassment, and assault.

Moreover, mentors also benefit from these relationships. For senior mentors, mentees are rising stars with new and interesting perspectives. Mentees help expose mentors to cutting edge research topics, methods, and innovative teaching. Many of us love working with graduate students, helping them progress through the field. Peer mentors also gain substantially from engaging in relationships, as support is mutually constituted.

Where to Find Mentors

Just like the various roles for mentors, there are a range of places to look for mentorship. The first place to develop your mentoring network is within your department. The faculty in your department should form the core of your general mentoring network. Practically speaking, they are gatekeepers who monitor and approve your progress through the program.

Colleagues in your department are also a key source of peer mentors. Coursework provides a captive audience for building social capital necessary for your peer network. Building local peer networks can be as simple as asking a fellow student to chat over coursework or research over coffee or as involved as establishing a writing group with regular meetings where you read each other's work. You may also find mentors outside of your department on campus, especially in a broader school of Social Sciences or in the Humanities. This helps build networks around different topics or methodological approaches.

Mentors outside of your academic institution can also serve as a valuable source of information that is relevant for a wider range of situations. Formally, graduate students can participate in formal mentoring programs with the professional organizations listed at the end of this chapter to connect with mentors outside of their institution. Informally, finding a mentor can happen organically, such as through talking to fellow graduate students in your department/university or meeting someone at a conference panel or reception. Taking initiative, however, helps maintain these relationships by taking a single encounter and making it substantive.

We want to stress, however, that graduate students should not feel pressured to force a mentorship relationship with someone who is aggressive, unprofessional, or unsupportive. The most important feature of a mentoring relationship is that it provides productive support for the student. While mentors are there to provide advice, it can be difficult to accept that from someone that we do not trust to have our best interests at heart. More importantly, graduate students should not feel like the power imbalances require that they feel unsafe or suffer through disrespect, even if a potential mentor is "famous." Therefore, we strongly encourage graduate students to keep an open mind about who counts as a mentor and types of support. One person should not be your mentor for everything. Mentors are people too, with limits in time, energy, and capability.

Graduate students from under-represented backgrounds may not always have mentors who understand them. In some cases, a mentor might actively discourage these students or disregard how their circumstances influence their experience of the program. This should be a sign to widen your mentoring network and shift your expectations from that particular mentor.

Some students may worry that being proactive in developing mentoring relationships creates a burden for their mentors, especially mentors from under-represented backgrounds. However, these mentors often have invaluable expertise in navigating academia that can help students with similar backgrounds. This is also why we advocate for the network model, since it widens your community of support and reduces the likelihood of depending on just one or two people. Ultimately, mentors choose to participate in mentoring relationships, which may help alleviate some concerns about over-burdening, as well.

When and How to Develop New and Existing Relationships

There are many ways to develop one's mentoring network. Some will come naturally while others may feel awkward at first. Remember that network building and finding people who support you and your progress is a process. Begin as early as you can with the activities you are comfortable with. When you find a relationship that works well for you, invest in developing that relationship. Both the forms of network building and the substance of relationships change as you move across stages of graduate school. Below are actionable recommendations for how to develop mentoring relationships.

- Be an active citizen of your department. Many mentoring relationships, especially at the beginning of your graduate career, are in your own department. Attend workshops, ask relevant questions, and set up meetings with visiting scholars. Meet with faculty in your department even if you are not taking their class.
- Invest in getting to know other graduate students in your department. Hear of a more advanced graduate student whose research is interesting? Ask them for a chat over coffee.
- Take advantage of conferences. Attend panels and ask questions, either during the panel or afterwards when people stand around and chat. Schedule a meeting with someone whose work interests you. Most people will be excited about your interest. One easy way to start building relationships is to have them talk about themselves and their work. Look for formal mentorship opportunities during conferences.
- Ask for introductions. If you know someone who knows someone you would like to meet, ask them for an introductory email. Finding relevant mentors can be particularly difficult for students from under-represented backgrounds. Even one relevant mentor can unlock a series of connections that can dramatically widen a mentee's network.
- Act in good faith. Some students, especially from under-represented backgrounds, may feel apprehensive about reaching out for guidance. If someone tells you to "let them know if you need anything," assume this is a genuine offer. Take a chance and reach out. If they seem unreceptive or unresponsive, move on to the next person.

Conclusion

This chapter has provided a categorization of who mentors are, what they can do, where to find them, when early scholars might need them, why mentorship matters, and how to build a supportive network. While not comprehensive, we hope that this approach clarifies the importance of being proactive about filling out a supportive network early in your graduate career and that mentorship is not solely a formal affair.

Every student is different and a network approach to mentorship allows students to identify and develop mentoring relationships based on their individual needs when they need it. Graduate students from under-represented backgrounds stand to benefit from cultivating their networks, since this can help them benefit from the experience and expertise of senior scholars. Mentors also have different preferences. Casting your net widely ensures that you have multiple sources of support for facing different challenges, an essential practice to ensure that you not only survive, but thrive in graduate school.

Resources

General Resources
- National Center for Faculty Development and Development: NCFDD Mentor Map (https://www.facultydiversity.org/ncfddmentormap)
- University of Washington's Graduate Mentoring Materials (https://grad.uw.edu/for-students-and-post-docs/core-programs/mentoring/mentoring-guides-for-students/building-your-mentoring-team/)
- Shives, K.D. 2012. "Picking a Good Mentor." Inside Higher Ed. (https://www.insidehighered.com/blogs/gradhacker/picking-good-mentor)
- On building peer reader mentoring relationships: Sarnecka, Barbara. 2021. The Writing Workshop (https://osf.io/5qcdh/)

Professional Organization Programs
- APSA Mentor Program (https://www.apsanet.org/mentor)
- APSA Women's Research Mentoring Workshop (https://connect.apsanet.org/womensresearchworkshop/)
- ISA Committee on the Status of Women Pay it Forward Program (https://www.isanet.org/Conferences/Special-Convention-Programs/Pay-It-Forward#:~:text=Pay%20It%20Forward%20is%20a%20limited-attendance%20special%20workshop,their%20Ph.D.%E2%80%99s%20or%20early%20in%20their%20faculty%20careers.)
- WPSA Peer-to-Peer Mentors for Scholars of Politics, Groups, and Identities (http://wpsanet.org/virtual/p2p_mentor.php)

References

Argyle, Lisa P., and Tali Mendelberg. 2020. "Improving Women's Advancement in Political Science: What We Know About What Works." *PS: Political Science & Politics* 53 (4):718-722.

Cassese, Erin C, and Mirya R Holman. 2018. "Writing groups as models for peer mentorship among female faculty in political science." *PS: Political Science & Politics* 51 (2):401.

Fugate, Gregory A., Patricia A. Jaramillo, and Robert R. Preuhs. 2001. "Graduate students mentoring graduate students: A model for professional development." *PS: Political Science & Politics* 34 (1):132-133.

Lorenzetti, Diane L., Leah Shipton, Lorelli Nowell, Michele Jacobsen, Liza Lorenzetti, Tracey Clancy, and Elizabeth Oddone Paolucci. 2019. "A systematic review of graduate student peer mentorship in academia." *Mentoring & Tutoring: Partnership in Learning* 27 (5):549-576. doi: 10.1080/13611267.2019.1686694.

Marino, Francesco E. 2020. "Mentoring gone wrong: What is happening to mentorship in academia?" *Policy Futures in Education* 19 (7):747-751.

Monroe, Kristen Renwick. "Mentoring in political science." *PS: Political Science & Politics* 36, no. 1 (2003): 93-96.

8

Speak of the Devil and (S)he Appears: The Role of Academic Administrators During Graduate School and Beyond

Lauren C. Bell[1]

1. Randolph-Macon College

KEYWORDS: Administration, Board of Trustees, Chancellor, Dean, Department Chair, Provost.

Who Are Administrators (And Why Do We Need Them Anyway?)

Administrators have supervisory authority over a college or university unit—a college, a department, or an office. They set policies; they supervise staff (and, in the case of academic administrators, may supervise faculty members); they manage the unit's budget and may have fundraising responsibilities; they hire, train, supervise, and fire direct reports; they mediate conflicts between and among the constituents for their area; they must attend to the reporting requirements of their institution's governing board as well as requirements imposed by state and federal regulators and accreditors. Every campus has administrators with responsibility for enrolling students, providing a robust academic program, ensuring that students have a variety of services and supports outside the classroom, fundraising and institutional advancement, budgeting and finance, responding to state and federal reporting requirements, and athletics—and that only scratches the surface of what administrators are called upon to do.

In early universities, administrators were few and often included only a president appointed by a governing board (Gerber 2014). Gerber documents the professionalization of the faculty during the early-to-mid-twentieth century, and reports that as faculty members professionalized and the professoriate became an established career path, faculty members began to take on both instructional and administrative roles at universities and colleges. However, by the end of the twentieth century, concern about the usurpation of faculty authority by administrators became a common complaint among faculty members. For at least the last 30 years, university faculty members have been harshly critical of "administrative bloat," identifying increased expenditures on administrators as largely responsible for the proliferation of paperwork, reporting requirements, and bureaucracy that reduce faculty members' time for teaching and intellectual activity (Bergmann 1991). One need only look to Twitter's @ass_deans account to get a sense of the esteem in which administrators and administration as a concept are held by many faculty members these days.

There's certainly truth to the claims about the proliferation of administrators on college and university campuses. A quick glance at the University of Michigan's institutional organization chart, for example, reveals 82 separate administrative divisions, each with its own organizational chart.[1] And Michigan is no different from any other doctoral/research university. Ginsburg (2011) documents the growth of both administrative and staff ranks in higher education, noting that whereas the average faculty-to-student ratio has largely stayed flat over the last quarter century, the administrator-to-student ratio and staff-member-to-student ratio has fallen, indicating that greater numbers of administrators and staff members have been hired to do things like provide counseling services, student activities, and residential living support—all while faculty class sizes have burgeoned (Bergmann 1991) and tenure lines have been eliminated (Ginsburg 2011). However, even if they wanted to significantly reduce the number of administrators on their campuses, most institutions could not eliminate them for a whole host of practical and regulatory reasons. Indeed, institutions have been under pressure from the federal government to increase certain activities—and their reporting around them—in order to maintain their eligibility for federal financial aid (Smole 2009), and these mandates have sometimes necessitated additional administrator and staff hires. Changes in technology have also driven changes in the administrative and staff workforce on college and university campuses, with more informational and instructional technologists needed to provide support to faculty and students.

Finally, on some campuses, administrative growth reflects a reluctance among faculty to take on the increasingly tedious and complex work of administering the institution, shifting more authority to the administration and contributing to the growth in administrative hires. As the American Association for University Professors acknowledged in a 1994 statement: "Faculty members must be willing to participate in the decision-making processes over which a sound governance system gives them authority. If they do not, authority will drift away from them, since someone must exercise it, and if members of the faculty do not, others will" (AAUP 1994). Indeed, as Lewis and Altbach (1995) reported regarding the Carnegie International Survey of the Academic Profession, "very few faculty express an interest in taking on more administrative responsibilities. They see such chores as interfering with their teaching and professional commitments. They vociferously complain about not being involved, but consistently reject opportunities to have greater influence on campus affairs."

Figure 8.1: Who's Who? A Summary of Key Administrative Titles and Positions

Board of Trustees/Regents/Visitors: The multi-member governing body for a single campus or for an entire statewide system of higher education (e.g., Board of Regents for Higher Education).

Chancellor/President: Either term may refer to the chief executive officer on a single campus or refer to the singular leader of a multi-campus system in which each campus has its own president.

Provost/Vice President for Academic Affairs: An institution's chief academic officer, who is often considered to be the first among equals among the campus' vice presidents and who may stand in for the college or university president when the president is unavailable.

Dean: Within a university system, deans are the heads of the colleges and schools that make up the university (e.g., the College of Arts and Sciences, School of Performing Arts). On smaller campuses that may have only one college (e.g., many liberal arts colleges) there may be a Dean of the College or Dean of Academic Affairs that serves as the chief academic officer or that serves as the Associate or Assistant Provost.

Department Chair: The administrator with responsibility for a single academic department on campus. Typically reports to a Dean or Associate Dean. This is the administrator that graduate students are most likely to encounter and interact with regularly.

Pathways to Administration

An institution's size and type will influence its organizational chart and the pathways into administration. The example of the University of Michigan's vast organizational chart from earlier illustrates how large the administration might be at a flagship state university. Not surprisingly, a smaller, regional public institution like Kent State University in Ohio has a much smaller—though still fairly large—administrative footprint.[2] Hampden-Sydney College in Farmville, Virginia, which enrolls under 1,000 students has a considerably leaner organizational chart.[3] Institution size may also affect the ways in which an administrator enters the administration. At small, private liberal arts colleges, even senior administrators, particularly but not exclusively in academic affairs, may be hired out of the institution's own faculty; those faculty members often expect to return to the faculty after serving some number of years in the administration. As a result, they are incentivized to strive for good relations with their faculty colleagues.

On the other hand, many administrative positions at larger institutions are subject to a traditional hiring process that may involve search firms with special training in hiring for academic institutions. Candidates who are identified through these kinds of processes may have prior experience as a faculty member, but equally likely, they may have come up in their career through other pathways. For example, as tenure-track faculty positions have become scarcer over the last several decades, PhD holders in many fields turned to administrative work on university campuses as an alternative (Golde 2019). Other administrators come to college and university administrative work having completed an advanced degree in the academic field of higher education administration. They may not have a substantive background in another academic field and instead have been educated for the purpose of becoming administrators. Although faculty members tend to be broadly critical of administrators, particular vitriol is often directed at these professional administrators.

The pathway into administration almost certainly influences an administrator's view of their work and the work of the faculty at an institution. Professional administrators who lack any specific tie to an institution before being hired to serve in an administrative role will have a greater challenge earning the trust of faculty members than will an administrator who is elevated into an administrative role from among their colleagues. At the same time, however, administrators who enter the institution from outside and with specific training in higher education administration may be able to see and address problems that campus insiders have simply accepted as the status quo. In short, administrators' career pathways have important influences on the ways in which they work with students and faculty members.

Encountering Administrators

Graduate students may have limited opportunities to engage with university administrators, other than with the chair of their department and the administrators who oversee the university's graduate college who are directly involved in helping the student make progress toward degree. Students may interact frequently with their department chair, especially. The chair is typically a member of the faculty in the department who has been given a workload adjustment to take on administrative responsibilities. Such responsibilities may include: developing and managing the department's annual budget; compiling teaching schedules and planning course rotations; the recruitment, mentoring, evaluation, and retention of faculty; the development and implementation of strategies to diversify the faculty and departmental offerings; fostering a climate that supports minoritized and underrepresented students and faculty members; serving as a liaison between the department's faculty and the college or university administration; and interpreting administrative decisions back to faculty members in the department.

At most institutions, when a student experiences a problem with a specific faculty member, with course availability, with the climate in the department, or with access to resources, the department chair is the person to whom the concern should first be directed. Different departments will have different norms of communication, but should it become necessary to contact the department chair about a concern, requesting a meeting through the chair's administrative assistant (if they have one) or sending an e-mail to the chair directly to request a meeting is appropriate. It is a good idea to provide basic details of the concern at the time of the meeting request so that the chair can gather any necessary information prior to the meeting.

Beyond the department chair, it would be unlikely that most graduate students would have significant need to engage with graduate school deans or the institution's leaders—such as the provost or president—as these administrators are unlikely to be immersed in the day-to-day operation of the specific academic program in which the student is enrolled, although graduate students who find themselves with a particular problem to resolve may find that they need to elevate the issue to the college or university level. Graduate students who get involved in their department or university's graduate student government might also encounter these administrators in the course of their work to represent their peers (or those who participate in graduate student unions and other collective bargaining activities; see Chapter 33).

Once a student enters the academic job market, however, university administrators play an integral role in every part of the hiring process. Behind every job posting that appears on APSA's eJobs employment site[4] there have often been painstaking negotiations between the department and the dean, as well as consultation with any number of other administrative units, such as with the institution's human resources office and chief diversity officer. At smaller institutions, the provost, the institution's chief financial officer, and even the president may also be involved in the process to authorize hiring. Everything, from the timing of the search to the content of the ad, to the number of candidates a department is permitted to bring to campus will depend on the negotiations between and among the faculty members seeking to hire a new colleague and the administrators with authority over the hiring process—with the department chair squarely in the middle. (See Chapters 36-40 for information on applying to specific kinds of academic institutions.)

An invitation for an on-campus interview will likely include a meeting with the dean of the college in which the department is housed; at many smaller institutions, the provost and president may meet with job candidates or attend their job talks. Meetings with administrators during the hiring process are chances for job candidates to learn about institutional resources and opportunities that might be available to them beyond what the department can offer. Because the reappointment and tenure processes also involve deans, provosts, and presidents, meeting with these administrators as part of the on-campus interview also provides the chance for job candidates to get a sense of the vision and expectations that each of these administrators has for faculty members at the institution, and to gauge whether the candidate's vision and goals for their own work will likely be well served and supported by the institution's leadership. (For more on academic job interviews, see Chapter 45.)

If a job offer is made, it may come from the department chair or from the dean. At a smaller institution, an offer might come from the provost. Generally speaking, any negotiation that takes place regarding salary, benefits, or startup funds will require some level of institutional approval beyond just the department chair, even if the chair is the job candidate's only point of contact during the negotiations. (For more information about accepting an academic job offer, see Chapter 46.)

Communicating with Administrators

One thing that is important to remember is that administrators are often much less accessible than are the faculty with whom graduate students are used to working. E-mails directly to administrators are often read by administrative assistants, who generally serve as gatekeepers. Graduate students who have a need to meet with an administrator should always be scrupulously professional when working with administrative assistants, as they control access to the administrators they support. (More generally, it is essential to work toward engaging with all members of the university community in a professional way while in graduate school.) As noted previously, when sending an e-mail or making an in-person request for a meeting, it is good practice to provide at least a basic overview of the reason for the meeting. For one thing, no administrator enjoys being blindsided or feeling unprepared for a meeting. More importantly, however, if the administrator can gather pertinent information prior to the meeting, a resolution to the student's concern during the meeting is more likely.

The same is true for job candidates and new faculty members. College and university administrative staff members know who the faculty members are that engage with them in professional ways, and who treats them as second-class members of the academic community; the former will always be given more rapid attention and fuller support.

Summary and Conclusion

Administrators serve different roles than faculty members do. They have greater levels of responsibility to institutional boards and state and federal regulators than do individual faculty members, and administrators and faculty members have different levels of authority and autonomy. There are more administrators now than there used to be, resulting from an increase in the scope of services that colleges and universities now provide, as well as from changes in technology and even from faculty members' own reluctance to do the work of running a complex institution of higher education. How these administrators are educated and how they come into their roles affects how they approach their positions.

Typically, the administrator that graduate students will encounter most frequently is their department chair. In most cases, graduate students have little need to engage with high-level university administrators; this is generally a positive thing, because it means that the student is focused on their education and not on institutional bureaucracy. But, as graduate students become PhD candidates, and then job candidates, and then new faculty—or maybe even new administrators themselves—their engagement with the institution's administration increases by necessity. Engaging with administrators and their administrative staff members in a professional manner can help to support the establishment of a positive working relationship with the administration. Being thoughtful about the institutional and regulatory imperatives that operate on institutional administrators can help to contextualize the decisions they make, even those with which the faculty disagree.

Endnotes

1   See: https://spg.umich.edu/org-charts/organizational-structure.

2   See: https://www.kent.edu/president/organizational-charts.

3   See: https://www.hsc.edu/human-resources/organizational-charts.

4   The American Political Science Association (APSA) eJobs website (https://apsanet.org/eJobs) provides a link to job postings in political science, public administration, public law, administration, and non-academic related fields. Membership in APSA is not required to view job listings.

References

Altbach, Philip, and Lionel Lewis. 1995. "Faculty Versus Administration: A Universal Problem." *International Higher Education*, no. 2 (March). https://doi.org/10.6017/ihe.1995.2.6175.

American Association of University Professors. 1994. "On the Relationship of Faculty Governance to Academic Freedom." Available online at: https://www.aaup.org/report/relationship-faculty-governance-academic-freedom.

Bergmann, Barbara R. 1991. "Bloated Administration, Blighted Campuses." *Academe* 77, no. 6: 12–16. http://www.jstor.org/stable/40250269.

Gerber, Larry G. 2014. *The Rise and Decline of Faculty Governance: Professionalization and the Modern American University*. Baltimore: Johns Hopkins University Press.

Ginsburg, Douglas. 2011. "Administrators Ate My Tuition." *Washington Monthly*, September/October 2011. Available online at: https://washingtonmonthly.com/magazine/septoct-2011/administrators-ate-my-tuition/.

Golde, Chris. 2019. "Grad Students Should Consider Administrative Work." *Inside Higher Education*, August 5, 2009. Available online at: https://www.insidehighered.com/advice/2019/08/05/phd-students-should-consider-careers-higher-education-administration-opinion.

Smole, David P. 2009. "Reporting and Disclosure Requirements for Institutions of Higher Education to Participate in Federal Student Aid Programs Under Title IV of the Higher Education Act." *CRS Report to Congress*. Available online at: https://crsreports.congress.gov/product/details?prodcode=R40789.

9

When Do Titles Matter and Why? A Guide for Graduate Students in Political Science

Meg K. Guliford[1], Meena Bose[2], & Dan Drezner[3]

1. Drexel University 2. Hofstra University 3. Tufts University

KEYWORDS: Professor, Dr., Honorifics.

What Do You Need To Know?

What to call your professors might be the most minor and awkward topic addressed in this guidebook. To paraphrase Woodrow Wilson, perhaps the debate is so fierce because the stakes seem so small. After all, does it really matter? Many professors are explicit in how they wish to be addressed in their course syllabi. Most professors will gently correct a student who is too formal or informal in their interactions. Surely this kerfuffle is a superficial and insignificant part of graduate student training. The truth is more complex. As recent debates over how to refer to Jill Biden given her EdD suggest, questions of honorifics are freighted with meaning (Epstein 2020; Jabour 2020). Learning how to recognize and navigate multiple expectations for formal and informal professional interactions is essential for success in graduate school and post-graduate employment. How to address professors is a perfect example of the hidden curriculum contained within any PhD program (Margolis and Romero 1988).

Graduate school—and graduate students—occupy a liminal space between undergraduates and academics. The zones of uncertainty are considerable, as are the stresses involved in passing comprehensive exams, conceiving an idea for a dissertation, and researching and writing said dissertation. Clear guidelines on how to address more senior scholars in the field will hopefully free up your scarcest and most valuable resource—i.e., your brain—to concentrate on the more scholarly dimensions of your training.

Our golden rule is a simple one. Whenever there is any uncertainty in initial interactions with professors both inside and outside your department, default to formality and then adjust accordingly over time. In other words, when first contacting professors, begin by calling them "professor." It is the easiest, most risk-averse move. In many settings the honorific will quickly be set aside—but not always.

Why Does It Matter?

In many US political science PhD programs, graduate students are encouraged to call their professors by their first name.[1] The logic is straightforward: in training PhDs, professors are attempting to mentor students who will eventually become peers. One way to signal this process is to have everyone call each other by their first names. Why bother with formality in a collegial environment?

One reason, which applies to all the situations described below, is that not all graduate programs operate this way. In some graduate schools, particularly public policy programs like the Fletcher School at Tufts, the bulk of the students are pursuing a terminal master's degree. The assumption that these students will enter the academy does not hold.

Another reason is that some faculty may be less willing to disregard their honorifics. Whether one looks at citation patterns, student evaluations, or faculty surveys, the evidence for gender and racial bias in academic political science is considerable (Maliniak, Powers, and Walter 2013; Mitchell and Martin 2018; Chávez and Mitchell 2020). These biases extend to variations in the use of honorifics. Women and faculty of color are more likely to be called by their first name in professional settings (Files et al 2017). This jibes with first-person accounts by professors in these categories (Berry 2014). Using a first name without invitation could be viewed as an unintentional slight. Furthermore, junior faculty are also closer in age to that of the median graduate student. Honorifics can serve as a reminder of the appropriate boundaries that should exist between professors and graduate students.

What Should You Do?

Written Correspondence

Virtually all written engagement with professors will take place electronically. Therein lies a potential problem. As early as 1985, observers noted that compared to other forms of communication, electronic mail was far more likely to generate miscommunications, misperceptions, and impulsive emotional responses (Shapiro and Anderson 1985). For younger generations who are digital natives, the informalities of texting and social media are simply taken as given. Many professors also have social media accounts, blurring and multiplying the channels of communication even further. Switching from informal arenas to more formal modes of contact means that opportunities for unintentional missteps abound.

Given this kind of environment, the safest and surest way to proceed is to start any new interaction with a bias toward formality. In emailing professors both within and without your department for the first time, open with "Dear Professor [last name]" rather than opening with "Hi [first name]!" If they use their first name in any of their responses to you, then that is the appropriate social cue to reciprocate and use their first name in any future correspondence. If they do not, however, then that should be interpreted as a signal to continue using the "professor" honorific.

The worst-case scenario with this approach is a professor gently chiding you to call them by their first name. Opting for informality, however, can create a bad first impression. As Laura Portwood-Stacer (2016) observed: "An honorific is a title used to communicate respect for a person's position. Whether or not you, as a student, actually respect your professor's authority or position, it's a good idea to act like you do." If this seems like kowtowing to a professor's perceived insecurities, bear in mind that they earned their title by completing the very degree that you are now pursuing.

Are there exceptions to this rule in written correspondence? Over time, yes. If advanced graduate students show excessive deference, they might cause a professor at another institution to mistakenly believe that they are more junior than is actually the case. For example, if advanced graduate students are organizing conference panels and need to solicit faculty at other institutions, opening with "Dear [first name]" and adding "(if I may)" just afterward would be the best approach.

Use of Titles in the Classroom

As with written communication, having a bias toward formality in the classroom is recommended. Taking and teaching classes as a graduate student requires multiple levels of preparation, and determining how to address faculty—and be addressed by undergraduates—can be very stressful. Guidelines are helpful if provided by individual instructors, but, in the absence of official guidance, these informal recommendations can establish a comfortable and professional classroom dynamic.

Graduate seminars are very different from undergraduate courses in that there is an understanding that everyone in the group is actively engaged in classic and contemporary debates in the scholarly literature. Ideally, the professor will establish at the start what the protocol will be for names. Many graduate school faculty expect that "Professor" or "Dr" will be used until students complete their comprehensive exams, after which first names are more common while students conduct doctoral research. Some faculty may say first names should be used from the start, but if not, then using a title is recommended.

Do not assume, regardless of whether the professor has just completed their dissertation and started teaching, or is a senior scholar in the discipline, that use of first names will be welcome.

That said, attention to classroom dynamics also is important. Graduate students begin their programs with varying degrees of academic and professional expertise—some start directly after college, while others join a doctoral program after working for some time, or earning a graduate degree from another institution. They may have different assumptions about titles in the classroom, particularly if they have been working in a field where use of first names is standard. If some graduate students address faculty by first name and faculty do not object, then an informal norm of no titles appears to be established. Having the professor determine what the classroom protocol will be is preferred, and inquiring is reasonable. In the absence of clear communication, titles are recommended unless an informal practice of first names develops. In that case, using a title is still fine, but making sure that some students are not perceived as more senior than others because they use first names is important. Again, professors should establish guidelines, and if they do not, then asking is the best way to have clarity on the topic.

Graduate students who teach a small-group section of a course, or their own course entirely, should consider how they want to be addressed by undergraduates and make that clear from the beginning of the term. In a course with multiple sections, some discussion among graduate students and instructors will be helpful. Instructors who have completed their doctorate may prefer to use a title, while graduate students who are working on their dissertations may not object to first names. Above all, ensure that you are comfortable with the use of titles, or not, and then inform undergraduates accordingly to establish the classroom structure.

As with informal dynamics in a graduate seminar, graduate student instructors should be prepared to address the possibility that some undergraduates will assume that first names are acceptable. If this happens, then gently letting your students know that you prefer a title—professor, dr., etc.—is fine. Making this clear will be helpful for all students in the classroom, and students should follow your direction. If a student repeatedly uses your first name when you have requested otherwise, then a direct discussion may be productive. If there is continued resistance (unlikely, but can happen), then you will want to raise the issue with your department chair to determine how best to proceed.

Use of Titles in Individual Interactions and at Formal Events

Similar to the use of titles in classrooms and written communication, settings such as a seminar series, conferences, and workshops can also serve as sources of angst for graduate students about how to address faculty. Students begin encountering external faculty early in their programs, and, over time, students are called upon to introduce departmental and external faculty at different events. The same rules of the road outlined for written communications apply for occasions in which students individually introduce themselves to faculty, but more formal introductions require a different set of considerations. While no universal rules exist for the use of honorifics, following three general guidelines can help to avoid embarrassment or rebuke when introducing oneself to speakers or introducing speakers to others.

The same default to formality recommended for written correspondence represents the most conservative of the three guidelines for a graduate student's introduction to and of faculty. This approach conveys a degree of titular deference that minimizes the risk of a student being perceived as flippant or brazen. More importantly, it allows the senior person to set the terms of subsequent interactions by either accepting the formality or by responding with "Please feel free to call me [name]." From this exchange, students may adjust their language accordingly.

The second guideline is specific to the introduction of speakers at seminars, workshops, or conferences. It is the most effective method of mitigating confusion with introductions, but assumes the benefit of time. Graduate students often are charged with coordinating departmental seminar series and workshops and frequently serve as conference discussants. In such roles, they can and should use the benefit of time before the event to specifically ask faculty how they wish to be referenced during an introduction. The language then used in the introduction provides a strong signal for other graduate students to follow. There is a distinct difference between "It is my pleasure to welcome Professor [first name, last name] to our seminar. Professor [last name]..." and "It is my pleasure to welcome Professor [first name, last name] to our seminar. [First name]..."

Observing before acting serves as the final guideline for these interactions. This involves mirroring the language used by peer-level graduate students in their interactions with a faculty member. While an approach available to students, it should be considered a last resort, as it is fraught with ambiguity and does not provide important context. A fellow student may have an existing relationship with a particular faculty member that affords them liberties not available to other students. The student being observed could be a co-author with the faculty member and may be introducing them to another potential co-author.

Endnotes

1   This norm varies widely across the globe. In some locales, such as Australia, England, or Scandinavia, the norm is to always use first names. In other regions the norm is more formal.

References (and Further Reading)

Berry, Carlotta. 2014. "They Call Me Doctor Berry." *New York Times*, November 1. https://www.nytimes.com/2014/11/02/opinion/sunday/they-call-me-doctor-berry.html.

Chávez, Kerry, and Kristina MW Mitchell. 2020. "Exploring Bias in Student Evaluations: Gender, Race, and Ethnicity." *PS: Political Science & Politics* 53 (2): 270-274.

Choi, Matthew. 2020. "'One of the Things I'm Most Proud Of Is My Doctorate': Jill Biden Responds to WSJ Op-Ed." *Politico*, December 17. https://www.politico.com/news/2020/12/17/jill-biden-doctorate-wsj-op-ed-448037

Diehl, Amy, and Leanne Dzubinski. 2021. "We Need to Stop 'Untitling' and 'Uncredentialing' Professional Women." *Fast Company*, January 22.

Drezner, Daniel W. 2021. "My Completely Uncontroversial Take On What To Call Your Professor." *Washington Post*, July 21. https://www.washingtonpost.com/outlook/2021/07/21/my-completely-uncontroversial-take-what-call-your-professor/

Epstein, Joseph. 2020. "Is There A Doctor in the White House? Not If You Need An M.D." *Wall Street Journal*, December 11. https://www.wsj.com/articles/is-there-a-doctor-in-the-white-house-not-if-you-need-an-m-d-11607727380

Files, Julia A., et al. 2017. "Speaker Introductions at Internal Medicine Grand Rounds: Forms of Address Reveal Gender Bias." *Journal of Women's Health* 26 (5): 413-419.

Jabour, Anya. 2020. "Referring to Female PhDs as 'Dr.' Promotes Equal Treatment and Values Women's Work." *Washington Post*, December 15. https://www.washingtonpost.com/outlook/2020/12/15/calling-female-phds-dr-promotes-equal-treatment-values-womens-work/.

Margolis, Eric, and Mary Romero. 1988. "'The Department is Very Male, Very White, Very Old, and Very Conservative': The Functioning of the Hidden Curriculum in Graduate Sociology Departments." *Harvard Educational Review* 68 (1): 1-33.

Maliniak, Daniel, Ryan Powers, and Barbara F. Walter. 2013. "The Gender Citation Gap in International Relations." *International Organization* 67 (4): 889-922.

Mitchell, Kristina MW, and Jonathan Martin. 2018. "Gender Bias in Student Evaluations." *PS: Political Science & Politics* 51 (3): 648-652.

Portwood-Stacer, Laure. 2016. "How to Email Your Professor (without being annoying AF)" *Medium*, April 26. https://medium.com/@lportwoodstacer/how-to-email-your-professor-without-being-annoying-af-cf64ae0e4087

Shapiro, Norman, and Robert Anderson. 1985. "Toward an Ethics and Etiquette for Electronic Mail." RAND report R-3283-NSF/RC, July. https://www.rand.org/pubs/reports/R3283.html.

10 Relax! They're Important, But Not Defining Choices: Choosing Your Subfield and Committees

Mike Widmeier[1] & Joseph B. Phillips[2]

1. Webster University 2. The University of Kent

KEYWORDS: Subfield, American Politics, Comparative Politics, International Relations, Political Theory, Methodology, Race, Ethnicity, and Politics.

Introduction

Almost all political science PhD programs require their students to select at least one subfield specialization and populate a dissertation committee. These decisions tap two crucial questions in your graduate journey. First, what are you interested in studying and, given that, who do you wish to work with? You are already forming tentative answers to these questions when selecting a program that fits best with your interests (see chapter 2 on navigating the application process and chapter 4 on choosing a PhD program). However, even in the second or third year of a political science graduate program, people can and do take the opportunity to change their minds. Our goal with this chapter is to help you navigate these choices. After all, they are important. Which subfield you choose will affect which classes you take, what you read, which comprehensive exams you take, and which scholars you work with in your program. However, at the outset, you should know that these choices, while important, should not feel deterministic. The subfield you select will influence which literatures you are likely to contribute to, professional networks you build, and will be one indicator of suitability for specific academic jobs. The committee you form will shape the priority various aspects of your dissertation are given and the connections you will be able to tap during the job market. However, regardless of these choices, you can still contribute the research you want, and build connections with the people you want.

Selecting Your Subfield

The Subfields you Can Choose From

Most political science graduate programs organize themselves in similar ways. These subfield distinctions within graduate programs largely—yet imperfectly—resemble actual divisions in the discipline. Three subfields are almost universal across programs. They include:

- **American Politics:** The study of institutional processes, representation, and mass political behavior within the United States.
- **Comparative Politics:** Using cross-national comparisons to make generalizable inferences about political institutions and behaviors within nations (Clark, Golder, and Golder 2009). This subfield also includes scholars who specialize in the domestic politics of specific countries or regions that are not the United States.
- **International Relations:** The study of diplomacy and conflict between states and within international organizations (Clark, Golder, and Golder 2009). This can also include transna-

tional political behavior conducted by non-state organizations, as well as civil conflict within states.

Two subfields are quite common, but not universal:

- **Political Theory:** Approaching the study of the state and society with a philosophical and/ or normative lens. Some programs have stopped offering political theory as a major field in the last 20 years.
- **Methodology:** The development and application of statistical, experimental, and computational tools for political science. Most programs have introduced it, but not all, and the majority of programs that offer it will offer it as a minor subfield only.
- **Race, Ethnicity, and Politics:** The examination of how race and ethnicity shape political institutions, mass political behavior, and even international relations. It is often seen as a subfield within American politics, but can and does overlap with comparative politics and international relations.

These are not the only way to organize the discipline. Some graduate programs, particularly Duke and UC Merced, organize more specifically by topic (e.g., political institutions vs. behavior). However, these are going to be your likely choices.

The Immediate Decision Before you

By the second or third year of your PhD program, you will administratively declare specialization in one or more subfields. The administrative requirements for programs across the discipline vary considerably. Out of the PhD programs for which we could find student handbooks (n=109), a significant plurality will require you to declare a major field and a minor field. Under this configuration, your major field is the one you will give the most attention, while your minor field is meant to supplement your expertise through exposure to another subfield. It is also common for you to have to select two major subfields on equal footing, sometimes with one or more minor fields attached. It is less common, but still possible, to select only one field or select more than two from a large list. Since the choice varies so much, you will want to find out the specific requirements for your program.

The subfields you choose have three likely administrative consequences. The first is the classes you take. In programs where you select one clear major field, most courses you take will fall into that field. Your coursework will certainly not introduce you to all the literature you will use in your graduate career, not even close. However, the literatures you discuss for years with professors and other graduate students will be easier to digest. The second is which comprehensive exams, if any, you will take. During the semester or two before the exam, you will live, eat, and breathe the required literature across the subfield(s) you choose to pass the exams (see chapter 12 on comprehensive exams). Finally, at least in some programs, your choice of subfield parameterizes who you can choose to be your advisor and who you can put on your dissertation committee.

The best way to approach these decisions is to work backwards from one key question. What are you ultimately interested in studying during your time in the program (and maybe beyond)? This is a daunting question, as you are likely still deciding this. The good news is that the answer does not need to be hyper-specific. You just need to know about your range of interests. They all have some non-zero chance of being your dissertation topic someday. If they clearly fit into one subfield, then think no further about this question. If they fit into two, the good news is that most programs accommodate that by having you declare two subfields. However, in many cases, you do have to figure out which to prioritize. Faculty who are more familiar with the workings of the graduate program can give you valuable insights and advice, as can graduate students who are further along that faced the same decision as you.

The academic job market in political science is tough, and so it can be tempting to try to select a subfield and research program that looks like it would perform well on the market. However, there are two reasons you should not take the market into account when deciding. First, the market is nearly impossible to game—what is popular one year is not going to be popular in another, seemingly without much rhyme or reason. Second, the academic job market is extremely tight, and very few people who

Relax! They're Important, But Not Defining Choices: Choosing Your Subfield and Committees

59

seek tenure-track employment are able to secure it. Navigating the market is hard enough—at least make it easier on yourself by doing what you love.

What Does this Mean for your Career?

Your choice of subfield does have some consequences for your career. It impacts which academic jobs you are likely to get. In a market where hundreds of people apply for the same job, whether a candidate specializes in the same subfield as the job ad is an easy way to whittle down the number of applications search committees need to look at. It also affects what search committees expect of you when it comes to classes you are willing and able to teach and which types of students and university activities you are likely to advise. In non-academic jobs, the distinctions are going to matter less than the skills you bring to the table, but it can still help you make your case on substantive knowledge.

However, your subfield does not seal your fate. No one you want to talk to at a conference is going to know what you administratively declared in your program. Not all jobs will be in a specific subfield, either. Some jobs are "open field"—that is, open with respect to your specialization. Others may specialize in more specific topics such as public policy, judicial politics, political behavior, etc., without regard for the initial subfield. No matter what you choose, these jobs are open to you. Additionally, once you build a research and teaching portfolio, these will be much more important signals than an administrative declaration. Finally, it is still possible—though don't bank on it—to get a job in a different specialization than the one you did in graduate school.

Forming a Dissertation Committee

Another incredibly important step in your graduate journey will be forming your dissertation committee. The most important part of this will be settling on an advisor (see chapter 13 on selecting an adviser vs a mentor). However, there are clear considerations you need to make about populating the rest of your committee (the typical graduate program will require two to four more members). In some cases, you will have a trial run at forming a committee with a master's Thesis. In others, you will be forming a committee for the first time. Here is our advice.

Think About What You Want Out of a Committee

By the time you have to form a dissertation committee, you will have had two to three years to figure out how you work best in an academic setting. You may like to work closely with your advisor and only consult committee members once key features of a project are done. In this case, you want to select people who won't present headaches for you. Alternatively, you may want input from all committee members at fairly regular intervals in the process. In this case, you will want to think much more carefully about how committee members complement one another. Regardless, your committee will be useful for feedback and for networking on your behalf, particularly if you plan to go on the academic job market.

You need to think about two things carefully: working style and topical fit, in that order. The best committee members don't always do exactly what you do. However, they can still be great social scientists who engage with your work meaningfully. They can still spot ways in which your approach could use some improvement and show you how to attain that improvement. They can still offer encouragement when you are stuck on a project, or the results did not turn out how you hoped. Topical fit is important too—someone who studies international organizations, as helpful as they may be to students studying international relations, might be a stretch for someone studying mass political behavior. However, if the tradeoff is between someone whose interests fit perfectly but falls short on mentorship vs. someone whose interests fit less well but whose mentorship is superb, pick the good mentor.

Listen to Other Peoples' Experiences

If you are unsure about how to populate your dissertation committee, ask faculty (particularly your advisor) and further-along graduate students. Other faculty can give you a good sense of how much time a given faculty member can give to you on your dissertation and their suitability on the topic. Other graduate students can give you fairly honest feedback about what it is like to work with that person. We cannot stress this enough: if multiple people warn you about putting a certain person on your committee, especially if it comes with stories of bad experiences, listen to them. You don't want to bank on being one of the few with a good experience—chances are, you're not the one (see chapter 65 on navigating things that can go wrong). To a lesser extent, if multiple people speak the absolute world of a potential committee member, think carefully before foregoing that person.

Committee Conflicts of Interest

Second, in an ideal world, faculty will put aside their differences with one another for the benefit of their students. We do not live in such a world. Whether it is for personal reasons, disagreements over methodological approaches, departmental politics, or something else, faculty members can and do have friction with one another. Sometimes this friction means you get competing and irreconcilable sets of advice from different committee members.

Furthermore, that same friction might not lead faculty members to find a way to synergize their feedback, and it's left to you to affirm one person's vision or another. This leaves you in the middle to decide which faculty member to affirm. If you're alerted by multiple other graduate students or faculty members themselves about the possibility of such a dynamic, avoid it if at all possible.

Not All Mentors Need to Be on Your Committee

The average committee has three to five people, and you probably don't want more than that. Having too many people in a formal advisory role increases the odds of faculty members having competing visions for your project that you are left to reconcile. It also just creates more issues in terms of getting signatures on paperwork. However, if you are in the lucky position of having many (potential) mentors, remember that not all of them must serve a formal role. Acknowledgement sections of dissertations are filled with gratitude for faculty members (and graduate students, for that matter) who don't have official roles on the project. The acknowledgement section of your dissertation can look the same.

Don't Waste that Outside Member

A common requirement of most PhD programs is that someone on your dissertation committee must be outside of your department. In some instances, this person can be outside your university. All too often, the outside member, through nobody's individual fault, simply serves as a rubber stamp, asking a handful of clarifying questions at the dissertation defense and signing paperwork. However, in our view, that is such a waste. Scholars from other disciplines have much to offer. Rarely is it the case that political science is the only discipline concentrating on your research question, and an outside member can plug you in to that literature (especially if it uses different terminology). New methods applicable to what you're interested in might come to other disciplines earlier, in which case an outside member from that discipline can alert you to it. So, if you can, don't select an outside member as a perfunctory step, select strategically! It can come in handy.

Conclusion

Selecting a subfield specialization and dissertation committee are unavoidable during your PhD program, and each choice can be daunting for its own reasons. Selecting the wrong subfield means wading through a lot of literature that you don't find interesting and doing so at the expense of reading work that piques your interest. Selecting the wrong dissertation committee can add dysfunction to a step in your academic life that already comes with some inherent stress. It is easiest to get this right the first time.

However, take some comfort. Both decisions are reversible. It is not unheard of for people to change their subfield in the second year of the program. If how you designed your committee is not working for you, virtually all departments allow you to change the composition of your committee.

Second, neither decision fully defines you. Even after graduate school, people can pivot subfields. One of the authors of this chapter was trained as an Americanist but is currently a post-doc in a psychology department studying the public opinion of British adolescents and adults. Additionally, your committee are not the only people who get to speak for you when you look for jobs. In the next few years of your graduate journey, you will attend conferences and workshops and meet all kinds of people (see chapter 21 on how to conference). The more people know you through first-hand experience and less through second-hand recounting of your committee members, the less you will need your committee to vouch for you. So go forth! You will make many more decisions than these along your journey.

References

Clark, William R., Matt Golder, and Sona N. Golder. 2017. *Principles of Comparative Politics*. Washington, DC: CQ Press.

11

Does an Internship Have Value for Political Science Graduate Students?

Susan E. Baer[1]

1. The University of Kansas & Walden University

KEYWORDS: Transferable Skills, Paid Internships, Unpaid Internships, Signed Memorandum of Agreement.

Introduction

The discussion regarding political science internships often concentrates on undergraduate internships (Berg 2014; Donavan 2011; Van Vechten, Gentry, and Berg 2021), and the literature about internships for political science graduate students is scarce. Nonetheless, political science graduate students may also have the opportunity to complete an internship, depending on their university and department (Marando and Melchior 1997). A political science graduate student needs to consider multiple factors when deciding whether to complete an internship. This chapter begins by describing several tensions related to internships for political science graduate students, including issues of transferable skills, paid versus unpaid internships, and the need for a signed memorandum of agreement.

Tensions Related to Internships

Transferable or generic skills are professional skills applicable outside the university (Bos et al. 2017; Craswell 2007; Gilbert et al. 2004). It may seem obvious that graduate students in vocational fields such as medicine need to develop transferable skills, but one tension related to political science graduate students completing internships involves the question of whether they also need to cultivate transferable skills during their program of study. Examples of transferable skills that political science graduate students may develop include the ability to work in teams, communicate effectively with nonacademic public audiences and policymakers (Gilbert et al. 2004), and use new software, among others.

According to APSA (2019), the percentage of nonacademic placements among persons entering the job market with a PhD in political science has increased over the past eight years. In 2017–2018, approximately 11% of those earning a PhD in political science accepted a nonacademic placement. Given this trend, it becomes increasingly essential for political science graduate students to build transferable skills, which an internship may help to advance.

Even if a person earning a PhD in political science accepts an academic appointment, possessing transferable skills such as the ability to communicate effectively with nonacademic audiences proves necessary given the teaching, research, and service expectations in academia. As an example, in a previous academic appointment I served as a co-principal investigator for a research study involving a pilot harm reduction program. One of my responsibilities included conducting a focus group of residents who lived in the neighborhood where the pilot program operated. I also helped to design a survey instrument about the program that was administered to community residents. These responsibilities required successful communication with nonacademic audiences, both verbally and in writing.

A second tension that applies to internships for political science graduate students involves the issue of whether an internship is paid or unpaid, and this chapter briefly highlights three criticisms about unpaid internships. First, internship providers may exploit students completing unpaid internships to get free labor (Perlin 2012; Perlin 2015; Smith 2006; Yamada 2021). Although the possibility for internship providers to exploit students in this way certainly exists, and all interns should ideally be decently paid, not all unpaid internships are necessarily exploitative or harmful. For example, in a survey study, Crain (2016) found that recent graduates rated unpaid internships as significant in helping to better understand academic coursework, while they did not rate paid internships as significant in this area. Second, unpaid internships receive criticism because they advantage those students who can afford to work for free (Yamada 2021), thus creating an issue of inequity for students who cannot afford to work without pay. Third, unpaid internships may present complex legal implications. As one example, people who do not receive compensation for their work may not be afforded legal protections from workplace harassment (Rothschild and Rothschild 2020). For a more detailed discussion of legal considerations surrounding unpaid internships, see Rothschild and Rothschild (2020) and Yamada (2021).

Whether the internship is paid or unpaid, it is not enough for political science graduate students to use an internship solely to enhance transferable skills. Political science internships must enable students to learn something significant about politics and political phenomena (Berg 2014; Hindmoor 2010), because the goal of a graduate political science internship should be to address students' substantive research interests in the field of political science.

Ensuring that internship responsibilities will be substantive involves legwork on the part of the political science graduate student and the instructor or faculty mentor responsible for internship placement. Specifically, students need to work with the instructor to attempt to ensure that internship responsibilities will provide an effective way to learn about some aspect of politics before they accept an internship placement. One way to accomplish this is by creating and signing a memorandum of agreement that delineates the responsibilities of all parties in the internship relationship (Marando and Melchior 1997).

Benefits of Completing an Internship as a Graduate Student

When evaluating whether to complete an internship, political science graduate students must also consider the potential benefits of completing an internship. According to Marando and Melchior (1997), the benefits of internships for political science graduate students include the opportunity for students to evaluate political theory, develop research agendas, implement research skills, and broaden real-world experiences. This section briefly describes these benefits.

A beneficial nexus exists between internships and political theory (Marando and Melchior 1997; Moon and Schokman 2000). Specifically, an internship as a form of site-based experiential education offers a different vantage point for political science graduate students to critically engage with political theory learned in the classroom and deepen their understanding of political theory. The relationship appears reciprocal, because students may also use their existing knowledge about political theory to better understand substantive political phenomena examined during an internship.

Completing an internship may also help political science graduate students to develop a research agenda. According to Marando and Melchior (1997), observing the dynamics of political phenomena as an intern may provide valuable insight that assists political science graduate students in creating a research agenda that builds on earlier research. Auerbach (2021) describes a more formal approach for undergraduate political science interns to develop their agenda, including required attendance of a research skills seminar. The more formal training offered by an internship may greatly assist graduate political science interns in developing their research.

In addition, completing an internship may enable graduate students to participate in applied research projects. These projects may positively impact society, and students may gain a sense of satisfaction by participating in them. Participating in applied research may also impart knowledge about how to create high quality research in a shorter period of time than generally occurs in a traditional academic setting (Bos et al. 2017; Krull et al. 2001).

Graduate students who complete an internship may also benefit by further improving and implementing their research skills (Bos et al. 2017; Marando and Melchior 1997). When completing internships, for example, political science graduate students may learn how to ask better research questions that will lead to more meaningful research results. Students may also have the opportunity to develop both qualitative and quantitative research skills. Additionally, internships may enhance political science students' knowledge about public policy if interns can effectively gather and use data related to the policymaking process (Moon and Schokman 2000). Graduate students who participate in internships may also learn new forms of research dissemination that reach a far wider audience than academia (Bos et al. 2017).

Internships may also benefit political science graduate students by broadening their real-world experiences. Broadened real-world experiences may subsequently help students to become better teachers (Marando and Melchior 1997). Another benefit of broadened experiences includes graduate students being able to network and collaborate with people working in their field of study (Krull et al. 2001). Networking opportunities may lead to an additional reference for the graduate student from outside academia, or to the student securing a future nonacademic position. In addition, an internship allows graduate students to see the relevance and significance of their work outside academia (Bos et al. 2017).

Recommendations and Reflection

If political science graduate students decide to pursue an internship, I strongly recommend they attempt to ensure that it is properly structured before accepting an internship placement. As discussed in this chapter, a student must work with the instructor or faculty mentor responsible for internship placement to confirm that internship responsibilities will be both substantive and provide an opportunity for the student to learn something significant about politics. To best accomplish this, all parties in the internship relationship, including the student, instructor, and internship provider, should sign a memorandum of agreement that outlines the general responsibilities of all parties before the student accepts an internship placement.

Based on my own experience completing an internship as a political science doctoral student, I regard internships for political science graduate students as beneficial. My two areas of specialization as a PhD student in the government and politics department at the University of Maryland, College Park were urban policy and political theory. I was motivated to pursue an internship because I believed it would offer a real-world vantage point to learn about urban policy and politics, and could potentially inspire new research ideas in this subfield.

I worked with my internship faculty mentor, who was a professor in the government and politics department and supervised the department's graduate internship program, to identify an appropriate internship provider. When I was ABD in the PhD program, I completed my internship at the Charles Village Community Benefits District, which is a special taxing district in Baltimore, Maryland. Created in 1995, this special taxing district provides supplemental sanitation and safety services within district boundaries in addition to services the City of Baltimore provides (Charles Village Community Benefits District 2021).

My internship experience at the Charles Village Community Benefits District met my expectations and produced benefits that Marando and Melchior (1997) outline. As a result of my internship, I began to develop a research agenda that extended beyond my doctoral dissertation and applied political theory to understand the political process involved in creating community benefits districts in US cities. The initial stage of the research agenda setting process was relatively informal and involved discussing my internship observations with my internship faculty mentor. At the time I started to develop this research agenda, I was not sure whether I would pursue an academic appointment or a nonacademic position after earning my PhD. During a brief stint working in a nonacademic position immediately following graduation, I decided to pursue a career in academia.

In terms of unexpected gains from my experience, I did not expect to have the opportunity to co-author two peer-reviewed journal articles with my internship faculty mentor as a result of the research agenda I began to develop during my internship. While most political science graduate students may not have the opportunity to collaborate on research projects with their internship faculty mentor, it is crucial for students to attempt to build a constructive working relationship with their faculty mentor. Intern mentoring is defined as "the interaction of a faculty sponsor with an intern in order to facilitate learning" (Berg 2021,62). The internship faculty mentor's main responsibility is to help the graduate student intern learn political science, and both the student intern and faculty mentor need to be actively engaged in the mentoring process for effective learning to take place. This means that students should attend and actively participate in all classes or meetings with their internship faculty mentor, as well as successfully completing all assignments related to the internship.

I also did not anticipate that the research agenda I started during my graduate internship would have such a positive ripple effect on my academic career. I was awarded a postdoctoral appointment at Indiana University's Workshop in Political Theory and Policy Analysis due to my research proposal to examine the political process involved in creating the Charles Village Community Benefits District. During my postdoctoral appointment, I co-authored my first peer-reviewed journal article, which examined the creation of the Charles Village Community Benefits District using polycentrism (Baer and Marando 2001). I subsequently accepted a tenure-track assistant professor position at San Diego State University (SDSU) where I co-authored a peer-reviewed journal article that analyzed the creation of the Charles Village Community Benefits District using transaction resource theory (Baer and Feiock 2005). In addition to teaching, other research activities, and service to the university and community, the publications stemming from my internship experience made a positive contribution toward my successfully earning tenure and promotion to Associate Professor of Public Administration at SDSU, where I was previously employed.

Conclusion

This chapter described issues related to internships that political science graduate students should contemplate. The chapter discussed tensions related to internships as well as benefits of internships. Drawing on both the literature and my own internship experience as a political science doctoral student, I believe internships can have great value for political science graduate students. I encourage graduate students to seriously consider completing an internship if their university and department offer this experiential learning opportunity.

References

American Political Science Association (APSA). 2019. "2017-2018 APSA Graduate Placement Report." https://apsanet.org.

Auerbach, Arthur H. 2021. "Constructing a Research Internship Program to Promote Experiential Learning." In *Political Science Internships: Towards Best Practices*, eds. Van Vechten, Renee B., Bobbi Gentry, and John C. Berg, 71-78. Washington, DC: American Political Science Association.

Baer, Susan E., and Richard C. Feiock. 2005. "Private Governments in Urban Areas: Political Contracting and Collective Action." *The American Review of Public Administration*, 35(1), 42-56. https://doi.org/10.1177/0275074004271717.

Baer, Susan E., and Vincent L. Marando. 2001. "The Subdistricting of Cities: Applying the Polycentric Model." *Urban Affairs Review,* 36(5), 721-733. https://doi.org/10.1177/10780870122185064.

Berg, John C. 2014. "Two Threats to Political Science Internships: Press Attacks and Incorrect Student Assumptions." Paper presented at the American Political Science Association, Washington, DC.

Berg, John C. 2021. "Mentoring Interns." In *Political Science Internships: Towards Best Practices*, eds. Renee B. Van Vechten, Bobbi Gentry, and John C. Berg, 61-69. Washington, DC: American Political Science Association.

Bos, Daniel, Robin Finlay, Peter Hopkins, Jenny Lloyd, and Michael Richardson. 2017. "Reflections on the ESRC Internship Scheme for Postgraduates." *Journal of Geography in Higher Education,* 41(1), 106–118. http://dx.doi.org/10.1080/03098265.2016.1260099.

Charles Village Community Benefits District. 2021. Accessed November 10, 2021. https://www.charlesvillage.org/about.

Crain, Andrew. 2016. "Exploring the Implications of Unpaid Internships." *NACE Journal*, 26-31.

Craswell, Gail. 2007. "Deconstructing the Skills Training Debate in Doctoral Education." *Higher Education Research & Development*, 26(4), 377-391. doi: 10.1080/07294360701658591.

Donavan, Janet L. 2011. "Designing an Intellectually Challenging Internship Program." Paper presented at the annual meeting of the American Political Science Association, Seattle, WA, September 1, 2011.

Gilbert, Rob, Jo Balatti, Phil Turner, and Hilary Whitehouse. 2004. "The Generic Skills Debate in Research Higher Degrees." *Higher Education Research & Development,* 23(3), 375-388. doi: 10.1080/0729436042000235454.

Hindmoor, Andrew. 2010. "Internships Within Political Science." *Australian Journal of Political Science,* 45(3), 483-490. doi: 10.1080/10361146.2010.499186.

Krull, Ira S., Hongji Liu, Kavita Mistry, and Sarah Kazmi. 2001. "Industrial Internships (Co-ops) in Graduate School—How, When, Why, and Where?" *Analytical Letters*, 34(1), 1-15. https://doi.org/10.1081/AL-100002700.

Marando, Vincent L., and Mary Beth Melchior. 1997. "On Site, Not Out of Mind: The Role of Experiential Learning in the Political Science Doctoral Program." *PS: Political Science & Politics*, 30(4), 723-728. https://doi.org/10.2307/420400.

Moon, Jeremy, and Wykham Schokman. 2000. "Political Science Research Internships and Political Science Education." *Politics*, 20(3), 169-175. https://doi.org/10.1111/1467-9256.00127.

Perlin, Ross. 2012. *Intern Nation: How to Earn Nothing and Learn Little in the Brave New Economy.* Verso.

Perlin, Ross. 2015. "Interns, Victimized Yet Again." *The New York Times*, July 3.

Rothschild, Philip C., and Connor L. Rothschild. 2020. "The Unpaid Internship: Benefits, Drawbacks, and Legal Issues." *Administrative Issues Journal: Connecting Education, Practice, and Research*, 10(2), 1-17. doi: 10.5929/2020.10.2.1.

Smith, Sonia. 2006. "Biting the Hand That Doesn't Feed Me: Internships for College Credit Are a Scam." Slate, June 8. Http://www.slate.com/articles/news_and_politics/hey_wait_a_minute/2006/06/biting_the_hand_that_d oesnt_feed_me.html.

Van Vechten, Renee B., Bobbi Gentry, and John C. Berg, eds. 2021. *Political Science Internships: Towards Best Practices.* Washington, DC: American Political Science Association.

Yamada, David C. 2021. "Major Legal Considerations Pertaining to Internships." In *Political Science Internships: Towards Best Practices*, eds. Renee B. Van Vechten, Bobbi Gentry, and John C. Berg, 31-42. Washington, DC: American Political Science Association.

12 | The Explicit, Implicit, and Unknown: Comprehensive Exams

Samantha R. Cooney[1] & David O. Monda[2]

1. University of New Mexico 2. Adelphi University

KEYWORDS: Comprehensive Exams, Advisers, Implicit or Explicit Biases.

Introduction

This chapter addresses the explicit, implicit, and unknown obstacles that PhD and master's students will encounter in preparing for their comprehensive exams. Comprehensive exams can either be oral or written. They are supposed to check "knowledge" like a traditional exam but are also supposed to ensure students are properly socialized—that they can write and talk about literature in political science as a colleague would. Some comprehensive exams cover a broad subfield, while others cover more narrow areas of expertise. Both authors of this chapter completed comprehensive exams or "comps" as a part of a doctoral program. Thus, the advice within this chapter is written with such students in mind. The suggestions within this chapter may or may not apply to you. Each graduate program is different with varying dynamics. Therefore, what is helpful to a student in one department may not be useful for a student in another. Some programs may have a more difficult environment than others or may have easier expectations. While the guidance within this chapter provides a good starting point, we recommend speaking to graduate students in your own program. Students who have taken and passed their own comprehensive exams may provide more tailored advice.

Practical Thematic Space

This section of the chapter will address some of the unexpected issues that arise in studying for the comprehensive exam from a practical thematic premise. These include planning study schedules, meeting with graders, fear and nerves, mental and physical health, and study groups.

Study Schedule

When you embark on your comprehensive exams journey, plan a study schedule. Remember that you have been studying for these exams the entire length of your program. You are not beginning this preparation in a vacuum. You have many semesters of classes under your belt. You have studied and learned in each of these courses. Keeping this in mind, beginning your road to comps with a planned schedule and strategy is wise. When creating your study schedule, think about the fields you will be taking your comprehensive exams or "comping" in. Which one will require more study time? Which one needs more practice exams? Within your department, most fields will have a reputation. Whether they have an easy reputation or hard varies by university. The more intimidating fields will most likely call for more practice exams and meetings with graders. The fields with more confusing theory will need longer study sessions to parse through the reading material. To determine the reputation of each field, do not be afraid to ask the students who have taken and passed their own comps.

Setting a start date for your study schedule is an important decision. Most exams occur in the spring semester of the third year. For us, the exams were in the middle of the sixth semester in the program. Beginning a study routine at the start of the fifth semester worked well. For others whose exams are at the beginning of the sixth semester, starting the summer after the second year may be better. As a rule, beginning your comps studying six months before the exam is a smart decision. Giving oneself a lengthy period of time to study each field also gives one the opportunity to apply spaced repetition learning (Cepeda et al. 2006) or other learning methods. Starting too early can be as bad as starting late. This lengthens the amount of time your body spends under stress. Additionally, starting early makes it more likely for your brain to forget the subjects you studied in the beginning. Around half a year should be long enough to tackle all the needed sections of each field without adding extra strain. Due to the many expectations and challenges during the exam process, if you have caregiving responsibilities or work in addition to attending graduate school, make sure to make alternative arrangements or take time off as needed (chapter 16 may provide helpful suggestions for how to balance caregiving and studying).

When planning your schedule, consider which fields you have preferred and which you find to be more arduous. Study those that you do well in and those that you dislike or find more difficult. This will help keep your mind from tiring out. Similarly, it is helpful to spend around one month at a time on a specific comprehensive exam field. This strategy helps keep certain theories in one field from muddling another field's theories and paradigms. However, allowing some leeway to adapt your fixed learning schedule to your needs will give you an advantage (Mettler et al. 2016).

Meeting with Advisers and Graders

Meeting with advisers and exam graders is often a good strategy for preparing for comps. If your program is transparent about which professors will be grading the exam, it is best to meet with them at least twice before the scheduled exam. Ask questions about the literature that they themselves teach or research. Not only will this help resolve questions that form when studying, it will show faculty that you are taking the exams seriously. These meetings should exhibit effort to accumulate knowledge in their field. Besides meeting with potential graders, meet with previous professors you have taken classes with. The subjects within these courses are often fair game for the exam. If your department is not upfront or does not appoint exam graders in advance, it is best to meet at least once with each professor that may grade the exam.

When meeting with potential graders, it is helpful to inquire about their expectations for the exam in addition to substantive questions regarding their expertise. This can help shape how you answer the exam questions. Most professors prefer a structured essay with a clear argument rather than an answer that simply presents everything learned. This is helpful to know to prevent "brain dump" answers.

Fear and Anxiety

Comprehensive exams are a fear-inducing process. In fact, for us, the fear and anxiety leading up to the exams was worse than the actual exams themselves. It is normal for you to feel immense apprehension during the months before your comps. Every graduate student is nervous about the exams. Comps carry a weight that provokes not only anxiety but also insecurity. This can cause major hurdles including hesitancy to share practice exam answers or meet with professors. However, one must keep in mind the many students that had the same feelings yet were successful. Oftentimes, we are our own worst critics. What you believe to be inadequate preparation or poor note taking is competent and satisfactory to another. If the strain becomes debilitating, consider seeking support from mental health counseling or other resources on campus, as described in chapter 69.

Study Groups

The use of study groups in supporting graduate students prepare for exams and conduct research has begun to receive increasing attention (Maher et al. 2008). In forming study groups, it is important for candidates to create groups that include participants who have good relationships with each other. They should be no more than four to five participants to reduce the likelihood of personality conflict, freeriding, and cliquing. Study group members should hold each other accountable for weekly contributions to the study group. This expectation can be accomplished by assigning chapters and/or writing summaries to individual group members that are due on a weekly basis for presentation to all group members. Freeriding should be discouraged and nipped in the bud either by a first warning or removal from the study group for repeated violations. Freeriding is disempowering, creates conflict in the group, and negates focus on the ultimate goal of preparing the group to meet the challenges of the test.

Mental and Physical Health

Part of mental and physical health is having a good routine to pace yourself. According to Birch (2011), there is a global increase in mental health disorders. Pacing yourself over the short few weeks before the exam is an important ingredient for success. This helps you reduce stress, more thoroughly comprehend the material, and avoid last minute panic memorization that may lead to failure. Pacing yourself not only helps manage the volume of reading and writing the candidate needs to do but allows candidates to scaffold their work building up to the ultimate success of passing the comprehensive exam while keeping sane in the process.

In terms of practical activities associated with mental and physical health, be available to do leisure activities and hobbies you enjoy in a group or individually. Movies, down time, exercise, and meeting with friends are essential elements to reduce the stress of studying for a major exam. You cannot read and study every minute of the day. Your mind needs a break, and you also need to sustain your social network. Be available to do extracurricular things you enjoy doing. Talking to other students who have taken the comprehensive exam helps demystify the exam. It assists you to appreciate the real and nuanced human experiences students go through in preparing for the comprehensive exam. In addition to this, get enough sleep before the exam so your mind will be in top shape to respond to the tough questions on the test. Sufficient sleep seems obvious, but many students forget the place of sufficient sleep in good mental and physical health. For more in-depth tips on achieving a healthy balance in graduate school, consider consulting chapters 62-69.

Theoretical Thematic Space

This part of the chapter will highlight some of the unexpected issues that arise in studying for the comprehensive exam from a theoretical thematic space. These include note taking, faculty biases, reading lists, and practice exams.

Note Taking

Your notes will be an essential tool throughout your comprehensive exam preparation. Create a folder for each exam you will be taking, then further divide those notes by each field, theory, and paradigm. This will help organize your studying. For example, if you were to study International Relations, creating an outline on Realism would be useful. Furthermore, gather each syllabus from classes you attended in graduate school. Use each of these courses to study for your comprehensive exams. Review the syllabi and gather any notes you took during those courses. Remember, you have been preparing for your comprehensive exams since the beginning of grad school. You have been studying for them your entire graduate career. Old notes can refresh your memory of what you already know.

If you are reading this guidebook as a first or second year, begin taking thorough notes and store them in an online cloud or drive that will keep them safe. These notes will be invaluable when it is time to prepare for your exams. While handwritten notes have some advantages (Aragón-Mendizábal et al. 2016), typing your notes and storing them in an online folder will save yourself an immense amount of time later on.

Sharing notes is a common practice in some programs and is sometimes encouraged. Yet, it is frequently frowned upon. If you are fortunate enough to find yourself in a program with graduate students who readily share their notes, it is best to be discreet. Some professors may view note-sharing as a plagiaristic practice. Use notes procured from other students as a starting point only. Understand that each student will have different viewpoints, distinct arguments, and varying preferences. Your comprehensive exam answers may argue something vastly different than your colleague's exam. That is favorable. Each scholar has a different view of the world and that is where new ideas and theories are birthed. So, take your own notes even if you receive notes from others—as their notes will not be as useful to you as your own.

Faculty Biases

It is important to consider the individual opinions of faculty members and the implicit and/or explicit bias that comes with them. When working with individuals, different personalities and relationships often dictate environments within academia. Hence, interactions with faculty members are an essential component of your preparation. Keep in mind as you interact with faculty, nothing exists in a vacuum—inherent biases and perceptions can be formed without intention. Therefore, meetings with faculty members can be used to discern what they think of your ideas and arguments. For example, a conversation with a professor may lead to them divulging their viewpoint of a specific ontological debate. Knowing how each faculty member views the theories within your field will help you form your exam arguments.

Reading Lists

Acquire a range of reading lists that provide a diverse and broad coverage of political science pedagogical, methodological, and disciplinary lenses to understanding the field. According to (Giblin et al. 2008), comprehensive examination reading lists have a significant impact on scholarship. With this in mind, make the effort to apply these readings to core subfields of political science. In organizing your reading lists, make notes next to those readings that best apply to case studies, theories, and concepts you anticipate writing about during the comprehensive exam. Remember, the comprehensive exam is timed. You will need to give sufficient time to each question in order to answer it effectively and give the examiner unshakable faith that you know the content and you can expertly apply it. Develop the savvy to read the reading list and highlight contrarian arguments to the established traditional norm or classics in the field of political science. Make sure to have a good balance of readings on your list that speak to classical authors in political science from Western Europe and North America. Also be well versed on the readings of authorities in the field from the Global South to provide you with a good balance of the field of political science. Show an independent understanding of the theory and concepts nascent in the readings and their theoretical premises.

Practice Exams

Stewart-Wells (2020) emphasizes the reality that comps have become a staple in doctoral programs as a way for students to express their understanding of academic material, for faculty to assess their learning, and for students to apply that learning to their fields of study. The old adage goes "practice makes perfect." With this in mind, practice exams are the best way for students to mimic actual exam conditions, attempt different exam taking techniques, and master skills that will make them successful in taking the final comprehensive exam.

Comprehensive exams are essential hurdles to overcome in the journey towards candidacy for doctoral students in political science. Use chapter summaries of different readings as it will be impossible to cover everything. Once you have a good understanding of the core tenets of each of the books or readings you have not been able to go through individually, attempt some practice exams. Time yourself taking the practice exam to see how much time it takes you to comprehensively complete each question.

You may want to recruit another graduate student to grade a practice exam in exchange for grading theirs or passing on the favor for another student later. Alternatively, if you enroll in a directed readings or independent study course with a professor, they too may be willing to administer a practice exam to you. Practice exams should ideally be done after you have had a chance to go over a majority of the readings. You should be in a commanding position to ably tackle the questions on each section of the comprehensive exam. An essential element of preparing for the comprehensive exam is knowing the student cannot read and memorize everything. As a result, reading chapter summaries, understanding and applying the material through practice exams, are all critical to success on the comprehensive exam.

Conclusion

While comps can be a point of adversity and tribulation for graduate students, they also provide a moment to expand your knowledge and improve yourself as a scholar. There will be both expected challenges and unexpected issues that arise during your comp preparation. Though, when one takes the time to maintain a well-balanced lifestyle during preparation and forge connections with professors and students, preparing for comps can be a less daunting and more fulfilling experience. Much of the advice in this chapter is often learned during the comps process rather than known beforehand. We hope this guidebook chapter sheds light on the explicit, implicit, and unknowns of the comps process and provides you with more wisdom than the authors of this chapter had before their comprehensive exams.

References

Aragón-Mendizábal, Estíbaliz,Cándida Delgado-Casas, José-I. Navarro-Guzmán, Inmaculada Menacho-Jiménez, and Manuel F. Romero-Oliva. 2016. "A Comparative Study of Handwriting and Computer Typing in Note-taking by University Students." *Comunicar* 24 (48): 101–107.

Birch, Michael. 2011. *Mediating Mental Health: Contexts, Debates and Analysis*. 1st ed. Milton: Routledge.

Cepeda, Nicholas J., Harold Pashler, Edward Vul, John T. Wixted, and Doug Rohrer. 2006. "Distributed Practice in Verbal Recall Tasks: A Review and Quantitative Synthesis." *Psychological Bulletin* 132: 354–380.

Maher, Damien, Lemie Seaton, Cathi McMullen, Terry Fitzgerald, Emi Otsuji, and Alison Lee. 2008. "'Becoming and Being Writers': The Experiences of Doctoral Students in Writing Groups." *Studies in Continuing Education* 30 (3): 263–275.

Giblin, Matthew J. and Joseph A Schafer. 2008. "Comprehensive Examination Reading Lists as Indicators of Scholar Impact and Significance." *Journal of Criminal Justice* 36 (1): 81–89.

Mettler, Everett, Christine M. Massey, and Philip J. Kellman. 2016. "A Comparison of Adaptive and Fixed Schedules of Practice." *Journal of Experimental Psychology: General* 145 (7): 897–917.

Stewart-Wells, A. Gillian, and K. Mallery Keenan. 2020. "Assessing Doctoral Students: A Background on Comprehensive and Authentic Assessments." *The Journal of Continuing Higher Education* 68 (2): 84–100.

Tabibian, Behzad, Utkarsh Upadhyay, Abir De, Ali Zarezade, Bernhard Scholkopf, and Manuel Gomez-Rodriguez, M. 2019. "Enhancing Human Learning via Spaced Repetition Optimization." *Proceedings of the National Academy of Sciences of the United States*, 116 (10): 3988.

13 Selecting an Adviser: Professional and Personal Considerations

Chris Macaulay[1], Mary McThomas[2], & Alisson Rowland[2]

1.West Texas A&M University 2. University of California, Irvine

KEYWORDS: Adviser, Long-Term Professional Goals, Mentorship.

Introduction

For graduate students, no individual is as important to their education or career as their *adviser*. Virtually all graduate programs require that students select a "committee chair," whose formal job is to serve as the leader on their dissertation committee. However, beyond this formal role is the informal role of adviser throughout the entire graduate school process, from the earliest stages of taking classes, guiding the student through comprehensive exams, crafting, and editing their dissertation and, ultimately, helping the student find employment. Finding an adviser who can fulfill all these roles can be difficult, and graduate students should consider each of these roles as they seek and assess potential advisers.

Given the crucial nature of this position, and its centrality to every aspect of the graduate school experience, there are few decisions as impactful as a graduate student's choice of adviser. This chapter will offer advice for graduate students in making this decision, outlining the importance of factors such as a potential adviser's prestige and expertise, ability to commit time to their students, ability to foster publications, capability to provide emotional and moral support, and the degree to which they help network and build the professional career of their advisees. This chapter will further explore the need to have multiple individuals fill the above roles, and address some of the potential inequities and issues that can face students in the adviser-advisee relationship.

Picking an Adviser

The choice of an adviser can understandably be difficult, and often students are given little direction in the process. Many institutions require a choice to be made early and formally, while others wait until the dissertation stage to require such a formal commitment. While it remains a perfectly acceptable option to change advisers at any point during graduate school, repeated changes may be undesirable and impede graduation, and thus it is advisable to find a good fit for adviser as soon as possible.

One of the most used tactics by departments when deciding which students to admit to their department is how well their research aligns with current faculty. Research fit can be incredibly helpful in choosing who to work with. However, be cautious about this being the sole deciding factor in a mentor relationship. While you may share the same substantive focus as a faculty member, it is highly unlikely you will be using the same methodologies and frameworks as them or be asking the same questions. Depending on the type of research you will be conducting, it is important to consider what your strengths and gaps are to know where mentoring will be the most appropriate. This may require talking to multiple professors and basing an advising relationship on factors aside from research fit.

While there are many factors to consider when choosing an adviser, students are often tempted to select an adviser with significant name recognition and influence, but in doing so must consider their overall availability. Choosing a prestigious or well-known adviser may be beneficial, as prestigious advisers may carry with them some weight on the job market and may be able to assist a student in networking and building their future career. This is particularly helpful when they share a similar research interest or subfield as the advisee, as their familiarity with their work will only serve to enhance the eventual dissertation. However, other factors must be considered, as advisers with considerable prestige may also have considerable time commitments beyond advising, limiting a student's ability to benefit from their tutelage. Particularly for newer professors and those seeking either tenure or promotion, the commitments of research on top of teaching and service may limit an adviser's availability, and potentially lower their available time as well as the overall quality of their advice.

It is thus advisable for graduate students to investigate the reputation of potential advisers, by speaking to their current advisees, colleagues, and others familiar with their personality and availability. One unfortunate factor to consider is the faculty member's reputation and track record of working with non-traditional students. As discussed below, unconscious bias can lead to false determinations about a student's ability. This, in turn, can translate into an adviser paying that student less attention. (See the section on "Strategies for Addressing Implicit Bias, Harassment, Assault" for advice for minoritized groups, and Chapter 65 for more on things that can go wrong). Often, potential advisers are more eager to expand their pool of advisees while others have pre-existing advising commitments or little time due to other academic demands and understanding this should help inform graduate students' choices.

Habits of good advisers are many and can be improved and expanded at the suggestion of the advisee. These habits include regular meetings to maintain contact, updating an adviser regularly on progress made at every stage of graduate school, not only during the dissertation writing process. These can be excellent opportunities to begin collaborative work, ensure continued progress on non-dissertation endeavors, plan for conferences and networking, and find emotional and social support that might otherwise be lacking. Ultimately, inquiring whether advisers have engaged in these habits with previous advisees, and suggesting and reinforcing them once the adviser is chosen, are vital to ensuring success in graduate school.

Networking

As with other professions, forming connections with those more senior in your field is essential for your growth and success. Your adviser plays a critical role in helping you shape your academic network in several ways. Conferences are a very common method for networking, and having your adviser attending with you, at least for the first few, can aid in positive conference experiences by introducing you to others doing similar research. These relationships may lead to further opportunities, such as invitations to chair panels, to work on collaborative projects, and sometimes even for job postings. While conferences are one avenue for such opportunities, there are less formal spaces to create these connections. Your adviser will have a much broader network due to their experience in the field, and they will be made aware of calls for proposals or grant applications and should be forwarding these to you for you to either pursue or not.

It is important to recognize that the adviser-advisee relationship is mutually beneficial, benefiting the adviser as well as advisee. Advisees should endeavor to assist their advisers in research projects, bolstering their publications and learning vital aspects of the research process, and otherwise demonstrate their skills and abilities. Advising itself provides considerable value to the adviser, and the gratitude and demonstrated effort of an advisee will only continue to benefit both parties. That said, it is important for advisees to ensure they are not being exploited in this process—advisees should ensure adequate representation in publications and other endeavors. This means ensuring that advisees are accurately and appropriately represented as author in any publication, commensurate with their efforts. Under no circumstances should an adviser pressure an advisee to complete tasks or otherwise assist them without compensation. The ultimate goal of an adviser is to assist a graduate student in graduating and finding employment—any tasks that go against this goal should be resisted, reported, and a new adviser should be sought. See Chapter 7 for more on networking.

Long-Term Goals

An additional consideration when picking an adviser is that of *long-term professional goals*. This can be an incredibly important factor in a supportive mentoring relationship. Even if you are not sure early on in your academic career what your plans are, consulting your adviser can help shape your path and direct you towards helpful resources. On the other hand, if you find your long-term goals shifting, this may direct you towards other faculty and that is completely normal and expected.

Being clear with your expectations for a mentoring relationship, knowing that research fit fluctuates as your research progresses, and being open to consulting other people as your long-term goals solidify are all important aspects to consider as your relationship with your adviser progresses.

Communication

Building a professional rapport with an adviser is extremely helpful. However, issues can arise with your adviser, even when they are providing all the benefits listed above. Advisers have varied styles just as students have different needs. For example, one student may want their adviser to proactively contact her to check in on her progress; another may find this anxiety-inducing and prefer to connect with her adviser only when she has something to discuss. Similarly, some students prefer weekly meetings while others find such regular meetings too burdensome. It is crucial to communicate your needs and preferred style to your adviser. Some programs use adviser contracts where both the student and faculty member indicate their expectations and commitments. A more informal discussion can satisfy this goal as well.

It is important to be realistic about what your adviser can and is willing to do. It may be that your preferred primary adviser is not willing to take on a more intense mentorship, especially if they have multiple advisees. It is then up to you to decide if it is worth it to stay with that person (for the reasons discussed above), find another primary adviser, or ask additional faculty members (perhaps those on your dissertation committee) to support you. Another issue that can arise is a lack of responsiveness on the part of your adviser. This can manifest in not returning emails or failing to provide comments in a timely manner. Students can be overly deferential and worry about following up with faculty so as not to "bug" them. However, this is the first step you should take. If, after multiple attempts, you are still not getting a response, you may bring this to the attention of the department's Chair or Director of Graduate Studies so that they can intercede on your behalf.

One unfortunate cause for communication breakdowns between advisers and advisees can be due to implicit (unconscious) bias or a lack of shared cultural, social, or embodied experience. Beyond the selection of advisees, unconscious bias can impact ongoing evaluations of the student's work, willingness to aid in networking, and levels of support when writing letters of recommendation. Exactly because this is an unconscious process, it can be hard to identify and root out when such bias is occurring. We all tend to use shortcuts or schemas when evaluating situations and people. This can lead to erroneous snap judgments; especially when stereotypes are at work. Such stereotypes can lead an adviser to project unwarranted positive or negative attributes onto a student based on the student's race/ethnicity, gender, disability, or sexual identity.

This is further problematized when advisers favor students that remind them of themselves. Also, an unconscious process, people tend to see themselves in those that share their identity, similar attributes, or backgrounds. Because the discipline is still predominantly white men, white male students may benefit from replicating existing faculty demographics. Meanwhile, other students may have a harder time finding an adviser who they feel takes them and their work seriously. This process works both ways. Underrepresented students often feel more comfortable with faculty that share their attributes and experiences. This often results in those faculty members taking on larger advising loads than their colleagues which, in turn, can lead to less time spent with each advisee. While the increasing diversity of faculty may eventually counter the preponderance of these unconscious processes, both advisers and advisees should be aware of the role of implicit bias, its consequences, and ways to counteract the effects.

Multiple Mentors

Given the many roles an adviser can play, it is rare to find all the *mentorship* you need embodied in a single faculty member (for more on mentorship, see Chapter 7). You may have chosen your primary adviser due to your research interests; but discover that she isn't as useful when it comes to professionalization or providing emotional support. As a result, many departments organize professionalization workshops. Such a centralized approach has the benefit of equalizing graduate student training given the uneven mentorship that can occur as a result of differing advising styles. In terms of emotional support, peers—especially those that are going through the same program with you—can play a huge role. Previous cohorts can often provide students with advice based on their own experiences. Some programs have initiated cascading mentorship models in order to encourage this transmission of experience-based knowledge. Building horizontal networks among other graduate students is also a good idea as, assuming you stay in the academy, you will continue to be in each other's orbit for the rest of your career. For example, current fellow graduate students may one day be responsible for reviewing your manuscript, conference abstract, grant proposal, etc.

Your dissertation committee will provide varying insights into your research; but can also be leveraged for professional advice and other forms of mentorship. In addition, you will typically need at least three letters of recommendation when you go on the job market, and it helps to have all writers know you and your work well. It is also helpful to build your mentorship network beyond your primary adviser to other faculty members both within your department and at other universities. Several professional academic organizations—such as the American Political Science Association and the Association for Political Theory—have developed programs to match graduate students with a mentor on another campus. Some programs, recognizing ongoing issues within the academy, specifically provide support for women and underrepresented students. For example, the International Studies Association "Pay it Forward" program is designed to mentor early career women. External mentors from these programs help students to grow their network and provide an outsider's view of the issues one may be facing. It is often easier to vent to a faculty member that is not within one's own department. In addition, they have experience with multiple institutions—through their own graduate education and various job placements—so can provide insight into different approaches and norms. Finally, academic conferences offer a great opportunity to meet potential external faculty and peer mentors as there is a good chance that those attending the same panel have similar interests to your own.

Another issue that can arise is if an adviser retires, dies, or moves to another institution. Professors Emeriti will often continue to serve on dissertation committees after retirement. However, there is no obligation to do so. Similarly, the ability of faculty to take their advisees with them when they accept a new position is increasingly rare. While students can ask a potential adviser about plans to retire or move, the faculty member may genuinely not be able to predict what will happen over the course of the student's graduate training. In any of these scenarios, the student will need to choose a new adviser. For this reason, it is wise for an incoming student to assess her fit with more than one faculty member prior to accepting admission into that program. Even if the primary adviser does not change, students will want to identify multiple faculty members that can serve on their dissertation committee and provide additional mentorship.

Conclusion

This chapter has discussed the various aspects of professional and personal development to consider when selecting an adviser or mentor and has emphasized the importance of such a decision. Considering aspects as varied as rapport, availability, prestige, research fit, and professional support are essential throughout the process, and should all be weighed according to each students' preferences and needs. While the authors provide strategies to craft and make the most out of this support system, it is a long-term working relationship and there will be boundaries to create and expectations to set. The sooner each student begins these conversations, the better grasp they will have on how their adviser operates and how they would like their student to operate as well.

Resources

- https://www.apa.org/gradpsych/2014/11/mentoring-benefits
- https://www.nature.com/articles/d41586-019-03535-y
- https://www.isanet.org/Conferences/Special-Convention-Programs/Pay-it-forward
- http://www.aspanet.org/mentor
- https://associationforpoliticaltheory.org/

References

Noy, Shiri & Rashawn Ray, "Graduate Student's Perceptions of Their Advisers: Is There Systematic Disadvantage in Mentorship?" in *The Journal of Higher Education*. Volume 83, Number 6, November/ December 2012, pp. 876-914. https://muse.jhu.edu/article/488574

14

Getting Started on the Doctoral Dissertation

Brady Baybeck[1]

1. Wayne State University

KEYWORDS: All But Dissertation, Narrative, Research Timeline.

"The hardest part is getting the first foot out the door." –Old runner's proverb

Introduction[1]

Achieving *All But Dissertation* (ABD) status is a milestone of graduate school. This status is attained when a graduate student has completed coursework, passed exams, and maybe even named a committee. The only thing missing at this point is a completed dissertation—an extended, independent research project. ABD status is also a bit of a danger zone—it is the point at which most attrition occurs. How hard could it be to execute a brilliant study that makes an original contribution, and then write it up in concise and engaging prose in no more than 300 pages? Put that way, it seems like an intimidating process, and maybe it should not be a surprise that many students find it a challenge. But it need not be an insurmountable challenge.

Many students get stuck at this point because it is difficult to get started! In any subfield, there are so many unanswered questions, but at the same time so much interesting work has already been done; there are a seemingly infinite number of research approaches, but you only can choose one; and ultimately even if you have a supportive and directive advisor and committee, the work must be your own. It is perhaps no wonder that students have trouble even getting started. But it does not have to be intimidating, if you have the right tools and a good process with which to get started.

This chapter aims to help you get over that hump by giving you a template with which you can start your project. Although the discipline of political science is diverse, there are some basic principles that exist across all subfields, and thus a student in the dissertation process should consider them when getting started. While the format of your dissertation prospectus is ultimately determined by your advisor, committee, department, and/or university (see chapters 13 and 15 for additional information), the template suggested here could be used as a "first first draft" to share with your advisor in your early meetings.

First Principles of the Dissertation Process

There are three things to keep in mind as you begin the dissertation process. First, a dissertation is not just a list or description of research findings. It is a *narrative* of the way you framed an important research question—of how you set it up and how you are making a contribution. It is also a report of the techniques and results of your original research, with a description of the research design, methods, and findings. The narrative is a good place to start with a big project such as a dissertation, as you need to justify spending potentially years of your life dedicated to what is likely a narrow research question. In other words, you need to demonstrate that your project "matters" and you need to do this early on in the process.

Second, it is a good idea to start with a relatively concise draft of what you hope to do; perhaps thinking of it as a proposal of a proposal may help. Expecting a fully formed prospectus or proposal to emerge the first time you try is a recipe for disaster. As many political scientists know, an incremental approach is a good strategy to achieve success. Thus, an early version of your thoughts, such as the one proposed here, should use succinctness as a guiding principle.

Third, the narrative is the most challenging aspect of the dissertation project, but it is crucial to stick with it: The only way to get to a completed written dissertation is to start writing and keep at it! It is so easy to set things down for a while to deal with other distractions—and then you find that three weeks have passed by and you have not thought about the project. The strategy and template proposed here breaks the various aspects of the dissertation project into manageable chunks (a "workflow") so that you can plug away at one section at a time. You can also expand each section as you proceed, eventually building them into the prospectus format required by your program, and then into the dissertation chapters. (For additional tips and suggestions about the larger dissertation process, see chapter 15.)

The Narrative Template

Constructing the narrative requires the following components (the appendix contains a specific organizational outline). To stick with the principle of succinctness, each section contains specific length limits. In these beginning stages, try to keep within these limits; being able to express your project (relatively) briefly is crucial to building the narrative and makes things more manageable. There will be time to expand things as the project expands. At least in the beginning, use the suggested headings.

1. Here's My Question

Two to Four Paragraphs

This is the introduction. The first paragraph introduces the issue, providing the motivation for the study: why are you doing this project, and why should others think it interesting? The second paragraph states your central research question as clearly and simply as possible. After that statement, you can pose some important sub-questions. If you believe you need more than two paragraphs, you may use more, but be as concise as possible.

2. Here's Why Answering the Question Matters

Two to Four Paragraphs

In this section, discuss the reasons that the topic is of importance in practical and academic terms. For the practical side, use one to two paragraphs to describe what impact this research will have on the world. How could it possibly lead to policy change, a better society, or something along those lines? For the academic side, take one to two paragraphs to describe which academic tradition, subfield, and/or literature to which your research will contribute. What will you learn that is not already known? How will your work help to move the subfield forward?

3. Here's What We Know

Try to Limit to Eight Paragraphs

At a relatively high level, review the scholarly literature and, if needed, other publications and media related to your topic and question. What are the knowns and unknowns in the area? What research has been done in the past? The purpose of this section is not to exhaustively summarize every work ever written on the topic, but rather to build the contours of your question and point to a gap that needs to be filled. Remember that you are building a narrative here, meaning that in the next section you will frame your question as a puzzle that has yet to be answered. In your dissertation, potentially even in your prospectus, you will expand this into a (relatively) exhaustive literature review, but for now keep your focus on the big picture, perhaps by focusing on the most influential works.[2]

4. Here's What We Need to Know

Two to Four Paragraphs

Building upon the previous section, identify the gaps in the literature, the puzzle that needs to be answered. Explain why the question you identified in the section, "here's why answering the question matters," is especially in need of answering and amenable to finding an answer. Be sure to connect the puzzle to the question. What is unknown that needs to be known? Do not be afraid to repeat or restate your question. Repetition is not always bad, particularly if it is in service of clarifying and connecting.

5. My Plan for Answering the Question

Five Paragraphs

In this section, describe the research approach you will take to close the gap you described in the previous section. Specifically address the following points with hypothetical or real examples from your research area, as sometimes an example can provide more clarity than the abstract reasoning. Examples can also help you think through complex challenges in your topic. The subsections are described below.

5a. Unit of Analysis

One Paragraph

Describe what kinds of events or action you will need to examine or observe to answer the question from the previous section. Are you examining an aggregate phenomenon or an individual one? Do you plan to focus on countries or people, or perhaps some other unit? If there are multiple levels of analysis, not that, but make sure you are clear in doing so. You should also provide the time period of the events or actions you plan to study. If you plan to examine them at a single point in time—if you plan a cross-sectional analysis—be sure to note this.

5b. Evidence Available

One Paragraph

Describe the kinds of evidence available to help you answer your question. In this context, "evidence" means much more than data, although it can be that, too. Other types of evidence include historical writing, mathematical theorems, and case studies. The need for evidence depends on the question you ask, your subfield, and the approach you plan to take. Think of this section as the realm of possibilities for your research project.

5c. Evidence to Collect

One Paragraph

Regardless of your question, subfield, or approach, you will need to collect some form of evidence, but you will not be able to collect all that exists. In other words, you will need to make choices. Use this section to select from the available evidence and justify your choices. You should consider your resource constraints, but it is important to remember that not all resource constraints are insurmountable, and you may not need to limit yourself just yet.

5d. Defend the Choice of Evidence

One Paragraph

Building upon the previous two sub-sections, explain why the evidence you chose is adequate to address the question. Provide some reasons why the specific evidence you intend to collect can be extrapolated to a more general understanding of the phenomenon you hope to explain. Do not dwell on potential shortcomings, rather make an affirmative case as to why your approach would be adequate.

5e. Analytic Technique

One Paragraph

Describe the analytical techniques that you will use to evaluate your evidence and answer your question. The technique you use necessarily depends upon the question you are addressing, the subfield or tradition in which you are working, and your inclination and resources. It is fair to say, though, that this section should rely upon your methods training, where the term "methods" is broadly defined to include approaches taken across all subfields. In other words, do not limit yourself.

Other Components

Other items to include in this initial draft include an outline of a Table of Contents, which will give you and your potential committee a good idea of what the organization of your dissertation. You should also draft up a Research Timeline that provides the dates by which you hope to compete the work. This is likely an aspirational document, subject to significant change, but as with everything else, it is a good idea to put things in writing to clarify things.

Once you compile the document described above, take it to a potential advisor or committee.[3] It is important to note that the document described above is not a legally binding contract, to be approved by your committee and enforced by law. That is in some sense what a prospectus is supposed to be. Rather, the document described here, and outlined in the appendix, is a starting point for a constructive discussion about your project. Only with a written document such as this can you begin the journey ahead.

Below, please see the template for getting started on the narrative component of your project. Use this as a guide if you like.

Concluding Remarks

As far as ABD is concerned, it can be hard to get started on your dissertation, but once you begin, you'll be happy you did. Getting started and keeping the momentum going is easier when you have a plan and process in place that provides guidance. Hopefully, the plan and process outlined in this chapter will help you get that proverbial foot out the door.

Resources

1. Reference Management / Research / Writing Tools:

- Endnote: https://endnote.com/
- Mendeley: https://www.mendeley.com/
- Zotero: https://www.zotero.org/
- Scrivener: https://www.literatureandlatte.com/

2. Dissertation Proposal:

- Knopf, Jeffrey W. (2006). Doing a Literature Review. *PS: Political Science & Politics*, 39(1), 127-132.
- May, Peter J. (2002). Constructing the Prospectus. *PS: Political Science & Politics*, 34(4), 843-844.
- Most, Benjamin A. (1990). Getting Started on Political Research. *PS: Political Science and Politics*, 23(4), 592-596.
- Rothman, Steven B. (2008). Comparatively Evaluating Potential Dissertation and Thesis Projects. *PS: Political Science & Politics*, 41(2), 367-369.
- Useem, Bert. (1997). Choosing a Dissertation Topic. *PS: Political Science and Politics*, 30(2), 213-216.

Appendix: Sample Template

Here is the suggested format for getting started on your dissertation:
1. Title page (including your name, affiliation, and date of the draft)
2. Here's my question (two to four paragraphs)
3. Here's why answering the question matters (two to four paragraphs)
4. Here's what we know (eight paragraphs)
5. Here's what we need to know (two to four paragraphs)
6. Here's my plan for answering the question (five paragraphs)
    a. Unit of analysis
    b. Evidence available
    c. Evidence to collect
    d. Defend the choice of evidence
    e. Analytic technique
7. Outline a table of contents
8. Outline a research timeline through the dissertation defense
9. Bibliography or references cited page

Endnotes

1. The idea for this comes from Dave Robertson, Curator's Professor at the University of Missouri–St. Louis, who sadly passed away in October 2020. Dave was a productive and influential scholar, and a great mentor to many successful PhD students. He would give his students a two-page "tip sheet" to get started, and this is adapted from that. This chapter is dedicated to him.

2. If you haven't already, now is the time to start using a reference management tool like Zotero, Mendeley, or EndNote. Keep track of all you have read by entering the citation in your library as soon as you read it.

3. Whether you talk to potential advisors before setting out on this particular journey is your choice, and something you should discuss with your academic advisor and peers. See chapters 13 and 15 for additional information about selecting an advisor and consulting with your advisor during the dissertation phase of study.

15

The Doctoral Dissertation and MA Thesis: Managing the Process, Your Life, and Your Data

Michael W. Widmeier[1] & Dessi Kirilova[2]

1. Webster University 2. Qualitative Data Repository

KEYWORDS: Original Scholarship, Prospectus Defense, Data Management.

Introduction

The master's thesis and doctoral dissertation commonly serve as the final step in the process of the respective graduate degrees in political science. These written works of original research serve as evidence that degree candidates can think like political scientists, exhibit expertise in the field, and illustrate their capacity to produce independent, novel intellectual work that contributes to existing knowledge in the discipline. Here we outline the general process for both, as they share many similar steps. We also touch upon some work-life balance considerations and discuss additional responsibilities outside of the dissertation/thesis, awareness of which will equip you to successfully manage what is expected of graduate students during that stage of their degree. Then we discuss some key points specific to the master's thesis and end with a section of data management advice that we think applies to all types of research projects.

Managing the Process

Typically, the start of the dissertation and thesis work marks a critical juncture in graduate student training in political science—the transition from coursework to producing *original scholarship*. PhD students will commonly embark on that research journey following the successful completion of comprehensive (or field) examinations as well. The subsequent sections outline the pathway through the dissertation and thesis process, from topic conception through defense and publication.

Choosing a Topic

The dissertation process commences with the choice of a topic. Ideally, students begin to think about potential dissertation topics during their coursework. As students work through courses, have conversations with faculty regarding areas of interest, present early research at conferences, and form advisory committees, they will need to closely consider the niche areas of research within their chosen subfields that excite them (or at least pique their interest). As the time comes to begin work on the prospectus, students should have settled upon a topic. It is important to note that, in most departments, the choice of topic is not etched in stone. There will be flexibility needed on the student's part to adapt to feedback given by the committee; this will inevitably involve the focus of the dissertation shifting to some degree. For example, it may become apparent to the student and committee during the prospectus phase that the agreed-upon data collection plan is either too ambitious given time and resource constraints or simply not feasible. Students should be aware that shifts in project design can happen, even if their specifics are not always foreseeable. While such changes can and do occur, students should strive to settle on and commit to a topic they are truly invested in as soon as possible. This serves a strategic purpose, as committees in many departments would like students to move through the dissertation as quickly as possible. This also serves to benefit the students' well-being, as working on a dissertation that one is passionate about will be a better experience than trudging through a project one does not enjoy or feel engaged with.

A challenging scenario that students sometimes find themselves in is when they feel the need to change their topic completely. While most (if not all) students working on a thesis or dissertation experience fatigue and become less excited about their topic at various points (or feel they suddenly dislike it!), only a small portion of these scenarios merit a wholesale change in topic. In cases where students have become worn out and need a break (but still have interest in their project), they should unplug and step away from dissertation work for a week or two if possible (see the section on "Health and Wellbeing in Graduate School" in this volume for more advice). Ideally, they come back refreshed and invigorated, ready to tackle their project again. On the other hand, sometimes students have truly lost interest in the topic or realize their research focus has moved in a different direction entirely. In this case, a topic change may be warranted. Conditional upon the approval of the committee (an adviser change may be prudent in some of these cases; see the next section), a new plan can be developed to either "start from scratch" or begin a new project that incorporates pieces of the existing project. In all likelihood, the timing of the change will be one of the (if not the most) important aspects of whether the topic change is the best decision. Due to funding and job market considerations, moving from a dissertation in its advanced stages to a new topic may not be worth the cost. In this case, there may also be ramifications for the coherence of the student's research agenda. Thus, our general advice would be to consider the potential negative consequences associated with a topic change, which exist along a spectrum—the closer (in time) one is to the *prospectus defense* and the fewer number of dissertation chapters completed, the less risky a topic change will be.

Choosing Advisers

While the decisions relating to selecting a topic have a direct impact on the shape of the project, the choice of advisers (and specifically the committee chair) also has a significant influence on the nature of the document that will be written (for advice on choosing advisory committees, see chapters 10 and 13 in this volume). A number of variables need to be considered when choosing an adviser, including both their personal and professional characteristics. One should consider personality. Does a potential adviser have a personality that will mesh well with one's own? This is an oft overlooked aspect of the process for students. The personal and professional relationship that develops between a student and formal advisers needs to be one that works for both parties. Central to this relationship are factors such as communication style, expectations and how they are communicated, delivery of feedback, networking and advocacy approaches, among others. Further, does the potential adviser have a reputation for truly mentoring students, or for serving in a more limited role? Having a mentor is a vital component of the dissertation or thesis process, so seeking mentorship from a chair not comfortable or accustomed to that role can lead to a student needing to find mentorship elsewhere (for a discussion of advisers vs. mentors, see chapter 13 in this volume). From a research perspective, choosing an adviser (and particularly a chair) who is well-versed (if not expert) in your topic of interest is critical. As mentioned above, students can (and do) change topics over time, whether it be minor project tweaks or wholesale shifts to new topics. As such, you will need advisers who have expertise in your broader areas of interest.

There are also cases in which students feel the need to change their main adviser. This is a big decision that can have substantial and wide-ranging effects on one's dissertation and academic future, so it should not be taken lightly. First, we recommend that you identify an alternative adviser before making a change, speak to this person, and get their assent to the idea of becoming your new chair. Additionally, it would be very beneficial to speak to other members of your committee or other trusted faculty to gain perspective on the dynamics and effects of a potential change. Making an adviser change at the prospectus or dissertation stage will entail bringing in a faculty member that may have different ideas about the direction of your dissertation. You should ask yourself if this is a good thing or not. If you are only looking to make a small change to some aspect of your research agenda that your current adviser is not on board with, the wholesale changes involved with a new adviser may not be worth the change. Of course, if you are wishing to make a change due to irreconcilable differences with the existing adviser (personality, advising relationship, disagreements over content or direction of dissertation), then a move to a more like-minded faculty member will likely be necessary and the decision may be clear. However, in scenarios not involving incompatibility or conflict (i.e., topic change), the costs and benefits should be weighed closely. You must consider differences between the potential advisers' contributions in a variety of roles: mentors, conduits for networking in your area of research, co-authors, letter-writers for the job market, or general advocates for you throughout your career (particularly the early stage). This is not intended to be an exhaustive list of the pros and cons of switching advisers, but to give a general sense of what may be gained and lost when making this critical decision.

The Prospectus and Proposal

The next step in the process is the prospectus/proposal. The size and format of this document varies widely across departments, but the general purpose of the proposal is to produce a plan for the goals and structure of the research work to follow. In most cases, the proposal is reviewed by an adviser or a committee; on the doctoral level it is also typically then subjected to a formal defense, after which the student moves forward with writing the dissertation itself.

In its simplest form, the proposal serves as a general outline of what the broader research work will accomplish and how the student will execute the project. The document should outline the structure of the dissertation project—will it take the form of a book project, or an article-based framework? The book format involves structuring the dissertation as one cohesive project, with each individual chapter providing a component piece of an overarching theory and empirical testing of the hypotheses. An article-based dissertation entails writing several standalone, though related, chapters that can be (relatively) easily modified to submit to journals for individual publication. This decision is likely to be determined by departmental or advisers' preferences, but should also take into account the size and scope of the proposed project. The proposal should include many of the basic elements of any research project in political science—a review of existing literature, identification of how the work contributes to that literature, a discussion of the theoretical contribution, and a proposed research design for how analyses (quantitative, qualitative, mixed-method) will be conducted. See chapter 14 in this volume for additional details on writing a prospectus/proposal.

Across departments and both types of graduate degrees, a fundamental expectation of all advisers is for students to justify the relevance and contribution of the proposed project. After all, any given department: (1) may be investing funding in the graduate student for several years (at least), and (2) stands to benefit from a job placement perspective with more competitive candidates who have exceptional research projects. Thus, the onus is on the student—whether a master's or PhD candidate—to make a convincing case in the proposal as to why the project is innovative or contributes to the extant literature in a meaningful way.

This brings us to the prospectus defense, which will typically involve a presentation of the prospectus to the students' committee followed by a question-and-answer period. This is almost always a formal requirement in doctoral programs and only sometimes (and might be less formal) for others. Typically, the entire committee has already reviewed the final prospectus draft, ideally with feedback given on prior iterations of the document. However, there are instances in which the dissertation chair is the only individual to have seen the draft in advance of the defense. In either case, the student should expect a critical and forthright examination of the project by the committee, with feedback given on how the project design should be modified to facilitate the best possible dissertation project. Contingent upon a satisfactory level of effort and quality, the committee decides upon a successful defense and the student moves on to the dissertation work itself.

Data Collection

An important aspect of the early phases of the dissertation concerns data. Given the assumption that empirical analyses will be conducted for most dissertations, you will need to gather data for theory building and/or hypothesis testing. Regardless of whether the data are qualitative or quantitative, you must decide whether your project requires the generation of original data. Based upon this choice, you must then decide if fieldwork is necessary to gather the requisite data (for advice on fieldwork, see chapter 20 in this volume). If fieldwork is necessary, but not feasible due to time or funding constraints, you will need to adjust and find alternative existing data sources. In cases where fieldwork is not necessary, but original data will be coded, the student must create a codebook to guide the process and a plan for gathering primary, secondary, or internet-based sources. Generally, students will forgo completing fieldwork for data collection purposes if limitations on time and/or funding prohibit doing so or sufficient data can be collected via desk research, using existing and accessible data sources. In all instances, making a clear plan for handling the various types of data you might need in ways that keep them well-organized, safe, secure, and easily findable is something that should come early in the process. (For further recommendations on data management planning and implementation, see the separate section later in this chapter.)

Dissertation Defense

Though we discussed the prospectus defense above, we will make several additional points regarding the final project defense here. First and foremost, students need to determine what is required for a committee in their department to schedule a defense date. This is the point at which the committee or chair has determined that the work has been completed to a sufficient extent to warrant a defense. This may vary across committees, as some may need to see the dissertation completed in its entirety, while others may schedule the defense well in advance with the expectation of a final chapter or sections being completed. The defense day is a significant moment in the life of an academic, as it is the culmination of the long and difficult process of earning a PhD. However, in many instances, the defense process itself can be fairly straightforward, even a formality in cases where a committee has found the progress of the work to be exceptional. The quality of the draft and the general tone of committee feedback across its previous iterations (individually reviewed chapters or sections) are likely to be significant determinants of the level of criticism faced by the student during the actual defense. To this point, it is important to have conversations with fellow students as well as your advisers well in advance about the general conventions and procedures for defenses in your department. For example, you should be aware of whether (or how often) others have failed their dissertation defenses—is this a common occurrence, or will committees generally not schedule defenses if a successful defense is unlikely? While much of this information can ideally be gleaned from conversations with your committee chair (or adviser), it is beneficial to have a general understanding of the department culture regarding the faculty's approaches to dissertation defenses.

Final Steps

Upon successfully defending your project, several final steps remain. First, it is possible that your committee will request revisions to be made to the manuscript as a condition of passing the defense. The requested revisions may be substantial or minor in scope, conditional upon the state of the work prior to the defense. Once the revisions have been completed, you must confront the process of formatting the final document per university or intra-university college/school division guidelines. While most students are elated to be so near the finish line, the formatting process can be extremely time-consuming and frustrating for many, particularly if they have only become aware of the formatting expectations post-defense. Formatting guidelines typically range from broad instructions regarding how the overall document is structured, to extremely narrow guidelines concerning the font, capitalization, and spacing of the table of contents. The best approach you can take would be to become familiar with formatting expectations as you begin to write your thesis or dissertation. In this case, you can format the document as required from day one, thus leaving little to no work to be done in this regard before final submission.

And finally, the dissertation must be formally submitted to your school, after which it will be placed in the university's institutional repository for theses and dissertations. At this point, the document has been "published" online and made publicly available.

Managing Your Life

Setting Goals

Writing a master's thesis or, even more so, a dissertation, requires many hours, including ones filled with frustration and stress, as you face the uphill battle of producing (often) a book-length manuscript of original scholarship for the first time in your academic life. Taken from this macro-level perspective, the task is daunting. Thus, when it comes to sitting down in front of a computer and actually writing, it is advisable to establish bite-size goals that can facilitate progress and minimize the potential for the paralysis students feel when unable to make significant leaps forward. The process of goal setting is closely connected to the degree of structure that is a part of the student's workflow. Students able to initiate by themselves a structure or guidelines for meeting daily, weekly, or monthly writing goals are well-positioned to make incremental, but consistent, progress on the thesis or dissertation. In many cases, structure is externally imposed by the one's main adviser, particularly those that manage students at a relatively micro-level. For those students that benefit from structure (as well as those with less hands-on advisers), it becomes imperative to self-impose a work schedule that creates manageable goals at the daily and weekly level. Students can generally use the prospectus (and any guidance received during incremental review meetings or at the prospectus defense) as a starting point for a work plan.

As you move forward toward the final draft, you will need to implement other goal-setting techniques. These can include targets for daily or weekly written word counts or uninterrupted hours worked each day. While larger targets such as chapter deadlines will largely be determined by the chair, the small and intermediate goals often have to be independently determined and have the most meaningful impact on your progress. Seeking additional feedback from the chair and your committee on smaller portions of the work is an additional way of implementing completion goals and providing for more detailed revision. In sum, incremental progress is quite often the best progress, and consistent incremental progress will lead to a finished dissertation. For more on time management during the dissertation process, see chapter 17 in this volume.

Protecting Your Mental Health

One aspect of the graduate school experience that has received a much-needed increase in attention concerns student mental health. While this topic is addressed further in the "Health and Well-being in Graduate School" section of this volume, we wish to briefly address this notion in the context of completing your graduate project here. As dissertations and master's theses are, by definition, solo projects, you will spend countless hours working alone. Thus, the experience can become very difficult, lonely, and isolating. As such, we recommend that you seek out support networks and self-care in whatever form you are comfortable with—you do not have to do it alone. Chapter 63 in this volume has advice on finding one's collective, which can help you feel less isolated and build camaraderie into the writing process, as well as facilitate the incremental work schedule we advocate. Other examples of support networks include university-sponsored dissertation/thesis boot camps, department cohort-based groups, family and friends, and mentors beyond your designated advisers for the project. If you feel the need, seeking professional counseling or therapy can be very beneficial in providing temporary or ongoing support throughout the process.

Balancing Other Demands

An important facet of the intense writing process you should consider is what other responsibilities are expected of you as part of your program during this time. For master's students, it might be the case that they are working on their terminal research project during semesters of regular coursework.

At the departmental or university level, all graduate students may be responsible for teaching courses or working as teaching or research assistants. This dynamic is tied to the structure and availability of funding for graduate students, but often these assignments are also needed by students from a personal financial perspective. Those who have the opportunity to pursue dissertation fellowships from either within or outside of the university should definitely do so, as the time commitment is much smaller relative to teaching or research assignments. See chapter 3 in this volume for more advice on funding. In the case of doctoral students, you should be clear on whether your main adviser expects you to be producing additional research—e.g., working on projects outside of the dissertation, presenting research at conferences, or submitting this work for publication. In such cases, these additional expectations can be extremely burdensome and difficult. The time and effort involved to teach or produce other research often comes at the expense of dissertation progress, and creates more pressure for students, particularly those expected to complete the dissertation quickly.

Having a publication record has become necessary for many PhD candidates to be competitive on the academic job market. Furthermore, the expectations regarding the quality and quantity of candidates' peer-reviewed publications continue to rise. In many cases, students can devote time to presenting their work at conferences and workshops and submitting dissertation chapters to journals while working on their dissertation. These pursuits are made much easier in cases where students' dissertation project is built upon work they started prior to comprehensive exams. Clearly, this period of a PhD candidate's life can be very demanding and stressful, so having a clear understanding in advance of what academic life will look like during this stage can help you to be prepared to best manage the workload that will come. Adapting to dissertation-caliber work is a challenging transition for many students, so having an awareness of what one's broader academic life during the dissertation phase will look like can make for a smoother adjustment.

Differences Between a PhD Dissertation and a Master's Thesis

In many respects, a dissertation and a master's thesis are very similar. Both use the foundation of knowledge obtained via coursework, selecting a committee and a chair, and result in the production of high-level scholarship that is subjected to a defense in front of faculty. The primary differences between the two projects are defined by time, size, scope and function. First, the dissertation—like the doctoral program as a whole—involves a much greater time investment. Not only do PhD students typically spend more time in coursework than master's students (two to three years rather than one year), but PhD students also complete comprehensive exams in a number of subfields prior to beginning the dissertation. Note that some master's programs offer the thesis as optional, with a form of a comprehensive exam as an alternative. In that case, students will need to consider the added value of completing a thesis for their career goals versus the time it will take to complete. In terms of time spent on writing the two manuscripts, most programs will expect master's students to complete the thesis in their second and final year of the program. As mentioned above, in most cases, master's students may not have a dedicated period of time in which to write the thesis, but work on it alongside coursework. Dissertation time to completion varies widely, but most PhD students will spend at least two years on their dissertation, including research design, data collection, data analysis, and writing.

Second, a dissertation will be a substantially larger project. A book-format dissertation will often include two to three theoretical chapters, each having an accompanying chapter with empirical analyses, as well as introduction and conclusion chapters. On the other hand, the master's thesis will likely consist of only one theoretical and empirical chapter. In terms of the expectations for scope and depth, a master's thesis generally focuses on a narrower topic within an existing body of research and does not require the collection of original data (although some master's students might choose to do that). A dissertation is expected to break new ground in terms of theory, data or methodology, while the main goal of a master's thesis is to show command of previous knowledge. Given that, in the social sciences, significantly more PhDs than those with master's degrees continue on with careers in academia, the dissertation plays a much more prominent role post-graduation than does the thesis, hence the focus on originality.

Managing Your Data

As is clear from our prior discussion, in the context of your dissertation or master's project, data loom large. Data take a wide variety of forms and here we use the term in the broadest possible sense: the record of empirical observations which undergird any knowledge claim. Whether you need to access data already collected by others or generate your own (or a combination of both), you will benefit from early data management planning for the whole project lifecycle, from collection and subsequent cleaning and analysis to publication and potential data sharing, which allows others to engage the same data for new research.

The concept of Research Data Management (RDM) describes the "caring for, facilitating access to and adding value to research data throughout its lifecycle." (Edinburgh University Information Services n.d.). Due to space constraints, here we only flag key RDM conventions (Briney, Coates and Goben 2020) to consider as you embark on your first large independent scholarly project, and then provide resources for further self-guided learning. Once aware of the core concepts, you can consider the unique aspects of your own project and record explicit choices in a Data Management Plan (DMP) to serve as a personal reminder of your procedures, as well as a reference for team members (including your chair or other advisers) who might also need to process or make sense of your data. Your DMP is also an important document that accompanies and contextualizes the data, should you choose to share them to enhance the transparency of your research for independent secondary use or methodological training.[1]

The key RDM activities are: (1) storing and keeping your data safe, (2) organizing your data, and (3) documenting the research and data handling process, including the connection among the forms of data which might be produced (e.g., by digitizing, translating, re-formatting, deriving new variables).

To prevent data loss, you should follow the "3-2-1 rule": keep three copies of each digital file (a main one you use and two backups), saved in two different media (or for most purposes, devices), with one copy off-site (or on a remote server) for disaster recovery. Additionally, you should set up backups that are regular, incremental, and ideally automated, and you should periodically check that your backups are working as intended. Over the long-term, data files need to be copied to new media every three to five years—something that can be handled by professionals if you archive your data with a digital repository after the end of your project.

How you organize your files will depend on your research design and personal preferences, but using a combination of meaningful folder structures (e.g., top-level folders for the different geographic sites you study) and comprehensive file naming conventions (e.g., which embed the date on which a given survey response was produced or a suffix that distinguishes recorded interview audio file from its transcript, from a de-identified version of the same) are key strategies.

Documenting all these choices, as well as project-level (contextual, methodological and procedural) and file-level details (e.g., name of interviewer and speaker tags, or variable attributes) in real time will allow you to retain information that makes the data more easily accessible and understandable when you return to them for analysis and writing. Furthermore, the documentation record accompanying a shared data collection will make the data and the research based on them reusable and verifiable by others. The guiding question you should try to address in your documentation effort is "If using these data for the first time, what would someone new need to know to make sense of them?"

Researchers must develop, enhance and professionalize their research data management skills in order to solve the various data-related challenges they will encounter during their master's level, doctoral dissertation or other projects. This subject matter is rarely taught in graduate programs, but you can find expertise and advice from a variety of research-related sources. Your university library data services can be a great first stop for general RDM guidance and one-on-one consultations. The IT department supporting your school can provide configuration assistance for back-ups and advice on services authorized or provided by the university. If you are contemplating data sharing in any form (whether to meet funder and journal requirements or because you want to be a cutting-edge science practitioner), reaching out to the personnel of relevant repositories—ICPSR and QDR are a good fit for curated social science data[2]—as early as possible will also allow you to adapt your ethics board application and informed consent script if you will engage with human participants in ways that address issues of access controls and confidentiality (ICPSR, Guide to Social Science Data Preparation, Sixth ed.; QDR, "Human Participants"). A few self-study options also exist online, such as the comprehensive MANTRA course out of the United Kingdom (EDINA n.d.) and the SSRC-supported course (SSRC and QDR n.d.) that specializes in qualitative social science data.

Data underpin all the scholarly claims and conclusions you make in your dissertation or master's thesis. Creating or gathering data is likely to be expensive, both in terms of money and your time. Spending a bit of time and effort at the very beginning of your work to detail relevant RDM steps, can save you time, frustration and in some cases even the data themselves. You will end up with better quality data that are more useful and usable—to you and others—which will enhance the quality and rigor of your published research.

Conclusion

For many students in graduate programs, the master's thesis or PhD dissertation is the first large-scale independent research project they undertake. The process of designing, conducting, writing, and defending the research is long and might seem daunting. Knowing what to expect, how to plan for the different expectations, and how to pace your work so that you are making steady progress should reduce the stress that otherwise can result. In all aspects of your preparations for this important phase of the MA or PhD, the mantra "make a plan, document it, seek expertise and support from others while following your plan" should help guide you in doing the best possible work you can do.

Endnotes

1   Understanding the importance of early data management planning, many social science funders—prominently the National Science Foundation—have started requiring a formal DMP as part of funding proposals. Whether you need to write a formal DMP or not, creating one would benefit you first and foremost. While you can start drafting one as casually as a set of handwritten notes, you can also take advantage of existing institutional templates by visiting the online DMPTool wizard (https://dmptool.org/).

2   Other self-deposit venues used by political scientists for sharing and finding data are Dataverse (https://dataverse.org/researchers) and the OSF Platform (https://osf.io/), although these are not professionally curated.

References

Briney, Kristin A., Heather Coates and Abigail Goben. 2020. "Foundational Practices of Research Data Management." *Research Ideas and Outcomes* 6: e56508. https://doi.org/10.3897/rio.6.e56508.

DMPTool. www.dmptool.org

EDINA and Data Library, University of Edinburgh. *MANTRA: Research Data Management Training.* https://mantra.ed.ac.uk/. Accessed on December 28, 2021.

ICPSR. *Guide to Social Science Data Preparation and Archiving: Best Practice Throughout the Data Life Cycle.* Sixth Edition. https://www.icpsr.umich.edu/files/deposit/dataprep.pdf. Accessed on December 30, 2021.

Qualitative Data Repository. "Human Participants–General Guidance" https://qdr.syr.edu/guidance/human-participants. Accessed on December 30, 2021.

Social Science Research Council and the Qualitative Data Repository. "Managing Qualitative Social Science Data." https://managing-qualitative-data.org/. Accessed on December 28, 2021.

16 Balancing Pregnancy, Parenthood, and Graduate School

Kimberly Saks McManaway[1], Regina Bateson[2], Marty P. Jordan[3], Karen M. Kedrowski[4], & Kyle Harris[5]

1. University of Michigan-Flint 2. University of Ottawa 3. Michigan State University
4. Iowa State University 5. Central Michigan University

KEYWORDS: Graduate Student Parents, Pregnancy, Parenting, Infant Feeding, Childcare.

Introduction

While some scholarly articles and reports examine the needs of faculty parents (Bassett 2005; Colbeck and Drago 2005; APSA CSWP 2016; van Assendelft et al. 2019), graduate student parents remain largely ignored in academia. The number of graduate students with children is increasing (Mason 2009; Perry 2021), and the lack of support for such students may contribute to the "leaky pipeline" in academia (Windsor and Crawford 2020). This chapter aims to recognize the needs and existence of graduate student parents.

The authors represent a diverse set of experiences and perspectives. Some of us were pregnant and/ or had children while in graduate school, were expectant on the job market, or gave birth to children as non-tenured assistant professors. One of the authors underwent fertility treatments, two of the authors suffered multiple miscarriages and a third suffered one, and two of the authors had twins. We offer our viewpoints juggling the competing demands of our academic and domestic responsibilities. However, we acknowledge that our perspectives are finite; they do not fully encompass everyone's intersectional identities and experiences as graduate student parents. Nevertheless, we hope the guidance here serves as one source of information for those on this journey.

Pregnancy, Childbirth, and Adopting Children

Making the Decision to Have Children as a Graduate Student

Today, there are more parenting and pregnant students in higher education (Brown and Nichols 2012). Pregnancy and parenting are profound choices that can significantly impact an academic career itself in its infancy. Women are particularly disadvantaged given societal and cultural expectations surrounding parenting and household work (Correll, Bernard, & Paik 2007; Dillon 2012; Utami 2019). All student parents find themselves in situations where the expectations of their academic programs conflict with parenting in a way that can lead to significant stress (Utami 2019).

Conventional wisdom encourages individuals to forsake parenting until after graduate school and often until tenure is attained (Kennelly & Spalter-Roth 2006). If you decide to have a child or children during graduate school, there are several competing factors to consider. In addition to concerns about fertility, graduate students must also weigh their own values and goals, the needs and wishes of spouses or partners, and more. For those who choose to explore parenthood, the structure of graduate school offers some advantages, like a somewhat flexible schedule and a community of other students who may be on a similar journey.

Like any expecting parent, pregnant graduate students can expect to experience a range of hopes and concerns. Upon discovering the pregnancy, graduate students should review their health insurance options, leave of absence policies, short-term disability benefits, and arrange suitable medical care. While many pregnancies are uneventful, others are marked by serious complications requiring frequent prenatal visits, specialist appointments, invasive treatments, or even hospitalization. The physical toll of pregnancy can also be significant. For example, about 70% of pregnant people experience nausea or vomiting in pregnancy, with symptoms persisting into the third trimester for nearly a quarter of them (Einarson, Piwko, and Koren 2013). It is also important to note that women of color—especially Black, American Indian, and Alaskan Native women—disproportionately experience health inequities, including maternal and infant death, due to long-standing racial injustice (CDC 2019). This is an additional burden on the minds of expectant graduate students of color.

Some graduate students may choose to tell their advisor about a pregnancy in its early stages, especially if they experience disruptive symptoms. Others may wait longer. No matter when you share your news, it is natural to feel apprehensive. In our experience, pregnant students' worry about telling their advisors is typically worse than the actual discussion. See chapter 13 for suggestions on selecting supportive advisors. Pregnancy and parenting in graduate school are more common than one might think; for example, a study in the University of California system found that approximately 12% of male graduate students and 14% of female graduate students were parents (Mason, Goulden, and Frasch 2009). Your advisor has likely encountered a pregnant student or colleague before. If you are clear, direct, and positive, they are likely to react neutrally or supportively. Cosme (2016) recommends that you "try to keep the conversation centered on your work:" explain how your pregnancy will affect your academic responsibilities and share your plans for the next several months.

Advanced graduate students may also wonder whether a pregnancy will affect their job prospects. Some research suggests that women who have children in graduate school may not be disadvantaged when finding a tenure track job, presuming they manage to finish their degrees (Kulp 2016), but large-scale studies are largely absent. When on the academic job market in 2012, one author conducted a small informal experiment. At the time of her interviews, she was somewhat visibly pregnant. She randomly disclosed her pregnancy to only half the schools where she interviewed. This choice appeared to make no difference in the outcome of the searches, or the way she was treated during campus visits. Some pregnant job candidates may feel more relaxed if they are fully transparent with search committees, especially if they may need some accommodations. Other job candidates may prefer to keep their status private. Either choice is justifiable, reasonable, and unlikely to substantially affect your career trajectory.

Additionally, fertility issues pose a conundrum for graduate students. The ideal childbearing years tend to coincide with graduate school years, especially as the median age for women at degree completion is 33.6 years (Hoffer et al. 2006). Fertility treatments, including IVF, may be covered in whole or part by certain institutions, making coverage under their health insurance policies an ideal time to seek out such treatments. You may find that the considerations in favor of going through fertility treatments now are worth the balancing that you will need to do in your academic life. Juggling academic and treatment-related responsibilities may be stressful and necessitate a leave of absence or a scaling back of participation. The very real physical effects of fertility treatments can be unpredictable and intense. Understanding these potential pressure points and, to the extent possible, timing fertility treatments over breaks and away from finals and conferences may help you attend to both.

Adoption has its own timeline and considerations that take years of planning and a certain degree of flexibility to adapt to changing situations. These issues are often stigmatized in society and doubly so in academia as they represent challenges to the traditional graduate student role. Court dates, paperwork, and the unexpected call that a child is available for placement complicate the graduate student experience because they appear out of nowhere for advisors and peers unless the student notifies them of their journey ahead of time.

Many happen upon pregnancy unexpectedly. Some pregnant students may decide to have an abortion. In some countries and some US states, abortion is a simple procedure that is easy to arrange, that may be covered by insurance or offered on a sliding scale fee. In other places, abortion may be illegal or very difficult to access. For some people, the time, mental energy, and emotional stress involved in choosing to terminate a pregnancy can be considerable. Others may feel a sense of relief after having an abortion. There is no right or wrong reaction.

The decision to continue an unplanned pregnancy is also complicated. Students who experience an unexpected pregnancy have no input on the timing of the pregnancy. Moreover, pregnancies that are not discovered until later in gestation may have additional medical considerations. Surprise pregnancies may force graduate students to rapidly re-organize their lives. When she became pregnant, one of the authors moved out of an apartment full of flaking lead paint, found new health insurance, and moved to another city to be closer to her partner—all within the span of just a few weeks.

Graduate students who endure miscarriage and infant loss have needs that are often underreported and unsupported. Whether you have been trying to achieve pregnancy or not, the emotional toll of pregnancy loss is unfathomable until you have to endure it. While it may be difficult, these are times that call for a meeting with an advisor or trusted faculty member to discuss extensions, leaves of absence, mental health resources and other accommodations (such as Employee Assistance Programs, or EAP) that are available to graduate students through the university. It is also possible that resources may be accessible to you via the university health system or healthcare plans. Feelings of self-doubt and blame, depression, guilt, and anger are normal but they are also often stigmatized and borne in silence (Winegar 2016). Take time to mourn your loss and draw on your network of support for your future academic success, and more importantly, your own wellbeing.

Parenting in Graduate School

Infant Feeding in Graduate School

For students who become parents in graduate school, infant feeding will consume many hours of their days and nights. Because infants are so dependent on their caregivers for food, your infant feeding choices will need to be integrated into your life. To be clear: there is no right or wrong way to feed an infant. Either breastfeeding or bottle-feeding is fine, but it might be beneficial to consult with a physician to determine the best choice for you. Here, we outline some of the options and discuss your rights.

The Breastfeeding Option

Breastfeeding rates are on the rise and in 2018, over 80 percent of newborns in the US have "ever been" breastfed (CDC 2021). The American Academy of Pediatrics recommends that infants be breastfed exclusively for at least six months, breastfed for a minimum of one year, and that the breastfeeding relationship should continue as "mutually desired" by the lactating parent and infant (2012). There are good reasons to support parents who choose to breastfeed as a matter of personal choice and bodily autonomy. Breastfeeding parents may find that the relationship helps them establish and deepen a bond with their new child. Aside from the health benefits, breastfeeding is a low-cost food source. There are costs, though, that are disproportionately borne by the breastfeeding parent, such as time spent nursing and pumping, lost sleep, additional food, supplements, and supportive supplies.

Breastfeeding is widely recognized by law as a right for the lactating parent and the infant. Title IX prohibits discrimination against pregnant and breastfeeding persons in educational settings and requires that institutions provide excused absences for pregnancy and childbirth for as long as medically necessary, usually several weeks postpartum (US Department of Education Office of Civil Rights n.d.). This period should allow most lactating parents the opportunity to establish their milk supplies. All 50 states, the District of Columbia, Puerto Rico, and the US Virgin Islands have laws that specifically protect breastfeeding in any public or private location (NCSL 2021). The Patient Protection and Affordable Care Act of 2010 (ACA) requires employers to provide "reasonable" unpaid break time to non-exempt employees to express milk. This applies to all employers with at least 50 employees (US Department of Labor n.d.). Employers must also provide a space other than a restroom to express milk. While these provisions may technically exclude many graduate students whose work is considered "exempt" (i.e., salaried, not eligible for overtime), some states have additional employment protections for lactating parents that may address this gap.[1] Moreover, if full-time employees are receiving these benefits, odds are that you can ask for access to them as well.

Parenting graduate students may be eligible for SNAP (Supplemental Nutrition Assistance Program) and WIC (Women, Infants, and Children) benefits, depending on their state's eligibility criteria. WIC may be useful to breastfeeding, combination feeding, and formula feeding parents. Eligible lactating parents also may receive an enhanced WIC benefit for up to one year (US Department of Agriculture n.d.). In addition, the ACA requires most health plans to cover the cost of a breast pump (Lee 2014). Finally, WIC offers breastfeeding support, such as peer counseling and connection to lactation services.

Job interviews and lactation can be difficult to manage. If you are comfortable disclosing your breastfeeding status, ask for one or two extended 20-minute breaks and/or an extended meal break to nurse or express milk. Some unscheduled time to prep a research presentation might also allow time to pump. Bring your breast pump and cold packs to preserve the milk; snacks and water to help maintain the milk supply, and breast pads to absorb any leaks. If that's not feasible, a five-minute break to hand express milk may help relieve some pressure until one can pump fully. Related to travel, most airports have lactation rooms for pumping, and breastmilk is allowed on flights as a carry-on so long as it is contained in 3.4-ounce bottles or less.

Formula and Combination Feeding Option

Breastfeeding is a demanding proposition and may not be the right choice for everyone for a multitude of reasons. The inability to pump or nurse regularly can lead to engorged breasts, mastitis, and/or a dwindling milk supply. Some graduate students may find that the demands of academic life do not accommodate the physical demands of exclusive lactation. Others may exercise their bodily autonomy in choosing not to breastfeed. Infant formula is a perfectly reasonable form of feeding an infant either exclusively or as a form of supplementation. Millions of infants thrive on infant formula and grow into healthy children and adults. Formula feeding more readily allows others to share the responsibility for infant feeding as well.

Parents who use infant formula exclusively can spend $1,200-$2,000 per year on formula depending on the brand and ingredients (Simon 2019) and more if the child requires a specialty formula. In states where graduate students are eligible for SNAP and WIC, parents may use these benefits to purchase infant formula (US Department of Agriculture 2019). In most cases, health insurance does not cover infant formula. However, seventeen states cover specialized infant formula prescribed by a doctor for infants with severe food allergies (FAACT n.d.).

There is a great deal of stigma surrounding infant feeding, no matter which route you take. There is no shame in formula feeding, breastfeeding, or a combination of both. There is a fair amount of debate about the overall importance that infant feeding has on the lifetime outcomes of individuals (Jung 2015). Given the myriad of barriers that graduate students face already, shame should not be one of them. Fed is best, and whatever evidence-based approach you take that allows you to maintain your infant's health and your own sanity is what works best for you.

Supports and Considerations for Parents in Graduate School

While the maxim "nothing can prepare you for parenthood" is mostly true, graduate students should consider several factors to balance pregnancy, parenting, and academic studies. Different institutional and governmental resources, [2] leave policies, and childcare options may factor into your decisions. Graduate student parents may also need to navigate co-parenting with (ex-)spouses or (ex-)partners and build a support network.

Despite the growing percentage of graduate student parents, there is sizable variation in the scale and scope of universities' support services. Parental leave and childcare are likely the two top considerations for graduate students weighing or facing parenthood.

As shown in tables *16.1* and *16.2*, we have gathered data from the discipline's top 40 ranked US PhD programs and documented their parental leave policies, university-associated childcare facilities, and average monthly cost of childcare.[3]

As *Table 16.1* illustrates, the majority of surveyed universities provide leave from academic and assistantship responsibilities for pregnancy, childbirth, or adoption. The amount of time off varies significantly for birthing parents (six to 16 weeks) and non-birthing parents (two to 16 weeks). A few schools allow some students extended leave up to a year. Graduate students often cannot rely on the Family Medical Leave Act (FMLA) for twelve weeks of protected unpaid leave unless they are considered employees and have worked 1250 hours over a rolling 12-month period. International students may not be able to leverage FMLA even if it is available. Universities may accommodate students on an individual basis, (Mason et al. 2013) though that does leave open the opportunity for bias in how such accommodations are given.

Another complication is the unique university calendar. Some schools' guidelines specify that the leave occurs during the quarter/semester that the child is born/adopted while others provide leave for the next quarter/semester. Depending on timing, this could leave the student without any leave for a few weeks.

Protected leave might not be paid leave. Most universities surveyed provide some paid leave for birthing parents who are employed by the institution. However, a handful of these schools do not provide any funding during the temporary absence. For non-birthing students, a quarter of institutions surveyed do not offer any paid leave whereas others provide equal paid leave regardless of the student's role in the birthing process.

As *Table 16.2* shows, most universities have one or more affiliated childcare centers that cater to faculty, staff, and students. These facilities are generally accredited and offer high-quality, developmentally appropriate education for infants to pre-kindergartners. Most centers open at 8:00 am and close by 6:00 pm, which may or may not cover class meeting times, but they do ordinarily follow the university calendar. Daycare costs for one child are on par with or exceed the outlay for rent. For these forty universities, average monthly daycare costs at university-affiliated centers ranged from $620 to $3,069. The mean monthly rate for one child, averaging across all ages, is $1,733. Considering doctoral stipends range from $4,000 to $35,000 per year (Williams 2008, inflation-adjusted to 2021 dollars), daycare comes with a whopping price tag. Even with subsidies, discounts, or scholarships, the net expense remains sizable.

Although student parents often receive priority over other applicants, many daycare facilities' waitlists are six months to two years long. Expectant parents may want to add their names to the waiting list long before a child arrives. Many universities offer emergency childcare at a subsidized or discounted rate for a few days each semester if you are in a pinch. Parents looking for summer childcare options for their school-aged children might consider university day camps that are offered in areas like art, literacy, math, and science.

Housing and health insurance are two additional considerations for graduate student parents. Most universities offer on-campus housing for students with families, providing proximity to classes, university facilities, and affiliated childcare centers. University housing also yields a community of fellow graduate students with families that may serve as an extended support network. Student family housing usually comes at a premium rate, though most utilities are included. For example, nine-month university housing costs at public research universities and private research institutions in 2018 averaged $11,200 and $13,800, respectively (Urban Institute 2021). Off-campus housing may be more cost-effective.

Most universities also provide health insurance coverage for their graduate students on assistantship or fellowship, although the quality of coverage varies. Birthing parents should inquire about the anticipated out-of-pocket costs (e.g., copays, deductibles) for prenatal checkups, prescriptions, tests, and delivery. Parents should ensure that their providers are in-network to avoid paying higher costs. Often, universities do not extend coverage to students' dependents (Williams 2008). For universities that do, there is typically a considerable premium associated with each added dependent. Domestic graduate students may qualify for sizable subsidies to shop and pay for health insurance coverage via Medicaid or the ACA marketplace, depending on the family income. International students, however, cannot access these outlets. In addition, most universities offer free on-campus or telehealth counseling or therapy for students, as well as graduate wellness programs prioritizing students' physical and mental wellbeing.

Take advantage of these resources, which will benefit you and your family members.

Table 16.1: Parental Leave Policies for the top 40 Political Science PhD Programs in the US

University	Amount of Parental Leave for Graduate Students	Paid Leave for Birth Parents (in weeks)	Paid Leave for Non-Birth Parents (in weeks)
Columbia University	Birth or non-birth parents (12 weeks, with another 12-week extension possible)	12	12
Cornell University	Birth or non-birth parent (6 weeks, or 8 weeks if cesarean section delivery) or up to 1 year reduced academic load status	6 to 8	6
Duke University	Birth parents (9 weeks); Non-birth parents (2 weeks)	9	2
Emory University	Birth or non-birth parents (8 weeks)	8	8
George Washington University	No parental leave	0	0
Georgetown University	Birth or non-birth parents (6 weeks)	6	6
Harvard University	Birth or non-birth parents (12 weeks)	12	12
Indiana University—Bloomington	Birth or non-birth parents (6 weeks)	6	6
Mass. Institute of Technology	Birth parents (12 weeks); Non-birth parents (4 weeks)	12	4
Michigan State University	Birth or non-birth parents (8 weeks)	8	1
New York University	Birth or non-birth parents (6-12 weeks)	6 to 12	6 to 12
Northwestern University	Birth or non-birth parents (12 weeks)	12	12
The Ohio State University	Birth parent (6 weeks); Non-birth parents (3 weeks)	6	3
Penn State University—University Park	Birth or non-birth parents (15 weeks)	0	0
Princeton University	Birth or non-birth parents (14 weeks)	14	14
Rice University	Birth or non-birth parents (6 weeks)	6	6
Stanford University	Birth parents (12 weeks, up to 12-month extension); Non-birth parents (12 weeks)	12	0
Stony Brook University—SUNY	Birth or non-birth parents (12 weeks)	12	12
Texas A&M Univ. —College Station	Birth or non-birth parents (12 weeks)	0	0
University of CA—Berkeley	Birth parents (8 weeks)	6	0
University of CA—Davis	Birth parents (6 weeks)	6	0
University of CA—Los Angeles	Birth parents (6 weeks)	6	0
University of CA—San Diego	Birth parents (6 weeks)	6	0
University of IL—Urbana-Champaign	Birth or non-birth parents (12 weeks)	2	2
University of Maryland—College Park	Birth or non-birth parents (6 weeks)	6	6
University of MI—Ann Arbor	Birth parents (8 weeks, up to 12 month extension); Non-birth parents (6 weeks, up to 12 month extension)	8	6
University of MN—Twin Cities	Birth or non-birth parents (6 weeks)	6	6
University of NC—Chapel Hill	Birth or non-birth parents (6 weeks)	6	6
University of WI—Madison	No parental leave	0	0
University of Chicago	Birth and non-birth parents (10 weeks)	10	10
University of Notre Dame	Birth and non-birth parents (16 weeks)	16	16
University of Pennsylvania	Birth or non-birth parents (8 weeks, up to two semester extension)	8	8
University of Pittsburgh	Birth or non-birth parents (6 weeks)	6	6
University of Rochester	Birth or non-birth parents (8 weeks)	8	8
University of Texas—Austin	Birth or non-birth parents (12 weeks)	0	0
University of Virginia	Birth or non-birth parents (8 weeks)	8	8
University of Washington	Birth or non-birth parents (12 weeks, up to 14 if birthing complications)	12 to 14	12
Vanderbilt University	Birth or non-birth parents (6 weeks)	6	6
Washington University in St. Louis	Birth or non-birth parents (8 weeks, up to 15 weeks)	8	8
Yale University	Birth or non-birth parents (8–15 weeks, up to 12 months extension)	8 to 15	8 to 15

Table 16.2: Childcare Facilities & Monthly Costs for Top 40 Political Science PhD Programs in the US

University	University Affiliated Childcare Facility Name(s)	Daycare Avg. Monthly Cost (in $ per child)
Columbia University	The Rita Gold Early Childhood Center, Teachers College	$2777
Cornell University	Cornell Childcare Center	$1795
Duke University	Duke Children's Campus	$1468
Emory University	The Clifton School; The Early Emory Center for Child Development and Enrichment	$1326
George Washington University	Bright Horizons at L Street	$2750
Georgetown University	Hoya Kids	$1520
Harvard University	Botanic Gardens Children's Center; Oxford Street Daycare Cooperative; Radcliffe Childcare Centers, Inc; Harvard Yard Childcare Center; Peabody Terrace Children's Center; Soldiers Field Park Children's Center	$3069
Indiana University—Bloomington	Campus Children's Center; Campus View Childcare Center	$1228
Mass. Institute of Technology	The David H. Koch Childcare Center; Kendall Childcare Center; Lincoln Laboratory Childcare Center; Stata Childcare Center	$2628
Michigan State University	Spartan Child Development Center	$1202
New York University	N/A—they do not operate their own childcare facility, but help students connect to resources	N/A
Northwestern University	University Children's Center	$2229
The Ohio State University	The Ohio State University Childcare Program	$1034
Penn State University—University Park	Bennett Family Center; Childcare Center at Hort Woods	$1089
Princeton University	University NOW Day Nursery	$2220
Rice University	Center for Early Childhood Education	$1618
Stanford University	Children's Center of the Stanford Community; Stanford Arboretum Children's Center; Stanford Madera Grove Children's Center; Stock Farm Road Children's Center; Pine Cone Children's Center; Stanford West Children's Center	$2504
Stony Brook University—SUNY	Stony Brook Childcare Services	$1532
Texas A&M Univ. —College Station	Becky Gates Children's Center	$890
University of CA—Berkeley	Early Childhood Education Program	$2440
University of CA—Davis	Hutchison Child Development Center; LaRue Park Child Development Center; Russell Park Child Development Center; Perfect Tender Infant Care	$1724
University of CA—Los Angeles	The Krieger Center; Fernald Center; The University Village Center	$2400
University of CA—San Diego	Early Childhood Education Center	$1892
University of IL—Urbana-Champaign	Child Development Laboratory	$1434
University of Maryland—College Park	UMD Child Development Center	$1925
University of MI—Ann Arbor	Health System Children's Center; North Campus Children's Center; Towsley Children's House	$1980
University of MN—Twin Cities	YMCA Early Childhood Learning Center; Child Development Laboratory School; Community Childcare Center; Como Early Learning Center	$1305
University of NC—Chapel Hill	Victory Village	$1638
University of WI—Madison	Eagle's Wing; UW Child Development Lab; Walsman Early Childhood Program	$1728
University of Chicago	University of Chicago Child Development Center Drexel or Stony Island, managed by Bright Horizons	$1515
University of Notre Dame	Early Childhood Development Center at the University of Notre Dame	$620
University of Pennsylvania	Penn Children's Center	$1880
University of Pittsburgh	University Child Development Center	$1328
University of Rochester	The Children's School at URMC	$1262
University of Texas—Austin	Child Development Center	$860
University of Virginia	University of Virginia Child Development Center	$1307
University of Washington	UWCC at Portage Bay; UWCC at West Campus; UWCC at Radford Court; UWCC at Laurel Village	$1958
Vanderbilt University	The Acorn School	$1260
Washington University in St. Louis	Washington University Family Learning Center	$1800
Yale University	Bright Horizons; The Nest at Alphabet Academy	$2454

While many universities provide some benefits in the form of leave, insurance, counseling, childcare centers, and student-family housing—that is about all they offer. Universities and political science departments have a long way to go to cultivate family-friendly environments and provide needed resources for graduate student parents. Many graduate program directors and faculty are unaware of university policies and services available to graduate student parents. Fewer than one-quarter of the top programs we researched included any information for graduate student parents in their handbooks or on their websites. Expectant parents will need to be their own best advocates and read all of a university's (and department's) policies and timelines. While most graduate parents report receiving needed accommodations, these are often offered ad-hoc upon request rather than as part of a universal policy (Mason et al. 2013).

Balancing Parenthood and Academic Responsibilities

Graduate student parents will likely need to consider co-parenting with ex- or current partners. Deciding on a parenting style, managing care, coordinating schedules, and balancing competing professional responsibilities will require patience, communication, empathy, and grace for all parties involved. Regardless of best-laid plans, you will also have to parent during the unexpected. Children are bound to catch a cold, need to be picked up early from daycare, be up all night from teething or be unable to attend school because of a global pandemic. Consequently, you might be unprepared for class, miss an assignment deadline, forego a special lecture, need an extension, or receive a lower grade. All of the authors here faced similar opportunity costs.

You might be tempted to "go it alone" and not ask for help. This approach is ultimately self-defeating. All parents face genuine barriers to participation in and benefit from the non-class activities associated with a graduate education. We strongly recommend that you make your advisor aware of the tensions you face to the extent possible. This allows them to advise you on how to prioritize competing demands. A support network in and outside your program is key, especially around those high-pressure times like comprehensive exams and finals. Consider linking up with other graduate students to share childcare and support. Or rely on neighbors, family, friends, or other trusted caregivers for additional support in a pinch or as part of a long-term plan. If you have access to childcare, use it as frequently as you can, especially while writing the dissertation. The unstructured time that falls into your lap when it is your turn to be a scholar allows flexibility as much as it presents a way to neglect your research because, unlike a child, it cannot immediately cry out for attention. Try going outside of the home and school to find a place where your research can be your sole focus for a block of time. Try scheduling your research work around nap times and sleep schedules. Many graduate student parents are up after bedtime finishing work or shifting their routine in some unconventional way.

It is important to prioritize teaching and service obligations while in graduate school. If these obligations are ones where you can bring your child/ren with you to accomplish a task, then make it an adventure. One author vividly remembers carrying over IRB paperwork for her dissertation with her toddler twins in tow. Planning ahead—to the degree possible—helps here. Your institution might have intermittent childcare options or a friend can come with you and distract your kids while you attend to a task. Necessity breeds creativity.

Domestic life is not always bliss. Self-care may conflict with laundry, dinner, and caring for children. Nevertheless, making sure you are taking care of yourself is critical. Take the flight attendant's warning seriously: put on your own mask before you assist others with theirs. Find or create spoken versions of your readings that you can listen to in the car. Allow children free play or tablet time while you edit a paper. Set timers to do your reading and your housework. Find adaptive tools that work for you.

Childhood happens once. The adage that "the days seem long, but the years seem short," may sound trite, but it is ultimately true. You will want to watch your child grow, develop, and become their own person. It is inevitable that you will let people down sometimes. You cannot manage everyone's expectations. Learning not to internalize this as abject moral failings is key. If you are in a committed relationship, this can be tricky as partners may both be stressed. Attending to that relationship is also important as you balance their needs as well.

You will have to learn to master when to say no. Graduate life is full of amazing and interesting things. Not all of them would fit into your schedule without children, but they certainly will not with children. Having a trusted advisor and other student parents to poll about an opportunity's relevance to your success is helpful. Conversely, don't be afraid to say yes. Sometimes this is scary for student parents as it may change your work-life balance. Some opportunities are worth rebalancing. Talk to your partner, fellow student parents, advisors, or others in the field who can provide a sounding board and advice specific to you.

Conclusion

Whether you are a parent at the outset of your graduate school journey or you join the parenting ranks during your time in a program, the challenges are multifaceted. We offer the above advice to individuals navigating this journey that we have navigated ourselves in the hopes that it brings you some perspective and advice. But what we offer is only our perspective and what research has been done, so take what is useful for you in your journey. If nothing else, know this: you are not alone.

We also hope that this serves as a clarion call to political science programs that the time is ripe for a reckoning about how we fully include graduate student parents in our programs. Institutions and programs are equipped to do this kind of work and it is high time that such work begins in earnest.

Appendix

The resources available to pregnant and parenting graduate students vary by institution and location. In any case, be prepared to do some research on your own and to advocate for yourself. However, the following table may help you get started.

Table 16.A: Appendix—On Campus Resources for Graduate Students who are Pregnant or Parents

Need or Service	Sources	
	On Campus	
	Employee	Student
Health Insurance (self)	Employer-sponsored (self or spouse/partner)	Student health service. Possible add'l insurance available at group rates
Health Insurance (children)	Employer-sponsored (family coverage)	Possible child/family insurance available at group rate
Pregnancy and Postpartum Leave	As provided by employer	Title IX
Pregnancy Discrimination Laws	Pregnancy Discrimination Act	Title IX
Grief Counseling (after pregnancy loss)	As provided by employer or covered by health insurance	Student Counseling Services
Food Assistance		On campus food pantry (if available)
Legal Assistance	Employer-sponsored benefit, if offered, or referral. Human Resources office	Student Legal Services Office, Title IX Coordinator, Graduate College
Affordable infant furniture and clothing		
Free Car seats		
Breast pumps	ACA compliant employer sponsored plans	ACA compliant student health insurance plans
Housing	Employee housing available on some campuses	Housing for families with children available at some institutions.

Table 16.A: Appendix Continued—Off Campus Resources for Graduate Students who are Pregnant or Parents

Need or Service	Sources	
	Off Campus	
	Public (Government)	Private
Health Insurance (self)	Medicare (65+ or some disabled); Medicaid (in some states); https://www.kff.org/medicaid/issue-brief/status-of-state-medicaid-expansion-decisions-interactive-map/	Purchase via Healthcare.gov on sliding scale; https://www.healthcare.g
Health Insurance (children)	CHIP (https://www.healthcare.gov/medicaid-chip/childrens-health-insurance-program/) for eligible children; Medicaid (in some states) https://www.kff.org/medicaid/issue-brief/status-of-state-medicaid-expansion-decisions-interactive-map/	Purchase via Healthcare.gov on sliding scale; https://www.healthcare.g
Pregnancy and Postpartum Leave	Family and Medical Leave Act	
Pregnancy Discrimination Laws		
Grief Counseling (after pregnancy loss)		National Alliance on Mental Illness affiliates (free and low-cost services Online or local support groups; https://www.nami.org/findsupport
Food Assistance	Supplemental Nutrition Assistance Program (SNAP); Women, Infants and Children (WIC); School lunch program (school aged children)	Community based food pantries
Legal Assistance	Legal Aid; ACLU	Pro Bono work taken on voluntarily
Affordable infant furniture and clothing		Thrift shops, discount stores, mom-to-mom sales, Facebook groups, churches, pregnancy assistance centers, charities
Free Car seats		Free Car Seats, https://safeconvertiblecarseats.com/blog/free-car-seats
Breast pumps	Medicaid in some states	All plans purchased on the ACA Marketplace
Housing	Section 8 vouchers or subsidized housing (eligibility varies) https://www.hud.gov/topics/rental_assistance	Varies by the local market

Endnotes

1   In any case, many non-exempt employees have a great deal of professional autonomy in their work schedules, which should allow them to nurse or express milk as needed. The state level protections for breastfeeding rights do cover college campuses.

2   We have added resource *Table 16.A* in the appendix of this chapter with resources for graduate student parents on and off campus.

3   We would like to thank Kelli Bowers, Master of Public Policy candidate at Michigan State University, for her exceptional research assistance in helping to collect this data.

References

American Academy of Pediatrics. 2012. "Policy Statement: Breastfeeding and the Use of Human Milk." Pediatrics. 129(3) e827.

APSA Committee for the Status of Women in the Profession (CSWP). 2016. "Pipeline to Tenure: Institutional Practices for Hiring, Mentoring, and Advancing Women in Academia." American Political Science Association. Available: http://web.apsanet.org/cswp/wp-content/uploads/sites/4/2016/01/FINAL-Pipeline-Report-May2016.pdf.

Bassett, Rachel Hile. 2005. Parenting and Professing: Balancing Family Work with an Academic Career. Vanderbilt University Press.

Brown, Virginia and Tracy R. Nichols. 2012. "Pregnant and Parenting Students on Campus: Policy and Program Implications for a Growing Population." Educational Policy. 27(3): 499-530.

Centers for Disease Control and Prevention (CDC). 2019. "Racial and Ethnic Disparities Continue in Pregnancy-Related Deaths." September 6. Available: https://www.cdc.gov/media/releases/2019/p0905-racial-ethnic-disparities-pregnancy-deaths.html

Centers for Disease Control and Prevention. 2021. "Breastfeeding Among US Children Born 2011-2018, CDC Immunization Survey." August 2. Available: https://www.cdc.gov/breastfeeding/data/nis_data/results.html.

Colbeck, Carol L., and Robert Drago. 2005. "Accept, Avoid, Resist How Faculty Members Respond to Bias against Caregiving...and How Departments Can Help." Change 37 (6): 10–17.

Correll, Shelley J., Bernard, Stephen, and In Paik. 2007. "Getting a Job: Is There a Motherhood Penalty?" American Journal of Sociology. 112(5): 1297-1338.

Cosme, Cate. 2016. "So You Want to Have a Baby in Graduate School." Psychological Science Agenda, April. Available: https://www.apa.org/science/about/psa/2016/04/baby-graduate-school

Dillon, Patrick J. 2012. "Unbalanced: An Autoethnography of Fatherhood in Academe." Journal of Family Communication. 12(4): 284-299.

Einarson, Thomas R., Charles Piwko, and Gideon Koren. 2013. "Quantifying the Global Rates of Nausea and Vomiting of Pregnancy: A Meta Analysis." Journal of Population Therapeutics and Clinical Pharmacology 20(2): 171-83.

Food Allergy and Anaphylaxis Connections Team (FAACT). n.d. "Elemental Formula Coverage." Available: https://www.foodallergyawareness.org/government-relations/statewide-insurance-coverage-for-elemental-formula/.

Hoffer, T. B., Welch, V., Webber, K., Williams, K., Lisek, B., Hess, M., Loew, D., and Guzman-Barron, I. (2006). Doctorate Recipients from United States Universities: Summary Report 2005. Chicago, IL: National Opinion Research Center.

Jung, Courtney. 2015. Lactivism: How Feminists and Fundamentalists, Hippies and Yuppies, and Physicians and Politicians Made Breastfeeding Big Business and Bad Policy. New York: Basic Books.

Kennelly, Ivy and Roberta M. Spalter-Roth. 2006. "Parents on the Job Market: Resources and Strategies That Help Sociologists Attain Tenure-Track Jobs." The American Sociologist. 37(4):29-49.

Kulp, Amanda M. 2016. "The Effects of Parenthood During Graduate School on PhD Recipients' Paths to the Professoriate: A Focus on Motherhood." New Directions for Higher Education. 176: 81-95.

Lee, Nancy C. 2014. "Breast Pumps and Insurance Coverage: What You Need to Know." September 29. Office on Women's Health, US Department of Health & Human Services. Available: https://www.womenshealth.gov/blog/breast-pumps-insurance.

Mason, Mary Ann. 2009. "Why So Few Doctoral-Student Parents?" The Chronicle of Higher Education. October 21, 2009. Available: https://www.chronicle.com/article/why-so-few-doctoral-student-parents/.

Mason, Mary Ann, Goulden, Marc and Karie Frasch. 2007. "Graduate Student Parents: The Underserved Minority." Communicator: Council of Graduate Schools. 40(4):1-5.

Mason, Mary Ann, Marc Goulden, and Karie Frasch. 2009. "Why Graduate Students Reject the Fast Track." Academe, January/February. Available: https://www.aaup.org/article/why-graduate-students-reject-fast-track/#.YacNfvHMJR1.

Mason, Mary Ann, Nicholas H. Wolfinger, and Marc Goulden. 2013. Do Babies Matter?: Gender and Family in the Ivory Tower. Rutgers University Press.

National Conference of State Legislatures (NCSL). 2021. "Breastfeeding State Laws." August 26, 2021. Available: https://www.ncsl.org/research/health/breastfeeding-state-laws.aspx.

Perry, Liz. 2021. "Graduate Student Parents Are Having a Moment." Inside Higher Ed. September 2, 2021. Available: https://www.insidehighered.com/advice/2021/09/02/advice-graduate-school-parents-opinion.

Simon, Javier. 2019. "The Cost of Baby Formula." Smart Asset. May 7. Available: https://smartasset.com/financial-advisor/the-cost-of-baby-formula#:~:text=The%20cost%20of%20baby%20formula%20across%20popular%20brands%20can%20average,the%20health%20of%20your%20chil.

Urban Institute. 2021. "Understanding College Affordability." Urban Institute (blog). 2021. Available: http://urbn.is/2nPYxhg.

US Department of Agriculture. n.d. "What's In Your WIC Food Package?" WIC Breastfeeding Support. Available: https://wicbreastfeeding.fns.usda.gov/whats-your-wic-food-package.

US Department of Agriculture. 2019. "WIC Frequently Asked Questions." July 1. Available: https://www.fns.usda.gov/wic/frequently-asked-questions.

US Department of Education Office of Civil Rights. n.d. "Know Your Rights: Pregnant or Parenting? Title IX Protects You From Discrimination at School." Available: https://www2.ed.gov/about/offices/list/ocr/docs/dcl-know-rights-201306-title-ix.html.

US Department of Labor. n.d. "Fact Sheet #73: Break Time for Nursing Mothers under the FLSA." Available: https://www.dol.gov/sites/dolgov/files/WHD/legacy/files/whdfs73.pdf.

Utami, Ade Dwi. 2019. "Walking a Tightrope: Juggling Competing Demands as a PhD Student and a Mother." In Wellbeing in Doctoral Education, eds, Lynette Pretorius, Luke Macaulay, Basil Cahusac de Caux. Singapore: Springer.

Van Assendelft, Laura, Page Fortna, Claudine Gay, and Kira Sanbonmatsu. 2019. "Would I Do This All Over Again? Mid-Career Voices in Political Science." American Political Science Association. Available: https://preprints.apsanet.org/engage/api-gateway/apsa/assets/orp/resource/item/5d-9ca075a6490200117d298f/original/would-i-do-this-all-over-again-mid-career-voices-in-political-science.pdf.

Williams June, Audrey. 2008. "Graduate Students' Pay and Benefits Vary Widely, Survey Shows." The Chronicle of Higher Education. December 5, 2008. Available: https://www.chronicle.com/article/graduate-students-pay-and-benefits-vary-widely-survey-shows/.

Winegar, Jessica. 2016. "The Miscarriage Penalty: Why We Need to Talk More Openly about Pregnancy Loss in Academe." The Chronicle of Higher Education. November 29, 2016. Available: https://www.chronicle.com/article/the-miscarriage-penalty/.

17 | Practicing Effective Time Management

Samantha A. Vortherms[1] & Coyle Neal[2]

1. University of California, Irvine 2. Southwest Baptist University

KEYWORDS: Time Management, Priorities, Goals.

Introduction

An important difference between undergraduate and graduate education is the amount of time and effort you put into your work outside of formal, structured classes. As you advance in your program, your time becomes less structured. The more flexible your time becomes, the more you're expected to accomplish, driven by your own motivation and organization. Successfully managing different priorities and developing your research agenda in this context depends on *time management*. Mastering time management skills is essential for successfully completing graduate training.

While healthy time management skills are important for all students, they are particularly important for students who are not "traditional students"— i.e., students who have major work and life commitments outside of graduate school. When balancing work, family care, community responsibilities, and other time commitments on top of your coursework, research, and dissertation writing, the demands on your time grow exponentially in often invisible ways. Graduate school and its culture tend to assume none of these out-of-classroom responsibilities exist, so developing and investing both in yourself and in productive habits becomes especially important.

A quick search on time management will yield dozens of bulleted lists of time management tricks. The problem with focusing on time management hacks is the same problem with any healthy lifestyle advice: it is difficult to form new habits. The key to time management is finding strategies that match your *priorities* with your work style. Because of this, we center this chapter on understanding priorities and understanding yourself in how you work to maximize efficiency in work. We also discuss how investing time in yourself helps create balance in your graduate career. Once you identify your priorities and your work style, you can design habits and systems to help you work smarter and accomplish more in less time.

The Value of Time Management as a Practice

Time is a limited resource that must be budgeted. At any given point, you will need to be reading published research, writing drafts of papers, collecting data, applying for conferences, organizing a lesson plan, grading papers, and reviewing other people's work. Managing time efficiently is a skill that allows you to balance multiple, competing *goals*. But like any skill, time management is one that requires practice. Inevitably you will miss a deadline or targeted amount of reading. It is essential to allow yourself to adapt and adjust. Plans and goals must be flexible, and you must be willing to reassess and adjust as you learn about yourself and your work. The keys to effective time management are to know your priorities, know yourself, and invest in yourself.

Know Your Priorities

Identifying your academic priorities must come first in establishing good time management habits. This can be challenging given the structure of academia and the changing nature of priorities over your career. But defining your priorities helps you focus your time and efforts in the most productive ways. Below are four categories of priorities to consider.

Advancing in the Program Towards Degree Completion

Your first professional priority in organizing your time is advancement in the program. What do you need to advance to candidacy? What are the deadlines?

Priorities Before Candidacy

Success in graduate school is dependent on coming up with good ideas and then being able to follow those ideas to fruition. Before candidacy, your emphasis should be on developing your ideas for research. So how do you develop good ideas?

The first place to start is with your readings for your coursework. When you read, focus on comprehension and analysis, both of which should be sharpened by informal conversations with your peers outside of class, formal discussion in class, and direction by your professors. Coursework and additional readings culminate in preparation for comprehensive examinations (see chapter 12 on comprehensive exams). There are usually far too many texts to read before exams, but as you take classes and talk with professors and older graduate students, you should prioritize texts based on the centrality of the reading and your own research interests.

Reading is also one primary way to develop and refine your own methodological training. When reading, focus on not only the arguments being made but how the authors make them. Published articles are examples of research design and methods that passed peer review. Want to improve training in causal inference? Critically evaluate each class or exam reading for the research method they use and its effectiveness in identification and convincing you of the causal mechanism. Read a paper that uses a "fuzzy regression discontinuity design" and don't know what that is? Google it for some background information on the method then read their methodology section closely to see how they describe it.

Outside of comprehending and retaining information from your reading, pre-candidacy is the time to develop ideas for your future research. For example, if you decide you want to write your dissertation on political parties, you may have opportunities to write in your Congress class about the role of parties on legislation, in your presidency class about how parties affect nominations, in your political theory class about how parties have leveraged ideas about human nature into results at the polls, or in your media class about the relationship between partisan news sources and institutional party leadership.

Priorities After Candidacy

If the priority pre-candidacy is the generation of new ideas, the priority after candidacy is following through on those ideas.

Having finished your coursework and passed your comprehensive examinations, the amount of reading might not change, but how you prioritize materials should. Your reading priorities should now focus on three areas: your specific topic of research, how your specific research topic fits into the broader discipline, and general academic trends. Your professors can help guide you to broad areas of research to read, but this is also the time for you to take ownership of your own area of expertise.

The two other priorities after candidacy are completing research and writing. These two areas are likely to grow significantly compared to before candidacy. For example, empirical research involves identifying sources, collecting data, analyzing data, and writing all along the way. You may also need to write grant applications at various points (see chapter 23 on applying to grants and fellowships). All of these activities take time, and it is essential to balance your time so that you are making progress.

Graduate students are often tempted to spend too much time collecting data and not enough time analyzing or evaluating it. Other students continually apply for grants to support their research while neglecting the research itself. And this is all in addition to normal graduate production: developing and producing arguments, writing papers for conferences, refining papers for publication, and, of course, writing the dissertation. Balancing these priorities by setting limits on how much time you spend on each task while protecting time to advance towards long-term goals is essential.

Training for Post-PhD Employment

While PhD programs are primarily designed to train the next generation of academic researchers, academic research is not the only use of a PhD. As you advance in your program, think about what your career goals are to help define valuable and effective uses of your time. What activities and items on your to-do list most directly help you meet these priorities? For ideas on these types of activities, see chapters 34-48 relating to different elements of the job market.

Know Yourself

The only way to regulate your time according to your priorities is to fully understand yourself, how you work, and what you need to be productive. We propose the following questions to help you know what you need to be your most productive.

What Are Your Priorities?

Building off of the last section, what are the most important professional and personal priorities? Explicitly assign and protect time dedicated to your most important priorities.

What Do You Need for Focus?

We all have our preferences when it comes to the work environment. Are you a coffee-shop scribbler? A library regular? What is your "must have" writing kit? Sam's work kit includes headphones (above all else), scrap paper and colorful pens, and a tumbler for tea. Set yourself up to focus on work and only work during work time.

How Do You Best Absorb and Evaluate Information?

Pre-candidacy, most of your time and energy is spent on absorbing and analyzing information through reading. Because of its flexibility, you can squeeze reading in almost anywhere: public transit, waiting in line, in bed, while eating, anywhere you've got a free hand you can be holding a book or an e-reader. But be aware of what you need to read well and plan your reading accordingly. If you're the type who can retain and comprehend when reading in snippets, then plan to have a book with you at all times and read when you can. If you're the type who needs more time to get into the book, arrange your schedule accordingly.

What Time of Day is Most Productive for You?

Is the first hour of the day your most productive? Do you feel like your creativity peaks at night? As you work, pay attention to when work "clicks" more and when you find more resistance. Reserve your most productive time for your most important and most cognitively demanding tasks and plan on doing lighter work when you are naturally less productive.

What are Your (Unproductive) Rabbit Holes?

We all have them, the small tasks that tend to distract us and take more time than we should spend on them. You might be prone to the never-ending literature review search; re-reading source material "just one more time;" the siren song of a new project or paper; or, our personal favorite, cleaning data and document formatting. Spending too much time on one task that does not deserve it is the enemy of efficiency. Knowing yourself will help you take steps to offset this tendency, whether by setting strict limits on how long you allow for these distracting tasks, relegating them to the times when you are already less productive, or by whatever method works best for you.

Are You Experiencing Writing Resistance?

Situations where we pull away from what we should really be working on are symptoms of resistance to writing. We resist writing for any number of reasons, from fear of failure (I don't know what I'm doing and this article has no value) to fear of success (what if I can't live up to the hype of this grant award?). Just like rabbit holes, we tend to have repeating patterns, go-to procrastination outlets that waste time (searching for playlists, getting up from our desks for coffee, etc.). Identifying your distractions and time-wasting resistance strategies is necessary to work past them.

Invest Time in Yourself

Up until this point, this chapter focused on your professional time and the value of thinking of time management as a practice. But non-work time is also critical. Graduate school can be all-encompassing, and it is easy for work to seep into every hour of every day. But a 24/7, always-on lifestyle is neither sustainable nor efficient. Graduate school is a marathon, not a sprint. Inherent in the argument that time should be managed is that work time is a discrete part of your day and should be balanced with personal time. Time spent at the gym, developing a hobby, or investing in relationships with family and friends is essential for time management. Investing in yourself when not working prevents burnout—the bane of efficient productivity (see chapter 67 on rest).

Between work, personal, and financial pressures, having a balanced life as a graduate student can be very difficult. Nevertheless, this balance is crucial. As with your studies, you must think about the quality and efficiency with which you spend your personal time. What are the activities in your personal life that you find particularly fulfilling? What activities can you do in the evening that relieve stress and promote healthy living not only because you need to have a life, but also because a healthy personal life helps you be a more effective scholar? Healthy, balanced lifestyles promote long-term productivity and mental health in an often-challenging professional environment. You are a person first and a graduate student second.

General Tips

Below are some of the most common tips for effective time management.

Get Organized

You cannot juggle teaching, research, writing, emails, conferences, grant applications, and anything else along the way unless you have a way of tracking it. There are a plethora of free organizational tools such as Trello, Asana, and Microsoft to-dos, but sometimes good old paper planners are the best for your workflow. Invest time in finding a system that works for you (but do not let endless organization turn into a procrastination strategy!).

Make a Timeline and Target Deadlines for Yourself

Identify when your big program requirements are due and start to work backwards to make intermediary deadlines for yourself. Imagine you are planning on applying for the APSA Doctoral Dissertation Research Improvement Grant. The deadline is June 15th. For the application, you must have your advisor's support. This means they need to see a full version of your proposal well ahead of the deadline, so set a personal deadline of June 1 for the full final proposal. But you don't want to send your advisor an unedited draft of the proposal, so you set a deadline to send your draft to a friend for feedback mid-May. You can continue this process back through the very early steps of any project or deliverable. Intermediate deadlines will help keep you on track.

Make a Plan, Then Revise It, Then Revise It Again

Time management is a practice. Rarely do we make a master plan and follow it all the way through to completion perfectly. At the beginning of each term, sit down and write out your timeline for the term. Then every Monday morning, review your timeline. What did you accomplish last week and what did you not finish? Then adjust your plan. What has to get moved to the next week? Don't let yourself fall into the trap of rolling over projects constantly. Unlike budgeting money, time cannot be earned back. When you find yourself rolling over too many tasks, what can you cut out? Prioritize tasks and take off what is not going to get done, so you can focus more time on what matters most.

Break Large Tasks Into Smaller To-Dos

Smaller tasks are more actionable and can be completed in less time, allowing you to fill in gaps in your schedule with productivity. Plus, there is nothing more demoralizing than seeing "Write dissertation" day after day on a to-do list.

Set Aside Time Every Day to Read and Write

For reading, set a daily reading goal that is reasonable, then increase it slightly but regularly until you can't keep up with it, then back off a bit. This can be either page numbers or a time for reading, depending on your availability. For example, start with 25 pages per class per day. Then increase that to 30 pages, then 35, and so on until you find a maximum amount that you can routinely complete. If 40 pages per class is too much, drop back to 35 or so and hold there, daily. The goal is to develop a habit of reading that lets you cover enough material in your available time without sacrificing comprehension. If on a given day you get into a reading and knock out 300 pages, that doesn't count as next week's reading. Pick back up the next day with a new 30 pages. If you miss today, you don't get to make it up by aiming for 60 pages tomorrow. The missed day is gone forever—it's far more important that you build the habit of regular reading than that you hit a specific total number of pages.

Similarly with writing, block off your writing time and protect it. Actually block off writing chunks in your calendar as an appointment with yourself. Turn off as many distractions as possible and go to your writing "happy place." Some people like to set writing goals by word limits (minimum 500 words a day), others work by time (every day from 9am-11am). As with reading, word goals can be gradually increased over time as your graduate career advances. Pre-candidacy, use writing time to analyze readings and draft term papers. Post-candidacy, work on your dissertation, papers for publications, and writing samples for the job market.

Learn to Say No

While department events and activities in the discipline are essential for socialization, networking, and professionalization, you do not have to do everything. If you're asked to take part in events or organize groups of students, be strategic. How will the event help your personal and professional development? Be proactive but do not over-extend yourself. Learning to say no is particularly important for students from underrepresented backgrounds as you may receive more requests for participation on panels and campus discussions. We encourage you to prioritize a balance between what you want and what you need. Which of these activities do you find particularly fulfilling or provide you with additional support and which activities don't? Pick and choose what works for you while protecting the time needed to advance through your program.

Know Yourself and Your Priorities

A good practice is to track your time. How much time do you spend on any given task? Within one week, how much time do you spend on reading and how much on writing? How much time did you spend on teaching? Looking at that distribution, does it match the priorities of your program and your current stage? Are you dedicating enough time to the tasks that are worth your attention?

Understand Your Own Limits

Time is a valuable resource that you should budget and track like money. Very few graduate programs provide an infinite amount of time to complete programs, and everyone's successful to-do list is limited by both time and energy. Setting your goals too high can backfire, creating stress and anxiety that reduce your productivity and can lead to burnout. You won't be able to do it all, so it is important to learn to prioritize what matters. Then, by knowing yourself, you can work efficiently and effectively to reach your goals in a healthy and balanced way.

Professional Development—Scholarship

18

Professional Norms: Clearing a Barrier to Developing Meaningful Relationships

Benjamin Isaak Gross[1], Kevin M. Kearns[2], & Evan M. Lowe[3]

1. Jacksonville State University 2. Texas A&M-Corpus Christi 3. Arizona State University

KEYWORDS: Impostor Syndrome, Personal Comportment, Professional Conduct, Career Ambitions.

What You Need to Know

The academy and political science as a field are becoming more diverse and are taking actions to extend opportunities to historically under-represented groups. These changes promise to be a benefit to these groups as well as the discipline as a whole, but realizing those benefits depends upon graduate student socialization to the professional norms of political science. Moreover, regardless of your background, familiarity with professional norms is a competency that is essential to your success as a graduate student and professional political scientist. While norms may change to meet new circumstances and societal expectations, knowing how to conduct yourself appropriately in various professional circumstances clears the way for building meaningful relationships that will serve you well in professional pursuits. Encountering new and often unspoken norms may be daunting, but if one approaches the process of socialization into these norms as an active participant, professional interaction will become easier and more likely to lead to the cultivation of a collegial network that will be essential for your continued success.

Encountering norms with which one might be unfamiliar can be daunting and may contribute to a variety of negative feelings, but this unease should not be taken as a sign that one does not "belong" in the academic community. *Impostor syndrome* (the notion that individual achievements are undeserved or owe to luck) is widespread and may be detrimental to success in graduate school (Fernandez et al 2019). Moreover, these feelings and their consequences are most acutely felt by students from historically under-represented groups insofar as they may experience the navigation of these norms differently even within the same institutional environment as others (APSA 2011; Chrousos and Mentis 2020; Tormos-Aponte and Velez-Serrano 2019). Although student experiences will vary, some uneasiness is common and not an indication that you do not belong in the academy. (See chapter 50 for more advice on imposter syndrome.)

As you continue in your career as a graduate student and professional political scientist, you will encounter a variety of different people and, sometimes, will interact with those who do not adhere to the expectations of professional norms. Some people will not be respectful of different views, others may harbor prejudices toward female or minoritized individuals, and others may just be bad colleagues who require frequent prodding to do their job. The purpose of long-standing professional norms is to promote functionality and meritocracy while generally supporting a collegial atmosphere. As with any other profession, however, political science does not always live up to the expectations that we set for ourselves as professionals and human beings. We can, and must, do better because it is the right thing to do. Improving the professional atmosphere in which we operate is, however, inextricably tied to each of our individual behavior. The best way to create the environment in which we prefer to work is to learn and to embody norms that support inclusivity, respect for individual and intellectual diversity, and personal accountability.

Why It Matters

Like any profession, political science has norms that are vital to heed if you wish to be successful. Following professional norms is important, for example, for working successfully with faculty members (Benesh 2001), writing and defending a dissertation (Wuffle 1989), publishing in academic journals and presses (Cohen 2002), and navigating the job market (Hanley 2008). Of particular importance for the discussion that follows is that learning and practicing professional norms helps build and sustain academic relationships in your department and field that will be indispensable on your path to professional success (Gardner 2008; Kim, Lebovits, and Shugars 2021; Weidman and Stein 2003).

Awareness of professional norms is important and should be taken seriously from the earliest days in a graduate program. Not only will beginning to socialize yourselves into professional modes of conduct contribute to your future success, but transgressing these norms (even unknowingly) may also undermine your professional aspirations. The sheer variety of interactions you will encounter mean that this chapter cannot be comprehensive.[1] Rather, we intend for it to serve as a starting point and we encourage graduate students to seek out peer and faculty mentors who can help them along the way. Choose your mentors wisely, for as in any profession not all individuals rise to expectations. Find those whose behavior supports professional, collegial, and meritocratic standards of excellence and seek to learn and model that behavior so that we can continue to shape the profession into what we all want it to be.

What You Can Do

In this section we address concrete ways which you might prepare for professional interactions as a political science graduate student, and offer suggestions for how to turn those interactions into meaningful professional relationships. Since professional norms are applicable in such a wide variety of interactions, the authors are unable to address everything and have, instead, chosen to highlight a few different areas of your professional interactions. In each of these subsections, we try to provide concrete recommendations for appropriate behavior that may be understood to communicate an underlying principle that will manifest in a variety of different areas and ways. We begin with a section that is generally applicable and addresses your *personal comportment* and image. We then move into particular interactions to provide rough guidelines for *professional conduct* in specific situations.

Self-Presentation and Comportment

You are no longer an undergraduate student and are now beginning on a path toward being a political science professional. Whether you have experience in the workplace and are returning to graduate school, or are just out of your undergraduate program, the transition to being a professional in the academy requires a change of mindset toward active learning, engagement, consideration about how you appear to others, and holding yourself responsible for embodying professional norms.

This turn toward actively engaged professionalism begins in its most outward manifestation with your appearance. Although only a part of who we are, how you look is the first impression you give to others. Dress appropriately for the situation. In classes and meetings, be clean, neat, and composed. Other events (e.g. academic conferences) may require professional business attire (usually a business suit). (See chapter 21 for more advice on how to participate in conferences most effectively.) If you are uncertain about what the appropriate attire is for a particular event, err on the side of being "overdressed." We all want to be "authentic" and often choose to represent ourselves outwardly in our clothing choices, but it is generally best to dress relatively conservatively so that our intellectual and professional merit stand out to others rather than our appearance.

In your disposition and behavior, focus on cultivating a social environment that is civil and respectful. Avoid cursing, being unnecessarily aggressive, and acting in a manner that is overly familiar. You may develop relationships where different behavioral patterns are entirely acceptable to all parties, but begin each professional relationship by putting your best foot forward. Particular individuals have different personalities and comfort levels with different modes of behavior, and you should respect these. The mark of professionalism is to meet each new person on a common and generally acceptable ground. There are a variety of norms which are perhaps best captured in their principle rather than in particulars. The above social traits are examples, as are other broad notions: punctuality, respect for others' time and attention, being prepared, and so on. The particular manifestations of general principles are too much to be addressed here but in the sections that follow we endeavor to provide some clear suggestions for how to put these (and other) general principles into practice.

In Your Department and University

The life of the professional entails frequent communication, meeting deadlines, and participation in a variety of different types of meetings. Keep track of deadlines and meet or exceed them. As a professional norm, being timely or punctual not only demonstrates that you have respect for others' time, but it also benefits you. Whether you are engaged in a research project or doing committee work, frequent and prompt communication, meeting deadlines, and general punctuality helps build a good reputation as a scholar and a colleague. As a matter of organizational function, punctuality is a necessary component for the successful completion of large-scale projects, which often involve contingencies. The Registrar, for example, cannot process student grades until you have submitted them, and students are often dependent upon the processing of their grades to qualify for university athletics or scholarships. As a general rule, complete your work (whatever it is) on time or early, and keep in mind that delays in your work often makes more work for others. Just as being timely helps you develop a positive reputation that will serve you well, developing a reputation for not completing work on time can be a barrier to healthy and meaningful relationships that you need to build for your own professional success.

Despite our best efforts to manage our time and be mindful of others, however, sometimes exigent circumstances arise that prevent us from delivering on promises. In cases like these, you should turn to clear communication—inform those who need to know about the delay, and take on responsibility by suggesting solutions or outlining an adjusted timetable. Especially in situations like these, the honesty of our communication with one another is important. If, for example, you know that a project will take you a week to accomplish because of other obligations you have, do not suggest that you can complete it sooner; promising prompt turn-around is only a benefit if you can keep those promises. Honest and clear communication combined with taking responsibility to meet reasonable expectations treats others with respect at least insofar as it allows them to plan and manage their time according to their needs. These principles apply in all sorts of interactions in your professional life—from coursework with fellow students to book projects you may eventually undertake with co-authors.

The academic department is more than just an administrative subunit of the university. It has a life and culture of its own and may offer a great variety of programing for graduate students. Get involved in the social and intellectual life of your department by attending invited lectures, job talks, university-wide events, and the like. By participating and contributing to the vitality of your department, you begin to contribute to the maintenance of an active and engaging (and collegial) departmental culture that supports education and social responsibility. Without active engagement, these programs are often for naught. The same is true outside of your department as well. In professional organizations, for example, you should consider signing up for and participating in special "sections" or attending symposia in order to begin to develop what Kim, Lebovits, and Shugars (2021) call a "knowledge-based family." These connections not only help to support the profession but also begin to build a lively personal network that will help you succeed professionally. (Chapters 31 and 32 provide suggestions for department and disciplinary service activities you might consider undertaking while still a graduate student.)

Do be mindful, however, that you do not overextend yourself, as "burnout" is a real risk and participating in more activities than you have time to do successfully will inevitably lead to delays in meeting deadlines. Whenever we participate in events, we want our participation to be quality participation. Quality participation begins with being on time and prepared for the event, and preparation takes time. Your arrival should be punctual and you should be prepared to engage as a professional. When others are speaking, listen carefully and take notes so that when it is your turn to speak you may do so meaningfully and constructively. Be patient and do not speak over others. Comments or questions should not be aggressive or accusatory, and questions should come from a place of genuine and honest interest. Seek to build academic relationships with people, not to "compete" with them.

Lastly, the time that you spend with fellow graduate students will (hopefully) involve a lot of more informal interaction as well. In fact, the further you progress into the profession the more opportunities for informal interactions you will come across. With informal situations, especially where food and alcohol are present, it bears mentioning that it can sometimes be challenging to distinguish "between friendly social behavior that is appropriate […] and sexual harassment" (Sapiro and Campbell 2018, 6). If you find that another has transgressed acceptable norms in this way, consult with a trusted adviser, your institution's Title IX office, and/or APSA's ombudsperson. Likewise, it is incumbent upon each of us to be especially mindful that we maintain the level of professionalism and respect that supports collegiality and the comfort of all individuals involved—even in informal situations. (For more clarity on what constitutes discrimination and harassment, as well as how to respond appropriately to these types of situations, see chapters 51 and 52).

With Faculty and Advisers

The life of a faculty member is one that is marked by a variety of different interests and obligations that pull them in multiple directions. As a graduate student (and even as a professional), that can sometimes make your interactions with faculty members frustrating or unclear. The best way to navigate this environment is to take responsibility for what you do have control over and to be responsive and direct. If you receive an email, respond to it promptly and clearly[2]—even if only to say that a full and proper response is forthcoming within a specified time frame. While norms establish expectations that help guide our behavior, establishing what others might expect of us (and when they might expect it) is equally important. You should also keep your own records of what has been submitted when, when meetings are or need to be scheduled, and what suggestions or advice has been offered as well as about what commitments you have made. Keep a calendar and be proactive.

As any other professional, you should be respectful of faculty and your advisers' time, but being respectful does not mean being subservient or meek. Remember that your advisers are there to help you develop as a professional and a scholar. If you have questions or concerns—whether about course material, programmatic requirements, or professional expectations—you should seek out the advice and guidance of trusted advisers. You can—and should—assert yourself as you take responsibility for your development and growth as a professional, but doing so should be performed in a manner appropriate to professional interactions. Selecting an adviser with whom you work well is also important, and you should work together to develop clear expectations about how your individual relationship will work.

With Undergraduate Students

Developing a rapport with undergraduate students is essential, for your professional career as a political scientist will inevitably involve significant amounts of interaction with undergraduates. Perhaps more than anything else, beginning to develop the mode in which you will interact with undergraduates early on in your graduate student career will serve you well. The sort of rapport you keep with undergraduates significantly depends not only on your own personality but also the culture of your institution and the backgrounds of the students. Remember that you are no longer an undergraduate and that your behavior with respect to undergraduates should reflect that. Though it should be obvious it bears mentioning that you should not attend undergraduate parties, for example, and you should certainly not engage in anything that might be construed as inappropriate. Being a professional does not need to mean being "stuffy," but it does mean embodying propriety in speech and actions.

Whether you have realized it yet or not, you are in a position of authority with respect to undergraduates and that authority also implies responsibility. Being in a position of authority does not, however, necessitate that you be commanding or dictatorial. Finding the line between being approachable and understanding, on the one hand, and authoritative, on the other hand, can be difficult. Begin to figure this out now. Your authority is based on your position and knowledge, but that position also entails a responsibility for teaching and mentoring undergraduates on their path to life after graduation. Whatever balance you strike or approach you take to these interactions, the principles that are supported by professional norms should be foremost in your mind: collegiality, understanding, meritocracy, and respect. One of the best things that you can do is to observe faculty members to learn from their approach to interacting with students. See what works and what does not, and how you can begin to cultivate your own approach based on your observations and a self-assessment.

In Outside Interactions

As a professional, you represent not only yourself when dealing with individuals outside of your program, but you also represent your program and advisers. These interactions (e.g., academic conferences, invited talks) provide an excellent opportunity to cultivate a professional network, but it is common to feel somewhat anxious about interacting with strangers. What should you talk about? What should you avoid talking about? Whatever your comfort level with social interaction, it is a mistake to think of networking as "waiting to be invited." Think of networking as an exercise in actively building a community that consists of "horizontal" relationships with those who share similar experiences and "vertical" relationships with those who are at different stages of their career but share interests (Kim, Lebovits, and Shugars 2021). Cultivating both types of relationship is essential for building a well-rounded network of scholars to whom you might turn for letters of recommendation, research collaboration, professional development, and various kinds of support.

Lastly, since building relationships involves connecting with other people, graduate students should be prepared to talk about themselves. For advanced graduate students, this will usually mean having an "elevator pitch" that describes their dissertation and current research. Although new graduate students may not yet have a clear research agenda, you should be prepared to briefly describe your interests. Having a concise description of your interests will be essential for building a network of peers and future colleagues who will be able to help you grow and advance as a professional.

Conclusion

Successfully learning and adhering to the discipline's professional norms will serve you well by helping you feel comfortable in the academy and clearing the way to the development of meaningful professional relationships that will serve your *career ambitions*. Adherence to professional norms of conduct does not require that you become anyone other than who you are, nor does it mean that you must conceal your background or individuality. On the contrary, heeding professional norms allows you to be yourself and to bring all you have to offer to the table in a manner that does not inadvertently conceal you behind negative impressions. Of course, not all interactions will be perfect or even positive. Be mindful of others, but also charitable when others fall short. Reflect on individual interactions so that you can continue to grow as a professional as you pursue your professional ambitions with confidence.

Endnotes

1   Although there is a great deal of uniformity in the professional norms of political science, there are slight variations in norms by sub-field, region, and university type (research universities v. liberal arts colleges), for example.

2   Prompt and clear responses to email or phone calls is a norm that should be followed in all professional interactions.

References

American Political Science Association. 2011. "Political Science in the 21st Century." TF_21st Century_AllPgs_webres90.pdf (apsanet.org) (Accessed 10-20-2021).

Benesh, Sara. 2001. "The Key to a Successful Prospectus: Consult an Adviser Early and Often." *PS: Political Science and Politics* 34 (4): 853-854.

Chrousos, George and Alexios-Fotius A. Mentis. 2020. "Imposter Syndrome Threatens Diversity." *Science* 367 (6479): 749-750.

Cohen, David. 2002. "Surviving the PhD: Hints for Navigating the Stormy Seas of Graduate Education in Political Science." *PS: Political Science and Politics* 35 (3): 585-588.

Fernandez, Mariela, Jill Sturts, Lauren N. Duffy, Lincoln R. Larson, Joey Gray, and Gwynn M. Powell. 2019. "Surviving and Thriving in Graduate School." *SCHOLE: A Journal of Leisure Studies and Recreational Education* 34 (1): 3-15.

Gardner, Susan. 2008. "Fitting the Mold of Graduate School: A Qualitative Study of Socialization in Doctoral Education." *Innovative Higher Education* 33: 125-138.

Hanley, James. 2008. "A Primer on Applying to the Liberal Arts College." *PS: Political Science and Politics* 41(4): 809-812.

Kim, Seo-Young Silvia, Hannah Lebovits, and Sarah Shugars. 2021. "Networking 101 for Graduate Students: Building a Bigger Table." *PS: Political Science and Politics*. FirstView 1-6.

Tormos-Aponte, Fernando and Mayra Velez-Serrano. 2019. "Broadening the Pathway for Graduate Studies in Political Science." *PS: Political Science and Politics* 53(1): 145-146.

Weidman, John and Elizabeth Stein. 2003. "Socialization of Doctoral Students to Academic Norms." *Research in Higher Education* 44: 641-656.

Wuffle, A. 1989. "Advice to the Advanced Graduate Student." *PS: Political Science and Politics* 22 (4): 838-839.

19 | Balancing Expectations for Research Transparency: Institutional Review Boards, Funders, and Journals

Mneesha Gellman[1], Matthew C. Ingram[2], Diana Kapiszewski[3], & Sebastian Karcher[4]

1. Emerson College 2. University at Albany, State University of New York

3. Georgetown University 4. Syracuse University

KEYWORDS: Research Transparency, Replication Crisis.

Introduction

The discipline of political science has been re-engaged in debate about the value and challenges of research transparency since 2010.[1] Pursuing research transparency with respect to a piece of scholarship means striving to be clear and open about how you collected the evidence on which its claims and conclusions rest; detailing the steps you took and methods you used to analyze that evidence; and making that evidence available to the degree that you can do so ethically and legally. When disciplinary discussions about research transparency were reinvigorated in the early 2010s, some scholars who use quantitative data and statistical methods in their work were already accustomed to pursuing transparency, while most scholars who analyze qualitative data had less practical experience with making their research transparent.

Multiple dynamics triggered the regeneration of the debate about research transparency. A key driver was what was termed the replication crisis in the social sciences identified first in psychology (see Simmons, Nelson, and Simonsohn 2011), i.e., the discovery that research findings—including those advanced in well-known work built on by other scholars or used in policymaking—could not be replicated.[2] Greater transparency in the conduct of research, facilitating the assessment of scholars' data and methods, was seen as an antidote to that crisis. In addition, various government entities (e.g., the Office of Science and Technology Policy 2020; see also Holdren 2013) introduced policies and proposals to encourage research transparency and data sharing. Some foundations and other research funders also started to require that funding proposals include a "data management plan" (DMP) discussing how the data generated through the supported research would be disseminated more broadly (e.g., the National Science Foundation [NSF] 2011, 2019 and the National Institutes of Health 2003, 2019). Journal editors, in turn, began to develop stronger standards for transparency for the work published in their outlets.

In response to, and to advance, the conversation, APSA developed the "Data Access and Research Transparency"(DA-RT) initiative (Lupia and Elman 2014), which generated suggestions to update the American Political Science Association's *Guide to Professional Ethics* (2012) to clarify transparency principles.[3] The speed and content of disciplinary discussion, as well as steps journal editors took to instantiate principles of openness in their journals' standards and guidelines, generated hesitancy among some political scientists, especially scholars who use qualitative data and methods. The "Journal Editors Transparency Statement" (JETS), signed by more than two dozen editors between 2014 and 2015, caused particular concern.[4] In November 2015, almost 1,200 political scientists signed a public petition calling on journal editors to delay implementing new transparency guidelines until additional, more inclusive discussion could occur.[5] Shortly thereafter, in January 2016, 20 APSA past presidents sent a public letter to the 27 journals that had signed JETS expressing concern about the statement's language and requesting clarification on how it would be interpreted.[6] Discussion also continued on panels and roundtables at disciplinary conferences, via journal articles (e.g., Fujii 2016, Monroe 2018, Kapiszewski and Wood 2021) and symposia on transparency (e.g., in *Qualitative Methods and Multi-Method Research* [Spring 2015] and the newsletter of the Comparative Politics section of APSA [Spring 2016]), as well as through the *Qualitative Transparency Deliberations* (see https://www.qualtd.net/), which produced 14 individual reports, summarized in Jacobs et al. (2021).

As this discussion illustrates, research transparency has been a core focus of conversation among political scientists over the last decade, resonating with concerns about open science across the social sciences, natural sciences, and beyond (Baker 2015; OSC 2015; Baker and Penny 2016; Bohannon 2016; Zeiler 2016). To be sure, few if any scholars in the discipline have argued against transparency; as is well recognized, research transparency promotes inclusivity and robust research practices, accelerates discovery, reduces duplication of effort, and empowers collaboration.[7] Instead, the discussion has revolved around whether, and if so how, openness can be achieved ethically and in ways that honor scholars' epistemological commitments.

Given the centrality of this debate, it is critical for graduate students to understand how transparency affects the landscape facing them with regard to intellectual production, publication, and professional advancement. This chapter helps you to do so. In the next section, we discuss some of the central benefits of and challenges to actuating openness; we consider in particular the difficulties that sensitive human-participants data pose to pursuing transparency. In the third section, we offer concrete strategies that graduate students who use quantitative and/or qualitative data and methods can use to pursue transparency and interact productively with key institutional stakeholders, including Institutional Review Boards (IRBs), potential funders of their research, and academic journals; we give special attention to the question of how graduate students can both achieve openness and protect the people they involve in their research. We close by enjoining graduate students to join the conversation and suggesting an overarching orientation that they might adopt toward making their work transparent—"as open as possible, as closed as necessary" (European Commission 2016).

Benefits of and Challenges to Actuating Transparency

In this section, we discuss three central benefits of research openness and three key challenges to achieving it. To begin, pursuing research transparency offers a window on the inner workings of your scholarship, demonstrating its rigor and power. The limits that journals, in particular, impose on the length of the scholarship published on their pages often prohibit authors from showing all of the analytic work and evidence that support the descriptive and causal inferences they draw in their scholarship, or the claim they make to have achieved empathetic interpretation. Scholars who use quantitative methods, for instance, can rarely display in the text of an article all of the regressions and robustness checks they ran; scholars who use qualitative data can rarely clearly discuss the details of data collection, or deploy all of the evidence they collected that supports their points. Enhancing the transparency of your scholarship, for instance by adding a methodological appendix (see Grossman and Pedahzur 2021) or using Annotation for Transparent Inquiry (ATI),[8] gives you an opportunity to include that detail, making your work more persuasive to reviewers and readers alike.

Second, pursuing transparency brings your work into line with emerging expectations for high-quality political science research. Many journals have well-developed and long-standing requirements for openness for quantitative scholarship, and guidelines are beginning to emerge for qualitative inquiry. Moreover, a growing number of top journals (e.g., *International Organization* and *American Journal of Political Science*) engage in what they term "pre-publication replication:" they only publish work if its findings can be reproduced. It is only possible to carry out such evaluation on open scholarship. Likewise, as noted earlier, increasing numbers of funding organizations (e.g., the NSF as well as the Ford, Gates, and MacArthur Foundations) are calling on grantees to make the scholarship produced using their funding open, including, in some cases, sharing the underlying data. Meeting these expectations, within ethical and legal limits, allows your scholarship to be funded and published, and marks it as aligned with the broad disciplinary consensus on the value of openness.

Finally, being more open about how you generated your research results and sharing the empirical basis of your work—always within ethical and legal limits—allows your scholarship to be used more broadly and to achieve wider-ranging purposes. Scholars being transparent about their research practices and sharing their data helps members of research communities to identify synergies between each other's work and empowers collaboration. Also, open scholarship can be built upon more easily, and can be replicated, leading to an expansion of our knowledge about critical political outcomes. In fact, studies find that articles with shared data receive between 25 percent and 70 percent more citations than comparable articles without shared data (e.g., Piwowar, Day, and Fridsma 2007; Colavizza et al. 2020). Likewise, open scholarship can be used to teach research methods, helping future generations of graduate students to be stronger social scientists. Openness, in other words, serves as a bridge between your research and the broader benefits it can generate.

Yet achieving openness ethically and legally and in ways that align with your epistemological commitments also poses important challenges. A first set are practical and professional. Taking the steps necessary to make quantitative and qualitative research more open can be time-consuming. Scholars—and perhaps graduate students in particular—may feel that the time they could potentially dedicate to making one piece of scholarship more open would be better spent conducting more research or writing another manuscript. Likewise, scholars may face logistical challenges: if your research rests on jurisdictional details depicted in large maps that you pored over in a far-away archive, how can those "data" be shared? Moreover, there are few immediate and obvious professional payoffs for making your work more open.

Epistemological challenges also arise as scholars consider engaging in research openness. As disciplinary debate has recognized from the very start (Elman and Kapiszewski 2014), there can be no single approach to achieving transparency. Political science is a heterogeneous discipline: scholars adopt diverse approaches to study political phenomena, hold varying epistemological commitments, and use an array of methods of analysis. The approach to transparency taken by a scholar who employs quantitative data and methods should and will diverge greatly from that of a scholar who uses interpretive methods, given those scholars' very different beliefs about how we know what we know. Moving toward openness as a discipline requires that particular research or epistemic communities develop, discuss, and continue to refine norms for transparency. Yet not all research traditions have had robust conversations about these issues. This gap leaves uncertainty among scholars about what would be considered an epistemologically appropriate way to make their work more open.

A final set of challenges are ethical and legal, and impinge most directly on the data sharing aspect of transparency. Ethical challenges arise most clearly and acutely for scholars whose work involves "human subjects" (e.g., who conduct interviews, focus groups, surveys, or experiments). All scholars who engage with people and draw on the fruits of that engagement in their research presentations and products are ethically bound to solicit and secure those people's informed consent to participate in the research project, and to adhere strictly to the agreements they and participants strike with regard to how the information participants convey will be stored, used, and disseminated. If you promise your respondents confidentiality (that you will keep private the information they convey) or believe that you may put respondents at risk if you share that information, what strategies can you use for sharing data? Likewise, if the information underpinning your work is under copyright or proprietary (i.e., owned by someone else), what approaches can you take to sharing them more broadly?

Strategies for Actuating Openness

Fortunately, social scientists and information scientists are developing diverse strategies for pursuing research transparency and interacting productively with the institutional stakeholders with whom scholars engage as their scholarship traverses the research lifecycle. In this short piece we cannot do these emerging and evolving techniques justice; for useful overviews see Blair et al. (2019), Firchow and

Gellman (2021), Ingram (2021), and Kapiszewski and Karcher (2021b). Instead, we identify and discuss three overarching strategies that you can adopt as you consider how to engage in research openness.

First, it is critical that you begin to think about how you will pursue transparency—and start to plan your strategy—from the earliest moments of envisioning and designing a research project. The choices you make as you design and implement research significantly shape and influence how open you can ultimately make that study and how you can do so. Moreover, making your work transparent is much easier if you have had doing so in mind from the start—if you create a DMP; carefully document (describing and justifying) all the research design choices you make as you conduct your study; and keep your data safe, secure, accessible, and comprehensible. While taking each of these steps facilitates research openness, doing so also benefits you and the future you, and strengthens your work.

One context in which graduate students can learn and experiment with transparency techniques is in methods courses (quantitative and qualitative). For instance, in quantitative courses, you can learn practices to increase the transparency of your entire workflow—from data generation, through cleaning and analysis, to reporting. Ingram (2021) advocates a set of 11 practices,[9] and illustrates how they can be implemented in R and Stata, two common statistical software packages. For instance, command files (i.e., scripts) can be used in the same way research notebooks are used in other disciplines,[10] documenting all stages of a project. Sharing these files with collaborators (including advisors and co-authors) facilitates communication. Such files (or at least documentation of where they can be found) can also be submitted to journals prior to publication in fulfillment of their requirement for providing replication materials. Methods courses can also introduce the logic and basics of preregistration. Preregistering publicly your data collection and analysis strategies is quickly becoming a norm in particular for experiments (e.g., in the EGAP registry); it also holds great promise for observational and qualitative research (see Jacobs 2020). For qualitative research specifically, techniques such as interview appendices (see Bleich and Pekkanen 2015) and others outlined in Kapiszewski and Karcher (2021b) can also be taught in methods courses. If transparency practices are not covered in your methods courses, you should encourage your instructor to discuss them. Moreover, you should ensure that any methods courses you teach integrate transparency techniques (see, e.g., Ingram 2021) (see also chapter 29 for additional suggestions about your first teaching experience).

Second, avail yourself of available resources—on and off-campus—as you consider what strategies to adopt to make your work transparent. Your campus IRB (on which more below) and library (in particular data librarians) are wonderful places to start. If the funding organizations supporting your work have expectations about transparency, engage actively with them about those expectations; if you are unsure that you can meet them or how to do so, discuss your concerns with them and solicit their guidance and support. If you have a particular outlet in mind where you would like to publish your research, review any transparency standards or guidelines it has for the kind of work that you do and contact the editor with questions or concerns. As you interact with these different stakeholders, think actively about how harmonious their expectations are; if there are conflicts among them, enjoin the different parties to help you resolve the tensions. Reach out to organizations that focus on research openness and can offer guidance and assistance, such as the Open Science Foundation (OSF), the Berkeley Initiative for Transparency in the Social Sciences (BITSS), and data repositories such as ICPSR and the Qualitative Data Repository (QDR).[11] You might also contact scholars whose work is similar to yours to solicit their thoughts and input on how to pursue openness.

Finally, we offer some more detailed advice on how to engage productively with your campus IRB—and other IRBs with which you may need to interact—to simultaneously pursue openness and protect human participants you involve in your research. Some scholars experience confusion over how to secure approval for their human subjects research, particularly at research institutions with strict IRBs (Babb 2020: 77–83) or when an IRB's practices continue to hew to the medical model on which they are based. Nonetheless, creating a productive partnership with the IRBs with which you engage can help you to enhance the quality and transparency of your research, and deepen your ethical commitments. We consider each in turn.

First, IRB protocols and other materials can serve as an integral part of a transparent and effective research design, regardless of your methodology. Creating IRB materials can help you to define, clarify, and improve various aspects of the research process such as contacting subjects, sampling criteria, interview questions, and informed-consent protocols. You may recognize these as standard elements of grant proposals for dissertation research funding and of DMPs. Indeed, we recommend that you create these related documents simultaneously, allowing you to ensure that their content aligns: for instance, promises about data sharing and about confidentiality need to be reflected in both your DMP and your IRB materials. Creating solid documentation strengthens your research and empowers transparency.

Second, the practices that you describe in your IRB materials serve as a baseline or starting point for indispensable reflection on the ethics of human participant research and your obligations to the people you involve in your work. One excellent way to ethically increase the transparency of your research with historically and contemporarily marginalized populations is to engage collaboratively with research participants (Gellman 2021). In sum, while creating the materials required by IRBs requires time and work, the IRB process helps scholars improve their research, protect the people they involve in it, and enhance its transparency.

Conclusion

As the length and detail of this volume suggest, you have many competing priorities as you pursue a graduate degree in political science. A host of exciting challenges and wonderful opportunities lie on the research road ahead. Achieving research transparency should not be a weighty concern for you. Taking the steps necessary to make the products of your inquiries as transparent as you can within ethical and legal limits should simply be part of your standard operating procedures as a researcher. We encourage you to think carefully and critically about how to do so, and to avail yourself of the many resources that are available to help you consider options, make informed choices, and embrace the ethical pursuit of open science. Moreover, as we have suggested, discussions about transparency are still open and ongoing in the discipline, and we encourage you to join them, bringing new perspectives and insights. By working together, the many research communities that comprise our rich and heterogeneous discipline will arrive at epistemologically appropriate strategies to make all kinds of inquiry more transparent.

Endnotes

1   This discussion builds on decades of debate in political science and other disciplines; see e.g., King 1995.

2   A confusing array of terms is used to describe the various strategies that can be used to "reappraise" (Gerring 2020) research. In this piece we use the term "reproduce" to describe evaluating a study by reanalyzing the same data and using the same methods employed by the original author to see if the same results obtain; and "replicate" to describe evaluating a study by collecting new data (likely from the same population) and analyzing them using the same methods employed by the original author to see if the same results obtain.

3   In April 2020, the APSA Council approved a new "Principles and Guidance" document drafted by an Ad Hoc Committee on Human Subjects Research that APSA had charged in 2017 with identifying broad ethical principles that could guide research on human subjects.

4   The JETS text can be found here: https://www.dartstatement.org/2014-journal-editors-statement-jets

5   The petition can be found here: https://dialogueondartdotorg.files.wordpress.com/2015/11/petition-from-concerned-scholars-nov-12-2015-complete.pdf

6   The public letter can be found here: https://politicalsciencenow.com/letter-from-distinguished-political-scientists-urging-nuanced-journal-interpretation-of-jets-policy-guidelines/

7   The website of the Center for Open Science (https://www.cos.io/) offers excellent discussions of the benefits of research transparency.

8   You can learn more about ATI here: https://qdr.syr.edu/ati; see also Kapiszewski and Karcher 2021a.

9   These practices are: (1) setting a working directory, (2) using hierarchical subdirectories, (3) placing original data in the appropriate subdirectory, (4) creating relevant metadata and placing

it in the working directory, (5) using command files, (6) using relative file paths, (7) setting the computing environment, (8) tracking versions of materials, (9) saving results to files, (10) file naming, and (11) commenting extensively.

10   Command files include directory structure, computing environment (version, packages, etc.), loading original data, all steps for cleaning and organizing data, key steps in the analysis, and key steps in reporting, including tables and figures.

11   OSF: https://osf.io/; BITSS: https://www.bitss.org/; ICPSR: https://icpsr.umich.edu/; QDR: https://qdr.syr.edu

References

American Political Science Association. 2012. *A Guide to Professional Ethics in Political Science, Second Edition*. Washington, DC: American Political Science Association. https://www.apsanet.org/portals/54/Files/Publications/APSAEthicsGuide2012.pdf.

Babb, Sarah. 2020. *Regulating Human Research: IRBs from Peer Review to Compliance Bureaucracy*. Stanford, CA: Stanford University Press.

Baker, Monya. 2015. "Over Half of Psychology Studies Fail Reproducibility Test." *Nature* (Aug 27). https://doi.org/10.1038/nature.2015.18248.

Baker, Monya, and Dan Penny. 2016. "Is There a Reproducibility Crisis?" *Nature* 533 (7604), May 26: 452–454. https://doi.org/10.1038/533452a.

Blair, Graeme, Jasper Cooper, Alexander Coppock, and Macartan Humphreys. 2019. "Declaring and Diagnosing Research Designs." *American Political Science Review* 113 (3): 838–59. https://doi.org/10.1017/S0003055419000194.

Bleich, Erik, and Pekkanen, Robert. 2015. "Data Access, Research Transparency, and Interviews; the Interview Methods Appendix". *Qualitative & Multi-method Research* 13 (1): 8–13. https://doi.org/10.5281/zenodo.892386.

Bohannon, John. 2016. "About 40% of Economics Experiments Fail Replication Survey." *Science* (Mar 3). https://doi.org/10.1126/science.aaf4141.

Colavizza, Giovanni, Iain Hrynaszkiewicz, Isla Staden, Kirstie Whitaker, and Barbara McGillivray. 2020. "The Citation Advantage of Linking Publications to Research Data." *PLOS ONE* 15 (4): e0230416. https://doi.org/10.1371/journal.pone.0230416.

Elman, Colin, and Diana Kapiszewski. 2014. "Data Access and Research Transparency in the Qualitative Tradition." *PS: Political Science & Politics* 47 (1): 43–47. https://doi.org/10.1017/S1049096513001777.

European Commission. 2016. "Guidelines on FAIR Data Management in Horizon 2020." Brussels: European Commission Directorate for General for Research & Innovation. http://ec.europa.eu/research/participants/data/ref/h2020/grants_manual/hi/oa_pilot/h2020-hi-oa-data-mgt_en.pdf.

Firchow, Pamina, & Gellman, Mneesha. 2021. "Collaborative Methodologies: Why, How, and for Whom?" *PS: Political Science & Politics* 54(3): 525–529. https://doi.org/10.1017/S1049096521000330.

Fujii, Lee Ann. 2016. "The Dark Side of DA-RT." *Comparative Politics Newsletter* 26(1): 25–27.

Gellman, Mneesha. 2021. "Collaborative Methodology with Indigenous Communities: A Framework for Addressing Power Inequalities." *PS: Political Science and Politics* 54(3): 535–538. https://doi.org/10.1017/S1049096521000299.

Gerring, John. 2020. "Coordinating Reappraisals." In *The Production of Knowledge: Enhancing Progress in Social Science*, edited by Colin Elman, John Gerring, and James Mahoney. Cambridge: Cambridge University Press. https://doi.org/10.1017/9781108762519.013.

Grossman, Jonathan, and Ami Pedahzur. 2021. "Can We Do Better? Replication and Online Appendices in Political Science." *Perspectives on Politics* 19 (3): 906–11. doi:10.1017/S1537592720001206.

Holdren, J. P. 2013. Increasing access to the results of federally funded scientific research; https://obamawhitehouse.archives.gov/sites/default/files/microsites/ostp/ostp_public_access_memo_2013.pdf

Ingram, Matthew C. 2021. "Teaching Reproducibility: General Principles and Practical Considerations with Workflow Illustrations in R and Stata." In Jeffrey L. Bernstein, ed. *Teaching Research Methods in Political Science*. Series Elgar Guides to Teaching, Edward Elgar Publishing.

Jacobs, Alan M. 2020. "Pre-Registration and Results-Free Review in Observational and Qualitative Research." Chapter. In Colin Elman, John Gerring, and James Mahoney, eds. *The Production of Knowledge: Enhancing Progress in Social Science*, 221–64. Strategies for Social Inquiry. Cambridge: Cambridge University Press. https://doi.org/10.1017/9781108762519.009.

Jacobs, Alan M., Tim Büthe, Ana Arjona, Leonardo R. Arriola, Eva Bellin, Andrew Bennett, Lisa Björkman, et al. 2021. "The Qualitative Transparency Deliberations: Insights and Implications." *Perspectives on Politics* 19(1): 171–208. https://doi.org/10.1017/S1537592720001164.

Kapiszewski, Diana, and Sebastian Karcher. 2021a. "Empowering Transparency: Annotation for Transparent Inquiry (ATI)." *PS: Political Science & Politics* 54 (3): 473–78. doi:10.1017/S1049096521000287.

Kapiszewski, Diana, and Sebastian Karcher. 2021b. "Transparency in Practice in Qualitative Research." *PS: Political Science & Politics* 54 (2): 285–91. https://doi.org/10.1017/S1049096520000955

Kapiszewski, Diana and Elisabeth Jean Wood. 2021. "Ethics, Epistemology, and Openness in Research with Human Participants." *Perspectives on Politics* (early access Mar 15). https://doi.org/10.1017/S1537592720004703

King, Gary. 1995. "Replication, Replication." *PS: Political Science and Politics* 28: 444–452. https://doi.org/10.2307/420301

Monroe, Kristen Renwick. 2018. "The Rush to Transparency: DA-RT and the Potential Dangers for Qualitative Research." *Perspectives on Politics* 16(1): 141–148. https://doi.org/10.1017/S153759271700336X

National Institutes of Health. 2003. NIH data sharing policy and implementation guidance. https://grants.nih.gov/grants/policy/data_sharing/data_sharing_guidance.htm

National Institutes for Health. 2019. Request for Public Comments on a DRAFT NIH Policy for Data Management and Sharing and Supplemental DRAFT Guidance. Federal Register 84(217): 60398–60402. https://grants.nih.gov/grants/guide/notice-files/NOT-OD-20-013.html.

National Science Foundation. 2011. Dissemination and sharing of research results. http://www.nsf.gov/bfa/dias/policy/dmp.jsp

National Science Foundation. 2019. Dear Colleague Letter: Effective Practices for Data. NSF 19–069 May 20. https://www.nsf.gov/pubs/2019/nsf19069/nsf19069.jsp

Office of Science and Technology Policy. 2020. Request for Public Comment on Draft Desirable Characteristics of Repositories for Managing and Sharing Data Resulting From Federally Funded Research *Federal Register* / 85(12): 3085–87. https://www.federalregister.gov/documents/2020/01/17/2020-00689/request-for-public-comment-on-draft-desirable-characteristics-of-repositories-for-managing-and

Open Science Collaboration (OSC). 2015. "Estimating the Reproducibility of Psychological Science." *Science* 349 (6251). https://doi.org/10.1126/science.aac4716

Piwowar, Heather A., Roger S. Day, and Douglas B. Fridsma. 2007. "Sharing Detailed Research Data Is Associated with Increased Citation Rate." *PLOS ONE* 2 (3): e308. https://doi.org/10.1371/journal.pone.0000308.

Simmons, Joseph P., Leif D. Nelson, and Uri Simonsohn. 2011. "False-Positive Psychology: Undisclosed Flexibility in Data Collection and Analysis Allows Presenting Anything as Significant." *Psychological Science* 22 (11): 1359–66. https://doi.org/10.1177/0956797611417632.

20 | Fieldwork

Kelebogile Zvobgo[1], Charmaine N. Willis[2], Myunghee Lee[3], Anne-Kathrin Kreft[4], and Ezgi Irgil[5]

1. College of William & Mary 2. University at Albany 3. University of Copenhagen

4. University of Oslo 5. Swedish Institute of International Affairs

KEYWORDS: Physical Safety, The Field, Data Collection, Funding, Theory-Building or -Testing, Harassment.

Introduction

Despite fieldwork's importance in political science research, many PhD programs do not offer adequate training. This leaves graduate students on their own to locate guides and work by trial and error. Consequently, first-time field research is daunting for many. In this chapter, we define the object and purpose of fieldwork and offer practical advice on a range of topics, including planning fieldwork, sampling, networking, interacting with research participants, carrying out interviews, *physical safety* and mental well-being in the field, and research ethics. This guide is based on our experiences in a variety of settings and on different topics, and is based on the original article, "Field Research: A Graduate Student's Guide" (Irgil et al. 2021).

Fieldwork-related concerns arise from an unfortunate shortage in curricular offerings and instructional materials for qualitative and mixed-method research in political science graduate programs (Emmons and Moravcsik 2020). As a result, many early-career researchers are underprepared for the logistics of fieldwork, from developing networks and effective sampling strategies to building respondents' trust and moving about *the field* safely and ethically.

To remedy this, the five of us share a set of suggestions based on our own extensive field research. Our experiences differ in several respects, from the time we spent in the field (ranging from 10 days to several months), to the amount of time we had to prepare, to the locations we visited, to how we conducted our research. We have worked in countries where we have professional proficiency in the language, and in countries where we have relied on interpreters. We have worked in settings with precarious security as well as in locations that feel as comfortable as home.

In this chapter, we first define what fieldwork is and its application through different *data collection* methods. Then, we detail the purpose of fieldwork, followed by *funding* applications in the context of fieldwork. We then move on to the phase of entering the field and adapting to the field. Moreover, we address physical safety and mental well-being both during and after fieldwork, and we conclude.

What is Fieldwork?

Despite its prevalence in political science, fieldwork as a concept is not well-defined. Even symposia discussing the "nuts and bolts" of conducting research in the field within the pages of political science journals rarely define it (Hsueh et al. 2014). In this chapter, we define fieldwork as acquiring information using any set of appropriate data collection techniques for qualitative, quantitative, or experimental analysis through embedded research whose location and duration depends on the project (Irgil et al. 2021, 6).

First, despite often being placed squarely in the domain of qualitative research, fieldwork can also serve quantitative projects—for example, by providing crucial context, supporting triangulation, illustrating causal mechanisms or through quantification of data that are available only in the field (Jensenius 2014). For instance, Willis's research on the United States military in East Asia began with quantitative data collection and analysis of protest events before turning to fieldwork to understand why protests occurred in some instances but not others.

Second, while much fieldwork requires leaving the country in which one's institution is based, this is not a requirement. What matters is the nature of the research project, not the locale. For instance, some of us have interviewed representatives of intergovernmental organizations (IGOs) and international nongovernmental organizations (INGOs), whose headquarters are often located in the Global North countries in which we reside. The COVID-19 pandemic has further highlighted the relevance of remote fieldwork.[1]

Third, the appropriate amount of time in the field should be assessed on a project-by-project basis, depending on the research question, the data to be collected, available resources, and prior familiarity with the field site. Our own presence in the field has ranged from a few days (Kreft at the United Nations in New York) to a few weeks (Zvobgo's interviews with human rights NGOs in different research sites), to several months (Willis's research on discourse around U.S. military presence in overseas host communities).

Purpose of Fieldwork

Fieldwork allows researchers to use different techniques to collect and access original/primary data sources. These include, non-exhaustively: visits to archives to review (or quantify) historical documents, interviews to obtain in-depth information or better understand human behavior, surveys to understand opinion formation, or lab-in-the-field experiments to better understand decision-making.

But beyond data collection as such, fieldwork is also useful for *theory-building* and *theory-testing* (Geddes 2003). When studying the rise of a protest movement in South Korea for her dissertation, for example, Lee found that existing theories did not offer a convincing explanation for the movement. Based on interviews she conducted with movement participants, she developed an alternative theory that centralized the authoritarian past as a unifying and mobilizing factor in the protest participants' collective identity.

In terms of theory-testing, many political scientists turn their attention to conducting field experiments or lab-in-the-field experiments to reveal causality (Finseraas and Kotsadam 2017), or to leverage in-depth insights gained through qualitative or archival research in process-tracing (Ricks and Liu 2018). Of course, for most PhD students, some of these options are financially prohibitive.

Funding

For many fieldwork projects, procuring funding via grants or fellowships is a necessity, regardless of how long one plans to be in the field. (Readers interested in a more general discussion of research funding should see chapter 23 in this volume.) A few things are important to keep in mind when applying for funding for fieldwork. First, the time between applying for and receiving funds, if successful, can be quite long, from several months to a year. For example, after defending her prospectus in May 2019, Willis began applying to funding sources for her dissertation, all of which had deadlines between June and September. She received notifications between November and January; however, funds from her successful applications were not available until March and April, almost a year later.[2] Accordingly, we recommend applying for funding as early as possible; this not only increases one's chances of hitting the ground running in the field, but the application process can also help clarify the goals and parameters of one's research.

Second, while both large and small pots of funding are worth applying for, many researchers end up funding their fieldwork through several small grants or fellowships. For example, Willis's fieldwork in the Philippines, Japan, and South Korea was supported through fellowships within each country. Similarly, Irgil was able to conduct her fieldwork abroad through two different and relatively smaller grants by applying to them each year. The amount of funding needed, of course, depends on the nature of one's project and how long one intends to be in the field; for some projects, even a couple of weeks in the field is sufficient to get the needed information.

Preparing to Enter "the Field"

What kind of preparations do researchers need? To maximize time in the field, good planning is important but requires a longer time horizon. By the time one contacts potential research participants, the data collection instrument (e.g., survey, interview questionnaire, experimental design, etc.), the informed consent protocols, and whatever ethical approval is required should already be in place. This gives you a much clearer idea of the universe of individuals you would like to involve as research participants, how you intend to (ethically) do so, and for what purpose. A general piece of advice is to research your target population's preferred communication channels and mediums (e.g., phone, various messenger services) in the field site if email requests yield few responses.

Regarding ethics and review panels, we encourage readers to talk openly, honestly, and as early as possible with supervisors and/or funders about situations where a written consent form may not be suitable and might need to be replaced with "verbal consent." For instance, doing fieldwork in politically unstable contexts, highly scrutinized environments, or vulnerable communities might create obstacles for the interviewees as well as the researcher. The literature discusses the tension between preserving the interviewees' anonymity and confidentiality while also requesting signed written consent (Saunders et al. 2015). Therefore, in those situations, the researcher might need to take the initiative on how to act while doing the interviews as rigorously as possible.

Ethical considerations also affect the research design itself, with ramifications for fieldwork. For example, when Kreft began researching women's civil society mobilization in response to conflict-related sexual violence, she initially aimed to interview victims of this violence to examine variation among those who did and did not mobilize. As a result of deeper engagement with the literature on re-traumatization, conversations with colleagues, and critical self-reflection of her status as a researcher (with no background in psychology or social work), she decided to change focus and shift toward representatives of civil society organizations. This constituted a major reconfiguration of her research design and strategy, from one geared toward identifying the factors that drive the mobilization of victims to one that identified how women mobilized in civil society "make sense" of conflict-related sexual violence.

Finally, when one wishes to conduct research in a country where one has less than professional fluency in the language, pre-fieldwork planning should include hiring a translator or research assistant, for example, through an online hiring platform like Upwork, or a local university. More generally, establishing contact with a local university can be beneficial, either in the form of a visiting researcher arrangement, which grants access to research groups and facilities like libraries, or by informally contacting individual researchers. The latter may have valuable insights into the local context, contacts to potential research participants, and may be able to recommend translators or research assistants.

Adapting to the Reality of the Field

Flexibility is key. Despite careful planning, there may be obstacles that necessitate adjustments to one's original plans. While it is important to have a list of people to contact in the field prior to entry, some leads will not be as fruitful as anticipated and you will likely add contacts to your list via snowball sampling (e.g., meeting new contacts through other contacts). You may meet people you did not make appointments with, come across opportunities you did not expect, or stumble upon new ideas about collecting data in the field. These happenings are part of the process; they will enrich your field experience and your research. Similarly, researchers should not be discouraged by interviews that do not go according to plan; this is normal and may even present opportunities to pursue relevant people who can provide an alternative path to your work.

Zvobgo, for example, had fewer than a dozen interviews scheduled when she traveled to Guatemala to study civil society activism and transitional justice since internal armed conflict. But she was able to recruit additional participants in-country. Interviewees with whom she built a rapport connected her to other NGOs, government offices, and the United Nations country office, sometimes even making the calls and scheduling interviews for her. Through snowball sampling, she was able to triple the number of participants. Likewise, snowball sampling was central to Kreft's recruitment of interview partners. Several of her interviewees connected her to highly relevant individuals she would never have been able to identify, and contact based on web searches alone.

We note that conducting interviews is very taxing. Depending on the project, each interview length might differ. Hence, field researchers should make a reasonable schedule and plan sufficient time for each interview, including travel and time for reflection/writing of field notes. This helps one to avoid cutting off an interviewee, missing important information, or being too exhausted to have a robust engagement with a respondent who is generously lending you their time.

We would also like to highlight the importance of distinguishing things that can only be done in person at a particular site from things that can be accomplished later at home. Prioritize the former over the latter. Lee's fieldwork experience serves as a good example. She studied a conservative protest movement in South Korea. She planned to conduct interviews with the rally participants to examine their motivations for participating. But as she only had one month in South Korea, she prioritized things that could only be done in the field: she went to the rally sites, she observed how protests proceeded, and she met participants and had some casual conversations with them. Then, she used the contacts she made while attending the rallies to create a social network to solicit interviews from ordinary protesters, her target population. In a nutshell, it is sometimes most beneficial to use one's time in the field to build relationships and networks as it can be more difficult to do so from outside the field.

Interacting with people in the field is one of the most rewarding yet ethically challenging parts of the work that we do, especially in comparison to the impersonal wrangling and analysis of quantitative data. Field researchers often make personal connections with their interviewees. Consequently, maintaining boundaries can be a bit tricky. Here, we recommend being honest with research participants without overstating the researcher's abilities. This appears as a challenge in the field, particularly when you empathize with people and when they share profound parts of their lives with you in addition to being "human subjects" (Fujii 2012). For instance, Zvobgo was very upfront with her interviewees about her role as a researcher: she recognized that she is not on the frontlines of the fight for human rights and transitional justice like they are. All she could/can do is use her platform to amplify their stories, bringing attention to their vital work through her future peer-reviewed publications. Interviewees were very receptive. In some cases, this prompted them to share even more, because they knew that the researcher was there to listen and learn. This is something that all scholars should always remember: we enter the field to be taught.

As researchers, we recognize a possible power differential between us and our research subjects, and certainly an imbalance in power between the countries where we have been trained and some of the countries where we do field research, particularly in politically dynamic contexts (Knott 2019). Therefore, we argue, researchers should be concerned with being open and transparent with everyone with whom they come into contact in the field and committed to giving back to those who so generously lend us their time and knowledge.

Physical Safety

Researchers may carry out fieldwork in a country that is less safe than what they are used to, a setting affected by conflict violence or high crime rates, for instance. Insecurity is also often gendered, differentially affecting women, and raising the specter of unwanted sexual advances, street *harassment*, or even sexual assault (Gifford and Hall-Clifford 2008; Mügge 2013). In a recent survey of political science graduate students in the United States, about half of those who had done fieldwork internationally reported having encountered safety issues in the field, (54 percent female, 47 percent male), and only 21 percent agreed that their PhD programs had prepared them to carry out their fieldwork safely (Schwartz and Cronin-Furman 2020, 8–9). Preventative measures scholars may adopt in an unsafe context may involve, at their most fundamental, adjustments to everyday routines and habits, and restricting one's movements temporally and spatially.

Others have collected a range of safety precautions that field researchers in fragile settings may take before and during fieldwork (Hilhorst et al. 2016). Focusing on the specific situations of graduate students, we recommend establishing communications protocols with supervisors or others at one's home institution, granting a colleague or two emergency reading access to one's digital calendar, and putting in place an emergency plan, that is, choosing emergency contacts back home and "in the field," knowing whom to contact if something happens, and knowing how to get to the nearest hospital or clinic. Registering with your country's embassy in the field site and any crisis monitoring and prevention systems it has is also advisable. Finally, it is prudent to heed the safety recommendations and travel advisories provided by state authorities and embassies to determine when and where it is safe to travel. Above all, one should always be aware of one's surroundings, use common sense, and listen to locals. If something feels unsafe, chances are it is.

Mental Well-Being

Different sources of stress during fieldwork, such as concern about insecurity, linguistic barriers, or social isolation and loneliness, can be both mentally and physically exhausting. In addition, it is natural for field research on sensitive issues to affect the researcher's mental well-being, especially in the absence of their normal support network (Hummel and El Kurd 2020; Williamson et al. 2020). Emotional reactions may appear disproportionate or unwarranted at a specific moment, but they may simply have been building up over a long time. Our primary piece of advice is therefore to be patient and generous with yourself: accept your emotional reactions as legitimate. Second, remember to take breaks, embrace distractions and rest. Third, we cannot stress enough the importance of investing in social relations, prior to, during and after your fieldwork trip. Seeking the company of locals and of other field researchers alleviates anxiety and makes fieldwork more enjoyable. For more comprehensive discussions and advice see Williamson et al. (2020) or Hummel and El Kurd (2020).

Conclusion

Many of the substantive, methodological and practical challenges that arise during fieldwork can be anticipated. Nonetheless, there is no such thing as being perfectly prepared for the field. Some things will simply be beyond one's control, and newcomers to field research should be prepared for things to not go as planned. New questions will arise, interview participants may cancel appointments, and findings may not match with expectations. So, one should be ready to adjust research and data collection plans, interview guides, questionnaires etc.

Our discussion on fieldwork preparation is by no means exhaustive. Formal fieldwork preparation should extend beyond what we have covered in this article, such as issues of data security, funding, and preparing for non-qualitative fieldwork methods. We also note that field research is one area that has yet to be comprehensively addressed in conversations on diversity and equity in the political science discipline and the broader academic profession.

Endnotes

1   See Howlett (2021) for a more in-depth discussion.

2   In our experience, this is not only the general cycle for graduate students in North America, but also in Europe and likely elsewhere.

Acknowledgments

This material is based upon work supported by the Forskraftstiftelsen Theodor Adelswärds Minne, Knut and Alice Wallenberg Foundation (KAW 2013.0178), National Science Foundation Graduate Research Fellowship Program (DGE-1418060), Southeast Asia Research Group (Pre-Dissertation Fellowship), University at Albany (Initiatives for Women and the Benevolent Association), the Japan Society for the Promotion of Science, the Korea Foundation, University of Missouri (John D. Bies International Travel Award Program and Kinder Institute on Constitutional Democracy), University of Southern California (Provost Fellowship in the Social Sciences), Vetenskapsrådet (Diarienummer 2019-06298), Wilhelm och Martina Lundgrens Vetenskapsfond (2016-1102; 2018-2272), and William & Mary (Global Research Institute Pre-doctoral Fellowship).

References

Emmons, Cassandra V., and Andrew M. Moravcsik. 2020. "Graduate Qualitative Methods Training in Political Science: A Disciplinary Crisis." *P.S.: Political Science & Politics* 53 (2): 258–64.

Finseraas, Henning, and Andreas Kotsadam. 2017. "Does Personal Contact with Ethnic Minorities Affect Anti-immigrant Sentiments? Evidence from a Field Experiment." *European Journal of Political Research* 56: 703–22.

Fujii, Lee Ann. 2012. "Research Ethics 101: Dilemmas and Responsibilities." *P.S.: Political Science & Politics* 45 (4): 717–23.

Geddes, Barbara. 2003. *Paradigms and Sand Castles: Theory Building and Research Design in Comparative Politics.* Ann Arbor: University of Michigan Press.

Gifford, Lindsay James and Rachel Hall-Clifford. 2008. "From Catcalls to Kidnapping: Towards an Open Dialogue on the Fieldwork Experiences of Graduate Women." *Anthropology News* 49 (6): 26–7.

Hilhorst, Thea, Lucy Hodgson, Bram Jansen, and Rodrigo Mena Flühmann. 2016. *Security Guidelines for Field Research in Complex, Remote and Hazardous Places.* July 1. http://hdl.handle.net/1765/93256.

Howlett, Marnie. 2021. "Looking at the 'Field' through a Zoom Lens: Methodological Reflections on Conducting Online Research during a Global Pandemic." *Qualitative Research.*

Hsueh, Roselyn, Francesca R. Jensenius, and Akasemi Newsome. 2014. "Fieldwork in Political Science: Encountering Challenges and Crafting Solutions: Introduction." *PS: Political Science & Politics* 47 (2): 391–3.

Hummel, Calla, and Dana El Kurd. 2020. "Mental Health and Fieldwork." *P.S.: Political Science & Politics* 54(1): 121–5.

Irgil, Ezgi, Anne-Kathrin Kreft, Myunghee Lee, Charmaine N. Willis, and Kelebogile Zvobgo. 2021. "Field Research: A Graduate Student's Guide." *International Studies Review.* 23(4): 1495–1517.

Jensenius, Francesca R. 2014. "The Fieldwork of Quantitative Data Collection." *P.S.: Political Science & Politics* 47 (2): 402–4.

Knott, Eleanor. 2019. "Beyond the Field: Ethics After Fieldwork in Politically Dynamic Contexts." *Perspectives on Politics* 17 (1): 140–53.

Mügge, Liza M. 2013. "Sexually Harassed by Gatekeepers: Reflections on Fieldwork in Surinam and Turkey." *International Journal of Social Research Methodology* 16 (6): 541–6.

Ricks, Jacob I., and Amy H. Liu. 2018. "Process-Tracing Research Designs: A Practical Guide." *P.S.: Political Science & Politics* 51 (4): 842–6.

Saunders, Benjamin, Jenny Kitzinger, and Celia Kitzinger. 2015. "Anonymizing Interview Data: Challenges and Compromise in Practice." *Qualitative Research* 15 (5): 616–32.

Schwartz, Stephanie, and Kate Cronin-Furman. 2020. "Ill-Prepared: International Fieldwork Methods Training in Political Science." Working Paper.

Williamson, Emma, Alison Gregory, Hilary Abrahams, Nadia Aghtaie, Sarah-Jane Walker, Marianne Hester. 2020. "Secondary Trauma: Emotional Safety in Sensitive Research." *Journal of Academic Ethics* 18(1): 55–70.

21 | How to Conference

Kimbery Turner[1], Christina Boyes[2], Elizabeth Bennion[3], & James Newman[4]

1. Harvard Kennedy School 2. The Centro de Investigación y Docencia Económicas

3. Indiana University South Bend 4. Southeast Missouri State University

KEYWORDS: Interdisciplinary Conferences, Networking.

Introduction

You may never have attended a conference, but as your department approaches abstract submission deadlines for APSA, MPSA, or another major conference, you can feel the tension in the air. How do you know your work is ready? What happens at conferences and how do you network while there? How do you budget for conferences? What types of conferences exist? In this chapter, we answer these questions and help you navigate the hidden curriculum, find your community, and get the most out of your first political science academic conferences.

Terms like "workshops," "panels," "sessions," "roundtables," "posters," and "section meetings" can confuse first-time attendees. Workshops may be held before, during, or after the main conference and are focused on predetermined topics. They offer an opportunity to get to know other scholars who share your specific research interests. Panels and sessions both refer to the main portion of conferences, within which presenters give brief talks and receive feedback from the audience. In some conferences, discussants are assigned to offer constructive criticism on each presented paper. Roundtables offer participants the chance to ask expert input on a topic. Some roundtables are focused on professionalization while others center on a given topic or may address specific scholarly works. Posters, uncommon in political science, provide presenters an opportunity to talk about their projects in greater depth than presentations allow.

Beyond providing opportunities to share your work, conferences offer additional networking opportunities such as happy hours and receptions. Additional professional advancement opportunities exist at conference vendor or exhibitor tables and recruitment events.

Are You Ready to Conference?

Conference attendance and presentation of research are viewed as one of the most important activities for scholars. Conferences allow you to develop an identity in the discipline while gaining awareness of how your research fits into the larger body of literature. They also allow you to connect with scholars and mentors.

Ask yourself what conference is right for your work. If you are in your first year of graduate school, consider presenting at a state or regional conference. Master's level work is often presented at state conferences. Some state and national conferences develop panels composed exclusively of students without a PhD.

Do not overlook *interdisciplinary conferences* such as the Western Social Science Association. These conferences may have sections devoted to subfields related to your research. Presenting findings from your dissertation or other major research project is encouraged at most interdisciplinary and regional conferences.

Networking allows you to engage with scholars at all levels, offers access to resources, and provides you with critical advice about grants, workshops, and writing groups. It also gives you an opportunity to promote your research. This is particularly important for students from less prestigious institutions or who have limited access to institutional resources.

Network vertically and horizontally. Develop a wide and deep network of fellow graduate students who will be your future colleagues, editors, and reviewers. This network can act as a conduit into new streams of vertical networking; you now have access to their advisors and mentors as well. These friendships and collaborations can last decades; do not neglect them to seek out senior scholars who will soon retire or those at top universities. The majority of the professoriate is located outside of the small set of elite institutions. Avoid the inefficient and counterproductive networking tactic colloquially known as "name badging." This is when individuals initiate (or suspend) networking according to institutional prestige. Not only is it rude to immediately glance at someone's name badge to determine whether to continue a conversation, these are your current and future colleagues. This disrespectful practice can have major downstream consequences, as academics have long memories.

Assistant professors can offer crucial advice about the job market and the transition to the professoriate. They are integrated into whisper networks and often generous with inside information on salaries, toxic work environments, and living conditions.

Associate professors often have students and may have less bandwidth to take on external mentees. Still, watch Twitter prior to conferences, as many associate professors will hold open coffee hours. Many will offer to look over resumes and job files and offer market advice. Take advantage of these offers and meet as many scholars as possible. Many postdoctoral fellowships require advisory supervision at the associate level, so it is important that associate faculty know who you are and have heard of your scholarship.

Many full professors are often busy at conferences and have limited time for their own students, much less external students. In order to maximize the likelihood of successfully scheduling a meeting with a senior scholar, set up a coffee meeting weeks in advance. At the meeting, have a short agenda scripted for yourself of what you wish to discuss with them. Prepare to be interrupted as people they know come up to them. Be direct and make it clear how your research is connected to theirs in a deep substantive way, what new angle you are working, and why you want them to know about it.

Budgeting

Funding is a major conference issue, particularly for under-resourced students and those who have caretaking responsibilities. Graduate student stipends can make it difficult to attend conferences. Even when university grants or travel funding are available, they are often provided via reimbursement. Major conferences often offer highly competitive travel grants for attendees. These are worth applying for, but there are limited funds and larger conferences tend to be more expensive than smaller, regional conferences. There are, however, ways to attend conferences in your field without spending too much (if anything). Increasingly, conferences offer online options, too, though networking opportunities may be more limited in the online environment.

If a regional or topic-specific conference such as Indiana University's Ostrom Workshop on the Workshop Conference (WOW), Peace Science, or IPES is held at your university, student volunteers may be needed and receive free or discounted registration for their help. Additionally, these conferences may be easier for graduate students with caretaking responsibilities to attend without needing to make special arrangements. Some larger conferences may also offer discounted or free registration to students who assist with the conference preparations.

Why Does it Matter?

Conferencing provides crucial opportunities for funding, research collaborations, and professional service. Additionally, conferences expose attendees to new and useful developments in the field and offer skill development and networking opportunities for attendees (Oester et al 2017). Conferences provide a network of people who can offer advice and support during your academic journey and serve as reviewers or recommenders for later promotion decisions and grant proposals. First-generation graduate students, BIPOC (Black, Indigenous and People of Color), and women often face conference barriers and confidence gaps that reduce their likelihood to actively network. Conferences provide an opportunity to level the playing field by expanding your academic community and finding mentors (O'Brien 2020). Networking and being mentored, in turn, helps career advancement (Argyle and Mendelberg 2020).

Hidden Curriculum

Despite having navigated the underlying culture and norms at your home institution, you may be unfamiliar with the norms, channels, and access points of political science. Lack of transparency and information regarding prestigious workshops, mini-conferences, and inter-institutional seminars reduce the competitiveness of students without access to elite networks and channels. Networking can help compensate.

Speaking to other students about their activities and discussing new opportunities with faculty provides crucial information on opportunities and potential supporters, advisors, and advocates for your participation in new venues. Participation in these endeavors can be career-changing and provide a crucial platform for your work. For female-identifying and BIPOC attendees, these opportunities can be impossible to break into without the right "access," which is often provided via your social network. This is compounded for many marginalized and racialized attendees if they are first-generation, and thus, do not have the a priori networks and knowledge of their classmates and colleagues.

The ability to break into more "closed" conferences, such as Polmeth, is easier if you have a particular set of credentials. Attendance at the Inter-university Consortium for Political and Social Research (ICPSR), Empirical Implications of Theoretical Models (EITM) Institute, or the Institute for Qualitative and Multi-Method Research (IQMR) signals your skills and provides you with networks embedded in conference leadership. While some schools provide their students with information and funding on workshops, many do not. Information booths at conferences often inform students about available participation and scholarship opportunities.

What Should You Do?

If you have a course paper that has received feedback from the course's instructor and you addressed the feedback, the paper is likely ready for submission. While the paper may not be accepted at a national conference, it may be appropriate for state or regional conferences. Many states host annual conferences with lower registration and travel costs. As a doctoral student, a state or local conference is an obvious place to start, due to the high acceptance rate and reduced travel costs. Notably, some smaller state, local, and regional conferences are also free.

As you gain experience, presenting papers at a regional conference (e.g., the Midwest Political Science Association, or MPSA) is a good next step. You may want to present at a conference focusing on a particular subfield (e.g., state politics and policy). Your advisor should help you evaluate the appropriateness of a conference for your work.

While dissertating, aim to present your findings at national conferences. Doing so gets your project noticed and gives you job talk practice. Furthermore, papers presented at conferences such as APSA also have a significantly higher likelihood of being cited (Lopez de Leon and McQuillen 2020).

Graduate students, junior scholars, and underrepresented scholars often face additional access barriers to conferences that are financial and non-financial in nature. Sections will often sponsor student travel and/or membership fees. Conferences are increasingly providing nursing stations and scholarships for childcare services. Take advantage of the subsidized graduate student hotel rates. This block of hotel rooms often sells out on the first day, so make sure to consistently check when they become available. If you miss out, check Twitter for fellow grad students seeking roommates for the conference.

Dining out is expensive. Many publishers hold morning breakfast surveys or focus groups, offering a continental breakfast and easy cash. Conferences often host coffee bars-the one at MPSA is famous for its lavish coffee bar. Receptions are an easy way to eat dinner. Most receptions are open to all attendees, unless otherwise specified. If you made a friend at a university that is sponsoring a reception, text them you will meet them there. You can eat dinner, meet up with new friends, and network all in a single stroke.

Clothing is often a barrier for students with limited funds. Don't forget your university career closet! Also, on Twitter, there are often clothing swaps prior to a large conference. Traditional costs of conferencing, such as poster printing and business cards, have become obsolete. Your Twitter handle does more heavy lifting than a business card, and e-posters make the costly poster print no longer necessary.

Non-financial barriers to access also exist. Unfriendly environments, a poor sense of community, and even differential panel or poster acceptance can hinder underrepresented scholars. All of these issues can, to a limited extent, be mitigated via networking. Finding your "group," your set of friends, collaborators, or mentors can provide a sense of belonging, ground you in the discipline, and provide clear avenues of mentorship, publication, and career opportunities.

Networking Opportunities

Networking is a skill you need to hone. Traditional networking still exists, but more modern and casual events are increasing in popularity. In this section, we discuss formal and informal networking at political science conferences.

Conferences vary in the types of networking opportunities they provide, but all offer opportunities for attendees to become acquainted. Before the conference, strategically consider where and how you will spend your time. Review the program carefully. Highlight the sessions you need to see for your research and those you would like to see to support your colleagues and friends. Contact people you met online who you would be interested in meeting face-to-face and find out where and when they will be presenting.

Much conference networking takes place at receptions, in the hallways and lobby of the hotel, and in section meetings. Additionally, sponsored receptions are thrown by publishers, think tanks, organizations, association sections, working groups, and university departments for networking. There are national and regional conferences specifically tailored to BIPOC, such as the National Conference of Black Political Scientists (NCOBPS), and the Politics of Immigration, Race, and Ethnicity Consortium (PRIEC). One example of networking with publishers is the book fair at APSA's Annual Meeting. This extensive book fair exposes you to texts and other materials you may choose to use in your courses. The fair will provide you information about appropriate outlets for your research. This type of interaction with publishers is rare outside of a book fair. Additionally, larger conferences often include sections for various identity groups. Sectional business meetings and receptions can offer graduate students access to new sources of friendships, collaboration, and mentorship.

Once you have a good idea of your conference schedule, look at the social events. For smaller conferences, meals and happy hours may be group events that everyone attends. Join in, have fun, and mingle! If you are shy, remember that you are attending the conference because you and the other attendees are passionate about at least one thing in common—your research areas.

Receptions can be scary, especially at large conferences such as APSA or MPSA. Take advantage of first-timers' receptions. At MPSA, 5-7 graduate students are put at a table with a "host," a faculty member or senior graduate student very familiar with the conference, hotel, and city. It is a more relaxed, small-scale opportunity to meet other graduate students from around the world, socialize, and mingle. Large-scale receptions such as the President's or final reception offer more scholars to mingle with, but it helps to pre-arrange a reception partner.

Note that conferences act as the main social mechanism in political science. Conferences are where faculty and students have a chance to catch up with friends. Thus, they can be a difficult environment to make new friends. As the receptions often take place at the end of the conference, you have the time to make new friends with whom you can meet at the reception.

Much networking occurs in the hotel lobby and in the hallways before and after panels. Even occasionally in the elevator! It is useful to get to a panel early: seating can be limited, and a surprising amount of glad-handing is done while panelists situate themselves.

Once panels end, they often spill out into the hallways as audience members ask panelists questions. Panelists want people to engage with their work and are often happy to discuss their work in more detail after panels if they have time. If a panelist is in the hallway holding court, join. Listen, ask questions, get their information, and follow up. This is an excellent way to identify scholarship and scholars that you wish to engage with, and is a low-cost manner of networking.

At the panels you attend, do you repeatedly see the same faces? Introduce yourself and ask their thoughts on a few of the panels you both attended. You likely share research interests. The time before and after panels is ideal for this type of casual networking.

Do not forget the exhibitor hall! It is a great place to get swag, but also to network with representatives from programs like ICPSR and publishers. If your dissertation is in book format, it is never too early to begin asking questions about what publishers need and expect when transforming a dissertation into a book. Publishers also often have opportunities for early career scholars to conduct paid surveys, review textbooks, or contribute to test banks. A working relationship with a publisher can provide you with information, and potentially cash.

Section meetings are an excellent and under-utilized networking channel. Most graduate students assume section meetings are closed to them and offer little utility. Not true! Section business meetings are where new policies and programs are set for the sections you belong to or present panels on. Besides agenda setting, sections often give awards and offer travel scholarships for conferences. Few graduate students attend these meetings, but they can be useful spaces to introduce yourself to senior scholars you otherwise would have difficulty meeting.

If meals are not prescheduled, look for opportunities to join lunches, dinners, or happy hours for your sections or groups. In addition to providing networking opportunities, you can often save a little money on food by attending and may hear about opportunities to apply for grants, awards, or funds that may be section or group specific.

Organizations hold receptions to seek out new graduate student members. These organizations often hold lucrative fellowship and travel scholarship opportunities and conduct resume and writing group forums. If you plan to go the alt-ac route, meeting recruiters and leaders of these organizations is very useful. Perhaps you desire to go the publishing route. Use conferences to seek out new employment rather than publishing opportunities. For those interested in agency analyst positions, government agencies still recruit at some conferences, as well.

New Ways to Network

We discussed traditional networking in the preceding section. However, networking has evolved with the growth and popularity of political science Twitter. Hashtags such as #poliscitweets and #PSJMinfo are often the first sources of information on new conferences, journals, workshops, and jobs. Twitter is also a key community space during conferences. Graduate students and junior faculty often put out a call for hangouts, coffee meetups, knitting circles, or D&D meetups using Twitter. Informal meetups are an excellent way to grow your social and scholarly network. Informal meals and dine arounds can also be a great way to network, as can grabbing a coffee with someone who attended a panel with you. Most conference attendees have networking and sharing their work in mind.

Although networking can initially feel awkward, you share a common goal and interests. Do not be afraid to DM someone posting about a meetup, even if you do not follow one another. The poster's intent is to meet new friends! Perhaps you want to attend a reception, but it feels too intimidating to do on your own. In late afternoon, Twitter is often awash with "who is attending X reception?" posts. These posts make excellent ways to attend with and meet your fellow scholars (and you have their profile pic to help limit awkward introductions).

Caretaker Networking

If you are concerned about managing caretaking and conference responsibilities, keep in mind that many larger conferences offer childcare on site. Even if you cannot attend multiple meals or conference events, make an effort to attend at least one. Also inquire if family members are welcome at events. Often, for smaller conferences, family members are welcome at meals and happy hours.

What Not to Do at Conferences

In addition to knowing what you should do, there are also some things to avoid at conferences.

Do not: (1) ignore instructions from session chairs, (2) become defensive when listening to suggestions from the discussant, or (3) promise more than you can deliver.

Make sure that your proposed project fits your timeline for completion. It is okay to submit a work-in-progress that is part of a larger project, but do not promise a discussion of findings if you may still be collecting data when the conference date arrives. Similarly, volunteer for service roles (e.g., discussant, chair, roundtable participant), but try not to accept any assignments that you cannot fulfill.

Only participate in post-panel Q&As with constructive comments. The goal is to help panelists improve their work, not to show others in the room how many holes you can poke in the theory, research design, or data.

Avoid being rude or disrespectful to people from any rank or institution. Be the colleague people want to work with! You never know who your future research collaborator, grant/award committee chair, or hiring manager might be.

Be kind to yourself as you navigate your first conferences. Do not overthink awkward interactions or unpleasant experiences; not every conference is the same and persistently engaging in conferences can be highly rewarding. Such large-scale gatherings will exhibit the very best and worst characteristics of our discipline. Stay encouraged and positive about your work and yourself as a person and scholar. The next interaction may be life changing. We often meet our closest friends, collaborators, and occasionally partners at these events.

If you feel uncomfortable at larger conferences, take advantage of smaller ones. If smaller conferences are more difficult for you, consider larger or medium conferences. Be persistent and you will find a conference community where you feel welcomed.

After the Conference

Follow-up with people you met to thank them for their time and express your desire to work together in the future (if appropriate). Send hand-written thank you cards after requesting and receiving 1:1 or 2:1 mentoring over a meal. If you discussed collaborating with someone, express your enthusiasm for proceeding and eagerness to learn more about the project timeline and next steps. Save any notes, screenshots, or slides where you can find them easily; you don't want to forget the most relevant tips, information, and ideas you gathered!

References

Argyle, Lisa P., & Mendelberg, Tali. (2020). Improving Women's Advancement in Political Science: What We Know About What Works. *PS: Political Science & Politics*, 53(4), 718-722. doi:10.1017/S1049096520000402

Lopez de Leon, Fernanda Leite & McQuillin, Ben (2020). The Role of Conferences on the Pathway to Academic Impact: Evidence from a natural experiment. *The Journal of Human Resources*, 55(1), 164-193. URL: http://jhr.uwpress.org/content/55/1/164.full.pdf+html.

O'Brien, Diana Z. (2020). Navigating Political Science as a Woman. *PS: Political Science & Politics*, 53(2),

315-317. doi:10.1017/S1049096519002154

Oester, S., Cigliano, J. A., Hind-Ozan, E. J., & Parsons, E. C. (2017). Why Conferences Matter—An Illustration from the International Marine Conservation Congress. *Frontiers in Marine Science*, 4. doi:10.3389/fmars.2017.00257.

22

Hidden Expenses in Graduate School: Navigating Financial Precarity and Elitism

Devon Cantwell-Chavez[1] & Alisson Rowland[2]

1. University of Ottawa 2. University of California, Irvine

KEYWORDS: Internal Funding, External Funding, Direct Coverage, and Reimbursement-Based Coverage.

Introduction

When applying to political science programs, prospective applicants often consider tuition, cost of living, and assistantship stipends. (See chapter 3 for additional insight into these considerations during the application process, and chapter 23 for more insight about grant applications.) However, there are many "hidden" expenses that creep up during the course of a program which can create significant financial barriers for many students. This chapter discusses additional costs to anticipate throughout a political science PhD program, along with both traditional and creative ways to pay for these expenses. An important caveat is that the usefulness of this advice will vary pending many factors including your class background, documentation status, nationality, family obligations, and so on. Despite giving advice for successfully navigating these expenses, we strongly condemn systematic financial barriers to graduate school as they not only actively harm students' fiscal and mental well-being, but also limit access for historically marginalized groups. Hence we conclude by encouraging those in positions of power, including faculty, administrators, and organizational leaders, to promote reforms that minimize financial distress and increase access.

Funding Types and How to Use Them

Some funds are single-time applications, whereas others are renewable. Knowing the frequency, and form, of funding opportunities is necessary to choosing the best option for you. There are two primary forms of funds.

Internal funding sources refer to all opportunities found within your university, including: (1) department-based funds, (2) school-based funds, (3) university-wide funds, (4) grants associated with university-affiliated research centers and/or labs, and (5) one-off occasions offered by your university.[1]

External funding sources refer to all other opportunities, including: (1) funds associated with other research centers, (2) governmental or non-governmental organizations, or (3) professional bodies such as American Political Science Association (APSA) and International Studies Association (ISA).

As important as identifying funding sources is knowing the different ways you can receive these funds. There are two primary ways: (1) *direct coverage*, where the money is provided upfront and prior to needing to spend it; or (2) *reimbursement-based*, where you spend your own funds first, provide receipts to the designated party, then wait to be reimbursed for the total sum.

If funding is reimbursement based, you will need an accounting system to manage receipts of what was purchased, and when. We have created a template to reference when tracking expenses.[2] Regardless of the disbursement method, it is always a good idea to keep detailed account of the materials you submit, the notification timeline, how the money is meant to be used, and any other unique regulations or instructions.

While these are the two most common methods, funding distribution methods will vary by organization. The rising utilization of reimbursements means the reality for many is having to pay out of pocket to perform expected scholarly duties (e.g., conferences, invited talks, data collection). Reimbursement can take anywhere from a few weeks up to 8 or 9 months (@SchutzAustin 10:30 AM). This places disproportionate burdens on first-generation students and students from historically low-income backgrounds who may have less access to funds and safety nets, or who may even have significant responsibilities in providing funds to parents and other family members. (See chapters 54-61 in the section Strategies for Addressing Implicit Bias, Harassment, and Assault, which provide additional insight into the way financial concern affects students with different intersectional identities.) Failing to meet requirements to receive the reimbursement can result not only in lost funds, but also in an inability to apply for the opportunity in the next cycle. To help you decide when and how to use funds, we discuss standard and hidden fees associated with graduate school.

Standard Costs

Some costs are fairly expected, such as conference travel, workshops, or job interview expenses, whereas others like dissertation filing fees or research expenses can be unanticipated. Being aware of the different costs you may incur as you progress will maximize your financial autonomy, as these expenses are often not articulated to prospective and new PhD students.

Conferences and Workshops

Conferences are a recurring expense to consider. On average, you should try to secure funding to attend at least one conference or workshop per year. A guide and sample budget is listed at the end of this chapter.[3] Some conference expenses, such as hotel, flight, meals, and transportation, are obvious. However, there are other expenses that need to be factored in depending on your circumstances. These expenses include childcare, professional clothing, visas and other paperwork, poster printing, and business cards. Do not overlook potential temporary costs. For example, many hotels charge an "incidental fee" and hold that amount on your card for three-to-five days after check-out. Call the hotel in advance to ask about this fee, as the amount can range between $15-$300 (or higher). If you are paying with a debit card, the incidentals fee can sometimes be higher than it would be if you use a credit card. Common ways to offset the costs of travel are identifying internal and external travel grants, becoming a member of the sponsoring association, and registering early.

External Travel Support

For external travel support, a number of conferences, including APSA and the International Studies Association (ISA), offer travel grants. Some conference sections, which are groups dedicated to subjects or issue areas, also offer funding support. We have created a list of common funding resources.[4] Another way to receive fundings support is through volunteering. Some conferences, such as ISA, will issue calls for volunteers and offer to waive registration and possibly even membership fees. These methods of external funding are usually available multiple times, though some may provide one-time-only support across your graduate career. For funds that are only offered once, you may want to consider saving your application for an expensive conference (e.g., one that requires international travel or an extended stay in a high-cost city) or to attend at a strategic time, perhaps near the end of your program when on the job market.

Many conferences are hosted by professional organizations, which offer memberships. In addition to providing access to online forums, resources, and scholarships, membership usually also discounts registration fees. There are also conference mentorship programs such as the ASPA Founders Fellows program, the ISA Pay-It-Forward program, and the ISA Global South Mentorship program, which provide travel assistance along with mentorship. These programs, and others, can be found in the common funding resources guide. Finally, organizations like ISA are beginning to defray childcare expenses with both subsidized childcare services and grants to make attendance more affordable. Chapter 21 provides additional valuable tips on budgeting and grappling with the financial barriers of conferences.

Internal Travel Funds

In addition to external funding sources, institutional resources can play a major role in making conferences affordable. Dr. Anna Meier discusses variability in conference funding for students in her 2019 blog post on this topic. As of that year, as the graph below illustrates, respondents' institutions ranged from no guaranteed funding per year to around $2,200 per year (Meier 2019).

Figure 22.1: Guaranteed Funds Per Year, Political Science PhD Programs

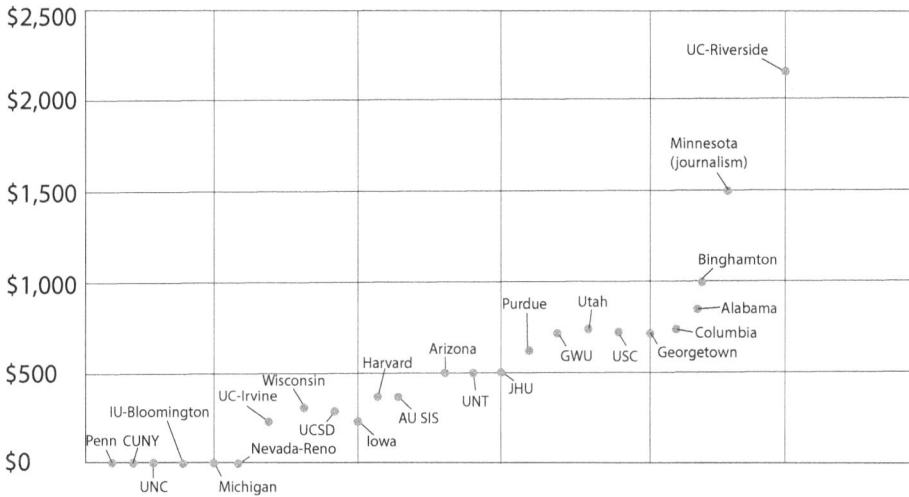

Source: (Meier 2019)

Although not a formal study, Meier (2019) provides a good picture of how varied institutional support can be and what to expect. Graduate divisions, colleges or schools, unions, and student government associations within your university may have a general pool of funds available for all graduate students to support their professional development. If you are a member of an ethnic or racial group that has been historically marginalized on campuses, you may also be able to access funding through ethnic and racial diversity resource centers (ex: Black Student Union, Movimiento Estudiantil Chicanx de Aztlán (MEChA)). These funds can be "once per lifetime" or renewable. If access is structured as first-come, first-served, you will want to apply for the funding as soon as you are eligible to apply. Often, you do not need to be accepted to your conference yet to apply for the funding, although check specific requirements at your institution. In other cases, there may be a lottery system to determine who receives funding.

Your area of study may also open you up to funding opportunities. For example, your university may have cultural and/or language centers. Teaching and learning centers may also provide grants if you plan to participate in pedagogy-focused professional development workshops. These centers often receive federal, state, and private grants and offer various opportunities for students to apply for funding throughout the year.

Finally, some professors may have research or conference funds that they may or may not be permitted to use to support their graduate students. If you are working closely with a professor on a paper that will be presented at a conference, it may be worth asking if funds are available to support your attendance. Research funds from professors can sometimes be used to cover travel costs until you can be reimbursed. Ask faculty about this option early to determine if this support is available to you, and to learn of restrictions or stipulations attached to it.

Stretching Out Your Dollars

Even in generous programs, it is unlikely that you will receive funding adequate to pay for the entirety of your conference participation. A common refrain graduate students often hear is "just put it on a credit card." If you have access to lines of credit, consider a credit card that rewards purchases with airline miles or a cash back percentage, which can help to defray future conference expenses. Small loans are a similar option. Note, educational loans will only be available to you if you have not met your full maximum, also called "cost of attendance," for the year. Unfortunately, both of these options pose immense difficulties for low-income, international, and undocumented students. While we are ethically and morally opposed to the financial power systems that pressure many students into taking on this additional debt, we do include it as an option in this chapter because it is a common way that graduate students make ends meet.

An option that is more accessible is sharing expenses with colleagues. You may also be able to reduce transportation costs by coordinating arrival and departure from the conference site and splitting expenses with colleagues, by taking public transportation, or by driving. As you will notice, it can be harder to find grants that cover the cost of food. The good news about conferences is that most of them are located in downtown locations with nearby convenience stores. Stocking up on snacks and caffeinated beverages is thrifty. If you are able to walk a few blocks, everything will be two-to-three times less expensive than near the hotel.

A catch-22 with funding is that the earlier you can pay for expenses, the cheaper it is. For example, there are usually early-bird registration fees that can save you hundreds of dollars. If you are tight on funds to pay for upfront costs, talk to the conference organizers. Some conferences require that you register by a certain date in order to remain on the program. If you reach out and explain that you cannot pay the registration fee until a later date, they can often work with you to pay the registration later when you have funds available.

Finally, you get what you pay for with discount travel airlines. Read your terms and conditions carefully because you might get nickeled and dimed for bringing a carry-on bag or choosing a seat. You may also have your flight itinerary canceled or changed, risking missing your panel. If you choose a discount airline that has these potential risks, you may want to consider adding travel insurance.

Hidden Costs

Beyond conferences, you will likely uncover an array of hidden costs before graduating. In this section, we will discuss some of the most common ones as well as options for covering these expenses.

First, even if you are "fully funded," your stipend and tuition waiver typically will not cover quarterly or semester fees. Sometimes these fees must be paid to the department, and sometimes the university. These fees may include expenses such as union dues and healthcare premiums, as well as various building, lab, or service usage fees. These expenses can range from a few hundred to thousands of dollars each term. Some universities assess the fees at the start of the term, others towards the middle or end of each term. Current students or department staff should be able to help you find the due dates and cost breakdowns for your specific program.

Second, books are often not provided. Some professors will generously assign articles or books that can be accessed through university library services. If this is not the case, they will often put course books on "reserve" at the library, which allows you to read and/or scan the chapters needed for class. You can also ask the professor or a student who has previously taken that course if they have an extra copy of the text that you can borrow. Another option is to split the cost of the books with one or multiple students and develop a system for sharing them.

Third, research software and fieldwork expenses are critical tools that you will need to complete milestones in your program. Research software costs can be mitigated with open-access statistical software options like R, Tableau Public, QGIS, but such options often come with limitations in either ease of use or function. Additionally, you may need specialty software like Stata, SPSS, Nvivo, Atlas.ti, and Covidence. Sometimes, your school may have a license for student use in a virtual lab, or for a discounted or free account. You may also be able to sign up for 30 to 90-day free trials, which may be an option for short-term projects. Librarians or staff will often help you navigate available software options that meet your needs.

Fieldwork and research expenses can also be significant. Some common expenses include survey or experiment incentives, travel costs, transcription costs, translation costs, and even publication costs (if you want to publish open access research). When fieldwork involves travel, some of the sources of funding in the conference section may be applicable. Small grants may also cover expenses.

Fourth, there are many costs that sneak up on graduate students at the finish line, including dissertation filing fees and regalia. You should reach out to recently graduated students from your program to ask about final year fees. Some graduate students have been able to negotiate the cost of regalia as part of their start-up package if they are expected to wear it while participating in convocations and graduation ceremonies. Many students will also manage expenses by renting or borrowing regalia. Finally, it is also important to pay attention to when you will lose access to health care and other benefits if you are a funded graduate assistant. Be sure to discuss this timeline with your dissertation advisor and schedule your defense and filing according to your needs.

Fifth, be aware that you may experience gaps in employment during your graduate career. If you are a funded student, your first paycheck may be delayed by several months into the term. Moreover, many graduate assistantships are nine-month positions that provide no financial support beyond the academic year. If you do not secure a summer teaching or research position, you may have a lapse in payment after the academic year ends, typically in May or June. Be sure to ask your advisor and professors about opportunities for summer employment to help cover expenses. If you pursue a traditional academic career, be aware that you will also likely have a lapse in payment between your last graduate paycheck and your first paycheck as a professor. If this lapse leaves you strapped for funds or affects your access to credit, make plans for how to cover moving expenses as you may need to relocate across the country (or the world). Most colleges and universities have historically reimbursed new employees for relocation expenses, but some are willing to negotiate a moving stipend or signing bonus in advance instead. Another potential negotiating tactic is to request a July 1st start date rather than August or September. (See chapter 46 for additional advice on negotiating your first position.)

Conclusion

This chapter offers an overview of the anticipated, and unanticipated, costs associated with doctoral programs and some strategies to reduce them. While some of these costs may be covered by your institution, many are not. Graduate school requires four to ten years, and stipends are rarely sufficient to make ends meet for one person, let alone those with other family or financial obligations. The practices outlined here amount to survival tactics to avoid extreme financial distress. The onus is on the academy at large to shift the culture around reimbursement, which is an elitist practice, towards direct cost coverage. In researching this chapter, we were startled to learn that even within universities, departments have actively chosen to retain reimbursement policies, even when they have the flexibility and resources for direct pay. Deans, chairs, and graduate studies directors can be pivotal in changing these policies and practices. Faculty can also take an active role in helping to minimize harm to graduate students by actively checking in with advisees about conference and workshop affordability, providing support for grant writing and identifying other funding opportunities, and assisting with cost coverage when feasible. It is not enough to admit marginalized and vulnerable scholars, the academy must also provide the necessary tools, resources, and practices for them to thrive. As students provide labor as teaching assistants and research assistants in addition to their own research output, universities should provide direct cost coverage for costs associated with these tasks; this includes conferences, professional memberships, course materials, dissertation filing fees, and tuition fees, among others. While there are other ways students are marginalized and forced out of the academy, financial precarity causes undue physical and mental stress, along with threats to livelihood. Adopting full cost coverage policies is a necessary and direct step in reducing financial precarity for graduate students.

Endnotes

1   This is not an exhaustive list of internal opportunities. Some other places to check at your institution include: graduate divisions, program offices, unions, student government, and individual professors.

2   https://bit.ly/ConferenceBudgetWorksheet

3   https://bit.ly/ConferenceBudgetGuide

4   https://bit.ly/ConferenceFundingResources

References

Meier, Anna. 2019. "Grad Student Conference Funding: A Preliminary Lay of the Land." (Blog). http://annameier.net/grad-student-conference-funding-a-preliminary-lay-of-the-land/.

Schutz, Austin (@SchutzAustin). 2021. "Hey everyone, welcome back to 'how do I gradschool?'" (Twitter). 12.13. 10:30 AM. https://twitter.com/SchutzAustin/status/1470461253378318338?s=20

23

Show Me the Money: Information, Strategies, and Guidelines for Applying to External Grants and Fellowships in Graduate School

Angie Torres-Beltran[1], Cameron Mailhot[1], Elizabeth Dorssom,[2] & Christina Boyes[3]

1. Cornell University 2. Lincoln University of Missouri 3. Centro de Investigación y Docencia Económicas

KEYWORDS: External Grants, Fellowships.

Introduction

Political science graduate students are encouraged to apply to *external grants* and *fellowships* during their academic careers. These grants and fellowships provide a myriad of benefits for applicants, including not only access to financial and institutional resources but also the opportunity to further clarify and improve your research agenda. However, identifying and applying to these external grants and fellowships is not always clear. In this chapter, we provide an overview of what external grants and fellowships are and the different purposes they serve, a snapshot of the awards themselves and how they may fit into the timeline of your graduate career, a discussion of the barriers and trade-offs you might encounter when applying, and a set of personal anecdotes delineating what the process entails.

What Are External Grants and Fellowships?

External grants and fellowships are awarded from an entity that is not your home institution. These awards are available from an array of institutions and offices, including research centers, private organizations, governments, think tanks, professional associations, and nonprofit organizations. Generally, fellowships are awarded to people, and grants are awarded to projects.

Applying to and successfully securing an external grant or fellowship is useful for a handful of reasons. First and foremost, external grants and fellowships provide you with the support you need to progress and advance your dissertation; this can include achieving language proficiency, conducting initial or primary-stage fieldwork, or completing your dissertation (for additional information, see chapters 15 and 20 on the dissertation and fieldwork, respectively). Second, external grants and fellowships may provide you with invaluable access to mentoring and networking opportunities by exposing you to potential colleagues, such as researchers or policymakers. Third, applying to external grants and fellowships may ultimately improve your understanding and explanation of your research agenda by providing you with opportunities to practice your descriptive writing skills and refining your narratives after receiving constructive feedback and successfully securing funding. Lastly, grants and fellowships signal a successful academic record. To be competitive on the job market, you need to display evidence of successfully obtaining and managing funding sources for your research; obtaining external grants and fellowships can signal a degree of professionalism and a third-party's support for your research agenda.

Pulling Back the Curtain on Fellowships and Grants

Regardless of your subfield or research interests, there are a wide array of fellowship and grants available to support you at different stages in your graduate career. Before pursuing an external grant or fellowship, you should consider the purpose that the grant or fellowship will serve and your overall eligibility. For what do you need the funding? How much is needed? When is the funding needed? By answering these questions, you can identify the type of grant or fellowship needed, the specific amount you may receive, and whether a specific grant or fellowship is appropriate for your needs.

Table 23.1 below provides a brief overview of external grants and fellowships according to the career stage for which the source is most useful and the general purposes they serve. We include specific examples in each category. While this is in no way an exhaustive list, the table should provide you with a general idea of what external grants and fellowships are available for you at different stages of your career.

Table 23.1: Stages, Purpose, Types, and Examples of External Grants and Fellowships

Stage in Graduate Career	Purpose	Award Type	Examples
Early-stage student	Preparation, relocation, personal moving costs, preparation for a new program, stipend	Fellowship	APSA Diversity Fellowship*
Early or mid-stage student	Long-term graduate training and support	Fellowship, grant	Ford Foundation Predoctoral Fellowship*, National Science Foundation (NSF) Graduate Research Fellowship Program (GFRP)
Early and mid-stage students and early candidates	Support for dissertation- relevant work: fieldwork, language training, data collecting and processing	Fellowship, grant	SSRC International Dissertation Research Fellowship, APSA Doctoral Dissertation Research Improvement Grants (DDRIG), Foreign Language and Area Studies Fellowship, American Institute for Southeast European Studies Graduate/Postdoctoral Fellowship, Horowitz Foundation for Social Policy Grant
Candidates	Dissertation completion, preparation for job market, contribution to another project, networking and professionalization	Fellowship, grant, pre-doctoral position	American Association of Women Dissertation Fellow Harry Frank Guggenheim Emerging Scholar Award, Mellon/ACLS Dissertation Completion Fellowships, United States Institute of Peace Peace Scholar Fellow
Any stage	Attend workshops and conferences; obtain additional methodological, technical, and language training	Grant	APSA Lee Ann Fujii Travel Grant, ISA Travel Grant, ICI Attendance Grant
Any stage	Service, policy analysis, publication	Fellowship, grant	APSA Public Scholarship Program Fellowship, Janne Nuclear Security Visiting Fellow at the Truman Cent National Policy

*Requires identification with one or more historically underrepresented groups in the academy.

Barriers and Trade-Offs

When applying to external grants and fellowships, you should consider the barriers and trade-offs you may face in the application process and once funding is secured. In this section, we review potential restraints in terms of timing and eligibility, and draw attention to strategies for attenuating the effects and implications thereof.

Barriers to the Application Process

External grants and fellowships often include distinct requirements and objectives as part of the application process. In these cases, eligibility may be restricted to a specific stage of academic career, or you may be expected to complete a certain set of criteria by the end of the award period. Some external awards may target applicants from specific (historically underrepresented) groups, depending upon one's socio-economic, racial/ethnic, gender, sexual, citizenship, or caretaker status. Other external funding sources may require research projects that focus on specialized topics (e.g., peacebuilding in post-conflict societies, the political behavior of racial and ethnic minorities, or experimental research in the Global South.)

First-time applicants may overlook or misinterpret what these requirements mean and entail; those from historically underrepresented groups, for example, may be doubly-disadvantaged as they navigate complicated application processes in addition to discovering the "hidden curriculum" of norms, soft skills, and informal knowledge that often makes applying to grants and fellowships much easier (Barham and Wood 2021; Calarco 2020). For example, students from underrepresented backgrounds are often expected to "trauma-dump" in their application statements in order to demonstrate their resilience and ability to persevere, despite their circumstances (Megginson 2021). This may pressure applicants from underrepresented groups to provide deep, emotionally exhausting personal experiences to demonstrate "worthiness" when applying. To mitigate these effects and develop strong applications, we suggest you reach out to advisors and mentors, senior graduate students, past (successful) applicants, or colleagues with similar backgrounds for assistance in writing application narratives. We furthermore suggest that applicants receive feedback on their materials from scholars who mirror potential reviewers.

To apply to certain external grants and fellowships, you must be at a certain stage in your graduate career. Some funding sources may restrict applications to pre-candidacy graduate students or to those with certain degree statuses. A common example of this is the NSF Graduate Research Fellowships Program (NSF GRFP). Others may only be available to individuals further along in their studies. For instance, dissertation completion fellowships, such as the APSA Doctoral Dissertation Research Improvement Grant (APSA DDRIG), require applicants to have completed and passed their comprehensive exams and dissertation prospectus defense before applying. Other advanced funding sources, such as predoctoral fellowships, may require applicants to demonstrate that they have made significant progress on their dissertation research. This may be demonstrated, for example, through either dissertation chapter(s) or stand-alone article(s) (for additional information, see chapter 15 on the dissertation). It is thus important to confirm your eligibility before beginning the application process.

Importantly, external grant and fellowship applications often take a significant amount of time to complete. When applying, you must consider if you can allocate your time efficiently to manage the workload of applying to a number of funding sources. For example, almost all applications require approval from an applicant's advisor or an endorsement from your graduate school. The former may simply require a signature, which may be received within a day, while the latter may require a submission of the full application to your graduate institution's fellowship office or equivalent for approval, which may take a week or more to obtain. Additionally, some applications require only a few supporting documents outlining your projects, while others require several statements justifying the dissertation, detailing the work to be completed during the funding period, and so forth. To streamline the workflow, create a work plan with the fellowship/grant's information and application requirements, deadlines, and stages of submission. This system will serve as a quick "go-to" guide as you go back and forth between applications. Rank-order and prioritize the grants and fellowships from which you will benefit the most. This allows you to strategically allocate your (limited) time when applying to funding sources you desire or require the most.

Trade-Offs After Successfully Securing an External Grant or Fellowship

The trade-offs you face after securing external funding are just as important as barriers to application. We outline the two most common impacts that grants and fellowships may have on you and your work.

First is the effect external grants or fellowships have on your institutional responsibilities. You may serve as a research or teaching assistant during your graduate career, as stipulated in the funding package that accompanied your acceptance letter (for additional information about teaching assistantships, see chapter 28). Securing a large external grant or fellowship may, however, "buy out" your requirements by supplanting the stipend and tuition rates that your assistantships ordinarily cover. This may be beneficial in that it allows you more time to focus on your own research; it may, however, be disadvantageous in that it prevents you from accessing these additional forms of professionalization. We therefore recommend that you take into consideration how awarded grants or fellowships affect your preexisting duties.

Second are the requirements that a grant or fellowship may present during or following the award period. Specifically, funders may require recipients to provide a set of outputs for their institution. For example, you may be asked to present your ongoing research at a conference or symposium during the award period. You may also be required to brief funders regularly on your research progress, as laid out in the application or letter of acceptance. This is the case for Peace Scholars serving at the United States Institute of Peace (USIP). Others may require you to provide a report or share a (academic or non-academic) publication at the end of their fellowship or grant period. The Horowitz Foundation for Social Policy, for example, has historically required grant recipients to provide evidence that they defended their dissertation, published their funded research in a peer-reviewed journal, or received an invitation to publish their funded research in a book (Horowitz n.d.). These requirements are often valuable and highly sought-after, as they provide researchers with unique opportunities to connect with policymakers or other researchers or advance their careers. However, in some instances – for example, during the early stage of your research or during periods of extensive fieldwork abroad – it may be difficult to meet these obligations. You should therefore consider how the requirements of the fellowship or grant fit into your timeline and impact your other obligations.

Personal Experiences

In this section we provide four of our personal experiences applying for and securing external funding as PhD students or candidates. We demonstrate strategies taken to secure funding based on the career timing, institutional status, and background of the authors.

Securing At-Large Funding to Conduct Candidate-Level Research

As a PhD candidate, one of your primary duties includes conducting independent research to move your dissertation forward. Doing so often requires securing funding to carry out independent research or to release you from your departmental obligations (often teaching or research assistantships). USIP's Peace Scholar Fellowship Program was able to serve this purpose for one of the authors.

Grants and fellowships for PhD candidates often require applicants to demonstrate that they and their research meet the goals and objectives of the funder. USIP's Peace Scholar Fellowship program provides financial and institutional support to a handful of PhD candidates conducting policy-relevant research in the fields of peace studies, security studies, or conflict management (USIP n.d.). Similar to many other candidacy fellowships, this program thus provides "at large" support for candidates whose dissertation research is centered around a specific theme, regardless of the candidate's background. As such, when applying for this fellowship, it was important for the author to demonstrate that he has conducted a (minimum) level of candidate-level research for his dissertation; it was also crucial for his successful application that he emphasized the ways in which his dissertation's research advances USIP's mission, instead of drawing attention to the ways in which he may meet certain demographic requirements (first-generation, low-income, and so forth), as is the case with numerous other grants and fellowships.

Utilizing External Funding to Secure Internal Funding

Financial and research support for graduate students is not equally distributed across all graduate programs: some departments not only expect you to secure external funding to support your progression through the program but also require you to apply for and secure external funding to obtain internal (institutional/departmental) funding. In this way, securing external funding may provide secondary, knock-on effects for you. This was the case for one of the authors, who was required to demonstrate her project's viability and fundability among external centers when applying for internal funding resources. In this case, applying for and successfully obtaining funding from an external institution for her research project assisted her in securing funding from her degree-granting institution as well.

Securing External Funding Prior to Graduate School

The American Political Science Association Diversity Fellowship provides financial and professional support for students from historically underrepresented backgrounds currently applying to graduate programs and those currently in their first or second year in a PhD program. When applying to this fellowship, the author, who is a member of historically underrepresented groups, sought out advice and support from past successful applicants. Given that the author was also new to political science and to research, her application focused on broad topical areas of interest versus homing in on a specific research question. The author was also able to leverage prior experience in research programs sponsored by APSA to distinguish herself from other applicants and to demonstrate her commitment to the diversity of the discipline.

Securing External Funding as an Early-Career Graduate Student

The NSF GRFP is one of the most highly sought-after external forms of funding for any graduate student. This program provides three years of support over a five-year fellowship period. For each of the three years of support, the NSF GRFP provides a stipend and cost of education allowance to the Fellow's institution. This fellowship relieves teaching and research assistance duties, providing time and financial support to complete the dissertation project and additional research. As an early-career student at an R1 University, one of the authors took advantage of the institutional support available to her as she prepared her application.

Since the NSF GRFP only allows applicants to apply once in either the first or second year of graduate school, the author chose to apply in her second year. This was strategically done for a number of reasons. First, the author was able to successfully obtain internal awards to signal her success as a researcher. Second, as a second-year student, the author was able to receive stronger letters of recommendation from professors at her institution. Third, the author was able to familiarize herself with the different forms of institution support available from various offices at her university. She was able to share her application with past successful applicants from different fields through a university-wide NSF GRFP workshop and review examples of past successful research and personal statements. The author also began her application months prior to the deadline, giving ample time to her advisor and colleagues as they read and reviewed multiple drafts.

Conclusion

You may hear regularly from your advisors, colleagues, and mentors how important it is to apply for and secure external grants and fellowships while in graduate school, yet it requires a significant amount of knowledge and expertise to understand which fellowships and grants you should consider, at what stage in your graduate career you should consider different fellowships and grants, and what considerations to keep in mind as you do so.

Our aim in this chapter has been to "pull back the curtain" on this "hidden curriculum" by providing further clarification along each of these dimensions. More specifically, we begin the chapter by providing a brief overview of what external grants and fellowships are and an outline of the different benefits available in applying for and securing them. We then provide a summary of the different purposes that grants and fellowships serve at different stages in your graduate career, providing a (non-exhaustive) list of some of the most well-known fellowships and grants within each category. We then move into a discussion of the different barriers faced and tradeoffs to keep in mind as you consider applying for external funds; we conclude with a set of vignettes highlighting the different purposes that these resources have served for the authors as they navigate their own graduate careers.

References

Barham, Elena, and Colleen Wood. 2021. "Teaching the Hidden Curriculum in Political Science." *PS: Political Science & Politics*. https://doi.org/10.1017/S1049096521001384

Calarco, Jessica McCrory. 2020. *A Field Guide to Grad School: Uncovering the Hidden Curriculum*. Princeton, NJ: Princeton University Press.

Horowitz Foundation. "Grant Information." Horowitz Foundation for Social Policy. Retrieved November 14, 2021. https://www.horowitz-foundation.org/grant-info.

Megginson, Elijah. 2021. "When I Applied to College, I Didn't Want to 'Sell My Pain.'" *The New York Times*. Retrieved November 14, 2021. https://www.nytimes.com/2021/05/09/opinion/college-admissions-essays-trauma.html.

USIP. "Peace Scholar Fellowship Program." United States Institute of Peace. Retrieved November 15, 2021. https://www.usip.org/grants-fellowships/fellowships/peace-scholar-fellowship-program.

24 | Political Science Publications: Charting Your Own Path

Shane Nordyke[1]

1. University of South Dakota

KEYWORDS: Peer-Reviewed Journal Articles, Field-Focused Articles, Articles on the Scholarship of Teaching and Learning.

Introduction

The political science discipline includes a broad diversity of publication types that scholars may contribute to as a part of their professional career. Each type has unique benefits and challenges for the scholar and most scholars will likely publish in more than one type of outlet at some point. Understanding the array of options can allow academics to craft a research agenda that is more personally fulfilling while still achieving their career goals. You may find certain types of scholarship more personally fulfilling than others and can carve out a larger share of your research portfolio for that type of work. You may also find that your personality and research skills are more relevant to one type than another. This chapter will briefly describe each while reflecting on some of the advantages and disadvantages they offer.

When considering publication types, it is important to have explicit conversations with your department about the specific expectations for publications within your research portfolio. When possible, look for opportunities to expand the work you are doing to multiple publication types. If there are findings within that program evaluation you conducted for a local non-profit that are potentially interesting for a broader academic audience, consider translating the work into a peer-reviewed publication. If there are specific findings from your published academic work that would be useful to practitioners, consider publishing a report or book that highlights the most important findings for those in practice. If your recent academic research touches on a currently relevant political debate, consider translating your findings to a popular press text or blog post. Within the parameters of your institution's expectations, experiment with multiple publication types to find what works best for you and your goals as a scholar.

Peer-Reviewed Journal Articles

Considered the cornerstone of research for most political scientists, *peer-reviewed journal articles* are the predominant publication type within the discipline. Peer-reviewed journal articles can be categorized as *field-focused* or *on the scholarship of teaching and learning* (SOTL).

Most graduate programs focus extensively on preparing students to author peer-reviewed single study papers that focus on the questions most pressing or relevant within their chosen subfields. Seminar paper assignments often mirror the expectations of these papers, which typically require an original contribution to a field of study. The contribution could be qualitative or quantitative, theoretical, descriptive, or empirical, single authored or co-authored, but will be written with an academic audience in mind and designed primarily to advance the current state of knowledge on a particular research question. Historically, most of this research has utilized a single study approach, but, increasingly, standalone literature reviews and meta-analyses are published as well.

Literature reviews provide an overview of the state of the discipline or research on a specific question. They often trace the development of the field or history of research on a specific question including theoretical approaches, methods, and substantive findings. Paternotte (2018) provides a good example of this approach. These literature reviews are sometimes accompanied by bibliometric analyses which evaluate the influence of specific studies within the discipline. Similarly, meta-analyses attempt to synthesize the findings on a specific question by statistically analyzing the results of multiple empirical studies to identify patterns, reveal biases, and estimate effects. Watkins and Gerrish (2018) provides a good example.

Finally, peer-reviewed journal publications also include SOTL research. Recognizing the importance of teaching within the discipline, SOTL authors apply the methodological tools they use to answer questions within their fields to evaluate the effectiveness of their pedagogy. This research may evaluate the impact of a single exercise, an entire course, or outcomes across a curriculum. The *Journal of Political Science Education*, APSA's primary publication for SOTL research, includes many excellent examples (see chapter 30 in this volume for more on APSA's Education Section). Graduate students are often well-placed to conduct meaningful SOTL research as they are still experimenting with their approach to their classes. Students interested in eventually working at institutions which are primarily teaching focused can utilize their SOTL publications to demonstrate both their research skills and their interest in evidenced based pedagogies.

While peer-reviewed journal articles are undoubtedly the primary currency for promotion within the discipline, increasing competition within publication outlets means authors can struggle to place good research in a timely manner. Articles are also most likely to be read by other academics, rather than policy makers or agency leaders. Thus, if it is important to you for your work to have public or policy impact, you may need additional outlets.

Chapters in Edited Volumes

Chapters in edited volumes often mirror journal articles in topic, approach, and method, though there is substantial variation in length and expectations. Many edited volumes also include a peer-review process. Some edited volumes are designed explicitly to be used as a resource for a course, such as Michael Nelson's *The Presidency and the Political System* (2021). Others are designed to capture a broad conversation about a particular area of research such as Daniel Cole and Elinor Ostrom's Property in *Land and Other Resources* (2012). Typically, edited volumes are populated through a solicitation process where the editor distributes a call for contributions from authors. This process provides an author a high level of confidence the work will be published if it is completed and also some assurance that it will be accompanied by other research that fits into a coherent structure on the topic. A benefit of this type of publication is potentially increased visibility of the piece to readers interested in the topic. However, many institutions do not place the same value on book chapters as they do journal articles, so it is important to know ahead of time how your work will be counted toward hiring, tenure, promotion, etc.

Applied Research and Technical Reports

While they often answer similar questions and use similar methodological approaches as journal articles, technical reports differ in many important respects. First, most applied research is designed to answer a question posed by an external stakeholder. This could be a state agency evaluating the effectiveness of a policy change, a non-profit agency evaluating programs, or a local government that needs to access public perspectives on performance. Public and non-profit agencies regularly issue grants and contracts to answer important questions about their agencies. Some of this work is done by for-profit research entities, but political scientists are also important contributors. This means the author may have less control over the exact question that is being addressed. Second, most technical reports do not undergo peer-review. While they are often published and can be replicated by other scholars, there is no independent review process of the scholarship before it is finalized. Finally, in most cases this research comes with funding to buy out course loads (i.e., reduce your required teaching), provide summer funding for researchers, or provide support for undergraduate and graduate research assistants. Applied research can be personally rewarding, as it is likely to be read by the decision makers that sponsored it and can lead to real-world policy or program changes. However, depending on the institution, it may not be given full or even any weight as research toward tenure and promotion and can instead be considered a part of public service.

Books

Political science books fall into four broad categories: original research, textbooks, practitioner-focused, and popular press. While full-length manuscripts are less likely to be required in political science than they are in other academic disciplines, they are still a common form of scholarship, especially in particular subfields. As with other publication types, it is important to know the expectations at your own institution.

Original research manuscripts are typically a close cousin to the PhD Dissertation. They include an introduction, an explanation of methodology, and the development or testing of hypotheses. There are multiple guides available online for recent PhDs on turning their dissertations into a research manuscript including some brief advice from Karen Kelsky on *The Professor Is In* blog (https://theprofessorisin.com/2016/02/26/how-to-turn-your-dissertation-into-a-book-a-special-request-post/), a guide from the publisher Palgrave McMillan (https://www.palgrave.com/gp/book-authors/your-career/early-career-researcher-hub/revising-the-dissertation), and the more detailed guide by William Germano, *From Dissertation to Book* (2013). Full length research manuscripts provide scholars the opportunity to explain their research contributions in greater depth and with a more comprehensive approach than the typical journal article will allow. The book *Agendas and Instability in American Politics* by Frank Baumgartner and Bryan Jones (2009) provides an excellent example of this type of text.

Textbooks are also a common publication form for faculty. Textbooks are written primarily for students and are often motivated by an instructor's frustration with the lack of a suitable text or the sense that they could explain the material in a way that would better resonate with students. Textbooks also offer scholars a way of translating the substantial time they have put into developing their teaching materials into a publication. This may be particularly important for scholars at teaching-heavy institutions that still require some research productivity. Whether textbooks are considered teaching or research varies from institution to institution though, so scholars will want to know how this will fit into their evaluation before spending substantial time on writing one. Writing a textbook may also improve the author's teaching, as it requires the author to prioritize the most important information on the topic and explain it in a way that will resonate with a broad audience. If widely adopted, textbooks may provide authors with a steady stream of revenue in the form of royalties and can be an especially creative outlook for faculty. Daniel Drezner's *Theories of International Relations and Zombies* (2014) provides an example of this.

Practitioner-focused books resemble textbooks in many ways but are designed more for the active practitioner in the field rather than a student in a course. These may be especially relevant for those scholars in public policy and public administration. These texts summarize the academic field of knowledge and apply it to relevant examples that are relatable to those serving in the public and non-profit sectors that may not have an academic background in political science. Dave Ammons and Dale Roenigk's *Tools for Decision Making: A Practical Guide for Local Government* or my own *Planning and Evaluation for Public Safety Leaders: A Toolkit* provide good examples of this type of resource. Practitioner-focused books may also be used as textbooks for more applied degree programs within the discipline. These texts can be especially rewarding to scholars that want to see their research utilized to improve decision making and policy outcomes on the ground, but they may not be given the same weight as original research manuscripts in hiring, tenure, and promotion decisions.

Finally, popular press books (e.g., Penguin Press), written for a broad public audience, have been a way for political scientists to communicate their findings since almost the inception of the discipline. Political Scientists often want their research to go beyond the ivory towers of the academy and shape the way potential voters and decision makers understand the field. Daniel Levisky and Steven Ziblatt's book *How Democracy Dies* (2018) provides a good example from the comparative politics subfield. However, the field still wrestles with how to appropriately weigh popular press books. They are typically not peer-reviewed or held to the same research standards as other types of publications. In order to be accessible to as broad an audience as possible, scholars often substantially reduce the nuance and complexity they provide in the text. And yet, these books serve an important purpose in elevating the visibility of our discipline to the public and ensuring our research remains relevant to decision makers. They apply the field's rich theoretical findings to current political debates. If popular, these books can generate substantially more royalty income than more purely academic publications, though increasingly scholars need to be social media savvy or already have a well-established reputation in order to be picked up by a press. Successful publication relies on a skillset that is not typically taught in political science PhD programs. As with other types of publications, it is important that scholars discuss how these publications will be factored into their evaluation before investing substantial time in their development.

Other Publications

Beyond the categories discussed above, there are many other types of publications that still frequently occur within the discipline but do not fit well into a particular category. Book reviews are short summaries of full-length manuscripts or textbooks that are helpful for other scholars in deciding which of the many books published each year are worth prioritizing. Many political science journals provide space for reflection pieces that offer thoughts on where the field ought to be headed or what scholars have learned through their teaching or research. While not empirical in nature, these reflections may inspire other scholars to empirically test or systematically evaluate the ideas presented and are an important part of the scholarly conversation. Blogs and even tweet threads have become a popular way for political scientists to communicate their expertise to the public without developing a full manuscript. The widely known Monkey Cage and 538 are both blogs started by political scientists that have gained national media attention to the methods and findings of the discipline. While few scholars will be able to populate their entire research agenda with these publications, they are a creative and productive supplement to more traditional types of research and can increase the impact of your work.

Concluding Thoughts

Some publication types are more common in specific subfields. For example, books are more common within comparative politics, and technical papers are more common for those within public policy and public administration. Institutions also value different types of publications in widely varying ways. At some institutions, SOTL studies and technical papers are given equal weight to peer-reviewed articles, at others, they are given only partial weight or counted as a part of teaching/service rather than research. As you begin to understand your skillset as a scholar, it is also worth evaluating how you might incorporate that into successful co-authored publications. If you are particularly adept at statistical analysis and writing up empirical results but find it more difficult to craft successful literature reviews, find reliable co-authors with opposite strengths and nurture those collaborations into a productive research agenda.

In short, do not fall into the trap of assuming there is only one type of research in the discipline or one role you can play as a scholar. Explore the multiple publication types and investigate how institutions value each type. This may even be one important factor you consider in deciding the type of institution you want to work for. Once you find the best fit for you and your institution, you may find your time spent on research more fulfilling than you thought possible.

References

Ammons, David N. and Dale J. Roenigk. 2019. *Tools for Decision Making: A Practical Guide for Local Government.* 3rd Edition. Oxfordshire, UK: Routledge.

Baumgartner, Frank R and Bryan D. Jones. 2009. *Agendas and Instability in American Politics.* 2nd

Edition. Chicago: University of Chicago Press.

Cole, Daniel H., and Elinor Ostrom, eds. 2012. *Property in Land and Other Resources*. Cambridge, MA: Lincoln Institute for Land Policy.

Germano, William. 2013. *From Dissertation to Book*. 2nd Edition. Chicago: University of Chicago Press.

Levitsky, Steven and Daniel Ziblatt. 2019. *How Democracies Die*. New York City: Crown Publishing.

Nelson, Michael ed. 2021. *The Presidency and the Political System*. 12th Edition. Thousand Oaks, CA: CQ Press.

Nordyke, Shane. 2021. *Planning and Evaluation for Public Safety Leaders: A Toolkit*. Oxfordshire, UK: Routledge.

Paternotte, David. 2018 "Coming Out of the Political Science Closet: The Study of LGBT Politics in Europe." *European Journal of Politics and Gender* 1 (1-2): 55-74.

Watkins, Shannon L., and Gerrish, Ed. 2018. "The Relationship Between Urban Forests and Race: A Meta-Analysis." *Journal of Environmental Management* (JEMA) 209:152-168.

25 | Turning Term Papers into Articles: Paths to a Productive Peer-Review Process

Michael P.A. Murphy[1]

1. Queen's University

KEYWORDS: Term Papers, Articles, Audience, Context.

Introduction

While the normative question of whether graduate students should publish as a matter of scholarly formation remains open, an emerging consensus holds that publication approaches necessity for employability in the hypercompetitive post-Great Recession academic job market (Hatch & Skipper 2016, 172). Recognizing this, many graduate school advice books offer guidance on the structure of articles and an overview of the review process (e.g., Berdahl & Molloy 2018, 125ff; Calarco 2021, 193ff), complemented by article-length guides for students on how to publish (Rich 2013; Van Cott 2005). Students can also draw on books on scholarly writing intended for a multidisciplinary audience (Belcher 2020; Silvia 2017; 2019). A second type of guidance from the graduate student advice literature identifies what source material might lead to a future publication. Karen Kelsky, for example, suggests that a master's thesis and doctoral dissertation chapters may provide preliminary material for submission (201), while other advice books suggest the adaptation of graduate-level term papers (e.g., Peters 1997; Semenza 2005; Hay 2017). These two types of publication-related advice are important supports for graduate students' first forays into academic publishing, and an important first step in building graduate student confidence is recognizing that a term paper might become an academic article (Arsenault et al. 2021).

This chapter focuses on the gap between how to publish and what to publish, drawing attention to the unique challenges that graduate students face in adapting their term papers for submission as academic articles. While this transformation is possible, it presents unique challenges that an established scholar might not face when preparing a conference paper for submission as an article. The first section of the chapter discusses the difference in genre, which we can understand as the difference between argument-first writing and contribution-first writing. The second section explores what graduate students can do, including both strategies for contribution communication and pre-submission checks for what I call "term paper-to-article red flags." The conclusion discusses how term paper revision can help prepare early career researchers to strengthen their contribution-first writing practices.

Term Papers and Articles: What's the Difference?

Whether in the form of a professor or teaching assistant, the term paper has a guaranteed audience, contractually obligated to read the work for the purposes of assessment and evaluation. Conversely, the article has an earned or an interested *audience*. While a journal with a strong sense of community may have an automatic set of readers for all articles, and other idiosyncratic motivators do emerge from time to time—a distinguished scholar's name may lure readers, and Google Scholar notifications may draw the attention of authors you have cited—the payoff for reading the work should be clear. It is not a matter of honing the argument and hoping an audience will arrive.

The guarantee of readership is closely related to the question of the term paper's contextual difference from the academic article. In the words of Eric Hayot, the "intellectual center" of a term paper "often lies somewhere in the set of questions and texts organized by the course's professor" (2014, 11). While this may be entirely acceptable—and even laudable—in the case of a term paper, this approach to writing neglects the earned audience that lies beyond the course enrollment. Indeed, "reviewers who encounter such essays as journal submissions recognize them immediately because the basic question they ask has an unspoken justification in the logic of the course for which the paper was originally written, about which the essays themselves cannot, of course, speak. (Hayot 2014, 11). The term paper, therefore, relies on the course it was written for in two specific ways that must be overcome in the transition from term paper to article—audience, and context.

Reliance on the course can be reduced by shifting the focal point of writing. By this, I mean to say that writing a term paper entails argument-first writing that externalizes the responsibility to connect with an audience and establish a context to the course itself. Conversely, writing an academic article entails contribution-first writing, wherein the author must earn the audience and articulate the context of the work. Foregrounding the contribution over the argument necessitates reflection on audience and context because the content and significance of the contribution can only become clearer once you have an audience in mind (whom are you writing for?) and a context for your intervention established (where does your contribution fit into the field of study?). The next section discusses different strategies for communicating your contribution.

Contribution Communication: Conceptual and Practical Strategies

Academic writing experts Wendy Belcher and Paul Silvia have slightly different approaches to how we can think about the contribution that we want our article to make. After reviewing these two approaches, I outline four practical strategies for putting these contributions to work.

Wendy Belcher (2019) suggests that authors consider their work in terms of significance, which speaks to the reason that a reader might read the article. Belcher offers ten types of claims to significance, visualized in *Figure 25.1* (Belcher 2019, 192-196). Paul Silvia offers similar guidance, suggesting that the structure of the introduction is crucial to establishing the purpose of an article. He offers four rhetorical models, describing the corresponding structure that each argument's introduction would take: "which one is right?," "here's how this works," "things that seem similar are different (or vice versa)," and "here's something new" (Silvia 2017, 86-95). Common to both Belcher and Silvia is a recognition that for the article to stand, its justification must be internal to the work and clearly expressed to the reader.

Figure 25.1: Belcher's Ten Types of Claims to Significance

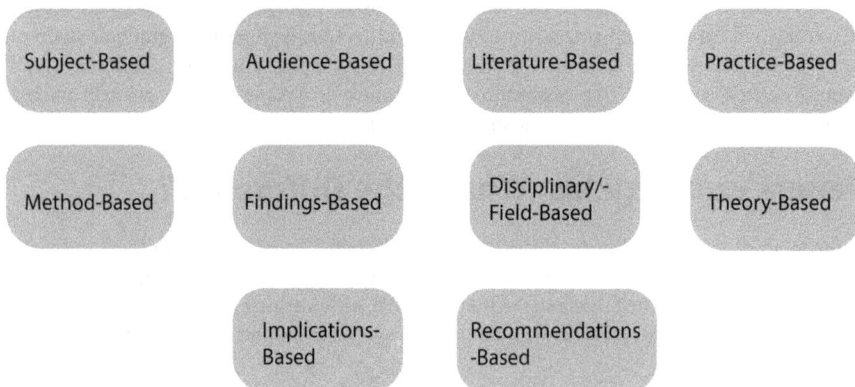

Subject-Based	Audience-Based	Literature-Based	Practice-Based
Method-Based	Findings-Based	Disciplinary/-Field-Based	Theory-Based
	Implications-Based	Recommendations-Based	

Journal selection is an important consideration in the submission process because it assists in targeting the primary audience. While students' interactions with journals in syllabi or comprehensive reading lists may communicate certain details about the prestige of one venue or another (Murphy & Wigginton 2020), assigned readings typically draw attention to the article as a self-contained text rather than situating the article within a broader conversation taking place within a specialist journal. An important realization along the path from student to scholar is that journals have unique features, foci, and familiar debates; recognizing the unique profile of journals—whether generalist journals seeking to cover all mainstream debates in a field or specialist venues that specific research communities call home—can set a submission process up for success.

There are four practical strategies to consider for putting an article's contribution in context of a given journal, summarized in *Table 25.1*. First, a journal can be selected for empirical fit, whether in terms of topical or regional empirics. A second strategy for journal selection can be through methodological or theoretical fit, where one or more elements of the research design provide the context for submitting to a particular journal. Third, some of the audience-earning and context-establishing requirements can be outsourced by joining a special issue of a journal. Finally, the fourth strategy is perhaps the simplest to begin and most difficult to complete: submitting to the journal that most frequently appears in the paper's bibliography. While this would indicate a likely venue, it requires the highest degree of effort to specify the contribution, which can only be identified on a case-by-case basis. While this piece of received wisdom is useful for the veteran scholar, I would suggest clearer guidance of the three earlier strategies for journal selection in the case of a first attempt at a paper-turned-article.

Table 25.1: Strategies to Consider for Putting an Article's Contribution in Context of a Given Journal

Strategy	Description	Example
Empirical Fit	• Select based on field of study or region discussed • Article contributes to scholars working on similar empirical area	A study on Canadian elections might be submitted to the *Canadian Journal of Political Science*
Methodological/ Theoretical Fit	• Select based on methodology or theoretical framework employed • Article contributes new empirical material to scholars using similar theories or methods	A project theoretically informed by critical security studies might be submitted to *Security Dialogue*
Special Issue	• Joins other articles on a shared topic or theme and articles share the audience-earning • Can be difficult for junior scholars to join, but open calls are posted to social media, listservs, and publisher websites	An article on the materiality of drone surveillance could take part in a special issue on research methods in surveillance studies
Reference List Frequency	• Select based on most frequent appearance on the article's reference list • No immediate path to contribution definition	An article frequently citing works from *Conflict & Cooperation* could identify its key audience in that readership

Term Paper-to-Article Red Flags

There is an additional stage of self-assessment that can help set the stage for the submission of a term paper-turned-article, which involves checking the manuscript for three common red flags. While each of these three issues can happen with works beginning as academic articles, they are particularly common in the case of term papers because of the assumed context and argument-first writing modality of the term paper genre. For each red flag, I offer an explanation of where the issue comes from, a guiding question to check your manuscript for this phenomenon, and finally, a way to rejoin the path to publication.

1. Over-Anchoring

Because many syllabi are designed to build from the beginning of the term to the end, courses often cover the early or 'big picture' works in a field that has little to do with developments in narrow corners of the present. While that kind of approach may be useful when contextualizing a novel research program for a generalist audience, over-anchoring is particularly egregious when intervening into an established debate in the pages of a specialist journal. There, a critique of certain aspects of older texts may well appear as preaching to the choir (at best) or an irresponsible allocation of page budget (at worst).

When revising the paper, over-anchoring can be identified by asking: "What context is necessary to situate my contribution for the journal's audience?" Reviewing articles on similar topics published in priority target journals is one strategy to determine what is appropriate for your intervention. Do these articles return to the foundations of the field, cite key works of general relevance, or proceed directly to the immediately engaged literature? Taking cues from works that have recently passed muster at the journal will offer direct and relevant guidance for your manuscript.

2. Overplaying the Hand

As the advice goes, the tendency of courses to assign the 'most important texts' on a topic can overexaggerate the contribution of a truly average article. In the words of Howard Becker, the actual threshold is not to say something earth-shattering but something "at least minimally new" (2007, 141). A key step in the path from paper to publishable is found in the recognition that a term paper might one day be an article (e.g., Arsenault et al. 2021), but this must also include a realistic assessment of the incremental contribution made by the vast majority of articles. Indeed, Becker warns against setting "ourselves up for failure by aiming at the impossible" (2007, 140), and instead suggests that we should aim – confidently and humbly – to make this kind of a contribution. Inflating the contribution that a paper offers risks raising the suspicions of reviewers and editors alike who may interpret the overplayed hand as a sign of arrogance rather than a desire to contribute.

The key question to check for the overplayed hand is: "Have I exaggerated the implications or novelty of my claims?" By replacing overstated claims with confident contouring of the contribution, recognizing the specific intervention while humbly admitting limitations, and graciously identifying prior efforts upon which the work builds, the paper becomes more publishable. And along that journey of publication and reception, the editors, reviewers, and readers will not see the work as under-delivering, but as accurately setting expectations for the impact of the work.

3. Overlooking the Literature

A course syllabus may well present a diverse set of readings encompassing important perspectives on the topic about which you write, but that does not mean that your specific topic of interest has been exhaustively covered. Revisiting the literature after the course is important because, assuming you have chosen a journal that is a good "fit," the editor may well invite recent authors on that subject to review your submission. As a matter of substance, engaging with recent work on your topic can help clarify your specific contribution in the context of the field's latest developments; as a matter of pragmatism and practicality, snubbing a potential reviewer is not in your interest!

A deceivingly simple question for this pitfall is "have I reviewed the literature?," but two qualifiers may help provide greater guidance—"have I reviewed the literature for my specific audience and in my desired journal?" The literature review may well seem like an unnecessary activity after a full semester of reading on the topic. However, this secondary and intentional review is an integral part of shifting from argument to contribution, because it ensures that the proper context for the discussion is established. If existing works are your landmarks in your argument's terrain, then specific and frequent references will help chart your clearest course.

Conclusion

The path to publication can be a difficult one at the best of times, and the unique pitfalls facing students seeking to publish term papers introduce new challenges that exceed the standard academic writing advice. It is my hope that this chapter's explanation of contribution-first writing, review of different strategies for contribution communication, and self-assessments for term paper red flags can help prepare early career researchers for a productive peer review experience. A recurring theme throughout this chapter has been the importance of the audience from contribution-first writing to journal selection, and keeping the audience in mind through the process of translating a term paper to an academic article can help prepare the author for a productive peer-review process.

References

Arsenault, Amelia C., Andrew Heffernan, and Michael P.A Murphy. 2021. "What is the Role of Graduate Student Journals in the Publish-or-Perish Academy? Three Lessons from Three Editors-in-Chief." *International Studies* 58 (1): 98-115.

Belcher, Wendy L. 2019. *Writing Your Journal Article in Twelve Weeks: A Guide to Academic Publishing Success, Second Edition*. Chicago: University of Chicago Press.

Becker, Howard S. 2007. *Writing For Social Scientists: How to Start and Finish Your Thesis, Book, or Article*. Chicago: University of Chicago Press.

Berdahl, Loleen and Jonathan Malloy. 2018. *Work Your Career: Get What You Want from your Social Sciences or Humanities PhD*. Toronto: University of Toronto Press.

Calarco, Jessica McCrory. 2021. *A Field Guide to Graduate School: Uncovering the Hidden Curriculum*. Princeton: Princeton University Press.

Hay, Iain. 2017. *How to Be an Academic Superhero: Establishing and Sustaining a Successful Career in the Social Sciences, Arts, and Humanities*. Gloucester: Edward Elgar.

Hayot, Eric. 2014. *The Elements of Academic Style: Writing for the Humanities*. New York: Columbia University Press.

Hatch, Trevor, and Antonius Skipper. 2016. "How Much Are PhD Students Publishing Before Graduation? An Examination of Four Social Science Disciplines." *Journal of Scholarly Publishing* 47 (2): 171-179.

Kelsky, Karen. 2015. *The Professor Is In: The Essential Guide to Turning Your PhD into a Job*. New York: Three Rivers.

Murphy, Michael P.A., and Michael J. Wigginton. 2020. "Canadian International Relations, American Social Science? Evidence from Academic Journals and Comprehensive Reading Lists." *International Journal* 75 (1): 5-23.

Peters, Robert L. 1997. *Getting What You Came For: The Smart Student's Guide to Earning a Master's or PhD*. New York: Farrar, Strauss & York.

Rich, Timothy S. 2013. "Publishing as a Graduate Student: A Quick and (Hopefully) Painless Guide to Establishing Yourself as a Scholar." *PS: Political Science & Politics* 46 (2): 376-379.

Semenza, Gregory Colon. 2005. *Graduate Study for the 21st Century: How to Build an Academic Career in the Humanities*. London: Palgrave Macmillan.

Silvia, Paul J.. 2017. *Write it Up! Practical Strategies for Writing and Publishing Journal Articles*. Washington: APA Books.

Silvia, Paul J. 2019. *How to Write a Lot: A Practical Guide to Productive Academic Writing, Second Edition.* Washington: APA Books.

Van Cott, Donna Lee. 2005. "A Graduate Student's Guide to Publishing Scholarly Journal Articles." *PS: Political Science & Politics* 38 (4): 741-743.

26 | Managing Online Harassment in the Academy

Angela X. Ocampo[1], Seth Masket[2], & Jennifer N. Victor[3]

1. University of Texas at Austin 2. University of Denver 3. George Mason University

KEYWORDS: Online Harassment, Community, Unregulated Space.

Introduction

Anyone can experience *online harassment*. A recent study by the Pew Research Center found that four in ten Americans have experienced online harassment and abuse (Vogel 2021). However, scholars who engage in public-facing work incur a greater risk of experiencing online attacks because of their heightened visibility and how readily available their information and profiles are. But even among scholars, the effects of online harassment are not equally distributed. Online harassment might be disproportionately experienced by certain communities, and it might also disparately impact scholars in a multitude of ways. In this chapter, we discuss differences in how harassment affects scholars and some strategies for how academics might handle it.

What We Know About Online Harassment

Research on online harassment is not especially well developed, and much of what exists is focused on cyber-bullying of school-age children. Beyond that, few studies of online harassment contain anything close to a comprehensive census of different types of harassment or the nature of their victims. Some studies are largely surveys of online users, asking respondents to self-report their victimhood. These results are nonetheless useful. Somewhat counter-intuitively, men are more likely to report being victims of online harassment than women are; however, women and people of color are more likely to report being harassed because of their sex, race, or ethnicity (Nadim and Fladmoe 2021, Vogels 2021). A recent social network study found that harassment directed at Latinas and Black women often contained racial stereotypes and epithets (Francisco and Felmlee 2021).

These attacks often have a particularly detrimental effect on women scholars and scholars of color, who are more likely than men to react by withdrawing from online public spaces or to self-censor (Chadha et al. 2020, Nadim and Fladmoe 2021, Veletsianos et al. 2018). Actress Kelly Marie Tran was subjected to an online harassment campaign after her leading role in the 2018 Star Wars film "The Last Jedi," leading her to delete much of her social media profile. As she later wrote in a New York Times op/ed, "It wasn't their words, it's that I started to believe them" (Tran 2018).

We wish to provide some advice to victims of online harassment, based both on existing research and on our own experiences. We should first acknowledge that, on a purely normative level, developing a reaction or a prevention plan for harassment isn't something users and scholars should have to do, but it has unfortunately become a necessity. In a better system, social media companies and policing agencies would take greater responsibility for this and not leave the burden on the user. Simply, you should be able to promote and argue your scholarly ideas online without needing to protect your identity or your life.

Furthermore, departments, institutions, and other organizations where scholars work and collaborate should provide tools and resources for those impacted by harassment. For example, departments and institutions should reassure scholars that they will not be penalized for backlash they might experience due to their public scholarship. They should also engage in public displays of support on behalf of victims by issuing statements. They can help victims of harassment by providing a safe physical workspace and by maintaining an appropriate professional profile for you on their websites, and offering you control over what information is included there (see "manage your experience" below). Lastly, our recommendation is that institutions also provide resources for scholars who might want to seek out counseling and other mental health services. In sum, chairs, deans, administrators, departments, institutions, and organizations where public facing scholars work should proactively work to protect and support scholars who are affected by online harassment.

Approaches for Dealing with Online Harassment

There's no single tried-and-true way to respond to or deal with harassment, in large part because there is a great variety of harassers and there is variation on the level and type of harassment. How one responds to a hostile tweet from a celebrity or high-follower-count Twitter blue check is different from how one responds to similar behavior from a colleague or stranger. It is also the case that one might need to take stronger measures against serious threats of violence or physical harm. It is difficult to provide a recipe for managing harassers because the specific context in which harassment takes place is important to consider when deciding how to manage it.

With that in mind, we provide a series of principles to follow and some specific examples of how the principles might be employed in different situations. While some of these strategies might be useful to some, they might not be for others. Our hope is that in considering these principles, scholars who face online harassment can have a set of start-up strategies and tools from which they might develop a more individualized approach based on their own needs, identities, and gravity of the situation.

Principle 1: Take a Moment

This may be the hardest principle to employ because it does not come naturally to most people. When you experience something harassing, abusive, or targeted in your public social media interactions, we recommend taking a moment to assess the situation and consider your options and potential response. Consider that off-the-cuff responses in the heat of the moment, driven by frustration and anger, may not necessarily be the most appropriate way to respond to the situation or yield the best outcomes. Depending on the kind and type of harassment you might need to take a different approach to deal with it. Taking a moment to assess the situation will provide you with a clearer picture of how to move forward. As you take a moment you might also want to reach out to others for support (see below on "having a squad"). If there is a threat of violence or physical harm, you want to report this to the authorities and the proper office at your institution. If the individual is a colleague, you might also consider your options for how to handle it through informal and formal reporting mechanisms available in your respective organization or university.

Part of taking a moment also means that it's okay to take a break from social media to care for yourself. When the things that we enjoy doing bring negativity and toxicity, this is bound to affect our self-esteem and overall well-being. Take a moment to turn to things that might help in dealing with the attack you have just experienced. We also recognize that many attacks are racialized, gendered, or prejudicial along other lines such as religion, ability, sexual orientation, among others, and as such these are deeply harmful to members of marginalized communities. We urge scholars who have been victims of harassment to do as much as possible to practice self-care and turn to whatever they might need in order to develop strategies for moving forward from the attack they have experienced (see chapter 69 on counseling and other resources).

Principle 2: Have a Squad

Online activity is individual; we conduct it using personal electronic devices and most often do it from personal accounts tied to our known identities. In this way, participating in public, online forums like Twitter, Instagram, or Facebook represents a vulnerability. When we post things, we are often revealing things about ourselves, even when we don't mean to. But just because posting is an individual activity doesn't mean that managing online responses needs to be. You'll have greater confidence in putting yourself out there if you know that there is a group of people who have your back. You'll be better equipped to respond to online harassment if you have a *community* to turn to.

This group doesn't need to be people you are friends with in real life, but they do need to be people you trust to some degree. They should be people who engage on platforms with a similar level of frequency as you, and people or accounts that you would defend or support if they were targeted. This group of people does not need to be like-minded on all things; rather they need to be like-minded about the rules of engagement and social norms of online behavior. Groups like HeartMob[i] have developed in recent years to provide such a resource for online scholars (Blackwell et al. 2017). However, in some cases and depending on the type of harassment, you might want to turn to individuals or friends whom you trust and have your best interest at heart, despite their level of online engagement. This is especially important if the harassment involves a person you know, a colleague or supervisor, or a more serious threat.

Principle 3: Document and Report

Keep a file of particularly threatening or persistent attacks. Do not only save websites or links but take screenshots or save them as PDFs, since some links expire or perpetrators might erase their posts. There are certainly limits to what a police department can or will do in these situations, but to the extent they are able to act, they'll want to know how specific any threats were and how traceable the harassers are. Your campus safety office may be able to help out here, even if this technically occurred off-campus. Local police may be interested, as well. If you're being attacked for work you published in a newspaper or on-line forum, it may be helpful to reach out to the editor or moderator to report the incident, especially if the attack violates the forum's code of conduct. Again, there's no guarantee they'll be able to directly help you or punish a harasser, but the more evidence you can provide, the more helpful they're likely to be.

Principle 4: Manage Your Experience

As we've noted, the managers of social media companies are not great about protecting users, and some companies (notably Twitter) have defined themselves by providing a largely *unregulated space*. But there are still ways to protect yourself while you're on there. Twitter, for example, offers a number of highly useful ways to customize one's account, allowing you to limit who can view your posts, who can comment on them, how much of your personal information they can see, and more. You can block accounts and content you don't want to see. You can report attacks against you and others and possibly get content and users removed in the process.

Managing your experience is not only about customizing your accounts but also taking measures to protect yourself if the threats involve violence or harm. For example, when one of the authors of this piece posts items on Twitter that they anticipate will be controversial or invite trolling or abusive responses, they adjust the settings on the post so that only people they follow are allowed to reply. This strategy significantly reduces the most corrosive response behavior from Twitter at-large.

Also, as a way to manage your privacy, you can request that your organization removes your office location information and any other personally identifiable information from the department or university's directory and websites. You can request changes to your classroom location, office location, among others. While you can't keep the hate from existing, you can limit how much of it gets to you and take measures to protect yourself from any harm.

Public Engagement: The Choice is Yours

If you become the victim of online harassment, you are not at fault regardless of any mitigation strategies you may or may not have followed. We encourage scholars to aggressively curate their social media feeds and control their experience using some of the strategies we have described. However, no scholar should feel compelled to participate in social media to advance their careers. While public scholarship is becoming an increasingly recognized and important medium for academic products, it is still the case that most elements of the academy value traditional peer-reviewed products over most other products, including high-profile media. In short, your dean may be thrilled if you wind up as a CNN Election Night analyst, but publishing books and articles is still the better path to tenure and advancement. Academic social media participation is still mostly a supplement to traditional scholarly work, not a substitute.

There is one approach we would strongly encourage you not to follow: to silence yourself, limit your valuable contributions, or change what you study to appease the harassers. We recognize that some scholars, especially those who are much more vulnerable and for whom the attacks might be particularly harmful and detrimental, need some additional time to self-care. It is perfectly okay to temporarily retreat from public-facing work to care for oneself. Despite all of the challenges and the ugliness, there are still very useful aspects of being an online scholar. Your work, expertise and perspective are incredibly valuable. You can actually engage constructively with journalists, activists, and other scholars about your work. You can gain positive attention that you just don't get from publishing articles and book chapters, advancing your career in valuable ways. You can develop an international support network that can see you through difficult times. But yes, it can at times be an unpleasant and even toxic environment. We hope the above advice can help you make the most of it.

Endnotes

1   https://iheartmob.org

References

Blackwell, Lindsay, Jill Dimond, Sarita Schoenebeck, and Cliff Lampe. 2017. "Classification and its Consequences for Online Harassment: Design Insights from HeartMob." Proceedings of the ACM on Human-Computer Interaction 1 (CSCW) 1–19.

Chadha, Kalyani, Linda Steiner, Jessica Vitak, and Zahra Ashktorab. 2020. "Women's Responses to Online Harassment." International Journal of Communication (19328036) 14.

Francisco, Sara C., and Diane H. Felmlee. 2021. "What Did You Call Me? An Analysis of Online Harassment Towards Black and Latinx Women." Race and Social Problems (May) 1–13.

Nadim, M., & Fladmoe, A. 2021. "Silencing Women? Gender and Online Harassment." Social Science Computer Review, 39(2), 245–258. https://doi.org/10.1177/0894439319865518

Tran, Kelly Marie. 2018. "I Won't Be Marginalized by Online Harassment," New York Times, August 21, https://www.nytimes.com/2018/08/21/movies/kelly-marie-tran.html.

Veletsianos, George, Shandell Houlden, Jaigris Hodson, and Chandell Gosse. 2018. "Women Scholars' Experiences with Online Harassment and Abuse: Self-Protection, Resistance, Acceptance, and Self-Blame." New Media & Society 20 (12): 4689–4708.

Vogels, Emily A. 2021. "The State of Online Harassment." Pew Research Center 13.

27

To Twitter or Not to Twitter?

Salah Ben Hammou[1] & Elizabeth Meehan[2]

1. University of Central Florida 2. The George Washington University

KEYWORDS: Social Media, Twitter, #PoliSciTwitter.

The Academic Twittering Machine

Recent years have seen an increased presence of academics across rank, discipline, and institutions on *social media*, particularly *Twitter*. Popular hashtags associated with online academic communities include *#AcademicTwitter* and our community of focus: *#PoliSciTwitter*. Several subcommunities exist within *#PoliSciTwitter*, often divided along subfields (i.e., International Relations and American Politics) or shared recreational interests (e.g., *#PoliSciRuns* and *#PoliSciCooks*). Scores of political science graduate students have joined these spaces with their own Twitter accounts, leading to greater interaction with faculty and peers worldwide. However, many graduate students choose to not create Twitter accounts or to not engage in online academic communities. Several reasons account for this choice, including caution over future employers surveying their online presence as well as uncertainty over how to start "networking" on academic Twitter. This chapter further unpacks the choice to use Twitter examining arguments for and against its use by graduate students.

We argue Twitter can serve several purposes for graduate students, emphasizing that Twitter usage need not follow a single formula. Specifically, having a Twitter account gives graduate students the freedom and versatility to follow several different pursuits in line with their own goals. Students can promote their ongoing or published research to a wider audience of academics while also learning about new or understudied fields of research. This pursuit can result in students networking with potential co-authors and collaborators while also remaining an active member in their research field's development. Conversely, students interested in non-academic careers can use the site to network with non-academic professionals. This networking is particularly relevant for individuals who want to transition from the academy to think-tanks and NGO positions, government positions, or other positions. A growing and accessible community of academics-to-practitioners is active on Twitter, providing tips and feedback on students' non-academic job market materials as well as general tips with networking outside the academy.

However, we also recognize common concerns about Twitter raised by non-users and other issues graduate students should keep in mind while navigating the site. Non-users generally raise concerns with Academic Twitter becoming a "time-suck" in line with other social media applications and argue they would be less productive if they participate in *#PoliSciTwitter*. Non-users are further concerned with the implications of their online presence. These concerns include potential employers using students' online content against them during the hiring process as well as digital harassment. (For additional insight on digital harassment, see chapter 26). In addition, non-users express uncertainty over

Twitter as a viable networking resource. While private social media usage has its own sets of norms, some non-users believe the norms behind managing more "professionalized" accounts are less clear. Ultimately, graduate students must weigh the pros and cons of setting up a Twitter account and decide what is best for themselves.

We proceed as follows. First, we further establish why Twitter has become salient to conversations about graduate school and academia more broadly. We use nascent scholarly research on academics' Twitter behavior to highlight six main applications among political scientists. Following this section, we lay out the nuts and bolts of Twitter: how to set up an account, how to tailor your account to your research interests, how to reach out to fellow academics, how to set boundaries on your Twitter account, and how to use Twitter's safety features to protect yourself. We briefly conclude with a summary of our main points.

Navigating the Bird App: Why Does Academic Twitter Matter?

For better or for worse, having an online presence is a baseline expectation for today's graduate students. Candidates on the job market are expected to have an accessible online presence documenting their research, expertise, and skill set for potential employers to survey. While students typically use personal websites or LinkedIn accounts to meet these expectations, Twitter has served as a viable supplement or alternative. This development fits into a broader discipline-wide trend: political scientists' Twitter use has grown dramatically since the platform launched in 2006.[1] Research conducted by Kim and Patterson (2021) finds that 41% of political science faculty at the top 50 US News and World Report graduate programs have identifiable Twitter accounts. Its microblogging format allows for many different types of engagement, from research conversations with fellow scholars to summarizing the politics of current events in real time. In short, Academic Twitter matters for graduate students because having an account is arguably becoming a necessity among political scientists.

Providing a Blue(check)²print: What You Can Do on Academic Twitter

Existing blogs and scholarly research suggest several main uses for academic Twitter. We base our uses for *#PoliSciTwitter* on research outlining seven networked practices of scholars on social media. These practices include kinship in community, self-directed learning, digital norms, navigating context collapse, career advancement, reputation management, and risk versus reward assessment (Pasquini and Eaton 2021). These practices are highlighted by Twitter users and non-users alike as motivations for their social media decisions. We suggest these practices are applied to at least six goals among political science graduate students: finding research, promoting research, asking for advice, networking, finding jobs, and teaching. Below we unpack each goal and offer practical tips and suggestions.

Finding Research

Graduate students have several useful resources for finding research relevant to their interests. Being an avid research consumer helps graduate students become better research producers, and Twitter can serve as a great means to stay up-to-date with work in your subfield. We recommend following all major political science journals and subfield-specific journals for your area of interest. For instance, the *American Political Science Review* (@APSR), *Comparative Politics* (@Journal_CompPol), and *International Security* (@Journal_IS) all manage active accounts. These accounts tweet out studies from their latest issues, making them rich resources for up-to-date work. We also suggest following scholars at all stages who work on your area of interest as well as academic blogs which regularly tweet out posts. Other accounts like @PoliSciRes automatically retweet any tweet containing *#poliscaresearch*. You can put all of these resources into a "list," which allows you to quickly glance through any research updates separate from your main Twitter feed (Twitter 2021).

Promoting Research

Students can use Twitter to raise awareness of their own projects and promote their work. Graduate students can opt to post research findings for a non-academic audience and walk through some implications of their work. Tweeting about your working papers and publications helps other political scientists to find you and your research. When tweeting, graduate students should summarize their research in a short thread with their research question, main contributions, and some implications (Taylor & Francis Author Services 2021). Recent research by political scientists finds that those who tweet about their research are more likely to be cited by others (Klar et. al 2020).

Like expectations for having an online presence, expectations for scholars to produce public scholarship have grown over time. Public scholarship includes different forms of public engagement, such as producing written work with outlets like the Washington Post's blog The MonkeyCage or Political Violence at a Glance or giving interviews to media outlets about one's research (Iber 2016). Graduate students can use Twitter to circulate their public-facing publications to a broader audience, often with a thread about the article's main arguments.

Asking for Advice

Graduate students are constantly learning and evolving, and Twitter offers an informal way to ask for help outside of your home institution for a variety of issues. We have observed graduate students requesting assistance concerning research and methods, the job market, pedagogy, and various discipline-specific problems. For instance, students can post questions to resolve coding issues, to find datasets, or to direct them towards bodies of literature they are unfamiliar with. Candidates on the job market can also reach out to faculty members or postgraduate individuals from other institutions for additional perspectives on their job market materials.

Many graduate students seek advice on coping with graduate school stressors, including feelings of isolation and imposter syndrome, drifting during the dissertation phase, and uncertainty over financial support. During the first year of the Covid-19 pandemic, we witnessed several informal groups emerge across #PoliSciTwitter where students and faculty alike could check in to alleviate isolation by holding informal Zoom hangouts and writing sessions. For many, sharing their stressors on Twitter reminds graduate students they are not alone on the PhD journey. (For further insights, see chapter 63).

Using Twitter to find solidarity and support is particularly relevant for graduate students from underrepresented groups. The site allows informal networks to emerge between graduate students passing tips and advice along about their own experiences navigating graduate school. When seeking advice, you can either tweet at the person or direct message them (where possible). Direct messaging scholars on Twitter can feel less formal than email and allows for casual conversation prior to a more formal meeting. Even commenting on scholars' Tweets and ongoing threads is a valuable way to offer your perspective and garner advice at the same time.

Networking

Twitter can serve as a resource for informal networking across the political science discipline and beyond (Drutman 2016; Kim, Lebovits, and Shugar 2021). While we acknowledge that Twitter networking is more informal than spaces such as LinkedIn, this does not diminish its value as a resource to connect with other professionals. In fact, the informal nature of Twitter engagement—as mentioned above—makes networking there more accessible than other more formal spaces. Broadly, students can integrate many of the same tips presented above (following relevant peers, scholars, journals, and outlets) to begin networking.

Graduate students can use several other available resources to maximize their networking potential on Twitter. Virtual writing and workshop groups based on subfield or topic are often formed on Twitter, allowing students to engage with scholars within their subfield or topic. Several Twitter accounts focus their networking efforts on underrepresented scholars, such as @1stGenScholars, @POCalsoknow, @womenalsoknow, and @Jam3a_MENA. POCAlsoKnowStuff and WomenAlsoKnowStuff allow students to log their name, rank, and expertise so that employers and media outlets looking to integrate underrepresented viewpoints can find them more easily as well. These accounts also tweet out the achievements and work of underrepresented students, broadening their outreach.

Finding Jobs

While Twitter is only one place to find academic jobs - the APSA job website, group listservs, and spreadsheets created and shared by current job market candidates are all invaluable sources—political science faculty increasingly share job postings via Twitter. Twitter job posting has become institutionalized over the last year, with the @PoliSciJobs account automatically retweeting any tweets containing *#PSJMinfo, #PolSciJobs, #PoliSciJobs* or *#PoliSciJobMarket*. Some faculty use Twitter to increase transparency in the job market by sharing their institution's progress on the job search and when their shortlist candidates have been selected. Some faculty also offer to review job market materials for first-gen and underrepresented scholars via Twitter, an offer we encourage graduate students to take.

On-the-market candidates can use Twitter to find alternative academic jobs in government and policy, in the private sector, and in NGOs and think-tanks. Through their own accounts, these employers also post job opportunities on Twitter prior to other outlets, giving followers an acute advantage. Similarly, graduate students can attract attention from different private sector organizations by posting their expertise or recent public engagement work, as mentioned above. Some Twitter accounts, such as @AltAcJobs and @HireHigherEd, provide job postings for relevant alternative academic jobs and send out newsletters with advice on navigating the non-academic job market. Other resources include accounts by individuals who successfully transitioned from the academy to industry and offer tips for others interested in alternative academic careers. (See chapter 41 on non-traditional options.)

Teaching

Finally, graduate students learn about how to improve their teaching on Twitter. Scholars often tweet what strategies they have found successful in the classroom or share their course syllabi, among other resources. Graduate student instructors may also use Twitter with their own students as a pedagogy tool, asking students to respond to Twitter polls or to hashtagged threads as part of their coursework (Blair 2013). For instance, Sweet-Cushman (2019, 763) found using Twitter in the classroom "provides a pathway for enhanced media literacy and deeper learning, makes learning about an issue more appealing, and engages students who are less interested in a traditional classroom delivery." Finally, graduate students can request guest lecturers with expertise on specific topics. This model can be particularly helpful for graduate students teaching a course for the first time or for those who want to give peers an opportunity to share their expertise with undergraduates.

Twittering Away: Account Setup, Boundaries, and Safety

For non-users who are considering whether to join *#PoliSciTwitter*, or for current users who are reassessing their accounts, we suggest using a checklist (Rust 2019; Academic Positions 2018) like the one below to ask yourself how and why you would use Twitter.

Would I (or do I) use Twitter to:

- Keep up with news, research, conference, funding, and/or job opportunities?
- Promote my own research?
- Find and share teaching and pedagogy tools?
- Bridge disciplinary boundaries with scholars from related fields?
- Network with political scientists or non-academic professionals?
- Ask for advice about graduate school life or research?
- Share parts of my life outside of academia?

If you will only use Twitter for one or two of these purposes, alternative tools are available, which makes setting up an account unnecessary. For instance, you can create a website to promote your research and teaching. You can sign up for email alerts about new publications in journals and conference solicitations. These are good practices regardless of whether you set up a Twitter account.

If you will use Twitter for multiple purposes, we suggest that you set up an account and tailor it to fit your goals. First, choose a Twitter handle (your username) that you would feel comfortable including on your CV. Write a short biography with your institution, subfield and topics of interest, and state you are a political scientist specifically to increase engagement. Include your website on your profile if you have one (Morajad 2020). Finally, select profile and banner photos that reflect who you are. Once your profile is set up, start by following political science journals, professional associations, and relevant workshop series. Use follower lists from these accounts to find faculty and graduate students working in your area. Hashtags like *#poliscitwitter*, *#polisciresearch*, and *#poliscicooks* can help you find other political scientists you want to connect with. You should also be mindful to promote accessibility and inclusivity when you tweet. Remember to caption images, include links to sources, reference someone's Twitter handle if they have one, and other citation practices to ensure many people can engage with your account.

If you set up an account, you must learn Twitter's safety features and use them to protect yourself (Doerfler et al. 2021). Muting, unfollowing, blocking, reporting, ending location sharing, and other tools within Twitter all exist for a reason. Junior scholars working on sensitive topics must utilize safety features like locking your account and restricting direct messages to protect them from attacks from state and non-state actors alike (Cox 2020). Using Twitter can lead to harassment from individuals to hate groups. Underrepresented scholars—women, BIPOC, and LGBTQIA+ individuals—are more likely to be harassed and to experience more severe harassment (Gosse et al. 2021). One of the authors has co-written a list of recommendations for how to protect yourself online before you publish an article[3] and for your online presence in general.[4] Relatedly, while there is debate over whether Tweets harm one's job prospects, using Twitter could contribute to employers discriminating against you for your online presence (Bateman 2017).

Set boundaries on your Twitter usage across multiple domains. Ask yourself if you would verbally say your tweet to someone's face. Recognize power dynamics, such as between you and your undergraduate students, and never punch down. You should also ask yourself if you want a piece of personal information about you in public. You can consider setting up separate personal and professional accounts if you want to share vulnerable details about your life. Balancing between wanting to share one's personal experience and finding solidarity with others while protecting your physical and emotional well-being is crucial. Moreover, Twitter is addictive (Brewer 2019; Flanagan 2021) and can take up a lot of time. Use apps like Freedom[5], StayFocusd[6], and RescueTime[7] to moderate your Twitter use. Alternatively, you can deactivate your account for short periods to meet deadlines (Meyer 2021). These boundaries help ensure a healthier relationship to Twitter.

To Tweet or Not to Tweet: It's Up to You

We emphasize that you do not have to be on *#PoliSciTwitter* to succeed as a political scientist. Graduate students who do join Twitter often find resources and communities they lack in their home institutions. These connections are often deeply rewarding and enriching, particularly in the context of the Covid-19 pandemic. Alternatively, graduate students can still obtain some of the benefits of Twitter, such as finding research and job opportunities, without having an account. Journal profiles and many scholars' profiles are public; you can make a list of helpful accounts that you check from time to time. Whichever decision you make now, you can always change your mind in the future.

Endnotes

1   Twitter does not have a built-in way to track and show trends of specific hashtags over time. Google Trends (https://trends.google.com/trends/explore?date=2006-01-01%20 2021-10-27&geo=US&q=Academic%20Twitter,Political%20Science%20Twitter) searches for AcademicTwitter and PoliSciTwitter increased initially and have been steady over time.

2   Verified accounts on Twitter have a blue check mark (https://help.twitter.com/en/managing-your-account/about-twitter-verified-accounts).

3   Cantwell, Devon, Elizabeth Meehan, and Rosalie Rubio. 2021. "Pre-Publication Digital Harassment Prevention Checklist." Retrieved January 3, 2022 (https://docs.google.com/document/d/1D1JaqTJRCiP8YAqIjN4x7364BX8P8iq_N-3d-9MqoQM).

4   Cantwell, Devon, Elizabeth Meehan, and Rosalie Rubio. 2021. "Dealing with the Digital Mob: Targeted Digital Harassment & What To Do About It." Retrieved January 3, 2022 (https://www.duckofminerva.com/2021/08/dealing-with-the-digital-mob.html).

5   Freedom. 2022. "Why Use Freedom?" Retrieved January 3, 2022 (https://freedom.to/why).

6   Transfusion Media. 2022. "StayFocusd - Chrome Application." Retrieved January 3, 2022 (https://chrome.google.com/webstore/detail/stayfocusd/laankejkbhbdhmipfmgcngdelahlfoji).

7   RescueTime. 2022. "RescueTime." Retrieved January 3, 2022 (https://www.rescuetime.com).

References

"A Guide to Twitter for Researchers." 2021. Author Services. https://authorservices.taylorandfrancis.com/research-impact/a-guide-to-twitter-for-researchers/ (November 1, 2021).

"About Twitter Lists." Twitter. https://help.twitter.com/en/using-twitter/twitter-lists (November 1, 2021).

Alstyne, Jennifer van. 2021. "A Guide to Twitter for Academics." *The Academic Designer*. Retrieved November 1, 2021 (https://theacademicdesigner.com/2018/academic-twitter/).

Bateman, Oliver. 2017. "Academics Are Stuck in Twitter Purgatory." *The Atlantic*. Retrieved November 1, 2021 (https://www.theatlantic.com/education/archive/2017/05/the-young-academics-twitter-conundrum/525924/).

Blair, Alasdair. 2013. "Democratising the Learning Process: The Use of Twitter in the Teaching of Politics and International Relations." *Politics* 33 (2): 135–145. doi:10.1111/1467-9256.12008.

Bateman, Oliver. 2017. "Academics Are Stuck In Twitter Purgatory." *The Atlantic*. Retrieved November 1, 2021 (https://www.theatlantic.com/education/archive/2017/05/the-young-academics-twitter-conundrum/525924/).

Brewer, Judson. 2019. "Addicted to Twitter? Here's Why." *Psychology Today*. Retrieved November 1, 2021 (https://www.psychologytoday.com/intl/blog/the-craving-mind/201902/addicted-twitter-heres-why).

Cox, Gloria C. 2020. "Dear Professor, Be Careful with Those Tweets, OK? Academic Freedom and Social Media." *PS: Political Science & Politics* 53 (3): 521–26. doi: 10.1017/S1049096520000219.

Doerfler, Periwinkle, Andrea Forte, Emiliano De Cristofaro, Gianluca Stringhini, Jeremy Blackburn, and Damon McCoy. 2021. "'I'm a Professor, Which Isn't Usually a Dangerous Job,' Internet-Facilitated Harassment and its Impact on Researchers." arXiv preprint arXiv:2104.11145.

Drutman, Lee. 2016. "On the Value of Fox-like Thinking, and How to Break into the Washington Policy Community." *PS: Political Science & Politics* 49 (3): 510–12. doi: 10.1017/S1049096516000858.

Flanagan, Caitlin. 2021. "You Really Need To Quit Twitter." *The Atlantic*. Retrieved November 1, 2021 (https://www.theatlantic.com/ideas/archive/2021/07/twitter-addict-realizes-she-needs-rehab/619343/).

Gosse, Chandell, George Veletsianos, Jaigris Hodson, Shandell Houlden, Tonia A. Dousay, Patrick R. Lowenthal, and Nathan Hall. 2021. "The Hidden Costs of Connectivity: Nature and Effects of Scholars' Online Harassment." *Learning, Media and Technology* 46 (3): 46:3, 264-280. doi: 10.1080/17439884.2021.1878218

Iber, Patrick. 2016. "How Academics Can Use Twitter Most Effectively." *Inside Higher Ed*. Retrieved November 1, 2021 (https://www.insidehighered.com/advice/2016/10/19/how-academics-can-use-twitter-most-effectively-essay).

Kim, Eunji and Shawn Patterson. 2021. "The Pandemic and Gender Inequality in Academia." *PS: Political Science & Politics* 55 (1) 109-116. doi: 10.1017/S1049096521001049.

Kim, Seo-Young Silvia, Hannah Lebovits, and Sarah Shugars. 2021. "Networking 101 for Graduate Students: Building a Bigger Table." *PS: Political Science & Politics* 1–6. doi: 10.1017/S1049096521001025.

Klar Samara, Yanna Krupnikov, John Barry Ryan, Kathleen Searles, and Yotam Shmargad. 2020. "Using Social Media to Promote Academic Research: Identifying the Benefits of Twitter for Sharing Academic Work." *PLOS ONE* 15 (4): e0229446. https://doi.org/10.1371/journal.pone.0229446

Meyer, Elaine. 2018. "To Tweet Or Not To Tweet: Twitter For Academics." IAPHS—*Interdisciplinary Association for Population Health Science*. Retrieved November 1, 2021 (https://iaphs.org/tweet-not-tweet-twitter-academics/).

Mojarad, Sarah. 2020. "A Beginners Guide to Academic Twitter." *Medium*. Retrieved November 1, 2021 (https://medium.com/@smojarad/a-beginners-guide-to-academic-twitter-f483dae86597).

Pasquini, Laura A. and Paul William Eaton. 2021. "Being/Becoming Professional Online: Wayfinding through Networked Practices and Digital Experiences." *New Media & Society* 23 (5): 939-959. doi: 10.1177/1461444820902449.

Rust, Niki. 2020. "A Nifty Guide for Academics on Using Twitter." *PLOS SciComm*. Retrieved November 1, 2021 (https://scicomm.plos.org/2019/06/18/a-nifty-guide-for-academics-on-using-twitter/).

Sweet-Cushman, Jennie. 2019. "Social Media Learning as a Pedagogical Tool: Twitter and Engagement in Civic Dialogue and Public Policy." *PS: Political Science & Politics* 52 (4): 763–70. doi: 10.1017/S1049096519000933.

"Why Academics Should Use Twitter." 2018. *Academic Positions*. Retrieved November 1, 2021 (https://academicpositions.com/career-advice/why-academics-should-use-twitter).

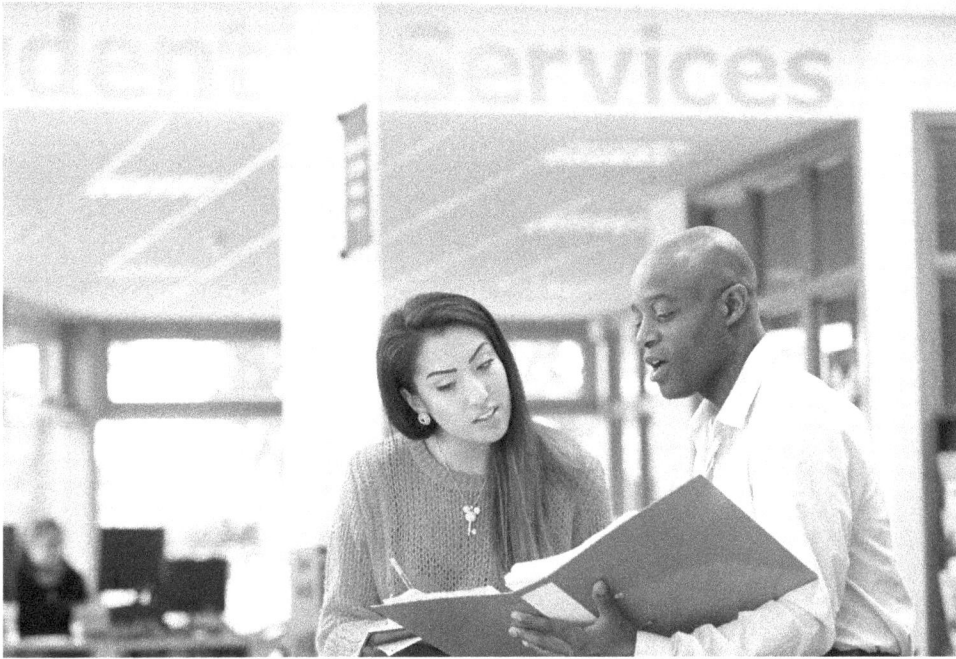

Professional Development— Teaching

28 Serving as a Graduate Teaching Assistant: Tips and Strategies

Zoe Nemerever[1] & Bianca Rubalcava[2]

1. Utah Valley University 2. University of California, Irvine

KEYWORDS: Teaching Assistant, University Resources.

Introduction

Many graduate students will serve as teaching assistants (TAs, also referred to as instructional assistants) during their time in graduate school. Teaching assistants are less common at liberal arts colleges and teaching-oriented institutions but are a crucial part of research universities where professors must balance their research agendas with teaching large courses. In addition to helping the department deliver courses to students, teaching assistantships are important components of graduate training (Darling and Staton 1989). Serving as a teaching assistant is an important opportunity to develop your teaching style, become comfortable in the classroom, and familiarize yourself with resources that will help you continue to develop as an educator throughout your academic career (Chiu and Corrigan 2019).

Expectations of the TA

The roles and expectations of a *teaching assistant* vary by institution, instructor, and course. These roles both lighten the workload of the instructor while also providing the TA with teaching experience. Most TAs will attend class, hold office hours, respond to student emails, grade assessments, liaise between the students and instructor, deliver guest lectures, and contribute to the development of syllabi, assessments, and rubrics. At larger universities, TAs may hold discussion sections.

It is beneficial to meet with the instructor before the start of the term to become acquainted and discuss expectations for each other, the students, and the course. Additionally, you should closely read the syllabus for information about the material covered in the course, as well as the types of assignments that you will grade. You should let the instructor know as soon as possible if you notice any difficult scheduling, such as grading a midterm the same week as your comprehensive exams (for additional information about comprehensive exams, see chapter 12).

As a TA you will work directly with the instructor and students to ensure that what is being taught in lecture is being understood by the students and then communicating with the instructor the needs and competencies of the students. Ask the instructor if they would like you to attend lecture. If it is your first time being exposed to the material, you may want to attend lecture regardless of the instructor's requirement. Mastery of lectures and assigned readings is essential for being able to assist students. The startup cost of learning a new course is high so serving as a TA for the same course multiple times is efficient.

Students will communicate with you via email, during office hours, and in-person before or after class if you attend. You should let students know how you prefer to be addressed—by your first name,

Ms./Mrs./Mr., or another salutation. Clear boundaries with students are essential so that they afford you the same respect they give the instructor and do not mistake you for a friend. Office hours are typically held in your graduate student office but can also be in the library or another public place like an on-campus coffee shop. If you meet with students in your office, be mindful of the door position. A student may feel more comfortable discussing sensitive information (e.g., disability accommodations, grades) with the door closed, whereas in other situations an open door may feel more comfortable to either the student or yourself. One strategy is to default to an open door and tell students that they're free to close it if they want.

Grading student work is your main responsibility. In addition to grading protocols specified by your instructor, here are some best practices. Activate the anonymous grading option on the course's online learning system. Grade one question at a time to maintain consistency and maximize efficiency.[1] If there are multiple teaching assistants, divide the exams by question as opposed to individually grading entire exams for a portion of the class. Ideally your instructor will provide you with a rubric of grading criteria and the desired grade distribution. If they do not provide a rubric, you should write your own (you can ask the university teaching center for assistance). Rubrics promote fairness and consistency and communicate to students where they lost/earned points.

Discussion sections (sometimes called "recitation sections" or just simply "sections") are smaller, discussion-based meetings that complement the larger and more passive lectures. In sections students can ask questions in a smaller setting, make connections between the course materials, and practice applying concepts from lecture. Leading sections may entail preparing slides that recap the week's lectures and readings, teaching supplementary readings, or something more casual like preparing questions for a discussion-based meeting. Research methods and statistics courses may require you to teach basic programming, such as Stata or R. Sections are also an opportunity to check in with students to see how they are progressing with assignments (for example, asking students to share their chosen topics for an essay due in two weeks) and to review their performance on exams (for example, going over the correct answers). Teaching sections is an important opportunity to practice facilitating classroom learning and leading classes. This experience will prepare you to your own course and/or pursuing an academic career (for more information about your first solo teaching experience, see chapter 29; for international students teaching their first class, see chapter 57).

The time commitment of your position will be outlined in the contract you sign with your department. If you are unionized there may be limits on how much you can work over a given week or academic term (for more information about graduate student unions, see chapter 33). Moreover, it is unlikely the hours you work will be consistent across weeks. For example, the week before an exam you may be overwhelmed with requests from students to meet while other weeks your office hours are unattended. The most demanding weeks will be the ones in which you grade assignments. You should ask the instructor how quickly you are expected to complete grading.

Resources to Address Diversity, Equity, and Inclusion in the Classroom

University resources are available to meet students' personal and life needs so that they may succeed in the classroom. You may consider asking students at the beginning of the course via an anonymous survey if they have consistent access to reliable internet, a quiet place to study, and/or personal, work, or familial obligations that may affect their ability to succeed in the course. Understanding the challenges that your students are facing will help you direct them to the proper resources, which may include a food bank, emergency housing, childcare, subsidized internet subscriptions, access to computers, legal clinics, and student health centers. Familiarizing yourself with campus resources and encouraging students to use them creates opportunities for students to thrive outside of the classroom. Checking in throughout the term shows your students that you care about their wellbeing and allows you to encourage interventions in a timely manner.

Universities contain myriad resources for academic support. Writing centers connect students with workshops and one-on-one consultations to improve their writing. There are also tutoring services and study groups available for students who need assistance beyond what you are able to provide in office hours. Students for whom English is their second language may benefit from the university's language assistance programs. Some universities also have resources for developing broader academic skills like time management and effective notetaking, which may be targeted towards first-generation or traditionally under-served student populations. If you want to provide students with additional academic resources, The Learning Center at the University of North Carolina at Chapel Hill has fantastic online resources that are freely available.[2] (See also chapter 30 for APSA and discipline teaching resources.)

Another important resource on every campus is the office of student disabilities (or a similar name). Although the instructor will handle formal arrangements involving the office of student disabilities, it is important to be aware of the process because students may disclose to you their personal situation. Any student with documented disabilities is entitled to accommodations according to their needs. Once the student provides university documentation of the designated accommodations, it is your responsibility to ensure that your student has access to these services. Beyond providing the designated accommodations to which students are legally entitled, you can use inclusive pedagogies to empower students (Scott et al. 2003). The APSA Educate website hosts an online library of teaching materials on inclusive course design. You do not need an APSA membership to access these resources.

A holistic and compassionate approach to teaching is the cornerstone of inclusivity. There is no comprehensive list of things to "check off." Everyday interactions signal to marginalized or disadvantaged students whether you are an ally. For instance, defaulting to they/them pronouns to avoid misgendering someone and avoiding culturally specific examples signal to students that they are welcome in your classroom. If you are teaching a discussion-based course, it is helpful to set community guidelines and review the campus' standards for inclusivity. Review microaggressions and acceptable language (e.g., LGBT+ people instead of "the gays") with your students on the first day of class. Your participation standards should address communicating respectfully, contributing to an inclusive learning atmosphere, and following the university's code of conduct.

Teaching Evaluations

Teaching evaluations are standard practice for educators in higher education. At their best, they offer feedback about what you are doing right and highlight room for improvement. At their worst, they can be a form of harassment and expose the intense gender and racial inequities in higher education (for a larger discussion, see chapter 49). Unconscious and unintentional biases about the race and gender of the instructor often results in lower evaluations than their peers with no true difference in quality of education (Peterson et al. 2019; Esarey and Valdes 2020). Nevertheless, it is common practice for academic job applications to require prior teaching evaluations, so it is important to strive for high scores. (For more information, see chapter 43 about job application statements and portfolios.)

Prior to students completing the official evaluations at the end of the semester you can facilitate anonymous and informal evaluation either by passing out notecards in class or an online survey. Suggested questions include: What is going well in this course so far? What could be going better? What can I do to facilitate your success? Students' feedback will help you adjust your teaching as necessary and will demonstrate that you value the opinions of your students.

In order to increase response rates on official evaluations you will want to email your students a reminder and talk to them in class about how evaluations are important for improving your teaching and securing future employment. You may also consider giving them time in class to complete the evaluations on their laptops.

Student evaluations often won't be available for instructors and TAs to view until after final grades are posted. Many people prefer to wait a couple weeks after the academic term to read evaluations because it gives them time to decompress and approach the feedback with fewer emotions and more neutrality. The course instructor, your advisor, or staff at university teaching centers can help you to understand the feedback and translate it into actionable changes for the next time you teach. Students' answers to open-ended questions will provide more insight than the quantitative scores. Finally, teaching evaluations are meant to improve over time. It matters more that you adapt to student feedback over the course of your graduate career rather than having perfect evaluations from the onset.

Common Challenges for TAs

Challenges are opportunities to develop new skills. We discuss two common challenges – facilitating classroom discussions and difficult interactions with students—but there are other situations that arise in or out of the classroom (Luo et al. 2000). The course instructor, your advisor, and your department chair likely all have many years of teaching experience and can help you troubleshoot these issues. The staff at the university teaching center will be able to support you as well.

Getting students to actively participate in classroom discussions can be challenging. Increasing participation in your class will require identifying why your students are not participating and devising a relevant solution. For example, some students do not participate because they fear being wrong will hurt their performance in the class. Address this by creating a classroom environment in which students feel comfortable taking risks and explain to your students that you do not expect them to always have the right answer. To help students become more confident speaking in front of the class, think-pair-share is a good tool for students to run their answer by a classmate before sharing it with the entire class. Additionally, students may want to participate but need more time to fully form their answers. When you pose a question to the class it can be helpful to set a timer for one to three minutes to allow them to think through the question. This can help mitigate the same person repeatedly being the first to raise their hand. There are many reasons beyond the ones mentioned here why students may not participate. If your classroom discussions are suffering from lack of participation, consider giving your students an anonymous survey inquiring what prevents participation in class and ask them what you can do as a teaching assistant to help them feel more comfortable participating.

Two types of difficult student interactions are those that occur in the classroom and those that occur in one-on-one interactions. Establishing clear standards of participation will help prevent disruptive classroom behaviors such as over-participation and disrespectful or offensive comments. Helpful rubric language to minimize overzealous participation may include "Participate actively without rambling consistently or dominating the room" or "Encourages and enables fellow classmates to participate." Some students do not act as respectfully towards teaching assistants as they do towards instructors. This disproportionately affects teaching assistants who are women and/or from racial and ethnic minority backgrounds. Strive for a friendly and professional hierarchical relationship with your students. It is important to always use your university email address when corresponding with students and to save all email correspondence at least until the end of the term. Additionally, office hours should be conducted with the door open so that you are never alone in a room with a student. Communicate with your instructor if any student interaction makes you feel uncomfortable or is problematic.

Conclusion

While much of graduate school is devoted to producing peer-reviewed scholarship, serious investment in pedagogical training and experience is crucial for those considering academic careers. Engaging in regular metacognition (Lin et al. 2005) and reflection will help you to improve your teaching throughout your teaching assistantships and be able to articulate a teaching philosophy when you draft materials for academic job applications. Keep a list of classroom successes and activities or materials that were especially beneficial for students so that you can incorporate them into future syllabi and discuss them during job interviews.

It can be tempting to put all your effort into being the perfect teaching assistant, but remember that your teaching should complement, not dominate, your research activity. Treat yourself like you would advise a student completing a major assignment – establish a growth mindset (Dweck 2006), establish S.M.A.R.T. goals[3] (specific, measurable, achievable, realistic, and time-bound) for yourself, and celebrate progress forward. A good rule of thumb is to try no more than one new pedagogical technique per class, and some techniques may require multiple classes to achieve proficiency. Remember that what works for other instructors and at other campuses may not work for you. This is not a reflection on your skill as a teaching assistant. If you are resourceful, enthusiastic, and persistent, you can learn to teach – and may even come to enjoy it, including both the humbling moments and the breakthroughs.

Endnotes

1   For more information on the mechanics of grading, see https://gsi.berkeley.edu/gsi-guide-contents/grading-intro/grading-efficiently.

2   "Tips & Tools" from the Learning Center at UNC Chapel Hill resources available at https://learningcenter.unc.edu/tips-and-tools/.

3   For more information, see https://www.ucop.edu/local-human-resources/_files/performance-appraisal/How%20to%20write%20SMART%20Goals%20v2.pdf.

References

Chiu, P. H. P., and P. Corrigan. 2019. A study of graduate teaching assistants' self-efficacy in teaching: Fits and starts in the first triennium of teaching, *Cogent Education*, 6:1.

Darling, A. L., and A. Q. Staton. 1989. Socialization of graduate teaching assistants: a case study in an American university. *International Journal of Qualitative Studies in Education*, 2(3): 221-235.

Dweck, C. S. 2006. *Mindset: The new psychology of success*. Random House Publishing.

Esarey J., and N. Valdes. 2020. Unbiased, reliable, and valid student evaluations can still be unfair. *Assessment & Evaluation in Higher Education*, 45(8): 1106-1120.

Lin, X., D. L. Schwartz, and G. Hatano. 2005. Toward teachers' adaptive metacognition. *Educational Psychologist*, 40(4): 245-255.

Luo, J., L. Bellows, and M. Grady. 2000. Classroom management issues for teaching assistants. *Research in Higher Education*, 41: 353–383.

Peterson, D.A.M., L.A. Biederman, D. Andersen, T.M. Ditonto, and K. Roe. 2019. Mitigating gender bias in student evaluations of teaching. *PLoS One,* 15, 14(5): 216-241.

Scott, S.S, J. M. McGuire, and T. E. Foley. 2003. Universal design for instruction: A framework for anticipating and responding to disability and other diverse learning needs in the college classroom. *Equity and Excellence in Education*, 36(1): 40-49.

Sharpe, R. 2000. A framework for training graduate teaching assistants. *Teacher Development*, 4(1): 131-143. DOI: 10.1080/13664530000200106

29

Preparing for the First Solo Teaching Experience: An Alternative to Learning as You Go

Christina Boyes[1], Mario Guerrero[2], Matt Lamb[3], & Mary Anne S. Mendoza[2]

1. Centro de Investigación y Docencia Económicas, DEI 2. California State Polytechnic University, Pomona
3. Texas Tech University

KEYWORDS: Graded and Ungraded Assignments, Student Resources.

Introduction

First-time instructors often lack necessary resources when preparing and teaching their first course, resulting in suboptimal outcomes for themselves and their students. Although introductory teaching programs can assist first-time instructors, access to these opportunities is unequal (McCormack, Gore, and Thomas 2007). Additionally, demographic and situational factors can hinder first-time instructors while preparing their first class. Consequently, graduate students and junior scholars are more likely to learn as they go during their first teaching experience, making them more susceptible to negative experiences while balancing research and service responsibilities (Assuncao Flores 2006; Gavish and Friedman 2010; Meanwell and Kleiner 2014).

We identify several aspects of course preparation for first-time instructors and address common situations which arise before, during, and after teaching your first course. Syllabus design is a necessary component of course preparation, but most graduate students are not taught how to do this. We provide points of consideration for the content and design of syllabi. During instruction, it helps when instructors have a sustainable means of lesson planning, while navigating various student issues and balancing teaching with research and service commitments. After teaching a course, instructors can benefit from spending time reflecting on how to develop their long-term teaching identity, especially focusing on how to be responsive to the needs of students.

Planning for course instruction should be intentional, since doing so makes it easier for instructors to teach a course that is designed in alignment with its stated outcomes. Planning also enhances student experience, since they are more likely to be engaged and do better when they know what to expect in a course. Lastly, teaching, like research, is a part of our job. We plan our research. Similarly, we should plan our teaching.

Writing the Syllabus and Determining Course Assessments

As a first-time instructor, you will be balancing teaching and research responsibilities. There are several ways you can write an optimal syllabus for student learning while accommodating time for your research agenda. Remember that you can determine assignments deadlines and exam dates according to your conference and research schedule. Additionally, you can create assessments that can be graded quickly and efficiently. In this section, we discuss the pros and cons of different types of assessments that can be scaled to accommodate time constraints and research schedules, while still optimizing learning outcomes.

Written Assignments

When teaching political science, one of the primary objectives is to assess the students' ability to synthesize and apply course content. Written assignments, such as essays, papers, and discussion boards, allow students opportunities to demonstrate a thorough understanding of the course material. They also allow you flexibility in assessing final grades for assignments as you can determine point allocation based on your expectations of the students. Written assignment prompts are also scalable to short and long form papers and can be used in multiple semesters. They may also alleviate exam pressure on students and allow for more in-depth examinations of topics.

For all their benefits, written assignments come with tradeoffs. They can be time consuming to grade, something that is especially difficult when trying to balance research responsibilities. Additionally, their evaluation involves subjective judgments on the part of the instructor. This could open up your evaluation to challenges by students. Students may enter a course with their own preconceived notions regarding course content, which could prove challenging as some students have difficulty separating pure opinion from well-supported analysis of course content. This is something about which instructors who identify as women and/or persons of color (POC) should be particularly mindful. Compared to white male peers, women and POC instructors are more likely to have their assessments challenged by students and to be rated negatively on student evaluations if those challenges do not yield results in favor of the student (see MacNell et al. 2014; El-Alayli et al. 2018).

Exams

If your goal is to assess content memorization, exams may be appropriate for your class. Exams can evaluate content knowledge through the use of multiple choice, short answer questions, or essays. They can be quickly and efficiently graded, especially if you use answer keys for short answer and essay questions. They are also less reliant on the subjective judgments of the instructor. Like written assignments, however, there are tradeoffs. Though exams take less time to grade than long form written assignments, they can take much more time to write. This is especially true if you are writing multiple-choice exams in that you have to write not only a multitude of questions, but also multiple answer choices per question. Exams also put more pressure on students and results may not accurately reflect how much they have learned in the class due to other mitigating factors such as class size and the intellectual propensities of the students (Leithner 2011; Towner 2016).

Projects

Projects can be a useful way to assess how well students process course content and apply it in original ways. They allow students to get creative and to turn the class into a collaborative experience. They also allow quite a bit of flexibility on the part of the students and the instructor. Like written assignments, projects can be scaled and altered for future classes. Some things to keep in mind, however, are that students may have different resources available to them. Any project that requires the use of technology or technical expertise may disadvantage some students, as access to technology outside of the classroom varies. Additionally, though group projects are a great opportunity to teach collaboration, they also increase the likelihood of intra-group conflict which may present difficulties in the process. For project and group activity based learning resources, see Oakley et al. 2004 or APSA Educate.

Backward Course Design

Backward course design focuses on course outcomes rather than course content, since finding content is often easier (Davidovitch 2013). For example, pre-existing syllabi from home departments or through APSA Educate can assist you immensely. The focus on outcomes leaves room for instructors to make choices in how to achieve them, making assessments or pacing a more open-ended process. It also leaves room for you to make changes throughout the semester or on an individual student basis.

Backward course design involves first asking what students should know once the course is done. These goals should be formalized into learning outcomes. Second, you should decide what students need to do to meet those outcomes. A guide for designing outcomes is in our Resources at the end of this chapter. Lastly, you decide on the activities that will meet these assessments. This will consume most of your course planning time. Reynolds and Kearns (2017) provide a helpful lesson planner if you want to align weekly activities with your course outcomes.

Identifying specific content and individual lessons is the last step (Michael and Libarkin 2016). At this point, first-time instructors may find it more useful to check whether sections from other syllabi align with the overall lesson goals. This is easier than selecting a mix of content before trying to find what makes it cohesive. Focusing on alignment with targeted learning outcomes ensures that students learn what is intended and have a better understanding of what is expected of them. Using learning outcomes to shape course design helps improve student engagement, since the syllabus will be clearer about why things are assigned (Strashnaya and Dow 2017).

It can be tempting to include many active learning techniques or the most recent academic articles in a course. You may want to update your course or entirely reject the traditional lecture model. However, be judicious. Always go back to your learning outcomes to determine if a particular reading, approach, or assessment helps you meet your objectives. The aim is to be effective, not just trendy.

You need to pace your course as part of syllabus design. Graded and ungraded assessments give students adequate scaffolding in the course. Scaffolding involves setting a foundation for students to practice skills or content and building towards a more complex task like an exam or paper. We recommend that you ensure your students practice their mastery of a certain skill or content in a guided way prior to grading their attempt. This helps instructors determine the pacing of their course, since students should have multiple opportunities to practice what they have learned prior to a major assessment such as a final exam, essay, or project. Additionally, consider the various weights attached to each assessment and if it is proportional to the importance reflected in the learning outcomes.

Aside from when assessments or content are introduced, plan out the behind-the-scenes work that is completed outside of lecture or assessments. It may be useful to not only plan for when students will take their midterm or submit a paper, but also when you will grade or provide feedback. Remember that you are balancing your teaching with research and service, meaning you will not want to be grading 25 papers the same week you are presenting at a national conference.

Handling Student Issues While Teaching

As a first-time instructor, you are likely closer in age to your students than other faculty. This can be beneficial since your students may be more open with you, but it can also be difficult as you need to maintain clear boundaries with your students. The Eberly Center at Carnegie Mellon University identifies two main causes for student issues: (1) issues tied to the course structure and (2) issues tied to individual student circumstances (Eberly Center 2021). Following the advice provided in the rest of this chapter, your course should be designed in a way that prevents structural problems. However, individual student circumstances may still arise. We do not address disruptive student behavior in this chapter, but resources for dealing with disruptive students can be found at this link: https://tomprof.stanford.edu/posting/1353. In this section, we focus on addressing individual student circumstances effectively. Individual student issues may be related to mental or physical health, academic struggles, cultural issues, or generational differences in expectations related to educational experience and respect for peers and instructors (Eberly Center 2021).

Student Resources

Some student issues, such as mental and physical health, are not your responsibility to address. However, most universities require instructors to serve as mandatory reporters of mental or physical health issues or incidents of victimization, offer institutional pathways for reporting students of concern, and provide various support services. Keeping a list of relevant on and off-campus organizations and services is helpful, since students may not know about all of them or in case students mention a concern that should be addressed by a professional. Some temporary concerns, such as relationship difficulties, stress, procrastination, or disruptive classroom behavior may be related to health struggles. Provide information on available services to your students without stigma, as cultural differences may make seeking help more difficult for some students. Additional training, as listed in our Resources at the end of the chapter, is also available for faculty interested in improving their awareness of the symptoms of mental health problems your students may be facing.

Office Hours

Hold consistent office hours and clarify the purpose of these hours. Many first-generation students are unaware of what office hours are for or have a negative perception of them. Yet, office hours attendance by political science students is correlated with academic performance (Guerrero and Rod 2013). To encourage attendance, consider offering multiple opportunities to meet each week as opposed to single blocks of time that may not work for many students. The purpose of office hours as a time for student support should be clearly stated, and office hours can be renamed 'student support hours' for this purpose. Reminders about the time and location can be automatically generated and sent to encourage attendance. Many students are intimidated by office hours or ashamed to admit they need help. Actively working to remove stigma from office hours and asking students who are performing poorly in class to attend office hours can significantly help these students, who may not attend otherwise.

Office hours are more than a tool for assisting students who are struggling. As an instructor, they help you gain student trust. Encouraging regular, active attendance at office hours can turn a classroom of strangers into a learning community as you and the students become acquainted. The development of professional student-teacher relationships can reduce behavioral problems and learning disruptions in the classroom (Decker et al. 2007). Furthermore, when students attend office hours, they may be more willing to share the specific issues they are facing, which in turn can help you to direct them towards appropriate resources.

Cultural and Generational Differences

Cultural or generational differences may lead to suboptimal student performance. Establishing clear expectations about classroom conduct, the purpose of lectures and activities, and actively seeking student feedback can help you to prevent many issues. Approaches to dealing with classroom disruptions vary across cultures (Lewis et al. 2005). Being cognizant of how international students' education in primary and high school impacts their expectations and behavior in the classroom can improve learning outcomes. Across the semester, international students may suffer from a decreased sense of social belonging, which may affect their ability to focus and potentially lead to disruptive behavior. Planning activities in the classroom that encourage communication and integration between students can help to alleviate issues related to social integration and may benefit domestic and international students (Van Horne et al. 2018).

Generational differences can also present challenges to new instructors. Though the "traditional" college student is typically 18 to 24 years old, there has been an increase in age variation in recent years due to the growth of early college high school programs, as well as an increase in enrollment amongst older students (Holland 2014). The increased age variation amongst students can also lead to differing expectations of the instructor, with some students expecting more structure while others desire more flexibility. Setting clear expectations and goals for the students early in the semester can help improve learning outcomes but showing a willingness to be flexible can increase the level of comfort that students feel in the classroom. Students of different generations can have different learning styles and varying comfort levels with educational technology (Williams, et. al., 2014). Additionally, the priorities of students of different ages can vary greatly. "Traditional" students may solely focus on their identity as college students, whereas older students may be juggling academic, professional, and familial responsibilities. Given that college student populations are much more diverse than ever before, fostering communication with students across the semester will be key to achieving desired outcomes.

Balancing Teaching, Scholarship, and Service

Most of your time as a first-year instructor will be spent on course preparation. Extensive course preparation often continues into the second or third year of a faculty appointment. You may feel some trepidation about spending a significant amount of your time focused on teaching, especially when you are excited about expanding research agendas or participating in university service. However, investing in teaching yields dividends in confidence in the classroom through the rest of one's career.

Effectively balancing teaching with scholarship and service commitments can be a nebulous task. It can take years to comfortably understand how one balances their workload. Part of this challenge rests in the wide variety of expectations found across institutions. Connecting with others who have been at your institution for a significant portion of time can provide a frank and honest assessment of how to approach these obligations, especially if expectations are not clearly delineated. See chapter 17 in this volume for more advice on time management.

Through the first year of teaching, take time to pause and reflect on your work in teaching, scholarship, and service. Reflecting upon your successes and commitments, even briefly, will help you discover that elements of your workload are inexorably connected. Bringing your research into the classroom allows you to complete publishable research projects while teaching, even perhaps in the *Journal of Political Science Education* (see chapter 30, which discusses publishing pedagogical research). As there is limited time to devote to teaching, scholarship, and service, finding these connections can lead to efficiency and your development as a scholar. Over time, it would be beneficial to cement these connections by joining the APSA Education Section or attending the APSA Teaching and Learning Conference, sharing your ideas with others in the discipline (also discussed in chapter 30). However, pausing to reflect on your efforts, typically in the summer months, also allows you to confidently assert and better articulate your own development as a teacher, scholar, and member of the university community.

Post-Course Evaluation

Successfully self-evaluating a course begins with setting appropriate objectives on the syllabus. These not only guide course assessments and content, but also the metric by which an instructor measures their efforts. The extent to which one successfully reaches these objectives can be measured through carefully designed assignments and assessments that facilitate student learning. Formal assessment work can be intimidating for first-time teachers, but a good start is keeping track of exams and essays to make small, responsive changes in each iteration of the class. However, the earlier in which one consciously thinks through course evaluation, the more consistently you can measure the success of your efforts in a class.

Student evaluations are often indirect instruments and not necessarily aligned with a course's specific objectives or goals. Biases can affect scores on student evaluations (Kreitzer and Sweet-Cushman 2021). However, some institutions still place a high value on these scores, so we encourage first-time instructors to adhere to the teaching requirements of their position. If your position does not require peer evaluations, getting feedback from a colleague who sits in your class is still valuable. For graduate students, getting an advisor to sit in your class is helpful–but can also provide a credible example of your teaching abilities in a job market letter. It can be difficult not to fixate on student scores, but we recommend focusing on being student-centered and ensuring that course assessments or assignments align with the objectives on the syllabus.

Conclusion

Building a course is a marathon, not a sprint. Prior to teaching the course, instructors need to determine the objectives that will guide the content and pacing of their syllabi. During the term, instructors need to encourage students to attend office hours and be prepared to navigate individual or course-level issues. After the term, instructors benefit from reflections and evaluations of what worked and what could be improved.

While instructors gain familiarity with course material after successive terms of teaching, this familiarity can still be fleeting since the students who make up a class change each term. A process of deliberate course design and syllabus construction with assessments that are aligned with objectives can help ensure a course's success, whether it is the first or tenth time you are teaching it. The three stages of course preparation and clear communication work together to ensure a successful course.

Resources

- APSA Educate (https://educate.apsanet.org/)
- APSA Syllabus Bank (https://www.apsanet.org/TEACHING/Syllabi-in-Political-Science/On line-Syllabi-Collections)
- APSA Teaching Simulations (https://www.apsanet.org/programs/teaching/simulations)
- Center for the Integration of Research, Teaching, and Learning (CIRTL) (https://www.cirtl.net/about)
- Mental Health First Aid Trainings (https://calendar.colorado.edu/event/mental_health_first_aid_3507)
- Dealing With Disruptive Student Behavior (https://tomprof.stanford.edu/posting/1353)
- Guide to Designing Learning Outcomes (https://teachingcommons.stanford.edu/explore-teach ing-guides/foundations-course-design/course-planning/creating-learning-outcomes)
- Template for Backward Course Design (https://wit.edu/sites/default/files/2020-10/UbD Design Template Quick Overview.pdf)

References

Assuncao Flores, Maria. 2006. "Being a Novice Teacher in Two Different Settings: Struggles, Continuities, and Discontinuities." *Teachers College Record* 108 (10): 2021-2052.

Davidovitch, Nitza. 2013. "Learning-Centered Teaching and Backward Course Design from Transferring Knowledge to Teaching Skills." *Journal of International Education Research* (JIER) 9 (4): 329-338.

Decker Dawn M., Daria Paul Dona, and Sandra L. Christenson. 2007. "Behaviorally At-Risk African American Students: The Importance of Student–Teacher Relationships for Student Outcomes." *Journal of School Psychology* 45 (1): 83–109.

Dewey, John. 1916. *Democracy and Education: An Introduction to the Philosophy of Education*. New York: Macmillan

Dewey, John. 1938. *Experience and Education*. New York: Macmillan.

Eberly Center. 2021. "Address Problematic Student Behavior." Eberly Center for Teaching Excellence & Educational Innovation at Carnegie Mellon University.

Gavish, Bella, and Isaac A. Friedman. 2010. "Novice Teachers' Experience of Teaching: A Dynamic Aspect of Burnout." *Social Psychology of Education* 13 (2): 141-167.

Guerrero, Mario, and Alisa Beth Rod. 2013 "Engaging in Office Hours: A Study of Student-Faculty Interaction and Academic Performance." *Journal of Political Science Education* 9 (4): 403-416.

Hebert, Edward, and Terry Worthy. 2001. "Does the First Year of Teaching Have to Be a Bad One? A case study of success." *Teaching and Teacher Education* 17 (8): 897-911.

Hepburn, Mary A., Richard G. Niemi, and Chris Chapman. 2000. "Service Learning in College Political Science: Queries and Commentary." *PS: Political Science and Politics* 33 (3): 617-622.

Holland, Kelley. 2014, Aug 28. 'Why America's campuses are going gray.' *CNBC*. https://www.cnbc.com/2014/08/28/why-americas-campuses-are-going-gray.html.

Jahanbani, Nakissa, Charmaine Willis, and Donnett Lee. 2018. "What We Wish We Knew: Reflections of Brand-New Teaching Assistants." *Journal of Political Science Education* 14 (3): 409-413.

Kreitzer, Rebecca J., and Jennie Sweet-Cushman. 2021. "Evaluating Student Evaluations of Teaching: a Review of Measurement and Equity Bias in SETs and Recommendations for Ethical Reform." *Journal of Academic Ethics*.

Leithner, Anika. 2011. "Do Student Learning Styles Translate to Different 'Testing Styles'?" *Journal of*

Political Science Education 7 (4): 416-433.

Lewis Ramon, Shlomo Romi, Qui Xing, and Yaccov J. Katz. 2005. "Teachers' Classroom Discipline and Student Misbehavior in Australia, China and Israel." *Teaching and Teacher Education* 21 (6): 729–41.

McCormack, Ann, Jennifer Gore, and Kaye Thomas. 2006. "Early Career Teacher Professional Learning." *Asia-Pacific Journal of Teacher Education* 34 (1): 95-113.

Meanwell, Emily, and Sibyl Kleiner. 2014. "The Emotional Experience of First-Time Teaching: Reflections from Graduate Instructors, 1997–2006." *Teaching Sociology* 42 (1): 17-27.

Michael, Nancy A., and Julie C. Libarkin. 2016. "Understanding by Design: Mentored Implementation of Backward Design Methodology at the University Level." *Bioscene: Journal of College Biology Teaching* 42 (2): 44-52.

Oakley, Barbara, Richard M. Felder, Rebecca Brent, and Imad Elhajj. 2004. "Turning Student Groups into Effective Teams." *Journal of Student Centered Learning* 2(1): 9 - 34.

Reynolds, Heather L., and Katherine Dowell Kearns. 2017. "A Planning Tool for Incorporating Backward Design, Active Learning, and Authentic Assessment in the College Classroom." *College Teaching* 65 (1): 17-27.

Strashnaya, Renata, and Emily AA Dow. 2017. "Purposeful Pedagogy through Backward Course Design." R. Obeid, A. Schartz, C. Shane-Simpson, & P. J. Brooks (Eds.) *How We Teach Now: The GSTA Guide to Student-Centered Teaching.*

Towner, Terri. 2016. "Class Size and Academic Achievement in Introductory Political Science Courses" *Journal of Political Science Education* 12 (4): 420-436.

University of Colorado Boulder. 2021. Mental Health First Aid Trainings. Health and Wellness Services. https://www.colorado.edu/health/trainings#mental_health_first_aid-267.

Van Horne, Sam Van., Shuhui Lin, Matthew Anson, and Wayne Jacobson. 2018. "Engagement, Satisfaction, and Belonging of International Undergraduates at U.S. Research Universities." *Journal of International Students* 8 (1), 351–374.

Williams, Chad J., John J. Matt, and Frances L. O'Reilly. 2014. Generational Perspective of Higher Education Online Student Learning Styles. *Journal of Education and Learning* 3(2): 33 - 51.

Wiggins, Grant P., Grant Wiggins, and Jay McTighe. 2005. *Understanding by design.*

30 Resources for Teaching Excellence: APSA's Education Section and the TLC

Megan Becker[1], Elizabeth A. Bennion[2], Colin M. Brown[3], & Eric D. Loepp[4]

1. University of Southern California 2. Indiana University, South Bend

3. Northeastern University 4. University of Wisconsin–Whitewater

KEYWORDS: Effective Teaching, TLC.

Introduction

This chapter covers the role of APSA's Political Science Education (PSE) Section and Teaching and Learning Conference (TLC) within the political science community. After outlining each institution, we discuss the benefits of joining the section and attending the conferences. These benefits are substantial, yielding professional and personal rewards for any political scientist who chooses a career that includes college teaching.

What Do You Need to Know?

APSA's Organized Section on Political Science Education is a formal community for political scientists interested not only in teaching excellence, but also in developing our discipline's tools, techniques, and norms around teaching. Formally stated, its purpose is "…both to promote exemplary undergraduate teaching within the political science discipline and to the scholarship of teaching. The section is especially dedicated to increasing the use of innovative teaching methods, particularly those rooted in experience (internships, service learning, simulations, and study abroad) and the evaluation of such methods" (APSA Connect Section 29).

The section helps coordinate panels at conferences and is active in the planning and organization of APSA's bi-annual Teaching and Learning Conference (*TLC*) and TLC at APSA—a mini-conference during the APSA annual meeting[1]. It also administers awards to recognize innovation in teaching and service to the pedagogical goals of the discipline. The section often advises the staff and leadership of APSA when they embark on new teaching and learning initiatives, like APSA Educate, an online platform for sharing classroom materials launched in 2020.

The goal of the section is to build a community to share teaching ideas and support the scholarship of teaching and learning (SoTL). Within the section, smaller communities support specific practices or issues that align with the "tracks" from TLC conferences (see below). Traditionally, the PSE Section has taken a strong interest in civic education, although as of 2020, a separate organized section has been established at APSA to focus specifically on such engagement both inside and outside the classroom.[2]

From its founding in 2005 until 2017, the *Journal of Political Science Education* was overseen by the PSE section. While this journal is now sponsored directly by APSA, section members remain well represented among the editorial board and contributing authors. The section's newsletter, the *PS Educator*, is published biannually and includes teaching tips and reflections, as well as informal reviews of teaching materials and texts.[3]

While the section does have nominal membership dues, graduate students do not pay section dues to join. All members must be active APSA members. Section leadership is elected by members at the annual business meeting held during the APSA Annual Meeting (with informal business meetings also held at TLC). All conference-goers, not just members, are encouraged to attend to learn more about the section.

Why Does It Matter?

Participation in the PSE Section and attendance at TLC are excellent ways to learn the latest pedagogical techniques. You are likely to teach sometime during your PhD program, either as a teaching assistant or as instructor of record. These experiences are valuable for near-term financial reasons (more potential teaching opportunities) and for longer-term development of important career skills.

Becoming an Effective Teacher (and Job Applicant)

You will be better prepared for the teaching expectations of a faculty position if you've spent time thinking about pedagogy and applying different approaches in your own classroom. Unfortunately, not all programs provide pedagogy training for PhD students, but attending TLC can help fill this gap. Hands-on workshops at the conference are particularly helpful in this regard. For example, conferences regularly feature workshops on using simulations and games in classes. In these workshops, attendees not only get instructions and associated materials for the games, but they actually play the games. It is easier to approach a new teaching method with confidence when you have practiced it beforehand and can anticipate how events will unfold.

Even without your own classroom, learning about pedagogy still has professional benefits. When applying for faculty positions, you will be expected to write a teaching statement explaining your classroom approach, how you design syllabi and assessments, and the goals you have for your students. Teaching statements can be especially important for new PhDs with little teaching experience, but who are interested in teaching-focused positions. Exposure to new evidence-based classroom practices and understanding current terminology is critical for crafting a compelling statement. In fact, past TLCs have had dedicated sessions for graduate students assembling application materials, and active PSE section members are helpful mentors for this aspect of the job market.

Teaching is a non-negligible (and incredibly important) part of nearly every faculty member's job. Being a good teacher is not an innate ability, but rather a skill that is learned and practiced. Starting that practice sooner rather than later, in a supportive environment like a TLC, can help you find and develop your identity as an educator and learn pedagogical practices that will have value for you, both as a PhD student and a faculty member.

Building New Networks

Most political scientists remember their first major conference presentation. Navigating to the proper room. Arriving early to quadruple-check the technology. Finally placing faces with names in their field. Advisors and peers often remind graduate students that attending conferences is not just about presenting research, it's about networking. Indeed, while major conferences like APSA's annual gathering incorporate a variety of networking opportunities, it is easy to get lost among thousands of attendees at a convention center. These events draw from across the discipline and are focused principally on the dissemination of research. This means that, despite a large quantity of potential contacts, many attendees at the major conferences work at research-oriented universities that do not represent the most common career trajectories for graduate students. Smaller conferences often lead to richer, more fruitful connections with potential peers, collaborators, and colleagues, with the quality of networking opportunities often more than making up for the lesser quantity.

APSA's teaching and learning events are a perfect example. As noted above, the stand-alone TLC is a separate entity from the larger annual conference and takes place every other year in the spring. It draws a more intimate crowd and affords some of the best opportunities for quality networking in the discipline, particularly for graduate students aspiring to academic appointments at more teaching-oriented institutions. A larger share of faculty attendees hail from smaller institutions that place less emphasis on research productivity and more emphasis on teaching. They are extremely collegial and are committed to both sharing and improving their pedagogy. Graduate students can mingle with leading pedagogy experts in the discipline in a smaller, less formal environment that lends itself extremely well to casual exchanges of teaching ideas between sessions, in addition to the more formal presentation of teaching and learning scholarship and innovations. Conversations often start during a scheduled session, continue at the coffee station in the hall, and then move to a restaurant at the end of the day.

The design of TLC also encourages productive networking. Rather than scheduling a series of panels over the course of the weekend and inviting attendees to pick and choose individual sessions, TLC combines traditional panel sessions with a "track" model. Participants select a track—such as civic education, technology and innovation, or simulations and games—and attend a series of panels during the conference with the same group of people. Rather than assigning specific discussants, all sessions include a moderator and significant time for open discussion focused both on the papers and on larger issues and take-aways. During that time, attendees can get to know their "trackmates" extremely well. It can also be a great opportunity to meet book publishers and other vendors sharing new educational products and tools.

Expanding Your Publication Options

Informal interactions often lead to productive collaborations and fulfilling friendships, even between people who have never met before. At the 2020 TLC, Eric, one of the authors of this chapter, first met Dan, one of the editors of this volume. During a casual conversation, Eric and Dan discovered a mutual interest in the pedagogy of teaching research methods. They soon connected with Julia, another editor of this volume, and formalized an edited book proposal that would ultimately become *The Palgrave Handbook of Political Research Pedagogy*. At the same conference, Colin, another author of this chapter, participated in rich conversations as part of the "Teaching Research, Writing, and Information Literacy" conference track that led to a cross-college collaboration where research methods students shared surveys and feedback with students on the other side of the country. Similarly, all three *Teaching Civic Engagement* books[4] published by APSA were launched at the TLC-based on connections forged at the conference and section meetings where chapter author Elizabeth met co-editors Elizabeth Matto, Allison McCartney, and Dick Simpson—along with current APSA President John Ishiyama who encouraged Elizabeth to edit the first volume and contribute two handbook chapters.[5] Similarly, Elizabeth contributed chapters to a book on civic education co-edited by two scholars she met through the PSE section,[6] and co-founded the Consortium for Intercampus SoTL Research with fellow conference-goer J. Cherie Strachan, another editor of this volume.[7] APSA books on assessment[8] and internships[9] were also conceived during track sessions, conference panels, and informal receptions for APSA's teaching and learning community.

Participation in APSA's Political Science Education Section and teaching conferences offers a wide range of opportunities for publication. Section members serve as editors and editorial board members for outlets like the *Journal of Political Science Education* and *PS: Political Science & Politics*, and many articles included in the journal were first presented at TLC or at APSA annual meeting panels sponsored by the PSE section. There are also relatively quick publication opportunities that enhance graduate school résumés while building one's reputation in the field. In addition to publishing full-length articles,[10] *PS: Political Science & Politics* publishes summaries of each of the TLC tracks each July, and track moderators often give preference to graduate student authors. All PSE section members are encouraged to share ideas about teaching through brief (1,000 to 1,500 word) essays in the *PS Educator*[11] and are frequently asked to write brief essays for APSA online platforms, including APSA Educate and Raise the Vote. It is important to note that some institutions (e.g., liberal arts colleges and regional comprehensive universities) will likely value these publications, and the scholarship of teaching and learning, more than other institutions (e.g., R1 universities). This is worth considering as you decide how much time to devote to such work. One of the authors, Colin, found such publications helpful in transitioning from a research-intensive PhD program to a teaching-focused faculty position.

What Should/Can You Do?

Graduate students interested in the PSE section have several ways to get involved. Perhaps most important is attending TLC and/or TLC at APSA, in order to see the range of pedagogical scholarship and practice. The section is eager to raise the importance and profile of teaching and learning in the discipline, and enthusiastically welcomes any political scientists interested in improving teaching. It is worth reaching out to anyone leading an interesting workshop or giving a paper on a topic of interest, as they are likely willing to share materials and introduce you to other members.

Joining the section is also an important way to get involved (and, again, it is free for graduate students!). Membership grants access to private discussion boards on APSA Connect and the *PS Educator* newsletter and also allows you to participate in section leadership.[12] As noted above, members wishing to write short reflections will find the *PS Educator* to be a relatively open outlet for writing about teaching practice and getting some early (non-peer-reviewed) publications. It is a great way to share ideas and build a reputation, especially when combined with the informal networking opportunities available at the annual TLC mini-conference at APSA and bi-annual standalone TLC.

Finally, there are a number of awards to recognize teaching excellence for graduate students, beginning faculty, and/or contingent faculty. At the section level, the Craig L. Brians Award for Excellence in Undergraduate Research and Mentorship emphasizes work encouraging undergraduate scholarship. There is also an award for best paper presented at the previous year's meeting. APSA presents two annual teaching and learning awards, the CQ Press Award for Teaching Innovation and the Michael Brintnall Teaching and Learning Award. Most colleges and universities have internal awards as well, and it is worth looking to your teaching and learning center or faculty development office for these opportunities; APSA also publicizes members who win campus teaching awards in *Political Science Today*. There are exceptions, but it is worth emphasizing that most academic awards not only accept but actively encourage self-nominations. The process of applying for these may not only recognize the hard work that graduate students and new faculty put into teaching but can serve as helpful opportunities to reflect on your own goals and accomplishments.

Conclusion

Teaching is an important part of most faculty jobs in political science, and teaching experience is highly valued by many institutions as they consider candidates for faculty positions. Liberal arts colleges, community colleges, and regional comprehensive universities often seek out candidates who have demonstrated an interest in teaching; such institutions pay greater attention to teaching statements and course evaluations as part of the job application process and may also require a teaching demonstration. Fortunately, there are many resources like the American Political Science Association's Political Science Education Section, Teaching and Learning Conference, and TLC at APSA available to political science graduate students interested in developing their teaching skills, networks, and philosophy.

Endnotes

1   TLC at APSA follows a similar structure as the stand-alone TLC event, but is smaller in scale. For graduate students who may only have funding for one conference per year, TLC at APSA is an ideal place to start.

2   For information about the Civic Engagement Section go to https://sites.google.com/view/apsacivic/home.

3   Past issues of the newsletter are available on the Teaching Civic Engagement website at https://web.apsanet.org/teachingcivicengagement/political-science-educator/.

4   The books include: Teaching Civic Engagement (2013) edited by Alison Rios Millet McCartney, Elizabeth A. Bennion, and Dick Simpson; Teaching Civic Engagement Across the Disciplines

(2017), edited by Elizabeth M. Matto, Alison Rios Millett McCartney, Elizabeth A. Bennion, and Dick Simpson; and Teaching Civic Engagement Globally (2021), edited by Elizabeth M. Matto, Alison Rios Millett McCartney, Elizabeth A. Bennion, Alasdair Blair, Taiyi Sun, and Dawn Whitehead.

5   Elizabeth A. Bennion. 2011. "Experiments." In 21st Century Political Science: A Reference Handbook, eds. John T. Ishiyama and Marijke Breuning. Thousand Oaks, CA: Sage Publications. Elizabeth A. Bennion. 2015. "Experiential Education in Political Science and International Relations." In Handbook on Teaching and Learning in Political Science and International Relations, eds. John Ishiyama, William J. Miller, and Eszter Simon. Northampton, MA: Edward Elgar Publishing

6   See Elizabeth A. Bennion (2015), "Partnering with Your Local PBS Station to Promote Civic and Political Engagement," and Cherie J. Strachan and Elizabeth A. Bennion (2015), "Moving the Scholarship of Teaching & Learning Forward: The Consortium for SoTL Research," in Civic Education in the Twenty-First Century, eds. Michael T. Rogers and Donald M. Gooch. Lanham, MD: Lexington Books.

7   For more information about the Consortium see J. Cherie Strachan and Elizabeth A. Bennion. 2016. "Extending Assessment beyond Our Own Programs and Campuses: The National Survey of Student Leaders and the Inter-Campus Consortium for SoTL Research." PS: Political Science & Politics 49 (1): 111-115.

8   See Michelle D. Deardorff, Kerstin Hamann , and John Ishiyama, eds. 2009. Assessment in Political Science . Washington, DC : American Political Science Association.

9   See Renee Van Vechten, Bobbi Gentry and John Berg, eds. 2021. Toward Best Practices in Political Science Internships. Washington, DC: American Political Science Association.

10   Pedagogy articles tend to be shorter than traditional disciplinary scholarship. At the time of writing, pedagogy articles at JPSE and PS are limited to about 3,000 words.

11   Submissions can be sent to editor.pse.newsletter@gmail.com, with deadlines usually falling in December/January and June/July.

12   Conference planning and award committees are good places for students or junior scholars wishing to gain or expand national service experience.

References

Bennion, Elizabeth A. 2011. "Experiments." In *21st Century Political Science: A Reference Handbook*, eds. John T. Ishiyama and Marijke Breuning. Thousand Oaks, CA: Sage Publications.

Bennion, Elizabeth A. 2015. "Experiential Education in Political Science and International Relations." In *Handbook on Teaching and Learning in Political Science and International Relations*, eds. John Ishiyama, William J. Miller, and Eszter Simon. Northampton, MA: Edward Elgar Publishing.

Bennion, Elizabeth A. 2015. "Partnering with Your Local PBS Station to Promote Civic and Political Engagement," In *Civic Education in the Twenty-First Century*, eds. Michael T. Rogers and Donald M. Gooch. Lanham, MD: Lexington Books

Bennion, Elizabeth A. Ed. 2022 (forthcoming). *Teaching Experimental Political Science*. Northampton, MA: Edward Elgar Publishers.

Deardorff, Michelle D., Kerstin Hamann, and John Ishiyama, eds. 2009. *Assessment in Political Science*. Washington, DC: American Political Science Association.

Matto, Elizabeth M. Alison Rios Millett McCartney, Elizabeth A. Bennion, Alisdair Blair, Taiyi Sun, and Dawn Whitehead Eds. 2021. *Teaching Civic Engagement Globally*. Washington, DC: American Political Science Association.

Matto, Elizabeth M., Alison Rios Millett McCartney, Elizabeth A. Bennion, and Dick Simpson. Eds. 2017. *Teaching Civic Engagement Across the Disciplines*. Washington, DC: American Political Science Association.

McCartney, Alison Rios Millett, Elizabeth A. Bennion, and Dick Simpson. Eds. 2013. *Teaching Civic Engagement: From Student to Active Citizen*. Washington, DC: American Political Science Association.

Mallinson, Daniel J., Julia Marin Hellwege, and Eric D. Loepp. 2021. *The Palgrave Handbook of Political Research Pedagogy*. New York, New York: Palgrave Macmillan.

Strachan, J. Cherie and Elizabeth A. Bennion. 2015, "Moving the Scholarship of Teaching & Learning Forward: The Consortium for SoTL Research," in *Civic Education in the Twenty-First Century*, eds. Michael T. Rogers and Donald M. Gooch. Lanham, MD: Lexington Books.

Strachan, J. Cherie and Elizabeth A. Bennion. 2016. "Extending Assessment beyond Our Own Programs and Campuses: The National Survey of Student Leaders and the Inter-Campus Consortium for SoTL Research." *PS: Political Science & Politics* 49 (1): 111-115.

Van Vechten, Renee, Bobbi Gentry and John Berg, eds. 2021. *Toward Best Practices in Political Science Internships*. Washington, DC: American Political Science Association.

Professional Development— Service

31

Academic Service and Flourishing

Anthony Petros Spanakos[1] & Ignangeli Salinas-Muniz[2]

1. Montclair State University 2. University of Michigan

KEYWORDS: Academic Service, Mentoring Responsibilities.

Introduction

No work environment functions, let alone flourishes, without some members engaging in services to others and the institution. *Academic service* is normally considered part of the responsibilities of a full-time tenure line faculty (often considered as factoring 10-20% of the evaluation towards tenure and/or promotion) and it is sometimes expected (and required) of non-tenure line and adjunct faculty. Departments often encourage graduate students to 'get involved' but also warn against taking on commitments that get in the way of their academic commitments (there are always cases of people who became very involved and never finished a degree). This advice is based on conventional wisdom that it is primarily publications and then teaching which land academic jobs for doctoral students.

Increasingly fewer students in doctoral programs in political science take tenure track positions upon defending their dissertations and most institutions of higher education need inspired and inspiring teachers (more than top-tier published authors). As more students move into less traditional professional academic employment and the field gives greater weight to job satisfaction and social emotional well-being, greater attention should be given to academic service (APSA 2021). This is because academic service can be a space for personal and professional development and happiness, and it can also open unexpected professional opportunities. Anyone who has served on an academic committee is unlikely to think 'this is the path to happiness,' but this essay will try to explain why graduate students and faculty should think carefully about and participate wisely in academic service. Of course, not all service opportunities are of equal value and people need to be careful not to overcommit or allow themselves to be pulled into too many service obligations.

An Apology for Service

Academic service is an ambiguous term, which can include multiple activities across a range of domains and on various levels. These activities may be research-oriented (organizing a seminar series), advising, organizing, mentoring, and governance. The domains might include the field (political science), subfields (comparative politics, American politics), professional associations (APSA, regional political science associations, Association for Asian Studies, Latin American Studies Association), local governance (Graduate Student Union representatives, Graduate Students of Color), or other spaces (associate editor on a journal, translator for legal clinic, advisor for a student association). The levels at which service can take place include the department, college or university, local (town or city), state, national, and international. The possibilities are rather limitless as service responds to the changing professional, social, and personal interests, responsibilities, and needs of diverse people operating over lengthy periods of time (whether several years for a typical doctoral student or several decades for some faculty members).

Academic service constitutes a quantitatively small part of faculty evaluations and, cynically, it can be said that good service does little to help an application; but bad service can be an excuse to deny tenure or promotion. The very engaged faculty member receives the same tenure as the one who just shows up and this can be discouraging. But the former is more likely to have better teaching evaluations and, more importantly, to enjoy teaching. Being more satisfied with teaching, which is disproportionately the primary responsibility for almost all professors in higher education, plays an important role in maintaining motivation as multiple articles pass through (or not) the slow process of peer-review. Greater motivation also contributes to continuing to engage in scholarship post-tenure, and it also encourages faculty to create new classes, work on new minor programs, and participate in departmental, college/university-wide, and professional programs (a program of Human Rights Studies, faculty development center, or division chair for a professional association). The happier faculty member may be on committees where one doodles and watches paint dry, but he or she can also choose committees where he or she cares about the subject and can make an impact.

Being a faculty advisor to a particular group of students, attending student recruiting events, serving as a mentor, being a leader in professional associations, serving on an editorial board for a journal, being a representative for the veterans' association, among other activities, can be very rewarding activities. They are not without their frustration. Mentoring involves prolonged discussions with students who struggle with very difficult, often irresolvable, challenges. But the reward of seeing students not give up and, sometimes, overcome challenges is considerable. Developing fellowship with other faculty and administrators who seek to help is critical for maintaining a sense of purpose and belonging. As a former chair once confided, being chair allowed him to help students more effectively than as a professor. Indeed, anyone in the field has opportunities to improve writing skills and analytical focus, but some advising scenarios allow faculty to contribute to improvement in more existential situations (e.g., retaining financial aid or responding to homelessness).

When faculty look through applications for a faculty position, full-time or adjunct, they look through a package that contains tremendous information (in what other field would it not be an offense to send a 25-page CV?). Although priorities vary in terms of how much and what sort of teaching and research is valued, academic service on CVs often stands out and gives occasion for a personal question in an interview, which can reveal more about a candidate than would a question about a dissertation. Search committees are not seeking soulmates, but they do not want to hire people who are not going to make their and their students' lives worse. And so, while many have written a dissertation that a dissertation advisor describes as 'brilliant' and possibly 'field-changing,' being the chair of the Graduate Women's Caucus for the last three years of a doctoral experience can truly stand out.

APSA reports roughly 26-27% of doctoral students get to all-but-dissertation status and roughly 32% report receiving a tenure-track position upon completion (APSA 2021). They may find tenure track positions later on but are most likely to work in other positions in higher education, think tanks, publishing, or other areas (See chapter 41 on non-traditional options). Academic service can, again, make a candidate stand out as being particularly qualified for a particular job. The person who as a graduate student was a Resident Advisor of the international dormitory can make an excellent case to be hired in a Global Affairs/Student Exchange unit. The coordinator of a speaker series can pursue positions in conference administration in a think tank or editorial work at a publisher. The graduate student who has been on the bargaining committee for the Union can look to other work in organized labor, government, or political advocacy. Importantly, all those positions may value the skills connected with service highly enough that being ABD or not (yet) completing the doctoral program may not be an obstacle to employment.

Of course, not all academic service will immediately open employment possibilities; but they certainly open the perspective to see the many and diverse possibilities for professional and personal engagement in an environment in which higher education training is a necessary but insufficient condition for long-term success and happiness. Understanding those possibilities and pursuing some through engagement in service can contribute to flourishing and to building resilience against the myriad forms of frustration that can occur during a career.

A Caveat

Not every service opportunity will be fulfilling, and one might need to experiment a bit to find what sort of service is more meaningful and enjoyable. You should be judicious in expectations with any service opportunity until you get a sense of what it truly entails, what is possible, and with whom you must work. People with different personalities may take on service differently, and there may be different expectations of participation for people of different backgrounds. You also need to be careful about how much of yourself you will devote to the role. Scholars who identify with one or more underrepresented groups often report outsized *mentoring responsibilities*. This can be especially exhausting, while also consuming time that could be spent on research. They also report a lack of support, which contributes to lower completion rates and higher levels of frustration (Tormos-Aponte and Velez-Serrano 2020).

Introverted students are less likely to engage in most types of academic service and may struggle with a sense of belonging, while extroverts are more likely to overextend themselves and risk having a reputation as a good departmental 'citizen' while not devoting sufficient attention to research. First generation students may be more likely to have a sense of 'imposter syndrome' and service, often more than research or being a teaching assistant, can give insight into the university while also contributing to a sense of membership (See chapter 50 on imposter syndrome). Indeed, the 'invisible curriculum' that is so vital to success and flourishing in graduate school and beyond is most easily visible to the participants in academic service, via their interaction with other members of the community (Gable 2021).

Particular advice is difficult as doctoral students are quite different and will pursue different paths. As such, you will need to figure out how to balance your various commitments, and overdoing service (or teaching or research) may mean different things to different people at different times. It may be impossible to quantify how much is over-doing it. But the conversations that emerge from academic service provide opportunities to dialogue with others to attain a better sense of what good balance looks like.

Service Opportunities in Graduate School

Most students enter into doctoral programs in Political Science already having been involved in a range of service activities (extracurricular activities). In orientations in their new programs, they are often told about great opportunities for involvement. Informally, however, mentors often express concern about becoming 'distracted' or too involved in activities that are far afield from a dissertation. The latter may be especially the case in doctoral programs that aggressively treat qualifying examinations or papers as ways of channeling out of the program people from whom the department sees minimal potential contributions. Focus on a dissertation and preparing for qualifying exams encourages students to strategically seek out people with similar interests, methods, subfields, and so on. And academic service can provide opportunities to go outside of a 'silo' and to have a better sense of the diversity within the field.

Perhaps the most obvious space in which graduate students can engage in service that overlaps with academic interests is through academic workshops. These are spaces where students and faculty present their work and receive constructive feedback, usually organized by sub-field or interdisciplinary workshops such as Peace and Conflict Studies and Race and Ethic Politics. Students may contribute in many ways, the lowest stake way is to attend frequently, listen carefully, and offer constructive feedback. Thus, students are in a conference-like scenario in which they learn about the field and develop professional skills. Since graduate students (especially in their first year) do not have classes with most faculty, workshops are spaces where students and faculty can learn more about each other.

A more active form of participation in workshops is to present work or to be a discussant for a presentation. Workshops cannot be sustained if scholars do not present their work. By presenting, you are not only improving your skills and receiving valuable feedback for your work, but you are contributing to your academic community by keeping these workshops active. Similarly, workshops need discussants.

Students often feel they do not have something ready for presentation and lack expertise to be a discussant. But the very same students, after participating, are often surprised by how well they tackle these assignments. Overcoming such fears is essential for many reasons. First, students need to learn that there is no moment where one has complete knowledge of a subject. Second, students must understand that participation in a scholarly community involves a dialogue of people who on any given day and any particular matter have different abilities and levels of interest. In the case of serving as a discussant, it is often easier to discern the value of and means of improvement of another's research.

Students may also organize workshops, which is more labor intensive and is often done by teams (say two to three students and one faculty member). This is a great opportunity to meet more faculty inside and outside the department. Organizing these workshops makes you part of the decision-making process. Furthermore, since workshops are such a key part of departmental culture, it could signal to future employers that you were an active participant. Creating workshops is more time consuming but it can be incredibly rewarding as you can create a forum for something not given sufficient attention. Such fora can provide opportunities to work one-on-one with a faculty member. You can even learn to apply for funding (a key skill!). Race and Ethnic Politics workshops are examples of recently created series and have usually been born out of this type of effort.

Another area in which students can be involved is in admission panels. Some departments reserve some seats on admissions committees for current graduate students. This is a great opportunity to shape the department in various ways, such as increasing diversity, or raising the profile of one theme or methodology. Depending on the subfield and the department, you will probably have to read from 40 to 200 graduate applications and take the hard decisions of choosing a few students from a big pool of excellent future scholars. This is usually done in the course of a few weeks to a month, which can be an intense demand on your time. Yet it is a great way to understand the admissions process and to signal to future employers that you know how it works. Being part of an admissions committee can prove invaluable, as it mirrors some of the same considerations that emerge in grant, dissertation award, and hiring committees. The experience of application review and relationship building with faculty has immediate benefits in terms of professionally relevant skills, while also contributing to a sense of membership and decision-making in a community.

Another area where graduate students often engage in service is through affinity groups such as a Political Science Graduate Student Association, Queer Political Scientists, Political Scientists of Color, and Women's Caucus. Departments tend to have a political science graduate student association, which carries a range of possible responsibilities such as governance issues, admissions, hiring, and union and/ or collective bargaining over research/teaching assistant contracts. Leaders in these groups learn quite a bit about their departments and the field while often take on mentoring roles as well. They do this through outreach in local initiatives, organizing, engaging in professional associations (MPSA, SPSA, etc.), and building networks of alumni among faculty and other professionals across the United States and beyond.

Extant groups could benefit from proactive members and there is space to form groups that do not yet exist. This might be a good opportunity to develop an affinity group with a few students. It might start out small and this could be a very difficult process. But if all goes well you can very likely get your department to fund your activities. Like workshops, students can contribute to departmental life by being an active part of these communities, including through taking on leadership roles. Such groups can play an important role in helping potential students to select a doctoral program, and they might be involved in recruiting and orientation events. Thus, building strong groups is important for creating the type of community you want.

Conclusion

There are many other areas in which graduate students can engage in academic service. Leadership while a graduate student is great preparation for professional and personal scenarios that follow a graduate experience, whether in the form of a tenure track faculty position, as adjunct faculty, a post-doc fellow, or some other role in higher education or another industry. Academic service often offers surprisingly important opportunities to contribute to flourishing via building social networks, maintaining motivation, developing a sense of membership, resilience, and responsibility, and giving insight into and agency in decision-making processes. Rather than being a distraction to be avoided or box to tick, it should be taken seriously. However, young scholars should prioritize the work they find most meaningful and enriching and should carefully consider the workload before accepting any service position.

References

APSA. 2021. "APSA Graduate Placement Report: Analysis of Political Science Placements for 2018-2020" American Political Science Association. https://preprints.apsanet.org/engage/api-gateway/apsa/assets/orp/resource/item/61649e5d8b620d1d574c4b7f/original/apsa-graduate-placement-report-analysis-of-political-science-placements-for-2018-2020.pdf (Accessed December 6, 2021), 1-23.

Gable, Rachel. 2021. *The Hidden Curriculum First Generation Students at Legacy Universities*, Princeton: Princeton University Press.

Tormos-Aponte, Fernando, and Mayra Velez-Serrano. 2020. "Broadening the Pathway for Graduate Students in Political Science." *PS: Political Science & Politics* 53(1):145–46.

32

Towards A More Holistic Graduate Experience: Professional Service to the Discipline

Courtney N. Haun[1] & Ivy A.M. Cargile[2]

1. Samford University 2. California State University, Bakersfield

KEYWORDS: Volunteer, Professional Network.

Introduction

Service during graduate school can amplify student learning outcomes and bolster relationships within the academy (McFadden and Smeaton 2017; Sinha 2014). However, at the same time, too much time devoted to service may lead an undue level of stress (Valovick and Swegle 2020). The type and amount of service one provides to the discipline can look different across graduate students and across the time in the academic program. With that said, weighing the pros and cons of service is important while completing graduate program work.

In political science, service may consist of volunteering at one's political science department as well as assisting with the various sub-groups, caucuses, and affiliated groups that are a part of the larger national organization, the American Political Science Association (APSA), and the smaller regional organizations. Some of these groups have specific positions for graduate students, while others do not but are open to having graduate students fill them. Some organizations, such as the Midwest Political Science Association, hire graduate students in order to help with membership and the planning of the annual meeting. While this latter opportunity is a paid one, as opposed to most which are volunteer based, it is still an effective way to get involved with the discipline outside of one's own institution. Similarly, at the APSA there is also the opportunity to be involved with a recently created group: the Graduate Student Status Committee. Its focus is to give graduate students a voice on important decisions made by the larger organization, as well as to provide professionalization opportunities. Then for some graduate students, there are other helpful pathways to partake in service that are paved by their faculty advisors. For instance, some graduate students have the opportunity to work with various journal editors (who are faculty) in managing the submissions of manuscripts for possible publications.

As a graduate student it is easy to fall into the trap of thinking that service to the discipline is not something to do, either because one has not yet finished the graduate program and thus has not yet secured full-time employment, or that it is simply not important. The latter is primarily driven by all of the different responsibilities that graduate students juggle—primarily those of course work, comprehensive examination preparation, dissertation creation, etc.—all while trying to publish manuscripts as an early scholar. However, providing service to the discipline of political science can yield important benefits that are worth considering.

By volunteering to conduct service, one of the immediate benefits is the opportunity to expand one's *professional network*, which can prove helpful not just in the immediate short term but in the long run throughout one's career. As a graduate student, it is valuable to know both faculty and graduate students who are not a part of one's own program. Not only does it lend itself to co-authorship opportunities, but also to hearing the perspectives and the experiences of professionals outside of one's institution. Another possible benefit is learning how things get accomplished within the discipline broadly, as well as the professional organizations that are vital to the academy. Lastly, it can also help with the development of leadership traits that can be useful as one journeys from graduate student to career professional. Overall, there are a variety of benefits from taking part in service, including but not limited to enriching a students' future career prospects, building professional networks, and providing a favorable impression among colleagues in the field.

Why Service Matters

Service to the discipline of political science is often on a *volunteer* basis. As such, what opportunities a student decides to get involved with needs to be carefully evaluated, especially when juggling course work, comprehensive exams, and teacher and research assistant duties. As a result, it is important that while giving their time, graduate students also be selective in what they choose to do. In a sense, graduate students want to be strategic and volunteer to do service work that will either enhance a skillset or that will help to take a "mental break" from school/academic work. Regardless of the reasons for deciding to complete service work, another reality to consider is that despite drawbacks such as losing time allocated for reading and writing, there also exist several benefits (Brock 2012).

By expanding one's professional network, it is possible to increase and vary the number of graduate students and faculty one is familiar with across various universities and departments. As previously mentioned, a wider network can not only result in opportunities to co-author with other graduate students or faculty who have shared research interests, but it can also result in the opportunity to learn about the numerous ways that other political science departments function, based on the experiences of those ones is meeting while serving. This can be beneficial when getting ready to go on the job market and figuring out what skills, approaches, and overall content should be highlighted in job packets. In addition, it is also possible to increase the level of knowledge one has about scholarships, fellowships, grants, and other assorted opportunities that assist, enhance, and help fund the graduate school experience.

The opportunity to serve as a graduate student can also enrich leadership skills (Brock, 2012). For instance, if the choice is to serve as a graduate student representative of a sub-group or affiliated group within the national or regional organizations, it is possible to get a behind the scenes look at how business meetings are run, and how award committees function. This kind of experience provides good insight into how to lead business meetings, how to feel confident in being in front of colleagues from different universities, and how to present important organizational information. While doing presentations is part of the training graduate students receive, leading professional meetings can be different. Especially when doing so in front of senior professionals who are not quite colleagues yet. By choosing to provide service in this way, graduate students have the chance to see how things are run and how others handle leadership in order to decipher for themselves how they want to develop as leaders. Additionally, there is also the possibility that some service roles may provide for the opportunity to advocate for better support and resources for students broadly and/or for underrepresented and underserved student populations.

Unfortunately, there are still many processes that are a mystery and are left untold, both when in graduate school and after graduation as one transitions from student to professional. However, this is why deciding to volunteer and engage in service to the broader discipline can be helpful. It provides insight and knowledge that one might not otherwise receive while in graduate school yet will be helpful in navigating one's career.

Interested in Service: Insight for Getting Involved

There are many different types of service opportunities that are available to you. However, not all of these activities and opportunities will be of interest to you, nor will they fit your future career outlook. In addition, there are unique professional service opportunities in the field of political science. As a graduate student in this field, it is important to spend some time figuring out the service opportunities that are available and would be of interest to you to get involved in. This requires "getting a lay of the land" in terms of the differing levels of service (i.e., at the department, college, and university levels as well as external organizational levels).

First, figure out what is going on within the department. This may or may not be covered during initial orientation before starting one's program. Take it a step further by meeting with the Department Chair to unveil professional service opportunities. Some examples include political science specific student organizations and societies (e.g., Pi Sigma Alpha), serving as a student representative on a hiring committee, or hosting an election conference. There also could be some service opportunities at the college/university one attends that would be of interest. During the meeting with the Department Chair, it is possible to ask about this as well as searching online.

Another action item is exploring service in external organizations related to political science. Discussion with other students, faculty, and research you conduct online will be beneficial. Although it is difficult to speak to the service available at the department and college/university level because of the uniqueness that comes along with each setting, political science organizations will be expanded upon. The following will highlight some of these by looking at some of the various associations, research outlets, and industry in general.

Political science associations, such as the American Political Science Association, are places where students can get involved at multiple levels. The following table provides a list of organizations at the international, national, and regional level. To note, there very likely other affiliated organizations at the state, local, and chapter level.

Table 32.1: Organizations Graduate Students Can Pick From

International	National	Regional
International Studies Association (ISA)	The American Political Science Association (APSA)	New England Political Science Association
International Political Science Association (IPSA)	Academy of Political Science (APS)	Midwest Political Science Association
Association for the Study of Nationalities (ASN)	National Academy of Public Administration (NAPA)	Western Political Science Association (WPSA)
	International City/County Management Association (ICMA)	Southwestern Political Science Association (SSSA)
	National Association of Schools of Public Affairs and Administration (NASPAA)	Southern Political Science Association (SPSA)
	National Conference of Black Political Scientists (NCOBPS)	

For those with a career outlook in academia, they may also be interested in serving journal outlets (e.g., *American Journal of Political Science, Politics Groups & Identities*) and conferences that are linked to the organizations mentioned above. There may be opportunities to review papers, help organize a conference or conference panels, lead in a local chapter, and more. Those who are interested in academia or going into industry may also see value in professional service through volunteer work or non-paid internships (see chapter 11 on internships while in graduate school). These opportunities vary based on one's particular areas of focus in the field of political science.

The biggest action that can be taken is making a list of these opportunities. Then, spending time narrowing that list down to the opportunities that are of most interest while aligning future career goals and objectives. After that, a clearer idea of what service opportunities are available and of interest will surface. This does not mean one should be involved with every single item on the list or that one will have the resources to do so. More on that below.

How to Plan for Service

When it comes to resources, there is only so much time and available funding for students. Service inevitably takes time. Membership in professional organizations inevitably costs money, although typically at a discounted rate for students. In some cases, departments are willing to cover student membership costs for organizations in which they are participating or serving. However, that is not always the case, and the student may have to incur that cost. With that said, the list from above and the opportunities you are interested can be further narrowed down with time and funding in mind.

Questions to ask oneself include:
- How much time do I have to give to service?
- How much funding is available to me to partake in service (if that is a requirement)?

Of course, service can be beneficial for networking, preparing for the job market, and achieving a better understanding of how the academy and political sciences in general function. However, there must be balance in how much service a student takes on.

A smart step to take is to create a "time budget" for service activities. For example, if in the process of completing course work then it is likely that there is time to serve at least one conference each academic year. It is important to test the time budget and modify accordingly. Each semester may look a bit different, with the budget increasing during one term while decreasing in another. In general, service lengths and time commitments do vary from a one to four hour need to review manuscripts, or two to three months for conference event preparation, or even a yearlong (sometimes multiple yearlong) commitments on a standing committee. These time allocations should be weighed with due diligence in order to avoid over committing and not spending enough time focusing on making progress towards finishing one's program. Also, it is important to not forget to keep a record of service activities by adding them to the curriculum vitae or resume and LinkedIn profile. Through service, there is the building of the professional network of current and future colleagues, as well as helping the field of political science prosper.

Personal Reflections

The authors' personal reflections of service are provided to help bring to light some examples of these roles during graduate school. In the academic setting, research mentors made it apparent that reviewing papers for conferences would be a good way to gauge quality of writing, learn more about the acceptance process, and volunteer for differing organizations. Reviewing papers for conferences typically took place once a year with one to three papers to review. The overall time commitment was three to five hours. This was a learning experience that illuminated how the review process works and the importance of volunteers for the conference to operate with academic integrity and rigor.

Another example is a service appointment that occurred through a conversation at a conference. Leadership was planning for the next year and made an announcement that they needed help with their website. This turned into a formal appointment with the statewide organization as Director of Communications, and it developed into various other leadership roles held within the organization during graduate school. Although two very different time commitments and roles, both service opportunities turned into strong relationships with colleagues, while cultivating experiences that paid dividends through aiding preparation for academic work, such as writing and publishing.

Other experiences the authors have had as graduate students include serving as the graduate representative for a standing committee organized by members of a regional conference. For this kind of service, the appointment was for an entire academic year. Yet in terms of actual time spent focusing on work for the committee, the expectation was a total of about four to six hours. The bulk of the work entailed working with the group's executive team to put forth ideas on recruiting more graduate students to join the standing committee. Additionally, attending the annual regional meeting, while not required, was definitely helpful for purposes of connecting with and reporting updates to the rest of the membership. Engaging in this kind of service yielded benefits that outweighed the costs, due to the ability to network with academics in various stages of their careers and receive valuable insight into life after graduate school.

It is important to also highlight that as a graduate student it is also possible to provide service to one's own department. One way to do this is through volunteering to serve as the graduate student representative on hiring committees of possible new faculty. This commitment does take time away from one's schedule. But it is usually for a period of about four to six weeks, with the majority of the work happening towards the end when application packets are due to the department. Reviewing job packets will consume time and so will the campus visits—especially if there is scheduled time for a student Q&A session. However, despite the cost in time that this opportunity demands, it is worth it given that it is possible to witness the hiring process and be privy to the conversations had by the committee about various issues such as fit.

Conclusion

Professional service is of extreme importance during the political science graduate school journey. Through service endeavors, students have the opportunity to build the foundation for their professional network, among other benefits. However, one should be weary of giving too much time to service commitments, as there are larger goals that should be the focus. There is a need for balance between program obligations (e.g., course work, assistantships, etc.) and service projects. In the world of political science, there are a vast amount of service engagement opportunities, including with the APSA as well as regional organizations, journals, and other various activities.

The "time budget" should be consulted while deciding if one should add and/or modify service commitments. In considering how much time there is to meet all the necessary deadlines it is also important to consider what benefits will be gained from deciding to volunteer time and energy towards a service project. Deciding to provide service to the broader discipline as a graduate student is a smart way to prepare and begin learning how to balance the different responsibilities that will demand time and energy once graduate school is over and the professional career, academic or not, begins.

References

Brock, Terry. "Professional Service: Getting Involved in Your Discipline." Gradhacker (blog), *The Chronicle of Higher Education*, April 08, 2012. https://www.insidehighered.com/blogs/gradhacker/professional-service-getting-involved-your-discipline.

McFadden, Amanda, and Kathleen Smeaton. "Amplifying student learning through volunteering." *Journal of University Teaching & Learning Practice* 14, no. 3 (2017): 6.

Sinha, Sharad. "The benefits of volunteering." IEEE Potentials 33, no. 3 (2014): 30-31.

Valovick, Kyra, and Kelsey Swegle. "The Effect of Volunteering on Stress Hormone Levels of Graduate Student Volunteers." (2020).

33 Community, Solidarity, and Collective Power: The Role of Graduate Student Organizations and Graduate Worker Unions

Samantha R. Cooney[1], Patrick J. Gauding[2],

Anna A. Meier[3] & Kevin Reuning[4]

1.University of New Mexico 2. University of the South 3. University of Nottingham 4. Miami University

KEYWORDS: Graduate Unions, Contracts, Activists.

Introduction

This encyclopedia is a compendium on how to survive and thrive in graduate school. In this section, we turn to the relationship between you and your graduate school as an employer, organization, and community. We first discuss the role of graduate unions, before discussing governance at the department and university level. We focus especially on how you can make change within your graduate program and university. Although this is drawn from our own experiences as graduate students and employees in US PhD programs, we believe it can still be of interest to those outside the United States.

Graduate Unions: What Your Union Can Do for You

A significant portion of the graduate school experience is the production of labor for money, whether as a teaching assistant, solo instructor, research assistant, or other role. In the United States, admission offers to PhD programs will generally include a description of the type of work to be expected, as well as the types and amount of support the admittee can expect to receive. When considering which graduate school to attend, we highly encourage applicants to be mindful of what labor will be expected, in what form, and at what rate of pay and benefits (see also chapters 2 and 4 on the admissions and application processes). The stress of graduate school is not just the amount of work as a student, but often has more to do with basic existence, high demands both in academics and labor, and inconsistent respect from supervisors and the institution, combined with low pay and poor benefits.

As a result of increasingly poor working conditions, graduate workers have formed *unions* to collectively advocate for themselves. The earliest unionization movement occurred at the University of California, Berkeley in 1965 as part of the larger Free Speech Movement, and in 1969, the University of Wisconsin–Madison became the first higher education institution to voluntarily recognize its graduate student union, the Teaching Assistants' Association (Singh et al. 2006). In 2016, the National Labor Relations Board overturned its 2004 decision and ruled that graduate workers at private universities also have the right to unionize (NLRB 2016). As of 2021, there are some 50 recognized graduate worker unions in the United States, including 12 at private universities, along with several other unionization movements that have not yet been recognized (GAU 2021; Chang and Xu 2021).

Graduate workers unionize for several interrelated reasons. First, the temporary nature of graduate employment can lead to employers not seeing graduate worker issues as worth seriously addressing.

Previous research has identified both the corporatization of the university setting, and the rapid expansion of the use of temporary labor, as predictors of graduate worker unionization (Wickens 2008; Dixon, Tope, and Van Dyke 2008). Individual workers come and go with time, and so the temptation for supervisors is to attempt to alleviate issues (or shut down the complainers) at the individual level, in spite of the possibility that that issue may be affecting many workers. Second, an individual graduate worker's capacity to advocate for themselves within the university bureaucracy is affected by how complex university policies and procedures tend to be. The time commitment necessary to understand how to file a complaint, the process by which that complaint might be adjudicated, and the energy needed to engage that dispute can easily be prohibitive (Lafer 2003). Additionally, graduate workers are also simultaneously graduate students, and so the demands of a student's curriculum are significant. Moreover, the person who may be the cause of a labor issue may also be the person grading the complainant's papers or writing letters of recommendation! Graduate worker unionization thus interacts with the university as an institution both in confronting the institution's treatment of labor, but also potentially moderating the relationship between faculty and students (Julius and Gumport 2002, cf. Hewitt 2000; Rogers, Eaton, and Voos 2013).

The prospect of union activity is something that universities generally work to avoid and may be willing to spend significant resources to prevent. This is because unions *work*: unionized graduate workers receive better pay, more academic freedom, and a higher level of personal and professional actualization (Rogers, Eaton, and Voos 2013; Kroeger et al. 2018). The permanent presence of a collective organization for workers and students who are often otherwise isolated from each other is essential to correcting issues and improving workers' lives. At a fundamental level, this formation of community can break through the isolation of graduate school and make workers aware that their concerns may not be one-offs or unique to them.

The second way unions alleviate difficult conditions is through a *contract*. Through a contract, the union becomes the recognized party empowered to bargain on behalf of graduate workers, which may include teaching assistants, research assistants, graduate student lecturers, hourly graders, or some combination. Insufficient pay, improper health insurance, or unclear, murky, or unfair disciplinary policies are common issues that graduate worker unions agitate against (Wickens 2008, Dixon, Tope, and Van Dyke 2008). The bargaining process provides the opportunity to workers to highlight the issues at hand and produce a binding agreement. The stability of the clarified terms of labor that is set down in a contract runs counter to the academic industry's preference for contingent labor, particularly graduate labor (Bousquet 2001, Lafer 2003). If anything, this stability is more valuable than the specific provisions within the contract, as this works to prevent disputes about the meaning of the terms of employment, or unequal treatment between similarly placed workers.

What You Can Do for Your Union

Unions do not just "exist" without the work of committed union volunteers. While the time constraints of graduate school are demanding, and the political situation at your workplace may initially discourage you from active participation, we want to highlight some of the benefits to both you and your fellow workers in serving as a union volunteer, however much or little time you can commit.

To begin, the existence of a union on a campus (or not) is a reflection of several things. Has there been previous organizing—in other words, have grad workers gotten together, talked about their shared struggles, and agreed to collaboratively agitate for solutions? If there is no union, is there a sense of dissatisfaction with workplace conditions that is common to graduate students? If a union is in place, what work does it do, and what work needs to be done? A union may also have suffered from turnover: on average, the unit of grad workers at a university will turn over completely within five to seven years. Thus, the imperative of union members, and particularly union leaders, is not just the work of the day, but also of preparing the next generation.

Activists, sometimes referred to as "rank and file" members, are the core of the union or organizing effort. These members serve in a multitude of roles, such as speaking with fellow workers about the union, volunteering time to whatever community outreach the union engages in or participating in demonstrations or advocacy to university or political officials. Nearly all unions will charge activists membership dues. These dues fund the union's activities, and depending on the structure of the union, may also help with the costs incurred by either a state federation or a national federation. Dues also provide the resources necessary to hire professional staff to support your effort, and may range as far as legal support in the event the union has a dispute with the employer, as well as covering lost pay after a strike.

Political Science Graduate Students and Unions

The political science graduate student brings special skills to the union that may be quite valuable. Perhaps you've worked on political campaigns in the past or are in the weeds with understanding how legislatures write policies. Whatever your experience or line of research, the way that political scientists are taught to think lends itself well to organizing, both externally and internally.

The union must be able to support itself financially, and so the perennial task of holding conversations with current and prospective members is a must. If you have experience with door-knocking campaigns, especially organizing them (cutting turf, training volunteers, etc.), you may find this task rewarding.

Similarly, for students of legislative or executive politics, each union will require members who are able to navigate bureaucracy, understand how and why actors in the university act and react as they do, and work to advance the interests of graduate workers by engaging in the political process, or through contract negotiations. Knowledge of Robert's Rules is a plus, and the opportunity to learn and apply that knowledge may be appealing to students of legislative politics. Others may find a conciliatory role a good use of time. Service as a steward will place you in contact with workers in need and allow you to serve the needs of the union in defending workers and the contract. This work may also help you feel that you are "doing something" practical, especially if your day-to-day research is more abstract in nature.

Strong leadership, the tolerance and skill to deal with the frustrations of resistance to progress, and the creativity and resourcefulness to "figure it out" are all skills worth developing in graduate school, and union leadership service will teach these skills with hard-earned experience.

Graduate Student Organizations

Whereas unions bring together graduate workers from across the university, departmental graduate student organizations (GSOs) can advocate specifically for political science grads. GSOs are created by political science students to represent themselves within the university-wide graduate student association/ senate/council. They can also be created in order to distribute funds from the university to individuals within their respective program. Chartered organizations with affiliation to the university's graduate student senate usually receive a distributed stipend based on the number of graduate students enrolled in the respective department. These funds can then be given to individuals or used by the student group. Chartered associations are also able to access grants and other sources of money that the university or graduate student council reserves for those specific groups. One author's departmental association had been a formally chartered organization for years and used university funds accumulated during that time to redistribute amongst students in emergency need during the pandemic.

Departmental associations can also be a way to raise concerns with faculty. The extent that these concerns will be heard depends on how formal the association is. Just because a departmental association is currently relatively weak does not mean that it cannot become more important in the future. For one of the authors, their departmental association changed from a group with no formal role in the department beyond organizing parties to a group that fought for graduate student representation on department level committees over the course of several years. This level of representation is important, because program decisions affecting graduate students should involve the input of those who will be directly affected.

Graduate student associations, specifically at the department level, may also be used to create a sense of community within a department. Graduate school can be a period of intense solitude, and this is especially true for the field of political science, where students do not have the opportunity to form connections with their peers within labs (Brandes 2006). In our own experience, departmental graduate associations have held semi-regular events of varying levels of formality, which can be a great way to meet people outside of your cohort. University-wide graduate student groups hold similar social events as well, although they tend to be more formal.

Departmental associations vary considerably between universities and programs. Though many are chartered organizations, as described above, others may be informal groupings of students within a department with no constitution or governing rules outside of created norms. The way they operate depends on both student needs and capacity. Some organizations may choose to host panels in order to share knowledge on publishing (see also chapters 24 and 25) or comprehensive exam studying (see also chapter 12), while others may focus on community-building through departmental socials and other more informal events. These can be important for morale in the department and are a good way to build networks with peers (see also chapter 7).

University Governing Bodies

Graduate students may also have the opportunity to sit on university governing bodies. It is common for universities to have some general governing body, often referred to as a senate or a council, to represent faculty (and sometimes staff) interests in the governance of the university. The authority of university councils varies significantly across institutions, and they are chiefly involved in making academic decisions. As policies engage more closely with budgetary decisions, university senate authority tends to shrink (Tiede 2021).

The final decision-making authority within universities rests not with senior administrators but instead with a governing board of trustees. These trustees will be the final decision-maker in any major financial decisions and will hire and fire the university president. For public universities, boards can be made up of individuals elected by alumni, elected by state residents, appointed by governors, or selected by state legislators. Boards sometimes have student representatives, including graduate students. While this can often be a role of title rather than substance, it is one way of obtaining direct contact and discussion with an administrative board. (For a larger discussion about academic administration, see chapter 8.)

What Are You Expecting to Get or Change?

There are a number of reasons one would choose to get involved with either a GSO or a union. If you are aiming to complete some university service, getting involved with the campus graduate senate would be to your benefit. If you want to help distribute university funds to yourself and your peers, your departmental graduate student association is where you should get involved. If, however, your interests lie in creating substantive change within the university—for example, wage raises or institutional changes for title IX reporting—the best way to utilize your time and energy is within a graduate worker union.

Friendship and comradery are often overlooked as a need in graduate school, but the isolation and self-depreciation that come with graduate degree programs make friends a necessity (for more information about overcoming academic isolation, see chapter 63). Both unions and GSOs are great ways to make connections with other students who are most likely going through the same trials and tribulations that you are experiencing. While departmental graduate associations may only connect you with students from your own program, graduate worker unions have members from different departments across campus. Additionally, the sense of comradery that you form within a union is hard to find elsewhere.

Activist Backlash

Though there are many benefits to joining a union or GSO, activism is not without its risks. Despite depictions in popular media, universities remain largely neoliberal institutions and as such do not take kindly to attempts at structural change. Graduate students involved in on-campus activism may be labeled as "difficult," "distracted from their research," or "not team players." Of course, the very concerns that graduate student activists fight for—a living wage, for example—are prerequisites to doing one's best work in other areas of the academy. Academics in secure positions may nevertheless feel unsettled by graduate students who challenge the individualized narrative of academia by working together. Faculty who have spent decades of their lives at an institution often feel a linked fate with that institution; thus, even faculty with histories of activism may not be supportive of your activism.

Costs can be especially high for non-cisgender male, non-white, and/or non-United States citizen graduate students. These can range from faculty disapproval to legal action by a student's home country for joining a union or participating in certain kinds of protest, and unions must take these possibilities seriously and prioritize protections for the most vulnerable. Nevertheless, historically excluded students tend to be at the forefront of activist efforts—after all, it is their well-being that is most directly on the line (for more discussions about concerns for minoritized and underrepresented groups, see chapters 54-61). For such students wanting to get more involved, we encourage cultivating community beyond one's home department and university. Despite appearances, many corners of the discipline are activist-oriented and can be found on Twitter and through more specialized conferences on race, ethnicity, and politics; gender; Marxism; and critical and postcolonial studies (see also chapters 26 and 27 on using academic Twitter and chapter 21 on attending conferences). Support from mentors and allies in the wider discipline can also protect activists who face backlash on their own campuses; unfortunately, the degree to which one's activism is tolerated may be contingent upon being perceived as a successful scholar.

Graduate students may further hear that mentioning their activism on the academic job market will hurt their chances. One of the authors found, to the contrary, that their activism helped them get interviews at liberal arts and community colleges, where wider campus or community involvement is expected. At the same time, they were branded a nuisance in their own department and written off by some faculty who could have been helpful in their job search. Other graduate students have faced far more serious backlash: one student-activist was even forced out of their program.[1] Activism is safer in numbers, but for individual tasks like going on the job market, whether or not to mention one's activism is a personal choice that comes at a potentially high cost (for additional information about the job market, see chapter 34). We encourage departments to see activism as a strength: student-activists bring invaluable experience in collective advocacy for policies that improve working conditions for all academics.

Conclusion

Graduate school is an isolating endeavor. Increasing focus on individual success, with ever-more-unrealistic standards for publications and grants achieved before a graduate student completes their training, can lead grads to feel that any challenges or roadblocks they face are their own fault. Graduate worker unions and graduate student organizations, in contrast, subvert this narrative by providing support and empowerment, underscoring that problems that appear personal are often caused by exploitative structures that treat grads as automatons rather than full humans with full lives. In this sense, unions and GSOs subvert a key narrative of the graduate school experience: that it must be pursued and completed alone.

Resources

Below we share a number of resources for those wishing to learn more about graduate worker organizing in the United States:

National associations
- Coalition of Student Employee Unions (CSEU) https://www.cseu-csee.org
- National Association of Graduate-Professional Students (NAGPS) http://nagps.org

National unions with locals representing graduate employees
- American Association of University Professors (AAUP) https://www.aaup.org
- American Federation of State County and Municipal Employees (AFSCME) https://www.afscme.org

- American Federation of Teachers (AFT) https://www.aft.org
- Communication Workers of America (CWA) https://cwa-union.org
- National Education Association (NEA) https://www.nea.org
- Service Employees International Union (SEIU) https://www.seiu.org
- United Automobile, Aerospace and Agricultural Implement Workers of America (UAW) https://uaw.org
- United Electrical, Radio, and Machine Workers of America (UE) https://www.ueunion.org
- UNITE HERE https://unitehere.org

General labor organizing help
- Labor Notes https://labornotes.org
- The Forge https://forgeorganizing.org

Endnotes

1   We thank this activist for sharing their story anonymously.

References

Brandes, L. C. O. 2006. "Graduate Student Centers: Building community and Involving Students." New Directions for Student Services, (115) 85–99.

Columbia University, 364 NLRB No. 90. 2016.

Chang, Cara J., and Meimei Xu. 2021. "'Our Success or Failure Is Tied Together': Grad Student Union Activism Picks Up in Biden Era." *The Harvard Crimson*, April 12. Accessed November 11, 2021. https://www.thecrimson.com/article/2021/4/12/grad-union-solidarity/

Dixon, Marc, Daniel Tope, and Nella Van Dyke. 2008. "'The University Works Because We Do': On the Determinants of Campus Labor Organizing in the 1990s." *Sociological Perspectives* 51(2): 375-396.

Graduate Assistants United. 2021. "Graduate Employee Unions in the United States." Accessed November 11, 2021. https://www.ufgau.org/graduate-employee-unions.html

Hewitt, Gordon J. 2000. "Graduate Student Employee Collective Bargaining and the Educational Relationship Between Faculty and Graduate Students." *Journal of Collective Negotiations* 29(2): 153–166.

Julius, Daniel J., and Patricia J. Gumport. 2002. "Graduate Student Unionization: Catalysts and Consequences." *The Review of Higher Education* 26(2): 187–216.

Kroeger, Teresa, Celine McNicholas, Marni von Wilpert, and Julia Wolfe. 2018. "The state of graduate student employee unions." Economic Policy Institute. epi.org/138028

Lafer, Gordon. 2003. "Graduate Student Unions: Organizing in a Changed Academic Economy." *Labor Studies Journal* 28(2): 25–43.

Rogers, Sean E., Adrieene E. Eaton, and Paula B. Voos. 2013. "Effects of Unionization on Graduate Student Employees: Faculty–Student Relations, Academic Freedom, and Pay." *ILR Review* 66(2): 487–510.

Singh, Parbudyal, Deborah M. Zinni, and Anne F. MacLennan. 2006. "Graduate Student Unions in the United States." *Journal of Labor Research* 27 (1): 55–73.

Tiede, Hans-Joerg. 2021. "The 2021 AAUP Shared Governance Survey: Findings on Faculty Roles by Decision-Making Areas" *Bulletin of the American Association of University Professors* 107(Summer):82-96.

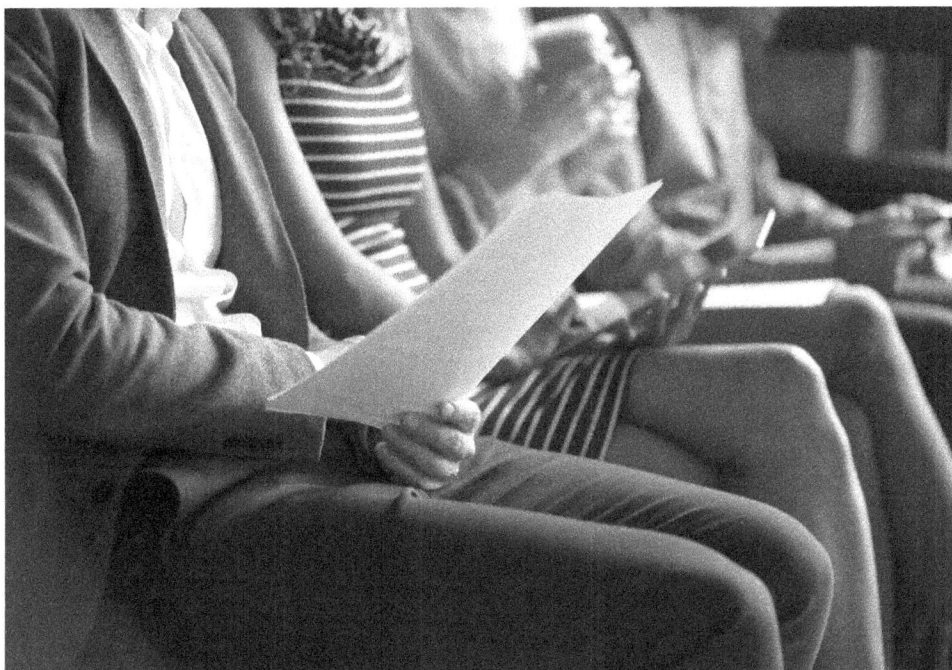

Professional Development—The Job Market

34

Expect the Unexpected: Choices and Challenges in the Political Science PhD Job Market

Bobbi G. Gentry[1], Kyla K. Stepp[2], & Jeremiah J. Castle[3]

1. Bridgewater College 2. Central Michigan University 3. Metropolitan State University of Denver

KEYWORDS: Political Science Job Market, Tenure Track.

Introduction

For most students earning a PhD in political science, the ultimate goal is to earn a stable, fair-paying job. For many decades, the modal employment opportunity for political science PhDs was a tenure-track job teaching political science. However, for reasons explored in this chapter, tenure-track jobs are becoming more scarce. It has become more common for candidates to spend time in post-doctoral fellowships, visiting assistant professor positions, or adjunct faculty positions before receiving a tenure-track offer. In addition, within the last decade or two, increasing numbers of political science PhDs have been turning to alternative employment opportunities, including private sector jobs (often labeled "alt-ac" careers). In short, the nature of the academic job search has changed considerably over the past few decades.

In this chapter, we provide an overview of the *job market* for political science PhDs. Our focus is primarily on the United States, but we also briefly cover opportunities in other countries. We begin by discussing trends in the political science job market, including an overview of some of the trends that have fueled the declining number of tenure-track jobs teaching political science. We then provide an overview of the timing of the market and the interview process, focusing mostly on the academic market. Finally, we give some practical tips for how students can prepare for the increasingly volatile academic market. Throughout the chapter we emphasize that the job market for political science PhDs is a decentralized and rapidly evolving one. While our discussion is centered around the "typical" experience, we recognize that individual experiences on the job market vary greatly. The solution for students is to prepare carefully, but "expect the unexpected."

Trends in the Political Science Job Market

Even prior to 2008, higher education was becoming more corporatized and relying more heavily on adjunct labor (see Williams 2013). However, the last two decades in higher education have been defined by two major crises, further diminishing the already fragile market for tenure-track jobs in political science. First, during the Great Recession, many states compensated for reduced tax revenues by implementing major cuts to public university budgets (Marcus 2017). The result was a decline in the number of tenure-track positions in political science from a high of 730 during the 2006-2007 cycle to just 445 during the 2009-2010 cycle (Diascro 2011). Budget constraints also led institutions to undergo program restructuring and faculty layoffs, further contributing to the tight labor market for political science.

Just as colleges and universities were recovering from the Great Recession, they were hit by the COVID-19 pandemic. The pandemic resulted in reduced revenues due to fewer students staying on campus and therefore fewer students paying for room and board. In addition, in fall 2020 the modal higher education institution experienced a 0.1% to 5% decrease in enrollment, and about one-fifth of institutions experienced an enrollment decline of 10% or more (Gardner 2021). Facing such financial pressures, many institutions instituted hiring freezes, laid off faculty (particularly adjunct and fixed-term faculty), and left vacant positions unfilled. In November 2020, The Chronicle of Higher Education reported that colleges had shed about 10% of their total workforce (Bauman 2020).

Given these financial pressures it should come as little surprise that an analysis of 2020-2021 postings in APSA's ejobs job advertisement system confirmed an overall decrease in the number of positions available. The number of positions that are *tenure-track* are decreasing, and non-tenure-track instructor positions and contingent visiting professor positions are increasing by 9% and 13.5% respectively (McGrath and Diaz 2021a, 9). One reason for the growth in non-tenure-track positions is that such positions represent significant cost-savings in terms of salary and benefits for institutions (for a comparison of salary and benefits data between tenure-track and non-tenure-track positions, see Davis 2019, 3-4).

Not surprisingly, the reduction in tenure-track openings means that students are finding it more difficult to secure a tenure-track job. Data on graduate placements in political science between 2018 and 2020 reveal that, "only 28.4% of candidates found a tenure-track position" (McGrath and Diaz 2021b, 10), which is far below the 11-year average. Trends suggest that there are more non-academic placements (10%) (2021b, 10), more years on the job market (2021b, 16), and more placement opportunities in post docs (2021b, 10). In short, the path from a PhD to a tenure-track position is neither as certain nor as linear as it was a few decades ago.

At the individual level, a handful of predictors exert a powerful impact on a candidate's placement prospects. First, candidates with their PhD "in-hand" were more likely to be placed than ABDs (All-But-Dissertation) (McGrath and Diaz 2021b, 14). Second, across many academic disciplines, the institution where candidates receive their PhD has a large impact on job prospects, particularly at research-focused universities (Han 2003). Within political science, Oprisko (2012) finds that, "eleven schools contribute 50 percent of the political science academics to research-intensive universities in the United States." Finally, demographic factors impact candidates' placement opportunities. While underrepresented groups are more likely to be offered tenure-track positions, post docs continue to be dominated by men from the top quintile of institutions in political science (McGrath and Diaz 2021b, 10-13).

Although tenure-track positions are declining in the United States, opportunities may be increasing abroad. In their study of APSA eJobs postings, McGrath and Diaz (2021a, 9) find that international positions now make up about 20% of total APSA postings. This growth is driven, at least in part, by strategic efforts from governments in Asia and the Middle East (Saiya 2014). Many of the institutions being founded in these regions are branch campuses affiliated with American universities, and therefore are interested in hiring faculty from prestigious institutions in the United States and western Europe. International positions have their own unique costs and benefits (Saiya 2014), and interested job seekers are encouraged to learn more about international positions prior to applying (see chapter 42 in this volume for more on differences between United States and international institutions).

The Timing of the Market: What You Need to Know

Unlike the "year-round" cycle that characterizes private sector hiring, the academic job market is seasonal in nature (Miller and Gentry 2011). The tenure-track job market in political science follows a predictable hiring schedule. The first jobs tend to post in May or June, with application deadlines in August or September (for jobs starting the following year). Many of the earliest postings tend to be at research focused R1 universities. The posting of jobs typically peaks during late summer or early fall. Positions at liberal arts colleges and teaching-focused public universities tend to post a bit later in the fall, with application deadlines in October or November. That said, some institutions also prefer to set application deadlines in January or February (or even later) (Miller and Gentry 2011, 578). While the posting of tenure-track positions generally slows to a trickle by mid-spring, it is common to see a few late-spring postings. The timing of the international market is quite different; many regions operate on the calendar year rather than the United States academic calendar (see Saiya 2014). Candidates seeking international positions are advised to become familiar with the customs in the regions where they are seeking employment (see chapter 42 in this volume for more on differences between United States and international institutions).

While the tenure-track job market in political science has long followed this relatively predictable cycle, several recent events create the potential for change. An important factor in many universities posting political science jobs relatively early in the season was a desire to have their advertisement "live" in time to conduct face-to-face first round interviews at the APSA conference traditionally held on Labor Day weekend. Given that APSA has moved its flagship conference back to after Labor Day (as late as October), institutions may shift postings slightly later in the coming years. In addition, the ongoing COVID-19 pandemic is likely to continue to disrupt academic hiring cycles for several more seasons.

There is even more variation in the hiring cycle for visiting assistant professor (VAP) and postdoc positions. Many research-driven institutions advertise prestigious postdocs relatively early in the fall cycle (at roughly the same time as tenure-track positions). However, peak hiring time for VAPs and teaching-focused postdocs is during the spring semester, with interviews happening roughly around spring break. Given the wide variation in postings, the best way to maximize your chances on the job market is to monitor the postings year-round until you have secured a stable position. See chapter 44 in this volume for more on adjunct, visiting, and fixed-term positions.

Most academic jobs in political science will be advertised on a small handful of websites. In the United States, the best source of jobs is APSA's "eJobs" platform. Other good sources for job advertisements are the International Studies Association's (ISA) website (https://www.isanet.org/Professional-Resources/Employment/Jobs), HigherEdJobs.com, The Chronicle of Higher Education, Insidehighered.com, and publicservicecareers.org. Adjunct positions tend to be less well-advertised than other types of academic positions. If you are seeking an adjunct position at a particular university, we recommend monitoring the university's own hiring website and/or contacting the department chair. For job seekers, we recommend setting up a spreadsheet with the application deadline, university name, any specific subfields mentioned in the ad, and a link to the job advertisement.

The Interview Process: What You Need to Know

Because the academic job market is decentralized, there is wide variation in how universities carry out the hiring process. While we do our best to describe the "typical" process, readers should be aware that their experiences may differ.

Given the shortage of tenure-track openings, it is not uncommon for tenure-track searches to yield hundreds of qualified applicants, meaning that an important step for hiring committees is to narrow down the pool of candidates to a manageable number. Most institutions handle this process in two stages: the "long-list" (roughly eight to 20 candidates deserving of a first-round interview), and the "short-list" (generally three to five candidates selected for on-campus interviews). That said, not every institution takes the process in two stages; some institutions proceed directly to on-campus interviews. In addition, some universities hire a candidate based on a first-round interview alone (especially for VAPs and postdocs).

First round interviews can take place in a variety of ways. Many institutions conduct interviews with "long-list" candidates via either phone or digital conferencing technologies like Skype, Zoom, or Webex. Another option for universities is to conduct face-to-face first round interviews at the APSA annual meeting. No matter the method, the goal for institutions is to use these interviews to get to know candidates and evaluate their fit with the institution. While interpretations of fit may differ, fit usually means easily matching the needs of the department in terms of research interests, publication record, teaching expertise, pedagogical approach, and diversity (Fuerstman and Lavertu 2005). Many common first-round questions are targeted toward determining fit, including inquiries about teaching philosophy, teaching experience, research interests, how candidates foster diversity, equity, and inclusion, and what makes the candidate a good fit for the institution.

Most second round interviews involve the institution flying three to five candidates to campus for a one to three day visit. The most stressful aspect of the on-campus visit for many candidates is the "job talk" or "research talk," in which candidates give a roughly 30–45-minute presentation of their current research followed by a question and answer session with attendees. Another increasingly common component of on-campus interviews is the "teaching demonstration," in which candidates teach a class. Candidates may be asked to "guest teach" a real class or a random selection of students; candidates may be given a topic (and reading) or may be given the option of teaching whatever they would like.

Beyond these key elements, on-campus visits can include a number of other events. Some of the most common include one-on-one meetings with members of the department, a meeting with the Dean, a meal with students, meals with members of the hiring committee, a benefits overview with human resources, a campus tour, and a "real estate tour" of the local town. Many academic institutions in Europe and elsewhere also include an intensive conversation with a panel as part of the interview process, and candidates from the United States may be asked about cultural differences in the classroom and how they will approach such differences (see Saiya 2014).

During interviews, candidates typically incur a few expenses for which they deserve reimbursement. Reimbursement procedures differ greatly from institution to institution. Many institutions will pay for the flight and hotel room in advance. However, the authors have also experienced situations where the institution asked candidates to purchase flights, hotel rooms, and rental cars and submit the receipts for reimbursement. In addition, the authors have incurred expenses like airport parking. Candidates should feel comfortable asking the department chair or search committee chair for reimbursement for interview-related expenses during or after their campus visit.

The largest post-interview concern for candidates is, of course, whether they will get a job offer. Once the final candidate leaves campus, the search committee votes on which candidate they would like to make an offer to. At some campuses, approval from the full department, department chair, and/or Dean may also be required. Some campuses may also have time-consuming human resources policies, including the need for representatives to confirm salary details for an offer. Therefore, the length of time between the interview and the offer varies between institutions. Stepp once received one offer while in the airport on the way home from an on-campus interview, while Castle's offer for his current job took several weeks. One way candidates can get a general sense of what to expect is by asking the department chair and/or search committee chair, "What does the anticipated hiring timeline look like?" At the same time, candidates should expect to wait at least a few weeks for an answer. Although waiting to hear back from an interview can be excruciating, candidates should try to redirect their focus to their teaching and research interests and use the interview as motivation for writing. For an in-depth conversation about advice for each stage of the interview process, see chapter 45 in this volume. See also chapter 35 for maintaining your mental health through the job market season. Finally, see chapter 46 for how to negotiate your job offer.

What You Can Do: Be Prepared

The best way to handle such an unpredictable and quickly changing environment is through preparation. One aspect of preparation is familiarity with both academic and non-academic career paths. In addition to the other chapters in this book, we recommend Kelsky (2015) as a universal primer on gaining employment as a PhD.

Candidates can begin preparing themselves by engaging in professional development throughout their time in graduate school. On the research front, candidates should publish their work, present at conferences, and embrace professional development opportunities like training on working with human subjects or grant-writing. When it comes to teaching, candidates should gain experience teaching college courses, either as a teaching assistant (TA) or (ideally) as the instructor-of-record (see chapters 28 and 29 in this volume for more on being a TA and teaching your own course). In addition, candidates can seek out pedagogical training, such as training for online teaching, through their campus teaching and learning centers. In short, candidates should take advantage of all the resources their graduate program and university-at-large has to offer.

As students get closer to completing their PhD, they should carefully consider when to enter the job market. Candidates generally enter the market the fall before their anticipated graduation date, but candidates should have candid conversations with their advisor and other trusted sources for individualized advice about the proper time to enter the job market. In addition, Kelsky (2015,70-71) provides a helpful list of ten indicators that a candidate is ready to enter the academic job market. Candidates should not apply to jobs that require a completed PhD by a particular date if they cannot be reasonably confident that all steps of the dissertation/graduation process will be completed in time.

Once you have made the decision to enter the academic market, preparing for common aspects of the application process is essential for reducing stress and achieving better interview performances. First, candidates should have candid conversations with potential letter of recommendation writers, send requests well in advance of application deadlines (one to two months is standard), and supply letter writers with a curriculum vitae (CV), sample cover letter, and sample working papers (see Carter and Scott 1998). See chapter 43 in this volume for advice on preparing these materials. Second, because many first-round interviews ask a predictable set of questions, preparing a few "stock" answers can help candidates do their best. Finally, candidates should extensively practice their job talks and deliver one or more practice job talks in front of peers.

Finally, candidates should recognize the possibility that spending multiple years in a national job search might have a negative impact on their mental health. Researchers are increasingly recognizing a mental health crisis among graduate students. Almasri, Read, and Vandeweerdt conducted a survey of political science graduate students at seven universities and found, "About 30% of respondents met the criteria for depression and only a third of those were receiving treatment" (2021: 1). Recognizing the prevalence of mental health issues, candidates should closely monitor their mental health and actively seek out adequate support networks. Those networks may be academic; for example, a team of political scientists have organized a Slack channel (http://supportyourcohort.com) for job market candidates (see Kim, Lebovits, and Shugars 2021). However, those support networks may also include family, friends outside academia, and professional therapists. For more advice on maintaining your mental health while on the job market, see chapter 35 in this volume.

Conclusion

Our central claim is that the job market for political science PhDs is changing rapidly from the expectation that candidates will move from a completed PhD directly to a tenure-track job into a much longer and more uncertain process. In such a competitive job market, candidates should distinguish between the factors that are in their control and the factors that are not. Candidates cannot change recent trends in the market, but they can understand such trends and plan accordingly. While in graduate school, candidates should focus on preparing themselves to be competitive when they enter the market. Such preparation will help candidates no matter whether they pursue a career in academia or take a new opportunity in the "alt-ac" market. In the face of a rapidly changing job market, preparation is the candidate's best resource in the event of the inevitable unexpected challenges.

References

Almasri, Nasir, Blair Read, and Clara Vandeweerdt. 2021. "Mental Health and the PhD: Insights and Implications for Political Science." *PS: Political Science & Politics*: 1-7. doi:10.1017/S1049096521001396.

Bauman, Dan. 2020. "Colleges Have Shed a Tenth of Their Employees Since the Pandemic Began." The Chronicle of Higher Education, Nov. 10. https://www.chronicle.com/article/colleges-have-shed-a-tenth-of-their-employees-since-the-pandemic-began

Carter, Ralph G., and James M. Scott. 1998. "Navigating the Academic Job Market Minefield." PS: Political Science & Politics 31 (3): 615-22.

Davis, Megan. 2019. "2017-2018 APSA Departmental Survey: New Hire Salaries, Benefits, and Professional Development Resources." APSA Preprints. https://www.apsanet.org/portals/54/apsa%20files/data%20reports/employment%20data/apsa%20departmental%20survey_new%20hire%20salaries%20benefits%20and%20resources_final.pdf?ver%3D2019-03-22-153716-087

Diascro, Jennifer Segal. 2011. "The Job Market and Placement in Political Science in 2009-10." *PS: Political Science & Politics* 44 (3): 597-602.

Fuerstman, Daniel, and Stephan Lavertu. 2005. "The Academic Hiring Process: A Survey of Department Chairs." *PS: Political Science & Politics* 38 (4): 731-36.

Gardner, Lee. 2021. "The Great Contraction: Cuts Alone Will Not be Enough to Turn Colleges' Fortunes Around." *The Chronicle of Higher Education*, Feb. 15. https://www.chronicle.com/article/the-great-contraction

Han, Shin-Kap. 2003. "Tribal Regimes in Academia: A Comparative Analysis of Market Structure Across Disciplines." *Social Networks* 25 (3): 251-280.

Kelsky, Karen. 2015. *The Professor is In: The Essential Guide for Turning Your PhD Into a Job.* New York: Three Rivers Press.

Kim, Seo-young Silvia, Hannah Lebovits, and Sarah Shugars. 2021. "Building a Bigger Table: Networking 101 For Graduate Students." *PS: Political Science & Politics*: 1-6. https://doi.org/10.1017/S1049096521001025

Marcus, Jon. 2017. The Decline of the Midwest's Public Universities Threatens to Wreck Its Most Vibrant Economies. *The Atlantic*, Oct. 15. https://www.theatlantic.com/business/archive/2017/10/midwestern-public-research-universities-funding/542889/?utm_source=atlfb&fbclid=IwAR-1SWOR2UkgL6Qk6dwqEYecW4JrPruZ5aH0uG8xteP8UnPmLgaEsHdqZQfs

McGrath, Erin, and Ana Diaz. 2021a. "2020-2021 APSA EJobs Report: the Political Science Job Market." APSA Preprints. doi: 10.33774/apsa-2021-xmm74.

McGrath, Erin, and Ana Diaz. 2021b. "APSA Graduate Placement Report: Analysis of Political Science Placements for 2018-2020." APSA Preprints. doi: 10.33774/apsa-2021-jmxt3

Miller, William J., and Bobbi Gentry. 2011. "Navigating the Academic Job Market in Treacherous Times." *PS: Political Science & Politics* 44 (3): 578-582.

Oprisko, Robert. 2012. "Superpowers: The American Academic Elite." *Georgetown Public Policy Review* 18 (Spring). http://gppreview.com/2012/12/03/superpowers-the-american-academic-elite/

Saiya, Nilay. 2014. "Navigating the International Academic Job Market." *PS: Political Science & Politics* 47 (4): 845–48.

Williams, Jeffrey J. 2013. "The Great Stratification." *The Chronicle of Higher Education*, Dec. 2. https://www.chronicle.com/article/the-great-stratification/

35 | Mental Health and the Job Market

Anna A. Meier[1], Adnan Rasool[2], & Annelise Russell[3]

1. University of Nottingham, UK 2. University of Tennessee at Martin 3. University of Kentucky

KEYWORDS: Job Prospects, Support Network, Job Candidates, Faculty Mentors.

Introduction

Next to finishing up a dissertation, one of the most daunting challenges any graduate student faces is 'going on' the job market. The process itself is grueling, challenging, and often heartbreaking. Yet, unlike the dissertation process, there has been little discussion about the mental toll the job market has on individuals. As academia in general and political science in particular become more competitive, especially as institutions of higher education slash jobs and cut funding, the mere thought of surviving the job market creates anxiety and extreme stress (see chapters 34–48 for various topics related to the job market). In this chapter, we address this daunting task many graduate students face and suggest ideas for individuals and departments to make it all a little less nerve-wracking.

So, why does this conversation even matter? Why did we find the need to talk about the mental health aspect of 'going on' the market in the first place? The harsh, oft-ignored reality of the job market is that it is a full-time job. Academia does not have a common application system like medical schools, where candidates fill out an application with their priority list and a match day occurs to inform individuals where they landed. Instead, each university or college has a very specific niche that they are trying to fill and expect a detailed targeted application for that position. A job seeker in this case must design a job packet for each job that includes a bespoke cover letter, their detailed CV, recommendation letters, teaching and research portfolios, writing samples, and at times diversity statements. That is tens of pages of application material for one job that the candidates have to vet and send in while coordinating with their recommenders. So, even if a candidate applies for twenty jobs in a cycle, this is a serious amount of work hours being spent on something that at best is a game of chance in those early stages.

Now add to this the fact that most candidates are 'on' the market in their final years of graduate school. They are sending out application packages while they are also trying to finish up their dissertations, apply for postdocs, and teach two or three classes given the kind of program they're in. Suddenly, the job market becomes a second job. But the difference here is that the second job decides your future. And that creates a level of stress and anxiety that seeps throughout a person's life—professional and private. And yet candid discussions on how it impacts us all are scant at best.

So, what if it all does work out? The stress surely goes down, right? Well, yes and no. The stress of knowing whether you will be able to have a career in the fall after you finish does go away if you are fortunate enough to land a job. But with that comes the additional load of work that needs to be completed before that stability comes to your life. Between when you receive the job offer, accept, and sign the offer letter and show up for your first day of work, you still need to complete your dissertation, defend it, find housing and then, in most cases, move at least a thousand miles away to a new state or country to start life over without a *support network* of family and friends. The job market is actually very long: it starts in July or August and the last-minute positions keep popping up till March or April. Even in the best-case scenario where you have accepted a job by the end of December, it means you have just six months to wrap up your dissertation, its defense, and essentially your whole life and find a place to move to cross-country. If you were fortunate to get a last-minute position, that means you often have less than 120 days to wrap up everything and move.

Now imagine, in the middle of all of this, you also must tactfully negotiate your salary and perks too. Most colleges and universities do not offer summer pay, which means even if you have an amazing job starting in the fall, for the months of May, June, and July, you are on your own without a steady paycheck. Negotiating other elements of the job are tricky too, i.e., there is no guide on how to do it. All you are trying to do is get the best deal with the constant fear that the university or college might pull out if you dig in too much. Just writing about it is anxiety-inducing; imagine what it feels like to be in the middle of it!

And remember, this happens if you have been extremely lucky and fortunate to have an offer on the table to begin with. If the job market cycle did not work out for you that year, that means you must figure out temporary work to make enough money to survive for the next academic year while you go back on the job market again. And while you do that, you need to figure out a way to deal with the heartbreak and disappointment of not landing a job this year. This severely hampers one's ability to finish up the dissertation and hurts one's confidence for the next market cycle.

There is an added layer of complication for international students who must figure out a way to retain their status in the United States to take another shot at the job market. To start with, their *job prospects* are slim given they can only apply to places that will sponsor them. This puts a large chunk of advertised jobs, especially late in cycle jobs, out of contention for them. And while they are dealing with the anxiety of this, they need to figure out their summer pay, fall plans, dissertation and its defense, and a way they can retain legal status. All of this has a serious impact on a person and their ability to survive the process.

That is why we believe it is important to have a candid discussion about mental health in relation to the job market. There are no silver bullets to erase the stress and anxiety from this process. Our intention is to present suggestions that can make this process a little less nerve-wracking. Below, we outline recommendations for both *job candidates* and institutions with respect to mental health on the academic job market. Many of the struggles of the market are structural, and thus responsibility cannot be placed solely on individuals to manage their mental health. At the same time, there are things you can do on your end to prepare for challenges you will face.

If you are not someone who has previously struggled with mental health, know that the market may test you in new ways. If you have ongoing mental health challenges, the market will likely exacerbate these due to heightened stress. And if you have had challenges in the past from which you have largely healed, be prepared for the market to trigger old behaviors. (One of the authors saw disordered eating return during the market, for example.) All of which is to say that you will likely need new sources of support, even if you do not think you do now, and there is no shame in pursuing them.

Advice for Job Candidates

One of the most exhausting parts of the market is having to explain your experience to people around you. Because of the academic market's unique cycle and lack of choice, family members and partners working in other industries may find it difficult to understand what you are going through, meaning your usual sources of support may be less available. This can make an already-isolating experience feel even worse. Thus, finding people who "get it" with whom you can talk is crucial.

You might think of your job market support network as a triad: peers, faculty mentors, and (insurance allowing) a therapist. First and foremost are peers who either recently went through the market or are on the market at the same time. The year-long referendum on your worth at the thing you've been doing for at least five years will wear anyone down, so it can be very helpful to have a job market "buddy" with whom you can commiserate. Having another person going through what you are going through and understanding exactly how it feels may not change the fundamentals of your situation, but it can lighten the load, because you no longer have to explain your excitement or disappointment. Peers can also help you feel less alone when you aren't sure how some part of the market works and remind you that your lack of knowledge is probably structural and a product of the hidden curriculum, not a personal failing.

Second, try to identify *faculty mentors* with whom you can speak openly about mental health issues. These may be different mentors than you have relied on in the past. Your dissertation chair may not have gone on the market in several decades, so you need to find faculty who have been through the process more recently. More senior friends can serve in this role, but so can mentors you may have cultivated through other networks (professional organization mentoring programs, conference connections, and so on). Resist the urge not to talk to faculty about your experiences: while peers are also important for support, the nature of the market may make you feel that you are directly competing with friends. In this regard, faculty can sometimes provide a safe and supportive outlet.

Third, seriously consider seeing a therapist, ideally as soon as possible. All of the authors went to therapy during graduate school, and for some of us, it was the single most helpful choice we made. Talking through your experience with someone who is invested in you as a person, but who has no stake in your professional success and does not belong to your broader academic community, can be a very relieving and cathartic practice.

We also recognize that therapists can sometimes do harm, especially to individuals with marginalized identities, and that finding a therapist who clicks with you can take time. Moreover, therapy in the United States is very expensive without insurance. Fortunately, therapy is often more accessible at universities than in the rest of the United States. Campus clinics may offer free sessions, although these are often in high demand and the number of visits may be capped. Therapists in the community may also offer sliding scale payments based on income. Ask more senior graduate students in your program if you are not sure where to start or whether your insurance (if you have insurance) covers therapy (see chapter 69 on counseling and other resources).

The last source of support, perhaps ironically, is yourself. Adding another task to your packed agenda may sound like the least appealing idea in the world while on the market but cultivating habits and hobbies now that build your self-worth gives you something to turn to when staring down rejection after rejection. We advocate devoting time to activities that let you create something on a shorter timeline than is typical in academia—this could include anything from cooking to art to community events—and move your body as much as possible. You may end up feeling too overwhelmed to continue these practices—one of the authors discontinued almost all of their outside hobbies while on the market because they simply didn't have the mental and emotional energy to pursue them—but the sooner you start prioritizing activities outside of academia, the longer before their benefits will wear off if you feel you have to disengage for a while.

Advice for Departments

Creating a less toxic and all-consuming job market experience can be buoyed by the departments supporting and recruiting candidates. Candidates often feel limited agency when on the job market, and changes to that experience also require institutional shifts in how we prioritize candidates' time and well-being. We highlight two potential sources of reform, one from the perspective of graduate students' home departments, and another from the hiring departments and committees themselves. The choices that get made about how to structure the experience will shape graduate students' experiences and expectations.

Departments recruiting candidates can structure their job search in ways that support candidates' mental health, prioritize their time, and limit anxiety over the uncertainty in the process. One easily implemented solution is requiring fewer materials for candidates upfront. Many job candidates feel overwhelmed by the materials required to "go on" the job market because across research statements, teaching materials, diversity statements, and other documents, an academic job application can total over 50 pages of material. Departments could save applicants considerable stress by asking for only a cover letter, writing sample, and CV during the first round, relieving most applicants of considerable work that goes into many of the statements that candidates put together. Letters of recommendation can also be a tool for final candidates rather than a requirement of all candidates. Similarly, departments should be as specific as possible about the position that they are hiring for. Searches that seek out the "best academic" regardless of rank or subfield can often turn away candidates who can't imagine ever rising to the top of the pool and often benefit traditionally advantaged scholars.

Uncertainty in the job market also manifests in the lack of transparency in the hiring process, where candidates often apply and never hear anything from departments or are given a formal notification from the university more than six months later. Universities are constrained in a number of ways through Human Resources and job listing regulations but offering candidates some information throughout the process can be helpful. Departments can be more transparent about where they are in the process, whether flyouts have been offered, and whether the position has been filled. This information can be communicated through social media channels or through our academic institutions.

Graduate student support from within a student's home institution can also mitigate anxiety by offering more resources, more information, and creating institutional norms for candidates that better address the realities of the job market. Departments with job market candidates should prioritize giving candidates the time and space to pursue the full-time job that is applying for full-time positions both within and outside academia. Adding another job on top of this, in the form of teaching or demanding RA work, means candidates simply cannot devote as much time to the market as they may need to, and the emotional costs can be debilitating. Departments should prioritize funding job market candidates with fellowships in order to minimize candidate stress, meaning resources with fewer requirements and stipulations for students' time. Additionally, if funding is an issue that would prohibit research assistant positions, creating an environment among the grad students and faculty to cover candidates' TA or teaching work as needed would minimize some of the stress.

Departments and faculty could also make a point to be upfront with the candidates and rationally explain to them the state of the job market and talk about the informal, unsaid rules of the market. Currently, many top programs offer just a one-hour info session that is given just once a year. Many of the most helpful conversations are done informally among graduate students, placing a higher burden on students, and advancing those with more extensive networks, resources, etc. Additionally, faculty should talk about their experiences, but more important than their market experience is their experience on a hiring committee. Finally, departments could better prepare candidates by having a seminar-style class that helps the candidates prepare for the market by working through their job market packet. A course like this would be beneficial the semester or year before candidates go on the market, so that when putting together final packets, students do not feel alone. Seminar sessions or workshops devoted to each part of the job packet were incredibly helpful for at least one of the authors.

Conclusion

Throughout the entire academic job market process, it is critical for departments, and candidates, to remember that job market candidates are people first, and the market will affect their personal lives and well-being. Prioritizing mental health—and, for departments, implementing structural changes with mental health in mind—can go a long way toward making the market less painful and helping candidates feel less alone.

36

What Your PhD Advisors Can't Tell You Because They Don't Know: Landing a Job at a Student-Focused Institution

Karen M. Kedrowski[1]

1. Iowa State University

KEYWORDS: Research Intensive Institutions, Teaching Philosophy Statement, Application Letter, Research Agenda.

Introduction

More than half of political science professors in the United States are employed in non-PhD granting departments.[1] While some of these are *research intensive* (R1 or R2) *institutions*, many more are institutions where undergraduate education is the primary focus (hereafter "student-focused" institutions). For faculty members who prioritize teaching and want to closely mentor undergraduates, student-focused institutions provide meaningful and rewarding careers.

At the same time, most PhD faculty have spent their graduate and professional careers in departments with doctoral programs at R1s and R2s. They may not provide very good advice for applying and interviewing for jobs at student-focused institutions because they have never worked at such an institution.

I spent a quarter century at a regional, master's institution in the South, where the regular teaching load was eight courses per year. I spent 20 years in administration, which included 16 years as department chair and dean. I participated in scores of searches and many issues came up repeatedly. This essay will provide concrete advice on how to prepare an application and interview at a student-focused institution from someone on the other side of the interview desk.

Be a PhD, Not an ABD

I knew what the time demands were for a new faculty member—with the mandatory trainings, multiple class preparations, grading, office hours, faculty meetings, assessment, and significant service requirements. I also had seen too many ABD candidates who joined the faculty and saw their defense dates delayed by a year or more. Sadly, some never finished, and consequently, did not earn tenure. Thus, I always pushed candidates to do everything possible to finish before they arrive on campus as a faculty member. (See chapters 14 and 15 for solid advice on starting—and completing—your dissertation project.)

Seek Teaching Experience

As a chair and dean, I wanted to see that candidates had been instructors of record with complete responsibility for every aspect of the course, from choosing the textbook to course design, creating student assessments, and responsibility for all grading. Serving as a teaching assistant with some grading responsibility in a large section led by a PhD faculty member is all well and good. However, this is not a substitute for classroom experience. Moreover, having one or more courses "in the can," so to speak, will make your life easier as a new faculty member.

If you are unable to teach your own course at your institution, consider a Visiting Assistant Professorship position or part time work with a community college. Other types of pedagogical instruction are also a plus, whether it's participation in a "Preparing Future Faculty" program, courses in education or pedagogy, online course development training, participation in APSA's Teaching and Learning Conference, or even, yes, secondary teaching certification. (For further insight into how to gain teaching experience, see chapter 28 on teaching assistantships, 29 on teaching your own class, 30 on APSA's Teaching & Learning Conference, and 44 on adjunct and fixed-term positions).

Craft Your Teaching Statement

Many student-focused institutions will ask for a *teaching philosophy statement*. Most that I read—and the ones I wrote—were pretty lousy. College teaching is a discipline unto itself, with its own literature, theory, and jargon. The strongest teaching statements are those that tap into this literature and also discuss the liberal arts skills that you emphasize, the pedagogical approaches you use, and the ways you measure student learning that go beyond rote memorization (chapter 43 provides advice on teaching philosophy statements, as well as on other types of statements increasingly requested by search committees).

Revise Your Application Letter

Prioritize your teaching experience and commitment in your *application letter*. Too many application letters read as though the candidate is applying for a position at a research-intensive institution (or R1). While I was interested in a candidate's dissertation, I'm going to hire based on the candidate's commitment to student learning and development.

Be sure to list the courses that you are interested in teaching. However, make sure that they are appropriate for a primarily undergraduate audience. Better yet, read the department's course offerings and list those courses already on the books that you have taught or have the academic background to teach.

Remember, too, political science and/or civic education are components of many liberal arts' general education programs. Your letter should also discuss your experience and/or ability to engage the apathetic nonmajor as well as your enthusiastic political science student.

You should include a description of your dissertation research and your future research agenda. However, it is secondary to the section on teaching and your experience or interest in service opportunities is tertiary.

Seek Tailored Recommendation Letters

When applying to a student-focused institution, make sure that at least one of your recommendation letters can speak to your classroom and/or online teaching and student interaction. This may not be one of your committee members, unless this person has observed you in the classroom or interacting online. The most tone-deaf letter I read said, "I haven't seen So-and-So teaching but I'm sure s/he will do fine." If none of your faculty mentors can speak to your skill as an instructor, ask a colleague to observe you and write a letter of support. Make it an additional letter if you don't want to replace a letter from one of your mentors and if the application portal allows you to.

Plan for Two "Job Talks"

Yes, you will present your research during your interview. However, you will probably teach a class too. This is important; prepare for it as intensely as you prepare your research presentation. You may, or may not, be able to teach on the topic of your choice. So be prepared for anything.

Have a Realistic Research Agenda

You will be asked about your *research agenda* during the interview. Your responses should indicate that you understand that you will have little time for research and writing and that student research assistants will be scarce. Your institution will probably not have an Inter-university Consortium for Political and Social Research (ICPSR) membership and the library, even with today's database subscriptions, will be smaller than at your PhD institution. You can still do excellent work and make your mark in the discipline. However, as an administrator, I wanted to see that the candidate had a plan that could be executed with the resources available.

Negotiate the Offer

Of course, salary is going to be front and center in your mind. Be realistic. Research salaries using public employee databases or resources such as Glassdoor. Also, be sure to account for the cost of living, which can make a huge difference in what your salary offer may purchase.

In addition, be sure to negotiate for more than salary. When you receive an offer is your best may be your best—or only—opportunity to secure resources to support your research agenda. (In my experience, STEM candidates were very good at this; social science and humanities candidates were not.) Consider asking for a course release, travel money, software, book allowance, data set purchases, support for undergraduate research assistants, technology, and more. Think creatively and long term. (See chapter 46 for additional advice on negotiating tactics.)

I recommend asking about domestic partner benefits and spousal/partner hiring practices when negotiating a position. However, be prepared for a "no." Consequently, you may need to explore the local community for employment opportunities for a spouse/partner. (See chapter 48).

Enjoy the Adventure

Working at a student-focused institution offers many rewards and opportunities. Not only are there many opportunities to mentor students and to develop long-lasting relationships with alumni, but these institutions also provide many opportunities to gain leadership skills and to learn about how universities work. Take advantage of these opportunities and enjoy the adventure.

Endnotes

1   Derived from Jackson, Rory and Betsy Super. 2018. "2016-2017 Departmental Survey: Faculty Composition Report." Washington, DC: APSA. Available: https://apsanet.org/Portals/54/ APSA%20Files/Data%20Reports/Employment%20Data/Faculty%20Composition%20Report%20 2016-2017.pdf?ver=2018-03-26-160737-587&timestamp=1522094866226 and APSA "2018 Community College Faculty Survey," Available: https://www.apsanet.org/Portals/54/APSA%20 Files/Data%20Reports/Charts/2018-June-cotm.pdf?ver=2018-06-25-094431-427). Extrapolating from Jackson and Super's study, approximately 2000 political science faculty in PhD granting institutions, and approximately 1500 at MA and BA-granting institutions. Thus, coupled with the 2600 political science faculty surveyed by APSA, I conclude that approximately 4100 political scientists are employed at non-PhD granting institutions.

37 | A Commitment to Teaching, Learning, and Student Advocacy: Community College Careers

LaTasha Chaffin DeHaan[1], Josh Franco[2], Verónica Reyna[3], & Randy Villegas[4]

1. Elgin Community College 2. Cuyamaca College

3. Houston Community College 4. University of California, Santa Cruz

KEYWORDS: Community Colleges, Hiring Committees.

Introduction

Community colleges are the most diverse institutions of higher education in the United States. The American Association of Community Colleges (Fast Facts 2017) reports that approximately 12 million students attend a community college throughout the country. Over one half, or 57%, of these students are women. When considering race and ethnicity, the community college student body is quite diverse: 27% are Hispanic, 13% are African American, 44% are White, 6% are Asian/Pacific Islander, and 1% are Native American. Additionally, 29% are first-generation, 15% are single parents, and 20% are students with disabilities.

Most graduate students in political science attend and receive their training at less diverse R1 universities where research is the main driver of pursuits (for a discussion of careers at R1 institutions, see chapter 40). With this experience comes an overwhelming emphasis on research and underwhelming experiences with teaching and pedagogy training. Some faculty members and advisors may push students to apply for jobs at R1 institutions while actively discouraging applications to community colleges or other teaching centered positions. On the contrary, graduate students in political science can thrive in community colleges, particularly if they love teaching, are dedicated to student success, and are committed to the student empowerment mission of community colleges. In this chapter, we will examine three areas: commitment to teaching as a career, commitment to teaching and student learning, and a commitment to student advocacy and communities.

Commitment to Teaching as a Career

A commitment to teaching is essential for any community college professor. Graduate students are mostly trained to be researchers, while their teaching knowledge, skills, and abilities are largely ignored. This is not surprising, given that students are trained by research faculty and not teaching faculty. However, community college careers are rewarding professionally, personally, and financially. Community colleges offer a viable and preferred career option for political science graduate students who have a commitment to teaching, learning, student advocacy, and to the communities in which these institutions serve.

Types of Community Colleges

There are at least six types of two-year *community college institutions*: public and private, union and non-union, and tenure and non-tenure (Smith 2021). Public community colleges are typically governed by locally elected Board of Trustees, who are members of the community, while private community colleges are run by non-profit or for-profit corporations. Some public institutions have faculty unions, which is largely determined by state laws that permit the right to organize and collectively bargain. Unions formally bargain with a community college district's administration for salaries, benefits, and working conditions. Finally, positions at community colleges may be tenured or non-tenured, which means there is assurance of long-term employment or not.

According to the National Center for Education Statistics (National Center for Education Statistics n.d.), from 2016 to 2017 the average annual salary for full-time instructional faculty at a two-year public institution was $67,684 compared with $53,017 at two-year private institutions. These averages were slightly higher for men versus women faculty members. The NCES suggests a geographical relationship with those higher education institutions that collectively bargain, in that the "the mid-Atlantic Census region and California contain 46% of all unionized faculty observations but only 26% of all faculty observation[s]" (Wassell et al. 2015, 9). As a result, unionized faculty are concentrated in specific geographical regions, and they tend to benefit from higher salaries.

The Competitive Community College Job Market

While searching for jobs within community colleges, competition is fierce. Take steps to ensure that you are prepared to hit the job market. First, make sure you check job postings via APSA eJobs,[1] HigherEd-Jobs,[2] and state-specific registries, such as CCC Registry.[3] Make an effort to seek out community college job sites, too, since many do not have budgets to advertise nationally. An often-overlooked aspect of applying to community college positions is to obtain your master's degree. PhD programs have different requisites for obtaining the degree, but typically a student is able to obtain their master's enroute to their doctorate after they successfully advance to candidacy. In order to teach at community colleges, you must obtain your master's degree; being "All But Dissertation" (ABD) is not recognized as a credential for teaching (see chapters 14 and 15 for more information about the dissertation and master's thesis).

Finally, do your best to earn teaching experience. Obtaining experience as an Instructor of Record for a class is required by community colleges, but even gaining experience as a teaching assistant can also help you prepare to lead a class on your own in the future. Ask your department if you are able to teach a summer school course once you have obtained your master's. Reach out to neighboring community colleges and apply to be placed into their adjunct pool. Although some faculty members may discourage students from teaching, these experiences can be crucial toward helping you earn the experience needed to be invited for an interview.

Advice for Your Job Application

As you find job opportunities, you should dissect each opportunity. The call for a position is one of the most important aspects to how you should craft your application materials. Most applications require you to submit an online application that should include: a cover letter; a teaching pedagogy and philosophy narrative (sometimes this is the same as the cover letter, sometimes these can be separate); a curriculum vitae or resume; unofficial copies of college transcripts; equivalency documents (if necessary); and two or three letters of recommendation.

While these may all seem like standard documents, create all application materials so that they speak directly to each of the minimum, desired qualifications of the position. For example, if the job description[4] has four minimum requirements and five desirable requirements, your cover letter should speak directly to each of those nine requirements. Committees sort through hundreds of applications, so it is very easy to rule out candidates based upon whether or not they followed directions or meet these qualifications.

What Are Community Colleges Looking for?

Teaching and service. Community college instructors are typically responsible for teaching a 5-5 course load during the academic year, and community colleges want to hire the best teachers. Highlighting your experience (and ideally experience as an Instructor of Record at a community college) is a must! Indicate service to any affiliated institution and to the community at large. Community college faculty are asked to serve on various committees, and the search committee will be looking for who is willing to contribute to these discussions on curriculum, campus planning, and equity. Whereas you might be tempted to highlight your dissertation or research publications, you should prioritize your teaching, pedagogy, and service.

What About Some "Don'ts?"

Generally speaking, do not ever state or even imply that this position is a "backup" position or a step-pingstone to another opportunity. Secondly, do not ask about a research budget, or how many teaching assistants are provided. Unless explicitly stated in the job description or the college's website, most community college positions do not require research and publishing, and most do not provide teaching assistants to assist with grading or classroom logistics.

What About Some "Dos?"

Make sure that your letter writers can speak to teaching and mentoring abilities, and to interactions with students and colleagues. Share student evaluations with those writing recommendations so they can cite what students are saying about teaching strengths. If there is little formal teaching, consider highlighting experiences indicating a future ability to teach. Be creative and honest about teaching experiences; not all forms of teaching are done directly in the classroom. Overall, the entire portfolio of materials must speak to the needs of the diverse academic, socioeconomic, cultural, disability, and racial and ethnic backgrounds of community college students.

What Are Hiring Committees Looking for?

Community colleges seek committed educators who embrace the realities of working with community college students. The *hiring committee* looks for these characteristics in the application materials, letter, the CV, and the teaching portfolio. In the application letter, make sure to convey the desire to teach courses allowed at the institution. Community colleges do not teach all political science subfields, so communicate through these materials the understanding of what courses are taught at the college and the ability to teach the courses offered. Know the modalities for courses offered and highlight training in online teaching. When listing courses taught as instructor of record, clearly delineate which and how many courses were taught each semester.

Another ability hiring committees look for in the application letter is knowledge about the community college's specific student body and how best to work with their students. Discuss training in inclusive course design and bandwidth recovery techniques. Share student stories that show how pedagogy and course design address the diversity of learners in a community college classroom. Are students' political histories incorporated into the curriculum? Are students empowered to participate in their democracy? Does course design support underrepresented students? Utilize a broad definition of diversity: growth areas for community colleges are dual credit or early college students, so indicate training or experiences teaching high school students.

Along with being committed to educating a diverse classroom, committees are looking for colleagues who are committed to institutional success. Express how you are a value-add for the department and what you can bring to the department and in service to the college. Be prepared to share ideas or experiences about mentoring, diversity and inclusion, professional development, rigor, or college success and transfer initiatives.

Finally, find out details about teaching demonstrations. Clarify expectations on the course topic, any specific teaching skills to incorporate, and other parameters for the demonstration. Can materials be given ahead of time to students, or can handouts be given to the audience? Will it be recorded? Are there any audience members with known ADA accommodations? Pro tip: inclusive, active learning is preferred to straight, PowerPoint lectures. Use this opportunity to highlight pedagogical and subject areas strengths! (See chapter 29 for information about preparing for your first teaching experience.)

You Got the Job, Now What?

Congratulations! As with all positions, academic or non-academic, take some time to celebrate this accomplishment! One of the first things to do is to read the union contract, if applicable. These contracts provide information about teaching loads, service expectations, contractual obligations, and salary schedules. Another important thing to note is to provide the years of teaching (whether K12, serving as a teaching assistant, or teaching as a graduate instructor) to Human Resources to make sure the salary schedule step reflects this experience. Check the Faculty Handbook to get familiar with the institution's procedures and rules.

Finally, find a mentor within the department or campus. Prepare for the school year and develop syllabi basing assignments, classroom activities, and assessments on class size, which can range from 25-50 students per course. The "base load" for most faculty members at community colleges is five to five, meaning five courses in the fall, and five in the winter/spring. It is generally advised to avoid service commitments during the first year to ensure time is devoted to improving your teaching and supporting the learning of your students.

Commitment to Teaching and Student Learning

At the heart of community college teaching is diversity, equity, and inclusion, and culturally responsive teaching. Community colleges commit to teaching excellence and to a social justice-driven duty to accessibility. Most community colleges have similar institutional characteristics as a result. For example, community colleges are open access institutions. This means that all students are accepted. Community colleges are low-cost to no-cost attendance institutions to make higher education accessible, too.

Community colleges are student-centered. This means that all employees focus on student retention and student success. Faculty success is defined by student success. Courses are offered online, face-to-face, throughout the day, evening and the weekend. Fundamentally, community colleges serve the entire distribution of students, not just the upper 10% of students like most four-year universities and colleges. Faculty must know how to educate military veterans, international students, English-language learners, teenagers and seniors, students with disabilities, students with families and full-time jobs, and students with GEDs to AP credit.

This means that professional development is continuous and should include pedagogy, diversity, inclusion, and bandwidth recovery techniques. Professional development can count as continuing education for states that require continuing education credits. Finally, professional development keeps us current. The commitment to teaching and learning implies striving to be a better educator and to recognize the social, economic, and political role community colleges play in the lives of their students.

When Research Serves Teaching and Learning

It is important to note that "teaching and research need not be mutually exclusive goals" (Wladis and Mesa 2019, 1591). In fact, "community college professors are educationally trained to conduct research as eighteen percent of all full-time U.S. community college faculty and 25% in education and social sciences have doctorates" (Wladis and Mesa 2019, 1593). As a result, there are many community college faculty members who are trained and have an interest in conducting research in their disciplines, pedagogical research, scholarship on teaching and learning along with civically engaged research (Jackson et al. 2021, 721).

The missions of community colleges center around faculty engaging in effective teaching practices, providing students with an excellent value for their educational financial investment and providing support services to recruit and retain students while helping them persist until degree completion. Community college faculty are not readily known as researchers engaged in the teacher-scholar model; however, many faculty members engage in research that aids their disciplines, colleges, communities, and students.

Faculty indicate that their reasons for not being as engaged in professional development activities and in research activities at community colleges are because of a lack of time, high teaching loads, that administrators, faculty, and staff do not value or reward these types of productive activities, and that some faculty have been dis-incentivized from conducting research (Wladis and Mesa 2019). Wladis and Mesa (2019) suggest that community colleges need to change their culture to incentivize faculty research by those who have an interest, are qualified, and are able to conduct generalizable/transferable education research. Colleges can consider providing faculty with small research grants and support faculty through providing set aside time or course load reductions for faculty members conducting research that will benefit their students, college, or departments.

Commitment to Student Advocacy and Communities

Community college faculty wear multiple hats: teacher, social worker, consigliere, career advisor, ombudsman, food banker and, most importantly, that of student advocate. Students are their best advocates, and faculty can amplify their needs and wants. For example, shared governance (Kater and Levin 2004; Reed 2017), the process of aggregating input from campus constituencies, is an important avenue for students to make their voice heard. For example, in California, all community college districts have campus committees where staff, faculty, and administrators discuss policies and issues affecting the whole campus. Faculty members can encourage students to serve on these committees, promote the allocation of stipends from campus-based funds, and support students who do ask questions and speak up during these meetings.

Co-curricular (Glass et al. 2017) and extracurricular activities (Schudde 2019), such as clubs and organizations, speech and debate teams, athletic sports teams, and community organizations are avenues for student engagement and skill development. Faculty can support these organizations by serving as unpaid or paid advisors, support the allocation of funding to these student organizations through campus budgeting processes, and attend events and competitions to support students. Additionally, faculty can encourage their college's communications teams and leadership to recognize students in campus newsletters and during governing board members. For example, Cuyamaca College President Dr. Julianna Barnes reported to the Governing Board that alumnus Ridwaan Mohamed was a featured speaker for Historically Black College/University (HBCU) Highlight Week hosted by the California Community College to HBCU Transfer Pathway.

A commitment to diversity and inclusion expands from the classroom to the communities in which students live. Understanding the social and economic realities of students should be reflected in course design details and in recognizing all students' needs influence success in education. For example, professors can pursue service-related roles in the college and in student communities. Some colleges offer a variety of resources for students including food pantries, mental health counseling, and sometimes even childcare. However, some offer few resources. Faculty can embed themselves in these conversations at the college and in community groups that create equitable resources to help students be successful in the classroom. Being a student advocate means being aware of college and local government resources to meet student needs.

Conclusion

Each of the authors teach at colleges with institutional and geographic diversity. The benefits of teaching at community colleges include having the ability as instructors to work closely with our students in primarily small class environments. We also enjoy the privilege of introducing our students to political science, many of whom may have never previously taken a political science course. As we are broadly trained in our discipline, most community college instructors are generalists teaching diverse political science courses including Introduction to Political Science, American Government, International Relations, and Political Theory. There are also opportunities to engage in training about equitable and effective teaching practices that enhance student learning outcomes. The salary and benefits are often competitive with liberal arts colleges and can be more lucrative depending on the negotiation efforts of the faculty member, whether the institution is unionized versus non-union, and whether the position is tenure-track or non-tenure track.

In bringing balance to the vast benefits of pursuing a full-time, community college career, there are also challenges to consider. While faculty members at community colleges provide service to their students, the campus community, and the community at large, as well as conduct pedagogical and disciplinary research, their primary focus is providing effective and quality teaching. Therefore, faculty teach up to five course preparations each semester, and can teach up to 250 students per semester. The grading and course assessment are the responsibility of the instructor. Additional challenges to consider are that some community colleges do not offer disciplinary majors or associate degrees in political science, and if they do, there may be a low number of declared majors. There may also be limitations on the curriculum offered, given state laws or regulations. Despite these challenges, however, teaching at a community college can be one of the most rewarding and fulfilling careers for graduate students in political science.

Endnotes

1   https://www.apsanet.org/eJobs

2   https://www.higheredjobs.com/faculty/search.cfm?JobCat=90

3   https://www.cccregistry.org/jobs/index.aspx

4   https://gocommunitycolleges.com/job-descriptions

References

"Fast Facts." 2017. https://www.aacc.nche.edu/research-trends/fast-facts/ (July 4, 2021).

Glass, Chris R., Peggy Gesing, Angela Hales, and Cong Cong. 2017. "Faculty as Bridges to Co-Curricular Engagement and Community for First-Generation International Students." *Studies in Higher Education* 42(5): 895–910.

Jackson, Jenn M., Brian Shoup, and H. Howell Williams. 2021. "Why Civically Engaged Research? Understanding and Unpacking Researcher Motivations." *PS: Political Science & Politics* 54(4): 721–24.

Kater, Sue, and John S. Levin. 2004. "Shared Governance in the Community College." *Community College Journal of Research and Practice* 29(1): 1–23.

National Center for Education Statistics. "Average Salary of Full-Time Instructional Faculty on 9-Month Contracts in Degree-Granting Postsecondary Institutions, by Academic Rank, Control and Level of Institution, and Sex: Selected Years, 1970-71 through 2016-17." https://nces.ed.gov/programs/digest/d17/tables/dt17_316.10.asp.

Reed, Matthew. 2017. "Community Colleges, Shared Governance, and Democracy." *PS: Political Science & Politics* 50(2): 428–29.

Schudde, Lauren. 2019. "Short-and Long-Term Impacts of Engagement Experiences with Faculty and Peers at Community Colleges." *The Review of Higher Education* 42(2): 385–426.

Smith, Ashley A. 2021. "California Community College Transfer Students Face Roadblocks to Bachelor's Degrees." *EdSource*. https://edsource.org/2021/california-community-college-transfer-students-face-roadblocks-to-a-bachelors-degree/656883 (June 24, 2021).

Wassell, Charles S., Jr, David W. Hedrick, Steven E. Henson, and John M. Krieg. 2015. "Wage Distribution Impacts of Higher Education Faculty Unionization." *Journal of Collective Bargaining in the Academy* 7(1): 4.

Wladis, Claire, and Vilma Mesa. 2019. "What Can Happen When Community College Practitioners Lead Research Projects? The Case of CUNY." *The Review of Higher Education* 42(4): 1575–1606.

38

More than Reordering the Cover Letter: Preparing for Careers at Small Liberal Arts Colleges

Kelly Bauer[1] & Shamira Gelbman[2]

1. Nebraska Wesleyan University 2. Wabash College

KEYWORDS: SLACs, Pedagogical Expertise.

Part 1: A Day in the Life

In contrast to institutions where tenure and promotion are awarded primarily on the basis of research credentials, small liberal arts colleges (*SLACs*) typically expect that faculty will excel as teachers, scholars, and leading members of their campus communities. This means that faculty members at SLACs carry out their own research agenda while teaching a variety of courses and investing in pedagogical development, navigating mentorship relationships with students, and working with colleagues from a variety of disciplines on all areas of college governance. As a result, daily life as a SLAC faculty member is varied, often featuring a vibrant—or even dizzying—mix of teaching, service, and research activities.

Teaching

SLACs are, first and foremost, teaching-focused institutions where faculty play a big role in supporting students' academic, personal, and professional development. Therefore, it is a rare day during the semester that a faculty member does not spend at least some time on teaching or other student-focused work, even for those who have classes only two or three days a week. Much of this daily work centers on the classes the faculty member is currently teaching—typically in the neighborhood of two to four distinct courses in a given semester. Class sizes can be quite small and seminar-style discussions and active learning activities are common. Preparing for class meetings comprises a significant part of the daily workload, as does meeting with students one-on-one or in small groups to discuss feedback on projects, help them master difficult course material, or talk more generally about class or other matters. Through this work, faculty provide "front line" support for students, helping to connect them with campus resources and, often, following up on those referrals.

In addition to their current teaching responsibilities, SLAC faculty members' daily schedule may include devoting time to developing courses they will teach in the future. Academic departments at SLACs can be quite small, with each faculty member responsible for teaching a broad portfolio of courses that cover much or even all of a subfield. Especially in their first few years on the job, this can mean creating and preparing many new or new-to-you courses. SLACs also often feature opportunities for teaching that extends or crosses disciplinary boundaries. These opportunities may include solo-teaching a topical course that brings political science into dialogue with other disciplines or co-teaching interdisciplinary courses with colleagues from other departments who share thematic teaching interests. They may also include teaching non-disciplinary courses as part of a freshman-year experience or other all-college curricular programs.

Because undergraduate teaching is so central to the SLAC mission, faculty dedicate time to their pedagogical development, and often participate in opportunities to improve their own teaching and contribute to departmental and faculty-wide initiatives to enhance the quality of teaching at the institution as a whole. Periodic activities in this vein might include attending workshops on pedagogical issues, presenting or writing about their own teaching innovations, or meeting with a colleague—whether in their own or another department—to discuss shared teaching challenges. Many institutions also have funding opportunities to support the pedagogical development of, for example, project-based learning, internships, service learning, or hybrid teaching on campus, and faculty spend time brainstorming, applying, researching, implementing, and assessing these teaching strategies. For additional information on two other resources—the APSA Education Section and the Teaching and Learning Conference—see chapter 30 in this volume.

Service

Departments and faculties at SLACs are relatively small, administrative and support staff are lean, and shared governance is highly valued. This can entail a good deal of service from individual faculty members, who are expected to contribute in significant ways to running both their own department and the institution of which it is a part. In addition, SLACs located in small towns or otherwise remote locations often serve as important cultural and informational resources beyond the campus walls. In turn, faculty may be encouraged to draw upon their expertise in service to their local community. Many SLACs also value disciplinary service and encourage and even reward faculty for professional activity such as peer reviewing, participation on professional association committees, or editorial board service.

What this means on a daily basis varies. Some days may feature no service work at all, or fifteen minutes here or there to complete an administrative survey or take a call from a local media reporter. Others may include an hour-long committee or department meeting, and yet others may entail sustained work to review job candidate files or prepare for an upcoming event. To the extent that SLAC faculty have significant responsibilities in student recruitment, retention, and mentorship, daily service tasks might also include advising, recommendation letter writing, meeting with prospective students, or participating in admissions or alumni events. Informal conversation with colleagues also drives institutional governance and community building, as relationships are a significant way that work gets done on a SLAC campus.

Research

As with teaching and service, SLAC faculty members carry out their research activities in an interdisciplinary, student-focused environment. On-campus research presentations—including job talks—may feature audiences that include undergraduate students and faculty from a broad range of disciplines in addition to political science colleagues. There may be opportunities for interdisciplinary research collaboration. And engaging students in meaningful research experiences, whether through participation in some aspect of a faculty member's research program or conducting their own independent research under faculty supervision, is often valued and encouraged.

Balancing research alongside teaching and service responsibilities can be a challenging part of SLAC faculty members' daily work life. For some, a solution might be to focus on different research tasks at different points in the academic year. For example, some might do background reading or code data while classes are in session and reserve more sustained writing for long summer and winter breaks. Others might designate small blocks of time for daily or weekly writing sessions, either on their own or alongside colleagues who help to keep each other on track for meeting short-term goals. Some faculty members find it useful to adjust their research program to include projects they can carry out more efficiently in the SLAC setting, especially while on the tenure track. Scholarship of Teaching and Learning (SOTL), research that can be done with limited travel or financial support, and projects that are amenable to collaboration with undergraduate students may be especially fruitful avenues to pursue (see chapter 24 on publishing in this volume for more details on SOTL research).

Part 2: Advice to Graduate Students

For those interested in pursuing this career path, we encourage preparing in four ways. Graduate students should consider this preparation for a career at a SLAC, not just for the SLAC job market, as demonstrating your preparation for the responsibilities of SLAC faculty is the best approach to succeeding at the interview stage.

Pedagogical Expertise

Graduate students should think early and often about their *pedagogical expertise* and experience, perhaps the most important qualification for SLAC positions. Graduate students interested in a SLAC career should develop teaching and mentoring expertise that scales over their graduate training. For example, you might observe different faculty undergraduate classes, lead discussion sections, hold office hours, develop a lecture and/or a full course, design and implement assessments of student learning, and reflect on curricular and pedagogical decisions (such as course assessment, recruiting). Certainly, the accessibility of these experiences varies widely—few if any graduate students will have this range of pedagogical experience during their graduate work (Ishiyama, Miles, and Balarezo 2010; Marineau 2018; Trowbridge and Woodward 2021)—and there are tradeoffs in dedicating time to teaching or making progress towards your dissertation defense. But, we encourage graduate students to take advantage of training and experiences available within the department and university, as well as less traditional teaching opportunities. These could range from adjuncting over the summer, guest lecturing, mentoring in a research lab (Becker and Zvobgo, 2020), or teaching in non-academic environments. Graduate students can also join the Political Science Education section of APSA and attend TLC (see chapter 30 in this volume). More teaching experience is not necessarily better. More important than the quantity of teaching experience is demonstrating commitment to teaching by learning and articulating two things: (1) your pedagogical priorities,[1] and (2) examples and expertise around these pedagogical priorities. Evidence of your teaching voice should structure your teaching statement, and your answer to a frequent interview question about what your classroom looks like.

SLAC Teaching and Research Trajectories

Often, the teaching and research happening at PhD granting institutions is very different from that in a SLAC, and a persuasive SLAC candidate will be able to translate their professional trajectory across institutional environments. While many graduate students will have specialized teaching experience, we encourage thinking through the courses you might teach at a SLAC environment. While bigger research institutions can support offering the same class content multiple semesters or even multiple sections the same semester, SLAC departments offer many content courses on one- or two-year rotations, meaning that faculty need a wide repertoire of courses. While graduate students certainly don't need to have experience developing and instructing all of the courses they expect to teach as faculty, they should think about what such a course rotation might look like. The rotation may include interdisciplinary courses and common SLAC curriculum like first year seminars.

In smaller departments, faculty are often responsible for teaching a wide range of writing, speaking, methodology, and statistical analytical skills throughout their classes. Pay attention to ways in which this skill development is and could be integrated across your teaching repertoire. Also seek out broad methodological training, experiences, or conversations to think through and equip yourself to work with students using diverse methodologies. Being able to teach a senior capstone course and advise student research across content and methodologies is desirable to most SLAC departments.

A common misconception is that SLAC faculty do not publish or maintain an active research agenda. Rather, most SLACs require research and/or professional productivity in traditional measures of research productivity, but also interdisciplinary journals, public facing work, scholarship of teaching and learning research, and collaborative research with students. Another misconception is that there are no research resources at SLACs. Certainly, these vary across institutions, but are less likely to facilitate long research trips off campus and time out of the classroom, and more likely to facilitate specific experiences and collaboration with undergraduate students. A search committee and faculty evaluation committee are likely to wonder if and how your research translates to those institutional priorities and resources, and if it can thrive in an interdisciplinary environment.

Networking

As evidenced above, a day in the life of a SLAC faculty differs greatly from that of faculty at PhD granting institutions, and networks greatly facilitate flows of information. While this networking certainly may happen at content-based panels at the larger disciplinary conferences, we recommend seeking out panels, roundtables, and conferences that are likely to overlap with the work of SLAC faculty. Some of our most meaningful networking with other SLAC faculty happens at APSA TLC, teaching panels and workshops, regional interdisciplinary conferences, and undergraduate conferences (ex: Pi Sigma Alpha, Model UN). See chapter 18 in this volume for more on networking.

Interviewing

As we suggest above, we encourage graduate students to prepare themselves more for a SLAC career than for the interview. From our experience on search committees, a few "tells" highlight which candidates are committed to and familiar with a SLAC career.

Prioritize Relationships with Students

Search committees at SLACs are often trying to understand how a potential new colleague will relate to, support, and challenge students in and out of the classroom, and on what content. You can help make your case by addressing these issues in your cover letter and teaching statement. Some institutions also include a student representative on the search committee, have candidates meet with a group of students, or solicit feedback from students who attend candidates' job talks. In the best-case scenario, a committee will understand which students to send to the candidate's office for additional resources and conversations, and trust the candidate is equipped and excited for those conversations.

Demonstrate Teaching Philosophy, Effectiveness, and Flexibility

SLAC search committee members know that graduate students' teaching experience is likely in a very different institutional context than their institutions. Accordingly, they are considering if the candidate is able to adapt and adjust their teaching to a new institution, department, students, and community. Candidates can demonstrate this by providing evidence of adjusting both content and pedagogical practices to improve student learning. Content adjustments may include transitioning away from a "canon" or narrow content. Pedagogical adjustments may include implementing different types of participation (for example, think/pair/share, fish bowl dialogues) and reflective (entrance and exit learning passes) exercises, and lesson plan organization (active learning, problem-based learning, case studies).[2]

Frame Priorities and Accomplishments in Terms of Intellectual Contributions to an Interdisciplinary Community

Many SLAC search committees are interdisciplinary, and interviews will likely involve meetings with faculty and administrators who are not political scientists. Candidates should think through and articulate their potential contributions to both the department and the college. Candidates who lead with the prestige of their graduate education, grants, or publication record may come across as missing the university's institutional mission. Those qualifications absolutely matter but are most impactful when the candidate can communicate how they translate into their broader intellectual contributions to a SLAC community. For example, perhaps an experience supports a research trajectory that students could be involved in, or brings field work experience into the classroom, or could be a support to students applying to prestigious grants.

Conclusion

SLAC faculty have a wide range of responsibilities that make their work very different from that of their dissertation committee members. While at times overwhelming, faculty careers at SLAC institutions can also be very rewarding. Students often take multiple classes (if not one most semesters!) with the same professor, allowing for rich mentoring relationships that continue after students graduate. Institutional service can visibly shift institutional culture, community relationships, and opportunities and resources for students and faculty. Departmental colleagues think deeply about creating and implementing curriculum to best serve student needs. Faculty in small departments often have more research interests in common with faculty outside the department, offering the potential for rich interdisciplinary conversations and collaborations. Certainly, this climate of community learning and exploration is an ideal no institution fully lives up to, but the potential is worth exploring.

Endnotes

1   In addition to specific content areas of expertise, persuasive SLAC job applicants are able to articulate how they teach content through specific pedagogical practices like active learning strategies, experiential learning, writing instruction practices, capstones, project based learning, flipped classrooms, and more. Vanderbilt's Center for Teaching Excellence and the AACU's work on High Impact Learning Practices (HIPs) have accessible primers on many of these conversations, and APSA Educate and the Journal of Political Science Education publish resources and articles that apply these practices to political science content and contexts.

2   For additional resources and ideas, see Finkel (2000), Bain (2004), Bean (2011), Lang (2021).

References

Bain, Ken. 2004. *What the Best College Teachers Do*. Cambridge, MA: Harvard University Press.

Bean, John C. 2011. *Engaging Ideas: The Professor's Guide to Integrating Writing, Critical Thinking, and Active Learning in the Classroom*. Hoboken, NJ: John Wiley & Sons.

Becker, Megan, and Kelebogile Zvobgo. 2020. "Smoothing the Pipeline: a Strategy to Match Graduate Training with the Professional Demands of Professorship." *Journal of Political Science Education* 16(3): 357-368.

Finkel, Donald L. 2000. *Teaching with Your Mouth Shut*. Portsmouth, NH: Boynton/Cook Publishers.

Marineau, Josiah F. 2018. "Life at a Teaching University." *Journal of Political Science Education* 14(2): 270-275.

Ishiyama, John, Tom Miles, and Christine Balarezo. 2010. "Training the Next Generation of Teaching Professors: A Comparative Study of Ph. D. Programs in Political Science." *PS: Political Science & Politics* 43(3): 515-522.

Ishiyama, John, Christine Balarezo, and Tom Miles. 2014. "Do Graduate Student Teacher Training Courses Affect Placement Rates?" *Journal of Political Science Education* 10(3): 273-283.

Lang, James M. 2021. *Small Teaching: Everyday Lessons from the Science of Learning*. Hoboken, NJ: John Wiley & Sons.

Trowbridge, David, and Jennifer Woodward. 2021. "Pedagogy Training among Political Scientists: Opportunities, Interest, and Obstacles." *Journal of Political Science Education* 17(sup1): 807-824.

39 | Preparing for a Career at a Regional Comprehensive University

Elizabeth A. Bennion[1], Monica E. Lineberger[2], & Eric D. Loepp[2]

1. Indiana University South Bend 2. University of Wisconsin-Whitewater

KEYWORDS: RCU, Research-1.

Introduction: What You Should Know about Regional Comprehensive Universities

Most casual observers think immediately of flagship research universities when they are asked about institutions of higher education. The association is understandable: these universities are extremely large and extremely visible, not only for their size and research productivity but for their athletic programs. Graduate students who did not attend regional comprehensive universities (RCUs) themselves are similarly more familiar with research institutions because they house most graduate programs. However, many—often most—academic positions graduate students survey while on the job market are not based at Research-1 (R1) universities or elite liberal arts colleges (SLACS); they are often located at RCUs. Indeed, in Wisconsin, where Eric and Monica teach (and research), most students in the University of Wisconsin System attend RCUs, not the more research-intensive universities in Madison and Milwaukee. Applying for jobs and working at RCUs is distinct in a variety of ways from employment experiences at other types of universities, yet graduate advisors may have limited knowledge with this type of university. In this chapter, we offer readers some things to keep in mind when considering positions at RCUs, as well as tips for curating a competitive application.

Regional comprehensive universities are public institutions that offer a wide array of bachelor's degrees, as well as some master's level programs, and potentially a few doctoral programs. Some are part of university networks, while others operate as standalone entities. They vary in size from (typically) a couple of thousand students to upwards of twenty-thousand students in some cases.

For faculty, the biggest difference between RCUs and R1 institutions concerns the ratio of the universal components of academic positions: teaching, research, and service. Relative to primarily research institutions, RCUs place more emphasis on teaching and less on scholarship.[1] Teaching four courses per semester is common, though it can vary between and within universities and university systems. Research expectations for promotion and tenure are lower than at more research-oriented programs, and more emphasis is placed on performance in the classroom. Increasingly, RCU faculty are also expected to be able to teach (well!) in a variety of modalities, including face-to-face, hybrid, and online.

It is important to note that teaching-oriented does not mean teaching-exclusive. Faculty at RCUs are still scholars! These universities have Institutional Review Boards, undergraduate (and graduate) research programs, sabbaticals, grants, labs, and even conference funding. True, these resources may not be as well-endowed as they are at more research-focused institutions, and teaching is the bulk of most faculty members' professional lives at an RCU, but many programs vigorously support the generation and dissemination of scholarship. Just as there are often fantastic instructors at R1 universities, there can be top-notch scholars who call RCUs home. Indeed, as we will discuss below, working at teaching-intensive universities provides unique research opportunities that scholars at other universities may not have.

Students at RCUs are incredibly diverse. These institutions draw applicants from a variety of socioeconomic and academic backgrounds. Among all types of four-year colleges, RCUs enroll the largest proportions of underrepresented students—including military veterans, adult learners, ethnic minorities, first-generation students, and immigrants (Orphan, 2018). Some are high achievers that would thrive at almost any institution of higher education; others are lower performers who would likely never gain admission to more selective schools. Many are paying for school themselves, and therefore work at least part-time; indeed, it is not uncommon to work with individuals who are full-time students and full-time workers. RCUs are also common destinations for first-generation and non-traditional students, and often draw a disproportionate number of Pell Grant recipients. This environment offers incredible opportunities for engagement; however, instructors must be prepared to deliver content to an audience comprising students with a variety of schedules, preferences, and needs. Working with students from diverse, and sometimes disadvantaged, backgrounds can be very rewarding, especially when you see firsthand the transformative effect of higher education students and their contributions to the broader community.

Applying For a Position at an RCU

A common mistake when applying to a regional comprehensive university is to treat the application as if it were for an R1 or SLAC. Search committees can easily identify applicants who are applying for the position because they are looking for a job, not because they are interested in the advertised position. Generally, RCUs are looking for applicants who are committed first to teaching and second to research. The application to an RCU should demonstrate this commitment by specifying your ideas on instruction, discussing your pedagogy, and demonstrating your knowledge of the university. If you have teaching experience, be specific about how you connect with students in the classroom, how you cover the course material, and how you have implemented ingenuity in your assignments. In addition, address how your overall pedagogy aligns with the department's or university's goals. Show that you are interested in the university by noting how your pedagogy serves the demographics of the student body.

Much like the application process, the department seeks a colleague who understands that teaching is a priority at their institution. While on the interview, it is necessary to demonstrate that you are the 'right fit' for the position by arriving prepared. The objective of the search committee is to identify the candidate that will be a utility player for the department. Resources are limited at RCUs and any way in which a job candidate can help fulfill roles will impress the department. Be prepared to discuss the specifics of your teaching strategies and the different classes or areas in which you would be interested in teaching. Search committees are looking for more than general ideas about your pedagogy, so the more detail that you can provide about the structure of your assignments, how you engage students in the classroom, and sometimes specific readings, will be important. If there are distinct ways you can help to connect the campus to the local community or serve the economic, civic, or cultural needs of the region, this is worth mentioning, too. Think broadly about your teaching, research, and public service.

Applicants should prepare a list of standard questions and institution-specific questions to ask during the interview. Standard questions include information about the position, teaching load, the tenure process, benefits, and the future of the department. It is also important to ask about the resources available to support teaching and research if that has not already been made clear to you during your visit. Institution-specific questions will vary depending on the interests of the applicant and the programs of the university and its surrounding community. Applicants should investigate programs distinct to the university that align with their scholarly interests. For example, Monica was interested in mentoring undergraduate student research and asked for additional information on those programs during her interview. Most likely, you will meet with at least one student, or a group of students, during the interview process. Student meetings present a wonderful opportunity to receive insight into the department's culture. Finally, ask for information related to your hobbies or interests within the community of your university's town. These queries help search committees gauge the likelihood that the applicant will remain at the university. Questions like these are mutually beneficial; to the department, they demonstrate a real interest in the position. To the candidate, these questions help identify how to engage at the university in a way that fulfills the applicant's personal and professional goals.

Negotiating an offer at an RCU bears some similarities to other institutions (see chapter 46 on negotiating an offer). Monica's dissertation advisor lent her invaluable advice for negotiating at an RCU. Create a list with three categories: (1) what you must have to be successful, (2) what you would really like to help you be successful, and (3) what would be an added bonus. By dividing up your negotiation list in this manner, you can prioritize items in column one during the negotiation. Categorizing your asks in this manner will also help you create justifications for those requests. Monica and Eric, for example, use Stata for nearly all their research projects and could spend a larger time discussing why this program would be necessary for successfully earning tenure.

RCUs generally have more latitude negotiating on one-time expenses like hardware, software, first-year course releases, start-up research funds, and moving expenses than they do on base salary. However, you should ask for what you need with the abilities of the institution in mind. For example, if you require a start-up fund to help you complete research projects, then that item should be categorized in column one. Be realistic and flexible when setting the funding amount. While rare, Deans who believe that candidates are inflexible about their requests during negotiation may rescind the offer.

Teaching at RCUs: More Classes Can Be a Good Thing

There is no doubt about it: RCUs are teaching-intensive institutions. Six to eight courses a year (not including summer instruction) is the norm, and many instructors manage three or even four different "preps" each term.[2] Other "teaching-adjacent" activities like advising may also be part of a professor's job duties at an RCU. Political scientists seeking appointments at RCUs need to love teaching and need to be prepared to be on-campus (if teaching fully face-to-face) more frequently than faculty at R1 universities.

It is important to note, though, that teaching more classes does not necessarily mean more total students. One of the benefits of teaching at an RCU is that the enormous, stadium-seating lecture courses for which many graduate students TA-ed are exceedingly rare! Instructors typically have classes in the twenty- to forty-student range. This more intimate setting provides several advantages. Most importantly, RCU faculty get to know their students on a personal level. In face-to-face courses, everyone is in a relatively small room where it is possible not only to learn names but routinely interact with a large share of the class on an individual basis. Indeed, classroom engagement can be higher in smaller spaces, and students are often more comfortable discussing challenging or sensitive material—like politics— in smaller groups. In addition, since RCUs are typically smaller than research-intensive universities, it is common to work with the same student over multiple years. Instructors get to know their students extremely well and mentor them both formally and informally. Internship placements, co-authoring, club advising, informal conversations, graduation or wedding celebrations, and joint community service are just a few of the ways these relationships develop.

The Research: It's Still Possible

Most RCUs expect faculty to be actively engaged in academic research leading to publication. Faculty contracts, teaching loads, and annual report templates reflect this expectation, with most institutions providing tenure track and tenured faculty with standardized assigned/release time for original research. At Indiana University's regional campuses, tenured and tenure-track faculty contracts typically specify a workload of 75% teaching and 25% research; faculty teach three classes per semester while the fourth course is replaced by "reassigned time" for research. In contrast, full-time lecturers teach a four to four load with no research requirement. Other RCU campuses (e.g., UW-Whitewater and Eastern Michigan University) assign tenure track faculty a four to four teaching load, while still expecting an active and ongoing research agenda. Unlike at community colleges, research is a significant part of faculty work, and promotion and tenure guidelines—and decisions—reflect the importance of balancing teaching and research commitments.[3] Faculty are expected to maintain an active research agenda by presenting their work at conferences and publishing their work in books and academic journals. Many RCUs are willing to consider the scholarship of teaching and learning and the scholarship of engagement as part of a faculty member's research portfolio (see, for example, Loepp 2018). Graduate students considering employment at an RCU should prepare specific questions about how various activities like SoTL and community-based research are factored into reappointment, tenure, and promotion decisions.

Creative faculty members will find ways to create projects that combine teaching, research, and service—providing opportunities for recognition across all three areas of faculty life. For example, Elizabeth's students served as field workers for a randomized voter mobilization field experiment in the neighborhood surrounding the campus. By studying the results of this get-out-the-vote campaign on voters, Elizabeth was able to publish in a traditional peer-reviewed political science journal (Bennion, 2005). By studying student learning outcomes, she was able to publish in a peer-reviewed SoTL journal (Bennion, 2006). Meanwhile, the mobilization campaign itself was a form of community service that led to a grant from Indiana Campus Compact, an organization supporting public engagement projects designed for community impact.

Increasingly, regional universities value scholarship designed to serve the region by addressing community-defined issues, problems, or opportunities by collecting, analyzing, and reporting data in a methodologically rigorous but accessible way. Media interviews, op-eds, expert testimony, and public workshops can help new faculty to build a "research everywhere" narrative at institutions with heavy teaching and service expectations. Regional comprehensives allow a good deal of latitude to conduct research related to politics, how to teach politics, or how to use politics to engage and serve the community most effectively.

Service Opportunities: Decide What's Meaningful to You

Service takes many forms at an RCU. At Indiana University's regional campuses, for example, faculty report on service to students, the department, the college, the campus, the university, the discipline, and the community. Service to students may include academic advising, club advising, letter writing, and other mentoring activities. Service to the department may include serving on a department-level committee (e.g., curriculum, assessment, PTR) or taking on a leadership role (e.g., chair or graduate program director). In larger departments, such positions may be full-time appointments, but in many others, the chair or program director receives a course release.

Service at the campus, academic unit, and campus levels usually involves committees and task forces that are central to the academic mission and to faculty governance. Job candidates should ask prospective department chairs and deans to determine the expected level, type, and amount of service required. Generally, department chairs will advise new faculty to limit their service as they adjust to the university, build their courses, and establish their research agenda.

RCUs often see themselves as "anchor institutions" and "stewards of place" based on their collective mission to provide access to higher education and to support the economic, civic, and cultural life of their regions (Scholars Strategy Network, 2018). Service-learning courses, community-based research, public service, and media interviews are just a few of the ways RCU faculty serve the public; many also serve on local (elected, appointed, or voluntary civic organization) boards. You will have time to identify appropriate service opportunities once hired. It is important to consider your teaching and research goals, how your service activities reflect your priorities, and the type of case you hope to build for tenure and/or promotion.[4]

Sometimes incoming and junior faculty are asked to assume significant administrative responsibility. If this is requested during your interview or first couple of years at an institution, consider how this service will affect your overall case for promotion. Also, consider the visibility of the work you perform on campus and in the community, and those who devote significant amounts of time may be eligible for grants and awards, and those who perform unusually high levels of service (e.g., advising all undergraduate majors or directing a campus-wide civic program) can (and should) negotiate for additional course releases.

Summary

For any number of reasons, a position at a regional comprehensive university may not be an applicant's first choice. The demand of higher teaching loads and provision of service while maintaining an active research agenda can appear taxing. Upon closer examination, RCUs offer a rich and fulfilling career that allows academics to explore and build upon a variety of their interests, without the pressure to publish frequently in top-tier journals under threat of losing their jobs.

This chapter discusses the perspective of faculty who have built their careers at an RCU. Many RCUs were designed to serve the needs of the regional community. Student bodies at RCUs are often diverse with respect to age, ethnicity, first-generation students, and immigrants. While low-performers at RCUs are also common, helping to transform these students' lives is extremely rewarding. Applying to and accepting a job at an RCU is technically similar to other applications, but substantively different. The application should reflect an explicit discussion of pedagogy, teaching interests, how the applicant can act as a utility player for the department, and what type of service the applicant might perform for the campus or larger community. Compensation offered is typically lower than at R1s and highly competitive liberal arts colleges, however many academics have found that negotiating on one-time expenses was successful.

Expectations about tenure and promotion are, generally, clearly defined and explained. The specific ratio between time allocated to teaching, service, and research will vary by institution, but a higher percentage—with rare exceptions—will be dedicated to teaching. Fortunately, many RCUs classify activities outside of the classroom under the category of teaching. Developing a research program is still valued at RCUs, despite it seldom being the top priority for achieving promotion and tenure. Guidelines on tenure and promotion often require service to be dispersed at the various levels of the university: to the students, the department, the college, the university, the campus, and the discipline. Service to the community offers additional opportunities to intertwine your personal and professional goals.

A successful career at an RCU requires a passion for teaching. An emphasis on teaching does not preclude academics from exploring other enriching professional activities. Those who support greater access to higher education and who are eager to actively contribute to the community in which they live will find a career at an RCU particularly satisfying. There are opportunities to combine teaching, research, and service in unique ways that are fulfilling both professionally and personally.

Possible Additional Resources

- https://www.insidehighered.com/news/2018/10/12/about-three-quarters-all-faculty-positions-are-tenure-track-according-new-aaup
- https://www.insidehighered.com/news/2016/08/22/study-finds-gains-faculty-diversity-not-tenure-track

Endnotes

1   In recent years R1 institutions have developed teaching-focused positions often known as teaching professors. There is variation between tenure track, full-time non-tenure track, and adjunct instructors within each college or university. We wrote this chapter with the assumption that most graduate students are interested in tenure track positions, but it important to recognize that, while 80% of all faculty positions were tenure-track in the 1950s, only about 20% are now, and minoritized faculty are still less likely than white faculty in the United States to be offered a tenure-track position.

2   A "prep" refers to a distinct course to prepare and deliver. Since instructors may teach multiple sections of the same course, the number of preps is often smaller than the number of courses, though not always! When talking to potential employers, graduate students should ask departments what a typical prep load is, not merely the number of typical courses taught. An additional prep is certainly more work, but it can be considerably less work than an additional (unique) course.

3   Annual reports also track student, department, college, campus, and public service, which is expected even when not explicitly included in the contract.

4   While community colleges base tenure decisions primarily on teaching performance and R1 universities base tenure and promotion decisions primarily on research, some RCUs offer more flexibility, allowing faculty to define their own area of excellence. At Indiana University, for example, faculty make a case for "excellence" in one area (teaching, research, service), plus "satisfactory" performance in the other two areas.

References

Bennion, Elizabeth A. 2005. "Caught in the Ground Wars: Mobilizing Voters during a Competitive Congressional Campaign." *The Annals of the American Academy of Political & Social Science*. 601 (September): 123-141.

Bennion, Elizabeth A. 2006. "Civic Education and Citizen Engagement: Mobilizing Voters as a Required Field Experiment." *Journal of Political Science Education* Vol. 2 (2): 205-227.

Loepp, Eric. 2018. "Beyond Polls: Using Science and Student Data to Stimulate Learning." *Journal of Political Science Education*. Vol. 14 (1): 17-41.

Orphan, Cecilia. 2018. "Why Regional Comprehensive Universities Are Vital Parts of U.S. Higher Education," July 25, 2018, *Scholars Strategy Network Online* [accessed December 14, 2021 at https://scholars.org/brief/why-regional-comprehensive-universities-are-vital-parts-us-higher-education].

40 | Succeeding at a Research Intensive Institution (R1 or R2)

Karen M. Kedrowski[1] & Benjamin Melusky[2]

1. Iowa State University 2. Old Dominion

KEYWORDS: R1 and R2 Universities.

Introduction

So, you're interested in working at a Research-Intensive institution? What do you put in the application? And how can you succeed once you're hired? This essay will provide some advice from two faculty members who work at institutions that are either R1 (Doctoral Universities, very high research activity) or R2 (Doctoral universities, high research activity) (Carnegie Classification).

Getting Started: the Application Process

Presenting Your Research Agenda in an Application

As one might surmise from the name, the major emphasis at *R1 and R2 universities* is research. This should be reflected in your application letter. The search committees will want to know all about your dissertation: your topic, your methods, your contributions, and equally important, your future research agenda. Your application letter should explain your project in some detail and emphasize in particular the contribution your research will make. Assuming a two-page application letter, the research statement should consume about one page. Describe your dissertation in one paragraph; note the contributions it makes in a second paragraph; and discuss your future research trajectory in a third.

The subject of your dissertation should be squarely in the advertised field. So, an Americanist who studies political behavior should not apply for a position that focuses on the Presidency, for example. A secondary interest or an "I can do that" statement will not be sufficient to land an interview—much less a job—especially in a competitive job market.

The search committee also seeks to assess the likelihood that you will succeed—in publishing, in securing research grants, and in bringing positive exposure to the department. Therefore, your vitae should include some publications. At this point, co-authored peer-reviewed publications are expected. However, the search committee will probably expect to see that you've presented some portion of your dissertation at a professional conference.

If your dissertation is complete, discuss your plans to publish it. If your dissertation is not complete, include your projected defense date. In either case, talk about what you intend to do after the dissertation. What is your next research topic? How does it build on your current work? The committee wants to see coherence in your research agenda, so the next big project should be related to the dissertation. This can be tough for individuals who have eclectic interests. However, our advice is to focus.

Also worth noting: do not go on the market prematurely. You should have your dissertation largely written with a firm defense date in hand. Do not waste time applying for jobs before that stage, even if you think you've found the perfect job.

What Else Should be in an Application?

The search committee is looking for other evidence of the quality of your work. External research grants, especially NSF, are the gold standard. However, any external grant is a measure of quality and external validation for your work. You can certainly mention internal grants and awards; however, they are less prestigious than external grants and awards. If you have any information about the competitiveness of the grants and awards—internal or external—include them on your vitae.

Remember that instruction occurs at research-intensive institutions as well. Discuss what courses you have taught or are willing to teach, and any experience you have as a teaching assistant or instructor. If you have the opportunity to instruct a course (or lead recitations), make sure that you have a faculty member sit in during one of your class meetings and observe your instruction. Many applications require evidence of teaching excellence, and a letter of review from that faculty member speaking to your teaching style and effectiveness is very beneficial. If you have already taught the course and/or this is not possible, another alternative is to have one of your letter writers speak to your teaching prowess and potential.

Building a Professional Network

Attending conferences is a great way to build a professional network (see chapter 21 on how to conference). Not only do you meet people on your panel, who are likely to share your research interests, you should join sections (when possible) and attend their business meetings. When you apply to a conference, very often there is a section which asks you to indicate if you are willing to serve as a discussant or chair. Do not shy away from this opportunity, as these positions afford you the possibility of connecting with people in your research area and engaging with them in conversation and developing connections beyond the panel. Further, your advisor(s) and committee members should also be able to introduce you to their friends and colleagues as well. Being acquainted with people will be helpful when you're applying, and your name is familiar.

The Road to Tenure

Once You're Hired

Having emerged from a very competitive, months-long job search process, you are anxious to begin the long journey to tenure. At this early stage of your professional career, tenure may seem very far away, but the planning process should begin as soon as possible. The following checklist will help you stay on track and succeed:

- To get tenure, you'll need to know what goes into a successful tenure dossier and how it is evaluated. The very first thing you should do is to meet with your department chair to make sure you understand the criteria for tenure. This should include what is written in the faculty handbook and the governance documents. It should also include any unwritten expectations or norms that the department may have. "Publishing in top peer-reviewed journals," for instance may—or may not—include interdisciplinary journals or those in other fields. Or it might mean "JOP, AJPS, and APSR only."
- If you are not assigned a mentor other than your department chair, find one (typically a member of your department who has gone through the tenure process at your institution and is able to read and evaluate your research). Then ask the mentor the same questions you asked your department chair. Seek clarification for any discrepancies.
- Take advantage of all the pre-tenured faculty professional development opportunities offered by your institution.
- Schedule time in your week exclusively for writing. This might include joining a writing group

for extra accountability (see chapter 17 on effective time management).

- Network within your university, department, and at conferences, and additionally, trade working papers with others in your field, to both develop your scholarly profile and solicit useful feedback to improve your research.
- Perfect and polish one or two courses before taking on new course preps. Course preparation, major revisions, and changing delivery modes (i.e., face to face to online) takes more time than one might think. If you are teaching two new preps at the same time, you will have little time left in your schedule for writing and service responsibilities.
- Be careful not to get lured into too many service opportunities. At the same time, you also need to be sure you engage in the requisite number and types of service activities required to earn tenure. Avoid any appointments that might lead you into controversies or those that take a lot of time. Do not overlook opportunities within professional associations. Ask your mentor and department chair for advice on what to pursue (see chapter 31 on university service and chapter 32 on service to the discipline).

Establish Your Research Pipeline

Although the demands at R1 and R2 institutions will differ on the criteria for publications, both are expecting you to be a productive scholar. As such, the pathway to tenure flows through a busy research pipeline. Yet, what does this mean?

As a junior faculty member on the tenure track, your main goal is to build a body of respected research which situates you within a small community of scholars. However, as you typically only have five to six years to develop a strong research file (and the peer-review process takes time and is fraught with uncertainty), you will want to hit the ground running from the start of your first semester to develop and shepherd a large number of papers from their first stages to their publication in respected journals (see chapter 25 on turning term papers to articles).

We recommend adopting the advice of Lebo (2016) to successfully manage your research pipeline and efficiently move your research from ideas to journal editor acceptance letters. This system involves thinking about the process of publishing a paper as eight manageable stages:

1. You develop your subject area, literature that will be addressed, data sources, and potential coauthors.
2. Your paper is outlined, and you have secured the necessary data.
3. You have completed a draft of the paper which includes your preliminary results.
4. Your paper has been presented at a conference (or two).
5. Your paper is under review at a journal.
6. You have been offered a Revise and Resubmit (R&R).
7. Your paper is back under review after the R&R.
8. Your paper has been accepted.

Thinking about all of your research in stages will allow you to prioritize and realistically maintain a pipeline towards tenure. Naturally, your research will be composed of projects which exist at various stages of this process. Ideally you should always have at least one project under review (Stages five to seven), several projects in progress (Stages two to four), and a multitude of ideas (Stage one) ready to begin when an earlier project reaches publication (Stage eight).

We also recommend that you understand how co-authored works are counted in the portfolio. Are they weighted the same as a solo-authored publication, or are they considered as fractions (i.e., two authors equal 0.5: three authors equal 0.34)? This is especially important in departments where the tenure criteria are numerical.

In addition, Lebo's stages apply, with a little adaptation, to writing book manuscripts as well. You might wish to break down the process, with steps one to three, for each chapter. As soon as you have two chapters solid and polished, start looking for publishers. Be sure to talk with your mentor(s) and department chair about presses. Does the department look for university presses only? If not, how are commercial academic presses evaluated? Do textbooks count? What about edited books? If the department uses numerical criteria, does a book translate to a fixed number of journal articles?

To keep track of your research agenda, it is recommended that you get yourself a whiteboard for your new office and organize your projects into a practicable timeline. Keep yourself accountable and prioritize the projects that have the greatest probability of landing in quality journals.

Of course, there are other publication options other than journal articles and books: research notes, peer reviewed letters (yes, that's a thing), and public-facing scholarship such as academic blogs. As you consider different types of outlets, find out whether and how they will count in your tenure and promotion portfolio.

The Pre-Tenure Review

One of the most important milestones on the road to tenure at an R1 or R2 institution will be the pre-tenure review. For this process you typically will prepare many of the same documents as you would for tenure, and members of the promotion and tenure committees at various levels will review your package. The goal of this process is to provide tenure-track faculty with feedback on their progress towards tenure, identify areas needing improvement, and provide guidance in preparing the professional portfolio to support the review for tenure.

It is understandable that for many this process produces a certain degree of trepidation and anxiety. However, do not fear the pre-tenure review, as it provides several key benefits:

- You will be assembling many of the same documents necessary for the tenure review process, thus allowing you to start crafting your tenure file. In doing so, you can take appraisal of the totality of your progress (research, teaching, service), providing personal validation of the hard work you have accomplished up to this point.
- Members of your department will review your pre-tenure file, becoming familiarized with your work. This will allow you to engage them in much more direct conversations after the fact where they can provide you with more informed answers and advice.
- You will get a concrete indication from the various tenure process decision makers as to how your efforts towards tenure are progressing – both in terms of where you are meeting expectations and where there is specific need for attention.

Coming out of the pre-tenure review, this is your last opportunity for significant course correction before you will submit your file for the tenure review. It is important to take all feedback and act upon it. Even the smallest piece of criticism can be indicative of a future issue with your tenure file. As such, seek out your Department Chair and faculty mentor to review and interpret the results of your pre-tenure review, and answer any questions you might have.

After these meetings, you will want to develop a specific plan to address each point of feedback from the pre-tenure review. Set concrete goals, practical steps to meet these goals, and deadlines to keep you accountable. You might even want to discuss these plans with your faculty mentor to ensure that they are consistent with your prior conversation and solicit any further recommendations.

Establish a Work-Life Balance

Irrespective of whether you are working at an R1 or R2 institution, the workload (research, teaching, and service) will be demanding and faculty burnout (e.g., the exhaustion, increased cynicism and negativity toward one's job, and reduced professional efficacy resulting from chronic workplace stress that has not been successfully managed (World Health Organization 2019)) presents a significant threat. From the beginning of your time in your new position, you will be inundated with meetings, grading, advising and other obligations which demand significant time and attention, in addition to the persistent specter of the tenure clock motivating a productive stream of research. There truly are not enough hours in the day, week, or semester to accomplish everything required of you both professionally and personally (see chapter 53 on the culture of overwork within the discipline and chapter 67 on rest and well-being).

As such, in order to truly succeed at your institution, you will need to find a way to balance the demands of your position with the demands of your life. To do this, you need to find a way to work smarter, not harder.

What this means is to establish boundaries for your life and decide how much you want to give to your position. Either that's enough for you to have a career and achieve tenure, or it's not. When you are working, give it your all during this time. Thus, outside of this boundary you can without professional guilt limit/restrict that which you can further give and can focus your time and attention to the demands of life. However, there will always be times when you will have to re-negotiate the boundaries between job and life. Anticipate that there are certain points during the semester and your tenure stream which will be busier than others. To best plan for this, utilize a calendar or planner to help establish these boundaries, create milestones, and keep ahead of that which is most demanding.

There will always be more work left at the end of any day, as such, planning well, prioritizing, and making the most of the time you allocate towards the demands of your job will allow you to find the proper balance, avoid burnout, and be successful.

Have a Nice Career

From applying to a position at an R1/R2 institution to successfully attaining tenure, it is a very long road with a steep learning curve. Yet, through proper planning, and a bit of luck along the way, you can have an enriching and successful career at some of the best research-intensive institutions in the country.

References

The Carnegie Classification of Institutions of Higher Education. Available: https://carnegieclassifica-tions.iu.edu/index.php.

Lebo, Matthew J. 2016. "Managing your Research Pipeline." *PS: Political Science & Politics* 49(2): 259-264.

World Health Organization. 2019. "Burn-out an "occupational phenomenon": International Classifica-tion of Diseases." May 28. https://www.who.int/news/item/28-05-2019-burn-out-an-occupation-al-phenomenon-international-classification-of-diseases

41

Pushing the Boundaries of Your PhD: Exploring Careers Outside the Ivory Tower

Danielle Gilbert[1], S.R. Gubitz[2], Jennifer Kavanagh[3], & Kelly Piazza[1]

1. United States Air Force Academy* 2. Kent Denver School 3. Carnegie Endowment for International Peace

*DISCLAIMER: The views expressed in this article, book, or presentation are those of the author and do not necessarily reflect the official policy or position of the United States Air Force Academy, the Air Force, the Department of Defense, or the US Government. PA#: USAFA-DF-2022-13

KEYWORDS: Traditional Tenure-Track Positions, Non-Traditional Academic Jobs, Professional Military Education, Postgraduate Service Schools, Private Sector Companies.

What Do You Need to Know?

Discussions about post-graduation career options for political science PhDs typically center around *traditional tenure-track positions* at large research universities and smaller liberal arts colleges. (See chapters 36, 37, 38, 39 and 40 for insights about working at different types of academic institutions.) However, these narrow discussions ignore the myriad challenging, fulfilling, and intellectually stimulating jobs beyond the ivory tower that are open to political science PhDs. In this chapter, we outline the reasons you might consider a "non-traditional" job, what some of those opportunities look like, and how you can best prepare to secure such a job.

Why Does It Matter?

There are several reasons why you might want to learn about career opportunities outside the ivory tower.

First, there are many *non-traditional academic jobs* that require doctoral degrees and are well-paying, policy-relevant, and service-oriented—from fellowships at think tanks to data science positions supporting diverse organizations. Given their own career trajectories, PhD advisors are often unfamiliar with the diversity of options available and so are unlikely to encourage those studying under them to consider or pursue these options. Plenty of people pursue a PhD without any intention of seeking a traditional academic job and, instead, work toward non-academic careers, challenging the notion that PhD programs are strictly "vocational schools" for tenure-track faculty positions.

Second, life circumstances and family obligations might dictate that you limit your job search geographically, and these constraints are often incompatible with the flexibility the academic job market requires. Considering non-traditional careers can open new doors and allow you to balance the work and non-work parts of your life more effectively. (Additional strategies for balancing these types of decisions are addressed in chapters 16 on parenthood and 48 on dual hires).

Third, and perhaps most obvious: academic jobs are scarce. Many PhD students have to consider alternative career tracks, even if they had originally hoped to land a traditional academic job. Over the past several decades, the National Science Foundation has repeatedly found that only a minority of PhD-holders are employed in tenure-track positions (McGrath and Davis 2019); a steadily decreasing minority of political science graduates secure a tenure-track position upon graduation (Opsomer et al. 2021). In such a difficult market, it is prudent that graduate students (and their advisors) consider other paths.

Thankfully, there are a wide range of alternative, exciting careers that will use and appreciate your training and expertise. Far from being "lesser" career options, many of these jobs remove the constraints that come with pursuing a tenure-track academic job, allowing you to live where you would like, make more money, influence policy, and give back to your country or community. If any of this sounds appealing, a job outside the ivory tower may be right for you.

While research, and sometimes teaching, are emphasized as important aspects of political science PhD programs, graduate school provides an opportunity to master a set of skills that make graduates appealing for "non-traditional" jobs. For example, you know how to:

- Absorb and synthesize information quickly
- Evaluate competing arguments and identify logical flaws
- Conduct research, including a mastery of methodological skills
- Communicate information to a less educated audience
- Manage long, complicated projects
- Ask big questions
- Interpret important, real-world political phenomena

All of these skills make you an attractive candidate for a wide range of alternative careers. (See chapter 50 on imposter syndrome if you need further encouragement.) Jobs in professional military educational institutions or pre-collegiate education are a great fit for graduates who love teaching. Policy-oriented positions, including government, think tank, and military institutions, are an excellent fit for graduates interested in policy engagement. PhDs who love co-authoring or working as part of a team will excel in policy-oriented or private sector jobs.

In what follows, we outline four categories of relevant jobs outside the ivory tower, from our own expertise: professional military educational institutions, pre-collegiate education, policy-oriented positions, and private sector jobs. For each, we outline the nature of the career; what characterizes the type of work, daily rhythm, and requirements for work; and relevant pros and cons. Then, we outline how graduate students in political science can become strong candidates for these jobs. Last, we offer details about the different application processes for each of these categories.

Academic Jobs "Off The Beaten Path:" Professional Military Education

The Basics: Working at a Professional Military Education Institution

Aside from traditional colleges and universities, *professional military education* (PME) institutions employ academics in wide-ranging disciplines to perform teaching, research, and service functions. While similar to traditional colleges and universities in many ways, PME institutions are unique in that they provide professional training, development, and education distinctly to military personnel. There are several categories of PME institutions in the United States: Service Academies, Senior Military Colleges, and Postgraduate Service Schools. The Service Academies, including the US Air Force Academy, US Coast Guard Academy, US Naval Academy, US Merchant Marine Academy, and the US Military Academy at West Point, are exclusively undergraduate institutions that train future military officers. The Senior Military Colleges similarly prepare undergraduates for military service albeit with Reserve Officers' Training Corps (ROTC) programs and corps of cadets that, together, create demanding military environments similar to those at the Academies (Today's Military 2022). *Postgraduate Service Schools* provide postgraduate education and training to officers in preparation for operational, command, and staff positions and encompass Service Schools, Staff Colleges, Senior Service Colleges, Joint Colleges, and Specialist Training Schools. These institutions are affiliated with one or more branches of the armed forces and include the Command General Staff College, the Air War College, and the Naval Postgraduate School, to name a few.

PME jobs are great options for political science PhDs committed to teaching, service, and policy relevance. At a military institution, you can expect to teach a heavy load with exceptionally bright, committed students and to carry a comparatively large service load that involves advising, scheduling, and participation in committees. At these institutions, traditional academic research prestige is less important than policy engagement, relevance, and impact. Note that at PME institutions, political science PhDs might also find jobs in interdisciplinary departments called "National Security Affairs," "Social Sciences," or "Military & Strategic Studies," to name a few.

Advantages and Disadvantages

Employment at professional military education institutions has both disadvantages and advantages as compared to more conventional civilian colleges and universities to which graduate students are exposed. Based on our experience as academics trained at prestigious civilian universities and currently employed at a nationally renowned service Academy, we outline those advantages and disadvantages here.

Advantages

For political scientists specializing in topics related to national and international security, American foreign policy, grand strategy, and strategic competition, professional military education institutions are extremely well connected, and opportunities to network with subject matter experts abound.

The specific mission of PME institutions lead them to be very student-oriented and to prioritize faculty-student interactions. The students are committed and bright and teaching them can be extremely rewarding.

Faculty positions offer highly competitive salaries and benefits packages, rivaling only the most prestigious academic institutions. Some institutions, like the Air Force Academy (Colorado Springs, CO), the Naval Academy (Annapolis, MD), and the Naval Postgraduate School (Monterrey, CA) are in exceptionally desirable locations. Job stability is extremely high at PME institutions, providing faculty with opportunities to pursue their passions, embark on new academic projects, and focus on other personal goals.

The intimate connection between political science course content and the job responsibilities of military personnel makes it easy to frame relevance of course content and to motivate students.

For those who are interested, faculty at PME are encouraged to engage with policymakers and the public and are supported in their efforts.

Disadvantages

While some disciplines at PME institutions receive substantial funding for research purposes, political science departments are often not as fortunate (unless, of course, research is closely connected to subjects of particular interest to the military). In addition, academics at PME institutions should not expect assistance from teaching or research assistants. Outside of class time, students who might fulfill these functions are preoccupied with military, athletic, and other obligations.

As an employee of the US Government, you might face restrictions on where and how you conduct your research. For example, in addition to pursuing research approvals through Institutional Review Boards, some human subjects research has to be approved by other government agencies, presenting hurdles to your work.

Faculty at PME institutions should expect to have their writing approved through a Public Affairs office before publication.

PME institutions often have robust core curricula which may translate into more oversight of teaching.

As PME institutions prioritize accessibility to students, there may be significantly less flexibility in work locations and schedules.

Government employees are required to complete a substantial number of administrative tasks, and this work takes time away from both teaching and research.

Finally, it is possible that the military mission may take precedence over academics.

How Should You Prepare?

You might prepare for a career in PME in much the same way you would prepare for a job at a civilian college or university with some added emphasis on policy-relevant research and of your familiarity with the distinct features of PME institutions. In your pursuit of these positions, you should keep in mind that: (1) PME institutions are typically primarily teaching institutions and interviews often include a teaching demonstration, much as a liberal arts college would; (2) policy engagement, policy-relevant research, and writing for public-facing outlets are desirable and can make you an attractive candidate; and (3) service and administrative tasks are non-negotiable and enthusiasm about these duties may help to set you apart from other candidates.

Pre-Collegiate Education

The Basics: Working in Pre-Collegiate Education

Many PhD programs and post-PhD careers place a heavy emphasis on research and somewhat less emphasis on the teaching component of the job. So, what is a PhD candidate to do when they are passionate about teaching and find themselves interrupted by research expectations, rather than the other way around?

Of course, there are several career paths for an aspiring educator in the academy. Small Liberal Arts Colleges (SLACs) offer some of the most rigorous education in the United States, and professors at these schools experience a lower threshold for research output (and fewer resources) than their colleagues at the large top tier research universities (or R1s). Community colleges can be found in nearly every mid-sized city in America, and one will be hard pressed to find more dedicated educators than the professors at these institutions. But positions in SLACs are perhaps even harder to come by than tenure-track positions at R1 universities. And while community college positions can be professionally rewarding, their relatively meager compensation packages can often dissuade those with serious financial considerations or familial responsibilities from applying. However, precollegiate education at independent schools can present the perfect opportunity for the right PhD candidate who is interested primarily in education as their end goal.

Independent schools—sometimes also called "private schools"—run the gamut from religious schools to secular day and boarding schools. The US Department of Education reports that there are over 30,000 independent schools in the country (compared to the nearly 100,000 public schools the Department tracks). Compared to the 4,000 institutions of higher education in the country, independent schools present a more plentiful, diverse, and readily available job market than in academia. But how does a PhD in Political Science translate to teaching high school students?[1]

First and foremost, it is important to understand what being an independent schoolteacher is and is not. If you fantasize about being an educator at a secondary school because you believe it will somehow give you more time to pursue research independent of any overbearing institution, you may want to look elsewhere. Being an independent schoolteacher means being an educator of children through and through; your job description begins and ends at teaching. You will be spending most of your time either grading, making lesson plans, sponsoring a student club, coaching a sport, or even talking to a concerned (or happy!) parent. If the thought of these things excites you, then you are the right sort of person for these positions. If not, then you may want to peruse the other sections of this chapter. Although it is possible to spend a year or two as an independent schoolteacher and then return to academia, the bottom line is that if you are interested in pursuing this career path long-term, your career in research is likely over.

Advantages and Disadvantages

Compared to positions in collegiate education, positions in independent schools come with many differences, both advantages and disadvantages. We outline some of those here.

As noted above, you will be educating children. Teaching children comes with its own unique challenges and rewards. To be blunt, educating a child is more about emotional and behavioral support than it is about the content you are probably used to emphasizing. While this may entail a host of responsibilities, it also means fostering incredible relationships with your students. As a teacher at an independent school, you are more than just their teacher. Indeed, schools have in loco parentis when parents drop their children off at school. In addition, you can help set the foundation on which your students will build their education.

Unlike the traditional academic job market, the market for jobs at independent schools is typically excellent. These positions come with excellent compensation, and compensation packages are incredibly negotiable. You will likely receive more interviews than you know what to do with and likely be presented with multiple offers. While many independent schools follow a pay scale based on experience, the definition of "experience" is itself negotiable. And the best part is that this negotiation is not only expected—it is encouraged to help with retention.

These jobs feature enticing benefits. Most schools offer matching contributions to retirement accounts, whether they are traditional 401k or TIAA programs. Additionally, these schools typically offer competitive health insurance policies, family leave policies, and even daycare programs in some cases. Finally, many independent schools offer their education to children of faculty for steeply discounted rates.

There has been much recent discussion about the equity of independent schools, with many arguing that they foster elite, privileged attitudes and worsen existing inequities. If you are interested in pre-collegiate education but share these concerns, there are a few things worth keeping in mind. First, independent schools often have generous need-based financial aid offerings for students who cannot afford the full tuition; indeed, some schools provide some form of aid to anywhere between a quarter to a third of their students. This means that these schools can diversify their student body. And while there is always room for improvement in this area, many are actively working toward this goal. School efforts in these areas are typically readily apparent and you can use this information to shape your search for employment. Independent schools are also smaller and more flexible than universities and opportunities abound for you to advocate for changes that you value. Furthermore, the children at these schools, regardless of their background, are often passionate about issues of diversity, equity, and inclusion and may be willing partners in efforts towards change.

How Should You Prepare?

Translating your PhD in Political Science to teaching at an independent school is probably easier than you think. Most high schools do not offer courses in "political science," per se. Instead, you will likely be applying for positions in social studies, history, social science, or civics programs. These are broad categories that cover everything from world history to US history to courses on economics and philosophy. That means that you need to translate that very specific thing you have been studying for years into this broad category; essentially, lead with your primary field and talk about your dissertation only when you are asked directly about it. Regarding your qualifications, these schools care about two things: (1) that you have the pedagogical skills to teach anything in their course offerings, and (2) that you have completed a PhD. When these schools hire PhD candidates, they understand that they are hiring a subject matter expert who can learn on the job and, most importantly, teach well.

The actual application process will look very different from that for jobs at R1s or SLACs and the materials you will need to submit will also be very different. If you pursue this career option, you will likely want to find a recruitment agency like Carney Sandoe and Associates or one of their competitors to help you navigate this job market. These firms help qualified candidates find employment in the wide-ranging independent school market and make money only when you accept a position somewhere (i.e., the school pays them a finder's fee or a subscription fee to access their candidate pool). Firms like these can help you tailor your application materials to this unfamiliar market; you can be assured that you are not their first PhD candidate.

Public Policy-Focused Opportunities

The Basics: Working in Public Policy-Focused Organizations

In addition to teaching jobs, there are also many opportunities for those with a political science PhD in the policy world. While pre-collegiate education allows candidates to focus on teaching almost exclusively, policy-oriented positions emphasize research and application. Research organizations and think tanks, advocacy organizations, non-profits, and federal and state governments are all looking for job applicants with the analytical and methodological skills as well as the substantive knowledge that political science PhD programs provide. Jobs in the policy-field are diverse and have varying requirements and demands. In this section we provide a broad description of some common jobs in this field, as well as advantages and disadvantages of policy-related careers compared to the traditional academic track. We also discuss things to keep in mind and pursue as you complete your degree that can help prepare you for a career in the policy world.

Although diverse, most policy-related jobs have some common characteristics:

- Most involve some sort of research and analysis responsibilities along with writing and publishing reports. There are also typically meetings with clients, seminars, data collection trips, as well as other activities and responsibilities.
- All are focused on using this research and analysis to inform, evaluate, shape, implement, or improve public policy. In many cases, the actual topics, questions, and research methods employed in the policy domain are not all that different from those in academia. However, the emphasis is always on identifying the policy implications or recommendations that derive from the research. This is not to say that work coming out of academia never informs policy. However, for policy-oriented jobs, the policy questions and needs are the driving focus of the research and in fact may shape the research questions and agendas themselves.
- Much of the work done at policy-oriented organizations and within the government involves working with interdisciplinary teams. While co-authoring and collaborating are not uncommon in academia, working in multidisciplinary teams is the widespread norm in policy work. In part, this is because the questions tackled by policy-oriented work are often broad and so require multiple lenses and larger teams. However, it is also just a different approach to tackling hard questions, geared more around a consultancy model.
- Most allow opportunities for other activities, like teaching as an adjunct at nearby universities. This can be a great way to continue teaching without pursuing a tenure track position or committing to a full-time teaching job.

Apart from these similarities, however, the type of work that you will do in the policy world will depend on the organization that hires you. Most obviously, the topics you work on will be determined by the focus of the think tank or organization. For example, there are research organizations focused solely on social and economic policy like the Urban Institute, those that focus largely on international and security-related work like the Center for Strategic and International Studies, and those that do both like the RAND Corporation. Similarly, there are NGOs focused on everything from international development to arms control to education. And of course, government agencies focus on diverse issues across sectors. If you are considering a policy-oriented career, the first step would be to determine the type of work that you want to do and then to identify the agencies and organizations that focus on the issues you are interested in.

Advantages and Disadvantages

Policy-oriented jobs come with a range of differences, challenges, and opportunities when compared to traditional academic jobs and even to each other.

The amount of control over research agendas[2] varies across organizations. If you are considering a policy or research career, you should determine how much flexibility you need, how much fundraising you want to do, and how much you are willing to have your research agenda set by external events, as this may influence the types of organizations you choose to target. Some organizations rely on grants and donations, which means that researchers will need to compete for Request for Proposals (RFPs) and be able to bring in money to support their research. Other organizations, including Federally Funded Research and Development Centers, have longer term government contracts. While these contracts provide more consistent funding, they also determine the client base and sometimes shape the research agenda. Research within government agencies is obviously government-funded with the research agenda being set by priority policy issues and senior leaders within those agencies.

Opportunities for external publication may be more limited and will almost certainly be of a different style than you are used to from your graduate career. You should consider how important it is for you to publish externally. While some organizations encourage their employees to publish commentaries and articles, at other organizations, especially those associated with the national security establishment, opportunities for external publishing are more limited and require special approvals. It is still possible to achieve a far-reaching impact, however, with unpublished work.

The style of policy publications may be very different from academic journals, and it may vary from organization to organization. This writing style is something you will likely learn on-the-job, but it is worth becoming familiar with how different organizations frame their research and the types of products they publish since knowing both may inform how you present yourself in a cover letter or at a job interview.

Organizations and positions vary in their relationship to politics and political parties. While some organizations are explicitly non-partisan, others have clear and known political affiliations or leanings that may be worth considering in the application process.

There may be variation in the amount of research and writing compared to more direct policy-oriented staff work or advising that is involved. Working in a think tank or research organization is likely to involve writing longer, research-intensive reports and commentaries, whereas jobs in government may include writing policy memorandums or preparing briefings For those working in government, there is also likely to be some amount of administrative or "staff work" which may be less stimulating, but is required to keep the organization functioning and to respond to near-term and emerging demands.

Compensation in policy-oriented jobs tends to be as high or higher than that of most comparable tenure track positions at R1s or SLACs, although there is variation across organizations. Many also offer flexibility in work style and location. While many policy jobs are Washington DC-based, there are policy-focused, advocacy, and non-governmental organizations in most major cities across the country and globe, and many organizations have multiple offices or flexibility for remote work. The one exception to such flexibility pertains to jobs in the national security sector which may require a security clearance and involve primarily in-person work in secure facilities (more on this below).

How Should You Prepare?

Preparing to pursue policy-related opportunities after graduate school does not require a radical departure from the path to academic jobs. However, there may be some things worth keeping in mind as you continue your graduate career that can help you be a successful candidate and ultimately successful in your chosen job.

It can be helpful to take some policy-oriented coursework or seek out policy-oriented opportunities on campus while you are a student. Organizations that hire political science PhDs do consider familiarity with the policy world when identifying promising applicants and will ask you to speak about policy issues, so having some experience can be helpful.

Methods courses are highly useful in this field. Since the work you do at policy-oriented research organizations may vary as policy issues and priorities shift, having a strong methodological toolkit that you can apply to a myriad of questions and topics can make you an appealing candidate.

Get used to framing your research projects around policy implications and ensure that your dissertation and/or job talk has a section on policy implications. It is easy to tell when policy implications have been appended at the last minute. Policy implications must be central to the project if they are to appear organic and lead to well-supported recommendations.

There are a number of summer, semester, and pre- or post-doctoral programs that you can use to prepare yourself for policy-oriented positions.

Training programs: The Bridging the Gap (BtG) Project's New Era Workshop (Bridging the Gap, undated), International Policy Scholars Consortium and Network (IPSCON) (Henry A. Kissinger Center for Global Affairs, undated), and the Clements Center's Summer Seminar in History and Statecraft (The University of Texas at Austin, undated) all provide extra-curricular training opportunities for graduate students interested in pursuing policy careers. These programs, ranging from three days (BtG) to a year-long program (IPSCON) are a fantastic way to network with like-minded junior and senior scholars while honing policy-relevant skills.

Summer or term internships: Many research organizations hire PhDs for paid summer internships that provide an opportunity to explore policy-related research for a period of time. These programs can be a great way to gain insight into what it is like to work in the policy world. Organizations with such programs often use them to identify potential permanent hires. Examples include the RAND Corporation's Graduate Student Summer Associate program (RAND Corporation, undated) or CNA's Research Student Summer Internship Program (CNA, undated).

Many think tanks and research organizations now have virtual connections for many of their events. Consider signing up to receive alerts about upcoming seminars at one or more organizations so that you can get a better sense of the issues discussed and the way questions and research findings are framed.

Spend time looking at the websites and publications of organizations where you think you might be interested in working. You will want to understand their research and writing style, what types of evidence and arguments they tend to use, and what types of graphics they tend to employ. These things can help you think about how you might communicate your research portfolio, skills, and strengths if you decide to apply.

Talk to people who work at organizations where you think you might like to work by reaching out to them directly or using conferences, whether virtual or in-person, as a meeting opportunity.

Policy jobs on the national security-side typically require a security clearance. This will be almost universally true of government jobs but may not always be true in the non-profit or advocacy space. Security clearance eligibility requires US citizenship along with a range of other factors. If you think you might apply to a job that requires a security clearance, it is a good idea to review the requirements and process (see for example, Indeed Editorial Team, 2021).

Private Sector Jobs

In addition to the opportunities discussed already, political science PhDs also have numerous opportunities at *private sector companies* serving in a range of capacities. Private companies like McKinsey, Boston Consulting Group, Amazon, Facebook, Google, Microsoft, and others often hire individuals with a political science PhD to support their consulting and other work with government clients, to conduct geopolitical risk assessments, to support the research arm of their organization (for example, Facebook employs PhDs to study their platform and to develop strategies for countering extremism), or to work in strategic planning. These organizations seek out political science PhDs for their methodological training, their systematic way of approaching complex questions, and also in many cases for their regional or substantive expertise. These companies offer exciting and well-compensated opportunities and can be found nationwide. These jobs and the optimal ways to prepare to apply for them are too diverse to adequately characterize here, but if you are interested in pursuing this path, you should feel confident in doing so with your PhD qualifications. To prepare and learn more, consider looking at company websites and seeking out contacts who might work at these places.

Conclusion

This chapter has described a range of non-traditional opportunities for political science PhD candidates and graduates to consider as they chart their careers. Although moving into one of the career paths described here is becoming increasingly common, limited information about these options is conveyed to students in PhD programs at major universities. This chapter provides resources for students to fill this gap. A key theme across the chapter is that your political science PhD makes you a highly sought-after candidate in a range of fields and offers you many paths to fulfillment and success, both in your career and outside of it. It is worth exploring these opportunities even if you think working at an R1 is what you want—you may be surprised by what you find!

Endnotes

1   This section focuses on high school education but could apply as well to middle or primary school.

2   Federally Funded Research and Development Centers "are owned by the federal government, but operated by contractors, including universities, other nonprofit organizations, and industrial firms." See Congressional Research Service, 2020.

References

Bridging the Gap. Undated. New Era Workshop, https://bridgingthegapproject.org/programs/new-era/.

CNA. Undated. Research Student Summer Internship, https://www.cna.org/careers/internship

Congressional Research Service. 2020. "Federally Funded Research and Development Centers (FFRDCs): Background and Issues for Congress." https://crsreports.congress.gov/product/pdf/R/R44629/6

Henry A. Kissinger Center for Global Affairs. Undated. International Policy and Scholars Consortium and Network, https://sais.jhu.edu/kissinger/ipscon

Indeed Editorial Team. 2021. "How to Get a Security Clearance." https://www.indeed.com/career-advice/career-development/how-to-get-security-clearance

McGrath, Erin and Megan Davis. 2019. "APSA Graduate Placement Report: Analysis of Political Science Placements for 2017-2018." *Political Science Education and the Profession.* July. https://preprints.apsanet.org/engage/apsa/article-details/5d2dd689f4cf65001aa0744b.

Opsomer, Jean, Angela Chen, Wan-Ying Chang, and Daniel Foley. 2021. "United States Unemployment Higher in the Private Sector than in the Education Sector for United States-Trained Doctoral Scientists and Engineers: Findings from the 2019 Survey of Doctorate Recipients." *National Center for Science and Engineering Statistics.* April. https://ncses.nsf.gov/pubs/nsf21319.

RAND Corporation. Undated. Graduate Student Summer Associate Program, https://www.rand.org/about/edu_op/fellowships/gsap.ht

The University of Texas at Austin. Undated. Clements Center for National Security, Summer Seminar in History and Statecraft, https://www.clementscenter.org/programs/clements-summer-seminar-in-history-and-statecraft

Today's Military. 2022. "Education & Training: Military Schools." https://www.todaysmilitary.com/education-training/military-schools?gclid=Cj0KCQiA2ZCOBhDiARIsAMRfv9IQbjvkU-i-DlpoZb3p4t-XSmE3Ci04yQsa_j3T7dFOM2LfqoVllUkaArdOEALw_wcB&gclsrc=aw.ds

42 | Weighing Up the Options: The Adventure of an Academic Career Outside of the United States

Dale Mineshima-Lowe[1], Pablo Biderbost[2], & Guillermo Boscán Carrasquero[1,3]

1. Birkbeck, University of London 2. Universidad Pontificia Comillas 3. Universidad de Salamanca

KEYWORDS: Studying Abroad, Specialist Knowledge.

Introduction

In considering one's prospects for a career in political science within and outside of the academy, there are good reasons for looking at wider options available in terms of programs beyond those within the United States. Previous studies have attempted to address the pedagogical as well as practical reasons for studying beyond one's "home" country and have focused on added value of intercultural exchanges to one's academic career (Asada 2019). Drawing on our collective experiences, we offer some insights about pursing academic opportunities outside the United States.

Collectively, we have found our experiences of studying and working outside of the United States have added a richness to our ways of learning, teaching, and research that is difficult to quantify. The experiences have also opened avenues of opportunities we would not have considered otherwise, through the development of more global networks. The enrichment of studying abroad at the graduate level can have a far-reaching impact on one's outlook and prospects beyond immediate considerations (Paige et al. 2009). This is something that is usually understated as it is more nebulous and doesn't demonstrate immediate impact. However, there are some key considerations and trade-offs, both short-term and long-term ones, to reflect upon before one takes the plunge. This chapter is by no means conclusive in its coverage, but more of an overview of key reflections with reference to our experiences from the United Kingdom and Spain to illustrate these insights.

Master's Level Studies Abroad

There are several key considerations for looking at an academic career outside of the United States, but a main one perhaps to reflect upon is, "What do you hope to get out of the experience?" Other top questions to consider: How long do I want to be abroad? What is the purpose of my studying? Is it to develop specialist knowledge for use in my current job? Do I want to change directions in my career? Or am I thinking about pursuing a doctoral study in political science but am unsure of what this will entail?

In terms of pursuing master's level studies in political science abroad, there are a wealth of reasons for studying abroad: international experiences, new contacts, different perspectives, regional / local specialisations, shorter time abroad, etc. However, perhaps if one is considering a master's program abroad, two key tips to consider are the duration and the focus of the programs you are shortlisting. For example, in the United Kingdom, while political science (referred to as "politics") courses can differ, most generally run for twelve-months (full-time). The difference is that some are taught courses (so specific topic courses taken along with then completing an independent research dissertation over a three or four-month period), while others are research-only courses (where you spend the entire time conducting fieldwork or research and writing to complete a dissertation). This distinction between "taught" and research-focused master's courses are similar in Spain and with similar durations for the completion of studies. With "taught" versus research-focused programs, the route one selects is dependent on one's reasons (building specialist-topic knowledge and methodologies versus conducting detailed research and fieldwork), along with one's academic background at the undergraduate level, and any other work/ life experiences.

In terms of the focus and types of programs available, in Spain there are master's level programs designed for different purposes. There are non-official master's degrees (or Títulos Propios in the Spanish academic jargon) that focus more on development of skills and knowledge for the professional market and are generally connected to labor opportunities. Other master's degree programs have been developed to let those who obtain their diplomas enter doctoral studies. In comparison to Spain, most United Kingdom master's degrees in politics serve the dual purpose of providing pathways towards professional development for those already working in policy making or business sectors, as well as a pathway for those who are interested in pursuing doctoral studies.

This understanding of how political science master's degree courses are designed and structured is important. In the Spanish and British examples, they demonstrate how the duration, structure, and rationale for these courses are developed and the audiences they are seeking to serve. These are important points to note in programs one is looking at, as while the prestige of an institution can be very useful, decisions should also consider whether the program is a good match to what you want it for in terms of your own career path and progression. This is the case for graduate programs in any country, however, thinking ahead about opportunities specific programs have with other parts of the world can provide added value to a choice of program. A good example is the strong connection of graduate courses in Spain to universities and other organisations outside of academia in both the European Union and Latin or Ibero America. Additionally, while program-specific benefits may be clear in terms of the cultural and personal benefits, it is also useful to consider within the context of the wider university and community where you will be based during your studies and if it is a good match to more personal needs and individual identities.

A Political Science Career Outside of the United States

A second important question one author was asked during her doctoral studies in the United Kingdom, which she totally valued at the time, was "Where do you want to establish your academic career?" This is a great question in our view, as sometimes we are so focused on the political science program that we are doing, that we do not think to contemplate where do I want to be when this is done? In addition, this reflection really links decisions about completing doctoral studies abroad and future career prospects. That said, there is nothing to say studying abroad negates taking up an academic post in the United States or vice versa; only that there are contacts and networks developed during doctoral studies that can help with finding and securing first academic posts (post-doctoral researcher or teaching ones).

While we were all discussing our experiences as doctoral students in Spain and the United Kingdom, some of the key tips we thought would be useful were focused on: the duration, the quality and recognition of program, added value of programs in each that perhaps were less known, costs and funding, and personal considerations in terms of dependents and for those who identify as part of minoritized populations.

One of the contrasting points to consider between doctoral programs within the United States and Spain or the United Kingdom, for example, is the duration of programs on average. Doctoral studies in both Spain and the United Kingdom can be completed in three years (full-time) and five years (part-time). This differs vastly from the United States, where many doctoral programs on average are undertaken in five years (full-time). We draw this point to start, as there are obvious balances to be had in terms of the duration of a program, entry into the academic career market, and financial costs associated with studying abroad based on the length of program and home/international fees to be paid and living costs.

As with any doctoral program, a key consideration is the quality of degree programs. While generally United Kingdom doctoral politics degrees are highly recognized, this recognition of quality is something that has also been increasing in recent years for programs in Spain. For both Spain and the United Kingdom, the quality of its political science programs has centered around the staff within universities based on their research and teaching competencies. In Spain for instance, professors must have a clear record of recent, good quality publications and material resources must be provided to the students (such as access to books, software licences, or support for participating in international conferences or for publishing with high standards in competitive journals). Likewise in the United Kingdom, the participation of universities in both the Research Excellence Framework (REF) to assess the excellence of research undertaken by staff, as well as the Teaching Excellence Framework (TEF) to assess the quality of teaching,[1] should provide indications about the quality of programs and staff.

In today's competitive graduate market, not only where and what is studied but also how to finance it, are major considerations. One the key tips in terms of finding funding for doctoral studies abroad, in general, is to start the process early. Funding applications need time, consideration, and in many cases, referees, or nominations as part of the process. While in the United States context there are many internal university grants and awards that one can apply for, this is less the case in the United Kingdom and Spain (for a United States-focused discussion, see chapter 23). Some institutions will have their own specific funding lines, but in general, these are limited to specific programs, research topics, or there are restrictions on the nationality of applicants. In both Spain and the United Kingdom, American students can also apply for grants and scholarships within the United States that allow for their use to fund doctoral studies abroad.[2] Additionally, one could apply and use the American federal student loan process and send those funds to the United Kingdom or Spain to cover course fees and living costs.

In addition to the above funding streams, there are opportunities for doctoral students to undertake part-time teaching, partly to fund one's studies but also to gain valuable experience as part of one's academic training. Not dissimilar to some of the opportunities available within the United States for doctoral students, in the United Kingdom doctoral students can serve as tutors (small group seminar leaders), as a university exams invigilator, or as a part-time research assistant on projects led by a member of staff in one's department. Other considerations for working in the United Kingdom while studying include being clear about your student visa conditions, applying for and receiving a British national insurance number (like the United States social security number used to track work and tax contributions), and considering the overall impact on one's ability to complete research and writing within the expected timeframe.

Another key point when starting one's academic career (vis-à-vis doctoral studies abroad) is to consider the support available for international students of diverse backgrounds, in terms of ethnicity, gender identification, sexual orientation, and family-dependents needs. These considerations are becoming more integrated with increased international student recruitment. In Spanish universities this is an important dimension to consider as diversity is a key criterion for universities looking to advance their rankings. Similarly, in the United Kingdom where international students are a part of its politics departments as well as the universities, diversity and inclusion has become a part of the university landscape. In the United Kingdom, the Equality Act 2010 provides guidance for universities, staff and students about legal protections in place for those studying or working who share a protected characteristic. [3]

The "value added" of undertaking studies abroad, as mentioned earlier, are the cultural exchanges, experiences, and new networks one develops. Related are the number of opportunities to participate in domestic (e.g., British or Spanish-based) political science networks. For example, within the United Kingdom, political science networks such as the Political Studies Association (PSA), University Association in Contemporary European Studies (UACES), and the British International Studies Association (BISA) all have dedicated graduate student networks connected to the main organizations' bodies, but run by graduate students to provide opportunities to network and develop one's academic skills beyond research and teaching (e.g., organizing conferences, workshops, delivering conference papers and collaborative publishing). Similarly, in Spain the connections between Spanish universities and those in Latin America and across the European Union adds value to studying abroad as these guarantee strong networks for participating in exchange programs. (For the value of networking in political science generally, see chapter 7.)

When considering a future career in academia outside of the United States, the above-mentioned points and tips (e.g., intersectional considerations, legal protections, developing networks, work visas, etc.) are also relevant for securing one's first political science academic post. Something to note, many universities (including in Spain and the United Kingdom) are seeking to diversify and internationalize their programs (Ortega-Ruiz et al. 2021). They are also seeking to be more inclusive, and many are actively encouraging applications from underrepresented populations (e.g., based on age, ethnicity/race, gender, sexual orientation, disability/ablism). This is supported through provisions by governments in both Spain and United Kingdom to provide visas for non-citizen academics taking up full-time positions, as well as support for dependent families and partners accompanying them (for a more general discussion about familial obligations while in graduate school, see chapter 16).

In electing to search for an academic position outside of the United States, there are expectations of what a new academic brings in terms of teaching experience, curriculum development, research and publishing, which are like those expected by political science departments in the United States. For example, in the Spanish context there are three typical activities expected of academics: teaching (with a clear mandate of "teaching innovation"), research (with the obligation of publications mostly in English but also in Spanish), and management (such as to be the tutor of a group of students, the director of a bachelor's degree program, or a coordinator of internship programs). This is similar for those seeking positions in British universities.

Additionally, it is worth noting that external accreditation (by quality assurance agencies) for both research and teaching are becoming a part of the job-seeking process in many countries outside of the United States. In Spain, for instance, this external approval is required for career progression in the academic arena (e.g., there is no promotion without a previous accreditation). External accreditation is used to evaluate the quality of the research, with university teachers evaluated every six years on the quality of their publication profiles. Impact of one's publication-research profile is reviewed within the Journal Citation Reports (JCR),[4] the SCImajo Journal Rank (SJR),[5] or journals published by the Scientific Publishing Institute (SPI). Similarly, in the United Kingdom the REF is a review process of research and publications by academics. The REF assesses submissions based on three elements: quality of outputs (so similar to use of the SJR), impact beyond academia, and on the research support environment of universities and their departments. This is used to determine a department's ranking against other similar universities in terms of research output and follows a seven-year cycle with the most recent REF review taking place earlier in 2021.

Along with the external accreditation of research and publications, many universities are also seeking candidates with a formal university teaching qualification. Within the United Kingdom, this is not yet mandatory in most universities prior to the start of a position, however, it is highly desirable of candidates seeking positions. In many instances, universities are requiring new staff members to acquire fellow status through the professional membership scheme promoting excellence in higher education run by Advance Higher Education (AdvHE). The alternative is the completion of a graduate certificate in higher education program during one's probationary period.

Lastly, an important part of the decision-making process of one's career prospects is to consider the earning capacity of political science positions in universities as compared to the private, governmental, or non-governmental sectors. Within the United Kingdom, academics on average earn less than their United States counterparts (Stevens 2020). This is similar in Spain, where average salaries for political science academic positions are less attractive in comparison to places like the United States and United Kingdom. However, like the United Kingdom, Spain boasts a good system of social healthcare and education. An additional bonus for academics seeking positions in Spain is that the cost of living is less than both the United Kingdom and the United States, so this can compensate for the salary levels particularly earlier in one's career.

Conclusion

There are some key take-aways to consider when looking at studying (master's level or doctoral) and searching for political science academic jobs abroad as mentioned in this chapter. The most important one to consider is "Why?" What is the purpose behind studying abroad and are you looking at it as a short-term experience or are you a bit more open to seeing where things lead? Leaving yourself time to reflect on these questions, as well as time for short-listing perhaps five programs you're most interested in, is key. Secondly, look at the duration of the program to complete on average, the costs, and the types of funding available (including American federal loans) to see what is a best fit. Do remember to consider the costs of living and not just the costs of studying alone, as unlike in the United States, not all universities provide clear ideas about the costs of living associated with where the university is located. And, again, leave yourself time to do your research on grants and other "free" money that you may be able to access (e.g., home-state scholarships, grants for specific ethnic groups, grants for specific programs and/or research topics, etc.). The time these take to find and complete are usually under-estimated. Third, as we will assume quality of research and teaching will be a key consideration in selecting a program, the next key consideration focuses on the extra-curricular opportunities available that will add value to the experience of studying abroad. These could be through the graduate program itself (e.g., work experiences, fieldwork, research assistant work, government internships, etc.), staff members in the department, or affiliate organizations.

All of these key take-aways are relevant for studying abroad are also very relevant for those looking to start their political science academic career abroad. Lastly, a great tip is to find a mentor who shares your research interests, affiliations, and that you like, who will be able to provide feedback and advice as you prepare to search for that first full-time political science academic job (for additional information, see chapter 13). Good Luck!

Resources of Interest

- British International Studies Association (BISA)—United Kingdom—www.bisa.ac.uk
- London School of Economics and Political Science (LSE): Fees and Funding Opportunities—United Kingdom—https://www.lse.ac.uk/study-at-lse/graduate/fees-and-funding
- Office for Students: Equality and Diversity—United Kingdom—https://www.officeforstudents.org.uk/about/equality-and-diversity/what-does-the-law-say/
- Political Studies Association (PSA)—United Kingdom—www.psa.ac.uk
- Postgraduate Funding—United States, United Kingdom & Spain—https://www.postgraduatefunding.com/search/results?los=1&sids=63
- Research Excellence Framework (REF)—United Kingdom—https://www.ref.ac.uk/about/
- Teaching Excellence Framework (TEF)—United Kingdom—https://www.gov.uk/government/publications/government-response-to-the-independent-review-of-tef
- University Association of Contemporary European Studies (UACES)—United Kingdom— www.uaces.org
- Advance Higher Education (AdvHE)—United Kingdom— https://www.advance-he.ac.uk/

Endnotes

1   Both measuring frameworks provide an evaluation of research and teaching undertaken at UK universities and in the case of the REF, this is used to inform the allocation of public funding for universities in research. The TEF is voluntary and publicly funded universities and colleges in receipt of a TEF award are allowed to charge tuition at a different level than non-TEF institutions.

2   Further details of sources of funding are listed in the reference section. Also check individual institutions (e.g., LSE – London School of Economics and Political Science in the UK) for details of individual institutional funding available. See also chapter 23 in this volume.

3   Protected characteristics under UK law include age, disability, gender reassignment, marriage and civil partnership, pregnancy and maternity, race, religion or belief, sex, and sexual orientation.

4   Journal report service that measures journal impact factor: https://clarivate.com/webofsciencegroup/solutions/journal-citation-reports/

5   Public portal that compares journal and country rankings for impact factor: https://www. scimagojr.com/

References

Asada, Sarah Renee. 2019. "Study Abroad and Knowledge Diplomacy: Increasing Awareness and Connectivity to the Host Country, Host Region, and World." *Compare* 51(3): 1-16.

Ortega-Ruiz, Manuela, José Real-Dato, and Miguel Jerez Mir. 2021. "Late but Not Least? Spanish Political Science's Struggle for Internationalisation in the Twenty-First Century." *European Political Science* 20(1): 159–82. https://doi.org/10.1057/s41304-021-00315-z.

Paige, R. Michael, Gerald W. Fry, Elizabeth M. Stallman, Jasmina Josić, and Jae-Eun Jon. 2009. "Study Abroad for Global Engagement: The Long-term Impact of Mobility Experiences." *Intercultural Education* 20(sup1): S29–44. https://doi.org/10.1080/14675980903370847.

Stevens, Philip Andrew. 2004. "Academic Salaries in the United Kingdom and United States." *National Institute Economic Review* 190(October): 104–13. https://doi.org/10.1177/002795010419000110.

Wood, J. 2021. "What's the Teaching Excellence Framework (TEF)?" *Complete University Guide*. Available: https://www.thecompleteuniversityguide.co.uk/student-advice/where-to-study/teaching-excellence-framework-tef [Accessed: December 21, 2021].

43

Making a Statement: Research, Teaching, and Diversity Statements for the Academic Job Market

Kelly Bauer[1], Colin M. Brown[2],

Maricruz Ariana Osorio[3], & Melissa L. Sands[4]

1.Nebraska Wesleyan University 2. Northeastern University
3. Bentley University 4. London School of Economics

KEYWORDS: Research Statements, Teaching Statements, Diversity Statements.

What Do You Need to Know?[1]

Research, teaching, and diversity statements are core elements of applications for faculty positions. In this chapter, we offer practical guidance for those developing these statements. We argue that the process of writing statements can play an important role in developing one's academic identity and plotting a trajectory. We offer reflection prompts for each statement and reiterate the importance of long-term reflexive practices and career preparation. The structural difficulties of the current job market raise the stakes of this process and limit the effectiveness of any strategy an individual applicant can adopt. Nonetheless, we hope the following allows students to approach their statements more confidently and prompts reflection on their professional identity.

Why Does It Matter?

Research, teaching, and diversity statements provide information beyond the CV. These statements bring a candidate to life and give the committee insight into how a candidate narrates their interests, ideas, and plans. They also signal to a committee the candidate's personality and motivations, which can help demonstrate fit to a particular type of position (e.g., an interdisciplinary focus or experience with a specific student population). The writing process is a way to reflect on your long-term goals and to detail the kind of scholar, teacher, and colleague you are now and are trying to become (Kaplan et al 2008, 243; Kearns et al 2010, 74). If started early, this drafting process may highlight aspects of your work to develop in the final year(s) of your graduate studies.

Below, we offer suggestions about how to think through and craft these three statements. But first, two caveats. First, we write this chapter drawing on our own experiences as applicants and search committee members, but we cannot represent the full variation across institutions, candidates, or even across search committees. Second, while these statements matter, search committees' deliberations are unobservable and therefore difficult to generalize, especially given the structural realities of the academic job market. There is no direct way to deal with this opacity, but we encourage candidates to seek advice and support from trusted colleagues, peers, and mentors on their statements as well as the ambiguities and unknowables of the process.[2] (See chapters 7 and 13 for more insight on seeking advice from advisors and mentors.) With these limitations, we offer some suggestions for this reflective drafting process.

What Should/Can You Do?

Research Statements

Writing research statements challenges applicants to articulate the broader empirical, theoretical, and/or methodological questions motivating their research. The research statement provides the committee with a holistic sense of you as a researcher, linking your CV to your overall trajectory. This document demonstrates that you have interesting ideas and projects, will "hit the ground running," and will ultimately make a strong tenure case.

The first few sentences typically summarize your scholarly identity by describing the "big questions" to which your work speaks and contributes, which should contextualize your writing sample(s). You do not need to describe every interest in the first paragraph. Use the remainder of the statement to describe your research interests, indicating the specific status and timeline of each project (e.g., about to go under review, published in [journal name], etc.) and any grant support. Anecdotally, the authors have repeatedly heard advice that statements from PhD candidates should devote 75% to work completed or in progress, and 25% to future work. Describing work in progress or planned is important for demonstrating an ongoing, productive research pipeline.

The research statement should signal the broader significance and impact of your current or planned work. Your statement will almost always be read by individuals outside of your subfield, so it is prudent to assume that your audience is not necessarily familiar with the state of your field. Avoid overly technical jargon and be relatively explicit about the contributions that your work makes (or is likely to make). For the same reason, we recommend that all research statements should speak across subdisciplines and observe that presenting research interests narrowly grounded in a specific subdiscipline carries a larger risk than being too broad.

How a committee reads these statements varies by department and university. For example, a liberal arts college (LAC) may read for a candidate's contributions to an interdisciplinary department. Others will read for whether the research is feasible with institutional resources, and implying needing start-up funds or extensive fieldwork may alienate potential colleagues at an institution that does not provide this type of support. Tailoring for individual universities probably has little impact, although there may be some benefit to having one statement for research-heavy universities (R1/R2) versus teaching-focused institutions or institutions with limited resources.

Some Helpful Questions to Ask Yourself

- Where would you situate yourself in the landscape of political/social science research?
- What is novel, unique, or innovative about what you do? How does your work push knowledge forward?
- What are the key contributions of your dissertation project? (Be sure to relay these in "everyday" language.)
- If a friend introduced you to a search committee member, how would they describe your research?
- What research questions will attract your attention in 5 years?

Teaching Statements

Teaching statements communicate your pedagogical priorities and experiences. Teaching statements should also clarify an applicant's teaching experience, and their range across disciplines, subfields, methodology, and level of coursework, and may include details about work outside of the traditional classroom environment such as sponsoring student organizations, overseeing undergraduate research collaborations, and mentoring or advising individual students.

Good teaching statements provide specific examples of how you put your teaching commitments into practice. Show evidence that you have developed your teaching methods by engaging with (and listening to) students and that you are capable of growth as an instructor. Those enrolled in a program that does not require extensive experience as a teaching assistant or instructor of record, but applying to teaching-focused jobs, may find it worth seeking additional teaching experiences or opportunities to craft teaching materials in order to develop and articulate their teaching priorities.[3] Some committees will ask for teaching evaluations (formal and/or informal), syllabi, lesson plans, assignments, annotated syllabi, and more. Keeping track of this type of teaching evidence throughout graduate school will provide useful evidence to reflect on in your teaching statement.

While there are some common understandings of what makes teaching statements successful, this is mostly "received wisdom" and has only occasionally been studied systematically. In the most extensive such interdisciplinary survey, Kaplan et al (2008) found five themes in successful teaching statements: 1) evidence of practice, 2) student-centered, 3) reflectiveness, 4) conveying the intrinsic or extrinsic value of teaching, and 5) clear writing. While these documents are often called "statements of teaching philosophy," and it is important to demonstrate some familiarity with broader ideas in pedagogy, successful teaching statements are more practical than "philosophical" texts (The Derek Bok Center for Teaching and Learning, "The Job Market").

Committees' evaluations of teaching statements vary widely depending on institutional priorities, departmental context, and the student population. At a LAC, for example, a teaching statement is likely expected to demonstrate an applicant's teaching repertoire and will likely be evaluated on whether the applicant's pedagogical priorities map on to those of the institution. Lecture-heavy classes are less likely to set a faculty member up for success in tenure and promotion reviews at one of the author's institutions, while an emphasis on "experiential education" is expected at another author's. Smaller departments will usually require faculty to teach regularly outside their subfield, while larger departments are more likely to want teachers who can diversify a catalog of more specialized courses. We do not suggest tailoring teaching statements to particular institutions, but having different versions for R1/R2 institutions, LACs, and community colleges may allow you to change emphases or highlight particular affinities if you plan to apply widely. Tailoring the teaching statement may be useful for positions with very specific missions, such as positions at minority serving or women's colleges, or for clinical or teaching professorships.

Many schools are likely reading a teaching statement for evidence that candidates show awareness of and/or implement inclusive teaching practices. Concrete examples include ensuring that assigned reading lists reflect diversity of various forms (e.g., gender, race and ethnicity, geographic region), providing for various forms of contact and participation with an eye towards accessibility, accommodating students who have caregiving or other responsibilities, and challenging exclusionary language.[4]

Some Helpful Questions to Ask Yourself

- What motivates your approach to teaching?
- What skills and content do you want students to take away from your courses, and how do you observe or assess that?
- How do you engage with students?
- What pedagogies—theories and methods of teaching and learning—have you used, and why did you implement them?

Diversity Statements

Diversity statements are a relatively recent addition to job applications, and as such norms around the content of these statements are less well-established.[5] In the authors' experiences, the most common advice is for candidates to balance a reflection on how their identities and/or experiences influence their work as a political scientist with evidence of their past, present, and future commitments to diversity, equity and inclusion (DEI) work. Golash-Boza (2016) suggests acknowledging obstacles and/or privilege in your life and using your personal story to reflect on how you work with students. Describe specific actions you have taken to help facilitate the success of students from historically excluded backgrounds; and demonstrate a practical commitment (including examples where possible) to supporting DEI work on campus. It is also important to demonstrate an awareness of the issues that face faculty members once hired; how will you show concrete support for fellow faculty from historically excluded groups,[6] and how will you help your department/unit actively promote and retain these colleagues? Diversity statements can be read as more political than other statements, so tailoring these statements may be more important or necessary than teaching and research statements. However, candidates do not know the level of proficiency or cultural competence among committee members or their understanding of diversity, so there are also inherent risks to trying to anticipate how they will be read.[7]

There are ongoing critiques of diversity statements. Hiring committees may value certain components of candidate identities for a number of reasons, including ability to connect with students in ways that the current faculty cannot. Diversity statements, however, may effectively require applicants to disclose legally protected information. They may also encourage applicants to disclose trauma that they may otherwise not wish to share, and that trauma may then become subject to legal scrutiny and other human resources processes. Furthermore, many highlight how these statements are representative of a common approach to DEI work not as a pursuit of justice, but rather tokenizing and reinforcing the burden on historically excluded groups to solve structural problems of exclusion themselves (Lerma, Hamilton and Nielson, 2020).

Self-disclosure is a particular difficulty for applicants. Disclosing one's identities, especially historically excluded identities, risks invoking the reviewers' implicit or explicit biases. For this reason, some have argued for limiting self-presentation in any kinds of application or interview materials (e.g., Lucas & Murry 2002) and at least one study has found a significant amount of self-concealment by post-doc applicants (Baker et al 2016). This is one unfortunate way in which the burden of adapting to potential discrimination ends up falling to the applicant rather than the institution and may also cause the candidate to downplay aspects of their application that could in fact be specifically valued (Kang et al 2016a, 2016b). Ultimately, self-disclosure is a personal decision. Should you choose to explicitly self-identify, it seems wise to describe how your background and experiences inform your approach to research, teaching, mentoring, and service and offer unique advantages in each of these aspects of your academic identity (Schmaling et al 2015).

Writing the diversity statement should also be a chance to reflect on the questions or concerns you have about the institution you are applying to. A good practice for applicants' preferred positions would be to invest time into reading institutions' strategic plans and diversity statements, if publicly available, before applying. Does the institution's approach to diversity reflect the actual promotion and retention of a diverse faculty? Does the institution appear to be inviting diverse applicants into a conversation, or expecting them to solve issues of faculty and student diversity on their own? Does the institution have specific DEI goals, processes, resources, and intended outcomes?

Some Helpful Questions to Ask Yourself[8]

- How or why is diversity important to your work in higher education?
- How does your commitment to promoting diversity manifest in your teaching and course design, research, and/or in your service to your department, school, or discipline?
- Does the language in your statement reflect a commitment to supporting and sustaining a diverse institution, and does it reflect a proficiency in the work that excluded scholars are doing to make the field more inclusive?
- In what ways will this institution provide you adequate support to actually promote diversity, equity, and inclusion efforts? And will it, really?

The following question may be helpful for personal reflection but introduces the issues of self-disclosure mentioned above:

- How do your identities impact your work, including your work with students?

General Advice

Imagine yourself in the shoes of a search committee member tasked with reading possibly hundreds of applications. How can the applicant make that work easier? Statements should be well-organized, clear, and concise, with a strong opening paragraph. Search committee members may be skimming a given statement or cover letter from each applicant, so make sure that the critical pieces of information are obvious on quick reading. And while each statement provides different details and emphases, the job packet should be cohesive with all of the documents reiterating and reinforcing the others.

As we suggest above, different institutions will look for different elements in these statements, and many candidates prepare a few versions of these statements. While tailoring to the type of institution can be useful (ex: R1 vs LAC vs CC), we advise against tailoring statements to specific institutions, which takes an extensive amount of time to do well, and is unlikely to significantly impact a committee's first-round evaluation. We recommend some degree of institution-specific tailoring in the cover letter, where an applicant might specify their interest in or connection to a specific institution. (Chapters 36-40 provide more in-depth advice about how to successfully apply for positions at different types of institutions.)

Applicants likely have a number of resources available to help them develop these materials, though the availability and quality of each will vary by institution and may be less accessible after leaving one's graduate program. The most obvious starting point are research advisors, graduate studies directors, and (in larger programs) placement directors, all of whom should in theory be available to help develop draft statements. Most faculty development offices or centers for teaching and learning will offer programs to develop teaching statements, and many grants and/or research offices will have programs or consulting to help develop research statements. APSA members may also participate in the APSA Mentor program, and academic meetings like the APSA Annual Conference also regularly sponsor professional development panels. Recent graduates of one's doctoral program may also be supportive mentors, and Twitter and Slack communities have begun to provide opportunities for advice and mutual support among applicants.

Ultimately, most job candidates find their time spent "on the market" to be rife with uncertainty and even anxiety since so much is beyond the candidate's control. We hope that this general advice gives candidates some assurances of having done all they can, despite the structural issues. Though easier said than done, it may help to conceptualize the process of preparing for the market as a period of intense professionalization. Authoring research, teaching, and diversity statements provides an opportunity for the candidate to introspectively reflect and plan for the future. In fact, these materials may become the basis for a promotion file, or for the next set of academic or non-academic job applications. We recommend approaching these specific statements through conversation and in community to adapt to the fluid nature of the market and to build long-term professional support.

Endnotes

1   The authors are grateful for insightful comments and feedback from Kerry Crawford, Daniel de Kadt, Meg Guliford, Tesalia Rizzo, and from the editors of this guidebook. A number of useful public Twitter conversations on these topics have helped inspire the authors as well; we are grateful in particular to posts by Leila Billing (@leilabilling), Meg Guliford (@mkguliford), Hakeem Jefferson (@hakeemjefferson), Anna O. Law (@UnlawfulEntries), and Olumuyiwa Igbalajobi (@olumuyiwaayo) for pointing us to resources and raising important questions about diversity statements.

2   Sometimes there are types of support that your professional or personal networks cannot provide; for these, consider utilizing your institution's mental health or other resources (Almasri, Read and Vandeweerdt 2021).

3   More specific recommendations are difficult because of the significant variation in how (and whether) graduate students teach in different graduate programs. For example, see Ishiyama, Miles, and Balarezo 2010; Ishiyama, Balarezo, and Miles 2014; Trowbridge and Woodward 2020.

4   We encourage applicants to familiarize themselves with current conversations happening around this work. APSA Educate frequently collates resources, such as "JPSE: The Inclusive Classroom Reading List," and "Teaching Black Lives Matter."

5   For additional context and resources, see Beck 2018. For specific guidance for international applicants, see Koutseridi 2021.

6 The use of "historically excluded groups" is intentional by the authors to acknowledge power dynamics inherent in these definitions.

7 Search committee members may have different understandings of "diversity" from each other. Michele Lamont, for example, has found that support for diversity on funding panels often balances very different ideas of gender, racial and ethnic, geographic, and topic diversity, while using the same language of "diversity" (2009, p. 212-214).

8 See also the "Job Market Do's and Don'ts" guide generated by the People of Color Also Know Stuff working group: https://sites.google.com/view/pocexperts/blog/job-market-dos-and-donts.

References

Almasri, Nasir, Blair Read, and Caroline Vandeweerdt. 2021. "Mental Health and the PhD: Insights and Implications for Political Science." *PS: Political Science & Politics First View*: 1-7. doi:10.1017/S1049096521001396.

Baker, Dana Lee, Karen Schmaling, Kathleen Carlisle Fountain, Arthur W. Blume, and Randy Boose. 2016. "Defining Diversity: A Mixed-Method Analysis of Terminology in Faculty Applications." *The Social Science Journal* 53 (1): 60-66.

Beck, Sara L. 2018. "Developing and Writing a Diversity Statement." Vanderbilt University Center for Teaching. 2018. https://cft.vanderbilt.edu/developing-and-writing-a-diversity-statement.

The Derek Bok Center for Teaching and Learning, "The Job Market," https://bokcenter.harvard.edu/job-market, Accessed Nov. 20, 2021.

Golash-Boza, Tanya. 2016. "The Effective Diversity Statement." Inside Higher Education. https://www.insidehighered.com/advice/2016/06/10/how-write-effective-diversity-statement-essay.

Ishiyama, John, Christine Balarezo, and Tom Miles. 2014. "Do Graduate Student Teacher Training Courses Affect Placement Rates?" *Journal of Political Science Education* 10 (3): 273-283.

Ishiyama, John, Tom Miles, and Christine Balarezo. 2010. "Training the Next Generation of Teaching Professors: A Comparative Study of Ph. D. Programs in Political Science." *PS: Political Science & Politics* 43 (3): 515-522.

Kaplan, Matthew, Deborah S Meizlish, Christopher O'Neal, and Mary C Wright. 2008. "A Research-Based Rubric for Developing Statements of Teaching Philosophy." To Improve the Academy 26 (1): 242-62.

Kang, Sonia K., Katherine A. DeCelles, András Tilcsik, and Sora Jun. 2016. "Whitened Résumés: Race and Self-Presentation in the Labor Market." Administrative Science Quarterly 61 (3):469-502.

Kang, Sonia K., Katherine A. DeCelles, András Tilcsik, and Sora Jun. 2016. "The Unintended Consequences of Diversity Statements" Harvard Business Review Digital Articles. https://hbr.org/2016/03/the-unintended-consequences-of-diversity-statements.

Koutseridi, Olga. 2021. "Decoding Diversity Statements for International Ph.D.s" Inside Higher Education. https://www.insidehighered.com/advice/2021/11/22/writing-diversity-statement-international-students-opinion.

Lamont, Michèle. 2009. How Professors Think: Inside the Curious World of Academic Judgment. Cambridge, MA: Harvard University Press.

Lerma, Veronica, Laura T. Hamilton, and Kelly Nielsen. 2020. "Racialized Equity Labor, University Appropriation and Student Resistance." Social Problems 67 (2):286-303.

Lucas, Christopher J. and John W. Murry, Jr. 2002. New Faculty: A Practical Guide for Academic Beginners. New York: Palgrave.

Schmaling, Karen B., Amira Y. Trevino, Justin R. Lind, Arthur W. Blume, and Dana L. Baker. 2015. "Diversity Statements: How Faculty Applicants Address Diversity." Journal of Diversity in Higher Education 8 (4):213-224.

Trowbridge, David, and Jennifer Woodward. 2021. "Pedagogy Training among Political Scientists: Opportunities, Interest, and Obstacles." Journal of Political Science Education 17 (sup1):807-824.

44

A Limited Time Offer: Exploring Adjunct, Visiting, and Fixed-Term Positions

Austin Trantham[1], Connor J.S. Sutton[2],

Margaret Mary Ochner[3], & Jennifer Lamm[4]

1. Saint Leo University 2. Anderson University 3. Montclair State University 4. Texas State University

KEYWORDS: Adjunct, Jobs, Visiting, Non-Tenure, Teaching.

Introduction

The diversity of non-tenure track (NTT) positions means there is no one-size-fits-all advice for graduate students in or considering such positions. However, we argue there are general principles that should be followed to maximize the utility of these roles in pursuing career and vocational goals. We first define and describe the roles and types of NTT positions and describe how graduate students should view NTT positions from both professional and personal perspectives. This chapter details the potential benefits and drawbacks of these positions to better prepare graduate students to navigate the NTT market. We illuminate crucial skills and experiences in NTT positions and highlight strategies for success in NTT roles for students throughout their graduate education and job search, as well as in leveraging these positions to obtain more secure positions. These include being strategic in choosing NTT positions and being strategic once in NTT positions. These positions can be extremely useful in developing teaching skills, building a marketable CV, networking, and assessing vocational goals, but these appointments are also often tenuous, low-wage, and time consuming. Hiring term-limited faculty is less regulated than the process for hiring tenure-track personnel. Like the market for postdocs, the NTT labor is "less transparent, less equitable, making it a bottleneck for improving diversity in disciplines as scholars move to more senior positions in the academe, a phenomenon known as the "leaky pipeline" (APSA 2005). Considering these factors, graduate students should be deliberate when considering NTT positions. Our goal is to guide students in developing realistic expectations for job searches during graduate school and enlighten students on core considerations in selecting positions.

What Do You Need to Know?

It is necessary to define and identify types of NTT positions prior to applying, as there are not only different hiring requirements, but different skills, benefits, and various other factors. For simplicity, we will discuss limited-term, part-time teaching positions under the umbrella term of "non-tenure track" or "NTT" positions pursuant to the American Political Science Association's (APSA) occupational studies of the discipline. NTT positions encapsulate a wide variety of teaching opportunities, including terms that frequently appear in job listings, as illustrated in Figure 44.1. The commonality between these positions is the fact that they are for a "fixed term" where the university is under no obligation to rehire at the end of the contract period unless stipulated otherwise.

Figure 44.1: Common Characteristics of NTT Positions

Position Title	Defining Characteristics
Adjunct Faculty	Temporary position that is paid a set rate to teach one or more courses in an individual semester. Based on departmental need/student demand.
Assistant Teaching Professor	Position primarily focused on teaching or teaching/service duties. May be eligible for eventual promotion to Associate and Full Teaching Professor.
Instructor	Most general term - implies nothing about education level or contact type. Typically lacking a terminal degree (PhD or equivalent) in the relevant field of study. Focused on classroom teaching.
Instructor or Professor of Practice	Positions for those with master's, PhD, JD, etc. Practitioners are sometimes hired on the basis of non-academic work and may include administrative duties (e.g., director of policy center, etc., usually 12-month contract)
Professional-Track Appointment	Position that focuses more on quality classroom instruction and service and does not require meeting defined benchmarks for scholarship/research output (e.g., usually 9-month contract.)
Visiting Instructor/Lecturer	Temporary appointment given to one without terminal degree. May be eligible for renewal for multiple semesters or academic years.
Visiting Assistant Professor	Appointment covering initial set-time frame but may be extended if needed. Preferred terminal degree (PhD/equivalent), but "All But Dissertation" (ABD) candidates may be considered.

As illustrated in *Figure 44.1*, NTT positions vary and are individually defined by institutions. This list is by no means exhaustive, as institutions continue to develop and proliferate fewer traditional tenure-track roles. We speculate that more of these roles will arise, especially with the rapid changes in integration of technology over traditional classroom settings. We recommend that applicants thoroughly review the hiring institution's faculty handbook in order to understand their rights and responsibilities as an NTT professor before accepting an appointment.

What does this mean?

Job Pipeline

Although many students do not begin a graduate program in political science with the goal of obtaining NTT employment upon graduation, it is important to understand how these academic appointments fit into the occupational landscape. If you aspire to a career in academia, it is more likely than not that you, members of your graduate cohort, and/or future colleagues will assume an NTT role at some point in your career, either during graduate school or upon completion. APSA's 2018-2020 job placement report illustrates that about one-half of graduates accept NTT appointments as "their first placement" after completing their PhD. Thus, it is crucial that applicants understand the stark differences between NTT and traditional tenure-track positions.

Qualifications for NTT Positions

It is worth noting that the labor markets for tenure and NTT academic appointments are highly distinctive. Hiring practices for NTT faculty are less stringent, and fewer credentials are necessary for appointment. Typically, hiring decisions for NTT's are made at the departmental level without significant involvement from higher-level university officials. Depending on the specific NTT position, the institution usually requires very limited, if any, research or writing expectations. NTTs do not always need a PhD, though some post-graduate degree is typically required. Relevant teaching and research experience in your field may be important, but often less so for tenure-track appointments. Thus, the NTT applicant may not have to submit the variety of scholarly materials (e.g., teaching philosophy and student evaluations) required for a tenure-track application, and the process may move quickly. (For additional information about application materials, see chapter 43.)

Benefits and Compensation

Full-time employment as faculty typically involves a consistent, simplified schedule, set office hours, and location on a daily basis. Additionally, it provides for health insurance, retirement plans, and increased job security. Therefore, the difference between working full versus part-time at an institution cannot be under emphasized. While part-time educators must perform many of the same duties as full-time faculty, the compensation offered is significantly less than that of full-time appointments. NTTs are typically not salaried but paid by semester, course, or credit hours. Additionally, there are often more stringent limitations on the number of classes a part-time NTT professor can teach per semester. This data should not be discouraging but serve as a guide for effectively planning your career choices.

Why Does It Matter?

How to View the Increase in Temporary Positions

The sharp increase in NTT faculty positions in political science (and higher education generally) over the last decade lends credence to the discussion within this chapter. This development should be considered by anyone assessing their career prospects in higher education, especially those who desire to teach. (For more general information about the political science job market, see chapter 34.) NTT appointments provide opportunities for candidates to gain teaching experience, build rapport, and focus on developing a publication record before applying to tenure-track positions. Because the NTT and tenure-track markets are intertwined, it benefits the applicant to understand the role of NTT educators in the discipline.

Opportunity Value

NTT appointments can be an excellent method for gaining practical experience in the profession. Developing pedagogical skills while completing temporary teaching assignments provides concrete evidence of classroom competence when applying for tenure-track positions. Thus, though an NTT role offers less financially, the opportunity for practice is invaluable. However, if one desires an alternative career path to academia or as a staff member (e.g., student advisor), but also enjoys faculty work or is uncertain where their passions lie, an initial NTT position can be a pathway toward future work. This experience allows the educator to fulfill vocational and personal goals, including staying current on changing trends in higher education while working with students and learning from their perspectives. Similarly, because NTT positions often have limitations regarding how many courses any employee can teach during any given semester, this allows the new teacher the opportunity to focus in-depth on crafting and completing one course, which is a rare opportunity. On the other hand, an NTT position can also lead to a "career" NTT. Though difficult to obtain and maintain, teachers may end up juggling NTT positions at several universities. Additionally, ad hoc teaching can be a supplement to non-academic vocations and these opportunities increase as new online mediums become more widely available.

What Will I Teach?

Graduate students should consider how these factors affect the job itself. It cannot be overstated that the appointments and specific assignments of full-time instructors (especially those with tenure) take precedence over NTT faculty. This means that fixed-term instructional appointments may be sporadic and may only be finalized weeks before the start of a given semester. Some NTT instructors are assigned courses after students have enrolled. This can be intimidating, but it is the nature of NTT work. Because of these factors, NTT faculty must be extremely flexible as course schedules may be assigned, changed, and/or removed quickly. Course preparation in drafting syllabi, creating assignments, and learning new subject matter is often extremely labor intensive, often on short notice.

Depending on the appointment, an NTT instructor may not have a choice in what class or classes they will teach, nor the textbook or supplementary materials used to teach it. NTTs are sometimes provided with samples and expected to teach the class a certain way or adopt a former professor's syllabi. However, other NTT positions may require the professor (who may have never taught, nor even taken, the course themselves) to develop relevant curricula and assignments and find scholarly materials on short notice. Often, instructors must teach themselves some of the subject matter at a rapid pace in order to effectively teach the course. Understanding and accepting these uncertainties should be considered when applying for NTT positions, and candidates should ensure this aligns with existing personal and professional obligations.

How Will I Teach?

Course assignments may be given in a wide array of instructional modalities. Non-traditional instruction is increasingly common. Online courses may include hybrid elements and may be conducted either synchronously or asynchronously. This may be beneficial in an NTT position, as it allows the professor increased autonomy while widening the range of available teaching positions without requiring travel. As early-career educators should know, teaching is perfected over time. The online element also creates unique challenges. Thus, before accepting an NTT position, it is important to consider individual practices regarding the use of instructional technology, creating innovative assignments, timely grading of student work, and ensuring equity and inclusivity in the classroom (For additional tips and suggestions, see chapters 29 and 30). Much of this is university-dependent and may continue to change and develop over time. Thus, flexibility is key, and it is wise to keep up to date on best practices in non-traditional classroom settings.

Finally, the impact of exogenous events on NTT employment should be mentioned. Depending on the location, instructors may be forced to accommodate for a hurricane, tornado, or other severe weather event disrupting the normal course schedule. Traditional classes may switch unexpectedly to a virtual modality due to a public health crisis and subsequent concerns of spreading illness in shared spaces or canceled altogether due to institutional financial cuts because of an economic recession or depression. These events may increase or decrease opportunities for NTT positions but often cannot be predicted and are outside the control of those in or seeking these roles.

What Should/Can You Do?

Given the significant financial and vocational challenges of term-limited work, as well as the time required to succeed in these positions, graduate students need to be strategic in two primary ways. First, they must be strategic in choosing NTT positions, and ensure they know the explicit purpose that any position(s) may serve in reaching their educational and vocational goals. Secondly, graduate students also need to be strategic once in NTT positions and make these positions as useful as possible in advancing their professional goals.

Strategy for Choosing Term-Limited Positions

There are significant benefits to NTT positions. NTT appointments are a low-stakes opportunity for self-assessment to see if teaching is a vocational calling. These positions allow individuals to teach and prepare classes that they may not have had the opportunity to—especially if a student did not have funding opportunities tied to being an instructor of record. Individuals have unique reactions to their first classroom experiences. For some, it confirms their vocational skills and career goals. For others, they realize working with undergraduates in the classroom should not be the defining feature of their career and would prefer more research-oriented positions, to work with graduate students, or pursue non-academic professions. (For additional information about your first teaching experience, see chapter 29.) Beyond vocation, NTT positions also make graduates more competitive on the job market, giving the chance to practice and reflect on teaching philosophies, compile evidence of teaching effectiveness (new syllabi, student evaluations, teaching demo lectures), and network with potential future collaborators, mentors, and employers.

Graduate students should also be strategic in saying no to certain opportunities. Given the diversity of term-limited positions, there is no one universal standard for making this decision. Full time NTT positions may provide competitive compensation while achieving opportunities for professional and personal development. Other positions pay very little without benefits for the same end on an ad hoc basis. Graduate students should be realistic in their assessment of opportunities. Some take term-limited positions and end up in tenure-track positions. However, this is hardly a rule. These positions should be considered for what they are, as defined in employment contracts, rather than what they could be. It is tempting to choose a position because it could become what they want it to be, but graduate students must prioritize timely competition of degrees and the pursuit of sustainable employment and vocation.

Figure 44.2: Dos and Don'ts for NTT Positions

Strategy in Choosing NTT Positions	Strategy in NTT Positions
Make vocational decisions	Cultivate mentors in teaching and scholarship
Recognize financial realities	Develop transferable course materials backed up outside of an institutional learning management system (LMS) - e.g., Blackboard, Canvas, Moodle, D2L, etc.
Consider NTT positions as means to an end	Build teaching philosophy with practical examples
Evaluate CV gaps for marketability	Compile evidence of teaching effectiveness
Prioritize degree completion and tenure-track (or non-academic equivalent) positions	Be effective but do not be perfect
Say "no" when appropriate	Design courses that minimize instructor time commitment while meeting pedagogical goals
Consider viable alternatives to NTT positions	Have explicit and purposeful boundaries

Strategy During Term-Limited Positions

NTT faculty need to be strategic once in these positions and maximize their utility. For the NTT instructor, perfect is the enemy of good. Many are called to teach because they love it and want to be the best teacher possible. Given the realities of NTT positions—variable pay, limited security, opportunity cost—it is not always advantageous to be the "best version" of a teacher. Rather than being the perfect teacher, they should focus on being the most pragmatic teacher. Instructors should be purposeful in approaching these positions as they are tremendous opportunities to hone teaching skills, develop reusable content, network with new colleagues, pedagogically experiment, and learn new subjects. Instructors should put in time and effort in teaching, but do not strive for perfection. This is the most difficult lesson for someone who considers themselves a teacher-scholar, in that order. This means prioritizing teaching in NTT positions to improve their lot in securing more sustainable appointments.

As there is not a one-size-fits-all model, we provide general considerations to make the most of NTT positions. First, build and maintain any and all teaching materials for portability (independent of the institutional LMS). Second, recognize instructors do not need to be masters of topics they teach. It is okay to be one step ahead of undergraduates, knowing that subsequent iterations will be better. Third, think about positions in terms of building teaching portfolios. The best teaching philosophies develop when practiced and when defended with evidence of teaching effectiveness. Fourth, know when to say "no." NTT positions may call for non-compensated work—informal/formal advising, lesson planning, curriculum drafting, faculty meetings, and mandatory training. Knowing what the benefits of these tasks vis-a-vis objectives is essential to knowing when to say no. Set personal and professional boundaries. Lastly, NTT positions often are less "plugged-in" than tenure-track positions and departments are less likely to invest in NTT professional development. This means that people in these positions must be more purposeful in pursuing networking and mentorship opportunities. These relationships may yield rich rewards but must be actively pursued (for a larger discussion, see chapter 7).

Conclusion

The direction of the field and market means that more political science graduate students will have to consider NTT positions in various forms. As such, students seeking careers in academia should be strategic while considering and applying for NTT positions. This is a highly personalized and fact-dependent choice, and graduates should keep their professional goals in mind while making decisions. NTT positions are excellent opportunities to be the instructor of record, to develop teaching skills, build their resume, and make informed decisions about their vocational preferences. Students need to be strategic once in NTT positions. These opportunities can be used either as a springboard towards a more permanent teaching career or appreciated for what they are. However, we encourage students to make strategic considerations when accepting or refusing potential job opportunities based on the strategies detailed above, as well as realistic standards for the job market.

References

American Political Science Association. 2021. APSA Graduate Placement Report: Analysis of Political Science Placements for 2018-2020. https://preprints.apsanet.org/engage/api-gateway/apsa/assets/orp/resource/item/61649e5d8b620d1d574c4b7f/original/apsa-graduate-placement-report-analysis-of-political-science-placements-for-2018-2020.pdf. Accessed October 18, 2021.

American Political Science Association 2019. APSA Statement of Student Evaluations of Teaching. https://www.asanet.org/sites/default/files/asa_statement_on_student_evaluations_of_teaching_feb132020.pdf. Accessed December 17, 2021.

American Political Science Association. 2005. Women's Advancement in Political Science: A Report on the APSA Workshop on the Advancement of Women in Academic Political Science in the United States. https://www.apsanet.org/portals/54/Files/Task%20Force%20Reports/Womens_Advancement_in_Political_Science_2005.pdf. Accessed August 16, 2022.

45 The Academic Interview/Marathon

Christopher Macaulay[1] & Michelle D. Deardorff[2]

1. West Texas A&M University 2. University of Tennessee at Chattanooga

KEYWORDS: Academic Interview, On-Campus Interview, Job Talk.

Introduction

The academic interview is a crucial part of the job application process, and typically serves as job candidates' first in-person interaction with their prospective employer and colleagues. Throughout the process, employers will evaluate candidates on metrics often difficult to discern through applications or virtual interviews. Interviewers take this opportunity to judge a candidate's skills and fit in their department, both in terms of teaching and research, as well as their ability to work well with potential colleagues and administrators. Similarly, this is an important chance for candidates to evaluate the match between the institution, position, and their own expectations. This chapter will use the style of a discussion between junior and senior faculty to help the reader better understand a typical interview process.

Chris is a fifth year assistant professor of political science. He is pretty new to the job application process, and his perspective is one of junior faculty and more recent job candidates. *Michelle*, Department Head and Professor, has served as a department chair at three very different kinds of universities, as a Dean of Arts and Sciences, and has coordinated a lot of faculty hiring over the last 30 years. So, her perspective may be a bit different than Chris', but the two hope to demystify this process a bit.

Pre-Interview

Preparation

Chris: Before I went to a job interview, I engaged in some thorough preparation rituals. Among those were mock interviews and job talks—some hosted by my institution, and others on my own—testing the timing of my presentations, prepping for difficult questions I might be asked, and practicing maintaining a professional and confident tone throughout the process. It definitely helped practicing in front of a real audience. I was hit by some good critiques and questions by my advisor and fellow grad students and appreciated having confident responses prepared. What sort of preparation do you recommend, Michelle, and have you had some interviewees that clearly did not prepare adequately for their interview?

Michelle: My primary advice is to study the website and investigate the department and the institution thoroughly. Review the advertisement and think carefully about how you contribute to their vision of an ideal candidate. I have met candidates who had confused us with another institution, thought they could teach whatever they wanted, or clearly communicated that we would be so fortunate to have them that they did not need to impress us. None of these candidates were successful.

Chris: I understand that different institutions have different expectations for their faculty, and not just in terms of teaching versus research. R1 institutions have higher research-related expectations compared to more teaching-oriented institutions, and it's important for applicants to understand and prepare for this. An R1 (research) institution will be much more interested in a job talk that outlines plans for future research, and makes clear the candidate's statistical training and ability to publish. A teaching institution (e.g., a small liberal arts college) will be judging an interviewee's presentation skills more thoroughly, as well as interactions with students. Since I interviewed at an institution that expected a good split of teaching and research credentials, balancing both facets was key, and I made sure that my research talk included elements that demonstrated my teaching effectiveness. See also chapters 36–41 in this volume for more specific insights into hiring at different types of institutions.

Michelle: If a campus is mission-driven—such as a religious institution, an historically black college or university (HBCU), or tribal-serving institution—and that mission is referenced in the ad, it is part of that campus' DNA and you must take it seriously. Think about your ability to contribute to that mission and how comfortable you would be at a campus where that is part of everything they do. I had candidates who interviewed at the HBCU where I taught who had not thought about what it meant to be in an Afro-centric program, focusing on primarily African-American students.

Virtual Interview

Chris: Let us not forget that for most prospective employees, the first step and first interaction with their future employer is not on campus, but over the phone or on Zoom. Typically, the committee conducts virtual interviews of a smaller pool of applicants, asking them a slate of questions in order to determine who is invited to campus. Any of the above regarding attire, confidence, and attitude applies, even without an in-person interaction. I treated my phone interview as seriously as the campus visit itself, and similarly prepped some questions to ask the interviewers as well. Compared to the campus visit though, it was relatively short and most of the questions were pretty surface level. It seemed as though the interviewers were more concerned with checking that I was a serious candidate, had an agreeable personality, and my credentials matched my application. They also asked a few clarification questions on some things that were vague or unclear in the application.

Michelle: The virtual interview can seem rote because committees are replicating the same questions every interview in order to control the potential of implicit bias, so you need to be specific in answering but not excessive, ensuring all questions are covered and there is time to ask your own questions. At teaching-focused institutions, it is always safe to ask the committee to talk about their perception of their student body, at research institutions ask about resources for new faculty, and at hybrid institutions you can ask both questions. Have some charisma—this is a bit of a performance. If you do not seem excited to be there, the committee will ask themselves why they should keep you in the pool. If asked to a campus interview, you should contact whoever invited you to inquire about the types of presentations you will make, forms of technology available, and who constitutes the audiences. While you should receive an itinerary beforehand, departments often do not clearly share their expectations with the candidates. Even if they promise technology is available, it does not always work, so have a plan B (handouts, etc). Candidates who react with grace to the unexpected and recover are viewed very favorably. If you have dietary parameters and no one asks you ahead of time about these needs, contact the itinerary coordinator so that they are aware of your needs as they plan your visit.

Campus Interview

Purpose

Chris: Once all your preparation is complete, it is time for the on-campus interview. The exact process and specifics may vary by institution, but typically the on-campus interview involves some social dinners, a teaching and/or research presentation, and some interviews or meetings with administrators and faculty. My graduate program made a point of something that might be unclear to others preparing to leave grad school—that it is important for the interviewee to ask questions of their prospective employers, not just the other way around. I had a list of questions prepared, with some already answered based on my research, but that I wanted to ask anyway. They included questions regarding teaching load, research and service expectations, travel funding or allowance, expectations for tenure, and other quality of life questions about living in the area. I always thought it important to ask some things, even if your own research or convention made the answer rather obvious, if only to ensure you get a clear response and have clear expectations for the job.

Michelle: I agree, asking questions signals your seriousness regarding the position. I encourage candidates to ask the same questions of the different people you interact with so you can gauge if you are receiving similar or very different answers. One such question might be: what is the reputation of the department on campus and in the community? Another important question that can result in different answers is: what is expected for tenure and/or promotion?

Chris: Obviously, the goal of the on-campus interview as a candidate is to convince the institution to hire you. However, what are the goals of the on-campus interview from the employers' perspective?

Michelle: One of the major goals is to gain a sense of how you will engage in the life of the department and assess your collegiality. For tenure-track jobs, the campus interview is like one blind date before you become engaged to be married. So, the faculty are asking will you "wear well" as a colleague and contribute to their needs longitudinally. Meals are a great way to get to know candidates in an informal setting and for candidates to gain a sense of the department's personality and environment. See meals as part of the interview and bring your "A" game. Everything you do and say will most likely be communicated to the larger department. I often have untenured faculty take out the candidate for the first meal in order to make it less stressful and gain a better sense of what the candidate is like in more informal circumstances. I have seen candidates be so relaxed with junior faculty that they forget these colleagues are part of the hiring committee—do not do that.

Chris: All of the above should be on the candidate's minds, and also, they should be evaluating the fit of the institution and its faculty as well! The meals and social interactions should be two-way, and the candidate should be asking themselves if they feel comfortable in that environment. If it is a tenure track job, in particular, this could be their working environment for 5+ years! I echo your call to remain professional and err on the side of formality—it is far more likely to be a problem if a candidate is too casual, rather than too formal.

Campus Norms

Chris: Another important thing to address—having the proper attire. While subtle, arriving to an interview dressed appropriately is crucial, as failure to do so can send a signal that the interviewee either does not take the job seriously, or will not fit in with their peers. It is always better to be a bit too formal than a bit too casual, especially at institutions that have more of a "conservative" culture when it comes to attire and professionalization. It is advisable to wear formal attire, including suits and jackets. I have heard stories from senior colleagues about interviewees who arrived in sandals and shorts, or other informal attire, and it sank their job prospects.

Michelle: Every campus and department has its own norms and culture; follow the lead of the department in terms of address. If you are referred to by a title, refer to everyone else by their title, but if you are called by your first name, reciprocate with others—you are there to be a colleague, not a student (see chapter 9 in this volume for more about titling). Dress more professionally than you probably would on a daily basis, realizing that some campuses—like HBCUs—are generally more formal in dress and address all the time.

Chris: It can be difficult as a junior faculty or ABD graduate student to address your colleagues by first name. I typically stayed on the side of caution by referring to my interviewers by title first unless otherwise corrected. Colleagues are not the only ones we need to think about in terms of professional interaction—what about students and administrative assistants or staff?

Michelle: I have found that one of the most telling indicators of what kind of colleague a person will be is in how they treat those they perceive as having little power. To that end, I ask the administrative assistant about their experience in working with each candidate—someone who treats the admin rudely or dismissively will not get the offer. You might be surprised how frequently this occurs. I know how candidates talk to me and treat me is not indicative of how they treat others they perceive to be "less important." First of all, as political scientists we should understand that the admin has tremendous implementation power in the department. Second, if someone is rude to the admin how will they treat our students? Alumni? Prospective students? Do not yell or snap at the admin or forget to thank them; they just want to help you.

Chris: I cannot agree more. Administrative assistants are vital to the job process and crucial to administrators and departments alike—treating them poorly is a very easy way to draw the ire of an entire department and impede the entire process. How quickly people forget who is handling the paperwork, entering the data, and otherwise helping interface between departments, colleges, and colleagues! That, and it's the basic human decency anyone should expect—and I certainly would not want to work with or under anyone who acts that way.

Engaging Students

Chris: While I have been more insulated from that aspect of job interviewee missteps, the one I have encountered more frequently is disastrous interactions with undergraduate and graduate students. Every institution cares deeply about its students, and while teaching may be more or less central to the candidates' desired position, positive interaction with students is vital. While a graduate student, we have had multiple job candidates with impressive resumes either bore the students with their lecture or outright demean or condescend to them. These complaints were forwarded to the hiring committee and almost certainly doomed their application, which was otherwise quite strong. At institutions where faculty are expected to mentor graduate students and serve as their advisors, demonstrating not just teaching effectiveness but the ability to positively interact with graduate students is essential.

Michelle: At institutions that define themselves as student-centric, the meetings with students—graduate and undergraduate—can make or break an interview. The students who participate in these interviews are often those with the strongest ties to the department and the closest relationships to the faculty. Once, we did not hire a candidate because the students felt he did not take them seriously and instead talked to them like peers. Show students you like them and are excited to teach them, listen and be accessible, and be the mentor to them you wished you had as a graduate or undergraduate student. Again, this is part of the interview and anything you say will go back to the committee. Please realize that the department cannot control what students say in an interview and that student perspectives are just that.

Job Talk

Michelle: I do want to say a few words about the job talk, as this is often very stressful for the candidate and in my experience very relevant for the decision of the department. Think about the nature of the institution as you design your talk. A teaching talk that is pure lecture with no student engagement may not send the right message; but a talk that is all small group work where faculty do not see your ability to engage students does not sell you sufficiently. Most graduate students find the research talk the easiest, but remember you are presenting your research to people from multiple subfields so you are giving this talk for generalists, not your committee. The hardest talk is the hybrid, where you present your research to undergraduates. In this situation, you want to demonstrate you can clearly communicate the significance and purpose of your research to a very elementary audience. Do not condescend to undergraduates. Instead, attempt to bring their knowledge into play in your presentations (theories, definitions of basic terms, key literature, etc).

Chris: My experience with the job talk was that it seemed to be a test by the faculty of the ability to present myself and ideas clearly, and their first real experience with me in a professional environment. I have attended other job talks where a candidate appeared excellent on paper but was not particularly effective at communicating their ideas—which reflects poorly on both their research skills, as well as their future teaching abilities. The job talk is the place to distinguish oneself from other equally qualified candidates, by demonstrating your value.

Michelle: There is a bit of a dance that is done at the interview. We want to sell our community, our campus, and our department in a way that meets your needs, but we are also (or should be) very aware of all the questions we cannot ask to learn what your needs may be (a partner's employment, children, religion, need for a welcoming community). So, sometimes departments try to anticipate your needs and guess wrong, or share personal things in the hope you will share as well. Sometimes these conversations are done with good intentions and sometimes not. If inappropriate questions are raised I would encourage you to alert the department. If it is the department head who is the offender, you can let the search chair know. If you directly report to the Dean or Human Resources, most likely that job will not be offered. You have some choices to make when inappropriate comments are made: you can alert people during the interview (see above); you can wait until the decision is made and then contact human resources; or you can do nothing. These are complicated decisions. If a comment is made in a public setting, watch how the others in the room respond–are they embarrassed? Act as if they expect this individual to behave this way? Surprised? Do they challenge him? Or are others oblivious to the problematic nature of the comment or question? The response of others in the room may help you decide how to navigate the complaint. In my experience, when inappropriate questions are asked, I used humor to indicate that I recognized the question was inappropriate and so I would not answer. After the interview, I evaluated the event to see how it impacted my relationship to the institution (to report or not report).

After the Interview

Chris: Once the interview is completed, and job candidates return home, they often consider the process complete and simply wait idly by for a response from the institution. Is that wise?

Thank You Notes

Michelle: I think the first thing a candidate should do upon returning home is write a thank you note to the people they have met. A note a few days after your visit is an excellent opportunity to remind the committee why they liked you and to stand out from the other candidates. You could send an email to everyone you met (they are all listed on your itinerary) or mail a handwritten note to the entire department. In your missive, discuss what you discovered in the interview about the department or university and why you are still excited by the position. This leaves a very positive impression with the department.

Decision-Making Process

Chris: Another source of anxiety for many candidates, myself included, is the waiting period following an interview. I know from experience that this can be lengthy through no fault of the institution. Even when my institution interviewed only one candidate, it took a week to gather the faculty and debate a final decision on whether to make an offer, then another week to get the necessary paperwork and administrative things together.

    Michelle: The time after the interview can be nerve-racking in that you expect a decision to be made immediately after the last candidate leaves. However, there are reference calls to make, feedback to collect from all of the participants in the interview, meetings to schedule with the search committee, and a department chair, dean, and maybe a provost to be convinced of the right decision. And so much documentation to file with the Office of Equity and Inclusion and Human Resources. This process can take much longer than you expect. So, no news, may simply be the complicated timetable of resolving these decisions. Once permission is given to make an offer, a phone call will be made to see if the preferred candidate is still interested. While candidates often want the offer in writing, institutions may not allow written offers until the candidate demonstrates that they are still interested.

Negotiating

Chris: While the offer is a moment of elation for many candidates, it also raises one last important hurdle—negotiations. I learned I was the only candidate to whom an offer was made, and likely missed out on a chance to get a slightly higher salary.

Michelle: Negotiating an offer can be tricky and this varies greatly from institutions. This is where your graduate faculty may be less helpful unless you are navigating an offer from an R1 institution. Be sure to research as best you can to obtain a sense of the salary range at the institution to which you are applying. Some institutions may be able to offer start-up funding, guarantee a teaching release the first semester or year, or have pre-tenure sabbaticals on offer. For other institutions, none of these things are possible and it would be tone-deaf to demand them. Your discussions with junior faculty during the campus interview may help you determine what are realistic asks. This is also the time to discuss spousal hiring, which is harder for smaller campuses to accommodate than larger. See chapter 48 in this volume for more on navigating spousal hires.

Chris: What are your thoughts on deferring a decision, and should candidates be open about their competing offers and ask for more time, or use it as leverage?

Michelle: Yes, if you are only asking for an additional week, I think that is fair to ask. If you have not had the other campus interview yet or it is several weeks away, you would have to truly be the only competitive candidate for a department to be able to wait that long. This is a decent time to be transparent and see what the response might be—but if you accept the position, you need to withdraw from the other search. Political science is a smaller discipline. You do not want to get a reputation for going back on your contracts and word. (For more advice on negotiation, see chapter 46 in this volume.)

Chris: Thank you so much Michelle! It's been fascinating to hear about the interview process from someone with such extensive experience on the hiring side! This definitely helped clear up some misconceptions on my part about the process, and hopefully will help guide job candidates at every stage of the process to a more professional and effective interview!

Michelle: The interview process is difficult especially when the power resides in the hiring party and if the candidate feels as if they have to accept any job that is offered. You combine the many different personalities that we have in academic departments and the situation can be stressful. The interview process not only tells the department about the candidate, but the candidate can learn a great deal about the department in the process as well. Listen to what you learn, so you can make the decision that results in the best outcome for you and your long-term career.

46

You Have an Academic Job Offer...Now What? Negotiating Advice from Two Perspectives

William O'Brochta[1] & Lori Poloni-Staudinger[2]

1. Louisiana Tech University 2. University of Arizona

KEYWORDS: Offer Phone Call, Job Contract, Negotiation Process.

Introduction

Congratulations on receiving a job offer! Any job offer is a time to celebrate and then to consider your next steps. Successful job negotiations establish a collegial relationship between the job candidate and the negotiating institution while at the same time providing an opportunity for the job candidate to ask for additional resources that help to ensure success at that institution.

Negotiating a job offer is a new experience for many graduate students, and the excitement of receiving the offer may provoke an urge to accept the offer immediately. Most job offers are extended on the phone, so we recommend conveying your enthusiasm about the position, asking to receive the details of the offer via email, and asking for some time to consider the offer. Negotiating institutions should be more than understanding of these requests—perhaps even offering to communicate the offer in writing and to give you time to consider the offer without you needing to ask. Negotiation is an expected part of the job search process and one that is critically important, particularly given known inequities in negotiation outcomes (e.g., Claypool et al. 2017).Salary, research funding, teaching load, sabbatical opportunities, and moving expenses are just a few of an almost endless list of potential negotiation items (see, for example, Farris, Key, and Sumner 2022). The exact list of items over which you negotiate depends on both your needs and the resources available at the negotiating institution.

This chapter discusses strategies for navigating the time between receiving an *offer phone call* and signing a *job contract,* drawing first on the experiences of a dean who frequently engages in negotiations and then from a faculty member who recently went through the negotiation process. We begin by discussing common pitfalls to avoid during the *negotiation process,* following this with strategies for making negotiation easier and more successful. We conclude by describing the process of accepting a job offer and signing a job contract.

A Dean's Four Negotiation Pitfalls

As an administrator with experience negotiating with new faculty across several disciplines and in several different types of administrative positions—department chair, associate dean, and dean—I have seen common patterns emerge related to the "dos and don'ts" of negotiation. I will cover four key pitfalls candidates often make here.

Be Confident, Not Condescending

You worked hard; you got a PhD; you should be proud. You should also remember that the person sitting across the proverbial negotiating table from you also has worked hard. They are likely in a senior position and most definitely in an administrative position. They most likely do not rest on the laurels of their advisor or their doctoral program; they have achieved success in their own right.

Why is this important? Most students come out of graduate programs of a higher rank than that where they are seeking employment. The person you are negotiating with has been in the profession for much longer than you. You should be confident in your skills, but you should not be condescending to the person with whom you are negotiating. Don't name drop. Be aware of your implicit biases and make sure these are not showing through in your negotiations. Implicit bias is when we have a preference for (or aversion to) a person or group of people (Perception Institute 2021). It is implicit because it is an unconscious attitude (see implicit.harvard.edu for more on implicit biases or to test your own). This is a sure way to start off on a bad foot with a person you will need later for everything from finishing up your negotiation to asking for indexing fees for your first book.

You want the administrator to leave the negotiation feeling like you are bright and confident, but not like you tried to "one up" them. At the same time, be aware that deans also come with their own implicit biases. For example, there is some research out of the corporate world that indicates that women can be "punished" for negotiating (Shonk 2021). When you are aware of these biases, you can use the negotiation as an opportunity to educate, to inform and to turn the negotiation in your favor.

If You Don't Ask, You're Not Going to Get It—But Don't Go Too Far

I tell candidates, "Give me your holiday wish list, but don't ask for a unicorn." In other words, be reasonable. Usually, a chair or dean will tell you if they can't budge on something like salary, but they are able to do more in start-up or summer funding. Often moving expenses are capped in public institutions based on state mandates. If you are coming up with nothing but no, ask where there might be room for negotiation. The institution has decided they want you, but in most cases, they aren't going to be willing to get you at all costs. The academic labor market is a market like any other market with supply and demand. Keep this in mind. Make a list of things you would like to negotiate on and be prepared to walk away from some of them.

At the same time, be prepared to ask. Some people, particularly women, have anxiety with negotiating (Barron 2003). Practice with a friend or with yourself in the mirror so that you can ask with confidence (see point one above). While advisors can be helpful with what to ask for, they likely were placed at an institution with a higher rank and more resources (your doctoral institution) than where you got your offer, and in most cases, they were negotiating under different market conditions. Reach out to peers from similar types of institutions to where you got an offer and seek their advice on areas where you can negotiate.

Keep Perspective on Your Place in the Institution and the Larger Institutional Community

It is important that you research and understand the larger institutional context. Is the institution mainly a teaching institution? If so, you may not be able to negotiate a reduced teaching load, but you may be able to ask for summer pay and an undergraduate research assistant. Does the unit have a graduate program? Could you ask for a graduate assistant for a period of time to help on a research project while also securing funding for a student? Understanding the institution also means understanding how your new department is situated in the larger institution.

If you are going into a unit that is expected to generate general studies seats for the institution, you may find better luck asking for software or grading help than a pre-tenure sabbatical. If instead you are entering a unit where grant writing is common and expected, negotiating that term off may be an easier sell. It is also important that you understand the financial situation of the institution. Has it suffered from years of budget cuts? If so, negotiating on salary may be difficult as it will likely cause salary compression with colleagues who haven't had raises in several years. In short, know your audience and ask for things that make sense in the context in which you will be embedded.

Have Perspective on the Unit

You should do your homework and see what other faculty's workloads and salaries look like. If you are negotiating with a public institution, this information is often available. Make sure that you are aligning your requests to be in line with what is common in your new department. Some administrators are very concerned with compression. This means there may be a top salary bar above which they absolutely won't go over because to do so would bring you in at a higher rate than colleagues with more experience. In these instances, seek alternative areas of negotiation.

The same advice goes for negotiating on teaching load. Be sure to understand what the norm is among your new colleagues. If all faculty are on a 3/3 load, three courses per semester, (or a 3/3/3 for an institution on a quarter system), asking for a 0/1 is probably not realistic. You would stand a better chance of getting a yes by asking for a 2/2 for the first year, 3/2 the second year, and 3/3 thereafter. Remember, these will be your future colleagues. You do not want to start off making an impression that you expected to be treated better or differently than others in the unit. You want to build a spirit of collegiality from the first moments of negotiation until you step on to campus. You do not want to start off making an impression that you expected to be treated better or differently than others in the unit. You want to build a spirit of collegiality from the first moments of negotiation until you step on to campus.

A Faculty Member's Strategies for Successful Negotiations

Given these potential pitfalls, what are ways for you as a job candidate to increase your chances of conducting a successful negotiation? My main suggestion is to plan for the negotiation carefully and strategically. This may seem like obvious advice, but each negotiation has its own set of circumstances, opportunities, and challenges.

Approach the Negotiation from the Perspective of a New Faculty Member and Colleague

You may end up accepting the job offer, so a confrontational negotiation process could create a negative first impression. You can avoid confrontation by clearly understanding who you are negotiating with and what their timeline is. You may negotiate with a department chair or a dean who then must take your list of negotiation items to someone else in the institution for approval instead of speaking with that person directly. In these cases, the person you are negotiating with is your messenger for the negotiation, so clearly explaining how each of your requests will benefit both you and the institution will help them to make your case to the approving authority. Confronting the messenger only serves to hurt your case.

Similarly, some institutions must end negotiations quickly for a wide variety of reasons. Aim for only one round of negotiations, so as not to drag the process along, especially when doing so presents challenges for the institution. Negotiating is rarely anyone's favorite part of the job search process, so keeping the negotiation friendly will improve your likelihood of success and reduce everyone's anxiety.

Negotiations often become confrontational when job candidates focus on negotiation items that institutions simply do not have the resources or ability to provide. As you view negotiating from the perspective of a new colleague at the institution, prepare yourself. Written offers often contain limited information. Some items that you may be interested in discussing during a negotiation—like parental leave or sabbaticals—may be listed in formal institutional policies or on the websites of various institutional departments. Salaries are often public information at many state institutions, and you may find that there is a state-mandated salary range. Checking for this information on your own before asking helps to show that you are taking the negotiation seriously and allows you to focus your requests on key items that the institution does not already provide to all employees.

One excellent way to find out about the norms surrounding negotiating at a particular institution is to informally ask faculty you met during your interview. Once they have decided to extend you a job offer, faculty members want you to come to their institution. Many times, they will reach out to you offering to talk or to answer questions about the position. Otherwise, reach out and ask to talk informally to faculty. This is a perfect time to get to know your new colleagues a bit better and to ask informally about negotiation items. Asking non-specific questions like "can you tell me a bit about what resources are usually provided to new faculty members?" or "I wondered if you had any advice as I discuss the details of the job offer with [my negotiating partner]?" provides willing faculty an opportunity to share their institutional knowledge. Listen carefully both to what faculty members say and what they imply. If faculty explicitly say that some items are non-negotiable (usually salary or teaching load), heed their advice. Explaining to your negotiating partner that you understand that a certain item is non-negotiable and, therefore, that you are not going to negotiate for it goes a long way in generating goodwill. If one of the non-negotiable items means that you are no longer interested in accepting the offer, you are better equipped to bring the item up in a sensitive way during the negotiation.

Gather Advice from Colleagues at Similar Institutions

Once you have learned all you can about negotiating at the institution, gather advice from as many colleagues as you can who work at similar institutions. Try to find institutions that match on as many characteristics as possible. For example, there are many research universities, but the advice most relevant to you comes from faculty at research universities with a similar size, location, cross-institution consortium, departmental degree offerings, departmental size and emphasis, and tenure standards. You may not know faculty at these "most similar" institutions: many faculty at these institutions will be responsive to an email explaining why you are contacting them and asking for advice. Alternatively, find faculty you or your advisors know that get as close to this list as possible.

Prioritize Asks Based on Your Own Needs

By now, you will have amassed a vast amount of information and advice about negotiating, with perhaps twenty or more items people have suggested that you ask for. There are also countless online lists of recommended negotiation items. Only you can prioritize. One way to do this is to stop collecting information a few days before the negotiation, therefore reserving some time to think about your priorities. Remember that you are the one who may ultimately accept the job offer, not those from whom you received advice. Consider the tradeoff between negotiating over one-time resources like a new computer and longer-term benefits like salary. At the same time, the financial costs of taking a new job are high; ask for resources if the institution has not offered to provide them and if they will help you.

Negotiate

The final step is conducting the actual negotiation, which most often occurs via phone. It may be helpful to prepare a script for yourself thanking your negotiating partner, expressing enthusiasm for the job offer, listing three or four negotiation items, and then describing each item in detail. The negotiation items you discuss should be your top negotiation priorities. It is good to have a mix of requests that you think that the institution can fulfill and items that may be a bit more challenging. Above all, choose the items that you need to be happy at that institution. Be clear about your intentions: are you almost ready to accept the job offer and these items are things you think will be beneficial or are these items required for you to accept? As you describe your items, focus on how each item helps the institution to succeed. For example, a course release benefits students because you have more time to carefully prepare appropriate teaching materials.

Post-Negotiation

End the negotiation by asking about what happens next in the hiring process. Usually, your negotiating partner will need to review the items you raised and get back to you with a revised job offer. At that point, if you are satisfied with the revised offer, signing the offer represents a formal commitment between you and the institution. Some additional approvals may be required, but those are typically pro forma. You can then turn your attention to getting ready for your new position!

You may decide that you are not interested in accepting the offer regardless of the outcome of negotiations or after the first round of negotiation. This too is a valid response to receiving a job offer, and you can communicate this to your negotiating partner via phone.

Conclusion

When you receive a job offer, you are undoubtedly excited. We recommend that you first pause and congratulate yourself on a successful search. Then, get to work on the negotiation. Negotiations that are approached strategically and collegially are going to be the most successful.

It will also be important for you to do your homework, getting to learn about your new place of work and your new colleagues. Both you and your future employer have an interest in maintaining collegiality throughout the process so that you start your new position with all sides feeling excited at the prospect of your employment. If you approach your negotiating process prepared and with realistic expectations, you will get off on the right foot as you start your career in academia. Employers will appreciate your reasonable approach to the negotiation process and you will leave feeling as if some of your needs were met. Good luck, and welcome to the academy!

References

Barron Lisa A. 2003. "Ask and you shall Receive? Gender Differences in Negotiators' Beliefs about Requests for a Higher Salary." *Human Relations*, 56(6): 635-662.

Claypool, Vicki Hesli, Brian David Janssen, Dongkyu Kim, and Sara McLaughlin Mitchell. 2017. "Determinants of Salary Dispersion Among Political Science Faculty." *PS: Political Science & Politics,* 50(1): 146-156.

Perception Institute. 2021. "Implicit Bias." *Research: Science & Perception.* https://perception.org/research/implicit-bias/.

Shonk, Katie. 2021. "Challenges Facing Women Negotiators." *Harvard Law School Program on Negotiation Daily Blog*, September 28. https://www.pon.harvard.edu/daily/leadership-skills-daily/women-and-negotiation-leveling-the-playing-field/.

47

Started From the Bottom, Now We're Here: Navigating the Job Market Without A "Top-Tier" PhD

Rachel E. Finnell[1] & Alexandra T. Middlewood[2]

1. Bethany College 2. Wichita State University

KEYWORDS: Top-Tier PhD, Desired Career Outcome.

Introduction

Being on the job market is one of the most precarious and daunting tasks one faces during their graduate career. Earning a PhD from outside a "top-tier" program may add additional—albeit often unnecessary—stress. As an upcoming graduate of a non-top-tier program, the challenges one faces can be dramatically different than others navigating the job market. Graduating from a top-tier program is not a requisite for success. Both authors graduated from a non-top-tier program and obtained tenure track jobs immediately, though at very different types of institutions—one author teaches at a small religious liberal arts college while the other teaches at a medium-sized R2 public university. Thus, we offer firsthand evidence and experience on what helped us be successful on the job market. Furthermore, we provide limited advice and tips on how to excel on the job market beyond the academic route, and we strongly encourage readers to refer to chapter 41 of this volume on non-traditional options for more extensive advice.

In this chapter, we discuss the quandary with program rankings, provide considerations for setting beneficial goals for tackling the job market, offer guidance on creating and utilizing academic networks, and discuss the teaching versus research debate.

Program Rankings

The ranking of one's doctoral program does not determine success on the academic or non-academic job market. Make no mistake, program rankings exist, and they do matter to some extent, but they are only one factor of job market success. Focusing on program rankings often overlooks what those rankings tell us about job market trends. The most recent report available, the APSA Graduate Placement Report: Analysis of Political Science Placements for 2017-2018, provides some insight into the state of the political science job market prior to the COVID-19 pandemic. While there is not an abundance of data available on political science graduate placements, this report does provide a glimpse into overarching trends in job market placements for the 2017-2018 academic year.

According to the report, top-tier programs are much more likely to place candidates into postdoctoral positions. In the top twenty percent of political science PhD programs—as ranked by the National Research Council—nearly 62% of candidates accepted postdoctoral positions for their first placement. The report indicates that these candidates were sixteen percent more likely to take a postdoctoral placement than a tenure track job. Of all job candidates that accepted tenure track positions, only forty-six percent were from those top programs. The remaining fifty-four percent of candidates who accepted tenure track positions came from non-top-tier programs.

These placements suggest that most PhD programs know their strengths. Top-tier programs tend to be heavily focused on research, and as such they encourage their candidates to seek out postdoctoral positions to further develop research skills and are quite successful in those placements. Additionally, it is well known throughout the discipline that top-tier PhD programs tend to hire job candidates from other top programs. Whereas the placements of non-top-tier candidates are more varied. PhD students at mid-range or lower ranked programs should expect to have greater chances of being hired at programs ranked lower than the one attended for doctoral studies. Most often, these candidates will be successful in political science departments without PhD programs. The sheer number of political science programs with only undergraduate or undergraduate and masters' programs far outnumber those that grant PhDs. There are certainly instances where mid-tier candidates do successfully get hired in PhD granting departments but doing so is often out of the norm.

Again, these trends speak to the fact that most PhD programs know their own strengths and utilize that knowledge to benefit their students on the job market. As such, non-top-tier students often take a different path throughout graduate school than their top-tier counterparts. Mid-tier and lower-ranked PhD programs tend to have a strong teaching focus alongside research. Mid- and lower-range programs know that their students will be most successful at institutions that emphasize teaching and often underscore the importance of getting this experience while in graduate school, especially as an instructor of record. When teaching-focused departments hire new faculty, having classroom experience can be extremely advantageous for job candidates. As this teaching emphasis is generally not found within top-tier programs, candidates from lower ranked programs have a distinct advantage over candidates from higher ranked PhD programs.

Knowing the job placements of prior graduates is helpful to setting job market goals. For example, the authors' doctoral program has been very successful at placing students into tenure track jobs at teaching-focused institutions and liberal arts colleges, with a few placements at R2 and mid- or low-tier R1 institutions. Recognizing this, we were able to set realistic job market goals and develop targeted experiences that ultimately helped secure tenure track jobs. If there is any uncertainty about previous job placements within one's department, it is advantageous to speak with other graduate students, the graduate director, professors, and one's advisor about this information.

Setting Beneficial Goals for the Job Market

When it comes to being successful on the job market, one of the most valuable things a PhD student can do is to set goals early. These goals should include deciding an area(s) of specialization and whether the goal is an academic or non-academic career path. The sooner these decisions are made, the more direction doctoral students will have throughout their graduate career and beyond. Not only will this help guide one's path towards the job market, but it will help align decisions throughout graduate school with one's job market goals—such as teaching vs. research.

These decisions can be made in consultation with one's advisor, mentors, or on one's own. Seeking advice from advisors, and other academic mentors, can help significantly with this goal-setting process. Some faculty are more attuned to academic trajectories while others to non-academic careers; some are more research focused while others put more emphasis on teaching. As a result, seeking advice from multiple advisors or mentors to gain different perspectives can be beneficial when making a decision.

We want to emphasize, however, that a PhD student's desired career outcome should reign supreme. If an advisor is not supportive of a student's goals post-PhD, then an alternative advisor, or additional mentors, may be necessary. Importantly, it is okay to find alternative mentors and/or advisors should a current one no longer be a healthy fit or supportive of the student's overall vision for their future—whether it be due to focusing on teaching, research, other professional choices being made, or possible personality clashes (see chapter 13 on selecting an advisor versus a mentor, and chapter 7 on building a supportive mentoring network).

First and foremost, choosing an area of study is particularly important. Generally, departments tend to specialize in certain research areas that graduate students will often gravitate towards. While it is of course possible to study a topic outside of one's advisor's specialty, we do not recommend it. The experience necessary to succeed on the job market with a research agenda outside the norm for the department and/or advisor does not always lead to disaster—some graduate students can and do excel in this type of environment. However, most benefit substantially by focusing on the research specialty of their department. Networking and co-authored publications are more easily attained when a graduate student's area of research aligns with their advisor. For these reasons, deciding an area of specialization as soon as possible is a critical step in the job market process (see chapter 10 on choosing a subfield and committees).

Academic and Non-Academic Career Choices

In addition, decide as early as possible about the academic versus non-academic career question. When choosing a career path, it is important to understand the diversity each of these paths provide. From different types of institutions in the academic realm to a blossoming job market in the non-academic sector, a graduate degree in political science is a valuable and useful asset for your future career plans.

The heterogeneity of institutions and career choices include everything from tenure-track to adjuncting, as well as institutions from R1 to community college. Regardless of the type of academic job, networking is critical. Frequently, the key to being hired for an academic job is having connections at several different institutions. This is especially true when graduating from a non-top-tier program. While there is no "right" way to network, regional networking is very effective for obtaining teaching-focused positions. These connections can be made through smaller regional and/or state political science conferences, online through Twitter or LinkedIn, and to some extent during large conferences (see chapter 21 on how to conference). Most non-top-tier PhD programs are very successful at placing graduates at regional institutions. As a result, networking with prior graduates, especially those who are employed at local colleges and universities, can be invaluable and even lead to job placement. Furthermore, it is common for PhD students in non-top-tier programs to adjunct at local institutions, including community colleges, during graduate school. Not only do these positions bolster curriculum vitaes, they also establish connections at several types of local institutions that can be beneficial when navigating the academic job market.

The choice to take an academic career path can often drive the need for outside teaching experiences—that is being an instructor of record at an institution outside of one's PhD granting institution. This experience is especially important for graduates from non-top-tier PhD programs. Being an instructor of record at an area community college, college, or university provides a more diverse skill set than only having experience as a teaching assistant. Students at large universities are generally quite different, in terms of their lived experiences and their academic and personal needs, from those who attend community colleges or small liberal arts institutions. When outside teaching opportunities are not possible—as is often the case for international students—teaching multiple courses as an instructor of record at one's own institution is extremely beneficial. Having this diverse teaching experience, as well as a background developing and teaching courses, signals to hiring committees that candidates will have less of a learning curve and as such this experience is immensely beneficial on the job market.

On the other hand, finding a career in the non-academic sector is a viable choice. In fact, several career opportunities are available for those who decide that teaching is not their goal. Most often, the private sector offers jobs centered around data analysis or other skills you have learned throughout graduate studies. The reality is being a social scientist prepares doctoral students well for the diverse challenges the world faces. Maybe you want to work for the government, a nonprofit organization, think tank, or large corporation? These are all excellent career choices for which a graduate degree in political science prepares you.

The Great Debate: Teaching vs. Research

Where should graduate students focus their time? Is it more advantageous to take on additional teaching responsibilities or should research be the focal point? The ultimate answer to these questions is it depends. It depends on the career goals discussed in the previous section—will it be academic or non-academic? Additionally, it is important to note that these are extremely broad categories and there is much variation within those silos. This variation, and the ultimate outcome, underscores why setting career goals early is essential for all PhD candidates. These choices provide costs and benefits that must be weighed as a graduate student. While research is important for one's work as a scholar and in the discipline, the authors know firsthand that research and publications do not define one's job market prospects. Every academic career is different.

Teaching Experience

If one chooses the academic route, one of the most important things a graduate student from a non-top-tier program can do is diversify the courses they teach and seek instructor of record opportunities. The reality is, there are more teaching institutions in the United States than there are research intensive universities. While most political science departments will have some research expectations, a majority will focus more, or equally, on teaching. These are the types of institutions where non-top-tier PhD students are most likely to be hired, and therefore starting to prepare for that experience while in graduate school is beneficial. To note, the decision to focus on gaining teaching experience can be a controversial one, mostly because it is a different path than faculty at PhD granting institutions experienced (see chapter 36 on what your advisors can't tell you because they don't know). If one's advisor is ill-equipped to offer advice on teaching experience, students should seek out mentorship from other faculty, either in their department, at conferences, or other academic social networking opportunities.

One key to a successful job market experience is to be the instructor of record for numerous courses. If these courses are across subfields, it is even more beneficial. Note that subfields do not need to necessarily be one's area of study. For example, most political science professors are needed for general education and degree requirement fulfilling courses like American Government. As a political scientist, one should be well equipped to teach an introduction to political science course that provides a general survey of the field itself, regardless of individual specialization. Courses such as these are useful additions to any teaching portfolio. Other introductory courses include Introduction to Comparative Politics and Introduction to International Relations. While those who major in these subfields are likely better equipped to teach the courses, having the ability to teach multiple introductory courses can give non-top-tier candidates a leg up, particularly with smaller-sized departments where all faculty teach introductory courses.

Courses beyond introductory are also helpful to teach as a graduate student. In fact, upper-level courses can be some of the most insightful and exciting courses professors teach. Often, these courses are focused on more specific topics and specialty knowledge—frequently from a dissertation topic or research agenda. For those graduate students most interested in teaching upper-level undergraduate courses and master's or PhD level courses, these courses can be particularly valuable in a teaching portfolio. From influencing the formation of a teaching statement to growth in teaching pedagogy, teaching is deeply beneficial for graduate students from non-top-tier programs. Diverse teaching experience should be highlighted as a unique strength in application materials. Further, speaking with one's advisor is a great way to decide which sorts of courses taught would speak to individual strengths and the current needs of the department.

While teaching and developing multiple courses during graduate school is a lot of additional work, it is invaluable to job candidates applying to teaching-focused departments. It shows the hiring committee that the candidate has experience developing coursework, teaching classes, and building rapport with students. It can also provide additional teaching evaluations to include with application materials.[1] While not the focus of this chapter, or even this publication, having teaching experience can also be extremely beneficial beyond graduate school. In an academic job, it serves the benefit of creating less course prep—we found this extremely helpful when trying to navigate new jobs and campuses. Additionally, teaching experience can also be beneficial in a non-academic job. Classroom teaching skills can easily translate to experience with meeting administration and conflict resolution, which are valuable in any career field.

Research Experience

While most non-top-tier PhD students are hired at teaching focused institutions, most still have some research requirements. Therefore, gaining research experience while in graduate school is still useful. Research allows new scholars to sharpen their skills and distinguish their dissertation and research interests within the field of political science.

Research skills develop most while writing the dissertation. When selecting a dissertation topic, it is important to choose a topic that is both enjoyable and interesting. Given the emphasis on teaching at most colleges and universities where non-top-tier candidates frequently obtain jobs, it can also be advantageous to choose a dissertation topic that is applicable to multiple subfields and teaching areas. For example: using mixed methods within a dissertation; choosing a topic that could connect to several types of courses, like public opinion or political behavior; or even choosing an interdisciplinary topic. The dissertation phase is the best time to be creative with research and figure out what is enjoyable. Choosing a dissertation topic will naturally extend beyond the research realm and into the classroom.

From the dissertation there are opportunities to present at conferences and publish. Networking at conferences is a great way to meet future coauthors, gain exposure to new research in the discipline, build confidence as an upcoming scholar, and create connections that can be helpful on the job market. Additionally, research completed during a PhD can sometimes count towards tenure, while also aiding in the development of knowledge in the field. Overall, having research experience in addition to teaching experience can only help one's job market chances as a graduate of a non-top-tier program and as such is worthy of time and effort while in graduate school.

Conclusion

Navigating the job market from a mid- or lower-tier PhD program is not as dire as it is sometimes made out to be. In fact, students can be very successful on the academic job market and graduating from a top tier institution is not a requisite for a tenure track job. The keys to success are setting clear obtainable goals, seeking outside teaching experience, and highlighting unique strengths and experiences in job applications. One of the most significant tasks necessary as a graduate student at a non-top-tier program is to network as much as possible. While following the advice presented in this chapter will not guarantee a job, we hope it makes the process less uncertain and provides graduate students from non-top-tier political science programs with a roadmap to help navigate the job market.

Endnotes

1   The authors acknowledge the vast depth of research that has been conducted on discriminatory bias and teaching evaluations (e.g. Chávez and Mitchell 2020), but unfortunately, evaluations are still currently used as a measure of teaching effectiveness and are often requested as part of academic job applications.

References

Chávez, Kerry, and Kristina M.W. Mitchell. 2020. "Exploring Bias in Student Evaluations: Gender, Race, and Ethnicity." *PS: Political Science & Politics* 53(2): 270–74.

McGrath, Erin, and Megan Davis. 2019. APSA Graduate Placement Report: Analysis of Political Science Placements for 2017-2018. *Politics and International Relations*. preprint. https://preprints.apsanet. org/engage/apsa/article-details/5d2dd689f4cf65001aa0744b (August 11, 2021).

48

Getting "Us" a Job: The Two+ Body Problem and the Academic Job Market

Tyler P. Yates[1]

1. University of Maryland, College Park

KEYWORDS: The Two+ Body Problem, Rising Cost of Living.

What is the Two+ Body Problem?

In the United States, more than half of relationships include dual career couples where both partners have their own respective jobs (Petriglieri 2019; Su 2019). For such couples, dual careers are often seen as both an issue of identity and economic need (Scurry and Clarke 2021; Blossfeld and Drobnic 2001). When an individual's career path has required years of education, ambition, and hard work much of who they are has become tied up in their career. Such investments are difficult for people to give up for any reason—especially if they have yet to reach their career goal. In the past, multiple career households may have been considered a luxury— an opportunity for greater economic freedom, but for many couples today having dual careers has transitioned into a necessity (Heckman 2011). The rising costs of living, inflation, stagnant wages, and the expenses associated with raising children create pressure for households to require multiple providers and sources of income. Under these conditions, job uncertainty has the potential to develop into near existential issues. Any career decision—especially those that involve relocation—must necessarily incorporate the career prospects and needs of the rest of the household. This two+ body problem occurs when an individual is seeking a new job with the added considerations of finding employment for a partner (LaFerriere 2017; Wolf-Wendel, Twombly, and Rice 2004). In such situations what is best for one person's career may not be in the best interest of their partners' career.

When it comes to the world of academia, dual careers—and the two+ body problem—have become increasingly prevalent, yet the academic job market and traditional hiring practices tend to compound an already difficult problem (Khan et al. 2021). This is because academic jobs are shaped around individuals rather than couples. Academia typically requires applicants to put position and opportunity over location and other factors. This is especially true for academics attempting to land a tenure-track position (Chait 2005). In any given year the supply of academic jobs almost always overwhelms the demand (Larson, Ghaffarzadegan, and Xue 2014). Most successful applicants will apply to tens, if not hundreds, of jobs before receiving a placement offer. The uncertainty inherent in this stressful process is intensified when the needs of a partner are added to the equation. The purpose of this chapter is to unpack and demystify the two+ body problem in academia. It is not a problem without solutions, though successful navigation requires compromise, patience, and long-term planning.

Why Does the Two+ Body Problem Occur?

The academic job process is not currently structured in a way conducive to alleviating or overcoming the two+ body problem. The application and interview phases of the job process focus on finding an ideal candidate and competition demands applicants frame themselves in a competitive way (Larson et al. 2019; Whitaker 2018). Though irrelevant to academic qualifications, sharing personal life information has the potential to influence job prospects negatively (Roberts 2017). Applicants are often advised not to discuss information about their partners, family planning, or other personal matters unrelated to a job's requirements as this can introduce bias into hiring decisions. Female applicants have historically faced discrimination related to concerns about pregnancy and their likelihood of staying in a position after childbirth (Rivera 2017). LGBTQ+ applicants face discrimination based on their sexual orientation and/or gender identity (Prock et al. 2019). (For further discussion on this topic, see chapters 54-61 on implicit bias and discrimination.) Federal and state law often explicitly forbid asking questions about an applicant unrelated to the job requirements for this exact reason (Roberts 2017). This prohibition often does not extend to questions asked by applicants, but since applicants know the potential ramifications of introducing personal matters into the interview process it is not in their best interest to do so.

For most individuals on the academic job market, it is difficult to fully plan anything substantial about the future prior to receiving a job offer (Diehl 2021; Roberts 2017). This is due to the number of applications required to land a job and the distinct locales of universities or colleges. Even limiting applications geographically by region or state can still find applicants looking at jobs varying across a range of hundreds—if not thousands—of miles. This inability to pre-plan is especially problematic for the partners of academics on the job market. The best time to introduce questions about spousal hire or help finding a job in the community for a significant other is after a job offer is extended (Kaplan 2010). Most programs place a short turn-around clock on job offers, making it almost impossible to work out anything substantial before a decision is required. Departments want to fill open positions as soon as possible and most operate in good faith to negotiate the needs of the applicants they select. Spousal hires, especially those that involve departments other than the one hiring the applicant, can be somewhat complicated (Wolf-Wendel, Twombly, and Rice 2004). Even adjunct hirings often require approval from both school administrators and the requisite academic department. In rare cases, tenure track or visiting professor hirings are possible, but these often take even more time to negotiate. It is common for departments to promise to the best they can to help with spousal placement, but few are able to put any such provisions into writing. In job markets of the past, strong negotiations on this front may have forced results, but large numbers of qualified candidates and shrinking academic budgets have mitigated candidates' negotiating leverage.

Once an academic job offer is extended, negotiated, and accepted there are usually only months before an expected start date. Quick relocation is difficult under ideal circumstances. The stresses of finding a place to live, moving, and getting settled are only amplified when finding a job for a significant other is added to the list. Most departments can be helpful with this process, but the best way to overcome the two+ body problem is to understand it and plan contingencies prior to the acceptance stage of the academic job process.

How to Best Navigate the Two+ Body Problem

There is no one-size-fits-all solution for the two+ body problem. Spousal hiring practices, as well as employment needs, vary across universities, while relationship dynamics, mental health, job prospects, and career path requirements vary across individuals. While it is impossible to plan for the outcome of the academic job market, it is possible to plan for the best way to handle the two+ body problem across circumstances.

Communication Between Partners

A key step towards navigating the two+ body problem is to understand the dynamics of one's relationship. This involves thinking through the needs and wants of everyone involved and ascertaining the limits of an acceptable work-life balance. Communication is key to preventing one partner's viewpoints from overstepping. Achieving career goals may be important to both partners in the relationship, but there can be differences in the cost each partner is willing to weather. Early academic careers can be exceptionally stressful and having a significant other nearby for venting and support, or to provide an escape will be incredibly important for some people (Hollywood et al. 2020). Others may prefer space during the more busy and stressful parts of the job, viewing some relationship responsibilities as a potential distraction better suited for breaks or when time allows. Neither of these approaches is necessarily unhealthy if they are communicated and acceptable to both partners. Things become problematic if partners fail to understand how each approaches the career-relationship dynamic. Presuming knowledge of how a partner feels is not the same as asking, and the consequences of incongruity between partners can be detrimental to one's relationship and career. Other concerns like children, pets, or distance to extended family should also be included in two+ body problem discussions. The more a couple discusses potential concerns ahead of time, the less likely they will face surprises later.

Communicate Career Goals

While attempting to find one's ideal academic job it can be easy to lose sight of the career goals of a significant other. The job application process can quickly become a part-time job in and of itself, forcing applicants to spend less time thinking about the particulars associated with any one job. For this reason, it is imperative for couples to discuss and understand each other's long-term career goals prior to the job application onslaught. In many instances, it will be clear that successfully achieving everyone's goals will require compromise and time. The academic job market is stochastic in any given year, meaning it is difficult to know what opportunities will be available (Diehl 2021). Non-academic jobs are more stable, but this stability can make relocating for a partner's academic job exceedingly problematic.

Set Expectations for Different Job Offer Outcomes

For dual academic couples both seeking jobs, it will be unclear for months what offers will come available and to whom. Prior to applying for jobs, these couples should discuss what types of offers they are seeking and the conditions under which they would reject an offer. This step can mean prioritizing a better job, allowing one partner to further their career now while the other partner puts their plans on hold. The other partner may seek temporary work at the same university as their significant other or somewhere else nearby. This trade-off may only be sustainable long-term if the partner who received the better offer now accepts that they need to similarly compromise in the future.

Understand What Each Partner's Career Requires

For couples featuring a non-academic partner, there may be more options to pursue both career goals simultaneously, though this will depend on location and the type of non-academic job. Since the norms and trajectories of non-academic jobs often differ substantially from academic jobs, it is important that partners fully understand one another's careers. Just because a job may seem easily transferable to another location does not mean that it is. If a career requires building a reputation and relationships over time, relocating may be a step backwards. The distinction between job responsibilities, education requirements, and overall qualifications can differ between locations. Long-term non-academic career goals are also worth taking into consideration. Career trajectories for certain corporate or professional jobs may eventually require relocation or a commute to a headquarters in a large city. Professions that require building a client base take time to develop and would be difficult to expand or sustain if a partner is constantly having to move for short-term academic jobs.

Academic Job Negotiations

Perhaps the most difficult aspect of the academic job market process for couples with the two+ body problem are the negotiations after one partner receives an offer. All candidates with offers have some leverage to negotiate but the conditions of the job market and the capabilities of a university will constrain its impact. It is important to be realistic and deferential when asking for additional hiring considerations—until an offer is signed it can be rescinded. Most of the people at the negotiating table understand the circumstances of academia and will be open to trying to help as much as they can. It is important to explain your circumstances and your ideal solutions. This is the only chance a candidate has to get any potential spousal appointment—or any other requests—in writing. Unless the spousal hire is a real line in the sand, do not frame your requests as obligatory demands. It is important not to do anything to needlessly jeopardize a job offer. Openness and respect go a lot further towards success in the negotiating process than reticence and demanding. (Consider reviewing chapter 46 to further prepare to negotiate your first academic job.)

Potential Solutions to the Two+ Body Problem

Beyond partners communicating about their relationship dynamics and career trajectories, there are some practical long-term and short-term solutions to the two+ body problem. One common solution is the long-distance relationship (Sahlstein 2004). In this scenario a couple maintains their relationship while living separate from each other either part or full-time. The distance between career locations, economic flexibility, and the scheduling requirements of partners typically dictate how this plays out. A long-distance relationship requires all parties to have adequate housing in their location. Apartments, especially those that come pre-furnished, are ideal for short-term long-distance relationships or for careers that do not require full time residency like academia. The associated cost of paying two rents, or a rent and mortgage, should be compared against alternative solutions to the two+ body problem. If the costs, both financial and emotional, of long distance are greater than what is gained by either of a couple's jobs, then it is likely not a good solution to pursue. Long-distance relationships can be exceptionally hard on couples and barring any obvious benefits they create more problems than they solve. For dual academic couples a long-distance relationship is often the only solution when both partners are pursuing competitive placements at the same time. Tenure-track positions are rare, and it is unlikely a couple lucky enough to get simultaneous offers will do so in the same geographic area. An additional solution for couples wanting to stay together geographically is for the partner seeking a job to examine opportunities outside of academia. Such careers may allow for individuals to utilize aspects of their degree while potentially making more money than many academic jobs. (Chapter 41 provides an overview of non-traditional options.)

Overcoming the Two+ Body Problem

The long-term goal for any dual career couple will be to find stable and secure employment in the same location (Wolf-Wendel, Twombly, and Rice 2004). The more career-related restrictions or requirements each partner brings to the table, the more time this goal may take to achieve. A partner may choose to utilize a long-distance relationship, maintain current employment, while they attempt to find a suitable new job in the locale their partner was hired. This helps ease the difficulty associated with the quick turnaround between academic job offers and start dates. It also removes pressure from needing to find a new job as soon as possible. For dual career academics, the ease of finding a job in the same location depends on both desired career trajectory and available job options. If one or both partners are willing to forego the more competitive tenure-track path, then it will be easier to find employment in the same location, though the contingency of non-tenured positions can create future job uncertainties.

For academic partners who seek both joint employment and tenure it is imperative that both do their best to remain competitive and desirable candidates. Even if compromises between a couple require a partner to take a less than ideal position in terms of their future career goals, it is important that they maintain impressive teaching, publishing, and networking within their discipline. The two-for-one package of academics is an easier sell if both have impressive CVs.

A Few Other Things to Remember

There are a few more things individuals facing the two+ body problem should keep in mind. Areas with large numbers of universities nearby should be key targets for dual career academics. More universities means more potential job opportunities in the future. Though it would be ideal to find a job in the same city as one's partner, commuting should not be overlooked as a viable solution. Expanding the range where one looks for employment increases the likelihood of finding something suitable. Advances in technology, as well as recent societal shifts, have made working from home a great option for both academics and non-academics alike. Remote work allows individuals the opportunity to continue working in a chosen field without geographic restrictions. Less traditional academic jobs like researcher, academic advisor, or journal editor may be less competitive than more traditional professorial positions while still allowing academics to keep their foot in the door. Though this may not be a long-term solution, these types of jobs may allow a couple to both find work at the same school.

Finally, due to the prevalence of dual career couples in academia it is highly likely that there are other individuals at one's hiring institution with two+ body problem experience. Such individuals are an invaluable resource for helping early career academics navigate the two+ body problem because they have the added benefit of sharing the same institutional background.

Ultimately, overcoming the two+ body problem requires careful planning, communication, and investment in a shared future. The academic job market as it currently exists can aggravate rather than alleviate the problem if one does not approach the process with a plan in place. Depending on a couple's agreed upon balance, dual careers may involve long-distance relationships, lengthy commutes, or short-term employment solutions. Flexibility is key since the job market plays an inequitable role in the opportunities available, making it necessary for couples to consider alternative routes that satisfy their preferred balance. A couple's ideal solution to the two+ body problem can take years to achieve.

References

Blossfeld, Hans-Peter, and Sonja Drobnic. 2001. *Careers of Couples in Contemporary Society: From Male Breadwinner to Dual-Earner Families: From Male Breadwinner to Dual-Earner Families.* New York: Oxford University Press.

Chait, Richard P. 2005. *The Questions of Tenure.* Cambridge, MA: Harvard University Press.

Diehl, Paul F. 2021. "Adapting to the Changing Academic Job Market." Political Science Today 1 (4): 13–15.

Heckman, James J. 2011. "The Economics of Inequality: The Value of Early Childhood Education." *American Educator* 35 (1): 31.

Hollywood, Amelia, Daniel McCarthy, Carol Spencely, and Naomi Winstone. 2020. "'Overwhelmed at First': The Experience of Career Development in Early Career Academics." *Journal of Further and Higher Education* 44 (7): 998–1012.

Kaplan, Karen. 2010. "Negotiating for Two." *Nature* 466 (7310): 1145–46.

Khan, Hassan, Elham Almoli, Marina Christ Franco, and David Moher. 2021. "Open Science Failed to Penetrate Academic Hiring Practices: A Cross-Sectional Study." *Journal of Clinical Epidemiology* 144 (April): 136-143.

LaFerriere, Tyler William. 2017. "Economics of Academia: The Two-Body and Dual-Hire Problem Revisited." PhD Thesis. Washington State University.

Larson, Lincoln R., Lauren N. Duffy, Mariela Fernandez, Jill Sturts, Joey Grant, and Gwynn M. Powell. 2019. "Getting Started on the Tenure Track: Challenges and Strategies for Success." *SCHOLE: A Journal of Leisure Studies and Recreation Education* 34 (1): 36–51.

Larson, Richard C., Navid Ghaffarzadegan, and Yi Xue. 2014. "Too Many PhD Graduates or Too Few Academic Job Openings: The Basic Reproductive Number R0 in Academia." *Systems Research and Behavioral Science* 31(6): 745–50.

Petriglieri, Jennifer. 2019. "How Dual-Career Couples Make It Work." *Harvard Business Review.* https://hbr.org/2019/09/how-dual-career-couples-make-it-work (December 12, 2021).

Prock, Kristen A., Scott Berlin, Rena D. Harold, and Sheryl R. Groden. 2019. "Stories from LGBTQ Social Work Faculty: What Is the Impact of Being 'Out' in Academia?" *Journal of Gay & Lesbian Social Services* 31(2): 182–201.

Rivera, Lauren A. 2017. "When Two Bodies Are (Not) a Problem: Gender and Relationship Status Discrimination in Academic Hiring." *American Sociological Review* 82(6): 1111–38.

Roberts, Laura Weiss. 2017. "Interviewing for an Academic Position." In L.W. Roberts & D.M. Hilty (Eds.), *Handbook of Career Development in Academic Psychiatry and Behavioral Sciences* (81-93). APA Publishing.

Sahlstein, Erin M. 2004. "Relating at a Distance: Negotiating Being Together and Being Apart in Long-Distance Relationships." *Journal of Social and Personal Relationships* 21(5): 689–710.

Scurry, Tracy, and Marilyn Clarke. 2021. "Navigating Dual-Careers: The Challenge for Professional Couples." *Personnel Review* (July 26, np).

Su, Amy Jen. 2019. "Finding Balance as a Dual-Career Couple." *Harvard Business Review.* https://hbr.org/2019/07/finding-balance-as-a-dual-career-couple (December 12, 2021).

Whitaker, Manya. 2018. "How to Be Strategic on the Tenure Track." *The Chronicle of Higher Education* (November 26, np).

Wolf-Wendel, Lisa, Susan B. Twombly, and Suzanne Rice. 2004. *The Two-Body Problem: Dual-Career-Couple Hiring Practices in Higher Education.* Baltimore, MD: John Hopkins University Press.

Climate and Culture in the Department and Profession

49

Climate and Culture in Political Science: Diversifying our Institutions, Methods, and Identities to Combat Implicit Bias and Microaggressions

Natasha Altema McNeely[1], LaTasha Chaffin DeHaan[2], & Verónica Hoyo[3]

1. University of Texas, Rio Grande Valley 2. Elgin Community College 3. University of California, San Diego

KEYWORDS: Discriminatory Biases, Microaggressions, Implicit Biases.

Introduction

Implicit bias, or unconscious bias, refers to *discriminatory biases* based on "outside conscious attentional focus" implicit attitudes or stereotypes (Greenwald and Krieger 2006). Implicit biases are directly unobservable, ingrained, automatic associations linked through social stereotypes to different groups and are traditionally considered stable through time and very difficult to change, if at all (Vuletich and Payne 2019).

Microaggressions are everyday unintentional or intentional, hostile, derogatory, or demeaning targeted remarks based on perceived marginalized or minority group membership. Microaggressions are often performed in a subtle, covert manner or as "deniable" offenses. Originally coined for racial acts (Pierce 1974), recent research has broadened the definition to go beyond race to include gender, sexual preference, religious, disability, and other statuses where there may be a perceived stigma and/or power imbalance (Williams 2020).[1] Microaggressions can also be used as tools for politicians to gain support for their political campaign; for example, microaggression cues are used by politicians to highlight cultural differences in order to increase divisions between groups (Gonzalez-Gorman 2018).

In this chapter, we focus on a behavioral approach to *implicit biases* and microaggressions in the higher education context and within the political science profession in particular. Newer research has emphasized the need to move beyond the "uncontrollable," and often "latent" mental structure aspects of biases in preference of understanding these phenomena as something that people "do" rather than "possess" (De Houwer 2019).[2]

This chapter is divided into three sections, with the first one shedding light on the potential roots of the problem: the existence of an "ideal" type of political science graduate student or faculty member that in actuality does not reflect the current composition of the student body or "expected" career paths in the larger discipline. It also provides an overview of what implicit biases and microaggressions may look like today for minority or underrepresented students and faculty in political science. The second section addresses the question of the impact of biases and microaggressions. The third section offers evidence-based recommendations on how to respond to, address or mitigate implicit bias and microaggressions. Finally, the chapter concludes with a brief discussion of our personal, perspective-giving lessons learned.

The Roots of Biases and Microaggressions in Political Science and their Impact

What does an "ideal" political scientist look like? Some would say that it would be a student or faculty member at one of the "best political science departments." Others would focus on research productivity metrics (Peress 2019). Perhaps some would even refer to the "biggest" subfield (American politics), a particular type of research method (quantitative vs qualitative), or a specific type of institution (private vs public, R1 vs others, etc.). The possibilities for all these implicit biases are endless as are the opportunities for microaggressions towards anyone who does not conform to these stereotypical types or clichés.

Two APSA surveys shed some light on relevant trends in the profession. First, the Graduate Placement Survey- Incoming Students Report revealed that the 2019-2020 cohort of incoming doctoral students was more diverse in gender, race, ethnicity, and country of origin than their peers currently on the market. For the 2019-2020 cohort, more women and more underrepresented racial and ethnic minorities received funding for graduate school, with the exception of Hispanic/Latinx students.[3]

It is encouraging news that the data show that political science graduate programs are consciously trying to increase diversity and funding opportunities for all grad students (Reid and Curry 2019; Sinclair-Chapman 2015).[4] However, the 2018-2020 Graduate Placement Report offers a different outlook; post docs and non-academic first jobs are on an upward trend while all other categories (tenure-track, academic non-tenure track, part-time, and full time, as well as academic administration placements) are either stable or decreasing.[5] In terms of characteristics by placement type, between 2018-2020 women and underrepresented minorities (URMs) were more likely to be placed in the increasingly less plentiful tenure track positions while the largest proportion of job market candidates who got postdoc positions were from top-ranked institutions (APSA 2021). The effects of the COVID-19 pandemic have yet to be examined but if political science follows similar trends in other labor markets, minorities may be further disproportionately impacted (Couch, Fairlie and Xu 2020).

Political science career paths have evolved; fewer than one quarter of the students will immediately move to a tenure-track position and what was once the "ideal" path is not as feasible today. Implicit biases that once held up non-Hispanic white, male, "Americanists" as the prototypical political scientist seem to be changing and the APSA surveys seem to provide reason for hope that our discipline is moving towards more balanced, diverse, and representative political science departments. A very different "prototypical" political scientist is in the making.

The impact of biases and microaggressions continue to affect women of color as they enter academia. Challenges include exclusion by their colleagues, hypervisibility and invisibility, tokenism, and sexual harassment. All these challenges are exacerbated not only in hostile departments and institutions but also in supportive departments (Brown 2019; Lavariega Monforti and Michelson 2020a and 2020b; Michelson and Lavariega Monforti 2021; Sinclair-Chapman 2019).[6]

It is imperative to incorporate an intersectional understanding of how various challenges affect students of color not only as they consider doctoral programs, but also as faculty positions. Intersectionality provides a comprehensive understanding of challenges encountered due to multiple identities which contribute toward multiple marginalities (Brown and Montoya 2020) (see chapter 56 for additional concerns for graduate students with intersectional identities). For example, intersectionality provides a comprehensive understanding of the gender gap between perceptions of challenges encountered by Latinas versus their male co-ethnic peers: Latina students identify familial obligations and the lack of good mentorship provided by Latino mentors and non-Latino male professors (Lavariega Monforti and Michelson 2008).

Some Consequences of Implicit Biases and Microaggressions

There are systemic biases embedded into the salary negotiation process (see also chapter 46) and academic tenure and promotion systems. Across all ranks, women make less than men and faculty, regardless of gender, at public institutions earn less compared to faculty at private institutions (Hesli Claypool et al. 2017). Researchers suggest that one reason that men earn more than women is because of their willingness to relocate for career opportunities. Additionally, women are less likely to negotiate at the time of a job offer or to procure competing job offers. Yet, when they do negotiate, assertive negotiation strategies are viewed negatively by employers who see them as not befitting of women's gender roles

Climate and Culture in Political Science: Diversifying our Institutions, Methods, and Identities to Combat Implicit Bias and Microaggressions

317

(Blackaby, Booth and Frank 2005; Hesli Claypool et al. 2017). When controlling for race, Hesli et al. (2017) found that non-Hispanic whites were paid more, especially at the rank of assistant professor. These data provide evidence that systemic biases have disparate impacts on women and minorities in tangible and substantial ways.

The prototypical political scientist model exacerbates implicit biases and microaggressions toward graduate students who do not fit that model. This manifests in several forms. First, implicit biases and microaggressions held by some faculty may contribute to the subpar and ineffective mentorship some students of color receive.[7] Second, biases and microaggressions experienced by graduate students of color in PhD programs cause increased perceptions of challenging departmental and institutional climate and culture and discrimination (Burnsma et al. 2017; Curtin, Stewart and Ostrove 2013; Gasman et al. 2008; Spalter-Roth and Erskine 2007; Stewart and Ostrove 2013). It is worth noting the low numbers of graduate students of color admitted to doctorate programs in favor of the "prototypical student" contributes to ongoing microaggressions and biases.[8] Unfortunately, the model of the "prototypical political scientist" also creates biases in the context of who should receive external funding. Ginther and colleagues (2011) found National Institute of Health (NIH) grant applicants who were Asian and Black/African-American were less likely to be awarded NIH investigator-initiated research funding compared to their non-Hispanic white counterparts.[9] These results have been recently confirmed and deemed "unacceptable inequalities," but, sadly, these systemic exclusionary practices persist within groups and especially when it comes to gender and race (Lauer and Roychowdhury 2021).

Dealing with Implicit Biases and Microaggressions

Constant exposure to implicit biases and microaggressions can trigger a long list of conflicting emotions: from shame, guilt, and anger, to insecurity and impostor syndrome.[10] (For a larger discussion about imposter syndrome, see chapter 50.) "Recent studies have shown that all these issues have a negative impact on the well-being....." and that a mental health crisis may be brewing for graduate students across several disciplines (Almasri, Read and Vandeweerdt 2021; Barreira, Basilico, and Bolonyy 2018; Gallea, Medrano and Morera 2021; James 2019). Longitudinal research on the stability of implicit biases on university campuses has shown that although interventions to remove or mitigate implicit biases may have a short-term impact, they are often completely ineffective in the long run (Lai et al. 2016). Despite this grim assessment, there is reason to hope; newer research reanalyzing the same data has highlighted that implicit biases reflect "biases in the environment rather than individual dispositions" and, as such, "changing the social environment" is more effective than attempting to eradicate individual attitudes (Vueltich and Payne 2019). This is particularly important for graduate students to know and understand since the recent proliferation of online information about how some political science departments have dealt with very visible cases of harassment, racism, bullying, and more sets a good precedent for how future cases may be handled. In short, history matters. Although social environments may be transformed, it takes time.

There are no single one-size-fits-all solutions to dealing with implicit biases and microaggressions. Research shows diversity training is not effective (Chang et al. 2019). So, what works? Intergroup contact reduces prejudices, explicit and implicit biases (Macinnis et al. 2016), as well as "perspective-getting" conversations (Kalla & Broockman 2020). Representation also matters; more diverse, better balanced, truly intersectional political science departments, graduate programs, and faculty would be integral in any effort aimed at reducing biases and aggressions.[11]

Evidence also suggests that peer-led, safe spaces to process the toll of implicit biases and microaggressions upon those on the receiving end and spaces to support like-minded people also help (Cassese and Holman 2018), as do listening to the personal stories of those who have gone through similar lived experiences themselves (Jaremka et al. 2020), in addition to self-care and self-acknowledgement (Grey 2020). The Women of Color in Political Science Workshop (WCPS), held at the APSA Annual Meeting, invited female graduate students and faculty from underrepresented backgrounds to participate and attend panels that provided guidance on how to pursue opportunities for professional and personal growth as well as solutions to overcoming challenges in graduate school and as faculty (Lavariega Monforti, 2020a, 2020b; Michelson and Lavariega Monforti, 2021).[12] Networking opportunities including "Women Also Know Stuff" (Beaulieu et al., 2020) and "People of Color Also Know Stuff" (Lemi, Osorio and Rush, 2020) have also been effective tools against biases and microaggressions experienced by women and scholars of color.

Our Personal Paths for "Perspective-Giving"

A final word on our personal paths.[13] As women of color with diverse backgrounds, we each have had different lived experiences. Here is what each of us would have recommended to our prior selves.

As an international female graduate student, implicit biases and microaggressions were a constant. From misconceptions, clichés, and racist comments about my country of origin to the "appropriateness of fit" of my own research interests to my background, they ran the gamut. However, they were also waiting for me when I got back home (turned in the opposite direction), so the moral of this story is: implicit biases and microaggressions will always exist, regardless of where you are, where you go, and where you have been. Second lesson for after you graduate: whatever you decide as your path, as your academic or non-academic career, know that regardless of everyone's unsolicited comments or well-intended advice, you are the only one who can evaluate and decide on your priorities. They may not conform to the "ideal" view of a political scientist, but know that whatever path you choose, if it works for you and is what you want, it is as successful or more than anything else you could have chosen. Success is in the eyes of the beholder.

As a minority woman academician, teacher, scholar, and political scientist I enjoy an intersectional identity. It is essential for the academy to recognize that teachers and scholars have important perspectives that are influenced by their race, culture, gender, and life experiences that add value to their teaching and the research questions they seek to answer within their disciplines. As a graduate student, I would have affirmed this sense of importance and value within myself. Minority and female graduate students are often faced with micro- and macro-aggressions within their departments and the discipline, and they do not always receive the affirmation that they are making important contributions. Given the lack of diversity in many graduate programs, in my own experience as a doctoral student I desired effective mentors who believed in me, my teaching, and what I was passionate about researching. Thankfully, I connected with such a mentor. I would advise graduate students to believe in yourselves and to proactively seek out effective diverse and non-diverse mentors, research and teaching opportunities within and outside your departments and disciplines, and outside of your home institutions.

As a woman of color, I have not only experienced microaggressions and biases while in graduate school but continue to experience them as a faculty member. Over the years, many of the recommendations discussed in our chapter have helped me deal with the consequences of these and other forms of discriminations. For example, attending the 2015 and 2017 WCPS not only allowed me to meet phenomenal female students and faculty of color, but each workshop also provided important information that helped me attain professional and personal successes. Outside of the WCPS, establishing a network of personal friendships with other women of color has also helped me create a safe space for myself with other women who have similar shared experiences while also exchanging ideas related to our research areas of expertise. The "Women of Color Know Stuff" and "People of Color Know Stuff" have also been very helpful to me.

One final statement about parenting in academia. Although we were no longer grad students when we became parents, we have personally witnessed the added hurdles of raising and tending to the needs of our families while also trying to succeed in our careers. It sounds commonplace, but it takes a village. Surround yourselves with a strong support network and be creative when problem-solving. (See also chapter 16.)

Resources

Implicit Bias & Microaggressions

- The American Bar Association (ABA): The ABA defines unconscious bias, implicit bias, and microaggressions and suggests strategies to address them. See the ABA's website: https://www.americanbar.org/groups/gpsolo/publications/gp_solo/2019/july-august/unconscious-bias-implicit-bias-microaggressions-what-can-we-do-about-them/

- National Education Association (NEA): The NEA Center for Social Justice provides resources and tools such as books, articles, and videos that deepen our understanding of implicit bias, microaggressions, and stereotypes. They also provide a list of partner organizations that are active in promoting racial justice, equity, diversity, and inclusion. See the NEA's website: https://www.nea.org/resource-library/implicit-bias-microaggressions-and-stereotypes-resources
- Project Implicit and the Implicit Association Test (IAT): Project Implicit is a nonprofit organization and collaboration of researchers who study implicit cognition. Project Implicit offers a free and optional assessment of implicit attitudes and beliefs. More information can be found regarding Project Implicit as well as a link to take the IAT at: https://www.projectimplicit.net/

Mental Health

Dealing with microaggressions and implicit bias on a recurring basis is exhausting and challenging. Some institutions offer regular workshops, thematic discussion (dealing with fear of public speaking, etc.) and support groups (LGBTQI+, international students, etc.), consultations, walk-in and emergency services ("crisis intervention"), some of which may be confidential and free. See examples of mental health resources at our institutions below:

- Elgin Community College Wellness Services: https://elgin.edu/life-at-ecc/wellness-services/
- UC San Diego Counseling Services: https://caps.ucsd.edu/services/grad.html
- UC San Diego Student Health & Wellbeing: https://studentwellbeing.ucsd.edu/
- UT-Rio Grande Valley Counseling Center: https://www.utrgv.edu/counseling/index.htm
- UT-Rio Grande Valley Mental Health Resources: https://www.utrgv.edu/counseling/services/mental-health-resources/index.htm

Endnotes

1   Pierce (1974), referring exclusively to racial microaggressions, described them as a "subtle, cumulative mini-assault."

2   This approach is useful when seeking to understand, "redirect," or "modify" them.

3   The survey is available at https://preprints.apsanet.org/engage/apsa/article-details/61015b730b093e2830e42b7a

4   Anecdotal evidence includes a sample of graduate student programs with clear diversity statements that have become more prevalent in recent years, see for instance: Stanford's here, CalPoly's here; UW-Madison's here, University of Illinois at Urbana-Champaign's here (efforts date back to 2019), amongst many others.

5   The survey is available at https://preprints.apsanet.org/engage/apsa/article-details/61649e5d8b620d1d574c4b7f

6   Despite public statements on their commitment to diversity, some allegedly "supportive" institutions have failed to provide resources and protection to minority and marginalized students and faculty who encounter microaggressions, biases, and harassment (including online). Beware of false allyship.

7   It is recognized that women faculty and faculty of color are often overly tasked with the responsibilities of mentoring and supporting students who are women and students of color in predominantly white institutions (PWIs) and in minority serving institutions (MSIs) where there may be a lack of resources devoted to student advising and counseling.

8   People of color still remain underrepresented both as students in doctoral programs as well as faculty due to various hurdles and challenging circumstances that cause many students of color to not pursue or finish their doctorates or later, while some faculty of color are unable to garner success during the tenure and promotion process (Lavariega Monforti and Michelson 2008; Tornos-Aponte and Velez-Serrano 2020).

9   Standard measures for NIH grant success such as previous grants and publications did not predict success across racial and ethnic groups. Even when controlling for demographic characteristics, education and training, research experience and productivity, the 10-percentage point gap between awarding NIH grants to non-Hispanic whites vs. African Americans was largely unexplained.

10   Impostor syndrome is defined as the feeling that you have ended up in a certain role or position not because of your abilities and competencies, but rather due to some oversight or stroke of luck. Succinctly put, it is feeling and thinking that you are a fraud or do not belong in a certain environment. Research shows that these feelings often have "contextual roots." That is, like microaggressions and biases, it is the environment, especially in the case of marginalized or underrepresented communities, that elicits these damaging feelings. See Feenstra et al. (2020).

11   A small but important caveat to insert here is that minority graduate students in political science should be mindful of not singling out specific ("niche") programs or departments as their only means to success. The latest APSA graduate placement reports suggest that funding and job market opportunities for Black males may be impacted by their focus on a more limited number of institutions to pursue their graduate studies.

12   The data gained through pre- and post-workshop surveys of participants have helped to advance our understanding of the experiences of female graduate students and faculty of color as well as the challenges they encounter within the political science discipline (Lavariega Monforti, 2020a, 2020b; Michelson and Lavariega Monforti 2021).

13   As former graduate students we would have liked to have heard more from the people before us, so we conclude this chapter with our own "lessons learned."

References

Almasri, N., B. Read, and C. Vandeweerdt. 2021. "Mental Health and the PhD: Insights and Implications for Political Science." *PS: Political Science & Politics* 1–7.

American Political Science Association. 2021. "Graduate Student Placement Report, Analysis of Political Science Placements for 2018-2020." https://preprints.apsanet.org/engage/apsa/article-details/61649e5d8b620d1d574c4b7f

American Political Science Association. 2021. "2018-2020 Graduate Student Placement Report: Incoming Students Report." https://preprints.apsanet.org/engage/apsa/article-details/61015b730b093e2830e42b7a

Barreira, P., Basilico, M. and Bolonyy, V. 2018. "Graduate Student Mental health: lessons from American Economics Departments." https://scholar.harvard.edu/files/bolotnyy/files/bbb_mentalhealth_paper.pdf.

Blackaby, David, Allison L. Booth, and Jeff Frank. 2005. "Outside Offers and the Gender Pay Gap: Empirical Evidence from the UK Academic Labour Market." The Economic Journal. 115 (501): F81–F107.

Beaulieu, Emily, Amber E. Boydstun, Nadia E. Brown, Kim Yi Dionne, Andra Gillespie, Samara Klar, Yanna Krupnikov, Melissa R. Michelson, Kathleen Searles, and Christine Wolbrecht. 2020. "Women Also Know Stuff: Meta-Level Mentoring to Battle Gender Bias in Political Science." *PS: Political Science* 779-783.

Brown, Nadia E. 2019. "Mentoring, Sexual Harassment, and Black Women Academics." *Journal of Women, Politics and Policy* 40(1): 166-173.

Brown, Nadia E. and Celeste Montoya. 2020. "Intersectional Mentorship: A Model for Empowerment and Transformation." *PS: Political Science* 784-787.

Cassese, E. C., and R.M. Holman. 2018. "Writing Groups as Models for Peer Mentorship among Female Faculty in Political Science." *PS: Political Science & Politics* 51(2): 401–405.

Chang, E. H., K. L. Milkman, D.M. Gromet, R. W. Rebele, C. Massey, A. L. Duckworth, and A. M. Grant. 2019. "The mixed effects of online diversity training." *Proceedings of the National Academy of Sciences* 116(16): 7778–7783.

Couch, Kenneth A., Robert W. Fairlie, and Huanan Xu. 2020. "Early Evidence of the Impacts of COVID-19 on Minority Unemployment." *Journal of Public Economics* 192:104287.

Curtin, Nicola, Abigail Stewart, and Joan M. Ostrove. 2013. "Fostering Academic Self-concept: Advisor

Support and Sense of Belonging among International and Domestic Graduate Students." *American Educational Research Journal* 50(1):108–37.

Feenstra, S., C. T. Begeny, M. K. Ryan, F. A. Rink, J. I. Stoker, and J. Jordan. 2020. "Contextualizing the Impostor Syndrome." *Frontiers in Psychology*. 11.

Gallea, J. I., Medrano L. A., and Morera, L. P. 2021. "Work-Related Mental Health Issues in Graduate Student Population." *Frontiers in Neuroscience*. https://doi.org/10.3389/fnins.2021.593562

Gasman, Marybeth, Aviva Hirschfeld, and Julie Vultaggio. 2008. "'Difficult Yet Rewarding:' The Experiences of African American Graduate Students in Education at an Ivy League Institution." *Journal of Diversity in Higher Education* 1(2): 126–38.

Ginther, Donna K., Walter T. Schaffer, Joshua Schnell, Beth Masimore, Faye Liu, Laurel L. Haak, and Raynard Kington. 2011. "Race, Ethnicity and NIH Research Rewards." *Science* 333(6045): 1015 – 1019.

Gonzalez-Gorman, Sylvia. 2018. *Political Speech as A Weapon: Microaggression in a Changing Racial and Ethnic Environment*. Denver, CO: Praeger.

Greenwald, A. G., and L. H. Krieger. 2006. "Implicit Bias: Scientific Foundations." *California Law Review* 94(4): 945-967.

Grey, P. 2020. "Four tips to ward off impostor syndrome." *Nature*.

Hesli Claypool, Vicki, Brian David Janssen, Dongkyu Kim, and Sara McLauglin Mitchell. 2017. "Determinants of Salary Dispersion among Political Science Faculty: The Differential Effects of Where You Work (Institutional Characteristics) and What You Do (Negotiate and Publish)." *PS: Political Science & Politics* 50 (1): 146 – 156.

James, B.T. 2019. "Staying in and Staying Healthy: Insights for Positive Mental Health in Graduate School." *The Behavioral Neuroscientist and Comparative Psychologist*. https://www.apadivisions.org/division-6/publications/newsletters/neuroscientist/2019/07grad-school-healthy#:~:text=The%20study%20found%20that%20graduate,et%20al.%2%202018.

Jaremka, L. M., J. M. Ackerman, B. Gawronski, N. O. Rule, K. Sweeny, L. R. Tropp, M. A. Metz, L. Molina, W. S. Ryan, and S. B. Vick. 2020. "Common Academic Experiences No One Talks About: Repeated Rejection, Impostor Syndrome, and Burnout." *Perspectives on Psychological Science* 15(3): 519–543.

Kalla, J. L. and D. E. Broockman. 2020. "Reducing Exclusionary Attitudes through Interpersonal Conversation: Evidence from Three Field Experiments." *American Political Science Review* 114(2): 410-425.

Lai, C. K., A. L. Skinner, E. Cooley, S. Murrar, M. Brauer, T. Devos, J. Calanchini, Y. J. Xiao, C. Pedram, C. K. Marshburn, S. Simon, J. C. Blanchar, J. A. Joy-Gaba, J. Conway, L. Redford, R. A. Klein, G. Roussos, F. M. H. Schellhaas, M. Burns, ... B. A. Nosek. 2016. "Reducing implicit racial preferences: II. Intervention effectiveness across time." *Journal of Experimental Psychology: General* 145(8): 1001–1016.

Lauer, M. S, Roychowdhury D. 2021. Inequalities in the distribution of National Institutes of Health research project grant funding eLife 10:e71712.

Lavariega Montforti, Jessica L. and Melissa R. Michelson. 2020a. "Building Our Communities: Women of Color Workshops in Political Science." *PS: Political Science & Politics* 53 (1): 141 – 143.

---. 2020b. "They See Us, But They Don't See Us," in *Presumed Incompetent: Race, Class, and Resistance of Women in Academia*. Eds. Yolanda Flores Niemann, Gabriella Gutierrez y Muhs, and Carmen G. Gonzalez. Louisville, CO: University of Colorado Press. 59-73.

---. 2008. "Diagnosing the Leaky Pipeline: Continuing Barriers to Retention of Latinas and Latinos in Political Science." *PS: Political Science & Politics* 41(1): 161-166.

Lemi Danielle C., Maricruz Osorio, and Tye Rush. 2020. "Introducing People of Color Also Know Stuff." *PS: Political Science* 52(4): 140-141.

MacInnis, C. C., E. Page-Gould, and G. Hodson. 2017. "Multilevel Intergroup Contact and Antigay Prejudice (Explicit and Implicit)." *Social Psychological and Personality Science* 8(3) 243–251.

Michelson, Melissa R. and Jessica L. Lavariega Monforti. 2021. "Elusive Inclusion: Persistent Challenges Facing Women of Color in Political Science." *PS: Political Science & Politics* 54 (1): 152 – 157.

Peress, M. 2019. "Measuring the Research Productivity of Political Science Departments Using

Google Scholar." *PS: Political Science & Politics* 52(2): 312–317.

Pierce, Charles 1974. "Psychiatric Problems of the Black Minority" in S. Arieti (ed.), *American Handbook of Psychiatry*. New York: Basic Books. 512-523.

Reid, R. A., Curry, T. A. 2019. "Are We There yet? Addressing Diversity in Political Science Subfields" *PS: Political Science & Politics* 52(2): 281-286.

Sinclair-Chapman, Valeria. 2015. "Leveraging Diversity in Political Science for Institutional and Disciplinary Change." *PS: Political Science & Politics* 48(3): 454-58.

Sinclair-Chapman, Valeria. 2019. "Rebounding on the Tenure Track: Carving Out a Place of Your Own in the Academy." *PS: Political Science & Politics* 52(1): 52-56.

Spalter-Roth, Roberta. 2013. "The Sociology Pipeline for Today's Graduate Students." Retrieved November 18, 2016 (http://www.asanet.org/research-and-pub- lications/research-sociology/research-briefs/sociol- ogy-pipeline-todays-graduate-students).

Tornos-Aponte, Fernando and Mayra Velez-Serrano. 2020. "Broadening the Pathway for Graduate Studies in Political Science." *PS: Political Science & Politics* 53(1): 145 – 146.

Vuletich, H. A., and B. K. Payne. 2019. "Stability and Change in Implicit Bias." *Psychological Science* 30(6): 854-862.

Williams, M. T. 2020. "Microaggressions: Clarification, Evidence, and Impact." *Perspectives on Psychological Science* 15(1): 3-26.

50 Feeling like a Fraud: Imposter Syndrome in Political Science

Thomas S. Benson[1], Bobbi G. Gentry[2], & Sarah Shugars[3]

1. University of Delaware 2. Bridgewater College 3. Rutgers University

KEYWORDS: Imposter Syndrome, Peers, Mentors.

Imposter Syndrome: What Are the Signs?

Many prospective and current political science graduate students experience imposter syndrome; however, imposter syndrome is not experienced equally or in a universal manner. Intersectional aspects of identity, including gender, nationality, and race can also shape and compound how imposter syndrome is experienced. Given this, we distinguish between two modes of imposter syndrome: (1) feelings of fooling others; and (2) anxiety from having to perform. But, broadly speaking, what is imposter syndrome? How do we characterize it? There are many assumptions about imposter syndrome, such as someone who does not want to work hard, or has feelings of not belonging, among other feelings of self-worth and anxiety. However, imposter syndrome is a psychological term that denotes a "pattern of behavior wherein people (even those with adequate external evidence of success) doubt their abilities and have a persistent fear of being exposed as a fraud" (Mullangi and Jagsi 2019, 403). Others have similarly defined this concept, noting that it is a very "real and specific form of intellectual self-doubt" that can feature anxiety and depression (Weir 2013), fear of judgment by colleagues (Evans et al. 2018, 283), and underestimation of "talents by ignoring evidence for those talents" (Slank 2019, 206).

The first mode of imposter syndrome—feelings of fooling others—can be characterized mostly by feeling like a fraud, feeling a lack of belonging to the department, believing that "success was obtained through luck," and fearing being "found out" to be an imposter (Slank 2019, 205-209). Within this, there is typically a concern that people perceived to be important will discover that graduate students (that feel like imposters) are not "capable" (Slank 2019, 209). Some of the feelings of fooling others comes from a lack of evidence about what others know about you but that you have full knowledge of. Meaning, you have evidence of your imperfection, but others do not. A colloquialism to this feeling is "fake it 'til you make it," meaning to act as though you understand what you are doing and saying in a setting until you feel like you belong in that setting. Anxiety can stem from the belief that others will see through your fake persona and see that you are actually not capable of graduate work or the ability to work in the discipline.

The second mode of imposter syndrome—anxiety from having to perform—is more closely associated with the realization that graduate students are expected to immerse themselves in the norms of the political science discipline, and the engagement that comes with this. For example, a graduate student may be invited to co-author with a member of faculty or be accepted to present at a conference. In these instances, the graduate student may experience self-doubt and be overwhelmed by these newfound responsibilities that can appear daunting. Fear of not meeting the expectations of a mentor, professor, or of members of the profession can hinder the ability to perform activities associated with being a member of the profession, such as writing, presenting, researching, and producing information to different audiences like peers, students, or the public. This mode of imposter syndrome, while closely tied to the first, can be debilitating and lead to negative health and professional outcomes. For this reason, we choose to distinguish between these two modes—acknowledging that in some sense we all "feel like imposters," but some people experience this feeling more acutely and with more dire consequences.

Within both of these modes, graduate students in political science are prone to compare themselves to others, and these comparisons can "foster self-doubt" and lead to "skewed" perceptions of oneself and others (Bothello and Roulet 2019, 857). Broadly, graduate students are also more than "six times as likely to experience depression and anxiety" compared to the general population, thereby exacerbating feelings associated with imposter syndrome (Evans et al. 2018, 282). In turn, these instances of self-doubt, skewed perceptions, and poor mental health can have significant impacts on graduate students' capacity to learn, conduct research, teach (as an instructor or teaching assistant), engage with colleagues, and pursue professional development. To combat the effects of imposter syndrome, graduate students must more openly discuss mental health challenges associated with these areas of development (Hummel and Kurd 2021), as well as re-examine their workload so as to prevent burnout, further self-doubt, and comparisons between oneself and others (Muller 2020, 1280). In addition to our chapter, see chapters 64 and 68 in this volume for more on mental health and burnout.

Impact of Imposter Syndrome on Graduate Students

As indicated in the preceding section, imposter syndrome can adversely affect mental and physical health as well as the capacity to operate effectively in the discipline of political science as a student, research or teaching assistant, instructor, and colleague. However, not everyone experiences imposter syndrome and, even among those who do, the experiences are not necessarily identical. Further, imposter syndrome is not limited to prospective and current graduate students, but can also be found among post-doctoral students, and even tenured faculty. This also means that imposter syndrome can 'look' differently at different stages of an academic career in political science. For example, prospective students may first consider how their academic backgrounds differ from their peers and that they feel less 'worthy' in the program. For post-candidacy students, it may be about how their peers have managed to publish a journal article while they have not. For those students on the job market, it may be a perception that peers are receiving more interest for their work along with a deep, but reasonable, fear that a long-term career in this field is just not viable. Graduate students who are women, gender minorities, racial minorities, international students, or from other populations which are underrepresented in political science are also more likely to experience imposter syndrome due to the additional challenges (e.g., discrimination, harassment, visas) they face given these intersecting aspects of their identity (Slack 2019, 207; Mullangi and Jagsi 2019, 403). It is also harder for these students to disambiguate between real or perceived negative feedback which arises primarily from discrimination, verses that which is actually warranted. Such disciplinary gaslighting can fuel fears of imposter syndrome as students worry that they are overthinking the role of discriminatory feedback and worry that their work may indeed deserve such negative reception. For more on many of the above issues, see the Climate and Culture in the Department and Profession and Strategies for Addressing Implicit Bias, Harassment, Assault sections of this volume.

Given the disparities in gendered and cultural norms, these particular underrepresented groups of graduate students may also suffer from imposter syndrome in silence out of concern for stigmatization, discrimination, and "potential damage to their careers" (Muller 2020, 1280). This may also result in a lack of pursuit of departmental opportunities for professional development, academic service commitments, or collaboration "due to feeling unqualified" (Mullangi and Jagsi 2019, 403). Consequently, those experiencing imposter syndrome can fall into a spiral of self-doubt, constantly comparing themselves to others, and questioning the "value" of their profession and status (Bothello and Roulet 2019, 858). Such a spiral can result in poor work performance, "lack of response to emails, unexplained non-attendance, [and] sudden indecisiveness and unreliability" (Muller 2020, 1280) and possibly exit from the profession. In these instances, imposter syndrome can appear unescapable, sometimes leading students to depart their graduate program and left feeling deflated at their perceived inadequacy.

Imposter syndrome is particularly common among high-achieving people. In dealing with imposter syndrome, people can experience anxiety, dysphoric moods, emotional instability, negative self-evaluations, and perfectionism (Rohrmann, Bechtoldt, and Leonhardt 2016; Wilson and Cutri 2019, 72). In addition to these effects, students may engage in behavior that, to some extent, can sabotage their success. For example, students may feel inclined to set high expectations for themselves and feel disappointed when they fail to meet these expectations. Even when success is recognized by others—faculty, peers, or family—there is a tendency for those experiencing imposter syndrome to downplay this evidence as insignificant. In settings outside academia, family, peers, and friends can introduce a mismatch of expectations, which can exacerbate feelings of being a fraud, lack of belonging, and anxiety to meet expectations from family, and friends outside academia.

Thus, the lack of self-confidence associated with imposter syndrome and the vicious cycle of self-doubt can result in students refraining from grasping opportunities that allow for academic and professional development. These may include not collaborating with faculty, avoiding on- or off-campus volunteering, not applying for fellowships or grants, and not applying to or attending conferences to present academic research. Moreover, those experiencing imposter syndrome may withhold information during meetings (not talking in graduate courses), engage in delay tactics when asked to perform (e.g., procrastinating when it comes to grading, completing assignments, meeting faculty), and make self-deprecatory comments. Breaking this cycle is undoubtedly challenging and fretting about breaking this cycle can only often lead to heightened psychological stress, whereby students engage in a culture of overwork and in behavior that results in burnout. Experiences of burnout, increased anxiety, loss of interest in hobbies, and poor sleep are likely symptoms that it is time for change. Given this, the next section focuses on how political science graduate students can best prevent or navigate experiences of imposter syndrome.

What to Do About Imposter Syndrome?

To manage or help others manage imposter syndrome, a number of recommendations are provided here. It is crucial that political science graduate students recognize what imposter syndrome is and remember that it can be experienced differently between people. Additionally, imposter syndrome should be normalized, not trivialized. This is a call for greater understanding that many people across the discipline of political science experience imposter syndrome but, at the same time, it should not be belittled as "everyone experiences it, [so it does not matter]" or downplayed as "it is just a process everyone goes through." As previously noted, there can be mental health concerns affiliated with imposter syndrome and it can seriously affect productivity and feelings of self-worth. Given this, imposter syndrome needs to be taken seriously.

It is also key to recognize the role that political science graduate students play in affecting imposter syndrome, should they themselves be experiencing it or seeking to prevent it. This begins with an understanding that departmental culture can strongly impact imposter syndrome. For example, an environment that encourages thinking about talent or capability or intelligence as malleable and teachable (Slank 2019, 214) may encourage better working conditions that halt the onset or development of imposter syndrome. As part of this, establishing a healthy work-life balance is crucial (Evans et al. 2018, 283), as is positive self-talk and affirmation (to combat feelings of self-doubt), and recognition of talents and achievements to realize what 'success' looks like, and that success is not necessarily a fixed goal or a binary. In many political science graduate programs, students are often informed that they will learn to perform as a political scientist, and this can lead students to develop a binary understanding of success. This happens when students perceive the outcome of being considered a political scientist a great contrast to their current standing—whether a prospective, pre-candidacy, or post-candidacy student—when, instead, they should understand that becoming a political scientist is a journey that begins with being admitted to a political science graduate program. It is a gradual process in which students will acquire a range of skills and talents, develop their knowledge, and adhere to the norms of the discipline.

Political science graduate students should also seek to collaborate with and uplift their peers. Although competition can be healthy, discussing class material with peers, co-authoring with peers, and talking about existing literature and academic service commitments can alleviate imposter syndrome. In this process, students can understand that they are most likely not alone in experiencing feelings of self-doubt or confusion. Thus, talking to peers enables students to build relationships that allow them to ask sensitive questions and gradually develop a "successful scholarly identity" (Cassese and Holman 2018, 2). On the other hand, students who isolate themselves and communicate very little with their peers are likely to experience more feelings of self-doubt as they fail to recognize that their peers share these feelings. Through collective discussion, students can support one another and feel united through "common academic setbacks and negative thoughts affiliated with imposter syndrome" (Wilson and Cutri 2019, 71). Further, students should organize their time to schedule regular breaks to establish an effective work-life balance that does not lead to burnout (Hummel and Kurd 2021, 4). These peer relationships also provide invaluable opportunities to praise and elevate the work of those around you and to help them overcome their own feelings of imposter syndrome. For more on finding your collective and overcoming isolation, see chapter 63 in this volume.

In a similar vein, mentors and advisers play a critical role. By regularly engaging (e.g., meeting once per month) with an assigned adviser, students can share their experiences with imposter syndrome, find support for their research, receive validation, and feel valued—all of which will positively impact a student's mental well-being (Evans et al. 2018, 283). Should a student lack an adviser who is supportive, they should contact the Graduate Director of their program to inquire about getting an additional or a new adviser (see chapter 13 in this volume for more on choosing an advisor versus a mentor). Students should have a supportive network of formal and informal advisers (Bothello and Roulet 2019, 859) given the range of expertise available inside and outside of the political science discipline. For prospective and first-year students, they may be assigned an older student in the program who will act as a mentor, who they can likely speak to in confidence about their experiences with imposter syndrome. If this mentoring does not exist formally, older students will likely offer insights (informally) into their own experiences navigating imposter syndrome. This can help to manifest a sense of community and a sense of belonging that can subsequently diminish feelings of self-doubt. Supporting each other is key.

Furthermore, students can find value in their research. For some, it is engaging directly with communities affected by their research—whether as part of the research process, or separately in discussing their findings with them (Bothello and Roulet 2019, 859). Participating (attending and/or presenting) in political science conferences—like the APSA Annual Meeting—can be great in further cultivating a sense of belonging by meeting like-minded scholars who share research interests. It is also important for graduate students to seek validation outside of academia (Bothello and Roulet 2019, 860), as this can help to ground students in an understanding that there are important events occurring outside of the discipline of political science, and there is value in non-academic or non-political science activity, too.

Should opportunities arise for political science graduate students to advocate for departmental changes, there are a few encouraging ideas for enacting positive change. First, faculty ought to ensure that they regularly reach out to students, ideally once per month, to meet one-on-one with their mentees to provide ongoing support and openly discuss imposter syndrome and its associated effects. This is vital for students who belong to the groups that are more likely to experience imposter syndrome—first-gen, women, minorities, and international students. Second, advisers and mentors should allow their mentees to "wander intellectually and develop a unique identity as scholars," rather than pushing for students to narrowly confine themselves early in the process of becoming a political scientist (Bothello and Roulet 2019, 858).

Third, advisers should "teach their students to cope with work-related stress," "support help-seeking behaviors," and "help in linking-up to mental health professionals or counseling" services on- or off-campus (Muller 2020, 1280). For political science graduate students who have assistantships, they will likely possess some healthcare associated with their employment. In turn, they will have access to on-campus facilities like therapy services, and counseling and well-being centers. Also, advisers can draw attention to the positive aspects of imposter syndrome for those students already experiencing it, highlighting how self-awareness in the journey of becoming a political scientist is helpful for ongoing reflection (Tewfik 2021). Knowing the challenges that graduate students face with depression, anxiety and imposter syndrome, faculty should advocate for more resources and university support for mental health services. Finally, imposter syndrome is not universal and is not experienced the same for everyone, remember that you are not alone and there are others out there to help you in this journey.

References

Bothello, Joel., and Thomas J. Roulet. 2018. "The Imposter Syndrome, or the Mis-representation of Self in Academic Life." *Journal of Management Studies* 56(4): 854-861. doi: https://doi.org/10.1111/joms.12344

Cassese, Erin C., and Mirya R. Holman. 2018. "Writing Groups as Models for Peer Mentorship Among Female Faculty in Political Science." *PS: Political Science & Politics* 51(2): 401-405. doi: https://doi.org/10.1017/S1049096517002049

Evans, Teresa M., Lindsay Bira., Jazmin B. Gastelum., L. T. Weiss., and Nathan L. Vanderford. 2018. "Evidence for a Mental Health Crisis in Graduate Education." *Nature Biotechnology* 36(3): 282-284. doi: https://doi.org/10.1038/nbt.4089

Hummel, Calla., and Dana El Kurd. 2021. "Mental Health and Fieldwork." *PS: Political Science & Politics* 54(1): 121-125. doi:10.1017/S1049096520001055

Mullangi, Samyukta., and Reshma Jagsi. 2019. "Imposter Syndrome: Treat the Cause, Not the Symptom." *Jama* 322(5): 403-404. doi: 10.1001/jama.2019.9788

Müller, Astrid. 2020. "Mental Health Disorders: Prevalent but Widely Ignored in Academia?" *Journal of Physiology* 589(7): 1279-1281. doi: 10.1113/JP279386

Rohrmann, Sonja., Bechtoldt, Myriam N., and Leonhardt, Mona. 2016. "Validation of the Imposter Phenomenon among Managers." *Frontiers in Psychology* 7: 821 https://doi.org/10.3389/fpsyg.2016.00821

Slank, Shanna. 2019. "Rethinking the Imposter Phenomenon." *Ethical Theory and Moral Practice: An International Forum* 22(1): 205-218. doi: https://doi.org/10.1007/s10677-019-09984-8

Tewfik, B. 2021. "The Impostor Phenomenon Revisited: Examining the Relationship between Workplace Impostor Thoughts and Interpersonal Effectiveness at Work." *Academy of Management Journal* 0. doi: https://doi.org/10.5465/amj.2020.1627

Weir, Kirsten. 2013. "Feel like a Fraud?" American Psychological Association gradPSYCH 11(4). https://www.apa.org/gradpsych/2013/11/fraud.

Wilson, Sue., and Jennifer Cutri. 2019. "Negating Isolation and Imposter Syndrome Through Writing as Product and as Process: The Impact of Collegiate Writing Networks During a Doctoral Programme." In *Wellbeing in Doctoral Education: Insights and Guidance from the Student Experience*, eds. Lynette Pretorius, Luke Macaulay, and Basil Cahusac de Caux, 59-76. Cham, Switzerland: Springer.

51

Discrimination and Sexual Assault: Resources and Options for Responding and Reporting*

Devon Cantwell-Chavez[1], Asif Siddiqui[2], & Christina Fattore[3]

1. University of Ottawa 2. NorQuest College, MacEwan University 3. West Virginia University

Content Warning: This chapter contains mentions of sexual assault, rape, mental health, institutional betrayal, and police.

KEYWORDS: Title IX, Title VI, University Ombuds, Equal Employment Office, OCR Complaint.

Introduction

In 2019, the American Association of Universities (AAU) conducted a study at 33 R1 universities. They found that 10.8% of graduate students experienced nonconsensual sexual contact by physical force or inability to consent, an increase of 2.8% since 2015. A 2019 Survey of Postsecondary Faculty and Researchers found that the highest rates of discrimination and harassment were experienced among disabled (46%), Indigenous (40%), bisexual and pansexual (42%) respondents. Moreover, many academics from historically marginalized backgrounds have shared their experiences with both systemic and individual instances of discrimination in the academy. These incidents impact the physical, emotional, and academic well-being of survivors, likely contributing to the leaky pipeline, which is the attrition of Black, Indigenous, People of Color (BIPOC), women, LGBTQ2SIA+[1] and other historically underrepresented scholars within political science. Over the past several years, there have been renewed efforts to name, address, and prevent these issues in academia broadly as well as within political science, specifically. Political scientists such as Nadia Brown, Jenn Jackson, Rebecca Gill, Vanessa Tyson, Valerie A. Sulfaro, Juliana Restrepo Sanín, Patricia Strach, Rose McDermott, Rosalee A. Clawson, J. Celeste Lay, Shauna Shames, Shayla C. Nunnally and countless others have documented, discussed, and raised awareness of the prevalence of sexual harassment within the profession (Brown 2019, 2021; Clawson 2019; Lay 2019; McDermott 2019; Nunnally 2019; Restrepo Sanín 2019b, 2019a; Shames 2019; Strach 2019; Sulfaro and Gill 2019; Tyson 2019). However, the prevalence of sexual assault and discrimination forces graduate students to be knowledgeable about the existence of these issues as well as how to respond to them—either as a survivor or a bystander.

In this chapter, we offer practical and adaptable approaches for responding to and reporting discrimination and assault, as well as resources to address the well-being of individuals directly affected by such incidents. (Discrimination and assault have a different legal standard than harassment, which is discussed in a separate chapter: Harrassment-Resources and Options for Responding.) While these issues are very different, institutional justice options are primarily granted through anti-discrimination legislation and policy (Title IX), which means there is some overlap between these two events. There are also many incidents in which sexual assault intersectionally overlaps with other forms of oppression and discrimination. Thus, we lay out legal definitions, options, and discussion of both within this same chapter.

A significant portion of the advice in this chapter will be specific to the context of institutions in the United States, but may also be applicable in some form to students at institutions outside of this context. These resources include institutional/organizational, departmental, and individual-level options. Furthermore, we provide bystander intervention strategies to help individuals better understand how to assist survivors[2] of discrimination and harassment. Finally, our intent is to provide easily accessible information, and it should not be construed as professional legal advice.

What Are My Options for (In)Action?

Once you are safe, you might begin to think about what your options are. One way to consider this is to ask yourself: what is your ideal outcome? This is critical to consider because there will be benefits and drawbacks to any approach you take, even if that approach is to do nothing. Some examples of possible outcomes that you might seek include protective orders from the perpetrator; an apology; formal university, professional, or legal repercussions; removal of the perpetrator from their employment, leadership, and/or mentorship positions; supportive measures for employment and academic success; access to counseling resources; cease and desist orders; or even financial compensation. In the following section, we will discuss the institutional, legal, and community-based options for responding to and reporting. We will also discuss what the pathway of not reporting may look like and resources to consider using in that instance. In addition to the resources we discuss in this chapter, we want to emphasize that experiencing sexual assault or discrimination can take a substantial toll on your mental and physical health. Thus, we recommend spending time exploring the section of this handbook in the section "Health and Well-Being in Graduate School," which includes chapters on counseling, isolation and anxiety, things that can go wrong, and deciding to leave.

Fundamental Steps

Although both assault and discrimination are vastly different issues, there are some common steps that we recommend in both instances. These include trusting your gut, gathering and keeping detailed documentation, and finding an advocate. First, trust your gut. If the situation that you are in doesn't feel right, it probably isn't. This is especially relevant in cases where something might be in a "gray area"-- ie: you aren't sure if it meets a cultural, legal, or administrative standard of assault or discrimination, but something feels off. In this piece, we broadly consider discrimination as unjust or differential treatment of people based on identity categories. We consider sexual assault as any non-consensual sexual act. We need to emphasize that these definitions are not formal, legal definitions and that these definitions can vary significantly based on institution and state. Later in this piece, we provide the US federal definitions of these terms. If you have experienced an incident, or even if you are at the stage where something just feels off, your next step is to document, document, document.

Documentation is incredibly important for several reasons. First, any type of hearing (Title IX,[3] Office of Equal Opportunity (OEO), and/or legal) will require evidence to be produced against the perpetrator to prove your case. Documentation can aid in building your case and seeking your ideal outcome, though there are many other factors in the power structure of institutions that may work against you in proceedings, regardless of the documentation presented. A lack of documentation does not mean you will lose your case or not get your ideal outcome, but it can present barriers down the road.

There are several methods that you can use to document issues. One option is to create a folder in a secure place (for example, a Dropbox, Box, or Google Drive account that only you have control of/access to) and upload screenshots or related documents. It's always better to over-document than under-document. Make sure this account is not related to your university-provided email address. Additionally, you might not want to access it from a university computer or any other university-owned device. In some cases, the university has the right to review anything you have accessed from your computer, not just files saved on it.

There are several types of things you will want to document. For discrimination, this would include email, text, or other written communications as well as written statements detailing particular meetings and topics discussed. When possible, these accounts should always include as exact as possible the following information: date, time, location, and those present. If others were present during conversations, ask them to also send you a short write-up of what they heard/saw during the meeting or incident. If you were the only one present, it's a good idea to send an email documenting what happened to the other party in the meeting to create documentation of what happened. You may also consider recording meetings or conversations, but you should check for the legal and policy stipulations around that.[4]

Third, you should make sure that you have at least one support person who can help you navigate the logistics and details of your situation. One option is seeking out a victim-survivor advocate (also called survivor advocates, victim advocates, or support advocates). These are individuals who are trained to support people who have experienced various forms of interpersonal violence, crimes, discrimination, and harassment. They are often highly knowledgeable about policies and resources relevant to your situation. They are also often able to be a support person during meetings and hearings. Furthermore, they can help take notes about your case and support you logistically in documentation and filing processes. A handout with various links and tips for documentation can be found here.[5]

Some universities have advocates that work with the specific campus population and are housed by a division within the university. In some cases, these advocates are confidential, which means that they are not mandatory reporters to the university. In other cases, they may have mandatory reporting responsibilities.[6] Generally, this is something you can check on the website of the center that houses advocates or ask during your email or call to set up an appointment. Not all advocates will be campus-based. For universities that don't have advocates on campus, there may be advocates based out of a community center or community provider or shared across multiple campuses. In other cases, advocates may be available through local or campus police departments.

If a victim-survivor advocate is not available to you or you don't feel comfortable using an advocate, another option is to find a trusted friend, colleague, or family member who can help you with these tasks. While you are experiencing the aftermath of assault or dealing with discrimination, you are also likely to be simultaneously dealing with school as well as other professional, personal, and family commitments. Many of the options for responding to and reporting discrimination or assault have multiple steps and strict timelines or deadlines for submitting paperwork. Having a support person can be critical to helping you process events and also navigate administrative channels for responding and reporting.

In the next two sections, we will discuss specific options for responding to and reporting discrimination and assault.

Discrimination

If you experience discrimination, you have a variety of institutional, legal, and community options. A critical starting place for figuring out what resources you are able to access and what type of relief you can gain from discrimination at your institution is understanding what is and what is not considered discrimination at your institution. There are some forms of discrimination that are barred by federal law in the United States. These protections are under Title VI (42 U.S.C. § 2000d) and prohibit discrimination based on "race, color, or national origin …under any program or activity receiving Federal financial assistance" (Department of Justice 2017).[7] Two other forms of discrimination are covered and overseen by the U.S. Department of Education: age and disability discrimination (Department of Education, Office of Civil Rights 2020b). Disability is protected by Section 504 of the Rehabilitation Act of 1973 and Title II of the Americans with Disabilities Act of 1990 (Department of Education, Office of Civil Rights 2020a). The Age Discrimination Act of 1975 provides protections against discrimination on the basis of age (Department of Education, Office of Civil Rights 2015).

Additionally, there may be other stipulations. The federal standard is that you must prove "intentional discrimination" (Department of Justice 2017). This is a different standard than harassment, which is discussed in the chapter "Harassment–Resources and Options for responding." Intentional discrimination can be proven with direct evidence or circumstantial evidence (Department of Justice 2017). Direct evidence can include things like someone making benefits or services available, or handing out punishment, on the basis of race, color, or national origin (Department of Justice 2017). Direct evidence also includes comments or behavior that demonstrate that someone has discriminatory motives (Department of Justice 2017). Circumstantial evidence can allege discrimination against an entire group using a variety of pieces of evidence that proves someone acted "at least, in part, because of race, color, or national origin" or that someone was treated differently than others in similar situations who did not share their race, color, or national origin (Department of Justice 2017). When considering group-level discrimination, statistical evidence is also commonly used to show a "pattern of discrimination, a racially disproportionate impact, or foreseeably discriminatory results" (Department of Justice 2017). Your university may have similar or additional standards of evidence to investigate discrimination claims and you should investigate what those standards are, especially as you work on documentation.

Title IX and Title VI also provide protection on the basis of sex in educational institutions. Title IX, which is the more common enforcement mechanism, is a federal civil rights law that states: "no person in the United States shall, on the basis of sex, be excluded from participation in, be denied the benefits of, or be subjected to discrimination under any education program or activity receiving Federal financial assistance" (Department of Education, Office of Civil Rights 2021).

Title IX policies work off of a similar evidentiary standard to the Title VI standards. This standard of proof is called "preponderance of evidence," which essentially means you need to prove that the events were more likely than not to occur. This is different, and a lesser burden of proof, than the typical United States legal standard of "beyond a reasonable doubt."

There are important categories that are left out of this definition, such as those based on religious belief, parental status, pregnancy, language, and LGBTQ2SIA+ identity. This volume offers several relevant chapters for members of each of these groups, as well as for women and members of minoritized racial and ethnic groups. See chapters: Concerns for Underrepresented Racial/Ethnic Students and Scholars and a Model for Inclusive Excellence, Political Science & LGBTQ Identity: Thoughts & Suggestions for LGBTQ Graduate Students, Gender and the Political Science Graduate Experience: When Leaning In Isn't Enough, Concerns for International Graduate Students in Political Science, Religious Minorities and the Graduate School Experience, and Disabilities and Chronic Health Issues for more insights into challenges and strategies of navigating various identities within the political science community. Your university or state may have legislation that provides additional rights for these identity categories. However, it is also possible that your institution may have a more limited scope of what it considers discrimination, especially if it is outside of the United States.

Institutional Solutions

Office of Equal Opportunity/Title IX

Once you know what your university, state, and federal policies on discrimination are, you can decide what institutional, legal, and community options make most sense for you to pursue. To begin, most universities have some sort of office that oversees all types of discrimination at the institution. The name may vary, but is usually something along the lines of "Office of Equal Opportunity" or "Office of Inclusive Excellence" or "Office of Equity, Diversity, and Inclusion." These offices are often umbrellas that include other offices such as the Title IX office and disability services. They may also include LGBTQ2SIA+ resource centers, international student services, women's resource centers, etc. When you report to these offices, you do often have a statute of limitations (usually around 90-120 days since the last incident), though these can often be extended if you provide a reason. These offices are also required to be neutral and cannot take sides. Many offices also interpret this neutrality standard as an equality standard, i.e., anything provided to the person reporting discrimination must also be provided to the perpetrator. The offices that handle these claims are also often able to (and in some cases required to) provide "supportive measures"—these could include temporary work or class reassignments, deadline extensions, staggered schedules, counseling, or other measures.

Finally, it's important to note that there are both formal and informal methods of resolution of discrimination. For formal resolution processes, the university will launch their own investigation into the facts and circumstances of the case to determine if they think discrimination has occurred. They are also able to assign their own determination of consequences at the conclusion of the process, which may or may not involve input from those who have reported and experienced that discrimination. While these consequences can be more severe and compliance is mandatory when assigned by the investigators, you will also generally have little agency in determining what these consequences are. The consequences may also be unaligned with the outcome that you desire. You can generally gain an idea of what these consequences typically look like by asking the office that handles investigations about what consequences for similar forms of discrimination have been.

Informal resolution processes require the involvement of both parties and it is an entirely voluntary process. In this process, the person reporting has more agency over the types of outcomes they would like to see in the case. However, the perpetrator must agree to those outcomes and has the power to deny any requests for outcomes or refuse to participate at all. Offices of Equal Opportunity and Title IX offices are not generally clear about this, but you have the right to do both processes simultaneously and you have the right to switch pathways at any time, for any reason. This means that if you try to go the informal resolution route and run into roadblocks with the perpetrator, you have the right to switch to the formal process and the office must honor that.

Although going through these offices may afford you institutional protections or more concrete remedies to discrimination, there can be some significant drawbacks to pursuing this option. First, the process is often quite long. Depending on the staffing and volume of complaints, it can take anywhere from 60-180 days for an office to come to a resolution on a discrimination complaint. Second, filing these complaints often requires filing dozens (if not hundreds) of documents and pieces of evidence as well as providing multiple statements. While several activists and advocates have been calling for universities to streamline their statement and evidence collection processes, many institutions still use outdated processes. These processes can be extremely time-intensive, triggering, and exhausting. Third, filing Title IX complaints can lead to negative reactions from people in your department or institution. Technically, this type of response is considered retaliation and is also barred under federal law, but it's often hard to be able to collect evidence for it and still happens quite frequently. Fourth, an unfortunate process that happens in discrimination investigations is a deep dive into the "character" of who is reporting. This is a recommendation that has been made by many consulting groups to universities. In these "character" investigations, the university will essentially try to determine if they think you are trustworthy or believable by talking to others in the institution and researching your reputation. This is an extremely invasive process and can have significant, negative emotional impacts on those reporting to read these "character" reports in the investigation materials.

Ombuds

In addition to OEO and Title IX offices, you may also be able to use a university ombuds. The ombuds is a neutral, confidential, conflict resolution resource. These offices are confidential by definition and can assist with clarification around policy. They cannot represent you or be an advocate for you, but they can be a good resource if you are unsure about your rights under certain policies or if you feel as if a university policy may have been applied in a discriminatory fashion. Ombuds services are not always provided to graduate students, so check with your university policies.

Human Resources/Equal Employment Office

Another thing that is important to keep in mind as you consider options is that you may be classified as a student, employee or both. If you are considered an employee, you also have the ability to report these issues to your Human Resources/Human Assets department and seek relief from federal agencies such as the Equal Employment Office (EEO). Additionally, if you are on a campus that is unionized, your union may be able to provide legal support or may be able to intervene on your behalf depending on the situation. See "Community, Solidarity, and Collective Power: The Role of Graduate Student Organizations and Graduate Worker Unions" on graduate student unions and organizing. You should note that if your perpetrator is also a member of the union, it is less likely you may have those resources available to you.

Professional Associations' Resources

Incidents of discrimination and assault occur not only on campus, but at annual meetings, conferences, and workshops sponsored by professional associations. Increasingly, academic professional associations have responded by hiring ombuds, as well as by adopting codes of conduct and anti-harassment policies and procedures. Consider familiarizing yourself with these resources and relying on the ombuds if an incident happens at an association-sponsored event.

Legal Options

OCR Complaint

You may also choose to forgo institutional options or may have an unsuccessful resolution of options through institutional avenues. In this case, you may consider legal options. This could include processes like independent arbitration or investigation (if applicable for your university), obtaining your own legal counsel, or filing a complaint with the Department of Education Office of Civil Rights (OCR). If you are pursuing legal options such as a lawsuit, some states may require that you exhaust all institutionally available options first. This means that you must go through every reporting and appeal process at your institution available to you, regardless of your likelihood of success. If you miss any steps (for example, not filing a discrimination complaint), the judge may rule that you did not exhaust your options. So, seeking legal options may require you to go through the full institutional processes regardless. Some firms may provide this support as a pro-bono service or, if they think the case is likely to be successful and result in a damages payment, as a service where they will collect their payment only if they win the litigation. In other cases, this option may require thousands of dollars to pursue.

Options like a complaint or request for an investigation by OCR has several advantages.[8] First, this is one of the few avenues that can actually change the entire policy or procedure a university uses. Second, the electronic complaint form is often less time-intensive and daunting than university paperwork and processes.[9] If the OCR needs additional information, they will send you correspondence requesting it after they make a determination as to whether they think your institution has violated federal law and engaged in discrimination. OCR complaints do require that you file within 180 days of the last incident/interaction or that you provide a reason why you are filing after the 180 day mark. You are also able to file this prior to engaging with your institutional processes. If you file as the process is ongoing, OCR may require that process to resolve and then file within 60 days of that decision (Department of Education, Office of Civil Rights n.d.).

Community-Based Support

You may also choose to seek out community-based support. In some areas, you may have a local civil rights group like Black Lives Matter or an Office of Multicultural Affairs that may take on cases and help push for corrective action through social and community pressure. Additionally, community groups may provide emotional and spiritual support—especially if you share any type of identity ties with the organization or individuals in the group.

Doing Nothing

Finally, you may choose not to report or directly address the situation when faced with discrimination. In these cases, looking into options for therapy or building a supportive network can be critical to healing and moving forward after discrimination. The chapters included in the Health and Wellness in Graduate School section may also be useful to consult as you process your situation.

Table 51.1: Summary of discrimination response and reporting options

Option	Advantages	Disadvantages
Office of Equal Opportunity/ Title IX	Free, decisions are generally binding and can provide protection.	Time-consuming, emotionally draining, long processing time (60-180 days).
Ombuds	Free, confidential resource, less time-consuming than filing a formal complaint.	No binding decisions, may not exist or be available for graduate students.
HR/EEO	Free, may provide quicker resolution and better solutions when the issue is work-related.	Not confidential, may not be available to graduate students if not classified as an employee by the institution or if the issue was not work-related.
Union	Free (except union dues), may be able to provide legal services or advocate for you to university or department.	Not confidential, may not exist.
Legal Counsel	May be free, an attorney can represent and fight for you and your rights specifically.	May cost thousands of dollars, is likely to burn bridges with your current department and/or university, litigation may bring many details to public light, may still require you to pursue institutional processes first.
OCR Complaint	Free, quick/easy process in comparison to many university forms, don't need to do university process first, may have quicker resolution than institutions.	Only covers some forms of discrimination, may not get you desired outcomes.
Community Resources	Free, may provide emotional or spiritual support while processing discriminatory incidents.	No enforcement mechanisms, may not be available or an option in very small communities depending on your identity, community resources may be highly limited in forms of support that can be provided.

Sexual Assault

In cases of sexual assault, there are also institutional, legal, and community options available to survivors.[10] Before we dive into these options, we will briefly discuss some common forms of documentation and evidence collection that occur.

Documentation

One of the most difficult parts of processing sexual assault is the time sensitivity in documenting events and evidence. You may want to consider having a sexual assault forensic exam, also known as a "rape kit." While these exams are most useful within 72 hours, there is still important evidence that can be preserved outside of that timeframe (RAINN n.d.). Getting an exam does not obligate you into filing charges or initiate any type of proceeding or investigation. It does preserve your options for doing these things in the future, however. These exams are free and you can stop, pause, or skip steps at any time during the exam (RAINN n.d.). For a more complete account of what this exam entails, check out RAINN's guide to forensic sexual assault exams.[11] In terms of other documentation, you may also want to work with a trusted friend or family member or victim-survivor advocate to help collect and document details about your sexual assault in case you need the information in the future. We would caution against using at-home or self-collected kits. The standard of evidence is unlikely to meet legal requirements, limiting your future options for reporting and justice, and they provide no healthcare benefit to survivors (International Association of Forensic Nurses 2019).

Institutional Options

Many of the institutional options available to survivors of sexual assault will be the same resources that are available to those experiencing sex or gender-based discrimination. To review those options see the section on Office of Equal Opportunity/Title IX.

There are some specific things to note around seeking institutional support when dealing with the aftermath of sexual assault that you should be aware of. First, Title IX regulations are currently in flux due to the transition from the Trump administration to the Biden administration. Under the Trump administration, new guidelines were put into place that required special hearings in cases of sexual assault and allowed perpetrators to directly cross-examine survivors (North 2020). While this provision has been recently vacated by a federal judge, it's likely that in future conservative administrations that these provisions may return (Cahill 2021).

Second, there has been a movement of litigation against survivors who are naming their assailants. This does not mean that you should hide your assault, but you should be aware of the climate that has allowed for and supported weaponized lawsuits (Bever 2016; Equality Now 2021). Furthermore, many perpetrators will exploit the neutrality of Title IX and Office of Equal Opportunity to turn protective orders or supportive measures against survivors (Nesbitt and Carson 2021; Tschanz n.d.). Often, when perpetrators of sexual violence are confronted with their behavior and presented with consequences for their actions, it is common for them to invoke DARVO, which stands for "Deny, Attack, and Reverse Victim and Offender" (Freyd 1997). Freyd explains DARVO as follows:

> The perpetrator or offender may Deny the behavior, Attack the individual doing the confronting, and Reverse the roles of Victim and Offender such that the perpetrator assumes the victim role and turns the true victim—or the whistle blower—into an alleged offender. (Freyd 1997)

DARVO has become more ubiquitous across society as a whole and has been especially present on many campuses. This phenomenon is not helped by the fact that many college administrators see themselves as neutral and responsible for the rights of both the perpetrator and survivor in these situations (Cruz 2021).

Third, many campus investigations into Title IX cases will not be led or handled by staff with formal legal training. Given the complexity of sexual assault cases, this often results in ineffective investigations and inconsistent application of university policies. There is also no standard protocol, guidelines, or qualifications necessary for Title IX investigators to abide by, which creates massive inconsistencies in practice from institution to institution. Even when these investigations are carried out well, the final say on the investigation, findings, and recommendations often lies with the office of the President or Chancellor.

Finally, there are many incentives for institutions to cheat in their data reporting. This reporting of data is governed by the Clery Act and requires three main components: timely notifications to the campus community of safety threats, maintenance of a crime log, and the publication of an annual report on security. These reports have become incredibly unwieldy and can span into hundreds of pages on some campuses (Davis 2020). As a result, campuses are often able to spin or bury troubling trends deep into the contents of these reports, to the benefit of institutions and to the detriment of faculty, staff, and students. There are also muddled definitions of what "counts" in Clery Act calculations which can drive how the university conducts its processes with handling and publicly reporting counts for crimes like sexual assault.

If you don't feel as if your institution properly addresses your sexual assault case, or if you think it is unlikely your institution will appropriately address the assault because of policies or procedures in place, you also have the option of pursuing an OCR complaint as described earlier in this chapter.

Legal Options

Aside from institutional options, there are also several legal options available to you. Unfortunately, in many cases, to pursue legal options, especially criminal prosecution, you may be required to talk to police or file a police report at some point. Additionally, many crime-victims services, such as access to healthcare, lease-breaking, victims' legal services, etc. require a police report filing as a condition for accessing those services, depending on your state and community. For those who are Black, Indigenous, Latine, people of color, LGBTQ2SIA+, disabled, undocumented, or belong to other historically marginalized groups, this may also pose a threat to your safety or exacerbate the circumstances of your assault. If this ends up being a step that you need to do or choose to do, victim-survivor advocates, as discussed earlier in this piece, can help significantly in streamlining and minimizing your interactions with police. You can meet with them first, record your story and details of the assault with them, and have them help you file the report. You can also request that your advocate be present in the room with you, as well as other emotional support (such as a parent, friend, significant other, or other supportive folks).

Community Options

Community resources and centers that deal with sexual assault can be an invaluable asset when it comes to sexual assault. If you are on a small campus, you may not have well-resourced offices that can support your material, financial, and emotional needs as you process. Community options such as rape crisis centers or domestic violence/family violence resource centers (in cases where the sexual assault was a result of intimate partner violence) can help provide you access to therapists, caseworkers, legal aid, victim-survivor advocates, and expertise. Aside from the justice aspects of handling sexual assault, you may need support in doing things like breaking your lease, getting access to temporary/safe housing, getting access to medical care or therapy, or other types of support. Community centers are often connected to other community providers and resources and can help you during the recovery process from assault.

Social media is also a popular method of seeking community and getting support after a sexual assault. There are many support groups that you can find through Reddit, Twitter, Facebook, and other social media sites that will connect you with other survivors. This can be a comforting option for those who need to connect with other survivors but would either like a degree of anonymity or can't physically attend support groups. Relatedly, some campus wellness centers will also do group therapy where survivors can connect with each other and communally process their experiences. Social media can also be useful for finding answers to questions regarding resources and policies. One example of this is the many campus Instagram pages for survivors to submit and share their stories (such as @shareyourstory, @metoomvmt, and their campus derivatives).

Unfortunately, many of the resources and discussions about responding to sexual assault in higher educational settings are disproportionately led by and centered on the experiences of white women. When Women of Color who identify as survivors of sexual assault have been interviewed, they have indicated that therapy options available to them on campus or covered by graduate insurance plans lack cultural competency (Harris, Karunaratne, and Gutzwa 2021). Alternatively, many of the women interviewed in this same study indicated that they found healing spaces through some groups of peers, space within their academic courses, and through body-based or somatic healing activities (such as yoga, ballet, and jiu jitsu) (Harris, Karunaratne, and Gutzwa 2021).

Table 51.2: Summary of sexual assault response and reporting options

Option	Advantages	Disadvantages
Office of Equal Opportunity/ Title IX	Free, decisions are generally binding and can provide protection, and may be able to receive supportive measures (like moving classes or campus ban) immediately.	Time-consuming, emotionally draining, long processing time (60-180 days), may involve invasive measures like direct cross-examination.
Legal Counsel	May be free, an attorney can represent and fight for you and your rights specifically, which may help you figure out how to avoid or navigate weaponized litigation by your perpetrator.	May cost thousands of dollars, is likely to burn bridges with your current department and/or university, litigation may bring many details to public light, may still require you to pursue institutional processes first.
OCR Complaint	Free, quick/easy process in comparison to many university forms, don't need to do university process first, may have quicker resolution than institutions	Only covers some forms of discrimination, may not get you desired outcomes.
Community Resources	Free, may provide material, emotional, financial support while recovering from assault.	May not be available or an option in very small communities depending on your identity, community resources may be highly limited in forms of support that can be provided, there may be significant waiting times for some types of support.

Bystander Intervention and Handling Disclosures

If you are a bystander in an instance of assault or discrimination, or if someone discloses these things to you, we have some recommendations on how to handle these situations based on best practices and input from those who have experienced these events.

   If you are present during an instance of discrimination or sexual assault, one common bystander intervention model is the four D's: direct, distract, delegate, and/or delay (American Friends Service Committee 2020). (Prior to engaging in any of the four D's you should assess the situation and determine that it is safe to intervene.) Direct stands for responding directly to the aggressor in the situation and telling them to stop their actions, words, or behavior. Distracting looks like asking a question, causing a commotion (spilling a drink, playing a loud song or video), pretending that you know the person who looks like they are uncomfortable or in danger. Delegating involves bringing in an additional person, usually someone with more power in the situation—a bartender, a manager, another professor, a staff member. If there is no third person to bring in, sometimes a cell phone recording (or perception of its recording) can do the trick. Finally, if there is no safe way for you to intervene at the moment, you can check in with the person who was being discriminated against or who experienced assault after the incident. You might ask something like "is there someone I can call?" or offer to take them to a safe location. These steps can help de-escalate or even prevent a situation of discrimination or sexual assault. You can find more information about this bystander intervention approach in a handout compiled by the American Friends Service Committee.[12] Bystander interventions are something you should practice at home before you ever need to think about using those approaches—especially if you are generally not someone to get involved in situations. You are far more likely to have the confidence to do one of the 4Ds if you have practiced this ahead of time, even if just in your head.

If someone discloses discrimination or sexual assault to you, there are several things you can do to support them. The following steps in this paragraph are adapted from Ending Violence's disclosure response guide (Ending Violence 2016). First and most importantly, believe them. It does not matter what they were doing, wearing, saying—it was not their fault. Discrimination and sexual assault are never the fault of the people experiencing it. Second, make sure that you are actively listening. Let the person disclosing take the lead on the order they tell their story, how much or how little information they share, and tell them that you are glad that you are sharing. While the person is talking, it's possible that they might be releasing many emotions or even have a panic attack. It is very important to give them physical space and not touch them. You can offer water, guide them through a simple grounding (name three things you see, name two things you smell, etc.), and/or help them do some guided breathing. Finally, ensure that you discuss options with them. They may disclose as a way to give context for things happening in class or their advising relationship with you. They may also disclose because they need help and are not sure where to turn for support. You don't need to provide all of these answers for them, but you should consider making sure you have at least one or two people that you might be able to "warm" connect students with (i.e., directly introduce) on your campus who handle sexual assault or discrimination if the student would like that type of support. For more detailed information on handling disclosures, read this resource from Ending Violence[13]: https://bit.ly/SA_Disclosure.

If you are considered a mandatory reporter on your campus (in some cases, this may also include teaching assistants or other staff positions), you may also want to remind them of this during the disclosure conversation. Many students may be unaware of what a mandatory reporter is or to whom that provision applies. University policies on mandatory reporting have been widely criticized by many activists and professors, noting that these policies often serve to protect institutions and may be actively harmful to survivors (Miron and Palacios 2018). It is a common misperception that these universal mandatory reporting policies are required when, in fact, Title IX does not require them and they are minimally effective for supporting survivors of sexual violence on campuses (Holland et al. 2021). Additionally, faculty have reported that they feel conflicted between a choice to "continue to teach about sexual violence, knowing that you will eventually be forced to betray a student's confidence, or simply stop teaching about sexual violence" (Holland et al. 2021). Additionally, mandatory reporting can unintentionally expose survivors to retaliation by their perpetrators, prevent them from fully engaging in course assignments and discussions, and fully engaging in mentor/mentee relationships (Lorenz, Shepp, and O'Callaghan 2021). One alternative to this universal mandatory reporting model would include a shift to a "responsible reporting" model, which offers survivors the option of reporting to Title IX if they want to, among other supportive measures (Holland et al. 2021; Kanik 2017). Centering effort and resources that prioritize healing for survivors, making room for transformative justice approaches led by survivors, and addressing the conditions that allow sexual assault and discrimination to uncontrollably fester (such as low wages, suppression of organizing, and threats to legal status) are all far more effective forms of support for students most vulnerable to these forms of violence (Holland et al. 2021).

Conclusion

Discrimination and sexual assault are far too frequent experiences for many graduate students. In this chapter, we have provided guidance for approaching responses and reporting of both discrimination and sexual assault. Additionally, we have provided some basic resources about bystander intervention and best practices for responding to disclosures of discrimination or sexual assault. College administrators must pay particular attention to survivor resources on campus and, in particular, ensure that the resources available to students who experience discrimination and sexual assault are culturally competent. There should also be serious consideration of revising or revoking mandatory reporting policies that trigger Title IX investigations without survivors' consent. While this article is far from exhaustive of the options out there for survivors, we hope that this will paint a fair picture of what survivors can expect (both the good and the bad) when taking different response avenues. Finally, we implore faculty members and programs to become proficient with these options that we have outlined and work with campus and academic communities at-large to respond to instances of sexual assault and discrimination. Institutional and discipline-wide policies are needed to help address and prevent this type of violence from occurring in the first place. This problem will not passively disappear. It requires diligent work by all members of our academic community to end this violence.

Endnotes

1   Lesbian, Gay, Bisexual, Trans, Queer and/or Questioning, Two-Spirit/2-Spirit, Intersex, Asexual, Plus

2   Many people who have experienced forms of discrimination or interpersonal violence have different terms or words that they prefer to use when referring to their experiences. For the sake of clarity and in alignment with our experience as the authors, we are choosing to use the term survivor while discussing sexual assault and discrimination in this chapter.

3   Title IX is a civil rights law that prohibits sex-based discrimination in any school or other education program that receives funding from the federal government.

4   https://bit.ly/RecordingLaws

5   https://bit.ly/DiscriminationDocumentationGuide

6   Mandatory reporters are people who are designated by institutions or state law to report certain crimes or abuses. In some states or institutions, mandatory reporting can be very narrow and only include abuse of vulnerable populations, such as children or the elderly and may only apply to people like doctors, nurses, police officers, or teachers. In other places, mandatory reporters can be anyone who receives a paycheck from the institution or is otherwise formally affiliated. This may mean that if you hold a teaching assistantship you are a mandatory reporter on your campus. Each campus has their own protocols for steps to take for mandatory reporting, so be sure to check with your department and/or HR about your mandatory reporting responsibilities.

7   https://bit.ly/TitleVILegalManual

8   https://bit.ly/OCRComplaintProcess

9   https://bit.ly/OCR_Form

10   We are aware of debates regarding using the terminology of victims vs. survivors. We have chosen to use the term survivors in this piece as it most closely resembles the current status based on our personal experiences as authors. Hopefully, later on, we can become thrivers using our (completely unwanted) experiences to make us stronger.

11   https://bit.ly/SAexam

12   https://bit.ly/FourD_Bystander

13   https://bit.ly/SA_Disclosure

References

American Friends Service Committee. 2020. "4Ds: Learn How to Distract, Delegate, Direct, and Delay." *American Friends Service Committee.* https://www.afsc.org/story/4ds-learn-how-to-distract-delegate-direct-and-delay (December 20, 2021).

Bever, Lindsey. 2016. "She Called the Man Who Sexually Assaulted Her a Rapist. Then He Sued Her for Defamation.—The Washington Post." https://www.washingtonpost.com/news/post-nation/wp/2016/10/03/i-felt-re-victimized-woman-sued-for-referring-to-the-man-who-sexually-assaulted-her-as-a-rapist/ (December 20, 2021).

Brown, Nadia E. 2019. "Mentoring, Sexual Harassment, and Black Women Academics." *Journal of Women, Politics & Policy* 40(1): 166–73.

———, ed. 2021. *Me Too Political Science.* First issued in paperback. London New York: Routledge.

Cahill, Ann J. 2021. "Still Harming: Why the Trump-Era Title IX Regulations Need to Go." Blog of the APA. https://blog.apaonline.org/2021/10/06/still-harming-why-the-trump-era-title-ix-regulations-need-to-go/ (December 20, 2021).

Clawson, Rosalee A. 2019. "#MeToo from a Department Head Perspective." *Journal of Women, Politics & Policy* 40(1): 184–89.

Cruz, Jacqueline. 2021. "The Constraints of Fear and Neutrality in Title IX Administrators' Responses to Sexual Violence." *The Journal of Higher Education* 92(3): 363–84.

Davis, Edward. 2020. "It's Time to Reform the Clery Act." *Inside Higher Ed.* https://www.insidehigh-ered.com/views/2020/05/15/clery-act-does-little-improve-campus-safety-even-during-pandemic-opinion (February 4, 2022).

Department of Education, Office of Civil Rights. 2015. "Age Discrimination Overview of the Laws." https://www2.ed.gov/policy/rights/guid/ocr/ageoverview.html (December 20, 2021).

———. 2020a. "Disability Discrimination." https://www2.ed.gov/about/offices/list/ocr/frontpage/caseresolutions/disability-cr.html (December 20, 2021).

———. 2020b. "Know Your Rights." https://www2.ed.gov/about/offices/list/ocr/know.html (December 20, 2021).

———. 2021. "Title IX and Sex Discrimination." https://www2.ed.gov/about/offices/list/ocr/docs/tix_dis.html (December 20, 2021).

———. "Questions and Answers on OCR's Complaint Process." https://www2.ed.gov/about/offices/list/ocr/qa-complaints.html (December 20, 2021).

Department of Justice. 2017. 42 U.S.C. *Section VI- Proving Discrimination- Intentional Discrimination.* https://www.justice.gov/crt/fcs/t6manual6 (December 20, 2021).

Ending Violence. 2016. "Responding to a Sexual Assault Disclosure." https://endingviolence.org/wp-content/uploads/2016/05/EVA_PracticeTips_UniversitiesColleges_vF.pdf (December 20, 2021).

Equality Now. 2021. "Weaponizing Defamation Lawsuits against Survivors Violates International Human Rights." https://www.equalitynow.org/news_and_insights/weaponizing-defamation-lawsuits-against-survivors-violates-international-human-rights/ (December 20, 2021).

Freyd, J.J. 1997. "Violations of Power, Adaptive Blindness, and Betrayal Trauma Theory." *Feminism & Psychology* 7(1): 22–32.

Harris, Jessica C., Nadeeka Karunaratne, and Justin A. Gutzwa. 2021. "Effective Modalities for Healing from Campus Sexual Assault: Centering the Experiences of Women of Color Undergraduate Student Survivors." *Harvard Educational Review* 91(2): 248–72.

Holland, Kathryn J., Elizabeth Q. Hutchison, Courtney E. Ahrens, and M. Gabriela Torres. 2021. "Reporting Is Not Supporting: Why Mandatory Supporting, Not Mandatory Reporting, Must Guide University Sexual Misconduct Policies." *Proceedings of the National Academy of Sciences* 118(52): e2116515118.

International Association of Forensic Nurses. 2019. "Addressing DIY Sexual Assault Exams: Protecting Our Patients." https://www.forensicnurses.org/page/DIYkits (December 21, 2021).

Kanik, Hannah. 2017. "UO Creates New 'Responsible Reporting' Policy to Support Survivors of Gender-Based Discrimination and Harassment on Campus." *Daily Emerald.* https://www.dailyemerald.com/news/uo-creates-new-responsible-reporting-policy-to-support-survivors-of-gender-based-discrimination-and-harassment/article_062c09d4-13b8-5a4d-9593-04772e29638f.html (February 4, 2022).

Lay, J. Celeste. 2019. "Policy Learning and Transformational Change: University Policies on Sexual Harassment." *Journal of Women, Politics & Policy* 40(1): 156–65.

Lorenz, Katherine, Veronica Shepp, and Erin O'Callaghan. 2021. "Title IX Mandatory Reporting Can Trigger Investigation Without Survivors' Consent." *Truthout.* https://truthout.org/articles/mandatory-reporting-can-trigger-investigation-without-survivors-consent/ (February 4, 2022).

McDermott, Rose. 2019. "Political Science's #MeToo Moment." *Journal of Women, Politics & Policy* 40(1): 148–55.

Miron, Rose, and Lena Palacios. 2018. "Mandatory Reporting Policies Protect Universities, Not Survivors." *Gender Policy Report.* https://genderpolicyreport.umn.edu/mandatory-reporting-policies-protect-universities-not-survivors/ (February 4, 2022).

Nesbitt, Sarah, and Sage Carson. 2021. *The Cost of Reporting: Perpetrator Retaliation, Institutional Betrayal, and Student Survivor Pushout. Know Your Title IX.* https://www.knowyourix.org/wp-content/uploads/2021/03/Know-Your-IX-2021-Report-Final-Copy.pdf.

North, Anna. 2020. "New Title IX Rules: Campus Sexual Assault Guidelines Released amid the Pandemic." https://www.vox.com/2020/5/6/21203255/new-title-ix-rules-campus-sexual-assault-betsy-devos (December 20, 2021).

Nunnally, Shayla C. 2019. "The National Conference of Black Political Scientists (NCOBPS): Organizational Empowerment Through Signaling and Valuing Women and Diversity During #MeToo." *Journal of Women, Politics & Policy* 40(1): 190–94.

RAINN. "What Is a Sexual Assault Forensic Exam?" https://www.rainn.org/articles/rape-kit (December 21, 2021).

Restrepo Sanín, Juliana. 2019a. "'I Don't Belong Here': Understanding Hostile Spaces." *Journal of Women, Politics & Policy* 40(1): 112–21.

———. 2019b. "#MeToo What Kind of Politics? Panel Notes." *Journal of Women, Politics & Policy* 40(1): 122–28.

Shames, Shauna. 2019. "Why I Do Activist Work within the Discipline." *Journal of Women, Politics & Policy* 40(1): 129–30.

Strach, Patricia. 2019. "What's Wrong with Us? Sexual Misconduct and the Discipline of Political Science." *Journal of Women, Politics & Policy* 40(1): 7–20.

Sulfaro, Valerie A., and Rebecca Gill. 2019. "Title IX: Help or Hindrance?" *Journal of Women, Politics & Policy* 40(1): 204–27.

Tschanz, Meghan. "Her Research Shows That Some Men Use Sexual Assault Allegations to Their Benefit." https://podcasts.apple.com/us/podcast/her-research-shows-that-some-men-use-sexual-assault/id1438368947?i=1000544194956.

Tyson, Vanessa. 2019. "Understanding the Personal Impact of Sexual Violence and Assault." *Journal of Women, Politics & Policy* 40(1): 174–83.

52 | Sexual Harassment in Academia: What Every Graduate Student Should Know

Valerie Sulfaro[1] & Rebecca Gill[2]

1.James Madison University 2. University of Nevada Las Vegas

KEYWORDS: #MeToo, Title IX, Betrayal Trauma, Bystander.

The Scope of the Problem

In the era of the #MeToo movement,[1] longstanding cultures that enable sexual harassment have been brought into the harsh light of public scrutiny. Despite the somewhat romanticized version of academic life visible to most outside the academy, sexual harassment is a significant problem in higher education. Indeed, as institutions of higher education have failed to address the problem adequately, current and former graduate students have turned to the same social media hashtags to try to build community and find healing (Kachen et al. 2019).

It's important for any potential or current graduate student to understand the scope of this problem in academia. While sexual harassment tends to be invisible to the casual observer, it is an underreported but pervasive phenomenon on college campuses. In this chapter, we introduce some of the research on sexual harassment and provide some thoughts from our own experiences navigating sexual harassment in the field of academic political science.

First, some clarification of terms is useful. Gender-based discrimination is an umbrella term that includes a wide variety of behaviors in which a person is treated "unfavorably because of that person's sex, including the person's sexual orientation, gender identity, or pregnancy" (EEOC n.d.). Gender discrimination can manifest itself in several ways, two of which are key for the purposes of our discussion: sexual coercion and gender harassment (NASEM 2018). A helpful way of distinguishing between the two is to view sexual coercion as a "come-on" and gender harassment as a "put-down," although the lines can be somewhat difficult to discern.

The term sexual coercion refers to an attempt to use a position of power to extract sexual favors, generally from a subordinate. This kind of harassment can include sexual coercion and unwanted sexual attention. Examples of these include quid pro quo harassment, which involves promises of professional rewards for providing sexual favors and/or threats of professional consequences for refusing sexual demands. By contrast, gender harassment is an attempt to disparage, discredit, harass, or otherwise treat you less favorably than others based on your perceived gender traits. Gender harassment can include unwanted sexual discussions, sexist insults, gender slurs, and other behaviors that can create a hostile work environment on account of gender.

In everyday discussion, the key components of sexual coercion and gender harassment are usually lumped into the category of sexual harassment. Indeed, the evolution of our interpretation of Title IX encourages this. Under Title IX, all the behaviors outlined above would be considered sexual harassment, provided they are severe or pervasive enough. When we discuss sexual harassment here, we refer to everything included in this broader definition.

Unfortunately, graduate school does not provide safe haven. Research shows that between ten

(Cantalupo and Kidder 2018) and thirty-eight (Rosenthal et al. 2016) percent of female students have experienced sexual harassment at the hands of faculty and staff while in graduate school. Female graduate students of color, despite their lower share of the graduate student population overall, are substantially more likely to experience instances of sexual harassment than are other students (Cantalupo 2019). But women are not the only targets of such abuse. Rosenthal et al. (2016) find that 38% of women and 23% of male graduate students reported experiencing some form of sexual harassment from university faculty and staff. In one study, harassment by fellow graduate students was reported by 58% of women and 39% of men in graduate school (Rosenthal et al. 2016). While men may also experience sexual harassment during their studies, women are generally the targets. The risk is particularly acute for women of color, members of the LGBTQ+ community, and international students.

As this discussion makes clear, anyone can be a harasser. Graduate students can be subject to sexual harassment from faculty, staff, or other graduate students. Faculty and staff may also be subject to harassment by graduate students, particularly early in their careers, or if they are adjuncts. Of course, the power dynamic in this instance is somewhat different, in that faculty ostensibly have legal protections against harassment in their place of employment, whereas graduate students have little recourse if a program chooses to terminate them for misconduct. However, there are situations where a graduate student with powerful faculty allies can have protection against accountability for harassing behavior. While this is not our primary focus here, it is important to acknowledge that the power dynamics in academia can operate in ways that a formal organizational chart might not predict.

Unfortunately, it is often difficult to recognize sexual harassment in academia. Even what is presumed to be a consensual intimate relationship may involve sexual coercion. Keller (1990) suggests that such relationships are often characterized by "implicit or explicit duress" that can push students into such relationships, whether they realize it at the time or not. The potential consequences of declining an unsolicited advance by a faculty member almost certainly influence the student's decision to engage—even if this is not obvious to the student in the moment.

This problem is uniquely acute for graduate students. Graduate students are far more vulnerable than undergraduates to such pressures because undergraduates are less reliant on specific faculty members to earn their degrees. Undergraduate students can often navigate around faculty harassers because their careers are generally not so heavily reliant on the support of one specific faculty member. Undergraduates can simply avoid faculty members in taking future courses or ask to be assigned a different advisor, mitigating (but not removing) the damage.

Graduate students are far more likely to need to establish and maintain a good working relationship with faculty members in their subfield (NASEM 2018). These faculty members are the ones from whom graduate students take more courses. Graduate students depend on subfield faculty consent to pass qualifying and comprehensive exams, to successfully complete their dissertation, and to receive necessary job references (O'Callaghan et al., 2021). Research has demonstrated that the more dependent a graduate student is on a faculty member, the higher the likelihood that they will experience harassment (Scott 1983).

While there is some variability in the rate of reported harassment in studies of different doctoral programs (see Bondestam and Lundqvist 2020), the common element across studies is that sexual harassment is a pervasive, enduring feature of the graduate student experience. That sexual harassment is endemic in higher education suggests that universities either have little interest in combatting the problem of sexual harassment in their ranks, or if they are concerned, they are pursuing the wrong avenues for addressing it.

In short, universities have created a climate friendly to sexual harassment and resistant to efforts to curb abuses. However, this should not be a surprise. Certainly, these institutions express commitment to the well-being of their students; most departments and their parent institutions make this commitment very clear in their public-facing material. At the same time, however, these same institutions have an ongoing commitment to maintaining the professional reputations of their faculty and their departments. This inherent conflict forces decision makers to weigh competing interests. Unfortunately, institutions of higher education often act in ways that favor preserving the reputation of the faculty over the safety of the students. Thus, there are powerful structural forces that allow sexual harassment to persist in academia.

The Consequences of Sexual Harassment

Sexual harassment in graduate school can be costly for its victims. Harassment acts as a "productivity tax" that affects the ability of women and others to be effective researchers, manage their time, receive academic support, and contribute to the diversity of ideas in their discipline (Zepeda 2018). It amounts to disparate treatment based on gender that disadvantages its victims vis-à-vis their peers. Put another way, those who can attend graduate school without experiencing sexual (or other) harassment experience a luxury akin to being raised in an affluent household—even if they are not cognizant of the benefits this creates for them.

Dobbin and Kalev (2019) argue that in a workplace setting, experiencing sexual harassment makes people more likely to quit their jobs. It's easy to see how harassment in an academic setting would produce similar results. Research suggests that students who experience verbal or physical mistreatment demonstrate a decline in their overall academic performance, and those who experience some form of sexual violence exhibit a higher rate of academic attrition than other students (Mengo and Black 2015; NASEM 2018). Victims experience a drop in motivation levels and suffer higher rates of career impairment than students not subject to sexual harassment (Bondestam and Lundqvist 2020).

The psychological and physiological effects of sexual harassment on those targeted for such abuse have been described as "severe" (Bondestam and Lundqvist 2020) and can include alcoholism, post-traumatic stress disorder, anxiety, and depression. Scholars offer varying theoretical explanations for why sexual harassment generates these outcomes. One such theory is imposter syndrome, wherein a victim of harassment feels less confident in her intellect and experiences a diminished sense of belonging in her discipline as a result of being targeted for abuse (see chapter 50 on imposter syndrome). In an article about imposter syndrome, one researcher describes the relationship this way: "What do one-off hand rubbing, leg touching, thigh grabbing, objectification remarks, or second-class status have… to do with research? Speaking from experiences, sexual harassments of all forms significantly dampen, if not completely kill, the research flame of victims" (Yao 2021, 41-42).

Other research finds that being harmed or exploited by a trusted mentor, a phenomenon known as betrayal trauma (Gomez 2019b), can have serious adverse psychological consequences for victims, including anxiety and depression, which may affect academic performance. Another variant of betrayal trauma theory is cultural betrayal trauma (Gomez 2019a). In this instance, a member of a racial or ethnic minority is targeted for harassment by a member of their own ethnic or racial community, who they might be primed to trust, and on whom they rely for mentorship. This type of traumatic experience is associated with post-traumatic stress disorder (Gomez 2019b).

Nadia Brown (2019) has related her own experiences with what she describes as "persistent sexual advances" from Black male co-workers during her first year at a tenure-track job. As a Black woman at a majority White institution, she was pressured to support her Black colleagues by enduring, and declining to report, this harassment, a phenomenon that creates distinct challenges for women of color. When the act of defending oneself against sexual harassment is portrayed as a form of racial betrayal, women of color may experience higher levels of guilt and trauma from abusive treatment by professors or colleagues in their department.

The damage of sexual harassment can extend beyond the immediate targets of harassment. Bondestam and Lundqvist's (2020) research finds that merely being a bystander to another person being sexually harassed can lead to adverse psychological consequences. Thus, even those who are not directly victimized can still experience a negative workplace environment if they are in a department where sexual harassment occurs. Ultimately, the climate of the department is at risk from such actions.

Yet, what goes unmentioned in these studies is the incentive structure for the sexual harasser. Those faculty who victimize their students may pressure their victims to leave an academic program in order to protect their own careers.[2] It may not take much pushing, given what we know about the negative effects of harassment on victims. The harassment itself can lead victims to feel isolated and ineffectual, and harassers can pile on by encouraging other faculty to view them in this way. Together, this can be a strong force that can lead victims of sexual harassment to abandon their studies. Colleagues who accept a faculty member's negative assessment of a student may not be cognizant of the underlying agenda of victim-bullying but may nevertheless find themselves participating in and maintaining this climate in the academic workplace.

How to Respond to an Experience of Sexual Harassment

Sexual harassment claims in higher education are often shrouded in secrecy. This makes it difficult for those who experience it to evaluate their institution's record of handling such complaints. Above and beyond the aforementioned adverse psychological effects of harassment, the process of responding can be retraumatizing, particularly if victims initiate the process expecting university officials to be focused on helping them find justice. Thus, seeking mental and emotional health support, whether on or beyond the campus, should be viewed as a critical part of your response (see chapter 69 on counseling and other resources). The formal institutional process for reporting sexual harassment is generally to file a complaint with your institution's Title IX officer. Each university has a different system, so it is important to understand your own institution's policies and procedures. This complaint usually must be made to the Title IX coordinator within 180 days of the incident on which the complaint is based.[3] It will typically require that the complainant identify themselves (Office for Civil Rights, n.d.), which results in the harasser learning the source of the complaint. You will be asked to provide a written description of the events on which your complaint is based and to offer names and contact information for any witnesses you might have.

It is also possible to file a third-party complaint (that is, to file a complaint on behalf of another person), but the target of the harassment must still offer written consent for such an investigation to proceed.[4] The accused will be permitted to offer their own narratives and their own witnesses and either party may appeal the outcome. While you will be entitled to a written report on the results of the investigation (that is, if your complaint was validated), you have no right to information about what type of discipline, if any, was imposed on the perpetrator.

Even this short description of the process makes it clear why many graduate students (and junior faculty members) decline to pursue the formal reporting option. Students may (rightly) worry about their ability to continue in their program (or even in their field) if their harasser learns of their complaint. However, there are options for seeking redress outside of this formal process.

A good place to start is to speak with the institution's ombuds. The ombuds can usually walk you through some of the reporting options at your institution. In addition to walking you through the formal options, the ombuds can provide informal counsel to help you consider the short and long-run consequences of the strategies you may employ to handle the situation, help you think through and practice difficult conversations, and when appropriate, connect you to other campus resources. The ombuds can also keep your identity confidential while you decide whether and how to proceed. Some universities employ third-party reporting services where victims or witnesses can report harassing behavior confidentially. These systems often allow complaints to remain confidential until such a time as additional complaints are received about a harasser; at that time, the third party can contact other victims to let them know that they are not alone. APSA currently uses this type of third-party reporting system, and this is yet another place where harassment in the discipline can be reported.[5]

Another option is to make a complaint directly to your department. The difference between making a complaint (formal or informal) in these alternative forms versus filing a Title IX complaint is that a Title IX complaint requires an impartial investigation. No such protection exists for complaints filed within a department, for example, where an academic unit head (AUH) is responsible for determining the validity of the claims and whether and how to discipline the offender.

While the risk to the careers of victims is high, the risk to the careers of harassers on the faculty is quite low. Despite the oft-expressed fears of false accusations ruining academic careers, vanishingly few faculty members are ever terminated outright for reasons of sexual misconduct. Well-known abusers in the discipline have even had their widely acknowledged harassing behavior minimized by their departments, all the while being promoted to higher administrative posts and within their own departments.

One such faculty member is Harvard Government Professor Jorge Dominguez, who was initially given a three-year respite from administrative duties in response to a substantiated complaint of several instances of sexual assault by a junior faculty member (Bartlett and Gluckman 2018; Fu and Wang 2018). It was only after Dominguez voluntarily retired that he was subsequently barred from campus and stripped of emeritus status (Berger and McCafferty, 2019).

The Dominguez case is not unique. Even when consequences do come to harassers while they are employed, these consequences are often quite lenient. Oftentimes, having a string of credible accusations across multiple years results in an earlier-than-expected retirement and a buyout package (Toppo 2018; Wolcott 2019; see also Academic Sexual Misconduct Database).

Sometimes perpetrators simply seek a job at a different institution to avoid the consequences of a harassment complaint. This leaves no paper trail for the hiring institution, leaving them in the dark about who they are hiring, and the risks this may entail for their students. Indeed, perpetrators may even receive glowing recommendations from their department, despite sexual harassment complaints, simply to increase the chances that another institution will take the problematic faculty off their hands. For the graduate student who experiences sexual harassment from a faculty member, this can be incredibly disheartening.

One positive development has been the recent set of principles adopted by the American Association of Universities regarding sexual harassment. Specifically, Principle 7 states: "In making hiring decisions, request or require applicants to provide written consent to release personnel information from their prior employer of substantiated findings of sexual misconduct, consistent with applicable law" (AAU 2021). However, the principles are not binding on member institutions.

Moreover, it is unclear what types of behaviors would constitute "personnel information" in this context. Would a pending complaint about sexual harassment be included? What about information about the existence of previous university investigations? Is such information limited to what is actually in an applicant's personnel file (which is likely to be scant) or is an AUH's knowledge of a sexual harassment complaint sufficient to constitute personnel information?

The new AAU principles are a step in the right direction, in that they acknowledge some of the problems in combatting sexual harassment in academia. However, it is not clear whether or how these principles will be implemented by member institutions. Departments and universities are still subject to the same reputational and political pressures that they've always been, so it's not clear that these principles create any new incentives to air an institution's dirty laundry.

This leaves a lot of factors to weigh if you've experienced sexual harassment. You'll need to know what to consider in making a decision about whether and how to respond. There's an inherent conflict for most victims. On one hand, victims have an interest in seeking justice for mistreatment and abuse. On the other hand, victims need to protect themselves and their future careers. Both are legitimate and worthy goals. If you have been victimized, you'll need to balance the costs of your potential response (which should include the likelihood of achieving the desired outcome) with the benefits you may accrue (and, again, with consideration of the likelihood of attaining such benefits). In making such calculations, we suggest some further considerations.

First, don't expect other faculty to know what's going on in their department—harassment and misconduct is often a "dirty little secret." In some instances, harassers may have a reputation for their bad behavior, but this is not always the case. Perpetrators generally harass others in private because there are social and career penalties for doing so in public. In our experience, the faculty (and others) we confided in were surprised to hear of what we'd experienced. Not all of them were convinced of the veracity of our stories. It can be devastating to reveal an experience of interpersonal violence and abuse to a trusted associate only to find that they are not believed. In fact, research suggest that such victims experience far worse negative health outcomes than those who do not face skepticism when reporting (Dworkin, Brill, and Ullman 2019).

Second, don't expect other faculty to be willing to go out on a ledge for you, even if this appears to be the ethical thing to do. Faculty have a long-term stake in the department and in maintaining a working relationship with their colleagues. By contrast, graduate students are transient members of the department community. As a graduate student (or junior professor), you don't vote on their tenure and promotion. Taking your side openly may endanger some fragile political alliances or put longstanding friendship networks at risk. Adjuncts and visiting faculty are in an even more precarious situation. Generally, contingent faculty simply lack the resources and political capital to advocate on your behalf. It's important to realize the politics inherent in any complaint that forces faculty members to choose sides— what their calculations of cost and benefit may be, and how these will influence their decision making.

Making a formal complaint about sexual harassment is, simply put, fraught with risk. Mandatory reporting of undergraduate confidential disclosures of sexual assault, for example, not only tend to result in a lack of institutional follow up and penalties, but also violate trust between students and those they confide in, making it far more difficult for students to seek out needed support to cope with the trauma (Holland et al. 2021).

In their study of graduate students who filed Title IX complaints regarding sexual harassment, Cipriano et al. (2021) found that the vast majority of complainants experienced what the researchers described as "severe, education-limiting consequences" as a result of their complaints, with institutions making little to no attempt to hold perpetrators accountable for their actions (see also Flaherty 2022b). Institutions have even improperly threatened students for speaking with anyone about their complaint (Bauer-Wolf 2018) in an attempt to deny them needed social and psychological support and to insulate the university from any outside accountability for their complaint process.

Given these risks, a reasonable person might conclude that filing a complaint would be counterproductive. This is not an unethical choice. Institutions should not rely on the most vulnerable members of their community to hold their employees responsible for misconduct. Rather, it is the institution's responsibility to create a climate that discourages and disincentivizes sexual harassment.[6] Being harassed doesn't obligate anyone to risk their education and their career.

At the same time, there may be psychological benefits to reporting your abuser, and those may help to limit the negative consequences of being victimized by a harasser. Carson et al. (2020) find that intentional disclosure of victimization may be an important means of dealing with post-traumatic stress and related consequences, whereas elicited disclosure doesn't offer such benefits.

In short, if you've experienced sexual harassment, we ask you to think carefully about your own needs before mounting a response. Is it important for you to receive psychological support from someone within your department (from faculty or from other graduate students)? Would you prefer to find such support externally (from a therapist or support group)? Are you interested in making a formal complaint against your harasser? If so, are there specific reasons for taking this action in the short term (i.e., are you worried about the damage your harasser is inflicting on your career right now), or are you better off waiting to take action (i.e., when you have more resources at your disposal and less at risk)?

What are the potential risks to your career from taking action in the short term in order to attain justice, and what is the probability that such justice can realistically be attained at your institution? Are you better off biding your time, documenting your experiences, and taking some form of action when you are less vulnerable to retaliation and derailment of your career, are more likely to be believed (if you have an established career), and when you have more political power to affect a positive outcome? Is there good reason to be optimistic that your institution's response could be robust, thereby protecting future graduate students from victimization? There's no one right answer here. Our key advice, however, is to center your own needs in this decision process.

Regardless of any decision you make about filing a complaint, it is important to document your experiences. We've spoken with numerous women who chose, for various reasons, not to file a formal complaint while in graduate school.[7] However, future scenarios may arise in which being able to document the behaviors of a harasser becomes more important to you. In the era of #MeToo, this most commonly happens when other victims of the same harasser come forward with their stories.

Sometimes, people find it easier to advocate on behalf of someone else than they do for themselves. In such a scenario, you can be an important witness in supporting claims of a pervasive pattern of harassing behaviors. So, try to make a note of any actions or comments that made you uncomfortable, in as much detail as possible, and keep a careful record of dates. Send this information to your own personal email account to preserve the records. This will enable you to seek accountability in the future if you choose to, either on your own behalf or on behalf of a future student who files a complaint against your harasser.

It's also important to document harassment that you witness as a bystander. As a graduate student, you may not feel safe intervening on behalf of a person you see is subject to sexual harassment. However, you can be an ally by keeping careful notes of what you've witnessed, by offering support to the target of the harassment, and simply by acknowledging what you've witnessed to the person who has experienced it. If a complaint is made against the harasser, you will be in a position to validate the experiences of the victim.

One of the best avenues for ensuring that your complaint isn't suppressed by your institution is to make it public. However, this strategy comes with significant risk. Such a strategy requires that you identify yourself and relate your experience to a wider audience. Strategies for this range from speaking up at a conference about a perpetrator, speaking with your campus newspaper, or a venue such as Inside Higher Ed or the Chronicle of Higher Education, which have a reputation for addressing problems of sexual harassment in academia. The more people that are aware of your experience, the more difficult it is for an institution to sweep abuse under the rug. However, speaking up about a powerful perpetrator carries risks, including potential retaliatory behavior from others in your discipline. You will need to carefully weigh your options here.

If you'd like to publicize your experience, either to warn other students about a perpetrator and/ or to generate pressure on your institution to respond to concerns about sexual harassment, but you'd like to do so anonymously, there are other avenues that you can pursue external to the formal complaint process. For example, you may consider creating a subreddit that references sexual harassment at your institution. You can use this forum to reveal your experiences and to allow other potential victims to share information. As a manager of a subreddit, you'll be able to control who adds and who deletes comments in the feed. That is, you can prevent your institution from deleting posts. Similar postings involving the media industry have led to greater awareness of serial harassers and sexual predators in this sector.

Dissatisfaction with an institution's response to reports of sexual misconduct has often led to other anonymous efforts to hold perpetrators accountable. In the 1990s, students at various institutions used a guerilla-style tactic for combatting the problem of date rape in campus. They made lists of date rapists on bathroom walls at their universities to inform other students of men who posed potential threats (Celis 1990; Culp-Ressler 2014; Pender 2021). Perhaps unsurprisingly, institutions condemned the lists and male students at Brown countered with "women who needed to be raped lists." However, these actions, over the long run, precipitated more serious discussions about sexual misconduct and led to substantial reforms in university policies (Pender 2021).[8] Nonetheless, blaming the victim for inviting abusive behavior is a problem that persists even in the #MeToo era.

In some instances, graduate students who have been permitted to unionize have used contract negotiations (and, in the case of Columbia, a work stoppage) to achieve better leverage in the complaint process (see chapter 32 on graduate worker unions). Columbia graduate students were able to get the university to agree to let graduate students avail themselves of mediation or arbitration for sexual harassment claims if they've exhausted the normal university complaint process with unsatisfactory results (Flaherty 2022a).[9]

Most of the well-publicized instances of sexual harassment involve numerous complaints by multiple students over an extended period, during which the institution took little or no action in response to such complaints. These instances remain rare but are notable for the type of public response they elicited. In the instance of Jorge Dominguez, Harvard alumna Elena Sokoloski spearheaded a social media campaign entitled #DominguezMustGo and rally where protesters dressed in black to protest the university's kid-gloves treatment of Dominguez in the aftermath of the Chronicle of Higher Education's narrative from one of his accusers (Fu and Wang 2018).

Sometimes, these tactics can have some positive results. An example of this is the unusual case of Professor Florian Jaeger from the University of Rochester. When numerous students filed public complaints about a particular faculty member, faculty members within and outside of the institution engaged in a campaign of public condemnation. After multiple students complained that Jaeger was a sexual predator who targeted females in his department, over 400 academics published an open letter advising potential female graduate students to avoid Rochester's program and pressuring the university to terminate his appointment (Toppo 2018; Open Letter to the University of Rochester Board of Trustees 2017). The university's investigation never found Jaeger guilty of sexual misconduct, and he remained in his position (Wadman 2020). However, litigation arising from this dispute led to a $9.4M settlement benefitting the victims, who argued the university retaliated against and defamed claimants (Murphy 2020; Wadman 2020).

Advice to Potential Students

For those students applying to graduate school, finding out in advance about the climate of a department can be a difficult task. Investigations of offenders tend to be confidential, and firings are exceedingly rare. Disciplinary actions taken against harassers may not be easily discerned, even by colleagues in the department. Thus, it is unlikely that there will be any data available for prospective students to evaluate when trying to make an informed decision about which institution to attend.

There are a few options available to prospective students to uncover circumstantial evidence of a program's level of tolerance for harassment. One way is to engage in conversations with female graduate students who are already enrolled in a program, particularly those who are near the end of their studies and may be more willing to discuss what they know. It can also help to contact female alumni of the department to ask them about the climate of the department. A department with a reputation for bullying is likely to be one that tolerates inappropriate behaviors more generally (Clancy, Cortina, and Kirkland 2020; NASEM 2018). It can also help to be attentive to the leadership structure of the department. Dobbin and Kalev (2019) find that more women managers in a workplace is associated with greater receptivity to sexual harassment training programs and to complaints made by employees. Thus, a department with a higher female to male ratio, or one where women occupy positions of leadership, may be more receptive to concerns about sexual harassment. Finally, prospective students may also consider searching the Academic Sexual Misconduct Database, which catalogues formal complaints against faculty members in all disciplines, although the database is limited to the US and does not include anonymous complaints that have not been subject to a formal complaint process. [10]

Ultimately, one of the most troubling aspects of sexual harassment, particularly when it involves a trusted mentor, is that it is difficult for graduate students to determine whether a potential mentor is a safe person to work with. Harassers and allies may initially present in similar ways—expressing an interest in you and your research and devoting resources to your career. Simply put, it's often impossible to predict which faculty are good mentors and which are perpetrators who may have a hidden agenda. There are often few warning signs to point you toward well-intentioned mentors and away from ill-intentioned ones.

As long as universities continue to protect harassers on the faculty, avoiding harassment will remain a challenge. One way to regain a sense of agency in this situation is to stay alert to potential signs of trouble. Warning signs may include a gradual introduction of sexual jokes into professional conversations or intrusive questions about your personal life. Another red flag is a mentor who expresses unreasonable anger if they feel slighted. Casual touching may also be a potential indicator. However, there are scant studies on the qualities and grooming practices of perpetrators of sexual harassment in academia. Rather, most studies focus on the victims. More research is needed on the behavioral traits of harassers so that we can develop evidence-based strategies for deterring such individuals from abusing those to whom they have a professional obligation. In the meantime, we must all stand committed to working toward transformative institutional change to push institutions of higher education to do better by the most vulnerable members of university communities.

Endnotes

1   The #MeToo movement gained public attention in October of 2017 following the use of the phrase on social media by actress Alyssa Milano. This movement builds upon the groundbreaking social justice work of Tarana Burke, who used the phrase in her extensive community organizing work to provide support for Black women survivors of sexual violence. For more information on

the movement, see http://metoomvmt.org.

2   Harvard Anthropology Professor John Comoroff is accused of sexually assaulting numerous students.When they filed complaints with their department and the Title IX coordinator, he is alleged to have called them into his office and told them that they would have "trouble finding jobs" as a result of their complaints (Flaherty 2022b).

3   Many institutions will investigate claims much older than this, but often such investigations are driven at least in part by public pressure when accusations are made in public. This is what happened in our own sexual harassment case (see Sulfaro and Gill 2019).

4   Technically, it is possible for a third-party sexual harassment claim to be investigated by a Title IX office without the consent of the target. However, without the participation of the target, such investigations are essentially pro forma exercises resulting in no findings of culpability.

5   APSA uses EthicsPoint reporting for this purpose. More information can be found at https://connect.apsanet.org/respect/submit-a-grievance/.

6   Bondestam and Lundqvist (2020) find that the most effective strategies for combatting sexual harassment are ones that proceed from the bottom up, rather than from the top down. Thus, a deliberate effort on part of departments to generate a no tolerance policy for harassment, and an inclusive climate, are more effective than university policies and sexual harassment training programs.

7   We, too, declined to report our own harassment during our graduate school careers (Sulfaro and Gill 2019).

8   Criticism of the rape list included media commentary by authors such as Joanne Jacobs (1990), who wrote an article in defense of men's rights, and belittled the concept of date rape, in the Baltimore Sun during this period.

9   In our own experience, making an accusation against Bill Jacoby at Michigan State University led to Jacoby's use of his position as editor of the American Journal of Political Science to post an open letter on the journal's website where he accused us of making false accusations against him (Aldhous 2018; Aldhous 2019). This act of public retaliation led to a letter signed by more than 85 MPSA members demanding Jacoby's immediate termination as editor. This letter was accompanied by resignations of multiple MPSA members, including a recently elected council member. Jacoby was ultimately stripped of his editorship at the AJPS (Flaherty, 2018).

10 Note that there is a clear pattern to the outcomes in this database—faculty are reprimanded, temporarily suspended, or they resign. There are few documented instances of terminations in this database.

References

Academic Sexual Misconduct Database: https://academic-sexual-misconduct-database.org/index.php/

Aldhous, Peter. 2018. "A Leading Political Scientist Used an Academic Journal to Deny Allegations of Sexual Harassment. Now He's Resigned as its Editor." *BuzzFeed News* (April 20). Retrieved Jan. 31, 2022. https://www.buzzfeednews.com/article/peteraldhous/william-jacoby-sexual-harassment-journal.

Aldhous, Peter. 2019. "He Denied Sexual Harassment Allegations in an Academic Journal. Now Two Universities Have Found Against Him." *BuzzFeed News* (Jan. 18). Retrieved Jan. 31, 2022. https://www.buzzfeednews.com/article/peteraldhous/william-jacoby-sexual-harassment-violations.

American Association of Universities (AAU). 2021. *AAU Principles on Preventing Sexual Harassment in Academia.* October 26. Retrieved Jan. 31, 2022. https://www.aau.edu/aau-principles-preventing-sexual-harassment-academia.

Bartlett, Tom and Nell Gluckman. 2018. "She Left Harvard. He Got to Stay." *Chronicle of Higher Education* (February 27). Retrieved Jan. 31, 2022. https://www.chronicle.com/article/she-left-harvard-he-got-to-stay/.

Cantalupo, Nancy Chi. 2019. "And Even More of Us Are Brave: Intersectionality & Sexual Harassment of Women Students of Color." *Harvard Journal of Law and Gender* 42(1):1-82.

Bauer-Wolf, Jeremy. 2018. "Subtly Silencing a Sexual Assault Accuser?" *Inside Higher Ed (*April 20). Retrieved Jan. 31, 2022. https://www.insidehighered.com/news/2018/04/20/james-madison-official-tells-student-who-alleged-sexual-assault-speaking-press-could.

Berger, Jonah S. and Molly C. McCafferty. 2019. "Harvard Prof. Dominguez Stripped of Emeritus Status Following Conclusion of Title IX Investigation." *The Harvard Crimson*. (May 9). Retrieved July 25, 2022. https://www.thecrimson.com/article/2019/5/9/dominguez-investigation-closes/

Bondestam, Fredrik and Maja Lundqvist. 2020. "Sexual Harassment in Higher Education: A Systematic Review." *European Journal of Higher Education* 10(4):397-419. Retrieved Jan. 31, 2022. https://doi.org/10.1080/21568235.2020.1729833.

Brown, Nadia E. 2019. "Mentoring, Sexual Harassment, and Black Women Academics." *Journal of Women, Politics, and Policy* 40(1):166-173. Retrieved Jan. 31, 2022. https://doi.org/10.1080/1554 477X.2019.1565455.

Carson, Caitlin Walsh, Sara Barbad, Elissa J. Brown, and Valentina Nikulina. 2021. "Why Do Women Talk about It? Reasons for Disclosure of Sexual Victimization and Associated Symptomology." *Violence Against Women* 27(15/16):3114-3135. Retrieved Jan. 31, 2022. https://doi.org/10.1177/1077801220978818.

Celis, William III. 1990. "Date Rape and a List at Brown." *New York Times* (Nov. 18). Retrieved Jan. 31, 2022. https://timesmachine.nytimes.com/timesmachine/1990/11/18/768991.html?pageNumber=26.

Cipriano, Allison E., Kathryn J. Holland, Nicole Bedera, Sarah R. Eagan, and Alex S. Diede. 2021. "Severe and Pervasive? Consequences of Sexual Harassment for Graduate Students and their Title IX Report Outcomes." Feminist Criminology. Preprint. Retrieved Jan. 24, 2022. https://doi.org/10.1177/15570851211062579.

Clancy, Kathryn B.H., Lilia M. Cortina, and Anna R. Kirkland. 2020. "Opinion: Use Science to Stop Sexual Harassment in Higher Education." PNAS 117(37):22614-22618. Retrieved Jan. 5, 2022. https://doi.org/10.1073/pnas.2016164117.

Culp-Ressler, Tara. 2014. "Columbia Students are Writing the Names of Accused Rapists on Bathroom Walls." ThinkProgess (May 14). Retrieved Jan. 31, 2022. https://archive.thinkprogress.org/columbia-students-are-writing-the-names-of-accused-rapists-on-bathroom-walls-a948e499c5c/.

Dobbin, Frank and Alexandra Kalev. 2019. "The Promise and Peril of Sexual Harassment Programs." *PNAS* 116(25):12255-12260. Retrieved Jan. 24, 2022. https://doi.org/10.1073/pnas.1818477116.

Dworkin, Emily R., Charlotte D. Brill, and Sarah E. Ullman. 2019. "Social Reactions to Disclosures of Interpersonal Violence and Psychopathy: A Systematic Review and Meta-Analysis." *Clinical Psychology Review* 72:1-14. Retrieved Jan. 5, 2022. https://doi.org/10.1016/j.cpr.2019.101750.

EEOC. n.d. "Sex-Based Discrimination." US Equal Employment Opportunity Commission. Washington, D.C. Retrieved Feb. 13, 2022. http://eeoc.gov/sex-based-discrimination.

Flaherty, Colleen. 2022a. "At Long Last: A Contract for Columbia Student Workers." *Inside Higher Ed* (Jan. 10). Retrieved Jan. 31, 2022. https://www.insidehighered.com/news/2022/01/10/columbia-student-workers-reach-contract-deal-end-strike.

Flaherty, Colleen. 2022b. "The Tip of the Iceberg." *Inside Higher Ed* (Feb. 9). Retrieved Jan. 31, 2022. https://www.insidehighered.com/news/2022/02/09/harvard-accused-ignoring-reports-against-anthropologist.

Flaherty, Colleen. 2018. "Editorial Malpractice?" *Inside Higher Ed.* (April 19). Retrieved July 25, 2022. https://www.insidehighered.com/news/2018/04/19/editor-prestigious-political-science-journal-uses-website-deny-harassment

Fu, Angela N. and Lucy Wang. 2018. "Forty Years in the Making: Dominguez and Sexual Misconduct at Harvard." *The Harvard Crimson* (May 23). Retrieved Jan. 31, 2022. https://www.thecrimson.com/article/2018/5/23/the-dominguez-case/.

Gomez, Jennifer M. 2019a. "What's in a Betrayal? Trauma, Dissociation, and Hallucinations among High-Functioning Ethnic Minority Emerging Adults." *Journal of Aggression, Maltreatment & Trauma* 28(10):1181-1198. Retrieved Jan. 5, 2022. https://doi.org/10.1080/10926771.2018.1494653.

Gomez, Jennifer M. 2019b. "Group Dynamics as a Predictor of Dissociation for Black Victims of Violence: An Exploratory Study of Cultural Betrayal Trauma Theory." *Transcultural Psychiatry* 56(5):10-27. Retrieved Jan. 5, 2022. https://doi.org/10.1177/1363461519847300.

Hill, Annie. 2018. "Reporting Sexual Harassment: Toward Accountability and Action," *The Gender Pol-*

icy Report, University of Minnesota, July 19. Retrieved Jan. 23, 2022. https://genderpolicyreport. umn.edu/reporting-sexual-harassment-towards-accountability-and-action/.

Holland, Kathryn Y., Elizabeth Q. Hutchison, Courtney E. Ahrens, and M. Gabriela Torres. 2021. "Reporting is Not Supporting: Why Mandatory Supporting, Not Mandatory Reporting, Must Guide University Sexual Misconduct Policies." *PNAS* 118(52):e2116515118. Retrieved Jan. 5, 2022. https:// doi.org/10.1073/pnas.2116515118.

Jacobs, Joanne. 1990. "Rape and the Bathroom Wall." *Baltimore Sun* (December 19). Retrieved Jan. 31, 2022. https://www.baltimoresun.com/news/bs-xpm-1990-12-19-1990353005-story.html.

Kachen, Axenya, Anjala S. Krishen, Maria Petrescu, Rebecca D. Gill, and Paula C. Peter. 2020. "#MeToo, #MeThree, #MeFour: Twitter as Community Building Across Academic and Corporate Institutions." *Psychology & Marketing* 38(3):455-469.

Keller, Elisabeth A. 1990. "Consensual Relationships and Institutional Policy." *Academe: Bulletin of the Association of University Professors* 76:29-32. Retrieved Jan. 22, 2022. https://lawdigitalcommons. bc.edu/cgi/viewcontent.cgi?article=1952&context=lsfp.

Mengo, Cecilia and Beverly M. Black. 2015. "Violence Victimization on a College Campus: Impact on GPA and Dropout." *Journal of Student Retention: Research, Theory & Practice* 18(2):234-248. Retrieved Jan. 5, 2022. https://doi.org/10.1177/1521025115584750.

Murphy, Justin. 2020. "UR Settles Federal Sexual Misconduct Lawsuit for $9.4 Million." *Democrat & Chronicle* (Mar. 27). https://www.democratandchronicle.com/story/news/education/2020/03/27/ university-rochester-federal-sexual-misconduct-lawsuit-settlement-9-4-million-jaeger-kidd-cantlon/2916365001/

National Academy of Sciences, Engineering, and Medicine (NASEM). 2018. *Sexual Harassment of Women: Climate, Culture, and Consequences in Academic Sciences, Engineering, and Medicine*. https:// www.nap.edu/read/24994.

O'Callaghan, Erin, Veronica Shepp, Anne Kirkner, and Katherine Lorenz. 2021. "Sexual Harassment in the Academy: Harnessing the Growing Labor Movement in Higher Education to Address Sexual Harassment Against Graduate Workers." *Violence Against Women*. Preprint. https://doi. org/10.1177/10778012211035793.

Office for Civil Rights, US Department of Education. N.d. OCR Complaint Form. Retrieved Jan. 31, 2022. https://www2.ed.gov/about/offices/list/ocr/complaintintro.html.

Open Letter to the University of Rochester Board of Trustees Regarding Sexual Harassment at the University of Rochester. 2017. Retrieved Jan. 31, 2022. https://sites.google.com/site/openletterunivof-rochester/

Pender, Caelyn. 2021. "'If We Don't Start Taking Care of Each Other, No One Will': How Women Started a Movement that Redefined How Brown Handles Sexual Assault." *Brown Daily Herald* (March 18). Retrieved Jan. 31, 2022. https://www.browndailyherald.com/article/2021/03/if-we-don-t-start-taking-care-of-each-other-no-one-will-how-women-started-a-movement-that-redefined-how-brown-handles-sexual-assault.

Rosenthal, Marina N., Alec M. Smidt, and Jennifer J. Freyd. 2016. "Still Second Class: Sexual Harassment of Graduate Students." *Psychology of Women Quarterly* 40(3):364-377. https://doi.org/ 10.1177/0361684316644838.

Scott, Deborah Deprez. 1983. "Sexual Harassment Behaviors, Management Strategies, and Power- Dependence Relationships Among a Female Graduate Student Population." Doctoral dissertation, Ball State University. Retrieved Jan. 23, 2022. http://liblink.bsu.edu/catkey/220228.

Sulfaro, Valerie and Rebecca D. Gill. 2019. "Title IX: Help or Hindrance?" *Journal of Women, Politics & Policy* 40(1):204-227. https://doi.org/10.1080/1554477X.2019.1565460.

Toppo, Greg. 2018. "Is Education Having its Own #MeToo Moment?" *USA Today* (Jan. 4). Retrieved Jan. 31, 2022. https://www.usatoday.com/story/news/2018/01/04/education-having-its-own-me-too-moment/1001889001/.

Wadman, Meredith. 2020. "University of Rochester and plaintiffs settle sexual harassment lawsuit for $9.4 million." *Science* (Mar 27). Retrieved July 26, 2022. https://www.science.org/content/article/ university-rochester-and-plaintiffs-settle-sexual-harassment-lawsuit-94-million

Wolcott, R.J. 2019. "MSU Political Scientist Tried to Trade Academic Guidance for Sex, University Finds." *Lansing State Journal* (Jan. 14). Retrieved Jan. 31, 2022. https://www.lansingstatejournal.com/story/news/2019/01/14/msu-um-find-political-scientist-propositioned-grad-students-sex/2558997002/.

Yao, Danfeng (Daphne). 2021. "Depth and Persistence: What Researchers Need to Know About Impostor Syndrome." *Communications of the ACM* 64(6):39-42. Retrieved Feb. 14, 2022. https://dl.acm.org/doi/10.1145/3437255.

Zepeda, Lydia. 2018. "Sexual Harassment and the Toll It Takes." *Science* (Jan. 4). Retrieved Jan. 23, 2022. https://doi.org/10.1126/science.caredit.aas9058.

53

What Do You Need to Know about the Culture of Overwork?

Thomas Benson[1]

1. University of Delaware

KEYWORDS: Overwork, Burnout.

Introduction

The culture of overwork is not a new phenomenon. Within the discipline of political science, focusing on scholarship holds out the promise of determining one's own schedule, but managing the array of tasks associated with an academic career presents an array of challenges that begin with the prospective graduate student. These challenges shapeshift throughout PhD students' experiences, suggesting that the culture of overwork does not remain static over time and shifts in accordance with progression throughout a PhD in political science. But what is the culture of overwork? Broadly, the culture of overwork has been encapsulated by the American Dream—although not a concept limited to the United States, as the problem has been shown to be endemic elsewhere, such as Japan, the United Kingdom, and Australia (Walsh 2013, 151)—in which people, through hard work and determination, are believed to be able to achieve wealth and status. Thus, it is believed that the most value is attributed to those who work long hours and appear omnipresent (or who display presenteeism) as these individuals are perceived to be the most diligent. It is also the normalization of long work hours, the erosion of personal and professional boundaries, the glamorization of always being consumed by work, and the romanticization of phrases like "rise and grind."

However, the culture of overwork can be characterized more specifically in the domain of political science. Here, the culture of overwork can be identified by its overlapping responsibilities for graduate students, especially those who are teaching or research assistants. In these roles, you are typically engaged in academic service (e.g., reviewing papers, presenting at conferences), university service (e.g., serving on university and graduate student committees), department service (e.g., helping your peers, administrative staff, and faculty members), funding (e.g., writing grants and fellowship applications), research (e.g., reading, writing, and submitting manuscripts to journals, undertaking fieldwork), and teaching (e.g., leading discussion sections, holding office hours, grading papers, responding to emails, advising students) (Guo 2014). In addition to all of these tasks, you may be constantly checking your emails and phone, writing policy reports, and performing community service. At different stages of your PhD program in political science, you can expect these obligations to change in intensity. For example, as a prospective student, you will be managing your transition into a PhD program and preparing for classes, but as a post-candidacy student, you will be focused on wrapping-up your dissertation, building a professional network, presenting at conferences, publishing research, and submitting job applications. Thus, your work will originate from multiple sources who rarely coordinate assignments and deadlines.

Given that the sources of work output are often independent, you will be left to your own devices to organize your time effectively and to balance these obligations. Expectations can seem especially burdensome when you receive critical student evaluations, teach challenging course material, have quick grading deadlines, experience journal rejections, fail to receive job offers, and more. Even while you are "acutely conscious of how little time" there is—and some mentors may assume all of your free time is available for responding to emails, reading academic literature, and working on class papers—and when peers engage in "busy-bragging" as a status symbol, rest assured there are ways to navigate the culture of overwork in academia (Robson 2021).

Why Does the Culture of Overwork Matter?

Before turning to the ways to navigate the culture of overwork, it is first important to understand why the culture of overwork matters. The culture of overwork can adversely affect your physical and mental health, which can subsequently damage your productivity. More specifically, overwork can make you susceptible to illnesses including sleeping disorders, heart problems, alcoholism, anxiety, depression, burnout, and panic attacks (Jongepier and Van de Sande 2021). Burnout has been described by the World Health Organization as a syndrome "resulting from chronic workplace stress that has not been successfully managed," and is characterized by "feelings of exhaustion, negative feelings about a job and reduced professional efficacy" (Lufkin 2021). And while caffeine can artificially and temporarily sustain you, it cannot sufficiently counteract the lack of sleep and near-constant expenditure of mental energy, thereby exacerbating your capacity to be productive. This state of existence can lead you to being physically and emotionally exhausted and result in a loss of passion for political science, which will only further dampen your efforts to be productive. (See chapters 64 and 67 for more in-depth discussions of wellbeing and rest in graduate school.)

Instead, your efforts ought to focus on producing good quality work and to recognize that you need not stay fixed on the "hedonic treadmill" in which your achievements pile up, one after the other, and become a never-ending cycle of overwork (Robson 2021). Similarly, you should avoid the "productivity trap," where you feel like you can "never truly escape the feeling that you should be doing more" (Robson 2021). Although both the hedonic treadmill and productivity trap can contribute to feeling like you are "in demand and scarce" and, therefore, important, the aforementioned physical and mental health issues associated with these efforts to be always productive will be to your detriment (Bellezza et al. 2016, 135). But what does overwork look like in practice? How do you know when enough is enough? Everyone has their own limits, and simply because your fellow graduate student works into the evening and on their weekends does not mean that you need to do the same if you are capable of fulfilling your obligations. Long hours—usually defined as being over 45 to 55 hours per week (Entrepreneur 2017; Headlee 2020; Walsh 2013, 153)—will only lead to fatigue and sharp declines in productivity and the quality of your work.

It is also crucial to acknowledge that the culture of overwork is not new, and that the notion of sleep as a luxury and valorization of wakefulness can be traced back in time. Emerging from mounting challenges to the United States' economic supremacy in the 1970s, there was a newfound commitment for the workforce to go "all-out" to ensure the country could continue to compete on a global scale (Derickson 2013, 20). In this process, there were "potent promoters of sleep deprivation" who reinforced the idea that a workforce was capable of "constant availability, ability to function competently" and that sleep-deprivation was necessary to succeed in a "24/7/365 society" (Derickson 2013, 1, 142-143). Fast-forward to the present day and you encounter the same level of pride found in tech entrepreneurs and corporate leaders who echo traits associated with the culture of overwork. With instantaneous communication, it has become even more challenging to 'switch off.'

However, it does not have to be this way. If you have experienced burnout as a political science graduate student, use it as a platform for change. Begin by recognizing that time spent in pursuit of non-political science and non-academic endeavors are important and enriching too. Such activities— going to the theater, reading a non-academic book, going to the gym, forest-bathing, spending time with family and friends, cooking a nice meal, or whatever activities you enjoy and value—can make you a more well-rounded person as opposed to someone who is consumed by all-things-political-science. Develop a more well-rounded identity that goes beyond your job title as a Graduate Teaching or Research Assistant of Political Science. It is not wasteful to rest, and the next section will outline ways in which political science graduate students can deal with the culture of overwork.

What Can You Do About the Culture of Overwork?

Generally, all political science graduate students should avoid "busy-bragging," or taking pride in being overworked. You should focus on time management to assist in organizing all your responsibilities to prevent you from feeling overwhelmed, and there are several ways to do this. If you struggle with self-motivation, you can utilize "Study with Me" videos on platforms like YouTube, especially ones that employ Pomodoro techniques to ensure you take breaks. Pomodoro is a timed technique where, for example, you study for 20 or 50 minutes and then take a 10-minute break. The process is then repeated with a larger break in the middle. In those breaks, productivity experts strongly recommended that you get up and move around. Whether you are in the library, working from home, or a graduate office, you should move away from your work and study space. Another tactic is to create to-do lists that create a sense of achievement and provide motivation to continue working. However, be wary of adopting too many big goals. Instead, break large projects down into smaller, more manageable tasks. You must learn to prioritize and, in doing so, you can make bigger strides by focusing on fewer goals that are smaller in size. More insight into time management is described in chapter 17, and these tips are especially important for doctoral students who have children or other care-giving responsibilities, as described in chapter 16.

In line with taking adequate breaks, ensure you are getting enough sleep—usually seven or eight hours—as well as adequate nutrition, exposure to sunlight, and exercise. While vitamin supplements and sunlight through a window can help, a healthy routine combined with regular exposure to nature is better. Do not be afraid to take a nap if you are sleep deprived or generally exhausted. Avoid screen exposure from your television and mobile phone too close to night-time, not only for the sake of the blue light negatively impacting your capacity to sleep, but to avoid reading emails that can wait until the morning. Consider putting your phone on silent or do not disturb mode. Further, if you are experiencing any mental health struggles, you should seek out your university's counselling, well-being, and therapy services. If these are not available and you have healthcare, you should assess what external services are available. Mental health resources commonly available to graduate students are described in chapter 69.

Moreover, recognize that your individual actions cannot change the culture of overwork, but nor are they without effect. The culture of overwork is endemic in many political science graduate programs, but you can cultivate habits and strategies to disengage from this culture that not only help you but normalize self-care for other graduate students. As part of this effort, if you are a Teaching Assistant, you should consider how your communication and demeanor may positively affect undergraduate students through discussion sections, grading comments, office hours, and email responses. If, however, you have other intersectional identities that result in implicit bias or undue scrutiny of your performance in graduate school, you may consider quietly implementing these work-life balance tactics, while leaving efforts to overtly challenge the norms in your graduate program to others. (See chapters 55-61.)

For example, women in graduate school are more likely than men to believe that "graduate school and parenthood are fundamentally incompatible" because of graduate schoolwork requirements (Mason, Wolfinger, Goulden 2013, 11). Those who do become mothers face challenges in navigating the fine line posed by the culture of overwork—choosing between the total dedication expected for academia and the total devotion expected for parenthood. This difficult position is compounded by the lack of faculty mothers, the perception that universities are not "family friendly," and stereotypes that women cannot "succeed as professionals while also having a family life" (Mason, Wolfinger and Goulden 2013, 16, 18). However, it is not all bad news. Some universities are offering mothers leave for a semester, with the ability to return to funded graduate positions without penalty, as well as grants for child-raising expenses, medical plans for student parents, and on-campus child-care facilities (Mason, Wolfinger and Goulden 2013, 23). Consider researching these types of policies as you decide which graduate program is a good fit for you. Additionally, in resisting the binary posed by overwork culture—to be a mother or a graduate student—student mothers can shift toward "and, and, and," to identify a balance between responsibilities (Guyonette 2018, 45).

For prospective students and first-year students who are acclimatizing to the PhD program in political science, you may feel burned out by your newfound responsibilities and the degree to which they differ from your previous educational experiences. This situation can seem even worse as a first-gen student and/or international student as there are new cultural and educational expectations to learn. (See chapters 57, 58, and 60.) Nonetheless, in your first year, you should identify a study space that is conducive for productivity and well-being—this may be a desk set-up in your apartment or house, a graduate office (sometimes shared), or your university's library. Additionally, you should collaborate with your peers, including students in the years above (Headlee 2020). If you are struggling with assigned literature in your political science program, talk to your peers to share your perspectives or what you found interesting. In doing so, you will more quickly learn to identify patterns in literature, and you can tease these out in your graduate seminars. You should also engage with your faculty adviser and mentor if you are struggling and ask for assistance or extensions if you truly need them.

For pre-candidacy students, the primary challenges are in balancing coursework with research and teaching obligations, in addition to emerging roles in applying for grants, fellowships, and conferences. By now, you will have hopefully identified a routine that works best for you in fulfilling your obligations without being overworked. If you find that your responsibilities as a Teaching or Research Assistant are taking more time than you are contracted for, typically 20 hours per week, then speak with your adviser about remedies (Headlee 2020). There may be times that you do not recognize that you are overworking, especially if you are committed to your activities, but greater self-awareness can help you prevent burnout (Walsh 2013, 156). Remember how far you have come from your first year and the progress you have made. Consider what the coming years hold for you and do not lose sight of the end goal of obtaining a PhD in political science. If you fall off the bandwagon—receiving a low grade, missing a deadline, or being unprepared for a presentation—you can recover and get back on track. (At these points in time, consider reading chapter 62 to help you reflect on why you initially pursued a doctorate.) Do not forget that you have time ahead to learn from these experiences and continually improve yourself, personally and professionally.

For post-candidacy students, attempting to strike a balance between data collection, fieldwork, dissertation writing, and job searches, with all the additional academic, departmental, and university service commitments expected at this stage, can be challenging. At this point, your established routine of attending classes will change dramatically, illustrating that work-life balance is dynamic. In order to ground yourself and create a new routine, you should consider joining or starting a weekly writing accountability group. Post-candidacy can be isolating, and such a group can help keep you focused (Ali 2021). Further, consider preserving your weekends or evenings and avoid spending all your time at your desk now that you have greater flexibility in your schedule. Be sure that your non-academic friends and family understand that this phase of your academic program is particularly rigorous and that they need to respect your boundaries (Ali 2021). If new teaching or research opportunities arise—choose wisely and carefully. Declining tangential opportunities can help you maintain progress toward degree completion, as spreading yourself too thin will likely result in poor performance across all that you do. As you enter the job market, save yourself time from endlessly searching by creating job alerts for commonly used higher education websites, including HigherEdJobs, LinkedIn, HERC Jobs, and APSA ejobs. Do not overlook your university's career and mentoring services, which can also be a valuable resource.

Finally, with all of this advice in mind, remember that you have gotten to where you are in your political science graduate program through your diligence and intelligence, among other skills. There may be times when you are burned out and all you can envisage is dropping out of the program, believing you are doomed to the downward spiral that is the culture of overwork. Keep in mind that many graduate students will feel this way at some point during their graduate program. With these solutions described above in mind, you can push back and persevere, establish a healthy routine, ensure mental and physical well-being, and be productive all at once.

References

Ali, Samina G. 2021. "6 Tips for the Final Year of Your Dissertation Marathon." *Inside Higher Ed* [website], October 18, 2021. https://www.insidehighered.com/advice/2021/09/21/tips-final-year-writing-your-thesis-opinion.

Bellezza, Silvia., Neeru Paharia., and Anat Keinan. "Conspicuous Consumption of Time: When Busyness and Lack of Leisure Time Become a Status Symbol." *Journal of Consumer Research* 44 (1): 118-138. https://doi.org/10.1093/jcr/ucw076

Derickson, Alan. 2014. *Dangerously Sleepy: Overworked Americans and The Cult of Manly Wakefulness.* Philadelphia: University of Pennsylvania Press.

Entrepreneur. 2017. "How the Culture of Overwork is Damaging Your Productivity and Your Health." *Entrepreneur* [website], October 18, 2021. https://www.entrepreneur.com/article/298956.

Guo, Philip. 2014. "Why Academics Feel Overworked." *Inside Higher Ed* [website], October 18, 2021. https://www.insidehighered.com/advice/2014/12/01/essay-why-academics-feel-overworked.

Guyonette, Kelly W. 2018. "The Undecided Narratives of Becoming-Mother, Becoming-Ph.D." In *Feminism and Intersectionality in Academia: Women's Narratives and Experiences in Higher Education,* eds. Stephanie Anne Shelton, Jill Ewing Flynn, Tanetha Jamay Grosland, 37-48. Cham, Switzerland: Palgrave Macmillan.

Headlee, Celeste. 2020. *Do Nothing: How to Break Away from Overworking, Overdoing, and Underliving.* New York: Harmony Books.

Jongepier, Fleuer., and Mathijs van de Sande. 2021. "Workaholic Academics Need to Stop Taking Pride in their Burnout." *Times Higher Education* [website], October 19, 2021. https://www.timeshigher-education.com/opinion/workaholic-academics-need-stop-taking-pride-their-burnout.

Lufkin, Bryan. 2021. "Why Do We Buy into the 'Cult' of Overwork?" *BBC* [website], August 9, 2021. https://www.bbc.com/worklife/article/20210507-why-we-glorify-the-cult-of-burnout-and-overwork.

Mason, Mary Anna., Nicholas H. Wolfinger., and Marc Goulden. 2013. "The Graduate School Years: New Demographics, Old Thinking." In *Do Babies Matter? Gender and Family in the Ivory Tower.* 8-25. New Brunswick, NJ: Rutgers University Press.

Robson, David. 2021. "How to Escape the 'Productivity Trap'." *BBC* [website], August 10, 2021. https://www.bbc.com/worklife/article/20210805-how-to-escape-the-productivity-trap.

Walsh, Janet. 2013. "Work-Life Balance: The End of the 'Overwork' Culture?" In *Managing Human Resources: Human Resource Management in Transition,* eds. Stephen Bach and Martin R. Edwards, 150-177. Hoboken, N.J.: Wiley-Blackwell.

·

Strategies for Addressing Implicit Bias, Harassment, and Assault

54

Concerns for BIPOC Students and Scholars and a Model for Inclusive Excellence

Aleena Khan[1], Jair Moreira[2], Jessica Taghvaiee[3], & Andrea Benjamin[4]

1. University of Illinois at Urbana-Champaign 2. University of Illinois at Urbana-Champaign
3. University of California, Irvine 4. University of Oklahoma

KEYWORDS: BIPOC Students, Macroaggressions, Microaggressions.

Introduction

As a discipline, political science, like other academic fields, has historically excluded racially/ethnically marginalized individuals. In the last 40 years there has been an increase in the number of faculty who are Black, Indigenous, and people of color (BIPOC) (Michelson and Lavariega Monforti, 2021). Still, when compared to their share in the population, BIPOC faculty remain severely underrepresented in the discipline (Garcia and Hancock Alfaro, 2021). In 2011, APSA released a presidential task force report entitled "Political Science in the 21st Century," which recommended specifically that "departments should expand their graduate training to include more of an emphasis on race and inequality. This may require the breaking down of traditional categories used to structure graduate training and rebuild areas in more substantive and social problem-solving categories" (APSA and Task Force on Political Science in the 21st Century, 2011, 2). As we take stock of the current data, we know that this is an area that still needs much improvement. APSA released data on the racial and ethnic make-up of the membership in 2018 in the Diversity and Inclusion Report and the findings were clear: only the non-Hispanic White membership is proportionally representative of its corresponding societal group (the non-Hispanic White population in the United States) (Mealy, 2018). Black and Latina/o/x populations are underrepresented, while Asian Americans membership is higher than the percentage in the United States population (ibid).

While these numbers are frustrating, we also know that membership in the association is only one way to measure the diversity of our discipline, and it may overlook those who are graduate students or those who cannot afford the membership fees. This lack of representation can have adverse effects on graduate students from underrepresented groups. In this chapter, we cover the lack of representation of BIPOCs students and faculty in political science, the climate of political science departments and programs, the personal hardships students may face in navigating graduate school, the limitations of current racial/ethnic politics work in the field and conclude with a set of recommendations that we believe can help improve the experiences of BIPOC graduate students in political science.

Navigating Graduate School as a Racially/Ethnically Marginalized Individual

In a field where students and faculty with marginalized racial/ethnic backgrounds are so underrepresented, navigating political science graduate programs as a BIPOC student can be a daily struggle. In the first place, individuals from historically underrepresented and racially or ethnically marginalized backgrounds face several challenges on the path to a political science doctorate. The research regarding that

Along with parental education, sources of financial support are an important factor for predicting doctoral study. A lack of funding influences whether students decide to pursue graduate studies and their ability to complete their doctoral degree (Tormos-Aponte and Velez-Serrano, 2020). Moreover, significant disparities exist regarding the primary source of financial support between doctoral recipients from different ethnic and racial groups (See *Table 54.1*). One note of caution ought to be mentioned when interpreting the results for Asian doctoral recipients. The "Asian" and "Hispanic/Latina/o/x" racial categories are considered "pan-ethnic" labels, as both populations are diverse in terms of national origin, language, religion, culture, and so forth (Junn and Masuoka, 2008; Jones-Correa & Leal, 1996). Therefore, we caution against understanding these populations' experiences as monolithic blocs and instead, encourage research that considers the distinct experiences of each ethnic group within the Asian and Latina/o/x populations.

Financial support to apply to and complete a doctorate is absolutely necessary. Upfront, the cost to apply to doctoral programs can cost hundreds of dollars, which can be particularly challenging for low-income students (Ramirez, 2011). Even after being admitted, students incur additional costs and must often compete for grants for travel, research, etc. In sum, graduate school is costly, from start to finish.

Challenges: During Graduate School

During graduate school, some of the challenges that underrepresented, and racially/ethnically marginalized groups face include the time to earn a degree, the lack of funding, ineffective mentorship, less opportunities for collaboration and co-authorship, and lack of social support (Tormos-Aponte and Velez-Serrano, 2020). This lack of support can manifest as macro- and micro-aggressions, imposter syndrome, and unique experiences that come with carrying identities facing intersecting forms of oppression (see chapter 49 in implicit bias and microaggressions, and chapter 50 on imposter syndrome). For instance, in the field of political science and government, the median is six years to earn a doctorate, but disparities still exist among different racial or ethnic groups due to the unique challenges that these groups may face. Therefore, it is important to explore what these difficulties are and provide recommendations for how to resolve them. This section discusses a few of those adversities and their significance.

Intersectionality

Alongside racial/ethnic background, there are other identities a student can possess that intersect and shape their experience of higher education, such as first-generation status, socioeconomic status, age, ability, wellness, sexuality, gender, immigration status, etc. The intersections of these different identities and how they shape the experiences of privilege vs. oppression that individuals face is called "intersectionality." The term intersectionality was first coined by Black feminist legal scholar, Kimberlé Crenshaw, in 1989 ("Demarginalizing the Intersection of Race and Sex"). A student's intersectional identity affects their graduate school application process, how they feel in their role as a graduate student, and how they navigate their interactions with other political science students, faculty, and the program overall.

Historically, academia as influenced by Western thought and traditions has served as a space of exclusion for the members of marginalized groups, including BIPOC individuals. As the statistics mentioned at the beginning of this chapter demonstrate, political science continues to struggle with the representation and inclusion of marginalized groups within the field. When you are a BIPOC student in political science, this continued exclusion can be felt in your classes, interactions with peers and professors, at conferences, program requirements, academic expectations, and how your research and validity as a scholar are perceived by the majority of the discipline.

Macroaggressions vs. Microaggressions

When you are a BIPOC in graduate school, even small things like the racial/ethnic makeup of your class, comments peers and professors make, or the feedback you receive on your research interests can make you feel unsafe or like you do not belong. Whether it is intentional or not, your peers or professors may make remarks or commit actions that are offensive or harmful to you or the communities you identify with, which can come in the form of assumptions of criminal behavior, treatment as a second-class citizen, underestimation of your ability, and cultural or racial isolation (Torres, Driscoll, and Burrow, 2010). These are microaggressions. Microaggressions occurring at the individual level are often a reflection of the macroaggressions occurring at the institutional and societal level. For BIPOC, microaggressions often perpetuate harmful and racist stereotypes or actions that further marginalize their communities.

Though microaggressions are difficult to identify, they shape the daily experiences of BIPOC individuals and over time "can take a real psychological toll on the mental health of their recipients. This toll can lead to anger and depression and can even lower work productivity and problem-solving abilities" (Desmond-Harris, 2015). Thus, student experiences with microaggressions can lead to less academic engagement and difficulties in completing their studies (Brunsma, Embrick, and Shin, 2017). Examples of microaggressions BIPOC students and faculty experience in political science programs can include: (1) a faculty mentor assuming a student should only study Latina/o/x politics because they identify with that community or, vice versa, that they cannot pursue such research since they hold close ties with that community; (2) a student asking a Black professor to explain their experience with police as a Black man; (3) a white male professor who only provides positive feedback on the discussion points made by white male students.

As psychologist Dr. Sue explains, these "remarks, questions, or actions [can be] painful because they have to do with a person's membership in a group that's discriminated against or subject to stereotypes" (Desmond-Harris, 2015). The culture of a classroom, political science program, or university more generally can create hostile and toxic environments for BIPOCs when they do not sufficiently address the micro/macro-aggressions taking place in these spaces.

Imposter Phenomenon

The macro/micro-aggressions discussed above can contribute to BIPOC student and faculty experiences of imposter phenomenon, commonly referred to as, "imposter syndrome." The imposter phenomenon may make some students question their deservingness to be a part of a certain space such as a political science PhD program. Much of this sense of not belonging is due to the way academic spaces perpetuate cultures and norms that continue to make BIPOCs feel excluded in these spaces. Examples of situations that may increase imposter phenomenon include: (1) being the only BIPOC individual in a classroom or program; (2) feeling discomfort in attending formal program events because of one's socioeconomic and first-generation status; (3) not understanding the terminology or references used by professors and peers in a course.

These experiences can lead to BIPOC individuals feeling like there is no room for them in their program or academia more generally. It is imperative that political science programs critically reflect on how the standards and culture of their departments may affect BIPOC faculty and students and their overall success.

Challenges: After Graduate School

Racial/Ethnic Politics Research Limitations

As we have shown, BIPOC graduate students face a unique set of challenges on the path to earning the PhD. Yet, there are often additional challenges to success beyond the degree program. While conducting research on race and ethnic politics is not limited to scholars who identify as members of underrepresented racial and ethnic groups, many BIPOC scholars study topics related to their communities. Our flagship journal, the American Political Science Review, highlights some of the challenges scholars who identify as members of underrepresented racial and ethnic groups and those who study race and ethnic politics may face. In 2019, the association selected an all-women editorial team to edit the journal. Their team submitted a proposal to helm the journal, in part because women, scholars of color, and those who study race and politics did not feel that their work was well received by the journal (American Political Science Review's incoming editorial team, 2019). The new editors credit their proposal's success to their stated commitment to "make the journal's scope more reflective of the wide range of crucial questions our discipline addresses" (Ibid).

While the discipline has journals that focus on Race and Ethnic Politics (Journal of Race and Ethnic Politics, Politics Groups and Identities, and The National Black Politics Review), there are still incentives to publish in the top journal. According to the new editorial team at the American Political Science Review, "in 2017, 88 percent of authors published by the APSR were white, and zero—none at all—were African American" and that between 2000 and 2015, only four percent of the articles were about race and ethnic politics (Ibid, 2). While we have seen gains in the number of BIPOC students earning their degrees in political science, we have not seen gains in representation in the top political science journals.

Publications are the currency in our field. They are used to evaluate job candidates and tenure cases. As our discipline diversifies and as the study of race and ethnic politics continues to grow, we must work hard to ensure equitable representation in those outlets. When the APSA Task Force on Political Science in the 21st Century challenged us to think about "substantive and social problem-solving categories," in 2011, they were really challenging us to incorporate the study of race and ethnic politics into our regular study and not treat it as a separate entity (American Political Science Association and Task Force on Political Science in the 21st Century, 2011, 2). That includes publications as well. The new editorial team at the American Political Science Review is a step in the right direction.

Recommendations

We advance three recommendations that the political science community as a whole, and marginalized graduate students and faculty as main stakeholders in particular, should pursue in order to increase diversity and student retention in the discipline. First, we recommend that the discipline increase its commitment to developing partnerships with programs seeking to diversify academia. This could be done by actively encouraging political science departments to work with underrepresented graduate recruitment programs that provide prospective graduate students from marginalized backgrounds with opportunities to learn and perform research under the supervision of a faculty member, while also exposing themselves to the culture and expectations of graduate programs in political science. Our political science departments should aim to participate in the programs already offered within the discipline, such as:

- APSA's Minority Student Recruitment Program (MSRP),
- Minority Graduate Placement Program (MIGAP),
- The Ralph Bunche Summer Institute (RBSI),
- Programs offered by their home universities:
    - Big Ten Alliance's Summer Research Opportunity Programs (SROP),
    - McNair Scholars Program,
    - Summer Research Programs (SRP) such as Leadership Alliance Summer Research Early Identification Program (SR-EIP) and the ones offered by the University of California system.

Second, we recommend that the political science community commit to mentoring students from underrepresented backgrounds on collaboration, co-authoring, finding funding, and preparing for the future. Lack of inclusive departmental and institutional climates along with a lack of strong mentee-mentor relationships have been associated with the "bait and switch" phenomenon, which occurs when academic departments present a positive image of their commitment to diversity to prospective students, an image that diverges considerably from the students' experiences once they are matriculated (Slay et al. 2019).

This occurs because academic departments and other institutions in the discipline tend to believe that their participation in organizational and structural diversity initiatives aiming to improve recruitment and admission practices is enough to reduce racial and ethnic inequalities in who enrolls and graduates. This focus on the number of students of color who enroll ignores the role of the educational process itself in successful educational outcomes among marginalized students (Milem et al. 2005).

Moreover, the "bait and switch" model has led to well-documented difficulties for undergraduate and graduate students of color in their attempts to find faculty mentors who are both willing and capable of providing the support necessary for developing and navigating graduate programs (Hurtado 1994; Nettles 1990; Noy and Ray, 2012; Thomas et al., 2007). In order to address the "bait and switch" issue, we would like to encourage the discipline, and especially senior marginalized graduate students and faculty members, to provide mentorship to first-year marginalized graduate students. More specifically, we recommend:

- That political science organizations establish mentoring programs that provide the ability for students to choose the length of their mentoring relationship and setting expectations beyond one-time meetings at conferences
- That political science departments hire more BIPOC and marginalized faculty in an effort to adequality reflect the identities and experiences of prospective graduate students.
- That a graduate student mentorship program be established for graduate mentors to assist and guide undergraduate students throughout their graduate school preparation (Juárez 1991)
- That graduate students be assigned (or the student chooses) a faculty mentor who supports and guides students through coursework, teaching, attending professional events, finding funding, and teaching norms of professional responsibilities while maintaining the cultural integrity of the student's background (Montgomery, Dodson, and Johnson 2014)
- That graduate students be assigned peer mentors that will help them transition into graduate school. First-year graduate students should be assigned two peer mentors who are at different stages of their doctoral study, one of which shares the mentee's subfield and gender.

Finally, we recommend that BIPOC scholars and graduate students take the following steps to navigate graduate school and beyond. First and foremost, we recommend they prioritize their health, self-care, and well-being. Graduate school can be quite challenging, stressful, and overwhelming. Students should seek help if they are facing any difficulties and make use of university mental health resources (see chapter 69 on counseling and other resources). Self-care and rest are also important for one's mental and physical health and overall well-being. Without it, students can burn out easily, which can impact quality of work and productivity, often producing a negative cycle (see chapter 67 on rest in graduate school). Once in the cycle, it can be difficult to break out, which leads to another tip: work/life balance. Finding and maintaining a work/life balance early on in one's doctoral study is crucial (see chapter 69 on counseling and other resources).

An important aspect to this step is time management (see chapter 17 on effective time management). At the beginning of graduate school, students often find themselves overwhelmed with coursework, reading loads, and teaching responsibilities. Many universities offer time management workshops targeted at graduate students. One such method is the Pomodoro Technique invented by Francesco Cirillo. While it is tempting to work all the time, that is not sustainable.

It is also important to rest and maintain personal relationships. Students should strive to build connections with fellow students and faculty both in the department and outside the department. It is easy to become isolated in graduate school, consumed in one's own coursework and research. Having social support and a life outside of work is important again, for one's mental health (see chapter 63 on overcoming academic isolation). Additionally, forming positive relationships with other students and faculty are important for networking and collaborations on research.

Conclusion

We have made some strides in terms of diversifying graduate programs in political science, but there is still more work to be done. As the discipline becomes more diverse, faculty and the political science community as a whole should rethink their approaches to students' professionalization, socialization, and mentoring to make them more inclusive. For example, in our mentoring, we should help students to build their confidence, teaching skills, and develop professional networks and long-term career goals (Brunsma, Embrick, and Shin 2017), while also being mindful of the barriers that underrepresented and marginalized students may experience.

Beyond academic work, mentors should care about their students' mental health, disabilities (physical and "invisible"), cultural practices, religious holidays (including those beyond Christian holidays, like Eid, Passover, Ramadan, Yom Kippur, etc.), and so forth. We also need to create research opportunities for promising BIPOC undergraduate students so that they can learn those skills early. For those BIPOC students that decide to pursue a PhD, it is not enough to simply admit those students to our programs and hope for the best. We need to create equitable and inclusive environments where they can receive effective mentorship, adequate financial support, and the skills needed to succeed in our discipline.

Descriptive representation without substantive change is no longer sufficient. We need drastic action to counter historical marginalization of BIPOC individuals and voices within the discipline. In order to do this, we need to critically reexamine department culture and that of the discipline more broadly. It is imperative that political science strive towards becoming an equitable space for the study of politics for both BIPOC students and faculty, as the future of the field depends on it.

References

American Political Science Association and Task Force on Political Science in the 21st Century. 2011. Political Science in the 21st Century: Report of the Task Force on Political Science in the 21st Century. Washington, DC: American Political Science Association. http://www.apsanet.org/imgtest/TF_21st%20Century_Allpgs_webres90.pdf (August 9, 2021).

American Political Science Review's Incoming Editorial Team. 2019. "We're an all-women team chosen to edit political science's flagship journal. Here's why that matters." *The Washington Post*. August 19, 2019. https://www.washingtonpost.com/politics/2019/08/29/were-an-all-women-team-chosen-edit-political-sciences-flagship-journal-heres-why-that-matters/

Brunsma, David L., David G. Embrick, and Jean H. Shin. 2017. "Graduate Students of Color: Race, Racism, and Mentoring in the White Waters of Academia." *Sociology of Race and Ethnicity* 3(1): 1–13.

Cirillo, Francesco. "The Pomodoro Technique (The Pomodoro).": 45.

Crenshaw, Kimberlé Williams. 1989. "Demarginalizing the Intersection of Race and Sex: A Black Feminist Critique of Antidiscrimination Doctrine, Feminist Theory, and Antiracist Politics." *University of Chicago Legal Forum* 140: 139–167.

Desmond-Harris, Jenée. 2015, February 16. "What exactly is a microaggression?." VOX. Retrieved from: https://www.vox.com/2015/2/16/8031073/what-are-microaggressions

"Doctorate Recipients from U.S. Universities: 2020 | NSF - National Science Foundation." https://ncses.nsf.gov/pubs/nsf22300/report/path-to-the-doctorate.

Garcia, Matthew Mendez, and Ange-Marie Hancock Alfaro. 2021. "Where Do We Begin? Preliminary Thoughts on Racial and Ethnic Diversity Within Political Science." *PS: Political Science & Politics* 54(1): 141–43.

"GRE General Test Fees (For Test Takers)." https://www.ets.org/gre/revised_general/register/fees/.

Hurtado, Sylvia. 1994. "Graduate School Racial Climates and Academic Self-Concept among Minority Graduate Students in the 1970s." *American Journal of Education* 102 (3) (May 1,):330-51. https://www.jstor.org/stable/1085740.

Jones-Correa, M., & Leal, D. L. (1996). Becoming "Hispanic": Secondary Panethnic Identification among Latin American-Origin Populations in the United States. Hispanic Journal of Behavioral Sciences, 18(2), 214-254. https://doi.org/10.1177/07399863960182008

Junn, Jane, and Natalie Masuoka. 2008. "Asian American Identity: Shared Racial Status and Political Context." *Perspectives on Politics* 6(4): 729–40.

Juárez, Carlos E. 1991. "Recruiting Minority Students for Academic Careers: The Role of Graduate Student and Faculty Mentors." *PS: Political Science and Politics* 24(3): 539–40.

Mealy, Kimberly. 2018. "Diversity and Inclusion Report." Washington, DC: American Political Science Association. https://www.apsanet.org/Portals/54/diversity%20and%20inclusion%20prgms/DIV%20reports/Diversity%20Report%20Executive%20-%20Final%20Draft%20-%20Web%20version.pdf?ver=2018-03-29-134427-467

Michelson, Melissa R., and Jessica L. Lavariega Monforti. 2021. "Elusive Inclusion: Persistent Challenges Facing Women of Color in Political Science." *PS: Political Science & Politics* 54(1): 152–57.

Milem, Jeffrey F., Mitchell J. Chang, and Anthony L. Antonio. 2005. Making Diversity Work on Campus: A Research-Based Perspective. Washington, DC: Association of American Colleges & Universities.

Montgomery, Beronda L., Jualynne E. Dodson, and Sonya M. Johnson. 2014. "Guiding the Way: Mentoring Graduate Students and Junior Faculty for Sustainable Academic Careers." *SAGE Open* 4(4): 215824401455804.

Nettles, Michael T. 1990. "Success in Doctoral Programs: Experiences of Minority and White Students." *American Journal of Education* 98 (4) (Aug 1,):494-522. https://www.jstor.org/stable/1085329.

Noy, Shiri, and Rashawn Ray. 2012. "Graduate Students' Perceptions of their Advisors: Is there Systematic Disadvantage in Mentorship?" *The Journal of Higher Education* (Columbus) 83 (6):876-914.

Ramirez, Elvia. 2011. "'No One Taught Me the Steps': Latinos' Experiences Applying to Graduate School." *Journal of Latinos and Education* 10(3): 204–22.

Slay, Kelly E., Kimberly A. Reyes, and Julie R. Posselt. 2019. "Bait and Switch: Representation, Climate, and Tensions of Diversity Work in Graduate Education." *The Review of Higher Education* 42(5): 255–86.

Sue, Derald Wing. 2010. *Microaggressions in everyday life: Race, gender, and sexual orientation.* John Wiley & Sons Inc.

Thomas, Kecia M., Leigh A. Willis, and Jimmy Davis. 2007. "Mentoring Minority Graduate Students: Issues and Strategies for Institutions, Faculty, and Students." *Equal Opportunities International* 26 (3) (Apr 3,):178-92. https://www.emerald.com/insight/content/doi/10.1108/02610150710735471/full/html.

Tormos-Aponte, Fernando, and Mayra Velez-Serrano. 2020. "BROADENING THE PATHWAY FOR GRADUATE STUDIES IN POLITICAL SCIENCE." *PS: Political Science & Politics* 53(1): 145–46.

Torres, Lucas, Mark W. Driscoll, and Anthony L Burrow. 2010. "Racial microaggressions and psychological functioning among highly achieving African-Americans: A mixed-methods approach." *Journal of Social and Clinical Psychology*, 29(10), 1074–1099. https://doi.org/10.1521/jscp.2010.29.10.1074

55

Political Science & LGBTQ+ Identity: Thoughts & Suggestions for LGBTQ+ Graduate Students

Monique Newton[1], Brian F. Harrison[2], & Edward F. Kammerer, Jr.[3]

1. Northwestern University 2. Carleton College 3. Idaho State University

KEYWORDS: LGBTQ+, Sexuality, Sexual Orientation, Gender Identity, Queer.

Introduction

The choice to pursue a PhD is among the most consequential professional decisions a person can make. That choice can feel even more daunting for a person who identifies as a member of the LGBTQ+[1] community because there are specific questions important to our community that are sometimes difficult to answer. The purpose of this chapter is to discuss some of the challenges and opportunities that come with pursuing a PhD from two perspectives: as an LGBTQ+ person and as someone who wants to conduct research on LGBTQ+ topics. Of course, both can be true!

This chapter begins with a brief discussion of pitfalls and potential solutions to the study of LGBTQ+ identity in political science, including the trajectory of the study of sexuality and gender as a part of the history of political science. Of course, not every LGBTQ+ graduate student will study topics related to LGBTQ+ identity. For those that do, political science has gradually become more open to including LGBTQ+ research topics but several obstacles remain.

The next section addresses concerns about campus climate. We start with general advice. Next, we provide specific information about choosing a graduate program that is the right fit for LGBTQ+ students. Then, we discuss considerations for the job market that are unique to LGBTQ+ identifying people as well as people who research LGBTQ+ politics. Topics include coming out during job interviews, how to ask questions during interviews that ensure the position will be safe and supportive for you, and how to navigate questions at a job talk surrounding your gender identity and/or sexual orientation (see also chapter 45 for more information about academic job interviewing).

The final section identifies networking opportunities and resources, including those available through the American Political Science Association (APSA), including the Sexuality and Politics section, the LGBTQ Caucus, and the Committee on the Status of LGBT Individuals in the Profession as well as others.

LGBTQ+ Inclusiveness in Political Science

Political science has not always been, and may never be, fully welcoming of LGBTQ+ political scholarship. Scholars who study LGBTQ+ issues may be members of the LGBTQ+ community but, of course, they may not be. The assumption, however, may well be that anyone studying LGBTQ+ politics is a member of the LGBTQ+ community. This assumption can be cause for concern for some graduate students, regardless of their sexual orientation and gender identity, as they begin to formulate a research agenda and choose a dissertation topic.

In 2007, the APSA Committee on the Status of LGBT Individuals in the Profession conducted a discipline-wide climate survey focused on LGBTQ+ issues (Novkov and Barclay 2010). The survey addressed both the climate for LGBTQ+ individuals and the climate for teaching and research related to LGBTQ+ topics. The data show progress in the years since an earlier climate survey conducted in the early 1990s (Ackelsberg 2017). Respondents in the 2007 survey reported less discrimination and marginalization compared to the earlier study; there were some areas of concern, however, notably around lower scores on student evaluations of teaching. The consensus of the 2007 survey was that teaching LGBTQ+ issues was appropriate for the discipline. Similarly, survey respondents clearly believed LGBTQ+ politics to be an acceptable area for research and scholarship, although there was some variation across subfields. Public law, American politics, and political theory were most supportive of LGBTQ+ research; international relations was the least welcoming.

Despite the generally positive responses in most areas, Novkov and Barclay (2010) note resistance to LGBT research.[2] Thirteen percent of respondents were concerned about how the discipline recognizes and values LGBT-focused research. A number of respondents (4.1%) appeared hostile to research on LGBT topics. Some of this hostility stemmed from homophobic views or a belief that LGBT researchers lack objectivity when studying LGBT issues: several respondents viewed work on LGBT issues as advocacy, not science (Harrison and Michelson, forthcoming). This concern can be traced even further back to the creation of the Status Committee itself in 1992. One of the charges given to the Committee was to ensure that research on sexual orientation issues be assessed by the same standards as other research in political science (Ackelsberg 2017). Ackelsberg, who served on the Status Committee, notes the assumptions buried in this charge: that such research was perceived as less rigorous or that it would lower the standards for assessing research in the discipline. Thankfully, these assumptions are less common today.

Research and scholarship on LGBTQ+ issues in political science has continued to grow. Tadlock and Taylor (2017, 212) refer to this as "an explosion" of research, across a host of topics. Scholars have shown how the study of LGBTQ+ politics enhances our understanding of questions asked throughout the field (Mucciaroni 2011). Research on LGBTQ+ topics is published in leading journals in the discipline as well as more in subfield or specialty journals. Tadlock and Taylor used keyword searches in the leading journals to determine how and to what extent LGBTQ+ issues are discussed in the articles published. Scholarship is increasing, with a slight majority of articles in their dataset published since 2007. Their study also looked at books addressing LGBTQ+ politics and find a similar increase in scholarship, with significant increases beginning in the mid-1990s. This demonstrates that LGBTQ+ topics in political science are increasingly accepted and fruitful areas for research. This trend is true across the full breadth of the discipline, although there remains significant variation in how common LGBTQ+ scholarship is in each subfield. There is also variation on topics within the broad LGBTQ+ umbrella: research on bisexual and transgender people remains less common than research on gay men and lesbians (Smith 2011). This discrepancy may shift, however, as the issues being addressed in government continue to single out transgender individuals for particularly harsh treatment. Whatever shifts may happen, we expect LGBTQ+ politics to continue to be an important part of the discipline.

Finding a Welcoming and Supportive Campus

Whether as an incoming graduate student or a candidate on the job market, one core issue remains the same: finding a campus community that will welcome and support you. This is true for all of us. But members of the LGBTQ+ community may face challenges on top of the normal ones associated with these processes. In this section, we address general concerns about campus climate and then shift to specific issues to consider at each stage of this process: starting graduate school and finding a faculty job.

First, you need to decide how open you want to—or can be—about your identity. This crucial decision affects how a person is perceived and treated by others in the department, the discipline, and beyond. It can also have important consequences for research and employment opportunities. Not everyone can be openly-LGBTQ+. For some, it is essential to stay closeted, particularly at certain religiously conservative institutions. Sometimes, scholars can be personally open about their identity but need to remain somewhat closeted professionally. LGBTQ+ scholars who do field work in areas that are hostile to LGBTQ+ people, like in areas where LGBTQ+ identity is criminalized or stigmatized, must think carefully about how much of their identity they share publicly (see also chapter 20). There may be other reasons to think carefully about how open you are about your identity and in which forums. You need to do what is best for you, at all stages of your career.

Although society has come a long way regarding the public treatment of members of the LGBTQ+ community, many departments aren't safe havens for all members of the community. Even if a department is welcoming for some LGBTQ+ people, you cannot assume that trans and non-binary faculty will be equally welcome or supported. Even today, people struggle to treat LGBTQ+ students and colleagues appropriately. People may form assumptions about how a person talks, the kinds of research topics a person may be interested in, how a person dresses, and the activities and interests of that person based only on their LGBTQ+ status.

Getting a genuine sense of a department can be challenging. Even in departments with clear, LGBTQ+ inclusive policies there may be disconnects between those policies and the everyday experiences of LGBTQ+ people in the department. While on campus or speaking with representatives of the department, trust your gut regarding how individuals interact with you. These conversations are essential for figuring out how you will be treated in your day-to-day life in that department. If you have interactions that make you uncomfortable or that give you a sense you would not be welcome, you need to think carefully about whether that campus is a good fit for you. Ask yourself if it is an environment where you can spend the next several years of your life.

As you navigate these decisions, there are some key considerations to keep in mind. First, it is a good general rule to consider whether you would be the only LGBTQ+ person in your cohort or department. Academia can be an isolating experience; having a community and a group of allies to lean on for support is important (see also chapter 63 for more on academic isolation). Look for department or university-wide LGBTQ+ organizations, either for graduate students or faculty. These organizations can help build community. Try to find out about campus life and LGBTQ+ life in the broader community. Many cities have thriving LGBTQ+ communities that can help supplement the campus community. In other areas, though, the LGBTQ+ community, both on and off campus, is smaller. You need to figure out what type of LGBTQ+ community is most important to you. Moving to a smaller town, with a small LGBTQ+ population (especially if you come from a larger urban environment) can be quite challenging. This is particularly true for single people looking for dating opportunities. They exist but can be hard to find.

Choosing and Navigating a Graduate Program

Choosing a graduate program can be complicated and stressful (see chapter 2 for more information). In addition to the issues common to all graduate students, and those noted above, there are specific issues prospective LGBTQ+ graduate students need to consider.

First is finding a supportive advisor. If you are able, ask potential faculty members with whom you may work, about whether they have worked with LGBTQ+ students in the past. This can be helpful in determining how easy it will be to find an advisor and build a committee. This is especially important if you want to study LGBTQ+ political issues. Not all departments will have faculty who specialize in LGBTQ+ politics, but they may have faculty who can apply their area of specialization to LGBTQ+ topics. (See also chapters 10 and 13 for choosing a subfield and advisor, respectively.)

If you can identify an LGBTQ+ graduate student already in the department, see if they are willing to have a frank conversation about their experiences, both on and off campus. You can also ask the department to put you in touch with a current, or recent, LGBTQ+ student. This conversation can help you address those climate concerns we noted above.

Academic Job Market

Of course, the goal of any graduate student is simple: to finish and get a job! The most important consideration in the job market is your health and safety. That supersedes all other elements of the job search. Yes, finding an academic position is important and there are numerous financial and personal concerns about finding a job. Any advice presented here, however, needs to be centered around your individual well-being, first and foremost. If being open about your identities is important to you and if it contributes to your continued health, then you should be open about your identities, provided it is safe for you to do so, even if it may be detrimental on the job market. Life is too short to not be true to yourself and to what you need. Self-care is always your first priority.

The reality of the job market is there are many aspects outside of your control: the other applicants, the needs of the hiring department, the expectations of the dean…just to name a few (see chapter 34 for further elaboration). An additional aspect out of your control is how you and your LGBTQ+ identity and/or research will be received by the search committee. There are steps to take to ensure you make informed decisions about self-disclosure during the job market process.

Sometimes it is unclear whether it's advantageous or even safe to be open about your identity during a job interview. On the one hand, it could highlight an aspect of yourself that can add to the diversity of a department. On the other, it might open you to explicit or implicit bias from department members (for more about navigating implicit biases within the profession, see chapter 49). Your goal should be to gather as much information as possible prior to an interview: ask with whom you will meet during a phone call or an on-campus interview and research each person. Have they made comments on-the-record about LGBTQ+ people or inclusion in general? What values can you glean from their research and teaching statements? Does anything in the general department and college/university website mention that diversity (including LGBTQ+ identity) is valued and cultivated? While there is rarely a perfect indicator, getting a feel for the values of the individuals, department, and college can provide clues about whether being open about your identity during interviews is a good idea.

There are concrete steps you can take while on a campus interview to discern whether the campus is a welcoming and LGBTQ+ affirming place. Many on-campus interviews will involve a meeting with a representative from the Human Resources department. (If there is not a meeting with HR personnel on your schedule, you may ask the search chair if you could add one.) During this confidential meeting, you can ask questions about existing policies that can support you and your family that will not be shared with the search committee. If you are comfortable, you can also request to add additional meetings. You can ask to meet with an LGBTQ+ faculty or staff member, a member of an on-campus LGBTQ+ group, or another person who might be able to answer questions about campus culture. Be aware that these meetings are generally not confidential so be sure to ask questions carefully and thoughtfully. Questions you could ask include how comfortable the person feels on campus and in their department; if there are ways the person feels they could be better supported as an LGBTQ+ person; whether the city or town is safe for LGBTQ+ people; and if there are groups or organizations on campus or in the community that are specifically oriented to LGBTQ+ people. If your research is on LGBTQ+ politics, you can also ask about research support and how valued LGBTQ+ research is on campus. Since it can still be difficult to publish LGBTQ+ research in the top journals, this may be a concern for tenure and promotion.

You are not required to disclose any aspect of your identity, even if you conduct research about LGBTQ+ issues or rights. Of course, others may assume you are a member of the LGBTQ+ community simply because of your research but you need not confirm or even respond if that question is asked. Remember that an employer cannot legally ask you intrusive personal questions during an interview, including questions about your sexual orientation, your family dynamics, or your gender identity. If questions are becoming too personal, you are within your rights to ask for that line of questioning to stop. If you have any questions, you can consult with someone in the Human Resources department at the college or university. These can be uncomfortable conversations. After all, you are the one trying to impress them, so they hire you for an academic position! It is important to consider, though, that there are boundaries that should not be crossed in a professional setting, and you are well within your rights to demand that you are treated with respect and within the parameters of employment law.

Sometimes your identity is closely intertwined with your research and a question may arise during a job talk. You should anticipate a question about the applicability of your research and develop a response that highlights the broad implications and importance of your work. You should also think about whether self-disclosure is an important part of that response. If someone were to ask about the normative importance of your work on LGBTQ+ rights, for example, you might choose to respond that the work helps to protect people like you from bias and discrimination. Personalizing the impact of LGBTQ+ research can have a meaningful influence on how your work is interpreted. However, others may try to dismiss your work because you are "studying yourself," known pejoratively as "me-search." This was a concern in the 2010 Novkov and Barclay study discussed above. Being able to pivot between the personal and the abstract will be useful depending on the campus environment in which you find yourself.

Thinking through these issues before a job interview or job talk can help you determine your comfort level with self-disclosure based on the prior research you can do about the department and the college or university and some of the questions you can ask while on campus. If you have questions and are not comfortable speaking with your advisor about these issues, you can reach out to the leadership of the APSA LGBTQ+ Caucus or Sexuality and Politics section for more specific advice. More information about these groups is listed below.

Name Changes: Keeping Your Publication Record Current

Another issue that can arise for scholars involves name changes on previously published work. It is important that scholars' entire body of work be clearly identified as their own. Yet, some scholars may not want to be linked to work with a previous name. This is particularly important for trans scholars who transition after they begin publishing. The Committee on Publication Ethics [3] drafted a statement of principles urging publishers to make this process easier, noting the hardship that a lack of name change policy creates for trans scholars. Thankfully, many journals now have a process to update author names on previously published work. The process for each journal varies and name changes may not be available at all journals. The Committee on the Status of LGBT Individuals in the Profession is currently working to ensure broad access to name changes for political science journals.

Resources and More Information

We want to close this chapter with information about the formal institutions within the American Political Science Association that exist to support LGBTQ+ scholars and research about LGBTQ+ politics. There are three main groups, each with a slightly different focus. The Sexuality and Politics section's primary focus is on scholars who study issues of sexuality; it is not limited to LGBTQ+ political scientists. The LGBTQ Caucus, on the other hand, is designed for LGBTQ+ political scientists (and their allies) regardless of their area of study. The APSA Committee on the Status of LGBT Individuals in the Profession has a focus similar to the Caucus but is more formally integrated into APSA's leadership channels and is an important advocacy voice for the community with APSA itself.

In 2007, the Sexuality and Politics section was created to provide a place for scholars working on LGBTQ+ issues as well as other topics related to sexuality (Wilson and Burgess 2007). The decision to name the section "Sexuality and Politics" rather than "LGBT Politics" was intentional, both to provide a name less likely to spark homophobic backlash and to provide a wider substantive focus to help maintain minimum thresholds of membership (Wilson 2017). Membership in the section has fluctuated over the years but the section continues to be a vibrant community for those engaged in LGBTQ+ research. Every year, the section sponsors or co-sponsors several panels at the APSA Annual Meeting.

The Sexuality and Politics section also sponsors two awards for research on sexuality and politics: the Cynthia Weber Best Conference Paper Award and the Kenneth Sherrill Best Dissertation Award. Along with the LGBTQ Caucus's Bailey Award (also for the best conference paper) and the Centennial Center's award recognizing the best dissertation proposal covering empirical LGBT politics, these awards demonstrate the understanding that scholarship on LGBTQ+ politics deserves serious recognition by the discipline. While the Sexuality and Politics section is the primary institutional home for research on sexuality and politics, many scholars are also members of the LGBTQ Caucus. The Caucus's primary focus is supporting LGBTQ+ political scientists, regardless of their field of study. In addition to that, the Caucus sponsors panels on LGBTQ+ research at the APSA Annual Meeting and recognizes the best work on LGBTQ+ politics with the Bailey Award.

Both the Sexuality & Politics Section and the LGBTQ Caucus strive to be welcoming for graduate students. Graduate students receive free membership in the Section. Caucus membership dues are voluntary and suggested dues are based on a sliding scale making membership affordable for everyone. The executive committee includes a graduate student representative and graduate students are welcome and encouraged to participate in leadership opportunities within the section.

For LGBTQ+ graduate students, or those who study LGBTQ+ politics, joining the Section and the Caucus can also provide invaluable mentorship. While there are more LGBTQ+ faculty in the discipline now than in decades past, they are not present in every department. Similarly, LGBTQ+ politics courses, while more common, are not offered everywhere. The Section and the Caucus can provide graduate students opportunities to find mentors, co-authors, or to discuss research ideas with a receptive and knowledgeable audience. In addition to attending the variety of panels on LGBTQ+ politics offered at APSA, graduate students can and should attend the business meetings for both the Section and the Caucus and the evening social reception jointly sponsored by the Section, the Caucus, and the LGBT Status Committee. These events help build community and can connect graduate students to important resources, particularly when students face challenges based on their identity or their research agenda. (For more information about networking and conferencing, see chapters 7 and 21.)

Finally, the Committee on the Status of LGBT Individuals in the Profession is another important resource for LGBTQ+ graduate students. The Status Committee is charged with advocating for the needs and concerns of LGBTQ+ political scientists, including graduate students, to APSA leadership. The members of the LGBTQ Status Committee work to ensure that APSA's policies take the needs of LGBTQ+ people into account and to encourage diverse voices to be heard. The Status Committee also sponsors grants to help defray the cost of attending APSA, with a particular focus on graduate students, contingent, community college, and other faculty who may lack resources for conference attendance.

Conclusion

LGBTQ+ scholars and scholars who study LGBTQ+ issues have a place in political science. While not every individual campus or department is a welcoming place, the discipline as a whole has become increasingly welcoming throughout the years. While much of the advice in this chapter centers around challenges and concerns, we do not want to paint a picture that LGBTQ+ political scientists cannot be successful in their academic careers. We have been and will continue to be. We hope the advice presented here helps make that success a reality for everyone.

Resources

Resources from APSA and Related Groups:
- APSA Sexuality & Politics Section: https://www.apsanet.org/section38
- APSA Committee on the Status of LGBT Individuals in the Profession: https://www.apsanet.org/statuscommitteelgbt
- APSA LGBTQ Caucus: https://connect.apsanet.org/lgbtq-caucus/
- LGBTQ Caucus Twitter: https://twitter.com/LGBTQCaucus
- LGBTQ Caucus Facebook Group: https://www.facebook.com/groups/apsalgbtqcaucus
- Centennial Center Sherrill Prize: https://connect.apsanet.org/centennialcenter/grants-awards/kenneth-sherrill-prize/
- ISA LGBTQ Caucus: https://www.isanet.org/ISA/Caucuses/LGBTQA-Caucus

Selected Resources for Scholars of LGBTQ+ Politics
- Queer Politics: https://www.queerpolitics.org/
- ONE Archive: https://www.onearchives.org/
- NY Public Library LGBT Collection: https://www.nypl.org/lgbtqcollections

- Williams Institute (UCLA Law School): https://williamsinstitute.law.ucla.edu/

Endnotes

1   While we use the term LGBTQ+ here, we acknowledge that the abbreviations and terminology used to refer to the LGBTQ+ community are constantly evolving and vary across subfields. Some may prefer a longer, or different, abbreviation. We do not intend to exclude those people from this chapter's focus.

2   Note the survey in 2010 utilizes the acronym LGBT so we use that acronym to describe the survey's findings here.

3   https://publicationethics.org/news/vision-more-trans-inclusive-publishing-world

References

Ackelsberg, Martha. 2017. "The Politics of LGBTQ Politics in APSA: A History (and Its) Lesson(s)." In *LGBTQ Politics: A Critical Reader*, edited by Marla Brettschneider, Susan Burgess, and Christine Keating, 177-197. New York: NYU Press.

Harrison, Brian F. and Melissa R. Michelson. Forthcoming. "LGBTQ Scholarship: Researcher Identity & Ingroup Positionality." *P.S.: Politics and Political Science.*

Mucciaroni, Gary. 2011. "The Study of LGBT Politics and Its Contributions to Political Science." PS: *Political Science & Politics* 44(1): 17-21.

Novkov, Julie and Scott Barclay. 2010. "Lesbians, Gays, Bisexuals, and the Transgendered in Political Science: Report on a Discipline-Wide Survey." *PS: Political Science & Politics* 43(1): 95-106.

Smith, Charles Anthony. 2011. "Gay, Straight, or Questioning? Sexuality and Political Science." *PS: Political Science & Politics* 44(1): 35-38.

Tadlock, Barry L. and Jami K. Taylor. 2017. "Where Has the Field Gone? An Investigation of LGBTQ Political Science Research." In *LGBTQ Politics: A Critical Reader,* edited by Marla Brettschneider, Susan Burgess, and Christine Keating, 212-233. New York: NYU Press.

Wilson, Angelia. 2017. "Our Stories." In *LGBTQ Politics: A Critical Reader,* edited by Marla Brettschneider, Susan Burgess, and Christine Keating, 157-176. New York: NYU Press.

Wilson, Angelia and Susan Burgess. 2007. "Sexuality and the Body Politic: Thoughts on the Construction of an APSA Sexuality & Politics Section." *PS: Political Science & Politics* 40(2): 377-381.

56 | Gender and the Political Science Graduate Experience: When Leaning In Isn't Enough

Maya Novak-Herzog[1], Alisson Rowland[2],
Kimberly Saks McManaway[3], & Tabitha Bonilla[4]

1. Northwestern University 2. University of California, Irvine 3. University of Michigan–Flint

4. Northwestern University

KEYWORDS: Woman-Identifying People, Gender Bias, Disproportionate Labor, Consciousness-Raising.

Introduction

In the fall of 2019, The Monkey Cage released a 10-part series of essays in The Washington Post highlighting the serious and unyielding nature of gender inequality ubiquitous in political science research by evaluating gender disparities in publications, course evaluations, journal submissions, and more.[1] While a glaring condemnation of inequity is a rare find on a mainstream news source, the article gives a statistical foundation to what every *woman-identifying person*[2] in the field of political science has experientially known for years: that being a woman in political science is an uphill battle.

Overwhelming quantitative and qualitative research has proven that despite women contributing more to teaching, mentoring, and administering in the discipline, they are less likely to advance and be recognized for their achievements (Alter et al. 2020). This runs deeper than inequity in publications and service distribution—which we address in this chapter—but rather, is seeded in the heart of departmental culture. For many female professors and graduate students alike, home departments can start to feel like a "Boys Club," inspiring feelings of immense stress and isolation for women (Schneider 2011). Furthermore, departments tend to place men[3] in leadership roles allowing them to control allocation of resources. Student bodies tend to be male dominated, leading to an overall competitive and often aggressive department culture (Niederle and Vesterlund 2011). These men often have a vested interest in maintaining institutional standards that do not serve women.

While we cannot rid every department on every campus of this deep-seated issue, there are tips and tricks we have collected to navigate our chosen discipline as women.

The Gendered Grad School Experience

Awareness and Sharing Stories

Radical feminists of the 1970s and 80s argued that *consciousness-raising* was the key to female empowerment and used consciousness-raising circles in order to turn what was seen as personal and individual struggles into collective understanding (MacKinnon 1982; Willis 1984). So too, we believe that coalitions among woman-identifying academics must push for recognizing issues in academia as institutional and structural problems instead of a deeply personal and individual experience. As a result, coalitions among women in political science can alleviate the shame of isolation, imposter syndrome, and harm done by misogynistic stereotypes. In this respect, coalitions are needed in academia. At the same time, we wish to acknowledge that not all coalitions represent or are for all woman-identifying people. We recognize and want to reaffirm that the experience of being a woman in academia is not homogenous. A woman's race, class, sexual orientation, age, and other identities can exacerbate or create different challenges that go beyond a shared gender identity (Collins 1998; Crenshaw 1991; hooks 1990). Here, we acknowledge different needs exist that have been identified by many intersectional feminist theorists. We encourage all prospective and current students to bring awareness to the diversity of experiences that exist within groups. While you are not alone in your struggle, it is important to be mindful of the most vulnerable among us and how to create space while uplifting those with the most needs (Hancock 2011).

Structures for Success

Too often, women (particularly women from underrepresented racial and ethnic groups) are admitted to political science departments in order to boost perceived diversity despite the departments' failure to provide structures necessary to help women succeed in the field (Teele, Kalla, and Rosenbluth 2018). At a base level, there are several institutional changes that we believe every department should have in place if they claim to care about their female colleagues.

The pressure for women to be caretakers in all kinds of capacities often puts an entire realm of invisible labor on them. Duties that are less rewarded in the academy are more likely to be feminized, with burdens of emotional labor often assigned to women (Bellas 1999). And, while men may be able to take summers and sabbaticals to work on research, women often go home to second shifts and full-time caretaking. Furthermore, childcare can sabotage tenure timelines.

Discrimination is also present against women who do not have children, particularly in hiring processes. Women are often told to hide their marital status or future plans during interviews for fear that departments will retaliate against women who might need to take time off.

Possible solutions to these barriers include advocating for parental leave for both genders, designated pump rooms in departments for those breastfeeding, and mandatory trainings for preventing gender discrimination in hiring and tenure review applications (see chapter 16 on pregnancy and parenting). While these processes require institutional support, there are also tools to navigate academia as a woman on your own. In this chapter, we have organized our thoughts into categories based on the three main categories graduate students will face once they are job candidates on the market as those categories are often replicated within the graduate student experience. These three categories—teaching, service, and research—are often new experiences for graduate students and present unique challenges based on gender. Therefore, we use those categories here as a structure to guide our advice both as a professional development tool and a practical guide.

Teaching

The art and practice of teaching are integral to a well-rounded graduate school experience (For more on teaching, see the section "Professional Development: Teaching"). Gaining this experience is not always straightforward and can be complicated by the barriers which woman-identifying people face in both the academy and society at large.[4] Two issues present themselves to woman-identifying graduate students: gaining experience and managing a classroom.

Getting Access to Teaching Experience

While some graduate programs do a thorough job of ensuring their graduates have various teaching experiences before graduation, others do not. If your institution is one of those that ensure such experiences for their graduate students, take advantage of those. In addition to volunteering to teach introductory courses, make sure to offer to teach courses in your subfield that are appropriate for a graduate student. Sometimes this may mean being a squeaky wheel—in other words, advocating for yourself may take continually drawing attention to your needs so you cannot be ignored. Often, women feel outside of the club for a variety of reasons. Make sure those who have the authority to distribute teaching assignments see you and know of your interest regularly.

If your institution is not one that offers such opportunities or if you feel left out of the available opportunities, there are a variety of ways you can ensure that you receive this type of exposure. Look for adjunct teaching roles at local institutions. Offer to lead a seminar or workshop to a local library or senior center about current political events. Find state and local organizations for civic engagement that need volunteers for mock trial and moot court competitions and coaches for mock legislative endeavors. There also may be a role for leading girls and young women in different contexts by volunteering for organizations such as the Girl Scouts and Girls on the Run that while they aren't teaching, do show the ability to mentor a group of students. These experiences and the development of content for a wide variety of audiences count as teaching experience and can often lead to other opportunities.

Learning how to Teach and Run a Classroom

The classroom may present unique challenges to woman-identifying people. Unlike cisgender men, woman-identifying people (especially women of color) may find that it is difficult to navigate the thin line between maintaining authority and fostering an open classroom environment where students feel like they can approach you with issues. A well-researched consequence of this is the tendency for women faculty to be rated as less effective than their cisgender male counterparts in student evaluations of teaching (Adams et al. 2021) This can be even more challenging for women of color (Pittman 2010). Though women are just as likely as men to engage in non-classroom student development (Cox et al. 2010), those experiences may be harder to navigate for women. Even identifying to your students how to address you—by Prof. [Name] or Ms. [Name] or by your first name—can be a complicated decision with no uniform answer for all women. Finally, you may find that your appearance takes on a different importance to your students and colleagues in a way that does not apply to men in your position.

These issues are not easily distilled into concrete advice that works for everyone. Instead, you must find what works for you and be prepared to shift if need be. While you should dress professionally, that term is often heavily used to establish gender-based standards and you can and should feel free to resist being guided by outdated advice. The authors of this piece have different expectations as to what our students call us and why we choose that route, but the one thing we have in common is that we make our preferences known at the beginning of the semester and reinforce them throughout. Finally, as for student evaluations, if you are concerned about unnecessary and harmful comments about your appearance or gender, you can work with a trusted friend to have them read the raw comments and filter the ones out that are harmful so that you can only see the ones that are important and reciprocate the same for that friend.

There is support available to help you develop your classroom style. First, look to your institution's center for teaching and learning. Most institutions have one (though the names may differ) and they often run a variety of programming throughout the year that is free and easily accessible. Second, talk to your instructors—especially your woman-identifying instructors—who you have found to be innovative teachers. Finally, reach out to professional organizations. The American Political Science Association has a journal dedicated to the scholarship of teaching and learning of political science called the Journal of Political Science Education (see chapter 30). Other journals, like PS: Political Science & Politics, have sections dedicated to the profession and the art of teaching. There are also other opportunities through non-political associations and organizations online to become certified in online and hybrid teaching methodologies for low cost or free.

Service

Often tacked on as an afterthought to a CV, service can be a valuable part of your graduate career. While at the graduate level service is often optional, it can help you develop skills for career advancement (inside or outside the academy), create opportunities for advocacy, and can be a primary mode of community-building. This section discusses how service can foster these rich communities within academia. Though service can be incredibly important, it is important to acknowledge the gendered and racialized aspects of it. It increasingly falls onto the shoulders of women and people of color to create these spaces, while also holding all other scholarly responsibilities. Additionally, service work is historically under-recognized. As such, we offer strategies to guide prospective and new students on when and where to put your energy as you balance your role(s) as mentor and scholar, but how service can be useful.

Service as Transformative Praxis

The word service acts as a stand-in for activities outside or related to, your department, university, or the discipline more broadly that have strong mentorship components. This can be advising students on research, serving on an editorial board, assisting in conference logistics, and much more. Participating in service can be a transformative praxis, in which your skills as a mentor and researcher are honed while you do the same for others. These activities can also be confidence builders! Offering to assist undergraduate research hones your skills as a mentor and increases your leadership potential. In this way, it can also make you a more competitive applicant on the job market. Finally, one of the biggest benefits of engaging in service is the opportunity to foster a supportive community and make lasting partnerships. Great research projects have blossomed from being in the right place at the right time, and those participating in the same forms of service as you will have other commonalities. Academia can be isolating at the best of times, so it is important to take an active role in creating your community.

We offer suggestions on how to build communities of care within academia. Within your department, you can play an important role in advocating for your fellow woman-identifying graduate students. This may, but does not always include, establishing department-specific women's lobbying groups. It is at the discretion of the members whether to include trusted people who are not woman-identifying. When organizing, you may want to address functional concerns in the department such as transparency in service hours, funding, teaching requirements, childcare services, and so on to ensure requirements are equitably distributed and supportive of gendered concerns. At the institutional level, you may find opportunities and support from the Office of Diversity and Inclusion, the Title IX office, childcare services, and other entities on campus that seek to support students holistically. Finally, you can propose guest speakers that are women who have successfully navigated these barriers to learn how they did so, coordinate conference panels that address gendered graduate experiences, and foster interdisciplinary mentorships outside of your home department. Although not a primary purpose of these exercises, this type of work is well-suited for inclusion in application materials that call for diversity and inclusion statements.

Service as Tokenization

Often, there is an expectation in academia for cascading mentorship—PhD students advise undergraduates, early career scholars advise PhD students, and so on. However, the distribution of service is often far from equal, in its practice and effects. The success of people whom academia was not made with in mind, particularly among historically excluded and disadvantaged communities, is lauded to prospective students. This signals to both current faculty and prospective students that they are 'rare' individuals who 'beat all odds' to be at their institution (Guinier 1990). Far from the flattering image this is meant to create, it pressures scholars who are in already-precarious positions to support others who find themselves similarly marginalized. While such support can and does form organically, it should not be their sole responsibility to change the culture. These inequitable power structures can lead people to burn out more quickly and feel overwhelmed by their responsibilities (McIntosh 1989).

Additionally, the pressure to succeed can foster a climate where 'no' becomes a forbidden word. Breaking this cycle where people are expected to overcommit, especially graduate students and non-tenured faculty, can lessen the tendency for service to become burdensome rather than transformative. The next section discusses the importance of creating boundaries for one's mental and physical well-being.

Setting Boundaries

The myth of meritocracy in academia creates pressures to say yes to opportunities at the expense of mental well-being. Participating in service activities can be an incredibly beneficial experience for fostering community and engaging with passionate individuals. But, as the previous section highlighted, these opportunities should not come at the expense of your other obligations or cause undue stress. That being said, everyone's personal calculus for what service acts to commit to and what to say no to will be different. This section proposes aspects to keep in mind when deciding.

If you are a PhD student, committing to service cannot take precedence over advancing to candidacy, defending, and dissertating. Prioritizing this time to develop as a researcher is critical. This is not to say do not engage in service, but to be cognizant of other competing responsibilities. Additionally, while these can be great experiences for developing interpersonal skills and creating spaces to transform inequitable power structures, it should never come at the expense of your mental and physical well-being. In this regard, it is important to practice grace with yourself; saying no can be difficult, but it can also be the right call to make.

Research

To the end of developing internal support structures for research, we focus on shedding light on the "hidden" curriculum that is often not something one learns from class material. While some of the curriculum stems from how to find resources, another key portion of this curriculum is about how to identify and problem-solve needs and resources.

Imbalances in Rank, Publications, and Methodology

While the graduate student experience is wrought with many challenges, an outlook for women graduate students suggests that women "lean in" and work harder (Alter et al. 2020) but face the difficulties of a leaky pipeline due to several factors (Teele and Thelen 2017). Indeed, although women are over-represented in undergraduate programs, by the time we look at tenured, full professors, they are seriously underrepresented in the profession (Teele and Thelen 2017). And, as one might expect, woman-identifying scholars are also underrepresented at the top ten journals in the profession (Teele and Thelen 2017) and underrepresented in citations (Shames and Wise 2017).

If rank and citations contain gender imbalances, so too does representation of women across subfields and methodology. Women are more likely to publish research with qualitative data than quantitative. This, of course, limits the type of journals that accept manuscripts for publication, but also becomes a self-reinforcing problem where general interest journals are less likely to publish quantitative data and authors are less likely to submit them. Beyond this is a general attitude that non-mathematically based methods lack "rigor" and are "discredited" (Poete and Ostrom 2005).

While we want to recognize the external structures that add barriers to women graduate students and their research, we believe the focus for research should be on creating internal structures and systems that create support for research. Importantly, these challenges are also likely to intersect with women who are also historically underrepresented due to race, ethnicity, religion, gender expression, sexuality, language, or another identity dimension (Hancock 2011).

Keeping Your Eyes on the Prize

Although students applying to graduate school often have a vision of what their ideal research agenda looks like, this knowledge may vary due to past lived experience (including in previous employment), shifting interests as learning progresses, and a need to pivot a research agenda due to various obstacles. The most important recommendation we might have is to create a graduate-student mission statement or values statement where the ideas and interests that brought you to graduate school live, and which you can use as a decision-making tool to navigate various challenges across their graduate experience.

Second, creating a structure of how to move your research forward is critical. At the top level is mapping out (as early as you are able) the key research milestones you need to be aware of as a graduate student. As students move through the program, and as research progresses, continue to add specific goals and deadlines needed to make these steps. Several programs exist to help provide structure for this process, breaking it down into term plans or article level goals (e.g., Belcher 2009). Institutions may have access to resources or be able to purchase membership for you with places such as the National Center for Faculty Development and Diversity. There are also free support resources such as Mirya Holman's Aggressive Winning Scholars newsletter[5] and Raul Pacheco-Vega's Blog.[6] Whichever resources one has access to or prefers to use, the goal should be starting to create a formalized structure for your own expectations of progress.

Finally, we recommend creating informal structures to help reach smaller milestones. Writing groups or retreats (even if just in a conference room on campus for a few hours a day) can help support writing goals. Some writing groups are created with the goal of offering feedback on written work, other writing groups are created to provide community while one navigates writing. Still other groups exist simply for goal setting, checking in, and as accountability mechanisms for weekly or semi-weekly progress. By making formal the in-formal, the process of progressing through graduate student research should become more transparent and more focused.

Identifying a Network of Mentors and Supporters[7]

Ideally, one can choose a graduate program with faculty that they have already identified (and talked to about being) potential mentors (see chapters 13 and 7 on mentorship and networks). Even in a best-case scenario, where one finds abundant mentorship at their home institution, students should look to expand their networks beyond their home institution. First, graduate school is about learning how to cultivate a network of knowledge and scholars with relevant research interests will be found at many other places. Second, faculty at other institutions can help provide additional knowledge, information, and other types of support. We recommend using all available resources including introductions from mentors or other contacts, organization caucuses (such as the Women and Gender Caucus or any other affiliations you may have),[8] and other networks—particularly those attentive to issues of women (such as WomenAlsoKnowStuff).[9] However, networking can pose particular challenges for women ranging from a lack of representation (e.g. the network explicated in Lazer 2010) to harassment as #MeTooPoliSci details (Brown 2020).

While cultivating relationships, graduate students should also remember to cultivate lateral relationships as well—students in their own program, in other programs at their university, and with students at other universities. These lateral relationships can be useful for building comradery, feedback on early drafts, and writing and accountability groups. For women, these peer support networks can be particularly helpful in providing validation, information, and material support (Macoun and Miller 2014).

Conclusion

Ultimately, the experience of being in graduate school can be an isolating one—and potentially more so for women. Alter et al. (2020) demonstrate that women "lean in" to the discipline—and sometimes without reward. We hope that our focus and advice on three specific areas of importance—teaching, research, and service—can be a guide for women in any stage of their program. In particular, the advice here is not simply intended to be instructions about how to "lean in" further, but to thrive while the systems that ask women to do and be more are dismantled. Although we hope the advice here affords readers ideas for how to simplify demands, problem solve solutions, and potential ways to cultivate safe and supportive structures that help facilitate success, we acknowledge that background, context, and access to various supports discussed here may differ and recommendations may not be applicable. In parting, we recognize that these suggestions may not be applicable to everyone and the level of support within each program may vary. Like we have discussed, overlapping identities, and axes of marginalization are sure to conflict with and impact the utility and relevance of this advice. Here we say: take what works and leave the rest!

Endnotes

1   2019, April 23. Introducing the Monkey Cage Gender Gap Symposium. The Washington Post. Retrieved November 24, 2021, from https://www.washingtonpost.com/news/monkey-cage/wp/2013/09/30/introducing-the-monkey-cage-gender-gap-symposium/.

2   We use the conventional spelling of woman/women, but we want to think inclusively about any woman- or womxn-identifying individual. We use "woman-identifying" to acknowledge the nuances in gender expression and self-identification and to push beyond gender binaries and conventional performativities of gender. Every mention of "women" and "female persons" in this article implies the inclusion of female-identifying people without the restriction of traditional gender norms.

3   Please note that while we recognize the mention of "men" and the "male" gender, we do not wish to ignore male-identifying people or constrain anyone to a gender binary. We do, however, want to consider the social positioning of cisgender men as differential than that of those with other gender identities.

4   Multiple chapters are dedicated to teaching in this volume. Here, we are specifically calling attention to the issues that women face in gaining teaching experience while in graduate school.

5   https://miryaholman.substack.com/

6   http://www.raulpacheco.org/blog/

7   There is a chapter fully on advisors, mentorship, and networking in this volume and we recommend looking there as well, though there are unique considerations for women in these contexts.

8   These affiliations typically also provide funds for travel to and from organizations or funds that can be used for research activities. While these pools of funds are typically small, if universities have matching or separate grant opportunities, combinations may help fund research and conference travel.

9   https://www.womenalsoknowstuff.com/

References

Adams, Sophie, Bekker, Sheree, Fan, Yanan, Gordon, Tess, Shepherd, Laura J., Slavich, Eve, and David Waters. 2021. "Gender Bias in Student Evaluations of Teaching: 'Punish[ing] Those Who Fail To Do Their Gender Right." *Higher Education.* https://doi.org/10.1007/s10734-021-00704-9

Alter, Karen J., Jean Clipperton, Emily Schraudenbach, and Laura Rozier. 2020. "Gender and Status in American Political Science: Who Determines Whether a Scholar Is Noteworthy?" *Perspectives on Politics* 18(4): 1048–67.

Anderson, Laurel, and Amy L. Ostrom. 2015. "Transformative Service Research: Advancing Our Knowledge About Service and Well-Being." *Journal of Service Research* 18(3): 243–49.

Belcher, Wendy Laura. 2009. *Writing Your Journal Article in 12 Weeks: A Guide to Academic Publishing Success.* Thousand Oaks, Calif: SAGE Publications.

Bellas, Marcia L. 1999. "Emotional labor in academia: The case of professors." *The Annals of the American Academy of Political and Social Science* 561, no. 1: 96-110.

Brown, Nadia E., ed. 2021. *Me Too Political Science.* First issued in paperback. London New York: Routledge.

Chtena, Natascha. 2015. "4 Reasons to Volunteer While in Grad School | GradHacker." *gradhacker.* https://www.insidehighered.com/blogs/gradhacker/4-reasons-volunteer-while-grad-school (November 12, 2021).

Collins, Patricia Hill. 1998. "It's All in the Family: Intersections of Gender, Race, and Nation." *Hypatia* 13(3): 62–82.

"Crenshaw–1991–Mapping the Margins Intersectionality, Identity P.Pdf." https://blackwomenintheblackfreedomstruggle.voices.wooster.edu/wp-content/uploads/sites/210/2019/02/Crenshaw_mapping-the-margins1991.pdf (November 15, 2021).

Crenshaw, Kimberle. 1991. "Mapping the Margins: Intersectionality, Identity Politics, and Violence against Women of Color." *Stanford Law Review* 43(6): 1241.

Cox, Bradley, McIntosh, Kadian, Terenzini, Patrick, Reason, Robert, and Brenda Lutovsky Quaye. 2020. "Pedagogical Signals of Faculty Approachability: Factors Shaping Faculty-Student Interaction Outside the Classroom" *Research in Higher Education* 51:767-788.

Guinier, C. Lani. 1990. "Of Gentlemen and Role Models." *Berkeley Journal of Gender, Law & Justice.* https://dash.harvard.edu/handle/1/12967843 (November 12, 2021).

Hancock, Ange-Marie. 2011. Solidarity politics for millennials: A Guide to Ending the Oppression Olympics. Springer.

hooks, bell. 1990. *Yearning: Race, Gender, and Cultural Politics.* 1st ed. Toronto, Ont., Canada: Between-the-Lines.

Lazer, David. 2011. "Networks in Political Science: Back to the Future." *PS: Political Science & Politics* 44(01): 61–68.

Levecque, Katia et al. 2017. "Work Organization and Mental Health Problems in PhD Students." *Research Policy* 46(4): 868–79.

MacKinnon, Catharine A. 1982. "Feminism, Marxism, Method, and the State: An Agenda for Theory." *Signs* 7(3): 515–44.

Macoun, Alissa, and Danielle Miller. 2014. "Surviving (Thriving) in Academia: Feminist Support Networks and Women ECRs." *Journal of Gender Studies* 23(3): 287–301.

Peggy, M., 1989. *White privilege: unpacking the invisible knapsack.* Independent School, 49(2), pp.1-4.

Poteete, A. and Ostrom, E., 2005, September. Bridging the qualitative–quantitative divide: strategies for building large-N databases based on qualitative research. In 101st Annual Meeting of the American Political Science Association (pp. 1-4).

Niederle, Muriel, and Lise Vesterlund. 2011. "Gender and Competition." *Annual Review of Economics* 3(1): 601–30.

Rancourt, Derrick. 2020. "PhD Students Can Benefit from Non-Academic Mentors' Outside Perspectives." *The Conversation.* http://theconversation.com/phd-students-can-benefit-from-non-academic-mentors-outside-perspectives-140988 (November 12, 2021).

Pittman, Chavella. 2010. "Race and Gender Oppression in the Classroom: The Experiences of Women Faculty of Color with White Male Students." *Teaching Sociology.* 38(3):183-196.

Schneider, Beth Z., William Carden, Alyson Francisco, and Thomas O. Jones. 2011. "Women "Opting out" of Academia: At What Cost?" *Forum on Public Policy Online* 2011 (2). https://eric.ed.gov/?id=EJ944197.

Teele, Dawn Langan, Joshua Kalla, and Frances Rosenbluth. 2018. "The Ties That Double Bind: Social Roles and Women's Underrepresentation in Politics." *American Political Science Review* 112(3): 525–41.

Willis, Ellen. 1984. "Radical Feminism and Feminist Radicalism." *Social Text* (9/10): 91–118.

57

Concerns for International Graduate Students in Political Science

Thomas S. Benson[1] & Silviya Gancheva[2]

1. University of Delaware 2. Wayne State University

KEYWORDS: Visa, Immigration, Graduate Record Examination.

Introduction

How do you choose which universities to apply for? How do you navigate political science departmental norms and expectations? What are your job prospects as an international student in the United States? These are a handful of questions that countless international political science graduate students—prospective, pre-candidacy, and post-candidacy—will need to consider at some point. There may also be language, cultural, and financial barriers to achieving a graduate degree in political science. Thus, this chapter is designed to provide helpful information to navigate these concerns.

Although research on international students in US academic institutions has expanded in the last 20 years, it continues to remain somewhat scarce. The prevailing focus has been on undergraduate students (Arafeh 2020), specific groups of students (e.g., Chinese students) (Ma 2020), or on retention rates (Haverila, Haverila, and McLaughlin 2020). Unfortunately, existing studies have hardly addressed what support is available for international students, especially for international political science graduate students. Given this, this chapter also seeks to provide ample advice.

Why is this Important?

The journey as an international political science graduate student is not without obstacles and challenges. Across all disciplines, there are "language barriers, loneliness and homesickness, identity issues, changes in eating habits…and financial setbacks," in addition to potential issues of racism and discrimination (Gautam et al. 2016, 503). Language barriers can also increase "academic stress, negative well-being, and feelings of isolation" (Gautam et al. 2016, 506; Stegall 2021, 725). Given these challenges, it is crucial for prospective students to identify universities to apply for that not only have courses in political science that interest them to sustain their passion, but also feature an office for international students and events that are dedicated to international students to help negate potential isolation and loneliness.

Further, interaction between international students and American students both inside and outside the classroom is also important because they can enhance understanding and knowledge of cultural disparities. In the United States, there is an emphasis on "individualism, assertiveness, and self-sufficiency over interdependence and relatedness" (Gautam et al. 2016, 506); thus, knowing how to navigate this terrain can be helpful to prospective students. And whilst being a graduate student in the United States can improve career prospects, there will be challenges throughout the course of graduate programs, such as language barriers, cultural idiosyncrasies, and alternative views on assignments and work-life balance—all of which will likely be compounded by financial, social, and religious aspects (Gautam et al. 2016, 520-521). Additionally, interactions between students from different cultures can enrich relationships and foster academic perspectives that are more nuanced. Therefore, for both international and US graduate students, the experiences can be challenging and enriching in cultural, economic, and career dimensions.

Advice for International Graduate Students in Political Science

Application Advice

For prospective students, you must navigate the application process, *visa* and *immigration* protocols, the completion of the *Graduate Record Examination* (GRE), and the identification of opportunities for on-campus employment (e.g., teaching and research assistantships) and housing with nearby amenities. In considering which universities to apply for, understand that prestige of the institution matters for post-graduate program employment prospects, especially if intending to remain in the United States, but give equal consideration to other aspects. For example, are the courses offered in the political science graduate program a good reflection of your own interests? Does the university have an office of international students that hosts social events? What are the costs of living? Are you eligible for a teaching and/or research assistantship, in addition to receiving funding for your tuition? If you do not find answers to these questions, consider contacting the graduate program director or administrative staff in the political science department (for a discussion about departmental and university organization, see chapter 8).

One of the biggest concerns for international students is the lack of appropriate matching with an academic adviser (Krsmanovic 2021). Having a clear career plan before and during the application process will help you considerably. Therefore, it is important to conduct research about the political science graduate programs available and the faculty you believe you would be interested in collaborating with, as well as your desired academic adviser who will be able to guide you through the norms of US graduate education. (For a larger discussion about choosing an adviser, see chapter 13.)

Financial Advice

Graduate school can be expensive, especially if you are paying for your own tuition. Consider other costs as part of the application process—GRE preparation and sitting the exam itself, university application costs, and visa and immigration processing fees. If English is not your native language, you will also need to present proof of proficiency in English (e.g., TOEFL, IELTS). Your capacity to work off-campus, if not employed by the university, is severely restricted in your first year (less so thereafter, but still very challenging) due to immigration and contractual limitations (often limited to working 20 hours per week during semester).

Immigration and Visa Advice

F-1 visas are the most significant as these are student visas for international graduate students. There are also J-1 visas for participants in educational and cultural exchange programs, but these are much fewer in number. There are other types of visas (M-1, F-3, M-3), but if you are applying to a graduate school in the United States, you will need an F-1 visa. In terms of process, you will need to apply for the F-1 visa after securing a place at an SEVP-approved (Student and Exchange Visitor Program), accredited United States university. You will need to demonstrate you have sufficient funds to come and study in the United States—a letter from the university outlining their coverage of your tuition fees and providing you with an assistantship or fellowship is usually sufficient. Your invitation from the university to participate in their political science graduate program should outline any offer for tuition coverage, assistantships, or fellowships, and the duration for which they will provide funding.

In your visit to the United States embassy or consulate in your home country—or in a neighbouring country if your home country does not have one—you will need to bring the aforementioned documents (applications for F-1 visas will outline what documents are required). You will have an interview for the visa that will generally query about your available funds, why you are interested in studying in the United States, and what you will be studying and where. As part of this process, you will need to familiarize yourself with I-20 forms, and SEVIS (Student and Exchange Visitor Information System) registration, the latter of which costs. Once all of these have been secured, you can arrange your travel plans and search for housing. You must also bear in mind that you may need to arrive in the summer—if the semester begins at the end of August or early September—for summer orientation programming for international students. This may involve further English language tests, teaching practice, social events, and learning about United States' cultural norms. In your spare time, you should prepare yourself for what will likely be a culture shock and understand how United States culture differs from your own—how people dress, interact, shop, learn, teach, and talk (Filonova and Barriga 2020).

Housing Advice

If possible, it is ideal for first-year international graduate students to secure on-campus accommodation as living off-campus without access to a vehicle can potentially lead to difficulties in commuting and navigating an unfamiliar setting. As part of this process, assess whether your desired university has a "dependable public transportation system" and that you can reside somewhere within reasonable distance of campus and amenities (e.g., access to food) (Gautam et al. 2016, 250). If you do not have a car (or dependable transport), you will likely face challenges given the car-centric nature of US city and town planning. Living on-campus might not be the optimal plan for your first year, but it may affect your chances of persevering in your graduate program, especially if it enables you to build close relationships with your peers.

As soon as you get accepted into the graduate program, apply early for on-campus housing, and plan your finances—paying rent from your monthly stipend or fellowship or savings will allow you to know how much money you are left with each month. It will take some to adjust as rent can be expensive in the United States. Create a chart with monthly expenses for food, rent, and miscellaneous costs as this will help to keep track of your expenses. If you want to live off-campus, consider your daily commute to campus, and research how to sign a lease for an apartment.[1] Additionally, you should consider the local culture that you are intending to move into and whether you would likely feel a sense of belonging. Some communities may oppose what they perceive to be "outsiders," even if you are only a student, and this could take a toll on your well-being. At the same time, if you come from a more traditional culture, US campuses can be liberating. For instance, female graduate students at liberal universities can experience open discussions about sex, sexuality, gender, and abortion rights both inside and outside the classroom. This can be life-changing, not just for you as a woman, but also a value you can take home to discuss these taboo topics (for a larger discussion about gender and graduate school, see chapter 56).

Language Advice

Language courses can be useful, but some may perceive them as a form of othering or marginalization (Peters and Anderson 2021; Sharma 2020). Nonetheless, learning to communicate clearly is critical, including subscribing to political science norms that are expected for publishing in journals in the United States (for additional information about academic publishing, see chapters 24 and 25). Some universities assume prospective students are proficient in academic writing, thus you should practice writing in advance, learn to share your own writing, and peer-review colleagues' work. Do not hesitate to utilize English proof-reading or writing centers on campus (should you need them) that will assist you with your course paper or manuscript—these services are often found in a university's library. They can guide you through the challenges of how to use the "Oxford comma," and cite and reference different sources of literature or material, among other things.

Cultural Norms in Education

International graduate students in the United States can encounter cultural shocks. The focus is often on international students adapting to the United States (Wang and Freed 2021). Nevertheless, there is need for adaptation on both sides. For international graduate students in political science—speak up!

It can be challenging to adapt to the direct and "blunt" way many United States citizens communicate, especially if you are from a culture that places value on being reserved or passive with your opinion (Ma and Garcia-Murillo 2018,270). Learning to speak up and share your critical opinion about political science texts in your courses is an essential component of the United States graduate system. Undoubtedly, learning to communicate your thoughts coherently and effectively will take time and is a learned skill. If you are especially struggling, speak with your adviser and peers.

Teaching

Discrepancies in teaching style across different cultures can create difficulties for international graduate students who are teaching assistants or instructors of record. For instance, research (Wang 2021) shows that international students more familiar with lecture-based and less participatory forms of education can lead to challenges in the American education system that is more focused on interaction. Additionally, entering a classroom of undergraduate students can be nerve-racking, but it can also be a fantastic opportunity for personal and professional growth.

Teaching or being a teaching assistant (e.g., grading, attending lectures, holding weekly office hours, responding to student emails, and sometimes leading discussion sections or seminars) will provide adequate funding to cover living expenses. These positions are usually limited to 20 hours per week and can be nine-month contracts (leaving summer as a period of "unemployment"), but the 20 hours will vary from week to week—some weeks you will only attend lectures and hold office hours, and other weeks you will be grading assignments and exams. If you get to teach your own class or discussion section, talk to your older peers who have experience, talk to your adviser, and utilize resources on campus—for instance, the campus center for teaching (variously named) can guide you.

Moreover, you should be aware that, as a non-US citizen, your authority may be challenged as an instructor or discussion section leader by undergraduate students. This is even more likely to be the case if you are female and/or not white. Students may mock or laugh at your accent. Nonetheless, be attentive in speaking with an accent and understand that US education is often very interaction-based, in which students are expected to respond to questions posed in the classroom. In smaller classroom settings (e.g., discussion sections), undergraduate students may engage in groupwork, actively write on chalkboards or interactive electronic screens, or participate in in-class activities (Stegall 2021, 725). If, however, you experience racism or discrimination, you should contact your instructor and adviser for support and resources to manage these incidents.

Prepare for your classes in advance by talking to your instructor (if you are a teaching assistant) or adviser. Consider what the appropriate student-assistant relationship looks like; how to report misconduct and plagiarism; if there is a dress code; and, most importantly, what your instructor expects of you in their lectures and what deadlines they have for grading (Stegall 2021, 732). Sometimes, undergraduate students will ask about your perspective on US culture or political system, and while you can share your honest views, you should be respectful. You may also find that undergraduate students address you by your first name or, despite your request to be called by your first name, they may insist on referring to you as "Professor" or using your surname.

Furthermore, consider visiting other (US citizen) colleague's classes and see how they lead their classroom and how they communicate. Request multiple syllabi from colleagues and see how they present the material. In your first session, you can always tell students about yourself—who are you and where you come from. This is also a good opportunity to engage US citizens about comparative political systems but be appropriate with what you teach to ensure it reflects the syllabus and meets students' expectations. (For additional tips and suggestions about your first teaching experience, see chapters 29 and 58. For more information about teaching assistantships, see chapter 28.)

Job Market and the PhD

For post-candidacy students, your greatest concern—beside your dissertation—will be navigating the political science job market. If you wish to work in the United States after completing your PhD, you will need to begin applying for jobs one year in advance and, if you do not secure a job by the time you graduate, you could take advantage of optional practical training (OPT) that will enable you to stay in the United States for up to one additional year to seek employment. In the United States, most political science jobs are posted in fall and will be hiring for fall next year. Closer to December, post-doctoral opportunities will begin to emerge and then, in spring, you can expect short-term, contractual roles (e.g., adjunct professors, visiting scholars). For OPT, you must apply for it in advance of graduating, so consult your office of international students to navigate this process. In the United States, there are no federal quotas or limitations on non-profit organizations—which include most accredited US universities and colleges—hiring non-US citizens. If you pursue an academic career in the United States, the Americanist field is, by far, the dominant field compared to others (e.g., Comparative Politics and International Relations). For methodology—which, for some universities, constitutes a field itself—quantitative skills are almost always in demand. Unfortunately, this leaves fewer opportunities for those who specialize in qualitative methods, but there are still positions available. Generally, the academic job market is very competitive, so you must take this into consideration (for a larger discussion, see chapter 34).

If you opt for the non-academic path, you will be subject to federal quotas on H1-B visas and, in most cases, only large companies will be willing to sponsor you as this process often leads the company to incur costs to hire you as a non-US citizen. These visas are for temporary workers—usually for three years and the possibility of it being extended for up to six years. In terms of non-academic jobs related to political science, you may want to consider a career in consulting, planning, public policy, research centers, thinktanks, international organizations, and philanthropic organizations. Remember that, as a non-US citizen, you will also be restricted from working for most local, state, and especially federal government organizations.

Endnotes

1   https://www.apartments.com/; https://www.realtor.com/advice/rent/rental-faq-renting-a-home-coronavirus/; https://www.realtor.com/advice/rent/can-you-break-a-lease-because-of-covid/; https://realestate.usnews.com/real-estate/articles/things-renters-should-do-before-signing-a-lease

References

Arafeh, Alia K. 2020. "Insights into Saudi Female International Students." *Journal of International Students* 10(4): 1087–1102. doi: 10.32674/jis.v10i3.1111

Filonova, Irina., and Paola Barriga. 2020. "Coming to America." *Inside Higher Ed* [website], October 29, 2021. https://www.insidehighered.com/advice/2020/10/12/advice-international-graduate-students-who-come-study-us-opinion.

Gautam, Chetanath., Charles L. Lowery., Chance Mays., and Dayan Durant. 2016. "Challenges for Global Learners: A Qualitative Study of the Concerns and Difficulties of International Students." *Journal of International Students* 6(2): 501–526. doi: https://doi.org/10.32674/jis.v6i2.368

Haverila, Matti J., Kai Haverila., and Caitlin McLaughlin. 2020. "Variables Affecting the Retention Intentions of Students in Higher Education Institutions." *Journal of International Students* 10(2): 358–82. doi: 10.32674/jis.v10i2.1849

Krsmanovic, Masha. 2021. "The Synthesis and Future Directions of Empirical Research on International Students in the United States." *Journal of International Students* 11(1): 1–23. doi: https://doi.org/10.32674/jis.v11i1.1955

Ma, Junqian. 2020. "Supporting Practices to Break Chinese International Students' Language Barriers." *Journal of International Students* 10(1): 84–105. doi: https://doi.org/10.32674/jis.v10i1.773

Ma, Yingyi., and Martha A. Garcia-Murillo. 2018. *Understanding International Students from Asia in American Universities: Learning and Living Globalization*. Cham, Switzerland: Springer.

Peters, Bethany, and Michael E. Anderson. 2021. "Supporting Non-Native English Speakers at the University." *Journal of International Students* 11(1): 103–21. doi: https://doi.org/10.32674/jis.v11i1.1200

Sharma, Emily. 2020. "Writing Support for International Graduate Students." *Journal of International*

Students 10(1): 220–22. doi: https://doi.org/10.32674/jis.v10i1.1013

Stegall, Jennifer. 2021. "Peaks and Valleys: The Lived Experiences of International Students Within an English Immersion Program Using the Integrated Skills Approach." *Journal of International Students* 11(3): 723–741. doi: 10.32674/jis.v11i3.2395

Wang, Xinxin, and Rebekah Freed. 2021. "A Bourdieusian Analysis of the Sociocultural Capital of Chinese International Graduate Students in the United States." *Journal of International Students* 11(1): 41–59. doi: https://doi.org/10.32674/jis.v11i1.952

58 | Teaching as an International Graduate Student

Irmak Yazici[1]

1. University of Hawai'i at Mānoa

KEYWORDS: International Graduate Students, Teaching Experience.

Introduction

This chapter addresses the unique challenges *international graduate students* of political science face as teaching assistants and/or instructors. A non-teaching path towards a graduate degree may not be an option for many international graduate students due to financial obligations and/or other disadvantages. Hence being aware of the material and non-material gains as well as challenges of teaching whilst working on a dissertation is crucial for international graduate students to be able to establish a healthy balance between teaching and research. This chapter outlines these gains and challenges and provides a roadmap for international graduate students on how to overcome such challenges whilst making successful progress towards their dissertation research. It also discusses the ways in which *teaching experience* offers a competitive advantage in their future academic endeavors.

Studying in another country as an international student expands one's perspective—both professionally and personally—and is useful especially for those working in the discipline of political science. Experiencing everyday life in another country broadens one's understanding of politics and how it disseminates into everyday practices, especially when one is an "alien." Although this comes with a set of challenges, the benefits can outweigh these challenges if students create a plan to pursue potential academic and financial resources available for them prior to the start of their program.

Gains and Challenges

Research shows that an increasing number of international students are seeking degrees in the United States and these students can experience difficulties stemming from a variety of factors including language barriers, academic differences, resource allocation, and finding support within their communities (Rodríguez et al. 2019). Among these, securing continuous and stable funding for graduate studies is one of the greatest concerns for international students since—due to visa restrictions—they are only allowed to work within the campus. In addition, some fellowships and scholarships require that the applicants hold US citizenship or permanent residency.

In 2021, the primary source of funding for 53% of international graduate students in the United States was personal and family resources (IIE 2021). For many other students, such resources may not be available, especially depending on the countries the students come from. For example, students who come from the countries in the global south will largely not have the opportunities those from the global north may have. This is reflected in the fact that in 2021, 40.2% of international graduate students relied on US college or university funds to pay for their studies (IIE 2021).

Graduate assistantships are among the few financial resources available to graduate students. These assistantships usually come with a full or partial tuition waiver as well as a monthly stipend. However, they are also highly competitive positions, and may come with certain restrictions depending on the institution's and/or departments' internal rules and regulations. For example, graduate students may be allowed to be a graduate assistant only for a limited number of years (e.g., 3 years in total) in one department/program. In that case, students must figure out how to fund the remainder of their time in the graduate program with fellowships and/or scholarships or find another graduate assistantship in another department/program.

There are a few other options for political science graduate students—aside from their home departments. They can also work in other social sciences or humanities departments as well as at the research centers within the university, depending on their research interests and availability. Hence, incoming international students can benefit from seeking advice from their potential adviser or the international student services office before starting the program. This would enable them to learn about the funding opportunities offered by the graduate program as well as the conditions of these opportunities such as, what sorts of expenses can be covered, for how long students would be eligible for financial support, and what other funding and employment opportunities are available for international graduate students on campus.

Gains

Working as a graduate assistant is advantageous for international students for several reasons. First of all, with a tuition waiver, students do not have to pay the out-of-state tuition fees, which are much higher than the in-state tuition fees. Second, students generally receive a stipend that helps cover their living expenses—at least partially. Also, depending on the institution, graduate assistants may be eligible for affordable on-campus housing. In addition, these assistantships come with health insurance, which otherwise may be another out-of-pocket expense for international students.

Aside from these material gains, serving as a graduate assistant also allows students to gain an "insider" look into academia. This is useful for realizing future career goals, especially for those considering entering the academic job market in the U.S. In this context, working as a graduate teaching assistant allows international students to become familiar with professional work etiquette across different levels by working with faculty and administrative personnel. As students apply for assistantships in different departments and research centers, they also gain experience in preparing applications for academic jobs and interviews—a valuable investment toward the job market.

Depending on the program and institution, as a graduate assistant you may or may not be required to teach a course as the sole instructor or assist faculty with teaching. As a teaching assistant, you will likely be responsible for grading assignments and exams, as well as meeting with students during office hours to discuss their progress and/or answer their questions regarding the course. You may also teach a few sessions as a guest lecturer. As a sole instructor, you will likely create your own syllabus and plan lectures, in addition to holding office hours and grading assignments (see chapter 28 in this volume for more on teaching assistantships).

You may be able to teach courses as a lecturer on a semester basis, otherwise known as being an adjunct or non-tenure track faculty member (see chapter 44 in this volume for more on adjunct teaching). These lectureships are different from graduate assistantships and applications are usually accepted on a semester basis. Meaning, these positions—and their associated funding streams—are not guaranteed for every semester owing to their competitiveness as well as departmental resources, demand for courses, and availability of funds. These lectureships do not come with health insurance and other benefits, so it is better to make sure you have a teaching or research assistantship whilst you can teach an additional course as an adjunct lecturer—either in your home department or in another department. This way, you can both gain teaching experience and make sure you have financial security and access to healthcare during your graduate studies. However, before committing to teaching more than one course per semester, it would be better to have completed any course work and, ideally, have passed your comprehensive exams. This way, you can manage your time more efficiently between teaching commitments and writing your dissertation (see chapter 17 in this volume for more on time management).

Challenges

It is also important to acknowledge the challenges international graduate students face while teaching. One challenge is that anything they may say can trigger controversy, especially because they may be seen as "outsiders" to discuss the political issues of the country where they teach. For example, if you are teaching American politics in the United States, you may face the threat of "callout" or "cancel culture," which can be described as "the desire to publicly shame and silence the offender" (Rom and Mitchell 2021), and consequently practice self-censure in order not to discuss potentially controversial topics even if they are essential to your course content. Nevertheless, it is important to maintain the classroom as a safe space for both the instructor and the students to share their thoughts on the course material and engage in constructive critique. In this regard, a useful pedagogical approach would be ensuring that not only multiple views on one issue are welcome "but also that multiple issues can be brought into discussion, even when those issues may be more important to one side of the political spectrum than the other" (Rom and Mitchell 2021). Using cases, narratives, and examples from disagreeing parties on a political issue can help encourage students to engage in dialogue rather than being defensive or aversive in expressing their thoughts. In addition, international graduate students can utilize the advantage of discussing similar political issues in their home country in a comparative perspective to expand students' understanding of politics, not as citizens of a particular country but as students of political science.

Given all the challenges graduate students face, it is not surprising that a recent study has revealed how political science graduate students are having "far worse mental health than other populations across a range of outcomes" (Almasri et al. 2021). One aspect of the study asked whether any aspect of the participants' identity or background made it difficult for them to feel supported, both professionally and personally, and found that 7% of the participants mentioned their "international status" affected this. This combination of being an international student and pursuing a graduate degree can exacerbate the already stressful academic experiences (see chapters 35, 64, and 68 in this volume for more mental health topics).

Making the Most of Your Teaching Experience

Teaching whilst working on your doctoral degree in political science can be both rewarding and challenging. In addition to financial security, students should seek a healthy balance between their research and teaching. This is easier said than done, but here are a few tips that may be helpful in finding that balance. Firstly, and most importantly, you should designate time slots to solely focus on your dissertation. During these slots, make sure not to check your emails or think about work that is associated with your teaching role. Keep in mind that, although teaching may provide you with financial resources and experience, without finishing your dissertation, you cannot receive your degree. It may be hard to focus on writing on the days you teach as all your energy goes into delivering the lecture, facilitating discussions, and answering questions. These days, instead of writing, it may be more productive to work on the following week's lecture, assignments, grading, and hold office hours. On the remaining weekdays, you can focus on your research and writing your dissertation (see chapter 17 in this volume for additional advice on time management).

Another useful strategy is finding ways to incorporate your research into your teaching. You may not be given the opportunity to choose a specific course to teach that completely overlaps with your research. However, whenever possible, you can draw on your research materials and assign these for your course. In addition, having writing workshops and retreats with students would not only allow you to work on your dissertation as part of your teaching role but also help your students improve their writing skills through peer reviews and constructive feedback.

It is crucial to have peer support groups where you can share your teaching "moments" with other graduate assistants as well as strategies to teach controversial topics, improve time management, and spare time for self-care or leisure activities. Peer support can be helpful in relieving stress and easing the feeling of isolation international students may face. Although teaching while writing your dissertation is often time consuming, it is important to make time for these social gatherings in order to sustain a healthy academic and personal environment (see chapter 63 in this volume for additional advice on finding your collective).

As an international graduate assistant and/or instructor, you will have endured many hardships and challenges by the end of your program. That being said, you will also have gained valuable experience not only in teaching but in other aspects of academic life, such as establishing professional relationships with faculty and other academic personnel, implementing pedagogical strategies, presenting your work and responding to questions related to it, to name a few. These experiences will be useful during your academic job search at the end of your program. Being able to draw upon your experiences and exchanges with your students in your teaching philosophy statement, rather than merely theoretical pedagogical strategies, will be noted by selection committees alongside your broader understanding of cultural differences and how to reconcile these differences within a constructive academic environment. Given that about half of the academic political scientists in the United States work in teaching institutions that do not offer doctoral programs (Hill 2021), teaching experience can help international candidates be more competitive on the job market. For more information about preparing for your first teaching experience, see chapter 29 in this volume.

References

Almasri, Nasir, Blair Read, and Clara Vandeweerdt. 2021. "Mental Health and the PhD: Insights and Implications for Political Science." *PS: Political Science & Politics* 1–7. doi:10.1017/S1049096521001396.

Hill, Kim Quaile. 2021. "Research Career Paths Among Political Scientists in Teaching Institutions." *PS: Political Science & Politics* 54 (4): 656–60.

Institute of International Education (IIE). 2021. "International Students by Primary Source of Funding, 1999/00–2020/21." *Open Doors Report on International Educational Exchange.* https://opendoors-data.org/data/international-students/international-students-primary-source-of-funding/.

Rodríguez, Claudia, Camila Restrepo Chavez, and Courtenay Klauber. 2019. "International Graduate Student Challenges and Support." *International Research and Review*, 8 (2): 49-64.

Rom, Mark Carl, and Kristina Mitchell. 2021. "Teaching Politics in a Call-Out and Cancel Culture." *PS: Political Science & Politics* 54 (3): 610–14.

59 | Religious Minorities and the Graduate School Experience

Sierra Davis Thomander[1] & Andrea Malji[2]

1. Stanford University 2. Hawai'i Pacific University

KEYWORDS: Religious Affiliation, Beliefs, Disclosure, Discriminitory Behavior.

Introduction

This chapter examines the challenges facing graduate students who are religious minorities, defined broadly. Specifically, it examines some of the prevailing concerns including dietary accommodations, socialization habits, cultural differences, and holiday/calendar differences. In particular, the normalization of Christian holidays and calendars, even in supposedly secular settings, has the potential to be exclusionary. Even within Christianity, there are minority religions that differ in practices, beliefs, worship dates, and holidays. Within the field of political science specifically, students may also have to navigate feeling called to be a representative or defendant of their religion, especially if others within the department are studying the political dynamics of their religion. Like other minorities, religious minorities may face discrimination, microaggressions, and unwelcome questioning or criticisms about their faith practices as well as outright harassment and assault. Students should be empowered to advocate for their rights and respectful treatment. Graduate school may also have certain socialization norms that are counter to the beliefs of certain religions, such as centering socialization around alcohol or assuming certain dates are free for scheduling.

We provide several recommendations for graduate students about using university resources, establishing boundaries and healthy dialogue, and proactively advocating for your religious needs. We also discuss the trade-offs of concealing or disclosing different aspects of one's religious identity in different contexts. We conclude with best practices for graduate students, both religious and non-religious, that will foster inclusion and respect among people of different beliefs, and additional resources.

Why Does It Matter?

Academia thrives when people from different backgrounds respectfully come together to learn, grow, and produce knowledge. Though individuals' religious backgrounds can and do inform their contributions in advancing scientific understanding, these backgrounds should not hinder opportunities and resources nor pose obstacles to completing a graduate degree. While civil rights laws have formally instituted these ideals in general, in practice discrimination occurs frequently. In one study, people who practice Judaism, Islam, and to a lesser extent Christianity report facing religious hostility, discrimination, and at times violence in their pursuit of scientific knowledge, as do other religious minorities such as Sikhs (Scheitle and Ecklund 2020). Even those lacking a religion can face discrimination (Scheitle and Ecklund 2020, 141). Even among Christians, discrimination occurs due to creed, denomination, and practices (Scheitle and Ecklund 2020; Rosentiel et al. 2007). Status as a religious minority may depend on the specific institutional and cultural context rather than population-based understanding of minority status. For instance, though the United States has more Catholics than Latter-day Saints, a Catholic attending the Latter-day Saints-affiliated Brigham Young University would effectively be a religious minority. Addressing this discrimination, both as individuals who navigate it and allies seeking to help, is critical to fostering an inclusive environment.

Addressing these concerns for graduate students is particularly important for both individual graduate school experience as well as the future of the discipline and its output. Graduate students deserve a respectful, open environment in which to learn, grow, and collaborate. Students at all levels benefit from the diversity that these environments create as well-supported graduate students become faculty. Admission of a diverse candidate pool is superfluous if the pipeline "leaks" such promising scholars due to religious discrimination and hostility.

Religious minorities in political science may also encounter a unique challenge related to the disciplinary study and analysis of religion. Unlike some fields, social sciences are inextricably linked to discussion of religion. From modern-day voting behavior to medieval state formation, religion often plays an important role in political science. While some scholars study questions that relate to their background, others do not. The intersection of backgrounds, beliefs, and research in addition to religious content can produce difficult environments. Students may find that scholars who study their religion seem distant or overly critical. This may make the student feel uncomfortable within the classroom, particularly when their religion is examined critically.

For example, Islam has increasingly been analyzed within the context of terrorism and extremism. A Muslim in a class reading articles about these topics, or engaging with classmates or faculty that study it, may feel their religion is being unnecessarily reduced to an analytical category. Likewise, Hindus, Sikhs, or Buddhists may feel similarly when religious nationalism in South Asia is discussed. This student may also feel marginalized or called to defend their religion from critique. At some institutions, people tend to assume that academics are secular/non-religious. This could potentially lead to microaggressions (see also chapter 49) or unwelcoming questions by non-religious persons regarding your spiritual choices. Because the best research often benefits from diverse perspectives and expertise, the political science discipline benefits when we focus on addressing these issues to create better environments while still exploring questions where religion and science intersect.

What Should/Can You Do?

The issues religious minorities face may range in severity. From insensitive comments to outright violence, these challenges can not only make an already difficult time even worse but may even impede progress and degree attainment. Strategies for dealing with these challenges depend on the severity of the challenge, the context, and the resources available. While graduate students can preempt some issues or easily solve others, some may take more formal pathways and resources. While we suggest first beginning with more informal and preventative approaches, graduate students should not hesitate to escalate concerns as needed. We discuss strategies in the following sections.

Disclosing Your Religion

Your *religious affiliation* and *beliefs* are personal matters. How public you make them is up to you. However, disclosing your affiliation/belief is often necessary to receive accommodations, explain your background and research interests, and engage in other opportunities. Universities often ask incoming students and applicants to indicate their religious affiliation, though you may opt to not disclose this information. Many graduate students fear disclosing their religion will result in discrimination and harassment. Your comfort level may also depend on your environment and affiliation. For instance, while you may feel apprehensive about disclosing your religious information when deciding between graduate schools, the feedback you receive by doing so can be highly useful in finding the right "fit." You may wish to use reactions to your religious information as a signal of each program's willingness to provide a positive environment and support for your unique circumstances. You may also need to disclose religious information to receive accommodations for religious holidays and worship. Talking with other religious minority students about their experience, if possible, is useful even if they do not share the exact same religion. It is also reasonable to disclose basic details about your religion while declining to discuss or disclose more specific details. You can exercise this right by simply saying, "I appreciate your curiosity, but I would rather not discuss that right now," in response to uncomfortable questions. Only you will know the right balance when it comes to *disclosure*.

Be Aware of Your Institution's Resources and Limitations

Specific characteristics of institutions often determine which resources, legal and otherwise, graduate students can use when facing challenges as a religious minority. Whether the educational institution is public or private is critical in understanding which laws, agencies, and resources are at graduate students' disposal. Prospective graduate students may wish to take public versus private status, as well as other factors such as religious affiliation, into consideration when applying for and deciding between graduate programs (for more about selecting a program, see chapter 2).

A variety of agencies and departments within the United States cover religious discrimination, often through different laws. Though none of the following information constitutes legal advice, the following agencies and resources can provide more information for individual graduate students. While the US Department of Education's Office for Civil Rights (OCR) enforces civil rights laws that protect against discrimination on the basis of race, color, national origin, sex, disability, and age, none of the laws OCR enforces explicitly covers religious discrimination. However, Title VI of the Civil Rights Act of 1964 (Title VI) protects students of any religion from discrimination, including harassment, based on a student's actual or perceived: (1) shared ancestry or ethnic characteristics, or (2) citizenship or residency in a country with a dominant religion or distinct religious identity (OCR 2020). The US Equal Employment Opportunity Commission (EEOC) covers employment discrimination based on religion, including harassment that creates a hostile or offensive work environment of adverse employment decision, which may or may not apply to graduate students (EEOC 2021). For on-campus housing, see the US Department of Housing and Urban Development's Office of Fair Housing and Equal Opportunity website (FHEO 2021). The US Department of Justice's Civil Rights Division also protects against some forms of religious discrimination in public school settings (US DOJ CRD 2015). Individual states may have additional bureaucratic and legal resources. See the Helpful Websites and Resources section at the end of this chapter.

While federal and state resources are useful, they often lack coverage of all issues and circumstances, particularly for attendees at private institutions. However, many individual institutions, regardless of public/private status, have their own resources and rules available to assist religious adherents in both practicing their faith and navigating challenges. While most academic institutions will cite civil rights requirements on their websites, some have additionally established offices for religious life, diversity, and inclusion offices and programs, and representatives in administration and student government. For instance, Stanford University has both a Diversity and Access Office and Office for Religious and Spiritual Life as well as Student Associated Religions (SAR) Groups, which provide resources and support to students seeking religious accommodation or facing discrimination (Stanford Earth 2021). You will need to explore which offices deal with religious issues at your educational institution. The extent to which these offices assist students with grievances differs by institution. If possible, discuss with current students before deciding on a graduate program (see chapter 2).

Addressing Diet, Schedule, and Socialization Issues

Religious minorities may encounter several challenges within their department and their university more broadly. Being aware of these challenges and devising strategies to address them early is critical. For instance, even in secular institutions, the academic calendar centers around Christian holidays. Meanwhile, universities rarely take the significant holidays for other religions into consideration. Universities and professors may not only expect religious minorities to attend class during their significant holidays but may also schedule important deadlines or exams during these times. Non-Christian students may also feel obligated to attend department holiday-themed celebrations which privilege, whether explicitly or implicitly, Christian holiday traditions. Furthermore, these events usually center around food which may pose additional challenges for students with religious dietary restrictions. Additionally, food-based social events may coincide with a period of fasting (e.g., Ramadan, Yom Kippur, Shivratri, etc.) or exclude people who abstain from certain food, drink, or preparation methods (e.g., alcohol, coffee, non-halal foods, non-kosher foods, non-vegetarian options). Others may also question or even mock the wisdom or necessity of religious lifestyle choices, such as covering one's hair, abstaining from alcohol, or marrying young. While such circumstances often arise out of ignorance, they nevertheless negatively affect graduate students in their ability to socialize, network, etc.

While everyone will have different levels of comfort disclosing religious information, students will likely find it necessary to advocate for themselves to receive accommodations. This is especially true with calendar changes. Contacting advisors and professors at the beginning of the semester to inform them of any scheduling conflicts, such as exams on religious holidays, is crucial. The same is true for any dietary restrictions at department and student events. You may find that providing suggestions for alternative food and beverage options can be helpful. The increase of vegetarian and vegan options for non-religious reasons may provide an easy option when certain meat and animal products are restricted. Do not hesitate to collectively address dietary accommodations with other students, even if their dietary restrictions and reasoning differ. Your university's Office of Inclusion and Diversity or Office for Religious Life may also have resources and advice when navigating these accommodations. The main takeaway is to be proactive; address your concerns early and with additional support if desired.

Graduate school can be an isolating experience. Recent studies demonstrate that as many as 15.8% of graduate students experienced suicidal tendencies in the previous two weeks, 30% met the criteria for depression, and 32% met the criteria for anxiety (Almasri, Read, and Vandeweerdt 2021). Inclusion is no substitute for adequate mental health resources and institutional support (see chapters in the Health and Wellness in Graduate School section). However, building an inclusive and safe graduate community may help dampen feelings of isolation that are common in graduate school. Graduate student social activity boards/committees help plan activities that allow students to feel engaged within the community. However, such social activities often center around alcohol and late-night settings. This may cause feelings of discomfort and judgment for those abstaining from alcohol and related settings. By volunteering for the social activities board, religious minorities can help provide more inclusive alternatives. Additionally, many individuals choose not to consume alcohol for non-religious reasons and may also feel uncomfortable in settings that include social pressure to drink. In fact, an increasing number of graduate students report substance abuse. Therefore, there are social benefits beyond the inclusion of religious minority perspectives. Having social activities that include religious minorities will help challenge the existing social activities paradigm. Consider serving on or offering to advise people on social activity committees/boards. Your contribution will not only benefit your own experience but also other religious minorities and future students.

Negative Interactions: From Difficult Conversations and Microaggressions to Harassment and Assault

Negative interactions, whether in the classroom, with an advisor, or with a fellow student, can cause harm mentally, socially, and even physically. As with many negative interactions, the reaction and response to such harmful *discriminatory behavior* depends on the extent of harm itself. For instance, microaggressions (commonplace slights, intentional or not, that communicate hostile, derogatory, or negative attitudes toward marginalized groups) may not require formal institutional action whereas assault and harassment should always involve university action (Sue 2010). While you should report harassment and assault immediately, other negative interactions that fall short of harassment are nevertheless harmful. For instance, fellow graduate students in a comparative politics seminar may continually label a Buddhist student's interest in fellow Buddhists' voting behavior as "too niche," or a professor may make jokes about religious clothing at the expense of a Muslim student in class. These examples and others, while individually falling short of the definition of harassment, nevertheless harm students in their ability to academically succeed, especially when occurring frequently. While any individual action may feel dismissible, the accumulation of these negative experiences is not.

There are a few approaches to dealing with microaggressions in academic settings. You should read through the following and may research further to decide which approach works best for you. Ronald A. Berk has created a trilogy of articles on microaggressions and approaches to dealing with them (2017a; 2017b, 2017c), which may apply well to microaggressions directed at religious minorities. Victims of microaggressions are understandably reluctant to address the situation, especially when feeling ambiguous as to whether a microaggression occurred or when the interaction catches you "off guard" (Berk 2017b, 75). However, failure to respond may inadvertently condone the microaggression. If unable to address the issue in the moment, a delayed response is better than none and may even allow you to gather your thoughts and provide the environment for a better response. The goal of your response, Berk argues, "should be correction and education, not retribution," with a focus on words and behavior rather than the actual person (2017b, 75-6).

The five generic strategies are: (1) say something on the spot so that the aggressor understands the harm caused, (2) address the aggressor privately after the incident has occurred, (3) offer to help and create an ongoing dialogue to educate the aggressor, (4) change the subject, and (5) engage in proactive "micro-resistance." Micro-resistance involves four steps (Ganote et al. 2016; Irey 2013; Rockquemore 2016). First, observe by stating in clear, unambiguous language what you see happening. Second, express what you think or what you imagine others might be thinking. Third, express your feelings about the situation. Finally, state what you would like to have happened—desire (Berk 2017b, 76). These approaches can foster honest communication, help others understand and validate your perspective, establish healthy boundaries, and avoid future microaggressions against yourself and others (77). The R.A.V.E.N. process (redirecting the conversation or interaction, asking probing questions, values clarification, emphasizing your own thoughts, and offering concrete next steps) is a similar approach that you may find useful (Harris and Wood 2020). Approaching trusted colleagues as allies can also help in navigating negative interactions. Repeated incidents may require more formal assistance. Any harassment or assault should always be formally reported. See chapters in the Climate and Culture in the Department and Profession section (especially chapters 49, 51, and 52) for more information.

Subject matter and discussions in political science may also pose challenges. Discussing something personal and sacred in a critical, academic context is often challenging even when others are being respectful. While you should address microaggressions and discrimination, it can be helpful to reframe these discussions and subject matter as opportunities to learn from other perspectives, to educate others through your perspective, and to deepen your own understanding of faith and scholarship. You may benefit from supportive groups with members of your own faith, religious leaders, and even licensed counselors or therapists. Maintaining the balance between critical analysis/discussion expected in academia with the need for respect is often difficult. One helpful tip is to frame contributions as your perspective rather than universal truth and encourage the same in others. Approach these topics with humility while encouraging the same in others, but also set boundaries that maintain respect. While you may not always receive respect, you signaled that you do not silently tolerate such behavior but are open to discussion and learning.

Conclusion

Religious minorities must be aware of the unique challenges they may face and be prepared to advocate for themselves in several capacities. It is also critical to note that students may face intersecting challenges related to their gender, race and ethnicity, sexuality, disability, etc. (See other chapters in the Strategies for Addressing Implicit Bias, Harassment, Assault section, especially chapters 54-56, for more information.) Strategies offered here are merely an overview, and each student will have individualized circumstances. Each student should investigate their specific program in detail to understand what resources they have available to help advocate for themselves. Being proactive for both yourself and fellow religious minorities will help mitigate major challenges and promote success.

Helpful Websites and Resources

- US Department of Education's Office of Civil Rights: https://www2.ed.gov/about/offices/list/ocr/religion.html
- US Equal Employment Opportunity Commission: https://www.eeoc.gov/religious-discrimination
- US Department of Justice Civil Rights Division: https://www.justice.gov/crt
- US Office of Fair Housing and Equal Opportunity: https://portalapps.hud.gov/AdaptivePages/HUD/about/index.htm#religion
- Allies and Microaggressions (How to be an Ally): https://www.insidehighered.com/advice/2016/04/13/how-be-ally-someone-experiencing-microaggressions-essay
- Ronald A. Berk's Publications on Microaggressions: http://www.ronberk.com/articles.shtml
- R.A.V.E.N. Process for Responding to Microaggressions: https://www.diverseeducation.com/opinion/article/15106837/how-to-respond-to-racial-microaggressions-when-they-occur

References

Almasri, Nasir., Blair Read, and Clara Vandeweerdt, C. 2021. Mental Health and the PhD: Insights and Implications for Political Science. PS: Political Science & Politics, 1-7. doi:10.1017/S1049096521001396

Berk, Ronald A. 2017a. "MICROAGGRESSIONS TRILOGY: Part 3. Microaggressions in the classroom." Journal of Faculty Development 31, no. 3: 95-110.

---. 2017b. "MICROAGGRESSIONS TRILOGY: Part 2. Microaggressions in the academic workplace." Journal of Faculty Development 31, no. 2: 69-83.

---. 2017c. "MICROAGGRESSIONS TRILOGY: Part 1. Why do microaggressions matter?" Journal of Faculty Development 31, no. 1: 63-73.

Ganote, Cynthia, Floyd Cheung, and Tasha Souza. 2016. "Micro-aggressions, micro-resistance, and ally development in the academy." Invited workshop presented at the National Center for Faculty Development and Diversity, Detroit, MI, April 7. http://www.faculty diversity.org/page/MicroAggressions/?src=IHEArticle

Harris III, Frank, and J. Luke Wood. 2020. "How to Respond to Racial Microaggressions When They Occur." Diverse: Issues in Higher Education Opinion Piece, May 5. Last updated May 6, 2020. https://www.diverseeducation.com/opinion/article/15106837/how-to-respo   nd-to-racial-microaggressions-when-they-occur.

Irey, Sayumi. 2013. "How Asian American women perceive and move toward leadership roles in community colleges: A study of insider counter narratives." Unpublished doctoral dissertation, University of Washington. https://digital.lib.washington.edu/researchworks/bitstream/ handle/1773/22898/Irey_washington_0250E_11343.pdf?sequence=1.

Office for Civil Rights. 2020. "Protecting Students: Religious Discrimination." US Department of Education, December 4. Accessed November 27, 2021. https://www2.ed.gov/about/offices/list/ocr/religion.html.

Rockquemore, Kerry Ann. 2016, April 13. "Allies and Microaggressions." Inside Higher Ed, April 13. Accessed December 12, 2021. https://www.insidehighered.com/advice /2016/04/13/how-be-ally-someone-experiencing-microaggressions-essay.

Rosentiel, Tom, Scott Keeter, and Gregory Smith. 2007. "Public Opinion About Mormons: Mitt Romney Discusses His Religion." Pew Research Center, December 4. Accessed November 24, 2021. https://www.pewresearch.org/2007/12/04/public-opinion-about-mormons/.

Scheitle, Christopher P., and Elaine Howard Ecklund. 2020. "Individuals' Experiences with Religious Hostility, Discrimination, and Violence: Findings from a New National Survey." Socius: Sociological Research for a Dynamic World 6 (January): 1 –15. https://doi.org/10.1177/2378023120967815.

Sue, Derald Wing. 2010. Microaggressions in Everyday Life: Race, Gender, and Sexual Orientation. John Wiley & Sons: Hoboken, New Jersey.

US Equal Employment Opportunity Commission. 2021. "Religious Discrimination." EEOC Employees & Job Applicants: Discrimination by Type, January 15. Accessed November 27, 2021. https://www.

eeoc.gov/religious-discrimination.

US Department of Housing and Urban Development's Office of Fair Housing and Equal Opportunity. 2021. "Religious Discrimination." Accessed November 27, 2021. https://portalapps.hud.gov/AdaptivePages/HUD/about/index.htm#religion.

US Department of Justice Civil Rights Division. 2015. "Educational Opportunities Section If You Have Been Discriminated Against." US Department of Justice Home: Civil Rights Division, August 6. Accessed November 27, 2021.https://www.justice.gov/crt/educational-opportunities-section-if-you-have-been-discriminated-against.

60

Concerns for First-Generation Political Science Graduate Students

Thomas S. Benson[1] & T. Mark Montoya[2]

1. University of Delaware 2. Northern Arizona University

KEYWORDS: First-Gen, Financial Resources, Intersecting Identities.

Introduction

Many political scientists remain unversed in the relevant and diverse experiences of first-generation college and university students, even if they themselves were first-generation (hereafter "*first-gen*"). This is likely the result of many first-gen academics failing to recognize their own experiences as anything other than 'normal.' However, first-gen political science graduate students often start in a predicament that differs from students whose parents attended and graduated with an undergraduate education; without the benefit of parental mentorship and advice with regard to resources, navigating application processes, transitioning into graduate education, reading unwritten rules, and the like.

A first-gen college student is one whose parents or guardians did not complete a four-year college degree (NASPA 2017). This is a near-universal definition, though the definition may be contingent upon program, department, school, university, or country. First-gen status is generally both a positionality and a topic many universities and colleges are interested in documenting for census-type reasons and for undergraduate programming. Moreover, because the significance of first-gen status will hold greater importance in graduate programs, we must also recognize concerns for first-gen political science graduate students.

While many of us have far greater clarity about first-gen identities, the first-gen label is not subject to aggressions that may often apply to race, gender, sexuality, and so on (to learn more about these aspects in political science, see chapters 54-59 in this volume). Still, first-gen status is often part of larger intersectional identities, meaning that many first-gen students may also hold multiple identities, of which first-gen is one of many. This means that first-gen experiences among political science graduate students are not identical. The primary issues that first-gen students face are often around cultural capital (social assets they may lack in college), imposter syndrome (self-doubts they may have in college), and survivor's guilt (experiencing opportunities not available to others back home). Further interconnected challenges include an absence of belonging, unaffordability of tuition and living expenses, and academic struggles (Azmitia et al. 2018, 93; Jehangir 2010, 534).

Moreover, first-gen students often face difficulties in negotiating access to higher education and navigating the academy all while usually working longer hours that often lead to lower grades and higher attrition rates (Bell and Santamaría 2019a, 7). Many of these concerns have more to do with structural issues than with first-gen political science graduate students themselves. What is further important to note is that first-gen graduate students have shared narratives of great resilience to persevere through college and in graduate school (Gardner and Holley 2011, 82). In short, first-gen identity is not a deficiency. Indeed, first-gen political science graduate students have the capacity to tell their stories, change the narrative, and hence create better conditions for themselves, their families, and their communities

(Bell and Santamaría 2019a, 7).

As such, learning how to navigate the various levels of higher education is imperative for most first-gen students. Specifically, first-gen political science students must try to make sense of curricular and pedagogical processes that are specific to political science as a discipline – processes which are both uplifting and daunting, otherwise they may be rendered invisible (Jehangir 2010, 536). Further, political science graduate programs are multifaceted, and the nuances and complexities of graduate school can make navigating the 'system' seem impossible, but it is not.

Why Does It Matter That You're a First-Gen Political Science Graduate Student?

If we seek higher graduation rates and greater success of political science graduates in the classroom, we need to understand why it matters that someone is first-gen. First, it matters that first-gen identity itself has only gained traction in the past decade. As such, first-gen students have quickly shifted from a deficit archetype (a perspective that suggests minority groups come into college with deficiencies compared to the dominant or majority group, in this case continuing-generation students) to an assets-based standard, which focuses on strengths (Ives and Castillo-Montoya 2020). In other words, first-gen students are resilient and are indeed worthy of entering and completing political science graduate programs. Second, it matters that first-gen political science graduate students are resilient because of the current realities most graduate students (both first- and continuing-gen) are currently facing, which will be discussed further below. Third, graduate first-gen issues matter because there remains the question of defining first-gen graduate students, especially as fewer folks have attended graduate school compared to completing an undergraduate degree (Van Galen and Sablan 2021, 1-2). For example, does a continuing-gen student become a first-gen graduate student if a parent did not receive a master's degree?

What we do know is that graduate students do not always receive the same type of support or have the same types of resources dedicated to their personal and academic growth as undergraduates at the university-level. Instead, most graduate programing is handled on the departmental-level or by a Graduate College, and the programing generally does not focus on status or positionality as a first-gen student. In graduate school, first-gen students can perceive that their peers already know the fundamentals of what is expected, whereas they can feel like imposters about how to navigate the system (see chapter 50 on imposter syndrome in this volume), which means they can end up studying "twice as hard to learn how to maneuver in and out of the system, how to work the system, [and] how to learn" (Gardner and Holley 2011, 84). Indeed, structural issues impact first-gen students.

Consequently, first-gen graduate students can be left to navigate a system they know little about, and this is compounded by feeling torn between two communities (home/community and graduate school), often a lack of *financial resources* to apply to graduate programs or take the GRE (if required), and generally transitioning into a graduate program in political science. Additional challenges include navigating convoluted structures of university, such as financial aid and housing (with little to no monetary help from families), all while maintaining home responsibilities. Notwithstanding, first-gen students regularly consider the desires of their families rather than their own personal goals. As such, family wishes manifest themselves in the course and programs they take, like political science (Jehangir 2010, 536). Simultaneously, families may fear the idea of "a new intellectualism" that pushes first-gen students to the margins at home and at university (Jehangir 2010, 537). This can critically impact how first-gen students feel. For instance, returning home after your first semester can be difficult when no one can understand what pressures you face or the new ideas you share. You may receive condescending comments, an inability to understand the questions you pose, or a failure to acknowledge the milestones you have reached. This can make you feel like you do not share the same values or beliefs as your family. If you are a prospective student, knowing you are first-gen can help prepare you for this. As an existing graduate student, take solace that you are not alone in these experiences and seek out shared first-gen spaces for a sense of community.

Furthermore, there exists a perception that a college degree is necessary for upward mobility (Azmitia et al. 2018, 90; Jehangir 2010, 534). While pursuit of a political science graduate degree may not necessarily be for post-PhD employment prospects, graduates do earn more than their undergraduate peers. This is important because 30-50% of US first-gen students drop out after their first year because they often feel unwelcome or like they do not fit in with the campus "ethos," experiencing heightened isolation (Azmitia et al. 2018, 92; Jehangir 2010, 534). The primary issue is that first-gen graduate students are more likely to be enrolled in graduate programs as part-time students than continuing-generation students, who are more likely to be full-time. They are also more likely to delay entry into graduate programs (Seay et al. 2008, 17-19). Ultimately, if first-gen students do enroll in postsecondary education, they are less likely to graduate from college (Graf 2019, 4). In light of all of this, there can be adverse mental health impacts which subsequently impact the capacity to learn (Bell and Santamaría 2019b, 195).

Excelling as a First-Generation Graduate Student

Our first piece of advice for prospective political science graduate students—especially first-gen students from low-income backgrounds—is that you should compare programs that offer fellowships and assistantships as these forms of financial support are often vital for success in graduate school (Gardner and Holley 2011, 86) (see chapter 23 in this volume for more on financial aid). You should also identify a faculty member who could be a potential adviser as they can play a critical role in helping you frame your research interests, strategize in letters of recommendation, and prepare you with mock interviews as part of the application process to study political science at the graduate level (Wagner, Alderson, and Spetz 2020, 346) (see chapter 13 in this volume on selecting and advisor and mentor). Additionally, pay attention to the value of the education on offer and the prestige among US universities and how these will affect your post-PhD employment opportunities (Gardner and Holley 2011, 84) (see chapter 4 in this volume on choosing a program).

For first-gen political science graduate students who have been accepted, you ought to consider preparing for your program. This will likely include ensuring that you are developing strong writing and communication skills, as well as some familiarity with data computation software such as Stata, R, SPSS, and Python. This also means having some familiarity with information acquisition, such as primary and secondary research methods, and qualitative and quantitative data collection and analytical methods (Seay et al. 2008, 20). In addition, you could begin reading foundational texts for classes that you will be enrolled in and this will ensure that the transition into political science graduate education is not as steep as it otherwise would be. You can identify these texts by reaching out to the Graduate Director of your department or faculty who will be teaching those classes. Most importantly, recognize the value that you bring to the discipline of political science. There may be times that you feel deflated, but you are worthy and able to embark on a graduate degree in political science just as much as continuing-generation students in your program (Gardner and Holley 2011, 83).

For current political science graduate students, you could participate in collaborative research opportunities with faculty members and these opportunities do not only assist in enhancing your employability and your research skills, but they also help to generate a sense of belonging, thereby offsetting the imposter syndrome that typically affects first-gen graduate students (Bell and Santamaría 2019b, 205). You should be proud that you 'made it' this far, despite major obstacles to being a first-gen student in applying to and attending graduate school to study political science. Moreover, if you are struggling in your program, you can seek out support from your university – support in writing, presenting, reading, citing research (e.g., Zotero), and publishing and broadcasting research (e.g., Google Scholar, ResearchGate, LinkedIn) – which can often be found in campus writing and learning centers, library services, and departmental professionalization seminars. There are also social media communities for first-gen students on platforms like Twitter and Facebook, but be wary—while these platforms can be fruitful sources of information and create a virtual sense of belonging, they can also be a source of toxicity that can adversely affect your mental health (see chapter 27 in this volume on Twitter). Given this, try to use social media in a balance that works best for you.

At some universities, short, one-credit classes are available for graduate students to boost their skills in these areas of professionalism, and these can be beneficial. Also, as a current student, you should not be afraid to seek support from your faculty adviser. If your adviser is not supportive, you should engage your department's Graduate Director, administrative staff, or Chair in seeking a faculty adviser who is more supportive and, ideally, understands the barriers you face as a first-gen graduate student (see chapter 65 in this volume for more on dealing with challenges that arise). For first-gen students, you may also find targeted financial support at conferences when it comes to presenting academic research. For example, the American Political Science Association (APSA) offers, every year, an Accessibility Grant to assist students in attending APSA for the first time. Some other political science conferences sometimes do the same—keep an eye out for grants in conferences that often take place in a cyclical fashion, in Spring and Fall.

To cultivate a sense of belongingness, you can volunteer in on-campus organizations that engage in campus politics or assist younger graduate students, undergraduate students or even high school students (Azmitia et al. 2018, 94) (see chapters 31-33 in this volume for more on service). This can also serve to retain first-gen students as you can provide mentorship and demonstrate that first-gen political science students can be successful and can attend graduate school. One example of engagement includes monthly coffee hours or forums with like-minded students and administrators to socialize and identify opportunities for improvement. Such opportunities may include requesting: on-campus financial resources for first-gen students to be clearer; appropriate guidance in navigating financial and well-being support; access to free or discounted printing credits, food, textbooks, prescription drugs, and health insurance; flexibility in extensions for academic papers and exams; opportunities for first-gen students to share their experiences in classrooms; and greater opportunities for interaction and collaboration with faculty. Further, we also recommend that you talk to your peers in your graduate program – whether they are first-gen or not – as this can help to address feelings of inadequacy, navigate cultural norms in the discipline of political science, and promote persistence and determination in achieving success in the discipline (Bell and Santamaría 2019a, 7; Seay et al. 2008, 20).

Finally, we acknowledge that first-gen students may also have multiple and often *intersecting identities*, such as being first-gen and LGBTQIA+, part of a religious minority, an international student, or part of a racial and ethnic minority, among other things. Thus, first-gen students and universities must both understand that challenges facing first-gen students cannot be isolated as they can be compounded by other issues, such as racism, and homophobia (see chapters 54-61 for more on these topics). As such, the first-gen identity becomes linked to other identities that can be equally or more important. Greater focus on navigating these other identities can be found in other chapters of this edited volume. And to conclude this chapter, we want to reiterate that you are worthy, as a first-gen student, of pursuing and completing a political science graduate degree. Further, we amplify the call for an asset-based approach that draws attention to the strengths and resiliency of first-gen students and the contributions they can make to the discipline of political science.

References

Azmitia, Margarita, Grace Sumabat-Estrada, Yeram Cheong, and Rebecca Covarrubias. 2018. "'Dropping Out Is Not An Option': How Educationally Resilient First-Generation Students See the Future." *New Directions for Child and Adolescent Development* 160: 89–100. doi: 10.1002/cad.20240.

Bell, Amani, and Lorri J. Santamaría. 2019a. "Introduction: Why Focus on First Generation Students?" In *Understanding Experiences of First Generation University Students: Culturally Responsive and Sustaining Methodologies*, eds. Amani Bell and Lorri J. Santamaría, 1-25. New York: Bloomsbury Publishing.

Bell, Amani, and Lorri J. Santamaría. 2019b. "Conclusion: Beyond Listening to First Generation Students." In *Understanding Experiences of First Generation University Students: Culturally Responsive and Sustaining Methodologies*, eds. Amani Bell and Lorri J. Santamaría, 191-218. New York: Bloomsbury Publishing.

Gardner, Susan K., and Karri A. Holley. 2011. "'Those invisible barriers are real': The Progression of First-Generation Students Through Doctoral Education." *Equity & Excellence in Education* 44(1): 77-92. doi: 10.1080/10665684.2011.529791.

Graf, Anne Jumonville. 2019. "First-Generation Students and Libraries: Beyond the Deficit Narrative." In *Supporting Today's Students in the Library: Strategies for Retaining and Graduating International, Transfer, First-Generation, and Re-Entry Students*, eds. Ngoc-Yen Tran and Silke Higgins. Chicago, IL: Association of College and Research Libraries, 3-21.

Ives, Jillian, and Milagros Castillo-Montoya. 2020. "First-Generation College Students as Academic Learners: A Systematic Review." *Review of Educational Research* 90(2): 139–178. doi: 10.3102/0034654319899707.

Jehangir, Rashné. 2010. "Stories as Knowledge: Bringing the Lived Experience of First-Generation College Students Into the Academy." *Urban Education* 45(4): 533-553. doi: 10.1177/0042085910372352.

NASPA. 2017. "Defining First-Generation." *Center for First-Generation Student Success* [website], October 20, 2021. https://firstgen.naspa.org/blog/defining-first-generation.

Seay, Sandra E., Donald E. Lifton, Karl L. Wuensch, Lynn K. Bradshaw, and James O. McDowelle. 2008. "First-Generation Graduate Students and Attrition Risks." *The Journal of Continuing Higher Education* 56(3): 11-25. doi: 10.1080/07377366.2008.10400158.

Van Galen, Jane A., and Jaye Sablan. 2021. "Introduction: First-Generation PhDs Navigating Institutional Power in Early Academic Careers." In *Amplified Voices, Intersecting Identities, Volume 2: First-Generation PhDs Navigating Institutional Power in Early Academic Careers*, eds. Jane A. Van Galen and Jaye Sablan, 1-17. Leiden, Netherlands: Brill Sense.

Wagner, Laura M., Alece Alderson, and Joanne Spetz. 2020. "Admission of First Generation to College Pre-licensure Master's Entry and Graduate Nursing Students." *Journal of Professional Nursing* 36(5): 343-347. doi: 10.1016/j.profnurs.2020.02.001.

61

Disabilities and Chronic Health Issues

Eun A Jo[1], Sally Friedman[2], & Alan Babcock[3]

1. Cornell University 2. State University of New York, Albany 3. Penn State, Harrisburg

KEYWORDS: Disability, Chronic Health Issues, Accessibility.

Introduction

The Covid-19 pandemic has made learning difficult for everyone—but particularly for graduate students with disabilities and chronic health issues. A recent article in the Washington Post documents widespread fears of being "left behind" as students returned to in-person instruction (Lai 2021). Frustrated, one student recounted: "I have to work 10 times harder than my classmates just to be able to succeed, and yet I'm not being supported" (Lai 2021).

In this period of transition, we seek to foster a conversation about disabilities and chronic health issues in graduate school. Drawing from our own experiences—as a graduate student with chronic health issues, a faculty member with a physical disability, and a university administrator in disability services—we identify some common challenges facing graduate students with special needs, point out available resources, and offer some recommendations for making academia more inclusive.

Indeed, disabilities can be more or less visible, and require different levels of ongoing medical interventions. Regardless of type, however, students with disabilities share challenges in balancing their needs against the pressures of graduate school, finding adequate institutional support, and confronting discriminatory actions including implicit bias. In this paper, we define disability. Then we document some common challenges and identify possible resources (institutional, legal, and social) that students may seek out in their respective departments, universities, and beyond. In doing so, we hope to acknowledge the unique needs of students with disabilities as well as inform, based on our lived experiences, how academia as a whole may better accommodate those needs. We also emphasize that disability is only part of the story: graduate school experience should be, first and foremost, defined by individual interests and aspirations.

That said, we begin with an important caveat: What works for one person may not work for another. Whatever insights you take away from this chapter should be tailored to your own needs and style. We point out common experiences, but we urge you to assess your own individual situation. We thus recommend that students, with intersectional identities in particular, seek out relevant advice in chapters 54-60 of this handbook.

Definition

We begin by discussing what counts and doesn't count as a *disability*. Without getting overly technical, what you should know is that more types of disabilities than you would expect are covered. Definitions go well beyond physical "impairments" to cover a wide range of visible and invisible disabilities.

The legal definition starts with the Rehabilitation Act of 1973, repeated in the original (1990) version of the Americans with Disabilities Act (ADA). The definition focused on "a physical or mental impairment that substantially limits one or more major life activities" (ADA 2008, Section 4(a)). When this definition proved limiting (for example, people with significant visual disabilities weren't covered if glasses could correct their situation; diabetics using insulin weren't included because their sugar levels could be appropriately regulated), the ADA as amended in 2008 broadened the number of people who were included: "the question of whether an individual's impairment is a disability under the ADA should not demand extensive analysis" (ADA 2008, Section 2(b)(5)).

One of the authors of this chapter, who works as a disability resource service coordinator, suggests simply to think of disability as barriers to overcome. His bottom-line question to the students is: "given your input of knowledge and level of effort, what gets in your way of performing the activities needed to do the work?" This should be the guiding question for assessing your challenges.

Challenges

We now point to four common challenges that students with disabilities and chronic health issues encounter: (1) accessibility, (2) discrimination and implicit bias, (3) awareness, and (4) self-doubt.

Accessibility: Can I, as a Student with a Disability, Have Equal Access to Resources and Opportunities?

We initially think of *accessibility* in a physical sense. Can students with wheelchairs easily get around their campuses? Do students with visual or hearing impairments have access to all parts of campus life, including the classroom experience? Are campus facilities such as parking and public transportation accessible to people who cannot walk long distances? To this, we add technology. How accessible are websites to users with visual impairments? Are browsers accessible by voice for people with mobility impairments? Even with this narrow definition of accessibility, however, universities often fail to adequately address student needs.

In fact, given the Americans with Disabilities Act (ADA), many in the United States tend to assume that questions of basic access have been solved. Yet, in the course of writing this short piece, we have run across too many stories where this is not the case. We have even encountered examples of professors who blanche at making even basic accommodations to students, including testing times and PowerPoint release.

The accessibility of the environment in which students live and work can be a game changer. One student noted: "I moved to Cambridge at a time when I was not worried if I would be able to walk the next day, when being wheelchair-dependent was not an imminent possibility. However, living with a degenerative condition and having passed through that very fog just before my arrival in Cambridge meant that accessibility and inclusivity are never far from my thoughts in this city" (Kaur 2018). For those with mobility considerations, whether chronic or temporary, environmental structures can make the world of difference.

At the same time, as another student's experience illustrates, a combination of cultural stigma and institutional barriers can make asking for these accommodations difficult: "I didn't tell anyone I used these accommodations.... I was so embarrassed. My university had a policy that you had to submit accommodation letters to faculty in person, and my anxiety would bubble just under the surface" (Singh 2021, np). Thus, while physical accessibility matters, we must also pay attention to people's perceptions of what it means to ask for accommodation.

Discrimination and Implicit Bias: Can I, as a Student with a Disability, be Treated Equally?

Discrimination—and relatedly, implicit bias—entail a variety of issues. Broadly, discrimination involves differentiating in favor of or against students on the basis of the groups or categories to which they belong. The ADA spells this out in greater detail: "individuals with disabilities continually encounter various forms of discrimination, including outright intentional exclusion, the discriminatory effects of architectural, transportation, and communication barriers, overprotective rules and policies, failure to make modifications to existing facilities and practices, exclusionary qualification standards and criteria, segregation, and relegation to lesser services, programs, activities, benefits, jobs, or other opportunities" (ADA 2008, Section 12101 (a)(5)). More subtly, implicit bias involves unconscious attitudes and stereotypes that shape how we think about what we deserve.

As graduate students with disabilities and/or chronic health issues, questions of equal treatment can arise in many contexts. Will I as a student be given equal opportunities as a teaching and research assistant? Will I be included in departmental functions and in all parts of department life? Will colleagues and even fellow students make assumptions about me and my abilities—that is, will people think I cannot do the work or expect less of me because they assume I will want to have things a little easier? In sum, discrimination and implicit bias are about equal treatment; if you think about it, there are a variety of ways, many of them subtle, unequal treatment can come into play.

Awareness: As a Student with a Disability, How Can I Know What I Need?

Awareness is the first step to realizing equal access and treatment. It concerns how students with disabilities and chronic health issues know what they need and how to ask for it. In general, students are expected to identify and communicate their needs, as well as request "reasonable" accommodations to meet them. Yet, this places a significant burden on students. Not only is it difficult to ask for help when you do not know precisely what you need, there is substantial mental and emotional labor that accompanies making decisions over how much information you must share.

This challenge is compounded by the fact that students' conditions and abilities can vary over time—how they feel or look on a given day may not fully represent the true extent of their needs. In fact, prior research shows that students tend to negotiate accommodations on a case-by-case, and often informal, basis rather than comprehensively through formal institutional channels that require full disclosure of disabilities; depending on the circumstances, they also often change how they identify as disabled (Castrodale and Zingaro 2015). This reflects institutional barriers to accommodation, which oblige a particular threshold of "awareness" on the part of the student at any given moment. It is not surprising that consistent, comprehensive demands for accommodation have been rare when the onus is entirely on the students to figure out and prove their needs.

These insights are captured in a recent blog post by a student with a disability: "[My advisor said to me:] 'Good luck to you. You're gonna have real trouble finding anyone willing to accommodate you in any way.'… Hearing this statement from him—with no advice on the matter, in combination with my experiences at that school—actually stopped me from applying for the jobs I wanted because at the time I was undiagnosed and did not know how to advocate for myself for a condition everybody kept telling me was fictional" (Anonymous 2021).

Self-Doubt: As a Student with a Disability, Do I Deserve to Get What I Need?

In graduate school—where "imposter syndrome" is already so prevalent (Edwards 2019)—students with disabilities and chronic health issues struggle with embracing their entitlements to care. Indeed, this becomes exponentially harder when they suffer from "invisible" disabilities and chronic health issues. Past research documents numerous and complex reasons why students with "invisible" disabilities—in particular, mental health problems and conditions with social stigma (Cunnah 2015; Grimes et al. 2019; Martin 2010)—choose to conceal their needs. This includes the administrative burden of paperwork, anxiety about sharing sensitive information, fear of denial of accommodations, and beyond (Matthews 2009).

Indeed, one student writer with a disability shared: "We're often taught to be ashamed of our needs, and to believe that they aren't reasonable. Is it just that we shouldn't be here? Whether or not the shame holds, there are times when being openly disabled just isn't practical—proving disability discrimination can be hard and encountering plausibly unrelated barriers as soon as we ask for accommodations is a common fear" (Hilary 2018). Her words suggest that there are deeper issues than, simply, challenges of "awareness": a culture of shame and delegitimization that prevents students from being "open" about their disabilities and chronic health issues.

Resources

Based on the challenges we have identified, we now point to some basic resources. While acknowledging the overlap of these categories, we divide resources into three groups, institutional, legal, and social. Overall, we want to leave you with the idea there's more "help" out there than you might think.

Institutional

Institutional support starts with your department. Your graduate school advisor as well as other political science faculty should become an important part of your life. You may interact with your adviser for all kinds of reasons: to learn to navigate the demands of graduate school; to determine the research in which you want to participate; to get help funding your research; and to assist you in finding internships. As makes sense for you, your advisor can also help you navigate your disability, for example, by helping you determine the types of accommodations you might need for the various things you will be expected to do.

Additionally, though they go by a variety of names, every university is required to have an Office of Disability Services. It is your responsibility to self-disclose that you have a disability; no one will reach out to you. Any communication you have is confidential and nothing will be shared outside the office without your permission. (For your security, you might want to clarify this confidentiality with the specific individual with whom you meet.)

A Disability Specialist will explain possibilities for auxiliary services and accommodations, both being determined on a case-by-case basis. For example, for someone who is hard-of-hearing, the auxiliary aids and services could include qualified interpreters, real-time computer-aided transcription services, assistive listening systems, closed captioning of videos, and/or note takers. These technological aids can be life changing.

Academic accommodations are changes to classroom policies and procedures to mitigate symptoms of your disability. For example, a professor might be asked to modify strict attendance requirements if your disability prevents you from attending. Your accommodations could change any aspect of the course as long as they do not change essential features or required elements. The goal of accommodations is to provide an alternative way to accomplish course requirements by eliminating or reducing disability-related barriers.

Legal

Going the legal route can take time and energy, and for many of us, it is a daunting undertaking, certainly not one you might take as a first step. The threat of legal recourse, on the other hand, may motivate your university to take the required action, and just knowing you have legal rights in the first place can be personally empowering.

The two federal laws of most relevance, and you've probably heard of them, are the Americans with Disabilities Act (first passed in 1990 and as amended in 2008), and the Rehabilitation Act of 1973 (section 504, in particular). Of additional interest is also The Fair Housing Act of 1968 which covers accommodations for service animals as well as architectural modifications, and some state and local laws should be checked out too—in some cases they are stronger than the federal legislation.

These laws are broad and inclusive, and stipulate that "physical or mental disabilities in no way diminish a person's right to fully participate in all aspects of society" (ADA 2008 (a)(1)). With respect to education specifically: "Both public and private colleges and universities must provide equal access to postsecondary education for students with disabilities." Title II of the ADA covers publicly funded universities, community colleges and vocational schools. Title III covers privately funded schools. All public or private schools that receive federal funding are required under Section 504 of the Rehabilitation Act to make their programs accessible to students with disabilities.

The schools can do this in several ways: by providing architectural access to buildings, including residential facilities; by providing aids and services necessary for effective communication, like sign language interpreters, Braille or electronic formats and assistive listening devices; and by modifying policies, practices and procedures, such as testing accommodations and access to school facilities for service animals" (ADA National Network 2021).

Social

There are also friends and allies all across campus. Reach out to build relationships with your peers, disabled and nondisabled alike. These social networks are crucial for many reasons, but two are of particular import in your context. First and foremost, they are a source of personal comfort and support. Most students with disabilities and chronic health issues prefer to seek help through their social networks before seeking formal channels of accommodation (Castrodale and Zingaro 2015). This suggests that being part of a community that helps you feel supported is very important, particularly in terms of meeting your immediate needs. Second, social networks provide information and an organizing mechanism. Especially support networks—formed around shared challenges—can provide you with practical advice on how to advocate for yourself or mobilize for broader institutional reform.

While social networks may look different depending on your personal circumstances, there are a number of online communities dedicated to promoting the rights of students with disabilities and chronic health issues.

Here, we identify four blogs, each of which also has a twitter page:

- Disabled in Higher Ed: https://disabledinhighered.weebly.com
- Disability Visibility Project: https://disabilityvisibilityproject.com
- Disabled Academic Collective: https://disabledacademicco.wixsite.com/mysite
- Chronically Academic: https://chronicallyacademic.blogspot.com

Though there is no formal webpage, Disabled in Grad School twitter page is a fantastic social media platform that deals specifically with the needs of graduate students with disabilities and chronic health issues.

In addition, several advocacy groups for various disabilities have sections geared toward academic environments. With respect to blindness, for instance, the two major advocacy groups, National Federation of the Blind and American Council of the Blind have divisions for college students and professionals in education. Such advocacy groups may provide you with more tailored advice and support.

Recommendations

The challenges described here indicate a need for change, and the key questions, along with the specific challenges and resources we have described, guide our thinking. What can be done, by all parties involved, to equalize the playing field to make things fairer for students with disabilities and health challenges? As a student first and foremost, know that you are more than your disability or health condition. You have been accepted to graduate school because you are good at what you do and because you seek to develop your capabilities within the field of political science. Beyond that as the above should have indicated, know there are more resources available to you than you might think—take advantage of institutional resources; know your rights; develop your social networks; and as you are ready, proactively seek out opportunities that will advance your academic and professional career.

You might even want to push your institution in directions of more disability awareness as there is a lot the institution can do to make your life easier. Is disability included in any official statement of university inclusivity? Does the college follow up with appropriate resources, and are these efforts visible to students? Are there efforts to recruit faculty, staff, and additional students with disabilities? Is the input of students with disabilities themselves considered? Positive answers to these and related questions can go a long way to helping students overcome the challenges described above, first and foremost providing the kind of welcoming environment needed so students feel heard and encouraged. What you can do as an individual student counts; top-down efforts from the institution can lead to long-run and significant change.

Finally, a simple language reframe—from thinking about the needs of students with disabilities as needing accommodation to one of providing equal access to resources and opportunities—can make a world of difference. It can take us a long way to enhancing everyone's understanding of the kind of equality that's really at the heart of concerns about disability and health challenges.

References

Americans with Disabilities Act of 1990, accessed 12/1/2021, https://www.eeoc.gov/americans-disabilities-act-1990-original-text

Americans with Disabilities Act Amendments Act of 2008, accessed 12/1/2021,https://www.eeoc.gov/statutes/americans-disabilities-act-amendments-act-2008

Anonymous, "Good Luck to You," *Disabled in Higher Ed*, December 16, 2021, accessed 12/1/2021, https://disabledinhighered.weebly.com/blog/good-luck-to-you

ADA National Network, accessed 12/1/2021, https://adata.org

Castrodale, Mark, and Daniel Zingaro. 2015. "'You're Such a Good Friend': A Woven Autoethnographic Narrative Discussion of Disability and Friendship in Higher Education." *Disability Studies Quarterly* 35(1).

Chronically Academic, accessed 12/1/2021, https://chronicallyacademic.blogspot.com.

Cunnah, Wendy. 2015. "Disabled Students: Identity, Inclusion and Work-Based Placements." *Disability & Society* 30 (2): 213–226.

Disabled Academic Collective, accessed 12/1/2021, https://disabledacademicco.wixsite.com/mysite.

Disabled in Grad School, accessed 12/1/2021, https://twitter.com/DisInGradSchool

Disabled in Higher Ed, accessed 12/1/2021, https://disabledinhighered.weebly.com

Disability Visibility Project, accessed 12/1/2021, https://disabilityvisibilityproject.com

Dolmage, Jay Timothy. 2017. *Academic Ableism: Disability and Higher Education*. Ann Arbor, MI: University of Michigan Press.

Edwards, C. W. 2019. "Overcoming Imposter Syndrome and Stereotype Threat: Reconceptualizing the Definition of a Scholar." *Taboo: The Journal of Culture and Education*, 18 (1).

Grimes, Susan, Erica Southgate, Jill Scevak, and Rachel Buchanan. 2019. "University Student Perspectives on Institutional Non-Disclosure of Disability and Learning Challenges: Reasons for Staying Invisible." *International Journal of Inclusive Education* 23 (6): 639–655.

Hong, Barbara S. S., and Joy Himmel. 2009. "Faculty Attitudes and Perceptions Toward College Students with Disabilities." *College Quarterly* 12 (3): 6–20.

Hilary, Alyssa. 2018. "Disabled in Grad School: How 'Out' Do I Need to Be." accessed 12/1/2021, https://www.insidehighered.com/blogs/gradhacker/disabled-grad-school-how-out-do-i-need-be.

Kaur, Amarpreet. 2018. "Pushing the Boundaries: Making the Exclusive Inclusive." *Chronically Academic*, October 22, accessed 12/1/2021, https://chronicallyacademic.blogspot.com/search/label/Disability

Lai, Stephanie. 2021. "In Return to Campuses, Students with Disabilities Fear They're Being 'Left Behind,'" *The Washington Post*, November 1, accessed 12/1/2021,https://www.washingtonpost.com/e%09%09ducation/2021/11/01/colleges-return-students-disabilities/

Martin, Jennifer Marie. 2010. "Stigma and Student Mental Health in Higher Education." *Higher Education Research & Development* 29 (3): 259–274.

Matthews, Nicole. 2009. "Teaching the 'Invisible' Disabled Students in the Classroom: Disclosure, Inclusion and the Social Model of Disability." *Teaching in Higher Education* 14 (3): 229–239.

Rehabilitation Act of 1973, accessed 12/1/2021, https://www.eeoc.gov/statutes/rehabilitation-act-1973

Singh, Manya. 2021. "Academia Won't Change by Itself." *Chronically Academic*, March 7, https://chronicallyacademic.blogspot.com/search/label/Disability

Health and Wellness in Graduate School

62

Why You're Doing This: Sustaining Joy and Inspiration in the Scholarly Vocation

Yuna Blajer de la Garza[1], Patrick J. Egan[2], & Sarah Shugars[3]

1. Loyola University Chicago 2. New York University 3. Rutgers University

KEYWORDS: Academic Work, Independence, Positive Contributions.

Introduction

A senior faculty member began his welcome remarks for new scholars by reminiscing of a time when, back when he was a graduate student, he and an older professor spent one Friday afternoon and early evening parsing through books and journals. They were searching, to no avail, for the proper reference for an elusive footnote. When they finally succeeded, relieved and exhausted, the then-graduate student picked up his belongings and headed to the door. To his visible surprise, the older professor walked back to his desk and uncapped a pen, readying himself to mark a pile of essays. Seeing the puzzled look on his mentee's face, the professor explained, "you know, a life spent in footnotes and marking essays is a pretty good life."

We are not going to romanticize the pursuit of a PhD in political science. Sometimes a doctorate will be exhausting and demoralizing, warranting the cautions and concerns detailed in other chapters of this book. And yet, you might notice that most of us penning these chapters have decided to pursue a career in academia. In this chapter, we thus want to explain why all these scholars, otherwise very good at diagnosing the shortcomings of the field, decide to continue being part of it. They could very well take their talents to other sectors, many of which provide better pay and more control over their job's geographic location.

Three Virtues of a PhD in Political Science

A PhD in political science has at least three virtues, which, combined, make a doctorate in political science the entry point to the "pretty good life" the senior professor spoke about. First, academic work is fundamentally *creative*, providing its practitioners nearly unparalleled opportunities to learn, generate, and share new ideas. Second, it is also quite *independent*, in that scholars—even during doctoral studies—enjoy a remarkable degree of latitude in deciding what to research and how to manage their time. And, last but not least, political scientists are well-suited to *contribute* to society through mentorship, research, academic leadership, public scholarship, and public service. Each of the three sections below discusses one of these virtues.

Before we move to those sections, however, we want to make two additional points. First, a life in academia is, at least to many of us, not only a job but (also) a vocation. It is replete of questions that nag us long after working hours, that drive us to scribble thoughts on paper napkins, and that we feel personally invested in. This feeling maps onto the etymological origin of a "vocation" as a summons. We all need something in life we are passionate about and most of us also need a job. Those two things need not be satisfied by the same endeavor, but in academia they often are. This has the benefit that we get to work on things we are passionate about and that draw us in, but can also compound some of the negative challenges of academia: rejection might feel particularly personal and maintaining healthy work-life boundaries can be hard (see chapter 64 on health and well-being and preventing burnout). But similarly, successes can feel incredibly validating and it can sometimes be invigorating to have a career you are so passionate about.

A second point: you are not stuck in academia. You always have outside options. If mid-way during your PhD, you realize that academia does not bring you joy or that overall you are enduring it more than enjoying it, you can always walk away (see chapter 66 on deciding to leave the program). We academics tend to forget this or treat it as a tragic change of heart. There is nothing tragic about it. Choosing to leave academia is most frequently simply a question of personal goals, needs, and priorities. We acknowledge that of course many people do not so much choose to leave academia but rather have the choice forced upon them, most typically by the vagaries of a precarious job market.

Whether you ultimately complete your degree or not, the education you receive during your doctoral studies will serve you very well to score terrific (and often more lucrative) jobs in other sectors: consultancy, non-governmental organizations, start-ups, or the public sector, for example. Many people with PhDs in political science have decided that they prefer to pursue a job in other sectors where they thrive. Below, we discuss three of the reasons why we decided we wanted to stay.

Creativity

As you slog through PhD admissions essays and GRE tests—and in graduate school, wrestle with response papers, problem sets and qualifying exams—it can be easy to lose sight of the fact that academic life is creative in myriad forms. Most obvious of these is the creativity that accompanies conducting research about a topic that you find compelling and worthwhile. If you're currently an undergraduate student, chances are you have not had many encounters with this particular joy just yet. Most of the assignments you're completing on the way to a bachelor's degree are designed to reflect the extent to which you have absorbed and integrated others' ideas.

By contrast, scholars generate their *own* ideas through a process that is by turns exhilarating, laborious, vertiginous—and ultimately deeply satisfying. Often, although not always, research projects are born from the ability to draw connections overlooked by others, imagine ways to approach questions that change our assumptions about the world, and think beyond established conversations. And it's not just the finished product—the dissertation, book, or article that results from your work—that yields gratification. Most scholars will say that it's also the creative steps taken on the way, like creating a graph, composing a particularly compelling paragraph, or unearthing a new dataset, that can make political science such a satisfying vocation.

Another attractive aspect of this creativity is that your ideas become part of a conversation with other scholars who share your curiosity and passion about your topic. This conversation unfolds in many places simultaneously, including academic conferences, books and journal articles, and online in arenas like blogs and social media platforms. It can be unnerving to have your ideas discussed, examined, and refined in this recursive process. But when conducted in a respectful, collaborative, and supportive manner, this peer discussion is a time-tested way that we as an intellectual community develop cumulative insight—and that you as a scholar get to contribute to a growing body of knowledge.

Research is just one of several avenues of creativity available to those who pursue the scholarly vocation. Teaching can be another tremendously creative endeavor, regardless of whether you're leading a small seminar or running a large lecture course. Typically, subject to minimal constraints, the material covered in the courses you teach will be pretty much up to you. The same can be said for how you present this material to your students, what you expect them to know, and the ways in which you evaluate their performance. One of the few upsides of the COVID era for academia is that creative teaching innovations—including flipped classrooms, online breakout sessions, and evaluations that go beyond the traditional in-class "blue book" essay format—have become more necessary and thus more welcome. Teaching isn't easy work: running a semester-long lecture course with hundreds of students can feel like producing, writing, directing, and starring in your own Broadway show. But the point is that it's your show, and each of these elements involve creative decisions that you get to make.

One more aspect of academic creativity in research and teaching is that your work is *your* work. It's your name that appears on the spine of your book, on the top of your syllabus, or in the byline of your op-ed. Over time, these creations accumulate into a body of work that is uniquely yours, allowing you to put your stamp on the world in a way that few other careers permit.

Arguably, many aspects of departmental, university, and disciplinary service can often feel less creative than teaching or research. There are only so many ways to run a meeting, adjudicate among applicants for fellowships and prizes, and engage in the other administrivia of many academic service commitments. But even here, opportunities for creativity can arise. New programs, majors, and degree requirements—or rethinking current ones—require creative thinking. And as any department chair or dean will tell you, a creative approach to problem-solving is often key to fixing the thorny issues that pose challenges for every academic administrator.

Independence

On February 26, 2016, the *Jewish Times* featured the story of Joaquín García, a Spanish civil servant due to receive a medal for decades of loyal work in public administration. But García was nowhere to be found. It soon became clear that he had barely set foot in his job for six whole years, all while collecting a paycheck. Instead, he had spent that time perusing the works of the 17th century philosopher Baruch Spinoza. David Graeber mentions García's story in his well-known book, *Bullshit Jobs* (2018), where he argues that a good fraction of the jobs in today's society are completely meaningless. Not only would it make no difference to the world if they suddenly vanished, but they provide no delight to those who perform them.

Discussing whether academic jobs contribute to the world in consequential ways occupies us in the next section. Putting aside the nonchalance with which García missed work or the fact that his job was (quite literally) unnecessary, let us pause on his decision to spend six years reading Spinoza. There is something quite joyful in imagining the feeling experienced by someone spending six years doing exactly what they desire. García had done what he wished for six years. And he had chosen to read Spinoza. The key term here is "chosen," for the ability to decide what to work on is a good predictor of happiness in a job. The Happiness Index is a survey instrument meant to measure overall happiness in multiple domains of life. It gauges happiness at work through six criteria: autonomy is one of them. Other survey instruments measuring well-being at work also center on autonomy, asking respondents whether they enjoy freedom in deciding how to perform their work.

Perhaps one of the greatest virtues of doing a PhD in political science is precisely that you will have remarkable leeway in choosing your research questions, and thus considerable autonomy in deciding how you will spend a good portion of your days. Just like García, you might opt to spend six years reading Spinoza. The difference is that doing it will be your job.

In contrast to most professional endeavors (and even PhDs in other fields wherein doctoral students work in the labs of senior scholars), students of political science enjoy much independence in deciding what they work on. Granted, you do not have full sovereignty and your advisors might steer you in certain directions or away from others. But, even in the initial years of a PhD, you are relatively free to choose what to study. This is rare in today's labor market, even in selective high-paying jobs. For example, corporate lawyers are bound to the interests of the clients they represent and the priorities of their firms.

You say you want to study bureaucrats in Argentina? You can probably do that. Voting patterns in Mississippi are more your thing? You can possibly do that too. You want to follow García's footsteps and read Spinoza for six years? Also a possibility. The independence trickles beyond research. Beside the requirement to teach undergraduate introductory courses, most political scientists imagine, design, and teach classes drawing on their own interests. One of us, for example, taught a course that paired classic punishment theory and discussions of slaughterhouses and pornography during her doctoral studies.

To be sure, while not having a boss (in the common sense of the term) and being sovereign over your own time and topics of inquiry can be liberating, it comes with its own challenges. You are mostly accountable to yourself. And since your research reflects your interests, putting it "out there" is often a vulnerable experience, wherein it is hard not to take criticism personally. Our research is, indeed, very personal to us. But the independence and flexibility that characterizes the job remains one of the joys of doing a PhD and pursuing a career in academia.

Contributing to the World

Last but not least, academics in political science also have valuable opportunities to make positive contributions to the world through their research, teaching, and service. Each of these dimensions make up an important part of a scholar's life and can provide unique pathways for impact. A scholar considering what types of contributions they want to make should consider all three of these potential outlets in conjunction with their personal needs, interests, and priorities. Importantly, in pursuing academia as a vocation, it's critical to embrace the fact that you are a whole person—your work does not define your life, but your life can shape and inspire your work.

While junior scholars, and particularly graduate students, should be intentional about not taking on too much service, this work comes with a subtle form of power that can have important impacts within the academy. Engaging in this work often comes with the benefit of being able to make decisions or implement policies which are capable of improving academic culture. If you find yourself being drawn to certain types of service—mentoring, organizing events, or participating on committees with important decision-making power—think about what specifically draws you to that service and think strategically about how you can use your time for maximal impact (see chapters 31 and 32 on academic and professional service, respectively).

For example, driven by a deep commitment to mentorship, Dr. Mirya Holman created the highly popular newsletter "Mirya Holman's Aggressive Winning Scholars." In doing so, she continually creates publicly available mentorship resources through which she can reach thousands of scholars while simultaneously protecting her time. Similarly, seeing a need for better support, community, and communication around the job market, a group of then-graduate students created Support Your Cohort—a group of hundreds of junior scholars who share resources, information, and support during this incredibly difficult time in one's career. These are just a few examples of how "service" can be used as a tool that makes academia better without absorbing too much of a scholar's precious time.

Teaching can also serve as an important outlet through which scholars can positively contribute to the world. Through teaching you are actively engaging with and shaping the next generation of global citizens and have real opportunities to help those students find their voice and agency, or to help them think about the world in new and surprising ways. Compared to many other subjects, the students who take political science courses tend to be drawn to work that has broad public impact. Among the students one of us has taught over 15 years in the classroom are alumni who are now early in their careers as advisors to legislators, government data analysts, political campaign strategists, and even elected school-board officials.

And finally, political science scholars have tremendous opportunities to make important impacts on the global world through their research. Public-facing scholarship, which works to make academic knowledge available beyond the ivory tower, is one potential venue for having this kind of impact. Through blogs, podcasts, or public reports, political scientists can help the public make sense of the day's most pressing issues around the world; providing important historical context, understanding, and insight into how events will unfold. Graduate students interested in making an impact through public scholarship have the opportunities to learn the skills and techniques of this public-facing work through APSA's Public Scholarship program (see chapter 26 on public scholarship). Additionally, scholars can make important impacts by building partnerships outside of academia, using their research to address community-identified needs. APSA's Institute for Civically Engaged Research can serve as an excellent starting point for this type of work, providing training in how to engage in this type of partnership. Additionally, the wonderful Research 4 Impact program (https://www.r4impact.org/) helps match researchers to community organizations in order to create mutually beneficial partnerships.

Conclusion

"Why am I doing this?" is a question almost every PhD student asks themselves on a regular basis. Indeed, this is an important question for us all to continually reflect upon as we consider graduate school, progress towards a degree, and advance through our years as scholars. While this question is frequently inspired by the true challenges of academia, the examination of why we do what we do is fundamentally constructive. We hope we have shown here that the answer to why you're doing this can embrace some combination of the creativity, independence, and public contributions that are uniquely made possible by a career as an academic political scientist. If these answers don't resonate, you may wish to consider the many other good options open to you instead of getting a PhD in political science—or, if you are already pursuing a PhD, in place of an academic career.

The challenges, barriers, puzzlements, and idiosyncrasies that accompany a life in academia are formidable. But for each of us it is rare that a week goes by without experiencing at least one moment of being slightly dazzled by the remarkable fact that we get to do this for a living. These are the moments that remind us that academia is more than a job, but is truly a vocation: a worthy calling that requires sustained dedication and brings genuine joy.

References

Graeber, David. 2018. *Bullshit Jobs: A Theory*. New York: Simon & Schuster.

Holman, Mirya. #MHAWS Mirya Holman's Aggressive Winning Scholars Newsletter. https://miryaholman.substack.com/

Support Your Cohort Substack: Political Science Market Resources. http://supportyourcohort.com/

63 | No Rapunzel in This Ivory Tower: Finding Your Collective and Overcoming Academic Isolation

Devon Cantwell-Chavez[1], Siobhan Kirkland[2], Hannah Lebovits[3], Maricruz Osorio[4], Natalie Rojas[5], Rosalie Rubio[6], Sarah Shugars[7], Rachel Torres[8], & Rachel Winter[9]

1. University of Ottawa 2. Government of Canada 3. University of Texas-Arlington 4. Bentley University

5. University of California, Davis 6. George Washington University 7. Rutgers University

8. James Madison University 9. Michigan State University, University of California, Santa Barbara

KEYWORDS: Isolation, Marginalized Groups, Patriarchal Structures, Supportive Communities.

Introduction

In March 2019, a sub-group of the authors (referred to as the FIRE Collective throughout this piece) began to converse with one another via the Twitter private messaging function. Conversations were initially focused on experiences of gender-based inequity in academia and graduate school, but over time, discussions extended to other parts of our personal and professional lives. When the COVID-19 pandemic hit a year later, the group members were prepared to support one another through the unknown. We are writing this piece to provide an understanding of the layers of isolation within academia, particularly for graduate students, and to empower others to create intentional communities. Most notably, our group has been successful in dispelling feelings of isolation and supporting one another during the most difficult times, therefore substantially enhancing our graduate and professional education. In this piece, we discuss the structural issues that contribute to feelings of isolation within academia, our experience addressing isolation through establishing a collective, and we provide advice for how graduate students can form their own collectives. Finally, we discuss recommendations to the profession as a whole for addressing isolation.

At its core, "*isolation*" is a psychological state: the knowledge and feeling that—no matter how many people you physically see or communicate with—you are deeply, existentially, alone. Feelings of isolation can be evident in daily life, and can be core elements contributing to a number of mental health concerns (Hawkley and Cacioppo 2010). Feelings of isolation are common in academia across disciplinary boundaries (Bloch 2002; Hunter and Devine 2016), which is perhaps unsurprising in a profession where one's personal and professional identities are so closely intertwined, and where individuals are trained to be personally and professionally tied to their knowledge output. Overcoming professional isolation requires more than the raw tools of virtual communication, such as a social media account or even a regularly scheduled virtual forum. Combating isolation requires a rethinking and reorientation toward finding and securing deeply personal and professional connections and support systems.

Extending Anderson's approach to nationalism as reflecting an "imagined political community" of disparate individuals who consider themselves compatriots through their shared dedication to norms and institutions (Anderson 2006), one might first consider an academic's community as their discipline or some segment of their subfield. Yet, a core challenge to this notion is the fact that, contrary to popular belief, academics function as humans outside of their professional interests. While academics have a great need to connect with scholars whose substantive knowledge is similar to their own, we have perhaps an even greater need to connect with others whose lived experiences are similar.

This is especially true of those whose personal identities are stigmatized within the academy. Women, gender minorities, people of color, first-generation college students, members of the LGBTQ+ community, disabled folks, and those with intersecting marginalized identities have unique experiences within academia and beyond. Yet none of these communities are monolithic, and there is no singular trait or experience that fully binds them together. This makes finding one's "community" in academia particularly challenging for scholars from marginalized groups. For these underrepresented populations, the colleagues who share the closest scholarly knowledge are unlikely to also share similar experiences of academic life.

Gendered and Racial Dimensions of Isolation within Academia

The most predominantly *marginalized groups* of scholars are women and people of color, and they face an industry that can be openly hostile to them, and discount their work. Academia's formal good-faith efforts to increase the number of our colleagues in these groups often fall short, even by our own standards (Devine et al. 2017). Women are more likely than men to leave higher education, and those who do manage to stay and continue to work are often promoted at lower rates (Brown and Samuels 2018; Key and Sumner 2019). The COVID-19 pandemic has only exacerbated demands on workload and caregiving, while also stripping away institutional support for women and other historically marginalized scholars within the discipline (Langin 2021). Recent work by BIPOC and women scholars illuminates the experiences of isolation and discounted labor in our discipline (O'Brien 2020). Specifically, the work of BIPOC scholars and scholarship that centers on the power dynamics of racial and ethnic discrimination continues to be underrepresented and marginalized in political science. This discounting is the artifact of many things that contribute to professional isolation, even in pre-pandemic times. To combat the intrinsic ostracism in academia, scholars turn to each other for support. Informal groups add space for vulnerability and growth, as well as physical and material assistance, which as Willoughby-Herard (2020) points out, is crucial to the success of scholars of color.

The FIRE Collective includes a number of women of color with different ideological leanings and research specializations. It also has members who are non-binary, queer, first-generation to college, and disabled, as well as several colleagues who are members of religious minority groups. In this group, we find strength in a diverse community that validates and encourages different experiences and insights. This community allows for open dialogue and discussion without the fear of "airing dirty laundry" when speaking frankly about our experiences with expectations in the academy. Graduate students who eschew or withdraw from support networks outside their programs are considered aspirational models for many programs. Subsequently, the strong implication is that upon entry into a graduate program, the identity of "graduate student" becomes the most paramount, prioritized over all others. Nonconformity in the form of family or care obligations, disability, financial limitations, and other circumstances put graduate students with multiple priorities at risk of being met with hostility and socio-professional sanctions from colleagues. Some in the FIRE Collective share concerns that we cannot speak freely about with academic colleagues; colleagues may conflate group memberships with our individual struggles and sharing our difficulties can lead to poor judgments of our personal communities as a whole. As an informal group, we can discuss the personal and professional struggles of building successful careers without the pressure to perform respectability politics by wrapping authentic concerns into palatable packages to gain legitimacy and sympathy. Leading with a strong respect for boundaries, we can candidly discuss issues with departments, friends, families, and communities that arise from our differences from the norm. We also trust that the experiences and perspectives we share will not be unfamiliar and dismissed, actions that often generate and contribute to feelings of isolation. We can also trust that feedback and challenges to our ideas are coming from a place of care for one another, and a desire to see each member succeed. This allows for intellectual growth on a personal level, and communal growth for members of the FIRE Collective as we seek to earn respect from one another instead of from outsiders.

Professional advancement is built on the evaluation, validation, and acceptance of an author's ideas. These criteria also isolate academics who choose to focus on theories of politics that center on race and gender. At present, scholars of color and women who research these aspects of access to power are especially disregarded as niche, denigrated as "activist scholars," and siloed throughout the publication process. In a discipline that heavily prioritizes publishing, researchers who are under-cited, even within journals that publish more non-male authors, find few receptive homes for their research (Dion et al. 2018). Many of the rejections from these journals complain that research projects focused on race and gender are not relevant to the entire discipline, but the murders of George Floyd, Breonna Taylor, other countless racial injustices, and the subsequent protests across the world show that these projects are urgent matters across the discipline's major subfields. Given continuous self-selected disassociation from the scholarship that addresses these questions, the top journals have been unable to supply the discipline or the community at large with explanations and frameworks for comprehending the racial tensions of today. It is possible to support this work; *Politics, Groups, and Identities* has an entire syllabus of readings from their journal and continues to create micro-syllabi on the most urgent research questions. The FIRE Collective has offered a space to process and situate this work and creates opportunities for intellectual exchange that is related to our own interests, personally or topically. We share and discuss resources like the PGI syllabus with each other, and collectively work to broaden perspectives in the field for ourselves, our peers, and our students.

Furthermore, any concerns that professional groups seek to exclude ignore the nature of mutual aid systems. Radically supportive networks provide intense, holistic, and constant support in the form of words of encouragement, peer review, and professional support, as well as direct aid for basic needs such as housing, food, and clothing when necessary. In order to provide this all-encompassing level of support—a level necessary because of the precarious, dismissive, and underfunded nature of graduate degree-seeking experiences—a group must spend significant amounts of time building trust. Intentionality and active participation are necessary for maintaining faith in the integrity of the foundation and sustaining the depth of the network. When groups get too large or members are too inactive, trust-building is far more difficult due to the diffuse and intermittent availability of support group members. Groups such as the FIRE Collective must focus on meeting the needs of its members and in doing so, maintain a higher threshold for member attentiveness. Members leverage their personal time, intellectual labor, and emotional effort to support one another on an on-call basis, which is practically difficult to do on a larger scale. While not intentionally exclusive, such personal investment in others requires a commitment to the cooperative space in the face of differing goals, personalities, and needs. Formed in response to the isolation graduate students from diverse social backgrounds experience in the academic space, the Collective provides radical and intense support beyond the conventional ideas of peer mentorship to directly address the ostracizing forces that hinder the professional advancement and success of its members.

Community Building as Pedagogy in Graduate Education

The *patriarchal structures* of graduate school and the larger social structures both isolate and disproportionately affect members of marginalized communities. This can make finding a community to help navigate feelings of isolation, discrimination, and exclusion difficult. Still, the ability to foster community with individuals with shared experiences and values is vital to an individual's success, and to the discipline at large.

There are limits to what a purely academic community can achieve since the academic system is built on structures that have long criticized, discriminated against, and experimented on marginalized groups. One way that marginalized scholars attempt to counteract this effect is through the formation of an extended support network. These networks are often initially formed in conference hotel lobbies or in brief coffee meetings with guest speakers. While these interactions are invaluable to development, in the midst of a pandemic and travel restrictions, marginalized scholars lose this contact as well.

Social media can become a tool by which individuals find and create new communities. The vast nature of the internet allows for individuals to expand beyond the physical parameters of their departments and institutions to meet new people. In this way, one expands their network while also avoiding the conference fees that are often prohibitive. We provide junior members of the academy with professional information regarding conduct that is not officially taught within graduate programs but has real consequences for success. Colloquially termed as the "hidden curriculum" of graduate school, these skills are essential to master. The Twitter accounts of social scientists like Kim Yi Dionne, Jess Calarco, Raul Pacheco-Vega, Mirya Holman, and Emily Farris have devoted significant time to demystifying the hidden curriculum, while countless others ask questions, share insights, and generate discourse around the hidden curriculum daily. For graduate students with more limited means, discussions of the hidden curriculum on social media open up new pathways of access for first-generation, BIPOC, low-income, and Global South students. Moreover, personal relationships are not siloed from professional ones, as friends can be key readers for a new project or create new connections with professional contacts. In this way, social media can act as a pivotal tool for diversifying political science networks. (For more information on the benefits (and challenges) of engaging on Twitter as a graduate student, see chapter 27. Additionally, Kim et al. (2021) provide a helpful guide for conceptually approaching networking.)

Graduate students often have limited access to information and perspectives on non-academic career paths and opportunities. As members of our collective have pursued different career paths after completing their graduate studies, including both academic and non-academic positions, we have helped provide the support that is often lacking in academia for those pursuing non-academic career paths, such as sharing job opportunities, interview advice, salary negotiation tips, revising resumes, and providing examples of cover letters. We have also remained connected even as we have pursued different career paths, and these connections have provided important perspectives on the relationship between academics and practitioners, highlighting the benefits of collaboration.

When our institutions and our disciplines cannot help us to overcome isolation, one can take to social media to create a new network. The difficulties of graduate school are only exacerbated when one cannot find their own Collective. Finding your group is important not only for handling the challenges of academia, but also remembering that outside of graduate school, you are also a person with emotional and social needs, and finding a means of personal and social fulfillment is imperative for success both within and beyond the discipline.

Creating communities online can be as simple as starting a group chat, a Slack channel, or setting weekly Zoom dates for chatting or coworking. What matters is that these methods of engagement are consistent, and encourage repeated interactions, going beyond one-off interactions in order to foster a true sense of community. For example, one member of our FIRE Collective has gone on to create several shared spaces online in an effort to build community with others facing similar isolation in their fields. She founded Jam3a, an online co-working space based on Slack that connects scholars and practitioners interested in the Middle East and North Africa. Similarly, she has applied this model to other groups to offer a platform that facilitates consistent interactions and community building.

Transforming the Discipline

Too often, efforts to build and nourish the types of communities capable of mitigating academic isolation are dismissed as distractions from the "real" academic work of research. It is not. It is absolutely essential to surviving and thriving in a discipline that is fundamentally designed for the archetype of a cisgender white man with no caregiving responsibilities. This archetype assumes that graduate students and faculty can spend unlimited amounts of time on teaching and research while discouraging boundaries on both time and labor. As such, institutions have implemented paltry support for caregivers as well as historically marginalized students and faculty. Additionally, many institutions continue to strip away the meager financial resources that exist. Collectives help fill in with support, advice, and even financial assistance where these institutions continue to fail.

Such *supportive communities* hold the power to change entire academic trajectories by reshaping who gets to stay in the academy, and who is forced out. It has the power to transform who gets to teach future generations. Building and participating in these spaces is a service to oneself and to the entire discipline. Our core recommendation then is that the discipline takes such service seriously. It is not an optional add-on, or a "nice to have'" feature of a scholar's profile.

For institutions and departments, this means valuing—during hiring and promotion decisions— the service scholars do in creating these spaces. It means supporting student attendance at conferences and actively teaching skills of lateral networking. It means building an expectation that members of your department will participate in external writing groups and support circles.

For individuals, this means allowing yourself time and space to enjoy meeting new people. The best way to find "your people" is to meet as many people as possible. Value each one of them as a human being whose stories and perspectives enrich the world. Don't think of "networking" as a utilitarian expectation, but as an opportunity to make someone else feel valued and welcome. Remember: you are somebody else's people too.

In a scholarly sense, isolation may be inevitable. When you're working at the forefront of human knowledge, you are likely pushing forward the boundary of your tiny section alone. But you are not alone. There are people out there who can understand you, who can support you, who can help you come closer to being the kind of scholar you want to be. And you can help them too. Community, in a very real sense, is the antidote to isolation, and we owe it to ourselves and our discipline to build, value, and support the propagation of such remedies.

References

Anderson, Benedict R. O'G. 1991. *Imagined Communities: Reflections on the Origin and Spread of Nationalism*. Rev. and Extended ed. London ; New York: Verso.

Bloch, Charlotte. 2002. "Managing the Emotions of Competition and Recognition in Academia." *The Sociological Review* 50 (2_suppl): 113–31. https://doi.org/10.1111/j.1467-954X.2002.tb03594.x.

Brown, Nadia E., and David Samuels. 2018. "Beyond the Gender Citation Gap: Comments on Dion, Sumner, and Mitchell." *Political Analysis* 26 (3): 328–30. https://doi.org/10.1017/pan.2018.14.

Devine, Kay, and Karen Hunter. 2016. "Doctoral Students' Emotional Exhaustion and Intentions to Leave Academia." *International Journal of Doctoral Studies* 11: 035–061. https://doi.org/10.28945/3396.

Devine, Patricia G., Patrick S. Forscher, William T.L. Cox, Anna Kaatz, Jennifer Sheridan, and Molly Carnes. 2017. "A Gender Bias Habit-Breaking Intervention Led to Increased Hiring of Female Faculty in STEMM Departments." *Journal of Experimental Social Psychology* 73 (November): 211–15. https://doi.org/10.1016/j.jesp.2017.07.002.

Dion, Michelle L., Jane Lawrence Sumner, and Sara McLaughlin Mitchell. 2018. "Gendered Citation Patterns across Political Science and Social Science Methodology Fields." *Political Analysis* 26 (3): 312–27. https://doi.org/10.1017/pan.2018.12.

Hawkley, Louise C., and John T. Cacioppo. 2010. "Loneliness Matters: A Theoretical and Empirical Review of Consequences and Mechanisms." *Annals of Behavioral Medicine* 40 (2): 218–27. https://doi.org/10.1007/s12160-010-9210-8.

Key, Ellen M., and Jane Lawrence Sumner. 2019. "You Research Like a Girl: Gendered Research Agendas and Their Implications." *PS: Political Science & Politics* 52 (4): 663–68. https://doi.org/10.1017/S1049096519000945.

Kim, Seo-Young Silvia, Hannah Lebovits, and Sarah Shugars. 2021. "Networking 101 for Graduate Students: Building a Bigger Table." *PS: Political Science & Politics*, September, 1–6. https://doi.org/10.1017/S1049096521001025.

Langin, Katie. 2021. "'On the Verge of a Breakdown.' Report Highlights Women Academics' Pandemic Challenges." *Science*, March 9, 2021. https://www.science.org/content/article/verge-breakdown-report-highlights-women-academics-pandemic-challenges.

O'Brien, Diana Z. 2020. "Navigating Political Science as a Woman." *PS: Political Science & Politics* 53 (2): 315–17. https://doi.org/10.1017/S1049096519002154.

Willoughby-Herard, Tiffany. 2020. "Conferencing Is Not a Luxury and Neither Is the Scholarly Life of Our Future Colleagues." *PS: Political Science & Politics* 53 (1): 146–48. https://doi.org/10.1017/

S1049096519001082.

64

Health and Well-being in Graduate School: Preventing Burnout

Thomas S. Benson[1] & Christina Boyes[2]

1. University of Delaware 2. Centro de Investigación y Docencia Económicas

KEYWORDS: Burnout, Health Challenges.

What Do You Need to Know About Health and Well-Being in Graduate School?

The Problem

Health and well-being are essential for political science graduate students who are aspiring to produce high-quality work, engage effectively in the profession, maintain healthy relationships and work-life balance, and—most importantly—be physically and mentally well. Unfortunately, Western society is experiencing a "mental health crisis" and "epidemic of work stress" (Väänänen and Varje 2019, 37). The discipline of political science is no exception to this (Lau and Pretorius 2019, 38). Overwork culture drives many graduate students to sacrifice health and well-being due to high workloads, isolation, competition for research funding, pressure to publish, career and financial insecurity, and lack of a support system (Lau and Pretorius 2019, 39). Additional duties include the pursuit of teaching excellence, community engagement, and managing familial expectations. (For a discussion about the culture of overwork in political science, see chapter 53.)

Collectively, these duties have led to many graduate students in the discipline to adopt their professional status as a form of identity that becomes all-consuming. This identity establishes an "exaggerated sense of duty," in which graduate students only feel they can relax once their duties have been completed but the "desk never becomes empty" and housework is seemingly never-ending (Pirker-Binder 2016, 108). By failing to conform to the norms constructed by the discipline, students subsequently feel as though their identity is being threatened (Dick 2019, 163-164). Those who experience their identity being threatened may encounter imposter syndrome – feeling as though they are inadequate and cannot achieve the incessant demands and high expectations placed upon them because they believe themselves to be frauds (Dick 2019, 171) (for a larger discussion, see chapter 50). Ultimately, then, political science graduate students can feel deflated, experience burnout, chronic stress, depressive symptoms, fatigue, irritability, suicidal ideation, and anxiety (Väänänen and Varje 2019, 38; Lau and Pretorius 2019, 40) – all of which can undermine health and well-being.

Stress from professional and personal demands and expectations attributed to the norms of the discipline can be understood as the "perceptions or feelings a person experiences when a particular environment taxes or exceeds the person's available personal or social coping resources" (Lau 2019, 48). Such stress is often triggered by "uncontrollable aversive challenge[s]" (Fink 2016, 4), including anxiety regarding conference presentations or teaching undergraduate students, conducting fieldwork, or sharing critical thoughts regarding political science literature or data in a classroom, among other things.

These stressful and anxiety-inducing situations can have physiological and cardiovascular consequences and are each influenced by a student's "perception of their ability to cope with the stressor," thereby suggesting that stress is subjective (Fink 2016, 5; Väänänen and Varje 2019, 39, 52). Stress and burnout also manifest as tiredness, muscle tension, and headaches.

The experience of health challenges during graduate study is normal. This does not demean the experiences of graduate students but acknowledges them. Experiencing these issues does not make you unfit to be a graduate student. Generally, graduate students are more likely to experience depression and anxiety than the general population (Evans et al. 2018, 282), and some have reported low quality of life, poor health, or feeling disconnected, depressed and overwhelmed by their workload (Yusuf et al. 2020, 468). There is a "mental health crisis" in academia (Lau and Pretorius 2019, 38). One study found that 15.8% of graduate students in political science at seven U.S. universities expressed thoughts of suicide in two weeks prior to the survey, 30% were depressed, and about 32% were experiencing anxiety (Almasri, Read, and Vendeweerdt 2021). (For larger discussions about these crises, see chapters 64, 68, and 69.) Given these challenges, we provide some potential solutions in the following subsection with greater emphasis on solutions in the final section.

Potential Solutions

Do not suffer in silence. Your adviser and graduate director should support your well-being, but they will not know you are struggling if you remain silent (Lau and Pretorius 2019, 39). Most faculty are supportive and open; speak to them about well-being, burnout, stress, anxiety, and imposter syndrome. It is likely that they—who were once graduate students—experienced the same issues. Similarly, you should speak openly with your peers—they are likely experiencing the same issues (Lau 2019, 49). Together, you can amplify concerns to your department or administration and address them as a collective, should there be lackluster resources available on campus (e.g., therapy, counseling, mental well-being services). If you have an assistantship, you likely have health insurance provided by your employer—if this is the case and your institution does not provide adequate support, consider off-campus resources. (For further information about mental health resources, see chapters 68-69. For additional commentary on academic isolation, see chapters 63 and 68.)

Being a graduate student in political science is job training in teaching, research and studying. Establish a work-life balance at the outset of your graduate program to keep your health and well-being on track. Maintaining work-life balance will likely have a positive impact on your quality of life (Yusuf et al. 2020, 470-471). As part of this, try different methods of note-taking, tracking deadlines, setting short- and long-term goals to keep motivated, building a support network (faculty, peers, staff, external mentors), identifying helpful resources, exercising, getting adequate sleep, going outside to get fresh air and sunlight, maintaining a healthy diet, staying hydrated, and being efficient with your time. However, be wary of advocates that call only for micro-level solutions as the culture of overwork is systemic, thereby warranting broader change in political science departments and academia as a whole (Väänänen and Varje 2019, 51). (For additional thoughts on sustaining your academic career for the long-term, see chapter 62.)

Why Does Health and Well-Being Matter in Graduate School?

The first step to developing an understanding of your health and well-being is to get tested and treated if you suspect you are experiencing any health challenge, be it chronic (e.g., chronic stress, back pain) or temporary (e.g., panic attack, sore throat). Identify any particular issues (e.g., OCD, ADHD, anxiety, depression, allergies, visionary challenges, chronic illness), so you can address them and prevent them from interfering with your quality of life. Remember: mental health is health too, and healthcare is confidential in many countries, including the U.S. Graduate students should not be concerned about stigma resulting from diagnoses, especially international students who may come from cultures that stigmatize mental or physical health issues. Recognize that you have basic needs as a human being and develop coping resources to maintain your well-being (Muniroh 2019, 155).

Poor health can adversely affect your capacity to work and study. This can further reinforce stress that you may already be experiencing (Lau and Pretorius 2019, 39), provoking a cyclical process of chronic stress (Lau 2019, 48) and sleep deprivation that can lead to "daytime sleepiness and cognitive impairments." Graduate students who reduce sleep to maximize study and work time can experience negative impacts on their success and quality of life (Lau 2019, 54; Calvo and Gutiérrez-García 2016, 143). However, not all stress is bad. Acute short-term stress (e.g., minutes or hours) can have some beneficial effects, such as memory consolidation (Calvo and Gutiérrez-García 2016, 142).

Burnout, conversely, is especially bad. Burnout has been described as being "comparable to a house that burns and consumes itself from the inside, without always leaving visible traces on the outside" (Kirouac 2019, 178). It has also been defined as a "transient mental illness" and a "state of fatigue or frustration" that stems from failure to meet your expectations (Kirouac 2019, 181-182). Symptoms of burnout include loss of positivity, decrease in the feeling of personal accomplishment, emotional exhaustion, and reduced productivity (Kirouac 2019, 182). Students who excessively compete with their peers may compound these issues by exacerbating imposter syndrome (Lau 2019, 50) (see, also, chapter 50).

Health challenges differ across groups. Some graduate students manage their own health and that of others (e.g., care-taking responsibilities for partners, parents, and dependents; see chapter 16). Issues vary across academic years too, with some third- and fourth-year students reporting comparatively higher levels of stress than students in their initial years (Rico and Bunge 2021, 180). This could be because of the increased focus on dissertation work, fieldwork, and job applications (on top of regular duties, such as teaching and research) compared to the class workload and research and teaching obligations for graduate students in their initial years (Rico and Bunge 2021, 180).

Due to poor cultural understanding by some healthcare providers, BIPOC and international student populations may experience misdiagnoses—this may also be problematic for international students who do not have English as a first language—that subsequently disincentivize future use of mental and physical health services (APA 2017a, 2). For example, many Asians are less likely to use mental health services compared to other racial and ethnic groups (APA 2017a, 2). Some populations are more likely to experience persistent depression, post-traumatic stress disorder and alcohol dependence (APA 2017a, 1) which can be exacerbated by avoiding treatment.

Women are more likely than men to experience PTSD, anxiety, suicide, depression, and eating disorders (APA 2017c, 1-2). Barriers to women's treatment include stigma, inability to find time (e.g., time off work, childcare, transportation) to seek help, and lack of insurance (APA 2017c, 2). Additionally, LGBTQIA+ individuals are more than twice as likely as their heterosexual counterparts to experience a mental disorder in their lifetime, and 2.5 times more likely to experience depression, anxiety, or substance misuse (APA 2017b, 2). Many report experiencing stigma and discrimination when using health services, which leads to delayed or foregoing necessary healthcare (APA 2017b, 3).

What Can you do About your Health and Well-Being?

Prevent Health Issues

Graduate school is a time when pressure is high and competition between cohorts and colleagues can be daunting. In the first year, anxiety and imposter syndrome typically complicate the scene. Later, qualifying papers, comprehensive exams (see chapter 12), conducting fieldwork (see chapter 20), and navigating post-comprehensive exam expectations each present their own challenges. While each major milestone in a graduate school program is challenging in different ways, being prepared can help prevent physical and mental health struggles from interfering with your performance.

One of the first steps to staying healthy in graduate school is preventing health problems and getting yourself tested if you suspect any problems. In your first year, identify existing resources and befriend those who are in the same position as you and commiserate with each other. However, do not let competition drive your interactions. There is no reason to compare yourself with others. Instead, recognize your own limits and focus on doing better every day. Focusing on the performance of your peers will likely only lead to you believing you are unfit to be a political science graduate student.

If you need to access support resources, on-campus facilities are likely to include stress, work-life balance, and productivity workshops, nutritionists, counseling, therapy, gyms, pools, and in some cases, short-term programs that feature emotional support dogs at the end of semester or recreational opportunities to destress. Take advantage of these resources!

Most faculty have faced their own health struggles and will view self-care as a sensible choice. However, not every department is supportive of student health struggles. If you are uncomfortable looking within your department for support, consider talking with faculty in other departments with whom you share good rapport. Additionally, within the field, the American Political Science Association offers many resources online, and conferences provide good opportunities for networking and identifying additional resources.

If your campus does not offer many health resources or recreational opportunities, does the surrounding community? Can you hike, bike, or run? Are there local health clubs available? Integrating into the community can also help you escape the stress of graduate school. Sometimes, being surrounded by others facing similar struggles can be beneficial, but it can also amplify anxiety around milestones like comprehensive exams. Not everyone is comfortable with public activities that are health-focused, which is fine. If you prefer not to utilize local resources, there are several options online too. Bloggers such as Mirya Holman[1] and Raul Pacheco-Vega[2] are accomplished political scientists who work to pave the way for future and early career academics by sharing tips on writing, reading, and organizing notes, as well as providing inspiration, motivation, and community for their readers. You can also find online support communities on Twitter, Facebook, and Instagram.

There are many independent activities you can do to reduce your risk of health issues. Several apps can help you cultivate a healthy routine for better academic productivity, such as: Calm; Headspace; iStudiez (primarily for undergraduates but still useful); Focus To-Do; Google Tasks and Calendar; Habit; FLIP; and Flora - Green Focus. Beyond apps, productivity methods such as Pomodoro, Eat the Frog, or the 3 Box Method/Ivy Lee can be useful. Many graduate students find using daily planners, to-do lists, and block scheduling helpful. The key to productivity is to find something that works for you that you use consistently.

If You Are Already Struggling

Much of what applies for prevention applies when you are already struggling. The preceding section offers some ideas that may be useful. There are additional ways to address existing health problems, which we focus on in this section.

Before making any changes to your routine, remember that sweeping changes may work for a bit but can be too difficult to maintain. Little, sustainable changes may be easier to continue in the long-term. Establishing accountability mechanisms and letting your support network know you are struggling can help. If you are new to your program, make sure that your Director of Graduate Studies and your adviser (or a professor you feel safe confiding in) are aware of your struggles. Also, keep relevant administrative personnel in the loop to ensure that you do not miss key deadlines. (For more information about academic department personnel, see chapter 8.)

Physical and mental health are impacted by nutrition, yet food insecurity is often an issue for graduate students (Coffino et al. 2021). If you are food insecure, look for on- and off-campus food pantries and check to see if your university has on-campus dining or food hall cards for student financial aid recipients. Healthy eating, regardless of how apparently healthy you seem, can be beneficial, helping resolve existing health issues and preventing further health problems.

If you are dealing with stress, anxiety, depression, or imposter syndrome, you are not alone. Health issues are prevalent among graduate students. Sometimes, sharing your struggles with your peers alleviates issues like imposter syndrome by creating a sense of belonging (Lau 2019, 53). Everyone struggles. Hearing you are not facing imposter syndrome alone can be cathartic. Many students also benefit from actively expressing and thinking through their problems, either orally, visually, or in written form. These creative processes may help you work through problems that can be resolved without external intervention (Muniroh 2019, 116). (For a larger discussion about imposter syndrome, see chapter 50.)

Regularly practiced mindfulness (potentially with the assistance of apps (e.g., Wysa, Headspace, or Smiling Mind)), self-compassion, support networks, counseling, regular exercise, good sleep habits, and a balanced diet can improve intrapersonal well-being (Lau and Pretorius 2019, 42; Lau 2019, 52). Having a life outside of the department is also a good way to improve well-being and decrease stress and anxiety. External friendship networks can remove you from the stress of graduate school and help you maintain a work-life balance. Finally, by integrating with your community and spending more time with friends and family or people who share your recreational interests, you can also tackle imposter syndrome through shared experiences of belonging (Lau 2019, 53).

Endnotes

1   See https://miryaholman.substack.com/

2   See http://www.raulpacheco.org/blog/

References

Almasri, Nasir., Blair Read., and Clara Vandeweerdt. 2021. "Mental Health and the PhD: Insights and Implications for Political Science." *PS: Political Science & Politics*: 1-7. doi: https://doi.org/10.1017/S1049096521001396.

American Psychiatric Association (APA). 2017a. "Mental Health Disparities: Diverse Populations." *APA* [website], December 12, 2021. https://www.psychiatry.org/psychiatrists/cultural-competency/education/mental-health-facts.

American Psychiatric Association (APA). 2017b. "Mental Health Facts for Lesbian, Gay, Bisexual, Transgender, Queer/Questioning (LGBTQ)." *APA* [website], December 12, 2021. https://www.psychiatry.org/psychiatrists/cultural-competency/education/mental-health-facts.

American Psychiatric Association (APA). 2017c. "Mental Health Facts for Women." *APA* [website], December 12, 2021. https://www.psychiatry.org/psychiatrists/cultural-competency/education/mental-health-facts.

Calvo, Manuel, G., and Aída Gutiérrez-García. 2016. "Cognition and Stress." *In Stress: Concepts, Cognition, Emotion, and Behavior: Handbook of Stress Series*, ed. George Fink, 139-144. Elsevier: Academic Press.

Coffino, Jaime A., Samantha P. Spoor., Rae D. Drach., and Julia M. Hormones. 2021. "Food Insecurity Among Graduate Students: Prevalence and Association with Depression, Anxiety and Stress." *Public Health Nutrition* 24(7): 1889-1894. doi: https://doi.org/10.1017/S1368980020002001.

Dick, Penny. 2019. "Understanding Stress as a Form of Institutional Maintenance and Disruption Work." *In Stress and Suffering at Work: The Role of Culture and Society*, ed. Marc Loriol, 155-173. Cham, Switzerland: Palgrave Macmillan.

Evans, Teresa M., Lindsay Bira., Jazmin B. Gastelum., L. T. Weiss., and Nathan L. Vanderford. 2018. "Evidence for a Mental Health Crisis in Graduate Education." *Nature Biotechnology* 36: 282-284. doi: https://doi.org/10.1038/nbt.4089.

Fink, George. 2016. "Stress, Definitions, Mechanisms, and Effects Outlined: Lessons from Anxiety." In *Stress: Concepts, Cognition, Emotion, and Behavior: Handbook of Stress Series*, ed. George Fink, 3-11. Elsevier: Academic Press.

Kirouac, Laurie. 2019. "Burnout in Quebec. Behind Psychological Suffering, Shifting in Social Representation and Relation to Work." In *Stress and Suffering at Work: The Role of Culture and Society*, ed. Marc Loriol, 177-190. Cham, Switzerland: Palgrave Macmillan.

Muniroh, Siti. 2019. "Maintaining Emotional Wellbeing for Doctoral Students: Indonesian Students' Mechanism of Thinking Out Loud." In *Wellbeing in Doctoral Education: Insights and Guidance from the Student Experience*, ed. Lynette Pretorious, 113-126. Singapore: Springer.

Lau, Ricky W. K. 2019. "You Are Not Your PhD: Managing Stress During Doctoral Candidature." In *Wellbeing in Doctoral Education: Insights and Guidance from the Student Experience*, ed. Lynette Pretorious, 47-58. Singapore: Springer.

Lau, Ricky W. K., and Lynette Pretorius. 2019. "Intrapersonal Wellbeing and the Academic Mental Health Crisis." In *Wellbeing in Doctoral Education: Insights and Guidance from the Student Experience*, ed. Lynette Pretorious, 37-45. Singapore: Springer.

Pirker-Binder, Ingrid. 2016. "The Working Human—The Exhausted Human." In *Mindful Prevention of Burnout in Workplace Health Management*, ed. Ingrid Pirker-Binder, 107-123. Cham, Switzerland: Springer.

Rico, Yvette., and Eduardo L. Bunge. 2021. "Stress and Burnout in Psychology Doctoral Students." *Psychology, Health & Medicine* 26(2): 177-183. doi: 10.1080/13548506.2020.1842471.

Väänänen, Ari., and Pekka Varje. 2019. "Epidemiological Transition and the Emergence of Mental Discomfort." In *Stress and Suffering at Work: The Role of Culture and Society*, ed. Marc Loriol, 37-54. Cham, Switzerland: Palgrave Macmillan.

Yusuf, Juita-Elena (Wie)., Marina Saitgalina., and David W. Chapman. 2020. "Work-life Balance and Well-being of Graduate Students." *Journal of Public Affairs Education* 26(4): 458-483. doi: https://doi.org/10.1080/15236803.2020.1771990.

65 | Things that Can Go "Wrong": Finding Our Own Way in Graduate School

Misbah Hyder[1], Dana El Kurd[2], Felicity Gray[3], Devon Cantwell[4],
& Alisson Rowland[1]

1. University of California, Irvine 2. University of Richmond 3. Australian National University

4. University of Ottawa

KEYWORDS: Structural Challenges, Mentorship, Faculty, Transferring.

Introduction

Graduate school was not designed for most of us. Students from marginalized backgrounds (BIPOC, LGBTQ+, certain socioeconomic backgrounds, those with disabilities) are less likely to have information about graduate school and academia, making them more likely to face challenges in navigating gatekeeping and moving through program requirements. Such students may also be at institutions that are unsupportive or hostile. While facing these obstacles, it might feel like something has gone "wrong." This chapter is intended to challenge that framing and guide you through these issues.

We start by acknowledging the various structural issues within graduate school and academia that are often the primary contributors to graduate student experiences "going wrong." These include faculty mentorship, hostility, and financial precarity. Then, we outline ways that plans might change for students, and how you can make choices when: changing your dissertation, subfield(s), and adviser; transferring programs; working additional jobs; taking a leave of absence; and caring for your mental health. As a supplement to this chapter, we have created a handout[1] to help you weigh options as you're navigating these forks in the road.

Structural Challenges of Graduate School

Faculty Mentorship

As Calarco (2020) notes, faculty mentorship is key to success graduate school. But it really is the luck of the draw whether you have an adviser that takes mentorship seriously, is not overworked or overcommitted, and has the professional ethics necessary to recognize this part of their job as an obligation. As a result, students may be susceptible to under mentoring, which seriously impacts their ability to graduate, perform well on the job market, and develop the networks necessary for success.

Marginalized students are less likely to know academic norms—the 'hidden curriculum'—and thus might not realize how much mentorship a faculty adviser owes them as part of their job. The hidden curriculum of academia is made clear for students with proper mentorship, whereas others learn, rather inefficiently, who to connect with, how to present at a conference and take advantage of the experience, where to publish, etc. (Barham and Wood 2021, Calarco 2020). Strong mentors often advocate for their students, facilitate funding, and identify opportunities to publish.

Students might also accept poor or inappropriate working conditions and not recognize that they are being exploited by faculty or administration (see chapter 53 on overwork and chapter 67 on rest). Much like other students in broader university settings, graduate students from marginalized backgrounds are less likely to ask for help, whether that be seeking feedback or extra funding. Alternatively, students from more privileged backgrounds will demand resources, which allows them to perform and produce at a higher level and have a more positive graduate school experience. This inequity in access and treatment often leads to the mistaken impression that marginalized students are just not on par when, in reality, some students have been set up to succeed while others have been left to falter (Calarco 2018).

It is important for you to know that these inequities exist and to recognize what students are owed by their mentors in their department. Departments accepted you on the basis that they would provide such training, oftentimes in exchange for underpaid labor. This understanding can help students seek solutions if they feel they are being short-changed in this area rather than endure such dynamics.

Faculty Hostility

Faculty can, unfortunately, show not only a lack of care for their students but also outright hostility. Racism and sexism in the academy are widely documented. BIPOC academics have discussed at length their experiences, and the "presumed incompetence" that colors their interactions with their colleagues (Muhs et al. 2012) (see chapters 54, 57, and 60 on concerns for underrepresented minorities, international students, and first-generation students, respectively).

Political science is no different; reports of racial and sexual harassment are continuous (Nair and Wang 2021, Flaherty 2018, Merhson and Walsh 2015). Hostility towards marginalized students can manifest directly, with harsh comments, aggressive or demeaning behavior, and general disrespect. Hostility can also manifest more indirectly, by isolating students, withholding financial support, and smearing their reputation within the department and within the discipline.

Dynamics between faculty members can also negatively impact your trajectory. Personality issues and competition between faculty can sometimes leave students in the awkward position of navigating grievances that have nothing to do with them, just to complete the requirements of their program.

Financial Precarity

The intellectual, social, and political challenges of graduate school are often compounded by material and economic pressures. Many graduate students are awarded stipends that fail to cover basic living expenses; this financial precarity then exacerbates other stressors (Fernandez et al. 2019, Acker and Haque 2014). A lack of support further entrenches economic, social, and racial inequalities, creating barriers to entry for those without access to familial financial support from pursuing graduate education. For those that do make it through the narrow financial door, the stipends provided come with strings attached, such as strict time limits on completion of a program, after which point graduate students receive no support, or are even required to pay the university themselves (Wong 2018).

Ultimately, a structural shift in the sector is necessary. Universities in North America (and globally) increasingly operate through a financialized business model that prioritizes revenue over the needs of students (Cellura, Akers, and Malas 2021). Part of this trend has been increasing reliance on a precarious workforce of graduate students, and this contingency is undoubtedly harmful. At the same time, contingency enables some collective leverage that is being used by students across the country.[2] Assessing and identifying how universities are accommodating (or curtailing) graduate student mobilizations for rights at work can be an instructive litmus test for prospective students (see chapter 33 on graduate worker unions).

A Note to Department Faculty, Chairs, and Directors

Oftentimes, the narratives about graduate school follow a linear trajectory that does not fit most graduate students' experiences in their graduate programs, and therefore, places unfair pressures on students. When advising graduate students, we urge you to take stock of various ways students have moved through your program, their financial situation, and how department climate contributes to their trajectories. Survey current and previous (graduated and non-graduated) students and ask if they always hit milestones within the timeline you've set or if they've changed trajectories. This way, you can ground your feedback to your future students based on the real experiences of students in your program.

Navigating Forks in the Road

Changing Dissertation Plans

The most common change that students will experience in graduate school is changing dissertation plans—which happens often. When your current adviser isn't working out, your methodology doesn't suit your questions, a pandemic derails your fieldwork, your research actually fits a different subfield, and/or you're uncomfortable with your research but don't know why—what do you do?

First, remember that your discomfort is often a product of a broader issue. If your adviser is hostile toward your work, it's very likely not about you or your topic. Do they have methodological preferences? Are there geographic regions they're more comfortable advising? Are there biases that you can identify in their own work and how they engage with students? Talk with the adviser's current and previous advisees—notice who they are and identify trends (what topics and methodologies they use) and whether you see yourself engaging with that work. If not, then you know that you might want to seek advising elsewhere.

If you're planning to change something about your dissertation, be aware that you will face gatekeeping. If you're choosing to move from a positivist methodological framework to an interpretivist one, for example, you'll need to communicate your research interests in interpretivist terminology to a potential adviser. If you're choosing to move from International Relations to Comparative Politics, you'll need to locate yourself within the authors and debates in your new subfield. Students working on your new research of interest can help you translate your thoughts to ensure faculty hear your research better.

Changing Advisers

Changing advisers is also a very common experience in graduate school. This might be: (1) voluntary, as you may change your dissertation topic (see above) or other reasons, including faculty hostility, and (2) involuntary, as your adviser take a position elsewhere or has passed away.

If you want to voluntarily change your adviser, oftentimes, it is mutually recognized if an adviser situation is not working out. If you face hesitation from the new adviser, this is likely due to interfaculty dynamics previously discussed. To help communicate the change to both faculty, it's important to "sell" your research to make it evident to others that it makes sense for your questions.

However, sometimes, an adviser may be possessive or otherwise hostile about changing. While this is rarer, it is, unfortunately, a reality. Before you decide to leave your current adviser, you should assess which outcome is likely by trusting your gut and speaking to others, including former or current advisees or the graduate director. Remember that other faculty may not clearly say that your current adviser is possessive or hostile due to collegiality norms. However, they may say something indirectly: "I'm concerned that you might not be able to finish your dissertation with" that individual, or that individual "may not be the right fit for you or your project." In some departments, you may be "locked-in" to an adviser after a certain point. You should be sure to research this policy as early within your department as possible.

If you are involuntarily forced to change advisers (i.e., the faculty member leaves), a few things can help soften the blow of the transition. Even if they have left your department/university, your current adviser may stay on the committee to help with continuity; clear this by both your department and current adviser. If they cannot (or don't want to), they may have ideas for other faculty that would be suitable replacements. If your adviser is leaving the institution, you should try to set up a transition meeting where your current and new adviser can get on the same page on your dissertation progress.

Working Beyond Graduate School

Students manage financial pressures in different ways, often through part-time departmental assistant-ships. For others, economic pressures can be so heavy that—when allowed by university policy—students will either pause programs to pursue full- or part-time employment in other sectors, or attempt to complete full-time graduate studies while working. Many students effectively leverage their subject-area expertise to pursue work in policy and practice related to their research. This hedging can lead to new research insights, deepening expertise, and creating new research networks. But in attempting to stay afloat financially, we risk sinking with the weight of these commitments, leaving little space for the creative thinking and rest that is so necessary to successfully and safely complete graduate school.

What can we do to stay financially afloat? This kind of advice is not new, but perhaps it bears repeating: being proactive from the outset is important. Be clear-eyed about costs, make a budget, and identify potential financial pressure points. For most students, supplementing one's stipend is necessary, and diversifying avenues for financial support can remove some of the pressure. Sign up for grant and funding notifications from your university and other repositories that collate this data. Connect with other graduate students in your field to learn about available supplementary funding. And ultimately, don't be afraid to pursue your graduate studies in a way that works for you—even if that means pausing your program or going part-time to pursue other kinds of work.

Taking a Leave of Absence

Sometimes, you might want to take a step back from graduate school. But make sure you remember one thing: this leave of absence is not an additional year of graduate school—it's a break from graduate school.

Each university structures its options for leaves differently; some consider parental leave (maternity and paternity) to be separate from a leave of absence, some consider medical leave to be in the same category as personal leave. Depending on the type available, the terms will differ. You might lose your stipend, on-campus graduate housing, and university-funded healthcare, for example, during your leave period (or, in some cases, it might jeopardize those entitlements after you return). Furthermore, for international students, your visa might not allow you to take a leave at all.

If you are considering this option, we highly recommend you speak with anyone on your campus who is familiar with your funding, including your department's director of graduate studies or other administrators who know about the funding structure of your program (a graduate student coordinator for instance). Be very direct about the questions that you ask and get any guarantees in writing. For example, if the university allows you to retain the year of funding that you are not using during your leave and adds it to your normative time, get that in writing. Don't hesitate to triple-confirm information about deadlines, funding, or stipulations post-leave—the university will not hesitate to retract those entitlements from you if it has the opportunity!

Transferring Graduate Programs

You might consider transferring out of your program due to program fit, a shift in research interest, departmental dynamics, regional boundaries (e.g., family considerations, diversity), program ranking, and many other reasons. Although transferring is often not discussed publicly, it is more common than people think!

Ask yourself first: why do you want to transfer, and why did you want to go to graduate school in the first place? Depending on the reason, it may not be the best option available to you. If you're transferring to be closer to family living elsewhere, you might consider a leave of absence or finishing your program remotely. Additionally, your goals may have changed, and you instead decide that you no longer want to be in graduate school. "Mastering out"[3] of your program can also be a good option. Answering these two questions will be useful for your transfer application and conversations with potential new faculty.

The timing of your transfer must also be considered. If you transfer early in your program, you may not add (as much) time in graduate school, and the transfer may be smoother. If you transfer later in your program, you may be able to negotiate qualifying exams, or you may carry more knowledge and research skills, making you an ideal candidate to work on a grant or for university-funded scholarships.

One of the challenges of transferring, depending on your situation, is obtaining letters of recommendation from at least two, and likely three, faculty. Identify allies in your department (faculty often outside of your field but are sympathetic to your situation). Although it is best to get letters from faculty in your current program, sometimes that is not an option. If there are no allies in your department to provide letters, you can reach out to faculty at another institution who does similar research and offer to collaborate on a project. Building networks through Twitter, conferences, and virtual communities can help you identify faculty for this purpose and programs to transfer into (see chapter 21 on how to conference and chapter 27 on academic Twitter). If your research is interdisciplinary, faculty from a different department at your university may have overlapping topics.

Caring for Your Mental Health

While graduate school can be a time for you to grow and thrive, it can come at a cost to your mental health (Forrester 2021). The financial precarity of graduate school, added pressure of balancing familial and personal commitments, and persistent structural inequities can all be very taxing (Macintyre et al. 2018).

Limited access to certain resources in departments or universities can slow your degree progress and can cause undue stress and imposter syndrome. Because of this, it is important to assess the resources offered by different campuses to support students and to make sure they speak to a wide range of academic, professional, and personal challenges that may arise.

If you do not feel adequately supported or that the barriers to completion are becoming too high, you can check in with your adviser, department chair, or other university officials and discuss available options. This could include additional resources tailored toward your specific needs, such as a career counselor or therapist, deferral, or even transferring to a different program/university (see chapter 69 on counseling and other resources). There is no shame in taking advantage of the resources you need to thrive and make sure to prioritize yourself in whatever way makes sense to you. This will take time and possibly multiple tries, but it is critical for your long-term growth.

Conclusion

Graduate school can feel isolating, but it is important to remember that those that have come before you, and those that join after you, also navigate through similar struggles. Building communities with others can help combat this isolation (see chapter 63 on overcoming academic isolation). Reach out early and often to individuals you have connections with—identify faculty allies and reach out to graduate students with diverse experiences. This can help ensure you get a broad view of possible graduate school and career trajectories.

Ultimately, this chapter is meant to equip you with knowledge of how "things that go wrong" are often not in your control and when some aspects might be, how you can navigate those forks in the road. We want to emphasize that making changes within your graduate career trajectory is part of learning from graduate school. In fact, we'd dare to say that, by observing and adapting to your circumstances, as well as building curiosity, you're doing something right! Find your own way in graduate school and pay it forward when you succeed.

Takeaways

You're here to learn; changing your topic and plans is completely fine and part of learning. Know that gatekeeping is common within academia—you're not doing anything wrong.
Not everyone comes to graduate school with certain privileges, including financial stability and coming from academic families, which pose financial constraints and different sets of obstacles as you learn the hidden curriculum of academia.
Departmental dynamics are often beyond your control. Ideally, make sure there are multiple faculty that align with your interests and identify allies.
Reach out to previous and current graduate students in departments to which you're applying (first-time or transferring). Note: (1) types of students in the program, (2) who graduates, and (3) who places. If you're in your program, reach out to those graduate students to strategize how to navigate challenges you're facing.
Facing obstacles can feel isolating, but you're not alone. If you face issues, you're not necessarily stuck with your situation—there are alternative options and sources of support.

Endnotes

1   Link to handout "Navigating Forks in the Road: Weighing Options and Question Guide": https://bit.ly/NavigatingOptionsGuide

2   See here a collection of articles on grad-student unions by The Chronicle of Higher Education: https://www.chronicle.com/package/grad-student-unions/

3   "Mastering out" means that you are leaving the PhD program after completing coursework (and likely other) requirements and have thus earned a master's degree in your enrolled program.

References

Acker, S., & Haque, E. (2014). "The struggle to make sense of doctoral study." *Higher Education Research & Development*, 34(2), 229–241.

Barham, E., & Wood, C. (2021). "Teaching the Hidden Curriculum in Political Science." *PS: Political Science & Politics*, 1-5.

Calarco, J. (2018) *Negotiating Opportunities: How the Middle Class Secures Advantages in School*. Oxford University Press.

--------. (2020) *A Field Guide to Graduate School: Uncovering the Hidden Curriculum*. Princeton University Press.

Cellura, P., Akers, C., & Malas, M. (2021). *The Financialization of Higher Education: At the University of Cincinnati. Roosevelt Institute*. Retrieved December 15, 2021, from https://rooseveltinstitute.org/publications/financialization-of-higher-education-university-of-cincinnati/

Fernandez, C., Webster, J., & Cornett, A. (2019). "Studying on Empty: A Qualitative Study of Low Food Security among College Students." *Trellis Research Series on Collegiate Financial Security & Academic Performance*. Trellis Company. https://eric.ed.gov/?id=ED601258

Flaherty, C. (2018). "Editor of prestigious political science journal uses website to deny harassment allegations." (n.d.). Retrieved December 15, 2021, from https://www.insidehighered.com/

news/2018/04/19/editor-prestigious-political-science-journal-uses-website-deny-harassment

Forrester, N. (2021). "Mental health of graduate students sorely overlooked." *Nature*, 595(7865), 135–137.

Macintyre, A., Ferris, D., Gonçalves, B., & Quinn, N. (2018). "What has economics got to do with it? The impact of socioeconomic factors on mental health and the case for collective action." *Palgrave Communications*, 4(1), 1–5.

Mershon, C., & Walsh, D. (2015). "How Political Science Can Be More Diverse: Introduction." *PS: Political Science & Politics*, 48(3), 441–444.

Muhs, G. G. y, Niemann, Y. F., González, C. G., & Harris, A. P. (Eds.). (2012). *Presumed Incompetent: The Intersections of Race and Class for Women in Academia*. University Press of Colorado.

Nair, M., and Wang, A. (2021). "Women Harassed by Domínguez Say Harvard's Investigatory Procedures Remain Insufficient | News |" *The Harvard Crimson*. (n.d.). Retrieved December 15, 2021, from https://www.thecrimson.com/article/2021/2/12/victims-criticize-dominguez-review/

Wong, A. (2018, November 27). "Graduate School Can Have Terrible Effects on People's Mental Health." *The Atlantic*. https://www.theatlantic.com/education/archive/2018/11/anxiety-depression-mental-health-graduate-school/576769/

66

Should I stay or Should I Go? Making the Decision to Leave your Graduate Program

Carmen J. Burlingame[1]

1. Samaritan Health and Living Center

KEYWORDS: Dynamic Factors, Adviser, Director of Graduate Program, Stopping the Clock.

Introduction

In 2020, the National Science Foundation's Survey of Earned Doctorates estimated that 637 individuals graduated from US colleges and universities with a PhD in political science (National Science Foundation, 2021). The attrition rate of individuals in doctoral programs is harder to calculate, though it is estimated that across all PhD programs, less than 75% of individuals who enter the program complete their doctorate (Council of Graduate Studies, 2021). Specifically, within the Political Science discipline, PhD program completion at the Top 20 Political Science programs (according to the National Research Council), is estimated to be between 40-50% of enrolled students (The Ohio State University, 2021). The proportion of women who graduate with a PhD in political science is fewer, with approximately 35% of women graduating from a Top 20 Political Science PhD program (The Ohio State University, 2021).

Despite attrition rates being higher than completion rates of political science PhD programs, there are nuances that can help individuals contemplating leaving their program successfully exit. While it seems oxymoronic to consider best-practices for not completing your degree, there are several factors to explore in your decision. This chapter will provide a roadmap for political science students considering leaving graduate school and resources to navigate the world beyond academia.

Reasons to Leave

You are not the same person you were when you applied for your program, and you will continue to have many dynamic factors in your life as the program continues. Many of your experiences will be like others in your cohort and it is through forming a community with them that you will find much of your strength (see chapter 63 in this volume for more on finding your collective).

There are other circumstances that you might experience that are more unique to your situation such as being an under-represented racial/ethnic minority (see chapter 54 for more on racial and ethnic minorities), an international student (see chapter 57 for more on being an international student), a member of the LGBTQ+ community (see chapter 55 for more on being an LGBTQ+ student), or a first generation graduate student (see chapter 60 for more on being a first generation student). As these authors address, you are not alone and there are resources available. If you experience harassment or assault, contemplating leaving would be normal, adaptative, and healthy; and there are resources to help support you in staying (see chapter 51 for more on discrimination and assault and chapter 52 for more on harassment). You will feel burnout at times in the program and while normalizing the experience doesn't make it less painful at the time, there are steps you can take to make it more manageable (see chapter 64 for more on burnout).

Mapping Your Exit

From the time that seeds start getting planted in your mind about wanting to leave the program (these typically start before you arrive on campus for orientation), it is important to include your adviser and the director of your graduate program in your department in the conversation. You are not going to be the first person who has ever left their program prior to completion, you will not be creating an untraveled road. There are often intermediary steps that your adviser may recommend, such as taking a leave of absence, or finding an option of "stopping the clock" on your path to program completion. Consider these options. They may be right for you and there is often limited consequence in choosing to take a pause. Prior to doing so, consider your life beyond the program such as health insurance, campus housing, funding, student loan deferment, etc., as it is possible that leaving can also have immediate implications on aspects of your living situation. There are other times when individuals choose to take a leave of absence, even when they have already made the decision to leave, but they are just afraid to say it. If you are truly at a point where you know this is not the right career path for you, make the decision and take the next step in leaving the program.

If you are in a doctoral program, it is possible that there is an option for a terminal master's degree, even if there is not a formal master's program at your institution. Stop to consider how far you are from meeting that degree criteria and what it would take to be able to "master out" of your program. Consider doing so, too, even if you already entered your doctoral program with an equivalent master's degree. Beyond having a really compelling post-nominal for your email signature, it can be helpful on your resume to account for the time you were in your PhD program, even if you won't be "using" that master's degree, specifically. It also signifies the work that you have done. Getting into a doctoral program is hard, leaving with a master's degree is a way to reflect the effort you put forth and the degree you earned.

You will also want to consider any commitments you have made to peers, colleagues, or professors for ongoing and upcoming writing projects or accepted conference proposals. Once you have left the program, with or without a master's, you can still follow through on any of the commitments you have made, you can still attend the next regional conference and you can complete the book chapter you have started. As you decide if there are projects you are going to abandon (such as not finishing your dissertation), check to see if there is anything salvageable that you might want to get published. You may be strategic in what you choose to continue to engage in, as you are going to need references for your next job. If your adviser can speak to the way you maintained commitment to your peers by presenting a research paper at a conference once you have already left the program, that speaks directly to your character and is something that any employer would respect. One of the arts of leaving your program successfully is to take as much with you as possible; in particular, invest time in exploring the transferable skills you have attained.

Life Beyond the Ivory Tower

Validate the Emotional Weight of this Decision

After you leave the program and you are reintegrating into life beyond academia, you will recognize that many of the ways that you have survived and thrived to this point are skills that will no longer serve you. Before Lin-Manuel Miranda, *The Federalist Papers* were rarely discussed, and certainly not sung about, outside of the political science world. So, you will have much to share at the *Hamilton* watch party and a lot of other information and skills that you will not access again once you leave your program. This is an obvious and anticipated loss that you will have already taken into consideration before leaving, but there are other habits and behaviors you have definitionally had to engage in to arrive at this point. Here are some examples of cognitive distortions that you will be thinking, by virtue of reading the next line, if they have not already been in your head: "I wish I had been as smart as [cohort member's name], then I could have finished." "I have spent the last [length of time in graduate school] working on this degree and now none of it matters." "I couldn't get my [master's or doctoral] degree, I will never succeed at anything." "I'm a dropout." "My professors think I am a flake." "Great, now I have a master's degree, big deal." "I should never have started that program; I took away funding from someone who would have been better." Each of these were generated from a list of examples from the *Encyclopedia of Cognitive Behavioral Therapy* and they have evolved from initial work by Richard Beck in 1967 through working with individuals with clinically diagnosed depression (Yurica & DiTomasso, 2005).

These examples of cognitive distortions are exaggerated a bit for this illustration; however, it is a reasonable estimation that some combination and variation of these statements will feel true to you. You are going to be feeling a wide variety of emotions after you leave, and a sense of grief and depression will be among them. Go to therapy, truly, even if just for a handful of sessions. You have just made a major life adjustment, are going to have a huge shift in identity, and are going to be alone in it. Your partner may be relieved that you will not have this struggle anymore and they won't understand your sense of failure. Your cohort members may want you to know that you are still their friend and they still want you to come over for Sunday Funday Game Night. You may go a few times, but gradually the invitations will dwindle, and their lives become distinct from yours. Aunt Marge will bake you a pie as she asks you what you intend to do about your student loan debt. It is going to be challenging. Go to therapy.

Marketing Yourself Now

Now that you have had therapy and you believe that you have value as a human, you need to transition your entire framework of your CV and make it into a resume that other individuals understand. You may choose to continue to keep a CV somewhat updated, especially if you are going to finish a few lingering commitments, but you will want to create a broader resume where you can speak to your transferable skills. If you are pursuing a position in business or sales, tell them you have marketed Karl Marx in the Intro to Political Theory and successfully kept 46/52 students awake for an entire lecture. If you are asked to describe how you would delegate tasks amongst a team, describe a project you collaborated on. The biggest struggle in successfully transitioning your experience beyond academia is thinking too concretely about your experience, you have done "it," you just need to think about how to frame it for the prospective employer. Included in the resources for this book is a list of links as resources to explore transferable skills that you have that you can reconceptualize your resume.

Conclusion

Being accepted into a graduate program is an accomplishment. No one can take that from you, regardless. The hours you spent coding research, grading exams, and reading countless pages all still matter, it just matters in a different way than it once did. If you have made the decision to leave, take a deep breath, and trust that you know yourself more than anyone else and you did what was best for you.

References

Council of Graduate Studies. (2013). *Master's Completion Project*. Alexandria: Council of Graduate Studies.

Council of Graduate Studies. (2021). *PhD Completion Project*. Council of Graduate Studies.

National Science Foundation. (2021). *Doctorate recipients, by major field of study: Selected years 1990-2020*. Alexandria: National Science Foundation.

Somerville, Leah. (2016). Searching for Signatures of Brain Maturity: What are we Searching For? *Neuroview, 92*(6), 1164-1167.

The Ohio State University. (2021). *Department of Political Science: Time to Completion*. Columbus: The Ohio State University.

Yurica, Carrie and Robert DiTomasso. (2005). *Cognitive Distortions. In Encyclopedia of Cognitive Behavioral Therapy* (pp. 117-122). Boston: Springer.

67

Rest in Graduate School: Boundaries, Care-Taking Labor, Racial Capitalism, and Ill Health

Pyar Seth[1] & Alexandra De Ciantis[2]

1. Johns Hopkins University 2. University of California, Irvine

KEYWORDS: Rest, Exploitation, Overwork, Marginalized Thought.

Introduction

Too often does the urgency to complete academic-related activities take priority over our health and well-being. The ability to choose rest, especially when it is needed the most, became even more challenging since the arrival of the novel coronavirus into our shareable world—a historical moment that not only dramatically reshaped the nature of our work-life but further exacerbated health inequities produced by racial capitalism (Laster-Pirtle, 2020). The graduate environment is a space that often relies on processes that reinforce commodification and reduce personhood to productivity, where our work is something to be merely bought and sold. Keeanga Yahmatta-Taylor (2021) discusses how the academy is so quick to disregard "what we think, what we fear, or how we get through the day."

And so, the question facing a graduate student in political science is: how exactly can one center their humanity, build solidarity, and prioritize their physical, mental, existential, and social health amid the constraining expectations of the discipline? We offer a collective rethinking of work culture by critically examining the institutional dynamics that have continued to push the centrality of rest, health, and community further afield. Although we do not offer a singular answer, we hope to provide a critical theoretical approach for thinking through overwork in graduate school.

Feeling Overworked: The Pervasiveness of Racial Capitalism

In *The Undercommons: Fugitive Planning and Black Study*, Moten and Harney (2013) describe how the university has a limited capacity to foster true learning, love, and empathy. For Moten and Harney, a university ranking is not an indicator of intellectual quality; rather, it is a signal that a particular institution has a distinct ability to create a labor force that can effectively serve both the state and the market. Many universities also have dark histories of exploitation in which Black and Brown communities have disproportionately undertaken excessive labor in the form of administrative responsibilities, research, and teaching without compensation (see chapter 54 on concerns for underrepresented racial/ethnic students). Meanwhile, it is all too common for those in graduate school to experience a precarious funding situation in which they live paycheck to paycheck. Time and time again, universities have prioritized self-interest and competition, not cooperation, to fuel their racial capitalistic impulse and force us into a condition of ill health.

Reflecting on their experience as a Black graduate student at Indiana University, Eric Anthony Grollman (2017) bluntly stated, "Racism is the norm in academe […] Your graduate program is not in the business of looking after your personal well-being, so do not rely on it to meet your personal, social, spiritual and sexual/romantic need." Here, the question is not merely how to establish an optimal work-life balance but rather, we must ask ourselves, how does one escape institutional obliteration? Racial capitalism embodies a theoretical notion that self-interest and competition, not cooperation and community well-being, should pervade each aspect of daily life. And the current work culture of academia is one that has continued to push the centrality of our health asunder.

Overwork not only implies excess labor but a "right amount" of work. When life or the body feel as though they seem to be crashing, does asking for a break come across as laziness? Each institution, department, advisor, to name a few, have likely derived their own criteria of where a student should be year to year of the PhD. To be frank, those criteria regularly work against us. Comfortably saying no to an unreasonable advisor or expectation can become harder as one progresses through the program and so, identifying when the phrase "I cannot say no" is steadily becoming commonplace as early as possible can be essential.

When our schedule is too demanding, not only does the quality of our intellectual engagement decline but so does our health. Fatigue can make us more susceptible to illnesses that caffeine alone cannot solve. Suddenly, the quality of your research is not the same. You start to have trouble learning and remembering course material. You move slower. You take a sick day. Then another. And another. There is a danger in prioritizing the amount of work you do rather than the quality of work done and your health.

On another hand, some enjoy having a full schedule and the pressure of overwork is not considered to be a direct result of graduate school. We do not mean to discourage against hard work or suggest that one should not be proud of the effort they expend. But unfortunately, in graduate school, the notion of hard work can quickly transform into a kind of "busy bragging"—an urgency to constantly share your overwhelming schedule. It could sound like the following: an insane amount of reading; another endless day of teaching and research; a conference presentation to prepare for; another panel discussion to attend.

To be fair, graduate school can be riddled with chaos, and sometimes venting or speaking aloud is necessary. It is also perfectly acceptable to share accomplishments and be proud of your academic success. The busy brag can be done consciously or unconsciously, but in either case, it is often accepted as "common" by the academic community to hide the depressive-oppressive environment of graduate school; it is not the badge of honor we presume it to be. Being selective with your time and creating a schedule that is conducive with relaxation is crucial.

The feeling of overwork is derived from a constraint placed on health and well-being, emotion, economic security (time, space, employment, wage), and institutional positionality. Overwork itself can become hegemonic, where underrepresented communities also take on affective labor disproportionately and at a lower value, sometimes with no value afforded at all. Selma James and Nina Lopez (2020) discuss how the pandemic created a "crisis of care—from the rise in the mental and physical ill health of children to the neglect of disabled and elderly people." Waged or unwaged, it became impossible to dismiss the significance of daily care-taking labor on which, pandemic or not, society is dependent on for survival. We desperately needed care but almost instantaneously, there was no way to provide it, receive it, or generate it—a relentless cycle of unmet physical and emotional need.

We continued to work, repressing each warning sign of ill health to impose a cure rather than commit to respecting and strengthening our bodies. In short, the experience of overwork in graduate school can differ from student to student, namely as we consider race, gender, sexuality, disability, class, to name a few. Not everyone is equally alienated, equally unwell, equally feeling the weight of social suffering, equally exploited, equally represented, and equally expected to follow the institutional procedure of academia.

Disciplined by the Pandemic

The COVID-19 pandemic also interrupted any sense of routine and normalcy. The sudden temporal uncertainty spawned a feeling of strangeness, where people across the globe quickly realized the extent to which our lives were previously scheduled and conditioned (Grondin et al 2020). To avoid a complete rupture of everyday life, we needed to create new connective tissue. Some took to baking. Some took to at-home exercise. Some took to artistic expression. Although we could provide texture to everyday life with new activities, we inevitably lost time or more acutely, a notion of time. Monday felt like Thursday. Wednesday felt like Saturday. Friday felt like Tuesday.

But the impression of losing track of time also went beyond the inability to remember a particular day of the week; for some, we also lost the ability to recall the past—our previous self. The normal was, in fact, abnormal at one moment. And so, we hope to draw attention to how a potentially unhealthy behavior, habit, or expectation in our present moment can be made to feel normal, ordinary, or mundane. Not every lifestyle change made during the pandemic should be absorbed or rendered as normal.

At the height of the pandemic, Veena Das (2020) urged the academy to contend with how social and personal suffering would shape the classroom experience as they did during the last recession when income declined, suicide rose, and divorce soared. In the face of a distinct world order, Das realized that what might have appeared to be an impersonal neutral question in the past moment would now likely touch a naked wound hidden behind a clothed body and smiling face. The pandemic came with a harsh realization that what we often characterized as normal was, in actuality, violence inscribed into the everyday. Disease, death, and despair felt unavoidable but nevertheless, many were encouraged to endure, hide their anguish and rage, and instead, focus on using the moment to generate new political science research.

Meanwhile, the discipline has also often "produced a decidedly incomplete portrait of political life" (Soss & Weaver, 2017) and of the experience of marginalized communities, where the over-representation of quantification and widespread neglect of theories of racism, sexism, homophobia, transphobia, classism, disability, to name a few, can induce a perpetual state of frustration as an aspiring political scientist. It can be incredibly difficult to establish a research agenda in a program that has remained deeply committed to archaic methodologies and vocabularies that bear limited meaning on communities that were never of interest to political science.

There is a cost to becoming a political scientist and learning the "canon." Immersing oneself into the bodies of thought, methodologies, and theories of political science has the capacity to determine our schedule, research interest, intellectual development, pedagogy, and relationship to our political world. It can become second nature to continuously value not only academic-related activities but the priorities of the discipline above rest and well-being. Social science and humanities research alike have long histories of racism and colonialism embedded into their epistemological processes and methodologies, where the act of immersing oneself into a particular discipline, to use the language of Katherine McKittrick (2021), can be a "dismal, suffocating" process that can ultimately hinder successful completion of the PhD. How does one locate space to research and write against a prevailing discourse? What exactly does it mean to become absorbed into the language and methodologies of political science?

Although there is a movement to "decolonize" the literature, for Robbie Shilliam (2021), it is also not enough to merely retrieve histories of imperialism or colonialism, nor is it enough to condemn the hidden and ignored colonial logic of a conventional argument. We have to create new modalities of seeing the world and introduce a far more expansive series of archival material and interdisciplinary methodologies to move the study of political science from the center of power to the margin. But where is the time? Here, there is a very practical concern, that is, for a graduate student, how does one actively unlearn the dangerous and harmful legacies of slavery and colonization amid coursework that does not share that same epistemic commitment?

Some also feel as though "decolonize" is nothing more than a buzzword and frequently deployed to quiet the recent call to include marginalized thought on syllabi. At the same time, having a "race week" or "gender week" over the course of a single semester is rarely comforting for a student that is actively looking to find a method or body of literature conducive with their research orientation.

It is unlikely that we can provide a single piece of advice on how to develop your academic voice and become confident in writing against a prevailing paradigm in graduate school. But maybe, Nikki Giovanni (2021) can serve as one starting point. In a recent interview with Public Books, Giovanni stated the following:

"I have a right to write what I believe. And I also have a right to write what I feel. I am going to say what I believe. I am not gonna make a joke out of you. I am not gonna lock the door to keep you in. You have a right to walk out that door. I have an obligation to say what I believe. This is how we get along […] A writer, by nature, is very arrogant. We do not often say that out loud, but we are. We believe in ourselves. So we write. I am not trying to change anybody, but we write what we believe in. That is the only thing that is really important. It is what you, what I, or what we believe. If you do not believe in your own writing, then I do not know where you will go. The main thing is that you have to trust your voice. Once you trust your own voice, then you are going to write well."

To a certain extent, one cannot become all too preoccupied with the expectation of the discipline. Sometimes, the answer is relatively straightforward. Say no. Write. Trust your voice. Each of which is certainly easier said than done. But there is a world of inquiry beyond the discipline of political science. Do not be afraid to question the boundaries of the discipline because it is likely that you have noticed something important—a serious theoretical contention, a methodological error, or poor organization. Establishing a broad intellectual horizon/community is necessary for success in graduate school. Again, to use the language of Nikki Giovanni:

"Where do you go to rest? Well, you should have a friend that you can go to. A friend that you can laugh with. A friend who is not going to laugh at you, who is going to be a part of you, who is not going to use you."

Rest: Embracing a New Vision

The political theorist Antonio Gramsci, who prioritized the development of critical pedagogies to overcome institutional oppression, understood culture as a learned way of shared being. Paolo Friere elaborated on this critical-pedagogical dimension of Gramsci's thought in Pedagogy of the Oppressed, wherein he delineated how oppressive, dehumanizing conditions can be transformed when new systems of education are created with and for empowering oppressed people.

In graduate school, the seminar room, the reading group, and the zoom-room workshop, which now transcends geographical boundaries, all underlie graduate student life and hold the potential to become a cooperative space for learning. Each space, structured by competitive individualism, the commodification of knowledge, and de-prioritization of well-being, could benefit from learning and teaching that is focused on critically examining power and institutionalized inequalities.

The complex entanglement between racial capitalism and academic overwork can produce a particularly deleterious assimilationist politics within the classroom, serving only to secure greater success for those already well-positioned within the institution. Academic overwork is inflected by race, gender, class, and sexuality and to prioritize our health, we must begin to center intersectionality within the academy, in order to secure real change. As we continue to participate in shared space and develop a clearer understanding of the restlessness of the current terrain, splintered by unhealthy disciplinary expectations, we can critically rethink a new form of work-life for the graduate student experience – one centered around cooperation and mutual-aid.

Academic overwork, in one way, is the prioritization of academic production over personal and social well-being. Creating a new and healthier culture, then, would require the acknowledgment that, while academic overwork may not be experienced by everyone in the same capacity, it is widely accepted as self-evident and good for academic success. But paradoxically, accepting overwork as self-evident and good is undermining associational life within the university and inducing disproportionate burnout, neither of which can be sustained over an extended period of time. But why do we continue to subscribe to an ethos of academic production? One response lies with the notion that culture is a shared way of learned being. Unlearning, then, would require the language of racial capitalism so that a space for rest may be opened.

Anything short of a prioritization of rest is a hindrance to success in graduate school. Rest, by nature, is a necessary moment for personal and social well-being and it has the potential to transform our shared academic space. Kevin Quashie (2012) described the quiet as a sovereign space of inner life, holding the potential for an expression of vulnerability, desire, fear, ambition, hunger; an internal oneness that is generated by a capacity to inspire collectivity (74). Rest, like the quiet, is neither still, nor silent.

Rest is pedagogical; it is an epistemic commitment to care and a learned way of sharing being focused on asserting our humanity.

What does it mean when someone who has historically been treated as nothing more than a resource lays claim to equal treatment or demands time for self-care? We can start to overcome the long-standing, entrenched expectation for marginalized graduate student communities to carry the extra-weighted burden of research, administrative responsibilities, and care-taking labor once rest is embedded into the meaning of graduate student success. As the academy and the other modalities of governance produce and exacerbate harm, a rethinking of our being, feeling, and knowledge is necessary for rest, precisely for a re-setting of our expectation of success in graduate school. We all have several personal and professional responsibilities to handle, but against the grain, centering a rest-based culture in critical opposition to overwork can begin to secure real change for our health.

Moving Forward: Building Practical Capacities

Both abolitionist studies and the field of critical pedagogy share a commitment to being guided by a wide, endless imagination and can be used to practically work toward providing institutional transformation at the level of teaching, learning, and research. They also offer fruitful ground for political science to engage in academic bridgework so that our specific disciplinary constraints can be examined, addressed, and overcome. We have offered a critical lens through which we can engage in a collective rethinking of academic work, especially how overwork perpetuates inequality according to the various power structures within the academy. From this vantage point, we can build a new vision of work-life in political science. Indeed, there can be no otherwise, however, without a collective re-imagining of graduate student life.

References

Das, V. (2020). "Facing COVID-19: My Land of Neither Hope nor Despair." *American Ethnologist*. https://americanethnologist.org/features/collections/covid-19-and-student-focused-concerns-threats-and-possibilities/facing-covid-19-my-land-of-neither-hope-nor-despair

Gadson, R. (2021). "There's No There There: Keeanga-Yamahtta Taylor On the Future of the Left." *Public Books*. https://www.publicbooks.org/theres-no-there-there-keeanga-yamahtta-taylor-on-the-future-of-the-left/

Grollman, E.A. (2017). "Playing the Game for Black Grad Students." *Insider Higher Education*. https://www.insidehighered.com/advice/2017/02/24/lessons-learned-black-phd-student-essay

Grondin, S., Mendoza-Duran, E., & Rioux, P.A. (2020). "Pandemic, Quarantine, and Psychological Time." *Frontiers in Psychology: Theoretical and Philosophical Psychology*.

Harney, S., & Moten, F. (2013). *The Undercommons: Fugitive Planning and Black Study*.

James, S. & Lopez, N. (2021). "An Income to Care for People and the Planet." in *Our Time is Now: Sex, Race, Class, and Caring for People and the Planet*. PM Press.

Laster Pirtle, W. N. (2020). "Racial Capitalism: A Fundamental Cause of Novel Coronavirus (COVID-19) Pandemic Inequities in the United States." *Health Education & Behavior*. 47(4): 504-508.

McKittrick, K. (2021). *Dear Science and Other Stories*. Duke University Press.

Quashie, K. (2012). *The Sovereignty of Quiet*. Rutgers University Press.

Seth, P. (2021). "The Love Story that Should Be Told About Black People: Nikki Giovanni on Rest, Love, and Care." *Public Books*. https://www.publicbooks.org/nikki-giovanni-on-rest-love-and-care/?utm_content=buffer6671b&utm_medium=social&utm_source=twitter.com&utm_campaign=buffer

Shilliam, R. (2021). *Decolonizing Politics: An Introduction*. John Wiley & Sons.

Soss, J., & Weaver, V. (2017). "Police Are Our Government: Politics, Political Science, and the Policing of Race–Class Subjugated Communities." *Annual Review of Political Science*. 20: 565-591.

68 | Mental Health and Well-Being in Grad School: Dealing with Isolation, Depression, Anxiety, and Turmoil

Nasir Almasri[1] & Dana El Kurd[2]

1. Massachusetts Institute of Technology 2. University of Richmond

KEYWORDS: Negative Self-Evaluation, Internalization, Boundaries.

Graduate School and Mental Health

Graduate school is an inherently stressful and taxing endeavor. Students are taking a leap of faith pursuing a graduate degree, often foregoing decent wages and more stable career trajectories in exchange for the chance of academic success. The process of taking specialized courses, attempting to publish, conducting dissertation research, and navigating the hidden curriculum of academia can take a toll on students, particularly those from less privileged backgrounds who are often not as well supported by their mentors and programs. Toxicity, abuse, and discrimination are also common and graduate students can be their most vulnerable targets. It is thus unsurprising that researchers have described academia as having a "mental health crisis" (Almasri, Read, and Vandeweerdt 2021). This has undoubtedly been exacerbated by the increasingly non-existent job market and the impact of the Covid-19 disruptions.

In this chapter, we discuss the ways in which the graduate school experience can lead to feelings of isolation, depression, and anxiety. We discuss this in terms of graduate school progress more generally, as well as in specific contexts such as fieldwork. We hope that by pointing out these issues and emphasizing that they are endemic to this institution, students and readers will avoid negative self-evaluation and internalization of these experiences. We also hope to sketch out what can be done when faced with such challenges.

What Do We Know About Graduate Student Mental Health?

Political science graduate students—and graduate students in general—are much more likely to struggle with mental health than individuals in the general population. In a survey, Almasri, Read, and Vandeweerdt (2021) show that there is a mental health crisis in political science akin to those found in other disciplines. About one-third of respondents have symptoms of anxiety and another third have symptoms of depression. Most strikingly, 16%of respondents reported that they had suicidal thoughts in the two weeks preceding the survey. The study was limited to a small handful of peer institutions, suggesting that there could be differential impacts of graduate school at different institutions.

There is suggestive evidence that the primary issues relate to the programs. Over a quarter of students who were not diagnosed prior to graduate school showed symptoms consistent with depression and anxiety. Well under half of students screened for depression (33%)and anxiety(42%)reported receiving treatment. Students with worse mental health were more likely to report thoughts of quitting their programs, often had thoughts consistent with impostor syndrome, and generally found little satisfaction, sense of accomplishment, or meaning in their work. See also the chapters in this volume on impostor syndrome (chapter 50), leaving graduate school (chapter 66), and sustaining joy (chapter 62).

The study concluded with a series of open-ended questions that allowed respondents to share their thoughts on what impacted their mental health. Many raised concerns about the long hours and low pay, lack of structure and consistent feedback, and job prospects, including the limited discussion about non-tenure track jobs.

Other Factors That Exacerbate Mental Health Struggles

Mental health issues can arise or become more severe given some of the conditions inherent to academia. The low pay and overwork that most graduate students endure can create situations of precarity, stress, and financial burden. All of these are correlated with negative mental health. Graduate programs that keep students contingent, evaluating their financial aid and scholarship packages regularly rather than guaranteeing such support upon entry into the program, actively increase the probability of students suffering mental health issues. Moreover, imposing high levels of work—through teaching or research assistant positions, for instance—while also expecting graduate students to conduct dissertation research efficiently can add a great deal of stress, further exacerbating mental health concerns.

These issues are not equally distributed among graduate students. Many students from marginalized backgrounds struggle to balance the pressures of graduate school with their research output without impacting their mental health. Ethnic minorities face greater challenges with their mental health in overwhelmingly white institutions, including higher education, because they must contend with subtle and covert forms of racism in addition to more direct acts of prejudice (Okazaki 2009). Racism in all its forms has been found to be directly correlated with "negative psychological states including symptoms of depression and anxiety, lower well-being, lower self-regard, and ill health" (Okazaki 2009, 105).

Implicit, and sometimes explicit, biases play a role in determining who will receive support from their graduate institutions (see chapters 54-61 on "Strategies for Addressing Implicit Bias, Harassment, and Assault" for more detail). The biases that plague departments in their interactions with, and evaluations of, graduate students have long-lasting ramifications which can affect marginalized scholars throughout their careers. It is for this precise reason that Buchanan (2019) refers to the academy as a 'running faucet' for Black women, who bear the heaviest brunt of these dynamics. This applies to varying degrees to the experiences of scholars from other marginalized communities as well.

For example, many institutions have processes that are purposely opaque. In some cases, the experiences and futures of graduate students are left entirely in the hands of the mostly white faculty who evaluate them. In one author's experience at their graduate institution, this meant that the students who received funding and support from the department were overwhelmingly white students. Students from other backgrounds often did not finish the program or struggled immensely to continue until graduation. The same author took on multiple jobs and commuting hours daily just to make ends meet, all of which was not conducive to achieving their research goals. This led to anxiety, symptoms of depression, negative self-evaluation, and burnout. Unfortunately, this is not an uncommon experience for marginalized students in that department or in political science more generally.

There are also stigmas around graduate students who are parents or become parents during their PhD program, with many institutions not offering any sort of support given that students are not technically workers or employees in many states. We know that schedule flexibility and childcare support can significantly reduce anxiety and stress, and we know this is the case within and beyond academia. However, given that fellowships and other flexible work arrangements are not distributed equally, this means those at greatest risk of adverse mental health effects are also the least likely to receive institutional assistance (see chapter 16 on pregnancy and parenting in this volume for more details).

First generation students who often come into academia with lower levels of income and generational wealth struggle in specific ways during their studies. These students face more stress and symptoms of depression than "continuing generation" students for two reasons: first, institutions are often built on a hidden curriculum that only the most privileged can navigate. First generation students are more likely to feel isolated, given that they must learn the norms and culture of academia without outside assistance (Barham & Wood 2021; Smolarek 2019; Jack 2016). Second, financial pressure limits the likelihood of success. Many such students may have to contribute financially to their families and cannot rely on familial support in the periods where graduate students are between semesters and often without steady income. This creates conditions that initiate or exacerbate mental health struggles (Ridley et al. 2020).

Moreover, issues can arise during graduate school that are unforeseen. Family issues, deaths, accidents, and political turmoil or repression can impact students. Both authors have found it difficult to focus and have exhibited anxiety and depression symptoms because of political events that impacted their home countries and extended families. One author also struggled with health issues and pregnancy loss during graduate school and did not think to seek accommodation or take a leave of absence. As is often the case, it is more likely that privileged students will know how to seek accommodation for such issues or that they can simply ask for support during such critical times. Thus, it is important that readers recognize the unforeseen circumstances that arise are a part of being a normal human being and that these are not issues that they must hide or "work through." To the extent possible, one must advocate for accommodations and work with their departments to delay deadlines while they get back on track. Attempting to work through these issues rather than take time to recuperate will likely lead to burnout and worse long-term outcomes.

The examples listed above are just some of the ways in which identity and personal circumstances can have an impact on a graduate student's progress through a PhD program. These are overwhelmingly outside a graduate student's control. Academic institutions are largely failing to make policy changes that would help mitigate the mental health issues that arise from such conditions. This means that graduate students who face such issues should put their mental health first and demand accommodation from their departments, recognizing that they are not alone in their struggles.

Finally, fieldwork can be a significant source of struggle for graduate students. Conducting fieldwork means leaving your home institution as well as your family, friends, and peer support networks (Hummel & El Kurd 2021). Fieldwork entails moving to a new place and learning new routines and being isolated from familiar environments, which are inherently stressful activities. If the field site is one with conflict or contentious politics, or if the research topic touches on sensitive issues, this adds to the instability and pressure on a researcher. For example, managing physical safety and well-being in a difficult field site obviously leads to stress. However, researchers that deal with post-conflict field sites or questions such as repression, gender violence, and other sensitive topics can also develop mental health issues even if they, themselves, remain safe. See the discussion on fieldwork in this volume for more details (chapter 20), as well as the literature on secondary trauma (Warden 2013; Loyle & Simoni 2017).

These issues are compounded for researchers depending on their identities and positionality. As El Kurd & Hummel (forthcoming) note, "researchers from historically excluded communities will likely experience more issues with access to the field site and to interlocutors, more doubt about research credentials, and microaggressions as well as more blatant forms of racism and prejudice." This can lead "to burnout, unfavorable self-evaluation, increased stress, and an array of other mental and physical symptoms" (El Kurd & Hummel forthcoming). Moreover, researchers studying their home countries or regions may face threats to their physical safety that other researchers might not, as well as internal pressures or obstacles that are community specific. Overall, fieldwork has the risk of initiating or exacerbating mental health issues, which means that researchers must plan to mitigate these risks. Several resources exist to help graduate students plan accordingly, such as the ARC bibliography on mental health, as well as the safety cards developed by Hummel & El Kurd (2020). Managing expectations is crucial. It is also important for researchers to set in place support networks they can reach out to during times of increased stress or crisis, both back home and whenever possible in the field site itself.

How Can New and Prospective Students Prepare?

We have shown that graduate school places individuals in a precarious situation. The work often feels personal and all-consuming, and departments across the discipline generally lack that ability to address the systemic determinants of mental health struggles such as funding, proper mentoring, and job placement support. Prospective students should be armed with the knowledge about how these issues will impact them, but we assert unequivocally that it is the job of department administrators and discipline-wide institutions to address these issues. These issues will take significant time and energy to fix. Until then, we offer prospective students five pieces of advice to help them prepare for graduate school and work to mitigate the impact of potential mental health struggles.

Graphic 68.1: Strategies for Mitigating Mental Health Struggles

Strategies for Mitigating Mental Health Struggles

- Protect yourself and your time
- Develop strategies to communicate struggles
- Establish boundaries between work and personal life
- Be familiar with mental health services available to you
- Develop work groups with your peers

The first and most crucial bit of advice is to protect yourself and your time. Your department, advisers, colleagues, and loved one—no matter how supportive—cannot do this for you. When opportunities to engage in extracurricular activities arise, learn when to say "no." Although you may be passionate about these opportunities or see some benefit in engaging in them, the time spent should never come at the expense of your well-being. The same goes for perfecting assignments. Submitting written work can be anxiety-inducing because it reflects on you as a thinker and writer, but all work—even published articles and books—are imperfect. Aiming to perfect your work before submitting is often not worth it! This does not mean that students should not try to do good work but rather that the tradeoff of spending extra hours perfecting a paper or assignment is not always warranted. More generally, learn to be a bit selfish with your time. Graduate school asks a lot of you, so be comfortable with setting limits.

Second, develop ways to communicate your personal struggles with professors and advisers. Hummel and El Kurd (2021) offer a set of exercises and practices that can help individuals manage their mental health struggles, including the use of mental health workbooks or journals. Communicating struggles does not need to mean opening up to advisers about personal problems and asking for advice. Instead, communication should indicate what kind of space and accommodation you need. We don't seek to minimize the difficulty of this task, however. Students often fear that they might appear weak or insufficient when asking for help or accommodations and, indeed, not all advisers are supportive to the same extent.

To do this, you have to decide how much information you would like to share. Simpler is better in most cases. Unless you feel comfortable or want to communicate the extent of your struggle, it is often sufficient to explain that you are struggling with a personal matter that you do not want to disclose and that you need an extension for a deadline, need to step away from work for a given amount of time, or simply need faculty to be patient with you. If the struggle is more severe, you should get a mental health professional to provide the necessary documentation and go through the more formal process of requesting a leave of absence (note: a number of institutions have, unfortunately, used such requests to force students to leave altogether. This should not deter you from taking leave, but this fact cannot go unmentioned. As a discipline, it is critical that we find ways to support colleagues who need leaves of absence).

Ideally, faculty will listen and support your decision to step away for the necessary amount of time. If you anticipate that this will not be the case, it is critical that you be prepared to indicate that this is necessary for your well-being and for the quality of your work and, perhaps more importantly, that you will be communicating the same concerns with a department chair, dean, or other official in your institution. This is not a threat as much as an appeal to authority. If you are unsure whom to approach, ask upper-year students who likely have more experience navigating the department and institution before you speak with the faculty member(s) in question. This strategy is, frankly, useful for everything in graduate school! Speaking with the appropriate person in your department or institution can help you identify the best strategy to ensure that you can focus on your personal struggles without the compounding effect of unempathetic faculty members.

Third, establish clear boundaries between your work and personal life. Graduate work can be all-consuming, and it becomes hard to separate your work from your identity as an individual. One strategy is to develop and maintain hobbies so that work is not the only significant activity in your life. Hobbies are often significant sources of release for graduate students. Although many graduate students in political science are activists, it is critical that hobbies go beyond this important but tiring work which often blends with our studies and research. One author, for example, plays and watches sports almost daily and their partner, also an academic, spends significant time knitting and is part of a book club. These activities provide release from the everyday stress of research and other academic activities. Another strategy is to prioritize scheduling personal time throughout your week before scheduling work. Students should also develop social circles that do not include friends from their programs. Even in social settings, conversations with classmates almost inevitably turn towards work. Finally, if possible, avoid living too close to your place of work. The physical separation can help create space between you and your work.

Fourth, become familiar with the mental health services available at your institution and, more importantly, commit yourself to using them. Not all students have sufficient coverage, so mental health care might not be affordable or accessible. Understanding if and how you can access mental health care throughout the course of your program can help you formulate a plan when the situation requires it. Most institutions have websites or, at least, health services staff that can explain where you can go outside the institute to access the care you need. Asking the department administrative staff members or upper-year graduate students about where to go is a safe bet, too. Although the discipline needs to work to de-stigmatize conversations about mental health struggles, some students are still hesitant to ask out of concern that this could reflect badly on them. One strategy to get around this is to ask about where you can go to get more information about health services in general. Health services staff at your institution are usually much more discrete.

There is also the option of online mental health services, through subscription services and their related apps. This has been found to be effective as well (Chandrashekar 2018). In some cases, health insurance covers a portion of the cost of such services.

Relatedly, do not be afraid to get the help you need! Unfortunately, advice about identifying mental health services is not often heeded. Most students know how to access mental health services, but many do not do so (Almasri, Read, and Vandeweerdt 2021). The tough truth is that graduate school is only likely to exacerbate and prolong any mental health struggle you experience. Waiting until later or weathering the storm might only make matters worse.

Fifth, develop a work group with your peers. Forming work groups is beneficial for several reasons. It can help with accountability in an otherwise unstructured job. It creates an avenue to get feedback on work prior to submission. And it can serve as a support group to discuss and resolve familiar grievances. Although your peers are not substitutes for good mental health practices or the expertise of mental health professionals, they can help ensure that graduate school is less isolating (Cassese and Holman 2018; Trippany, White Kress, and Wilcoxon 2004). See chapter 7 on building supportive networks for more details.

Each of these recommendations is far easier to verbalize than to act on. In formulating these recommendations, the authors are partially reflecting on their own successes and failures in managing their struggles with mental health. We urge new and prospective students to take these recommendations seriously and to consult mentors with experience navigating graduate school.

Conclusion

Students considering graduate school should recognize the many ways that the intensity and isolation of the programs can impact their mental health and do their best to shield against the potential negative effects. The mental health crisis facing graduate students is severe and has likely been exacerbated by the Covid-19 pandemic. Our goal is only to prepare students to deal with these potential struggles, but we reiterate that the onus is not on them to fix the systemic issues that have negative impacts on mental health.

Instead, we call on departments and the discipline to recommit to creating environments that can support graduate student learning and growth. As a collective, we must address the key stressors that impact the well-being of graduate students, including funding concerns, job uncertainty, lack of support for students from marginalized backgrounds, unclear expectations, and the feeling of never being "off" from work (Almasri, Read, and Vandeweerdt 2021). These issues cannot be written off as "part of the experience" of graduate school. They have severe and negative consequences for our colleagues and can be mitigated via strategies that prioritize efficient and effective mentorship, working conditions, and job preparation.

Many students enter graduate school aspiring to be top researchers producing valuable knowledge to change the world, but few exit graduate school on the same optimistic note. Protecting your mental health and well-being is critical to your ability to survive grad school and to maintain a safe and healthy personal life. We hope the discussion in this chapter helps new and prospective students to fully understand the intensity of graduate school and, more importantly, to carefully evaluate their strategies for dealing with isolation and mental health struggles.

References

Almasri, Nasir, Blair Read, and Clara Vandeweerdt. Forthcoming. "Mental Health and the PhD: Insights and Implications for Political Science." *PS: Political Science & Politics*.

Barham, Elena, and Colleen Wood. 2021. "Teaching the Hidden Curriculum in Political Science." *PS: Political Science & Politics*. doi:10.1017/S1049096521001384.

Buchanan, NiCole T. 2019 "Researching While Black (and Female)." *Women & Therapy*. Vol. 43(1-2): pp. 91-111.

Cassese, Erin C., and Holman, Mirya R. 2018. "Writing Groups as Models for Peer Mentorship among Female Faculty in Political Science." *PS: Political Science & Politics*. Vol. 51(2): 401–405.

Chandrashekar, Pooja. 2018. "Do Mental Health Mobile Apps Work: Evidence and Recommendations for Designing High-Efficacy Mental Health Mobile Apps." *MHealth* (4).

El Kurd, Dana and Calla Hummel. Forthcoming. "Mental Health, Identity, and Fieldwork." in *Doing Good Qualitative Research*, edited by Jennifer Cyr & Sara Wallace Goodman. New York, NY: Cambridge University Press.

Hummel, Calla and Dana El Kurd. 2020. "Mental Health and Fieldwork." *PS: Political Science & Politics*. Vol. 54(1): 121-125.

Jack, Anthony Abraham. 2016. "(No) Harm in Asking: Class, Acquired Cultural Capital, and Academic Engagement at an Elite University." *Sociology of Education*. Vol. 89(1): 1–19.

Loyle, Cyanne E and Alicia Simoni. 2017. "Researching under fire: Political science and researcher trauma." *PS: Political Science & Politics*. Vol. 50 (1): 141-145.

Okazaki, Sumie. 2009 "Impact of Racism on Ethnic Minority Mental Health." *Perspectives on Psychological Science* Vol. 4(1): 103–7.

Smolarek, Bailey B. 2019. "The Hidden Challenges for Successful First-Generation PhDs." *Inside Higher Ed*, October 9.

Ridley, Matthew et al. 2020. "Poverty, depression, and anxiety: Causal evidence and mechanisms." *Science* (New York, NY) vol. 370,6522.

Trippany, Robyn L., Kress, Victoria E. White, and Wilcoxon, S. Allen. 2004. "Preventing Vicarious Trauma: What Counselors Should Know When Working with Trauma Survivors." *Journal of Counseling*

& Development. Vol. 82 (1): 31–37.

Warden, Tara. 2013. "Feet of Clay: Confronting Emotional Challenges in Ethnographic Experience." *Journal of Organizational Ethnography.* Vol. 2(2): 150-172.

69

Health and Well-Being in Graduate School: Counseling and Other Resources

Mikaela Karstens[1] & Anne M. Whitesell[2]

1. Pennsylvania State University, The Behrend College 2. Miami University

KEYWORDS: Mental Health Issues, Counceling Centers, Community.

Introduction

In a 2019 Nature survey, over one-third of PhD students reported seeking help for anxiety or depression (Woolston 2019). Certain research topics in Political Science, such as those related to violence, death, or oppression, can traumatize researchers further, even on top of the baseline pressures of graduate school (Loyle and Simoni 2017). Preexisting anxiety and depression was exacerbated during the pandemic, especially for poor graduate students and underrepresented groups who must balance both academic and non-academic stressors. Those struggling with mental or physical health challenges such as these are not alone, but finding the right support can be difficult, time-consuming, and expensive. Moreover, what is in someone's best interest often seems to contradict the norms of academia, leading graduate students to neglect caring for themselves. In this chapter, we discuss the importance of mental healthcare and identify numerous resources and strategies you can use to meet your emotional and psychological needs.

Why Does Mental Healthcare Matter?

It is not uncommon for the stress of graduate school to cause pre-existing or undiagnosed *mental health issues* to (re)emerge (Siegal and Keeler 2020). Addressing one's mental health while in graduate school can feel like a lower priority—something to be pushed aside by a seemingly endless list of tasks and deadlines. Such a view, however, sets one up for a rocky if not impossible road through academia.

You cannot do your best work if you are ignoring your mental health. Graduate students struggling with mental health problems report disruptions in productivity and completion of their theses or dissertations (Wyatt and Oswalt 2013). Graduate students who teach their own courses or serve as teaching assistants may find themselves confronted with undergraduate students who are struggling with their own mental health. Graduate students who work with undergraduates are mandatory reporters under Title IX, and depending on the university, may be asked to report or intervene when their students display worrying behaviors. Taking care of your own mental health is essential to helping others.

Even if you could get through graduate school ignoring your mental health, you have a whole life after graduate school. It is likely that many of the stressors you encounter during graduate school (the pressure to publish, imposter syndrome and comparing yourself to others, work-life balance issues, etc.) will continue in your early career. Burnout, isolation, and imposter syndrome issues persist throughout and beyond grad school, further amplified by the ongoing pandemic (see chapter 50 on imposter syndrome, and chapter 64 on preventing burnout). More than half of faculty members surveyed by the

Chronical of Higher Education in 2020 said they were seriously considering changings careers or retiring early, a trend more prominent among women (Gewin 2021).

What Actions Can You Take?

So, you have decided you want to prioritize taking care of your mental health, but where do you start?

Find Affordable (Mental) Healthcare

As a graduate student, you should have access to your university's student health services. Large universities typically have both health services and counseling or psychological services. University counseling services often provide free or reduced-cost services (National Council on Disability 2017), making it an attractive choice for students. These same centers may offer group therapy, either geared towards specific diagnoses (anxiety, depression, eating disorders, etc.) or specific student populations. Group therapy sessions targeted towards graduate students may offer discussions and coping strategies based on problems unique to graduate students, such as the pressure to publish or being on the job market (see chapter 35 on mental health and the job market). At the same time, do not discount the value of meeting others, including undergraduates, who do not share an academic background with you but are experiencing similar challenges.

Due to the overwhelming demand for mental health services, on-campus *counseling centers* often have a limit on the number of sessions and serve as more as a triage system (Shaffer, et al. 2017). Centers with a triage system may ask students to fill out a questionnaire or participate in a short intake session to assess the level of concern. In a 2017 survey, 97% of four-year colleges reported having a waiting list for counseling services (National Council on Disability 2017), with wait times spanning from a couple days to over a month. Counseling services typically become busier later in the semester, so the earlier in the semester you can schedule an appointment, the easier it will be.

Furthermore, most counseling centers are open Monday through Friday during normal business hours. Depending on the flexibility of your class and research schedule, you may not be available during these times. The location of university counseling services, however, may make it easier to take an hour for therapy than traveling to visit a provider off-campus. If you are concerned about people within your department noticing your absence, you may want to schedule your therapy around lunch or at the beginning or end of the day to make your absence less conspicuous.

There may be other options available to you through the university. If you have an assistantship, you are also an employee of the university, so take advantage of any mental health services offered to employees. Employee Assistance Programs (EAPs) offer a range of services, from meditation and stress management seminars to 24-hour hotlines. If your university has graduate programs in psychology, social work, or other counseling-related fields, there may be services offered through those programs. The Association of Psychology Training Clinics has a list of more than 150 member clinics available on their website.[1]

There may also be affordable mental health options available in your community. Community clinics may provide care at a reduced rate. These services may be offered through a religious organization, so if you are not religious, this may not be a good solution.

Before scheduling with a therapist, check to see whether they accept your health insurance. If that is the case, you should only be paying a co-pay for each visit. If the therapist does not accept your insurance, check with your insurance provider about their out-of-network benefits. You may have to pay the cost of an appointment up front, which is not ideal. But depending on your insurance plan's benefits, you may be eligible for reimbursement. Due to mental health parity laws, your insurance provider must provide equal benefits for mental health care as medical care. You can also ask your provider if they have a sliding pay scale, where the provider adjusts their rate depending on the income of the client.

Advocate for Yourself

The work you do advocating for yourself will be just as important to your mental health as the work you do with a therapist or counselor. For many graduate students, the first place to start is by speaking with your advisor and/or dissertation committee. Supportive faculty can assist you in many ways, such as tailoring deadlines to accommodate your needs, structuring the advising relationship to fit your learning style, and helping you feel less alone.

That said, you should prepare yourself for the possibility that your advisor may not recognize the importance of mental health; graduate students often report feeling a stigma or culture of silence around mental health in their programs (Forrester 2021, Siegal and Keeler 2020). Do not let this deter you. In the long run, you will be better served by putting your mental health above the latest revision of a dissertation chapter, a conference paper, or job market materials. Your advisor may be demanding, but this is ultimately your life. If your advisor or committee members do not recognize the importance of mental health, you may wish to seek support or accommodations from other sources (e.g., campus support groups, other faculty, or fellow grad students).

Advocating for yourself can also take the form of meeting with someone from your university's student disability services (or the equivalent office) to make sure that you receive appropriate accommodations. This is particularly helpful in cases of formally diagnosed learning disabilities (such as attention deficit disorder or dyslexia) and psychological disabilities (such as depression or bipolar disorder). Accommodations achieved through such offices can include additional writing time for comprehensive exams, altered deadlines, alternative exam locations, or other changes to help facilitate your success. These accommodations do not mean that you are less capable of the rigors of graduate school – rather they are just modifications to allow you to complete the same work as your peers in a way that works for you.

Build Community

Caring for your mental health is more complex than just deadlines and counselors. Given that graduate school is difficult, stressful, and often isolating, everyone eventually finds themselves feeling broken down to some extent. Building community can help you maintain balance and provide support when you are feeling vulnerable (see chapter 63 on overcoming academic isolation).

For many graduate students, their cohort mates—or the other graduate students who entered the program at the same time—serve as the initial members of their academic community. Through orientation and shared first-year classes, your cohort mates are likely to understand and sympathize with what you are experiencing. Likewise, senior graduate students within your department can help provide guidance and support from the perspective of someone who recently experienced the same thing. Fellow political scientists are also more likely to understand emotional distress specifically related to your research interests.

You should not feel compelled to build close relationships with other graduate students in your department, however. You may experience heightened anxiety or feelings of imposter syndrome from being surrounded by other political scientists, especially if you are competing within your department for resources. It is not worth putting your mental health at risk to build ties within political science. Over time, you may realize that what you need most in community is not a shared academic interest.

There are benefits to including people outside of your department, and outside of academia, to your support network. Having a support system within academia provides you with a space to talk about issues specific to academia without having to provide additional context. Building a support network of people outside your department provides the solidarity of a common graduate school experience without feeling like you are in direct competition with your support network. It can also provide valuable perspective that what may be happening in your department is not the norm (and therefore warrants further action) or is typical of higher education (in which case you can commiserate together).

Building community with people outside of academia is equally important. You need time to stop working, and that includes time that you are not talking about political science or academia in general. You need interests outside of your research to create that fabled work-life balance. Community organizations (e.g., community orchestra), religious institutions, and volunteer services are great structured outlets to meet people outside of academia.

Students who come from traditionally underrepresented populations may wish to seek out those who share their identity. For example, queer graduate students can benefit from including other queer students or faculty in their support system. LGBTQ+ resource centers are a common fixture on campuses and often host graduate student events to help facilitate these connections. Likewise, non-American students may seek out co-nationals who share their culture, language, or experiences. Regardless of identity, those with a shared experience can help you feel understood and give you advice on how to navigate difficult situations.

Develop a Plan

It is difficult to address your mental health when you are in crisis, so try to plan ahead. When you are in a good head space, develop a plan to help yourself cope with negative emotions and feelings. These plans can take a variety of forms, but may include the following:

- What are the warning signs? This may include physical signs or symptoms, behaviors that you notice in yourself, or triggers that are likely to set you off.
- How can you take care of yourself at this stage? You need a list of coping strategies. These coping strategies will likely not solve your problems but will help you tolerate distress.
- Who can you reach out to for help at this stage? Identify people in your support system who you can contact and provide them with concrete actions they can take to help you. These people can range from mental health professionals to friends and colleagues to members of your family.

There can be various stages of your plan to help you recover from a range of challenges, from "having a bad day" to "full blown meltdown." The more detailed you can be in your plan, the easier it will be for you to put the plan in place when you are struggling. By thinking this through in advance, you may also be better equipped to communicate your needs to members of your support system (Hummel and El Kurd 2021).

Identify the Root Problem

The source of your mental health struggles may predate your graduate school experience, but the nature of political science research can cause emotional distress and trauma (Hummel and El Kurd 2021; Loyle and Simoni 2017). Graduate students conducting fieldwork, for example, may feel particularly isolated, and those studying topics related to violence and oppression may experience secondary traumatic stress or vicarious trauma (Coles, et al. 2014). Be cognizant of your research subject and take regular breaks.

Additionally, the environment of your department or college can exacerbate the stress of graduate school (Mackie and Bates 2019). While these issues cannot be addressed alone, graduate student associations, graduate unions, or other collective entities on your campus may be able to intervene on your behalf (see chapter 33 on graduate school unions).

Conclusion

The pressures of graduate school can create mental health challenges and exacerbate pre-existing conditions. Feelings of anxiety and depression are common among graduate students across disciplines; depending on your area of research and the environment within your graduate program, you may find yourself even more emotionally vulnerable. Preparation and prevention are essential in managing your mental health. With a combination of trained medical professionals, a strong support network, and self-advocacy, you can create a plan to succeed academically without compromising your mental health.

Endnotes

1   http://www.aptc.org

References

Coles, Jan, Jill Astbury, Elizabeth Dartnall, and Shazneen Limjerwala. 2014. "A Qualitative Exploration of Researcher Trauma and Researchers' Responses to Investigating Sexual Violence." *Violence Against Women* 20 (1): 95-117.

Forrester, Nikki. 2021. "Mental Health of Graduate Students Sorely Overlooked." *Nature* 595: 135-137.

Gewin, Virginia. 2021. "Pandemic Burnout is Rampant in Academia." *Nature* 591: 489-491.

Hummel, Calla, and Dana El Kurd. 2021. "Mental Health and Fieldwork." *PS: Political Science & Politics* 54 (1): 121-125.

Loyle, Cyanne E., and Alicia Simoni. 2017. "Researching Under Fire: Political Science and Researcher Trauma." *PS: Political Science & Politics* 50 (1): 141-145.

Mackie, Sylvia A., and Glen W. Bates. 2019. "Contribution of the doctoral education environment to PhD candidates' mental health problems: a scoping review." *Higher Education Research & Development* 38 (3): 565-578.

National Council on Disability. 2017. "Mental Health on Campus: Investments, Accommodations Needed to Address Students Needs." July 21.

Shaffer, Katharine S., Michael M. Love, Kelsey M. Chapman, Angela J. Horn, Patricia P. Haak, and Claire Y.W. Shen. 2017. "Walk-In Triage Systems in University Counseling Centers." *Journal of College Student Psychotherapy* 31 (1): 71-89.

Siegal, Jason T., and Amanda Keeler. 2020. "Storm, Stress, Silence: A Focus Group Examination of Mental Health Culture and Challenges Among Graduate Students Currently or Previously Experiencing Depression." *Journal of College Counseling* 23: 207-2020.

Woolston, Chris. 2019. "PhDs: the torturous truth." Nature 575: 403-406.

Wyatt, Tammy, and Sara B. Oswalt. 2013. "Comparing Mental Health Issues Among Undergraduate and Graduate Students." *American Journal of Health Education* 44 (2): 96-107.

Contributor Biographies

Adler, William D., PhD

William Adler is Associate Professor of Political Science at Northeastern Illinois University.

Almasri, Nasir

Nasir Almasri is a Predoctoral Fellow with the Middle East Initiative at the Harvard Kennedy School and a PhD Candidate in Political Science at MIT.

Babcock, Alan

Alan Babcock is the Assistant Director of Student Disability Resources at Penn State Harrisburg.

Baer, Susan E., PhD

Susan E. Baer is an Online Lecturer in the School of Public Affairs and Administration at The University of Kansas and a Contributing Faculty Member in the School of Public Policy and Administration at Walden University.

Bateson, Regina, PhD

Regina Bateson is an Assistant Professor in the Graduate School of Public and International Affairs at the University of Ottawa.

Bauer, Kelly, PhD

Kelly Bauer is an Associate Professor of Political Science at Nebraska Wesleyan University.

Baybeck, Brady

Brady Baybeck is Associate Professor of Political Science at Wayne State University in Detroit, Michigan.

Becker, Megan, PhD

Megan Becker is an Associate (Teaching) Professor of International Relations at the University of Southern California.

Bell, Lauren C., PhD

Lauren C. Bell is the James L. Miller Professor of Political Science and Special Assistant to the Provost at Randolph-Macon College in Ashland, Virginia.

Benjamin, Andrea, PhD

Andrea Benjamin is an Associate Professor in the Clara Luper Department of African and African American Studies at the University of Oklahoma.

Bennion, Elizabeth A., PhD

Elizabeth A. Bennion is a Chancellor's Professor of Political Science and American Democracy Project Director at Indiana University South Bend.

Benson, Thomas S.

Thomas S. Benson is a PhD Candidate and Princeton Dissertation Scholar in Political Science and International Relations at the University of Delaware.

Biderbost, Pablo, PhD

Pablo Biderbost is an Associate Professor of Political Science at the Universidad Pontificia Comillas, Spain.

Blajer de la Garza, Yuna, PhD

Yuna Blajer de la Garza is Assistant Professor of Political Science at Loyola University Chicago.

Bonilla, Tabitha, PhD

Tabitha Bonilla is Assistant Professor of Human Development and Social policy at Northwestern University.

Boscán Carrasquero, Guillermo, PhD

Guillermo Boscán Carrasquero is an Assistant Professor of Political Science at the University of Salamanca, Spain.

Bose, Meena, PhD

Meena Bose is Executive Dean for Public Policy and Public Service Programs, Director of Presidential Studies, Peter S. Kalikow Chair in Presidential Studies, and Professor of Political Science, Hofstra University.

Boyes, Christina

Christina Boyes is an Assistant Professor (Profesora Titular) in the Division of International Studies at the Centro de Investigación y Docencia Económicas (CIDE).

Brown, Colin M.

Colin Brown is an Assistant Teaching Professor in Political Science at Northeastern University in Boston, Massachusetts.

Burlingame, Carmen, J., MPA, MA, MSW

Carmen Burlingame is a Licensed Clinical Social Worker practicing psychotherapy at the Samaritan Health and Living Center in Elkhart, Indiana.

Cantwell-Chavez, Devon

Devon Cantwell-Chavez is a PhD candidate in Political Studies at the University of Ottawa.

Cargile, Ivy A. M., PhD

Ivy A.M. Cargile is an Associate Professor of Political Science at California State University, Bakersfield.

Castle, Jeremiah J.

Jeremiah J. Castle is an Assistant Professor of Political Science at Metropolitan State University of Denver.

Chaffin DeHaan, LaTasha, PhD

LaTasha Chaffin Dehaan is an Assistant Professor II of History & Political Science at Elgin Community College.

Chandler Garcia, Lynne

Lynne Chandler Garcia is an Associate Professor of Political Science at the United States Air Force Academy.

Chandra, Tara

Tara Chandra is a PhD Candidate in Political Science at the University of California, Berkeley.

Cooney, Samantha R.

Samantha Cooney is a PhD candidate in Political Science at the University of New Mexico.

Culver, Chris

Chris Culver is an Assistant Professor of Political Science at the United States Air Force Academy.

Davis Thomander, Sierra

Sierra Davis Thomander is a Political Science PhD student at Stanford University and a Graduate Fellow at the IRiSS Center for American Democracy.

De Ciantis, Alexandra

Alexandra De Ciantis is a PhD student of political theory and critical theory in the Department of Political Science at the University of California, Irvine.

Deardorff, Michelle D.

Michelle D. Deardorff is the Adolph S. Ochs Professor of Government and Department Head of Political Science and Public Service at the University of Tennessee at Chattanooga.

Dorssom, Elizabeth, MPA

Elizabeth Dorssom is an Assistant Professor of Political Science at Lincoln University of Missouri.

Drezner, Daniel, PhD

Daniel Drezner is Professor of International Politics at The Fletcher School at Tufts University.

Egan, Patrick J.

Patrick J. Egan is Associate Professor of Politics and Public Policy at New York University.

El Kurd, Dana, PhD

Dana El Kurd is Assistant Professor of Political Science at the University of Richmond.

Fattore, Christina

Christina Fattore is an Associate Professor of Political Science at West Virginia University.

Finnell, Rachel E., PhD

Rachel E. Finnell is an Assistant Professor of Political Science at Bethany College in Lindsborg, Kansas.

Franco, Josh, PhD

Josh Franco is an Assistant Professor of Political Science at Cuyamaca College in east San Diego county, California..

Friedman, Sally, PhD

Sally Friedman is an Associate Professor of Political Science at State University of New York at Albany.

Gancheva, Silviya

Silviya Gancheva is a Political Science PhD Candidate at Wayne State University and a Humanities Center Dissertation Fellow at Wayne State University.

Gauding, Patrick J., PhD

Patrick J. Gauding is a Visiting Assistant Professor of Politics at the University of the South in Sewanee, Tennessee.

Gelbman, Shamira

Shamira Gelbman is the Daniel F. Evans Associate Professor in the Social Sciences at Wabash College.

Gellman, Mneesha

Mneesha Gellman is Associate Professor of Political Science in the Marlboro Institute for Liberal Arts and Interdisciplinary Studies at Emerson College.

Gentry, Bobbi G.

Bobbi Gentry is Associate Professor of Political Science at Bridgewater College as a scholar of teaching and learning who focuses on improving student engagement in the classroom through simulations, policy problem/solution proposals, and research projects.

Gilbert, Danielle

Danielle Gilbert is an Assistant Professor of Military & Strategic Studies at the US Air Force Academy.

Gill, Rebecca D., PhD

Rebecca Gill is an Associate Professor of Political Science at the University of Nevada, Las Vegas.

Gray, Felicity

Felicity Gray is a PhD Scholar in international relations at the Australian National University specializing in civilian protection.

Gross, Benjamin Isaak

Benjamin Isaak Gross is the Director of the Tocqueville Lecture Series, Co-Editor of *Compass: An Undergraduate Journal of American Political Ideas*, and an Assistant Professor of Political Science at Jacksonville State University.

Gubitz, S.R.

S.R. Gubitz is an Upper School History Teacher at Kent Denver School.

Guerrero, Mario

Mario Guerrero is Professor and Department Chair of Political Science at California State Polytechnic, University Pomona.

Guliford, Meg K., PhD

Meg K. Guliford is an Assistant Professor of Political Science at Drexel University.

Ben Hammou, Salah

Salah Ben Hammou is a PhD candidate in Security Studies at the University of Central Florida.

Harris, Kyle

Kyle Harris is a MPA candidate at Central Michigan University.

Harrison, Brian F., PhD

Dr. Brian Harrison is a Visiting Assistant Professor at Carleton College in Northfield, Minnesota.

Haun, Courtney N., PhD, MPH

Dr. Courtney Haun serves as an Assistant Professor and the Director of the Healthcare Administration Undergraduate Program at Samford University in the Department of Healthcare Administration and Informatics.

Hoyo, Verónica, PhD

Verónica Hoyo is an Evaluator and a Research Associate at the Center for Comparative Immigration Studies at the University of California, San Diego

Hyder, Misbah

Misbah Hyder is a PhD Candidate in the Department of Political Science at the University of California, Irvine.

Ingram, Matthew C., JD, PhD

Matthew C. Ingram is Associate Professor of Political Science in the Rockefeller College of Public Affairs and Policy at the University at Albany, State University of New York.

Irgil, Ezgi

Ezgi Irgil is a Postdoctoral Research Fellow in the Global Politics and Security Program at the Swedish Institute of International Affairs.

Ishiyama, John, PhD

John Ishiyama is University Distinguished Professor of Political Science at the University of North Texas and Piper Professor of Texas. He also serves as President of the American Political Science Association (2022).

Jo, Eun A.

Eun A Jo is a PhD Candidate in the Department of Government at Cornell University.

Jordan, Marty P.

Marty P. Jordan is an Assistant Professor in the Department of Political Science at Michigan State University.

Kammerer, Edward F., JD, PhD

Edward F. Kammerer, Jr., is an Assistant Professor in the Department of Political Science at Idaho State University.

Kapiszewski, Diana

Diana Kapiszewski is Provost's Distinguished Associate Professor in the Department of Government at Georgetown University.

Karcher, Sebastian

Sebastian Karcher is Research Assistant Professor of Political Science and Associate Director of the Qualitative Data Repository at Syracuse University.

Karstens, Mikaela

Mikaela Karstens is the Commonwealth Postdoctoral Teaching Fellow in Liberal Arts at Penn State Behrend.

Kavanagh, Jennifer, PhD

Jennifer Kavanagh is a Senior Political Scientist at the RAND Corporation.

Kearns, Kevin M.

Kevin Kearns is an Assistant Professor in the Department of Social Sciences at Texas A&M University-Corpus Christi.

Kedrowski, Karen M.

Karen Kedrowski is Director of the Carrie Chapman Catt Center for Women and Politics and Professor of Political Science at Iowa State University, and Professor Emerita of Political Science at Winthrop University in Rock Hill, SC.

Khan, Aleena

Aleena Khan is an Associate Policy Researcher at the Bridging Divides Initiative at Princeton and a PhD student in Political Science at the University of Illinois at Urbana-Champaign.

Kirilova, Dessi

Dessi Kirilova is the senior curation specialist at the Qualitative Data Repository.

Kirkland, Siobhan

Siobhan Kirkland is a Research Analyst at the Government of Canada.

Kreft, Anne-Kathrin

Anne-Kathrin Kreft is a Postdoctoral Fellow in Political Science at the University of Oslo.

Lamb, Matt

Matt Lamb is an Assistant Professor of Political Science at Texas Tech University.

Lamm, Jennifer

Jennifer E. Lamm is a Lecturer in Political Science at Texas State University.

Lebovits, Hannah, PhD

Hannah Lebovits is Assistant Professor of Public Affairs at the University of Texas–Arlington.

Lee, Myunghee

Myunghee Lee is a Postdoctoral Fellow at the Nordic Institute of Asian Studies and the Department of Political Science at the University of Copenhagen.

Lineberger, Monica E.

Monica E. Lineberger is an Assistant Professor of Political Science at the University of Wisconsin-Whitewater.

Loepp, Eric. D.

Eric D. Loepp is an Associate Professor of Political Science at the University of Wisconsin-Whitewater.

Lorentz II, Kevin G., PhD

Kevin G. Lorentz II is Assistant Professor of Political Science at Saginaw Valley State University.

Lowe, Evan M., PhD

Evan M. Lowe is an instructor at the School of Civic and Economic Thought and Leadership at Arizona State University.

Macaulay, Christopher

Christopher Macaulay is an Assistant Professor of Political Science at West Texas A&M University.

Mailhot, Cameron

Cameron Mailhot is a PhD Candidate in the Department of Government at Cornell University.

Malji, Andrea

Andrea Malji is an Assistant Professor of International Studies at Hawai'i Pacific University.

Mallinson, Daniel J., PhD

Daniel J. Mallinson is an Assistant Professor of Public Policy and Administration at Penn State Harrisburg.

Marin Hellwege, Julia, PhD

Julia Marin Hellwege is an Associate Professor of Political Science and Director of the Government Research Bureau at University of South Dakota.

Masket, Seth

Seth Masket is a Professor of Political Science and Director of the Center on American Politics at the University of Denver.

McNeely, Natasha Altema, PhD

Natasha Altema McNeely is an Associate Professor of Political Science at the University of Texas Rio Grande Valley.

McThomas, Mary, PhD

Mary McThomas is Associate Professor of Political Science at the University of California, Irvine.

Meehan, Elizabeth (Bit)

Elizabeth (Bit) Meehan is a PhD candidate in political science at the George Washington University.

Meier, Anna A.

Anna A. Meier is Assistant Professor in the School of Politics and International Relations at the University of Nottingham, UK.

Melusky, Benjamin, PhD

Benjamin Melusky is an Assistant Professor of Political Science at Old Dominion University.

Mendoza, Mary Anne S.

Mary Anne S. Mendoza is an Assistant Professor of Political Science at California State Polytechnic University, Pomona.

Middlewood, Alexandra T., PhD

Alexandra T. Middlewood is an Assistant Professor of Political Science at Wichita State University.

Mineshima-Lowe, Dale, PhD

Dale Mineshima-Lowe is an Associate Lecturer in Politics at Birkbeck, University of London, UK.

Monda, David O.

David O. Monda is a Professor of Political Science at the City University of New York-York College.

Montoya, T. Mark, PhD

T. Mark Montoya is Director and Associate Professor of Ethnic Studies at Northern Arizona University.

Moreira, Jair

Jair Moreira is a PhD student in Political Science at the University of Illinois at Urbana-Champaign.

Murphy, Michael P. A.

Michael P.A. Murphy is a Banting Postdoctoral Fellow at Queen's University and Editorial Assistant at *Security Dialogue*

Neal, Coyle, PhD

Coyle Neal is an Associate Professor of Political Science at Southwest Baptist University.

Nemerever, Zoe

Zoe Nemerever is an Assistant Professor of Political Science at Utah Valley University.

Newman, James

James Newman is an Associate Professor of Political Science at Southeast Missouri State University.

Newton, Monique

Monique Newton is a PhD Candidate in Political Science at Northwestern University studying poor Black political behavior in American Politics.

Nordyke, Shane

Shane Nordyke is the Allene R. Chiesman Distinguished Professor of Democracy at the University of South Dakota.

Novak-Herzog, Maya

Maya Novak-Herzog is a PhD Candidate in Political Science and a Gender and Sexuality Mellon Cluster Fellow at Northwestern University.

O'Brochta, William, PhD

William O'Brochta is an Assistant Professor of Political Science at Louisiana Tech University.

Ocampo, Angela X.

Angela X. Ocampo is Assistant Professor of Political Science and Faculty Associate in the Center for Political Studies and the Latina/o Studies Program at the University of Michigan.

Ochner, Margaret Mary

Margaret Mary Ochner is an Attorney and Adjunct Professor in the Department of Political Science and Law at Montclair State University.

Osorio, Maricruz Ariana

Maricruz Ariana Osorio is an Assistant Professor in the Global Studies Department at Bentley University.

Phillips, Joseph B.

Joseph Phillips is a Postdoctoral Research Associate in Political Psychology at the University of Kent.

Phoenix, Davin L.

Davin L. Phoenix is an Associate Professor of Political Science at the University of California, Irvine.

Piazza, Kelly

Kelly Piazza is an Assistant Professor of Political Science at the United States Air Force Academy.

Poloni-Staudinger, Lori

Lori Poloni-Staudinger is Dean of the College of Social and Behavioral Sciences and Professor in School of Government and Public Policy at University of Arizona.

Rasool, Adnan

Adnan Rasool is an Assistant Professor of Political Science at the University of Tennessee at Martin.

Reuning, Kevin, PhD

Kevin Reuning is an Assistant Professor of Political Science at Miami University.

Reyna, Verónica L.

Verónica L. Reyna is an Associate Chair and Professor at Houston Community College.

Rodda, Patricia C., PhD

Patricia C. Rodda is an Assistant Professor of International Relations at Carroll University.

Rojas, Natalie

Natalie Rojas is a PhD student in Political Science at the University of California Davis.

Romo Rivas, Mishella

Mishella Romo Rivas is a PhD student in Political Science at Princeton University.

Rosebrook, Erika, PhD

Erika Rosebrook is Interim Director of the Master of Public Policy program and Assistant Professor of Political Science at Michigan State University.

Rowland, Alisson

Alisson Rowland is a PhD candidate in Political Science at the University of California, Irvine.

Rubalcava, Bianca

Bianca Sofia Rubalcava is a PhD candidate in the department of Political Science and an incoming

Assistant Professor in the department of Political Science at the University of the Pacific. Assistant Professor in the department of Political Science at the University of the Pacific.

Rubio, Rosalie

Rosalie Rubio is a PhD candidate in Political Science at George Washington University.

Russell, Annelise

Annelise Russell is an Assistant Professor of Public Policy at the University of Kentucky.

Sacco, Jennifer Schenk, PhD

Jennifer Schenk Sacco is a Professor of Political Science and Women's and Gender Studies, and chair of the department of Philosophy and Political Science at Quinnipiac University.

Saks McManaway, Kimberly

Kimberly Saks McManaway is Assistant Professor of Political Science at the University of Michigan-Flint.

Salinas-Muniz, Ignangeli

Ignangeli is a Political Science PhD student at the University of Michigan.

Sands, Melissa L.

Melissa Sands is an Assistant Professor of Politics and Data Science at the London School of Economics.

Schiff, Eleanor, PhD

Eleanor Schiff is currently an Adjunct Lecturer at The Pennsylvania State University after holding Visiting faculty positions at Bucknell University and Dickinson College.

Seth, Pyar

Pyar Seth is a Ph.D student in the Interdisciplinary Humanistic Studies Program at Johns Hopkins University pursuing a joint degree in Anthropology and Political Science.

Shugars, Sarah

Sarah Shugars is an Assistant Professor of Communication at Rutgers University.

Siddiqui, Asif, MA

Asif Siddiqui is a business instructor in the Faculty of Business, Environment, and Technology (FBET) at NorQuest College and a term instructor in the School of Business at MacEwan University in Edmonton, Canada.

Spanakos, Anthony Petros

Anthony Spanakos is Professor of Political Science and Law at Montclair State University.

Stepp, Kyla K.

Kyla K. Stepp is an Assistant Professor of Political Science and Public Administration at Central Michigan University.

Strachan, J. Cherie, PhD

J. Cherie Strachan is Director of the Ray C. Bliss Institute of Applied Politics and Professor of Political Science at the University of Akron.

Sulfaro, Valerie, PhD

Valerie Sulfaro is Professor of Political Science at James Madison University.

Sutton, Connor J.S., PhD

Connor J.S. Sutton is an Assistant Professor of National Security and International Relations at Anderson University.

Taghvaiee, Jessica S.

Jessica S. Taghvaiee is a PhD student in Political Science at the University of California, Irvine.

Torres-Beltran, Angie

Angie Torres-Beltran is a PhD Candidate in the Department of Government at Cornell University.

Torres, Rachel

Rachel Torres is an Assistant Professor of Political Science at James Madison University.

Trantham, Austin

Austin Trantham is an Assistant Professor of Political Science at Saint Leo University.

Turner, Kimberly N., PhD

Kimberly N. Turner is an International Security Program postdoctoral fellow at Harvard Kennedy School's Belfer Center.

Victor, Jennifer, PhD

Jennifer Nicoll Victor is Associate Professor of Political Science at the Schar School of Policy and Government at George Mason University, in Fairfax, Virginia, USA.

Villegas, Randy

Randy Villegas is a PhD candidate in political science at the University of California Santa Cruz.

Vortherms, Samantha A. PhD

Samantha A. Vortherms is an Assistant Professor of Political Science at the University of California, Irvine.

Whitesell, Anne M.

Anne M. Whitesell is an Assistant Professor of Political Science at Miami University.

Widmeier, Michael W.

Michael W. Widmeier is an Adjunct Associate Professor at Webster University.

Willis, Charmaine N.

Charmaine N. Willis is a PhD candidate in political science at Rockefeller College, University at Albany (SUNY).

Winter, Rachel

Rachel Winter is the Assistant Curator at the Eli and Edythe Broad Art Museum at Michigan State University, and a PhD candidate in the history of art and architecture at the University of California, Santa Barbara.

Yates, Tyler P., JD, PhD

Tyler P. Yates is a researcher for the Global Terrorism Database at the Consortium for the Study of Terrorism and Responses to Terrorism (START) at the University of Maryland–College Park.

Yazici, Irmak

Irmak Yazici is a Fellow and Lecturer in the Civic, Liberal, and Global Education (COLLEGE) program at Stanford University.

Zvobgo, Kelebogile, PhD

Kelebogile Zvobgo is an Assistant Professor of Government at William & Mary, a faculty affiliate at the Global Research Institute, and the founder and director of the International Justice Lab.

www.ingramcontent.com/pod-product-compliance
Lightning Source LLC
Chambersburg PA
CBHW080409270326
41929CB00018B/2952